READER'S DIGEST
THE STORY OF
WHERE YOU LIVE

READER'S DIGEST

THE STORY OF WHERE YOU LIVE

Published by the Reader's Digest Association Ltd
London • New York • Sydney • Montreal

Contents

TOWNEND CYCLES BEST VALUE IN THE WORLD.

TOWNEND Bros LIMITED COVENTRY. 1896.

Introduction

Every day of our lives is affected by where we live – in a house or flat, village or town, against a backdrop of fields, hills or coastline, or simply bricks and mortar as far as the eye can see. The people, places and events that entwine to make the story of our homes, our communities and our landscapes have built up layer upon layer of history over the centuries. *The Story of Where You Live* helps you to unpeel the layers, with the reward of discovering all the engrossing tales about the place that you call home.

Maybe you long to find out when your home was built, and why, and who lived there before you, or how the land it stands on was once used. Perhaps you are curious about the origin of some of the street names in your town; or what was made at a former factory before it was turned it into an arts centre; or who made the old stone-cobbled lanes that run over the moors. Whatever intrigues you, *The Story of Where You Live* is packed with the expert knowledge that will guide you towards the information you seek.

Incredible stories on your doorstep

The three main sections of the book, 'Landscape', 'Community' and 'Home', show how Britain's rural and urban landscapes have emerged from prehistoric times to the present day, how our villages, towns and cities, and all they contain, have developed, and how what we live in has evolved, from wattle and daub cottage to energy-efficient house and flat. There are thousands of stories and remarkable facts here that build into an understanding of why Britain is like it is. But, above all, *The Story of Where You Live* is a practical tool. It encourages you to get out and about in your streets and landscape and interpret what you see, and equips you with the information you need – records, websites, publications, places to visit – to become your own local history detective. You will be amazed at how much there is to learn about where you live.

Making the most of the book

The Story of Where You Live is easy to dip into so you can quickly find the information you need. Each spread covers a new topic or moves the story on, providing you with a comprehensive picture of how Britain has evolved and all the necessary tools to uncover the tales behind your own area.

1 The three main sections – on landscape, community and the home – are each divided into two parts: 'story' pages, crammed with absorbing history; and 'explore' pages, showing you how to interpret your surroundings and carry out your own research, whether at home or in archives.

2 Most 'story' pages include a time span, such as '1066-1500' or '1830-1910', which helps you to place the subject in a wider historical context.

3 'In Focus' features appear regularly throughout the book, offering an in-depth look at key topics.

4 Special feature boxes highlight interesting examples and case histories.

5 'Find out more' boxes list carefully researched sources – museums, organisations, books and websites – that will help you take your research further. When 'see DIRECTORY' appears in the text after a source of information, you will find contact details in the 'Directory of sources' on pages 332-339.

6 'Magnifying glass' symbols pinpoint specific clues to look out for, that might lead to the missing links in your story.

7 Maps appear regularly to show how historical and natural developments affected the regions of Britain, and even individual towns or cities.

TIMELINE OF EVERYDAY LIFE

Our history is as much about the domestic and local developments that changed daily life as it is kings, queens, wars, laws, and religious and political upheaval. Below, you can track those society-changing events in relation to the wider national picture.

MAIN EVENTS

0	AD100	200	300	400	500	600	700	800	900	1000

ROMAN BRITAIN | ANGLO-SAXONS AND VIKINGS

55 BC Julius Caesar lands in Britain, but soon leaves

54 BC Julius Caesar returns, defeats the tribes of southeast Britain and departs again

AD 43 Roman invasion of Britain

60-61 Native tribes rebel under Queen Boudicca and destroy Colchester and London

80 Romans invade Scotland, then withdraw south of the Forth ten years later

216 Britain divided into two provinces: Britannia Superior (south and west) and Inferior (north)

260-74 Britain becomes part of breakaway Gallic Empire, made up of Gaul and Britain

c.390 Angles, Saxons and Jutes begin to settle in parts of Britain

400-503 Colonisation of modern Argyll by the Scots from northern Ireland

410 Romans leave Britain

c.563 St Columba founds a monastery on Iona, which becomes the principal centre of Christianity in Scotland

597 St Augustine arrives in Canterbury to spread Christianity

793 Monastery at Lindisfarne is sacked by Vikings

843-58 Kenneth MacAlpin (843-58) unites the Picts and the Scots

865 Danes land in East Anglia and capture York and Reading

886 The Danelaw established by Alfred (871-99) to contain the Danes in the north and east of England

1016 Danish prince Cnut (1016-35) becomes the first Viking king of England

1018 Battle of Carham ensures Scottish possession of Lothian for Malcolm II (1005-34)

1058 Death of King Lulach marks end of the old Celtic kingdom; Kingdom of the Scots begins under Malcolm III (1058-93)

0	AD 100	200	300	400	500	600	700	800	900	1000

CHANGES TO EVERYDAY LIFE

c.47 Fosse Way Roman road laid out from Exeter (Isca) to Lincoln (Lindum Colonia)

c.50 Foundation of London (Londinium)

▶ **122-39** Hadrian's Wall built to mark northern frontier of Roman Empire

c.140-3 Antonine Wall built in an attempt to push frontier further north. Abandoned c.190

c.150 Roman landowners begin to settle in country villas such as Chedworth, Gloucestershire

270s First shore forts, such as Pevensey, built against the threat of Saxon invasion

c.597 St Martin's, the oldest parish church in England, established at Canterbury

▲ **c.630** First English coinage struck

c.790 Jarlshof prehistoric site first settled by Vikings

c.790 Offa's dyke constructed

c.800 Saxon farmers begin to use open-field system of crop rotation

890s King Alfred creates system of burghs (fortified towns) in Wessex

▼ **893** Anglo-Saxon Chronicle begun

0	AD 100	200	300	400	500	600	700	800	900	1000

The Norman invasion of England, depicted on the Bayeux Tapestry

| 1100 | 1150 | 1200 | 1250 | 1300 | 1350 | 1400 | 1450 | 1475 |

MIDDLE AGES

1066 Harold II (c.1022-66) defeats the King of Norway at the Battle of Stamford Bridge

▲ **1066** Triumph of **William the Conqueror (1066-87)** at the Battle of Hastings – beginning of Norman rule

1086 Domesday Book compiled

1096 First Crusade

1135 Stephen (1135-54) siezes the throne, beginning a civil war with his cousin Matilda

1170 Murder of Thomas Beckett

1215 King John (1199-1216) puts his seal to the Magna Carta

1237 Treaty of York between **Henry III (1216-72)** and **Alexander II (1214-49)** defines border between England and Scotland

1264 Rebellion of English nobles led by Simon de Montfort, who is killed at the Battle of Evesham in 1265

1272 Eighth, and last, Crusade

1284 Edward I (1272-1307) issues Statute of Wales to establish the Principality of Wales

1314 Robert I (1306-29) defeats the forces of **Edward II (1307-27)** at the Battle of Bannockburn

1328 England recognises Scottish independence in the Treaty of Edinburgh

1337-1453 Hundred Years' War

1348-9 The Black Death

1381 The Peasants' Revolt, led by Wat Tyler and John Ball, demands the abolition of serfdom

1399 Henry Bolingbroke – **Henry IV (1399-1413)** – siezes the throne from **Richard II (1377-99)**

1400-16 Owain Glyndwr leads revolt in Wales

1415 Henry V (1413-22) defeats the French at the Battle of Agincourt

1455-85 The Wars of the Roses

1468-9 Orkney and Shetland ceded to Scotland in lieu of Margaret of Norway's dowry

| 1100 | 1150 | 1200 | 1250 | 1300 | 1350 | 1400 | 1450 | 1475 |

1066 onwards Flemish weavers settle in England

1100 The White Tower, the original castle keep of the Tower of London, is built

1123 St Bartholomew's Hospital, London, founded

1128 First Cistercian abbey founded at Waverley in Surrey

c.**1150** Jew's House, Britain's oldest-surviving occupied stone house, built in Lincoln

1175-84 Canterbury Cathedral remodelled as the first Gothic cathedral in England

c.**1185** Oxford University founded

1209 Cambridge University founded

1209 London Bridge completed

c.**1213** St Thomas's Hospital, London, founded

1220 Old Bell, Malmesbury, said to be Britain's oldest hotel, opens

1220s First Dominican and Franciscan friars arrive in England

1230s First surviving manor court records begin

1253 Scarborough Fair established

▼ **1283-90** Harlech castle built by Edward I in Wales, one of ten castles, including Conwy and Caernarfon, erected to subdue the Welsh.

1290 Edward I expels Jews from England

1348-9 More than one-third of Britain's population dies, and thousands of villages are wiped off the map, during the Black Death

1362 English made the official language of Parliament and law courts; quarter sessions introduced

1377-81 Poll Tax levied

1382 Winchester College founded, Britain's oldest public school

1393 It becomes compulsory for every pub and inn to display a symbol on a sign

1411 Work begins on the London Guildhall

1412 Foundation of first Scottish university, St Andrews

1440 Eton College founded

c.**1450** Glass windows start to appear in many towns

1451 Foundation of Glasgow College of the Arts

1476 William Caxton opens the first printing press in England, in Westminster

MAIN EVENTS

CHANGES TO EVERYDAY LIFE

MAIN EVENTS

TUDORS AND STEWART SCOTLAND

1485 Richard III (1483-5) killed at the Battle of Bosworth and succeeded by **Henry VII (1485-1509)**

1493 James IV of Scotland (1488-1513) suppresses Lordship of the Isles and becomes the first king to rule the whole of Scotland

1513 James IV defeated and killed at the Battle of Flodden

1520 Henry VIII (1509-47) meets Francis I of France at the Field of the Cloth of Gold

1536 Henry VIII declares himself Supreme Head of the Church of England

1536 Act of Union between England and Wales

1536-40 Dissolution of the Monasteries

1547-53 Edward VI

1549 Thomas Cranmer (1489-1556) completes the *Book of Common Prayer*

1553 Lady Jane Grey rules for nine days

1553-8 Mary I

1558-1603 Elizabeth I

1578-80 Francis Drake (*c*.1540-96) sails around the world

1585 First English settlement in America, at Roanoke Island

1587 Mary, Queen of Scots (1542-87), tried and executed

1588 Defeat of the Spanish Armada

1600 East India Company is founded

STUARTS

1603 Union of the Scottish and English Crowns under **James VI (1567-1625)/ James I (1603-25)**

1605 Gunpowder Plot

1607 First permanent British colony in America at Jamestown, Virginia

1611 King James Bible, or 'Authorised' version, appears

1620 Pilgrim Fathers sail for the New World

1642-51 Civil Wars

1646 Plague in Scotland

1649 Execution of **Charles I (1600-49)**

1649-60 Commonwealth of **Oliver Cromwell (1649-58)** and **Richard Cromwell (1658-60)**

1660 Charles II (1660-85) restored to throne

CHANGES TO EVERYDAY LIFE

1489 The pound coin – 'sovereign' – is minted for the first time

1495 Foundation of Aberdeen University as King's College

1505 Royal College of Surgeons founded in Edinburgh

1512 Henry VIII establishes the modern Royal Navy when he builds the warships *Mary Rose* (1509-10) and *Great Harry* or *Henri Grace à Dieu* (1512-14)

1513 Deptford and Woolwich dockyards on the Thames founded to build warships

1538 Parish registers introduced in England and Wales

1540 Statute of Wills allows property in England and Wales to be bequeathed to those other than an heir

1547 English replaces Latin in church services in England and Wales

1553 Scotland's oldest surviving parish register – Errol, Perthshire

1554 St Andrew's golf course, Scotland, founded

1565 Royal Exchange founded in London

◀ **1570s** First county maps drawn up by Christopher Saxton

1572 First influx of Huguenots to Britain from France

1576 James Burbage opens first theatre in London at Shoreditch

1581 First presbyteries introduced in Scotland

1582 University of Edinburgh founded

1590 First paper mill in England established

1590 First known performances of Shakespeare plays – *Henry VI* and *Titus Andronicus*

1592 Presbyterian Church formally founded in Scotland

1598-1601 Poor Law Acts establish a system of parish levies to fund relief for the sick and the poor in England and Wales

1599 Erection of the Globe Theatre in Southwark, London

1605-10 John Speed (1542-1629) produces the first town plans of England and Scotland

1612 First Baptist church in England opens in London

▲ **1616** Inigo Jones (1573-1652) begins the Queen's House, Greenwich, Britain's first Classical building. In 1619 he starts the Banqueting House, his masterpiece

1617 Register of Sasines established in Scotland, recording the transfer of all land and property

1630s Dutch engineer Cornelius Vermuyden (1595-1683) drains much of the Fens

1632 First coffee shop opens in London

1634 Covent Garden market opens

1635 First public postal service begins

1638 The Pantiles laid out in Tunbridge Wells, one of the first spa towns

1646 First recorded cricket match takes place in Kent

1647 Society of Friends (Quakers) founded by George Fox

1649 Regular stagecoaches begin to run

1653 World's first public library, Chetham's, opens in Manchester

1655 Wilton carpet factory is built in Wiltshire

1656 Jews readmitted into England

1660s Bloomsbury Square, London, is laid out

1662 Theatre Royal opens in Drury Lane, London

1662-88 Hearth tax (1691-5 in Scotland)

1663 First turnpike tolls introduced

1665 Bubonic plague kills 70,000 people in London

1670s First sash windows start to appear

A round of golf in the 16th century

1675   1700   1725   1750   1775   1800

GEORGIANS

MAIN EVENTS

1666 Great Fire of London

1685 Duke of Monmouth's rebellion against **James II (1685-1688)** crushed at Battle of Sedgemoor

1688 'Glorious' Revolution – James II abdicates

William III and Mary II (1689-94)

1692 Massacre of Glencoe

1694 Bank of England founded

1695 Bank of Scotland founded

1702-14 Queen Anne

1707 Act of Union of England and Scotland unites their two parliaments and forms Great Britain

George I (1714-27)

1715 Jacobite rebellion

1720 Collapse of the South Sea Company – 'The South Sea Bubble'

George II (1727-60)

1730s Better-off Scottish highlanders start to emigrate to America

1745 Jacobite rebellion

1746 Jacobites and Prince Charles defeated at the Battle of Culloden; tartans and clans banned

1750s Industrial Revolution begins to gather pace.

1752 Gregorian calendar is adopted

1753 British Museum is founded

1756-63 Seven Years' War with France

George III (1760-1820)

1768 First of Captain James Cooke's voyages to Pacific

1775-83 War of American Independence

1780 Anti-Catholic Gordon Riots leave 700 dead in London

1783-1803 Many poor Scottish highlanders emigrate; those left behind forced onto new settlements

1788 First British convicts land in Australia

1793-1815 Revolutionary and Napoleonic Wars

1801 Act of Union unites Parliaments of Great Britain and Ireland

1805 Battle of Trafalgar

1807 Abolition of the slave trade

1675   1700   1725   1750   1775   1800

CHANGES TO EVERYDAY LIFE

1675 Christopher Wren (1632-1723) starts to rebuild St Paul's Cathedral in Baroque style; he finishes in 1710

1678 'Crown glass' first made, leading to larger window panes

1683 Ashmolean Museum, Britain's first public museum, opens in Oxford

1685 Edict of Nantes is revoked by Louis XIV and 50,000 French Huguenots emigrate to Britain

1689 Devonport naval dockyard is founded

1690 Presbyterianism becomes the official doctrine of the Church of Scotland

c.1690 Fort William built in the Scottish highlands, the first of three forts constructed by the government to quell Jacobite uprisings

1694-9 Poll Tax in Scotland

1696 Window tax introduced, causing the blocking up of many house windows

1698 Society for the Promotion of Christian Knowledge founded, establishing charity schools across Britain

1701 Jethro Tull (1674-1741) invents the seed drill and horse-drawn hoe

1702 *Daily Courant*, the first daily newspaper, is published

1706 First evening newspaper, *The Evening News*, is published in London

1707 Leonard Knyff and Jan Kip publish their drawings of estates and parkland in *Brittania Illustrata*

1709 Abraham Darby pioneers iron smelting at Coalbrookdale, Shropshire

1711 Ascot races established

◀ **1712** First steam engine built by Thomas Newcomen to pump water from a tin mine

1715 Claremont Gardens, near Esher, Surrey, one of the first landscaped gardens, is begun

1725 General Wade (1673-1748) begins a military road-building programme in Scotland

1728 John Wood the Elder (1704-54) starts his development of Bath with Queen Square

1730s Charles 'Turnip' Townshend (1674-1738) invents the Norfolk System of crop rotation

1732 Covent Garden Opera House opened

1733 Legal documents start to be written in English instead of Latin

1733 John Kay (1704-c.80) patents the Flying Shuttle, allowing cloth to be made at much faster speeds

1739 First Methodist chapel is founded by John Wesley (1703-91) in Bristol

c.1750-1850 Main period of parliamentary enclosure of fields

1759-72 Bridgewater Canal built to transport coal between the Duke of Bridgewater's mines at Worsley and Manchester

c.1760 Robert Bakewell (1725-95) introduces the selective breeding of cattle, sheep and horses

1764 James Hargreaves (c.1720-78) invents the Spinning Jenny, which allows a spinning wheel to operate eight spindles rather than one

1764 First houses in London numbered

1766 James Craig (1744-95) wins a competition to design Edinburgh's New Town

▼ **1766** Bristol Old Vic, Britain's oldest surviving playhouse, opens

1767-75 John Wood the Younger (1728-81) builds the Royal Crescent – Britain's first – in Bath

1769 Richard Arkwright (1732-92) invents the Water Frame, a spinning machine that could be powered by water-wheel

1769 James Watt (1736-1819) patents his steam condenser, which makes steam engines more efficient

▶ **1769** Josiah Wedgwood (1730-95) opens the largest china factory in the world at Etruria, Staffordshire

1770s Trade directories appear

1771 Richard Arkwright establishes the factory system at his textile mill in Cromford, Derbyshire

1775 Alexander Cummings patents the water closet

1779 Samuel Compton creates the Spinning Mule, allowing the spinning of finer cloth

1780 First Epsom Derby is run

1781 World's first iron bridge opens at Coalbrookdale, Shropshire

1784 Royal Mail coach service begins

1784-1850 Tax on the number of bricks used in buildings

1785 Power loom patented by Edmund Cartwright (1743-1823)

1787 Marylebone Cricket Club founded

1787 Steam engines introduced into Manchester cotton mills

c.1790s First chimney pots appear, creating a better updraught

1796 Pump Rooms built in Bath

1797 First £1 notes are issued

1800 Robert Owen (1771-1858) turns the cotton-mill village of New Lanark in Scotland into the first model industrial village

1801 First British census

1801 First crofts are created by the Duke of Argyll on the island of Tiree in Scotland

1805 Grand Junction canal between London and Birmingham opened

1805 House numbers become mandatory in London

1807 Gas lighting demonstrated for the first time, in Pall Mall, London

1675   1700   1725   1750   1775   1800   **11**

M A I N   E V E N T S

REGENCY

1811 George, Prince of Wales, is made Regent

1811-17 Luddite attacks in the Midlands and north of England on machinery in cotton and textile factories

1815 Battle of Waterloo

1815 Corn Laws passed to protect English farmers by restricting imports of cheap foreign wheat

1819 Peterloo Massacre in Manchester – 11 killed

George IV (1820-30)

1820 Cato Street Conspiracy – Jacobite plot to assassinate the Cabinet – is foiled

1820s Highland landlords encourage emigration en masse

William IV (1830-7)

1832 Reform Act marks the beginning of the democratic system of voting

1829 Catholic Emancipation Act removes restrictions and penalties on Catholics

1830 'Swing' riots hit farmers and landowners in southeast England

1833 Isambard Kingdom Brunel (1806-58) is appointed engineer of the Great Western Railway

1834 Tolpuddle Martyrs transported for taking an illegal oath to a labourer's union

1835 Municipal Corporations Act sets up the first local councils to replace the old boroughs

VICTORIAN

Victoria (1837-1901)

1837 Civil registration of births, deaths and marriages introduced; 1855 in Scotland

1840 Construction of the Houses of Parliament begins

1843 Free Church of Scotland founded

1845-51 Irish Famine

1846 Repeal of the Corn Laws

1850-60 Peak of the Highland Clearances in Scotland

1851 Great Exhibition held in the Crystal Palace

1853-6 Crimean War

1857-8 Indian Mutiny

1858 Raj established in India

1859 Charles Darwin (1809-82) publishes *The Origin of Species*

C H A N G E S   T O   E V E R Y D A Y   L I F E

1814 Dulwich Picture Gallery, the first public art gallery, opens

1814-53 James Pigot publishes the first national series of trade directories

1814 Gas street lamps installed in Westminster

▼ **1815** Thomas Telford (1757-1834) begins the reconstruction of the London to Holyhead road and the Menai suspension bridge

1816 John McAdam (1756-1836) devises a method of improving road surfaces using crushed stone and gravel

1818 Incorporated Church Building Society founded to build and restore Anglican churches

1819 First public cemetery, The Rosary, opens in Norwich

1819 Burlington Arcade, Britain's first arcade of shops, opens in Piccadilly, London

▲ **1823** Rugby invented

1823 Houses of correction and county gaols are combined to be called prisons

1824 First public 'bus' service operates between Pendleton in Salford and Manchester

1825 First passenger railway, the Stockton & Darlington, opens

1828 University of London founded

1828 Iron industry revolutionised by invention of hot-blast process by J.B. Neilson (1792-1865)

1828-42 Thomas Arnold implements reforms at Rugby that influence all other public schools

1829 Metropolitan Police formed

1830 Liverpool to Manchester Railway opens

1830s Influx of Irish workers to Glasgow

1832 National cholera epidemic – up to 7000 die in London

1832 First sheet glass is manufactured

1832 Durham University founded

1834 Hansom cabs introduced in London

1834 Poor Law Amendment Act creates Union workhouses in England and Wales

1835 Regent's Park opens, flanked by the elegant stuccoed houses of John Nash (1752-1835)

1835 William Henry Fox Talbot (1800-77) produces the first negative photographic image

1836-52 Tithe awards and maps drawn up for 11,395 parishes in England and Wales

▼ **1840** Penny Post is introduced, heralding the modern postal system

1840s 'Railway mania' begins as Parliament approves the building of 273 new lines

1841 For the first time, census information on names, ages, addresses and occupations is kept

1843 Theatres Act bans smoking and drinking in playhouses and spawns the creation of music halls

1844 Ragged School Union is set up by Lord Shaftesbury

1844 Railway Act forces rail companies to offer travel at a penny a mile

1844 First 'co-op' store opens in Rochdale

1845 General Enclosure Act provides the first 'allotments' for the landless poor

1846-7 Blight of Scottish potato crop leads to famine

1847 United Presbyterian Church is founded in Scotland

1848 Public Health Act aims to improve sanitary conditions in urban areas

1850s New brick-making machines allow cheaper bricks and more building. Damp-proof courses are introduced

1850 Factory Act restricts working hours of women and children and gives all workers Saturday afternoons off

1851 Window tax is abolished, leading to houses with more windows

1851 Caledonian MacBrayne, Scotland's ferry link to its off-shore communities, begins life as a steamer company

1852 First post box is introduced by the novelist and Post Office employee Anthony Trollope (1815-92)

1852 Burial Act closes urban churchyards and paves the way for municipal cemeteries

1853-76 Industrialist Titus Salt (1803-76) builds the model village of Saltaire in Yorkshire for his workers

1855 Repeal of stamp duty on newspapers leads to a cheaper press

1855 London Metropolitan Board of Works is set up to improve the capital's sanitary conditions

1856 Henry Bessemer invents his steel-making process in London, using the Bessemer Converter. His move to Sheffield two years later begins the age of mass-produced steel

1860　1870　1880　1890　1900

1865-6 Transatlantic cable enables Morse code transmissions between Britain and America

1867 Second Reform Act extends the vote to urban men who rent or own property valued at more than £10 – electorate doubles to 2 million

1868 Foundation of the Trades Union Congress

1870 Education Act paves the way for schooling for all children in England and Wales

1871 Trade Union Act gives unions official recognition

1872 Education (Scotland) Act introduces compulsory schooling for Scottish children aged 5 to 13

1874 Britain takes a 40 per cent share in the Suez Canal

1876 Victoria is proclaimed Empress of India

1879 Zulu War

1880 School made compulsory for all children up to 10; education is free from 1890

1884 Third Reform Act raises the electorate to more than 5 million

1885 Karl Benz tests the first motor car

1888 County Councils Act creates 62 county councils in England and Wales

1888 Jack the Ripper murders five prostitutes in Whitechapel, London

1890 General Gordon is killed in Khartoum, Sudan

1890 Forth Railway Bridge opens

1893 Independent Labour Party is founded by Keir Hardie

1894 Manchester Ship Canal opens

1897 Queen Victoria's Diamond Jubilee

1899-1902 Boer War

1860　1870　1880　1890　1900

1851 Great Exhibition

1857 Britain's first football club, Sheffield FC, is founded. The oldest surviving club, Notts County, starts life in 1862

1858 'Great Stink' in London results in Joseph Bazalgette building the city's sewers

1860s Gas lighting becomes common in homes. Gas-powered water-heating geysers appear

1861 William Morris (1834-96) opens a factory to produce fabrics, furniture, tiles and wallpaper

1862 George Peabody sets up a trust in London to provide housing for the poor and needy

1862 Land Registry is established

1863 First underground railway, the Metropolitan Railway, runs from Paddington to Farringdon

1863 Football Association founded

1863 Whiteley's, Britain's first department store, opens in Bayswater, London

1866 Dr Barnado's first home opens

1868 Artisan's Dwellings Act starts to tackle slum clearance

1869 John Sainsbury opens his first shop at 173 Drury Lane, London

1871 Bank holidays introduced

1871 Penny Farthing bicycle invented

1872 Wanderers beat Royal Engineers 1-0 at Kennington Oval in the first FA Cup Final

1875 Public Health Act stipulates good drainage and sanitation in all new houses

1875 Liberty's opens in Regent's Street, London, selling decorative ornaments and shawls from the Far East

1875-86 Bedford Park, west London, Britain's first garden suburb, is built

▶ **1876** Alexander Bell invents the telephone

1877 First Wimbledon Lawn Tennis Championship

1878 Joseph Swan gives the first public demonstration of an electric light bulb

1879 Britain's first telephone exchange opens at 36 Coleman Street, London

1880 Statute (Definition of Time) Bill is introduced to standardise time, based on Greenwich Mean Time, throughout Britain

1881 Electric street lighting is installed in Godalming, Surrey, the first town to have a public electricity supply

1882 First electric power station is built at Holborn Viaduct in London

1882 Suicides allowed to be buried in consecrated ground

1883 Cheap Trains Act allows affordable travel for workers

1884 Michael Marks opens his Penny Bazaar in Leeds

1884 Thomas Crapper develops the valveless water cistern

1885 Electric trams are introduced in Blackpool

1885 Cremation is legalised

1886 Crofters' Holdings (Scotland) Act gives crofters security of tenure for the first time

1888 William Heseketh Lever (1851-1925) founds the workers' town of Port Sunlight in Cheshire

1889 Britain's first purpose-built mosque opens in Woking, Surrey

1889 First electric power station opens in Bradford, Yorkshire

1890 World's first deep-level underground electric railway – the 'tube' – opens, connecting Stockwell and King William Street in London

1890 Housing of the Working Classes Act leads to first council houses in London, Liverpool, Manchester and Sheffield

1890s Beginning of a large influx of Jews, particularly to London, from eastern Europe

1890s Penny slot meters bring gas to the working classes

1894 Creation of Urban and Rural District Councils, setting up new townships and parish boundaries

1895 Northern Rugby Football Union is formed at Huddersfield. It becomes the Rugby Football League in 1922

1895 National Trust established

1898 Britain's first motor buses run in Edinburgh

1900 Eastman Kodak Co's Brownie easy-to-use camera leads to a new era of cheap family snaps

20TH CENTURY

Edward VII (1901-10)

1901 Guglielmo Marconi (1874-1937) sends first transatlantic radio signal

George V (1910-36)

1911 Parliament Act confirms the political primacy of the House of Commons over the House of Lords

1914-18 First World War

1916 Easter Rising in Dublin

1918 Women over the age of 30 get the vote

1919 First radio broadcasts by Guglielmo Marconi's company

1921 Irish Free State established

1926 General Strike

1928 Women over the age of 21 get the vote

1928 Alexander Fleming (1881-1955) discovers penicillin

1929 Wall Street Crash

1935 Radar invented

1936 Abdication of Edward VIII

George VI (1936-52)

1936 Jarrow March to London by 200 shipyard workers

1938 Munich Agreement between Neville Chamberlain and Hitler

1939-45 Second World War

1940-1 Blitz bombing raids on Britain

1944 Butler Education Act provides free secondary education for all

1945 Labour Party wins first overall majority in the general election

1947 School leaving age raised to 15

1948 National Health Service established

1948 Rail network nationalised

1948 SS *Empire Windrush* brings 492 Jamaican immigrants to London

1949 First commercial passenger jet, *Comet*, is built

1902 Cremation Act enables public burial authorities to provide and maintain crematoriums out of the rates

1903 First garden city, Letchworth, is founded by Ebenezer Howard (1850-1928)

1905 Electrification of the London Underground

1909 Cinematograph Act results in the creation of purpose-built cinemas

1909 First Lyons Corner House opens in London on the corner of Coventry and Rupert streets

1910-15 Valuation Office surveys, carried out by the Inland Revenue, record all land and property in Britain

1912 First automatic telephone exchange opens at 24 Station Road, Epsom, Surrey

1913 Stainless steel produced at Sheffield

1918 School leaving age raised to 14 years

1919 Forestry Commission created

1919 First commercial air service begins, from Hounslow, London, to Paris

1919 First Betty's Tea Room opens in Harrogate

1920 First petrol pump installed at Aldermaston on the road from Bath to London

1920 Croydon becomes London's first air terminal

1920s First metal-framed windows appear

1921 First public telephone boxes introduced. The red cast-iron box is designed by Giles Gilbert Scott in 1924

1921-32 Becontree Housing Estate, the world's biggest housing estate, is built in Essex

1922 BBC (British Broadcasting Corporation) established

1922 Britain's first crude oil refinery opens at Llandarcy, near Neath

1923 First FA Cup Final at Wembley, between Bolton Wanderers and West Ham United – Bolton win 2-0

1926 Foundation of the Council for the Preservation of Rural England

1927 First single white lines introduced to keep cars to the left-hand side of the road

1928 Harry Ramsden opens his first chippie in Guiseley, near Leeds

1932 Several thousand walkers stage a mass 'trespass' on Kinder Scout in the Peak District. The same year the Public Rights of Way Act is enforced

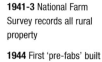

1934 Percy Shaw (1890-1976) invents 'cat's eyes'

▲ **1934** Launch of the *Queen Mary*

1935 The National Grid is completed

▼ **1936** First Butlin's holiday camp opens at Skegness

1936 Roll-on roll-off ferries are introduced on cross-Channel routes between England and France

◄ **1936** The BBC begins the first television broadcasts

1941-3 National Farm Survey records all rural property

1944 First 'pre-fabs' built

1944 Patrick Abercrombie's plan for London establishes the creation of a green belt zone around the city

1946 Heathrow Airport opens

1946 New Towns Act authorises the creation of a series of satellite towns around London. Stevenage is the first

1947 East Kilbride, the first new town in Scotland, is established

1948 Last workhouses in Britain close their doors

1949 Cwmbran, the first new town in Wales, is established

1949 Britain's first high-rise block of flats is built in Holborn, London

late 1940s First fully fitted kitchens appear

BUTLIN'S HOLIDAY CAMP SKEGNESS
IT'S QUICKER BY RAIL

ILLUSTRATED BOOKLET FREE FROM BUTLINS HOLIDAY CAMP (DEPT.R.P) SKEGNESS LINCS OR ANY L N E R OFFICE OR AGENCY

1950   1960   1970   1980   1990   2000   2010

MAIN EVENTS

1950-3 Korean War

1951 Festival of Britain

Elizabeth II (1952-)

1952 Britain tests its first nuclear bomb

1956 Suez Crisis

1956 Britain's first nuclear power station opens at Calder Hill in Cumbria

1964 Labour government starts to encourage the establishment of comprehensive schools

1969 Voting age is reduced to 18

1970s Around 30,000 Asians settle in Britain after expulsion from Uganda by Idi Amin

1972 British troops shoot dead 13 demonstrators in Belfast – 'Bloody Sunday'

1973 Britain joins EEC

1973 School leaving age raised to 16

1973 Edward Heath introduces the three-day working week

1978-9 'Winter of Discontent'

1979 Margaret Thatcher becomes Britain's first woman prime minister

1979 Government introduces the 'right to buy', allowing council tenants to buy their homes

1982 Falklands War

1984-5 Coal miners' strike

1989-90 Introduction of the Poll Tax

1990-1 Gulf War

1993 Introduction of the Council Tax

1994 Channel Tunnel opens

1997 Tony Blair is elected with the Labour Party's biggest ever majority

1998 Good Friday Agreement between political groups in Northern Ireland

1999 Devolution establishes a Welsh assembly and a Scottish parliament

1999 NATO forces attack Serbia and liberate Kosovo

2003 Iraq War

1950   1960   1970   1980   1990   2000   2010

1951 Peak District National Park becomes the first National Park in Britain

1951 First zebra crossing appears

1952 The Great Smog kills around 4000 in London

1954 Government lifts restrictions on private housing, leading to boom in house building

1955 Coventry's Upper Precinct, Britain's first traffic-free shopping area, opens

1956 Clean Air Act sets out to control air pollution

1958 Parking meters are introduced in Grosvenor Square, London; traffic wardens follow in 1960

1959 The M1, Britain's first full-length motorway, opens

▼ **1959** The 'Mini' hits the streets

1960 First motorway services open at Newport Pagnell

1960s MFI pioneers flat-pack furniture

1960s Dr Beeching closes 5000 miles of Britain's railways and 2000 stations

▷ **1961** Guildford Cathedral is built, the first in the post-war years

1964 The Bull Ring, the largest shopping precinct outside America, opens in Birmingham

1964 Terence Conran opens a Habitat store on Fulham Road, London

1967 First colour television broadcast, on BBC2 – tennis at Wimbledon

1969 Open University founded

1972 Victorian Oliver's Wharf building in Wapping, London, is coverted into warehouse flats

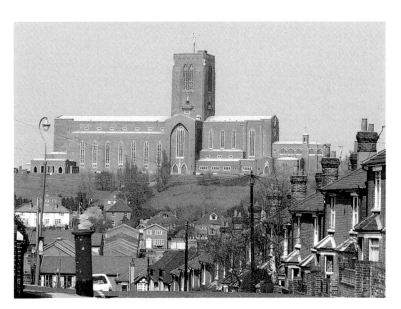

▼ **1976** Two Concordes take off simultaneously from Paris and London on maiden commercial flights

1978 Louise Brown is the first test-tube baby

1980 Newcastle's Metro opens, Britain's first metro outside London

1985 Opening of The Point, in Milton Keynes – Britain's first multiplex cinema

1987 IKEA opens its first store in Warrington, Lancashire

1991 First wind farm in Britain opens at Delabole in Cornwall

1992 Speed cameras appear

1996 Duchess of Northumberland begins to transform derelict land at Alnwick Castle into the grandest post-war garden

1999 Work begins on the Greenwich Millennium Village, one of Europe's largest urban regeneration projects

2000 Countryside and Rights of Way Act grants the right to roam in the open countryside of Britain

2002 Loch Lomond and the Trossachs becomes the first National Park in Scotland

2003 Village of Cwm Brefi in mid Wales becomes the last place in Britain to be connected to the National Grid

2005 New Forest becomes Britain's 14th National Park to open

CHANGES TO EVERYDAY LIFE

1950   1960   1970   1980   1990   2000   2010   **15**

GETTING STARTED

How do you start uncovering the story of where you live? What are the best lines of enquiry to follow, and places to turn to for finding out what you want to know? This section will help you to set out your goals, draw up a step-by-step plan of action, find the best sources of information, and gather together and present your discoveries.

The first steps

Start by asking some questions, and try to decide whether your main interest is in your community, your home and the buildings around it or your local landscape.

Why am I interested? You may just be curious about the history of where you live. Perhaps you would like to know more about an area you have just moved to. Or you may have decided to trace your family's involvement in the shaping of your community.

What exactly do I want to know? Decide where your main interest lies. Is it in people, events, buildings or the origins of a place and how it has changed over time?

How much time can I put into the project? You might even end up writing a full-blown history of your area, village or city, but it is best to start with more limited aims and see where your research takes you.

What do I know already? Write down what you already know, listing any areas of interest that arise.

Looking close to home

Before launching into a wide-ranging enquiry, first explore what is nearest to hand. A trip to your local record office (see pages 18-19) should start to satisfy your curiosity.

Who lived in your home before you? Local archives will hold the answer or you may have a copy of the deeds.

How has your neighbourhood changed? Ask when a new estate was built, or when a factory or mine closed.

What are the main features of your landscape? Do you know the history of any nearby woods or fields? Comparing what is on an old Ordnance Survey (OS), tithe, enclosure or estate map (see pages 26-27) with the details on a modern OS one may tell you a great deal.

What tales do the locals have to tell? Ask others what they know about the area you live in. Start with your own family and neighbours, but be sceptical of romantic stories about the past. It could be a good idea to take a walk around the local streets first, noting down any features that you might want to ask questions about.

What might old pictures reveal? Look at old drawings, paintings and photographs (see pages 212-213). Ask when they were made and by whom. Can any of the people or places shown be identified? Take your own photograph of the same sites for comparison – ask what has vanished, what remains and what is totally new.

Keeping records

A systematic approach will save time and help you get the most from your research.

- Keep a series of different-coloured notebooks, one for each topic. Then regularly transfer information that you gather into larger files or a computer database.
- Your files or database should be flexible enough to include drawings and photographs.
- Keep a large-scale map of the area you are researching, to refer to and to scribble notes on.
- Make a full record of where you find your information. If it is from a book, write down the page number, title, author and publisher. If it is from a document, note its reference number and which archive it is kept in.
- Also note any documents that you have searched and found of no use. You do not want to go back to them by mistake.

LOCAL ARCHIVES

One of the most exciting parts of revealing the story of where you live will be discovering and reading original documents. The ones that are likely to be the most useful will be found in local archives: at your local reference library, or your city or county record office.

Getting to know your local resources

Documents relating to the key changes and events in the development of your area will be held in local archives. Make them your first port of call when you are researching the story of where you live.

Local reference libraries Many reference libraries have a local studies section, where copies of records such as census returns, registers of voters, old maps and photographs, as well as books and publications about the surrounding area, are kept. Their contact details will be in your phone directory or on your local council website.

English and Welsh record offices All counties and most large cities and metropolitan districts in England and Wales have offices where civic records, such as registers of births, marriages and deaths, are stored along with other documents relating to the area they cover. Addresses, phone numbers and websites are given in the DIRECTORY (pages 332-339) under city or county name.

Scottish record offices Local archive offices in Scotland generally cover larger areas than those in England and Wales. Also Scottish national archives (see page 21) hold more local documents than is the case in English and Welsh national archives. Contact details are in the DIRECTORY under city or region.

Internet service On-line links to local record offices and other useful archives throughout Britain can be found on **www.genuki.org.uk/big**

What you can expect to find

Every city and county record office's archives hold collections of local records that cannot be seen anywhere else, as well as copies of important national records that relate to your district. Some offices produce booklets stating what is in their archives, or list such information on their website. The following is a list of what you are likely to find.

- Parish registers (see page 227) are held in all local record offices. Some offices also keep the archives of ancient dioceses, which include wills and probate inventories (see pages 324-325).
- Civic records, which include registrations of marriages, births and deaths in the area.
- Census returns (see pages 218-219) and the registers of those eligible to vote (see page 222).
- School and workhouse records (see pages 234-235 and page 227).
- Property records, which include deeds and planning applications.
- Papers that relate to court cases and disputes.
- Local council records, which include local tax and business registration documents.
- Manorial and estate documents (see page 322 and pages 318-319). Maps may be attached to many of these.
- Old maps, photographs and newspapers (see pages 214-215, 212-213 and 216)
- Collections of private letters and other personal documents are sometimes found in local archives.

Record office websites You may be able to check the indexes of your local record office on-line before paying a visit. Some also allow access to detailed catalogues and images of original documents.

Using a microfiche reader

Looking in the indexes

Your first visit

Most record offices provide clear instructions on how to search for documents, and experienced staff will always be on hand to assist you.

Before you go

It will help you to make the most of your visit if you do a little groundwork before you go.

- Ring to check opening hours and to enquire about procedures, such as how to order documents, how long you may have to wait for them and whether they can be pre-ordered by phone. Ask if you need to book a microfiche reader (see above) or a computer terminal. Heavily used documents, such as census returns and parish registers, and those that are fragile, may only be available on microfilm or on-line.
- Bring a notebook and pencil (pens are not allowed). A laptop computer can sometimes be used, but check first.
- You will be issued with a reader's ticket, for which some means of identification, such as a driving licence, will be required. Some record offices will also ask you for a passport-size photograph.
- Arrive armed with any information you have already gathered and with any questions you hope to answer.

At the archives

Record centres house a wealth of documents, so you should enjoy a fruitful visit, particularly if you come armed with some of the advice given below.

- Be aware that coats and bags will have to be left in the cloakroom. Lockers are usually provided for valuables.
- Even if you think you know precisely which documents you wish to see, and have pre-ordered them, take some time to familiarise yourself with the index and catalogue files. It is likely that your local archive can fill in far more of the story of where you live than you thought.

- Start with the place-name indexes. These are a good place to search for documents on your community.
- Most record offices ask you to sign a different order slip for each document and allow you to request up to three at a time. Documents will be issued one by one and you will have to sign a receipt and return the document to the counter when you have finished with it. This is to limit the risk of irreplaceable documents going astray.
- Always note the reference number on any document you are given. You might want to see it again later.
- You can usually buy photocopies of documents and print-outs of microfiche or computer records. Do not spend time deciphering unfamiliar handwriting (see pages 22-23) when you can study it at leisure later.

MUSEUMS AND HERITAGE CENTRES

Documents, such as trade and property records, and artefacts and machinery relating to the history of your area, may also be found in local museums and heritage centres. Admission to any run by the local authority is usually free, but if you wish to search through private archives, such as those of a large country estate like Chatsworth in Derbyshire, you may be charged a small fee. Keep an eye open for courses or special events that museums might run, and remember that you may have to give advance notice if you wish to view material not generally kept on display.

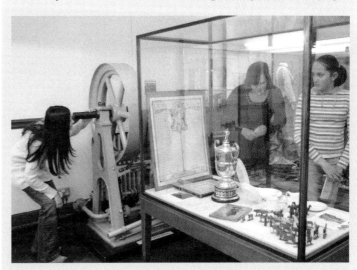

NATIONAL ARCHIVES

A visit to one of the national archives, of which Britain has some of the finest in the world, should help complete the story of your area. Records go back as far as the early Middle Ages: no other country has anything comparable with the 1086 Domesday Book.

England and Wales

Joint rule of the two nations goes back to the 13th century and most records of their shared history are held together.

The National Archives

The National Archives in Kew is the official record office for England and Wales (government records for the whole UK are also housed here). The name was adopted in 2003, upon the merger of the former Public Record Office (PRO) and the Historical Manuscripts Commission.

What it holds Among the thousands of documents, including Magna Carta and Shakespeare's will, there are many that should prove useful to a local historian.

- Lists of taxpayers range from those who paid poll tax in 1377-81 to those who were taxed on their hearths in Charles II's reign (see page 219).
- National census records (see pages 218-219) for 1871, 1881, 1891 and 1901 are available.
- Legal documents include wills and probate inventories (see pages 324-325) and records of cases judged in the Courts of Chancery, Exchequer, Requests and Star Chamber (see page 331).
- Medieval records contain information about charters, local markets, deer parks and licences to fortify houses.
- Tithe awards and maps (see pages 26-27 and 215), Valuation Office surveys (see page 130), and the National Farm Survey of 1941-3 (see page 130) are among the many property documents.

Using the archives The reception desk staff will offer guidance and answer any questions. Leaflets are also available on the main classes of records that are held.

- There is no need to book and entry is free, but proof of identity is required to obtain a reader's card. This must be shown on every visit and is valid for three years.
- Many indexes of the collections are available on-line (see 'Practical information', opposite, for website). It may be useful to search through them before your visit.
- Up to three documents can be ordered in advance to be ready for viewing by phoning 020 8392 5200. The website will help you search for their reference codes. There are charges for photocopying.

The National Library of Wales

The archives kept at the National Library of Wales hold many valuable collections, ranging from manuscripts and maps to photographs, sound recordings and films. Here you will find many parish registers, all the diocesan records for Wales, pre-1858 wills, a full set of Welsh census returns (1841-1901), along with copies of old newspapers, maps and business records and directories. Proof of identity is needed to obtain a reader's ticket. The Library's website (see 'Practical information', opposite) includes a full on-line catalogue.

On arrival at the National Archives, you will need to obtain a reader's ticket

NEW READERS   RECEPTION

Background material Most of the archives not only provide extensive research services; they also publish a range of leaflets and books relating to the various records in their collections. Details are often given on the websites (see 'Practical information', below) and it may be useful to order and read some of them before your visit.

Scotland

Despite sharing a monarch with England since 1603 and the formal union of the two parliaments in 1707, Scotland has always maintained separate records of its distinctive history.

The National Archives of Scotland

The records at the National Archives of Scotland in Edinburgh (formerly known as the Scottish Record Office) date from the 12th century up to the present day.

• Details of documents held are given on the Archives' website (see 'Practical information', below). They include local authority and court records, registers of sasines (land transactions) and property deeds, as well as private and business papers.

• Contact the Archives before you visit to check the availability of documents you wish to consult. Some are not stored in the main building, and you may have to give several days' notice in order to view them.

• A number of records are not held in Edinburgh, but in the locality they relate to, often with local authorities or in universities and colleges. For information about such documents and where they can be seen, consult the Archives' website.

• Access to the Archives is free, but there is a charge for any documents that you wish to photocopy.

• A list of all private Scottish archives – the National Register of Archives for Scotland – is available on-site for reference. It details records held by individuals, landed estates, businesses, libraries, colleges and clubs.

General Register Office for Scotland

Parish and civil records of births, marriages and deaths, and census returns, are kept at the General Register Office for Scotland. Visits must be booked in advance and there is a search fee (see 'Practical information', right).

National Library of Scotland

Scotland's largest reference library houses an extensive collection of books, early manuscripts and maps (housed in a separate building). Details of how to obtain a reader's ticket are on the website (see right).

Family Records Centre

Although mainly of use to family historians, many of the documents held at the Family Records Centre are relevant to local history research. The archives include census returns for England and Wales (1841-1901), the records of births, marriages and deaths in England and Wales since 1837, indexes of adoptions in England and Wales since 1927, and registers of wills and death duties. An on-line link to the archives of the General Register Office for Scotland provides access to Scottish records, including census returns, registers of births, marriages and deaths, and parish records dating back to the 16th century. The General Register Office for Scotland aims to open a Family Records Centre by the end of 2006.

PRACTICAL INFORMATION

• **The National Archives**, Ruskin Avenue, Kew, Surrey TW9 4DU, Tel. 020 8876 3444. www.nationalarchives.gov.uk

• **The National Library of Wales**, Penglais, Aberystwyth, Ceredigion SY23 3BU, Tel. 01970 632 800. www.llgc.org.uk

• **The National Archives of Scotland**, Historical Research Room, HM General Register House, 2 Princes Street, Edinburgh EH1 3YY, Tel. 0131 535 1334; and at West Register House, Charlotte Square, Edinburgh EH2 4DJ, Tel. 0131 535 1413. www.nas.gov.uk

• **General Register Office for Scotland**, New Register House, 3 West Register Street, Edinburgh EH1 4YT, Tel. 0131 314 4433. www.gro-scotland.gov.uk

• **The National Library of Scotland**, George IV Bridge, Edinburgh EH1 1EW, Tel. 0131 623 3700. www.nls.uk

• **Family Records Centre**, 1 Myddelton Street, London EC1R 1UW, Tel. 020 8392 5300. www.familyrecords.gov.uk/frc

OLD DOCUMENTS

Reading tax, legal and business documents, old letters and other texts could be part of your research. Whether the material has been printed or handwritten, you may need some help, as well as a little patience and practice, to decipher unfamiliar scripts.

Reading old text

When you delve into the archives for useful documents on your area or home, you may find you have some difficulty in understanding what you find. A few guidelines will help you on your way.

- Start with material written in the last 200 years and work backwards in time. You should be able to read most late-18th and 19th-century text quite easily, as modern 'copperplate' handwriting came into general use around 250 years ago.
- Another reason for not starting with early documents is that many were written in Latin. Except for the short period 1651-60, Latin was the language used for legal material, including manor court rolls (see page 322), up to 1733. An imperfect form known as dog Latin was often used in other documents, such as parish registers.
- Some spellings, even from as late as the 19th century, will surprise you. Once you get back to the 17th and 16th centuries, you will find that people generally spelt words as they sounded, with no regard for consistency.
- It helps to know the typical phrases that were used, so that you can anticipate what the document should be saying. For example, a will normally begins: 'In the name of God, Amen ...' and if the person who made it declares that he is 'seke in body but foole in mynd' this should be read as 'sick in body but full in mind'.
- Documents often include technical words, such as 'burgage' or 'appurtenances'. Inventories attached to wills (see pages 324-325) use many obsolete dialect words. You will need a specialist dictionary or glossary (see 'Find out more', opposite) to decipher these.

Interpreting a document

Do not think that because something is written down, it is an established fact. No single document can tell you the full story. It is just one version of what happened. Look at it critically, and compare it with related material.

- Enquire who wrote a particular document, when and why. You might not find precise answers, but posing the questions will put you in the proper frame of mind. Documents were not written for historians but for some immediate purpose, usually administrative or legal.

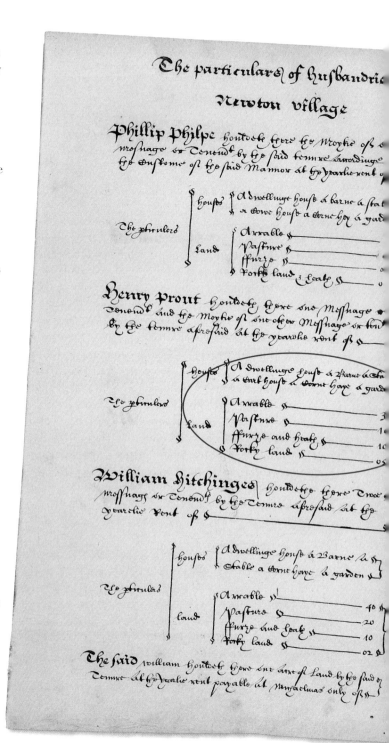

DECIPHERING SCRIPTS

When you first see a handwritten document from the Tudor and Stuart period (1485-1714), you may think that you will never be able to read it. Buy one of the packs on handwriting from different eras, which are usually on sale at your record office, and have relevant examples alongside you when going through your own document.

You will need to recognise the ways in which scribes tended to abbreviate words. A 'p' with a stroke through its stem was a common way of shortening 'par' (as in 'parish') or 'per' (as in 'person'). A wiggle over a letter 'm' signifies 'mm'. 'The' was generally shortened to 'ye', and apostrophes were widely used to indicate where letters had been missed out.

Some letters are harder than others to recognise, as they differ greatly from the way we write them today, or they have more than one commonly used form (see below). Capital letters are usually more difficult to decipher, as writers frequently used different styles, even in the same document.

's' at the beginning and in the middle of words usually looks like an 'f' without the crossbar.

A final 's' often looks like a number '6', leaning to the right.

'r' sometimes looks like a modern 'w', but can also be similar to an 'e' or even a 'z'.

'c' is generally written like a modern 'r'.

- You also need to analyse the information in a systematic way. A hearth tax return (see page 219) from the 1660s or 70s will list the householders and record the number of hearths on which they were taxed. From this, you can get a good idea of the social structure of a parish or township, based on the large numbers who paid for only one or two hearths, tapering upwards to richer families in larger houses with 20 or more. You might even be able to identify surviving houses and distinctive surnames. If you do this for the surrounding villages as well, you will see whether your community was different or typical.

- Some documents will be exciting finds, but most will merely add a little more to what you already know. Link the information from your document to what you have found in other sources. The people named in a tithe award (see pages 27 and 215) might also appear in a census return (see pages 218-219) or trade directory (see page 217). In this way, you will build up a broader picture of how your community grew and changed over time.

Working the manor In 1618, the rents paid by the tenants of the manor of Manorbier and Penally in Pembrokeshire were recorded (left). The resulting document not only tells us the names of the farmers and what they paid, it also gives us an idea of the property they held. Apparently one tenant, 'Henry Prout', rented 'A dwelling house, a barn, a stable, a cart house, a corn haye (a kind of enclosure) and a garden', along with 30 acres of arable land, 10 acres each of pasture and heathland (covered with 'furze', or gorse) and 5 acres of rocky land (see inset, above).

Letters of the law
The various styles of lettering that made up the Court-hand alphabet (above) will be seen in 16th and 17th-century legal documents. Be aware that handwriting could be just as individual as it is today.

FIND OUT MORE

- *Reading Tudor and Stuart Handwriting* (L. Munby, S. Hobbs and A. Crosby, British Association for Local History, 2nd ed., 2002)
- *The Handwriting of English Documents* (L.C. Hector, Kohler and Coombes, 1988)
- *Oxford Dictionary of English* (eds. C. Soanes and A. Stevenson, Oxford University Press, 2002) Includes definitions of many now obsolete words.
- http://yourhandwriting.ca/writing/oldhandwriting Gives numerous links to useful websites offering assistance, with examples, on the reading of old documents.

THE INTERNET

Computers have made it much easier to research into local history. Useful websites are mentioned throughout this book and you can track down many more with a search engine. There are also some key sites that will provide you with helpful links and general advice.

General links

There are several websites that you are likely to refer to again and again when tracking down the details of the story of where you live.

- Links to the websites of most organisations involved in local history research in Britain can be found on **www.balh.co.uk** the British Association for Local History's site. Also, a visit to **www.humbul.ac.uk/topics/localhistory.html** will give you similar links, plus details of research projects, and access to an on-line course in reading and understanding old documents.
- Although mainly aimed at family historians, Genuki at **www.genuki.org.uk** is another excellent place to look for links to local history material. It has a page for every county in the British Isles, as well as pages on many individual towns and parishes.
- A good site for links to information on specific topics of history is **www.history.uk.com**

Record offices and libraries

The most useful archives for researching the history of a specific area are usually found at local record offices and libraries (see pages 18-19). Most have websites giving details of what they hold (see DIRECTORY, under the relevant city or county name, for contact details). You will also find links to such websites on the Genuki site (see above).

- At **www.archon.nationalarchives.gov.uk/archon** you can view the ARCHON Directory, a definitive list of local archives. It gives opening times and contact details for every repository of records in the British Isles.
- The A2A database at **www.a2a.org.uk** catalogues material held at English record offices, libraries, museums and heritage centres, while the Scottish Archive Network at **www.scan.org.uk** does the same for Scotland.

- Many public libraries in Britain have a local studies reference section. You should be able to find out about any of these and what they hold from your local authority's website, which can be accessed via links on **www.direct.gov.uk/quickfind/localcouncils/fs/en** Familia at **www.familia.org.uk** also lists public library records that are likely to interest local historians and genealogists.

On-line research

The volume of original material that you can view on the internet grows rapidly. You can find out what is available on your area by logging on to **www.enrichuk.org.uk** and selecting the Browse option, then the Geographic option.

Documents

Many archives and research institutes now publish some of their records on-line.

- Census returns (see pages 218-219) are one of the most useful research tools for the local historian. Some for England and Wales are available on **www.nationalarchives.gov.uk/census** and sets for Scotland for 1881, 1891 and 1901 can be seen on **www.scotlandspeople.gov.uk** Note that not all census sites offer an address search, which makes looking for a specific street or house difficult.
- For the present day, the Office for National Statistics has data from the 2001 census on its Neighbourhood Statistics website at **www.neighbourhoodstatistics.gov.uk**
- One of the most important local history publications is the *Victoria County History*, a project that aims to compile a detailed account of every county in England throughout history. Volumes are available in some libraries, and there is a project to create an on-line edition. See the website at **www.englandpast.net** for details.
- Another major project, covering the whole of England and Wales, is the Digital Library of Historical

Directories at **www.historicaldirectories.org** which offers access to a selection of trade directories for 1750-1919.

- In Scotland the Statistical Accounts provide summaries at a parish level of life in the 1790s and 1830s. They can be viewed on **www.edina.ac.uk**
- Many individuals, history societies, heritage centres and universities now place the results of any research they carry out on the internet. Genuki (see above) is one of the best places to find links to these documents.

Pictures

The internet is full of sites displaying photographs, paintings and prints of Britain's towns and villages that help reveal how they have changed over time.

- Many local record offices and libraries have large collections, some of which can be viewed on-line (see 'Record offices and libraries', opposite, for details of websites).
- At **viewfinder.english-heritage.org.uk** English Heritage has assembled a large collection of photographs relating to local history in England, including pictures of buildings, industrial sites and community and social events from the 1840s onwards.
- One of the largest digital image collections is of works of art from the Guildhall Library's gallery and print room. More than 20,000 pictures, mainly engravings and paintings of London streets and buildings, can be seen by logging on to **collage.cityoflondon.gov.uk**
- Two useful sites for picture postcards are the Francis Frith Collection at **www.francisfrith.com/uk** and PastPix at **www.pastpix.com** Both are designed to sell prints of old photographs, but small scans are available free.
- There are also several websites of modern photographs of old buildings. The largest of these is the Images of England site at **www.imagesofengland.org.uk** run by the

National Monuments Register. It aims eventually to include a photograph of every listed building in Britain.

- The search engine Google also has an excellent facility for locating on-line photographs and pictures at **images.google.com**

Maps and plans

Tracing and viewing old maps on the internet can save a great deal of time, although in many cases digitised maps lack the clarity of the originals or of printed copies.

- The British Cartographic Society has a comprehensive on-line directory of British map collections at **www.cartography.org.uk/Pages/Publicat/Ukdir**
- Some of the best old maps are available on **www.old-maps.co.uk** which offers high-resolution scans of 6-inch Ordnance Survey (OS) maps (see page 26), from around 1870.
- The National Library of Scotland (see page 21) has an outstanding series of town plans in its on-line map collection at **www.nls.uk/digitallibrary/map/townplans** giving a high level of detail for 62 towns. It is also worth checking city and county record office sites (see above) for maps held in their archives.

Local history societies

There are countless local groups around Britain devoted to the study of their area and many have websites. A list giving full contact details is provided by *Local History Magazine* at **www.local-history.co.uk/groups**

If you want to get in touch with those who share your interests, there is bound to be a mailing list or on-line discussion group that covers the locality you are interested in. You will find links to a large number of these at **www.genuki.org.uk/indexes/MailingLists.html**

MAPS AND PLANS

By taking two maps of your area that were drawn at different points in history and comparing them, you will get an almost instant overview of how where you live changed during the gap in time that separates them.

Ordnance Survey maps

A modern Ordnance Survey (OS) map of your local area and the countryside and other settlements around it will place where you live in the context of its landscape. It should also help you to work out what it is you want to know about, such as street patterns, the relative size of communities, or what remains of past industries.

How to find OS maps The Ordnance Survey's website at **www.ordnancesurvey.co.uk/oswebsite/getamap** enables you to find and view a map from the current Landranger and Explorer series (see right) on-line. You can search by place name, postcode or OS grid reference. You can also buy a map from the on-line OS map shop.

Old OS maps The Ordnance Survey, Britain's national mapping agency, was founded in 1791 to map the south coast of England for defence planning. At the beginning of the 19th century, it turned its attention to general mapping, producing a series of 1-inch-to-1-mile maps – now known as the Old Series – that covered the whole of Britain. This was gradually replaced, from the early 1850s onwards, by the New Series of 6-inch-to-1-mile and 25-inch-to-1 mile maps, which was completed in 1897. In the meantime, extra information, such as new streets, factories and railway lines in areas not yet covered by the New Series, was added to fresh editions of the Old Series maps.

Walk with history Glancing at a copy of an early OS map as you walk your local streets may help to give you a sense of what it must have been like to live and work there just over 100 years ago.

Lie of the land The Ordnance Survey publishes nearly 700 up-to-date maps covering the whole of the British Isles. Choose from their two main series, depending on how much detail you require. A Landranger map, drawn to a scale of 1¼ inches to 1 mile (top, above), will help show how your community fits into the surrounding area. Then you can zoom in for a closer view using an Explorer map (bottom, above) drawn on a scale of 2½ inches to 1 mile.

How to find old OS maps The British Library holds the largest collection of OS maps in Britain (a catalogue of what is available is on **www.bl.uk/collections/map_os.html**). You can also order copies of all the Old Series and New Series maps on the Ordnance Survey website (see above). Other good facsimiles of these maps, some with a helpful commentary, include the Godfrey series (available from **www.alangodfrey.co.uk**) and around 90 of the post-1860, 1-inch Old Series maps, published by David & Charles. A large collection of 6-inch New Series maps for England, Wales and Scotland, dating from the 1850s to 1899, is available for viewing on **www.old-maps.co.uk**

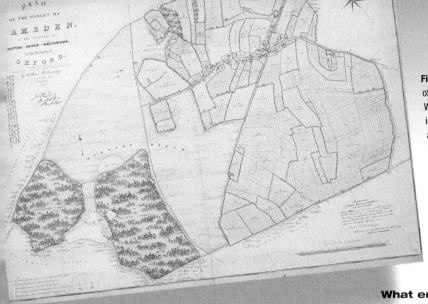

Fixing rents The tithe award for the hamlet of Ramsden in the parish of Shipton-under-Wychwood in Oxfordshire, drawn up in 1838, includes a map showing clearly how the land at the time was farmed. As well as numbering all the plots to correspond with the owners and tenants listed on the tithe award, some field names and crops are also noted.

Tithe maps

The Tithe Commutation Act of 1836 changed the ancient system of all parishioners paying a tithe – a tenth of their produce or income – to the Church into a cash payment or rent-charge. It involved the making of an award, which identified landowners, their tenants and the land they worked. By 1852, about 86 per cent of England and Wales had been surveyed and awards, with accompanying maps, had been made for 11,395 parishes or townships.

What tithe maps tell you Tithe maps, dating from the mid 19th century, are often the earliest detailed maps of many parts of Britain. The awards list that accompanies each map identifies the owners and occupiers of every piece of property in the parish. These properties were numbered and plotted on the map.

Where to find tithe maps Three copies of each award and its map were made. One was deposited in the parish chest and will now be in the archives of the local record office (see pages 18-19); a second went to the local bishop and should be in the archives of the ancient diocese, or in the case of Wales at the National Library in Aberystwyth (see pages 20-21); the third, central government, copy will be in the National Archives at Kew (see pages 20-21).

Enclosure maps

Many English and Welsh parishes have a map attached to a parliamentary enclosure award, most of which date from 1750 to 1850 (see pages 62-63). But some places had enclosed their fields and commons at a much earlier date. A private Act of Parliament was necessary where unanimity could not be reached, and the views of a minority were overruled. Altogether, 5341 awards were made for England and 229 for Wales. Most Scottish parishes were enclosed privately and few maps survive.

What enclosure maps tell you An enclosure map of a parish or township is likely to be the earliest one available of that particular place. Some, mainly those of upland districts, where only the parish commons and wastes were enclosed, do not include farmland. But those for areas where an open-field system (see page 146) was in use will give the owners and tenants of every piece of property.

Where to find enclosure maps Enclosure awards and their maps are kept in local record offices and reference libraries (see pages 18-19) and at the National Archives at Kew (see pages 20-21).

Estate and county maps

From the late 16th century, written surveys of manors or estates were often accompanied by a map, or 'platt'. The first, rather sketchy, county maps were being drawn up at around the same time, but it was not until the second half of the 18th century that a set of accurate 1-inch-to-1-mile scale maps of the English and Welsh counties was commissioned by the Royal Society of Arts.

What estate maps tell you You will discover how land was divided up and worked, as well as who owned and farmed it from an estate map.

Where to find estate maps The archives of national and local records offices, libraries, museums and heritage centres (see pages 18-19, 20-21) will include estate maps. Most date from the 18th or 19th century, but a few earlier ones survive: the National Archives (see page 20) holds around 60 pre-1603 maps for the Duchy of Lancaster.

What county maps tell you A sense of what the landscape was like before industrialisation can be gleaned from maps such as that of Staffordshire in 1775 (left).

Where to find county maps County record offices and reference libraries (see pages 18-19) hold copies. Some can also be viewed at the British Library (see DIRECTORY).

UNDERSTANDING PLACE NAMES

Every place has a distinctive name that tells you something about its past, whether it describes the landscape, a local industry, an ancient settlement or a feature, such as the Yarnbury Castle hill-fort in Wiltshire (above). Place names are perhaps the most telling records of Britain's history – Celts, Romans, Anglo-Saxons, Vikings and Normans have all left a mark on our maps. They tell a story of invasion, settlement, industrialisation and urbanisation – a story that continues right up to the present day.

Ancient names from the landscape Rivers were vitally important in the life of prehistoric settlers, and some of their names, thought to date back over 3000 years to pre-Celtic times, can still be found. Many simply mean 'river' or 'water', but the name of the River Dove (left), which runs through Staffordshire, Derbyshire and Yorkshire, means 'black', referring to the colour of the water.

The oldest place names were probably influenced by the Celts, the Iron Age people living in these isles two thousand years ago. They spoke two dialects: British, which later became Welsh and Cornish, and is thought to have included a variant spoken by the Picts (see opposite); and Gaelic (spoken in Ireland, north and west Scotland and the Isle of Man). With the arrival of the Anglo-Saxons and Vikings, the Celts in England for the most part stayed and learnt the languages of their conquerors. By contrast, in the extreme west around Cornwall, and in Wales and Scotland, Celtic languages continued to be spoken for centuries.

Many Celtic place-name elements bear a resemblance to Cornish and modern Welsh words, evidence of their linguistic links. For example, the Celtic word *penno*, meaning 'top', 'hill' or 'headland', is represented in both the Welsh and Cornish word *pen*. Examples are Penrith ('hill ford') in Cumbria, Pendleton ('farmstead by the hill') in Lancashire, Penzance ('holy headland') in Cornwall and Penarth ('top of the headland') in Wales.

CELTIC NAMES

The Celts were the native British people when the Roman conquered in AD 43-83. Celtic place names mainly describe landscape features such as hills and rivers, but there are also Celtic names for inhabited sites. Today, only a small proportion of Britain's place names have obvious Celtic roots, because many of the original names were replaced by the Anglo-Saxons.

Barr 'hilltop'. Examples include Great Barr, Staffordshire, and Barry ('place of the hill') in the Vale of Glamorgan.

Ced 'wood', as in Culgaith in Cumbria, and Culcheth in Lancashire (both 'narrow wood'), and Lytchett ('grey wood') in Dorset.

Creig 'rock' or 'cliff'. Examples include Creake in Norfolk, and Crayke in Yorkshire.

Crug 'hill', 'ridge' or 'barrow'. Variants are Creech in Dorset, Crich in Derbyshire, and Crick in Northamptonshire.

Eccles, from the word 'egles', meaning 'church'. Examples include Eccles in Lancashire, Ecclesfield in Yorkshire, and Eccleshall in Staffordshire.

Penno (see page 28, opposite).

Ross 'hill', 'moor', 'heathy upland'. Examples are Ross in Northumberland, Rossett ('place by the hill') near Wrexham, and Rossington ('farmstead at the moor') in Yorkshire.

GAELIC NAMES

Many Scottish place names have Gaelic roots. Gaelic originated in Ireland and came to southwest Scotland in the 5th century AD with the Irish *Dál Riata* tribe, who the Romans called *Scotti*. Viking invasions later encouraged the Gaels to move east, where they supplanted the Picts.

Baile 'farm' or 'homestead', as in Ballindalloch ('meadow homestead') in Moray, and Balerno ('sloe-tree homestead') near Edinburgh.

Beinn 'mountain'. Examples are Ben Nevis ('mountain by the River Nevis'), and Benbecula ('hill of the fords') in the Western Isles.

Cill 'church', as in Kilmarnock ('church of my little Ernon') in Ayrshire, and West and East Kilbride ('church of St Brigid') in Lanarkshire.

Dun 'fortress', as in Dundee ('fort of Daigh'), and Dunkeld ('fort of the Caledonians') near Perth.

Drum 'ridge', as in Drummond ('ridge') and Drumnadrochit ('ridge of the bridge'), both in the Highlands.

Gleann 'valley', as in Glencoe ('valley of the River Coe') in Argyll.

Inbhir 'river mouth', as in Inveraray ('mouth of the River Aray') in Argyll, and Inverness ('mouth of the River Ness').

PICTISH NAMES

Little is known about the Picts, who occupied the northeast provinces of Angus, Atholl, Fife, Strathearn, Mar, Moray and Caithness until AD 844, when sovereignty of these territories was taken over by the *Dál Riata* Scots (see 'Gaelic Names', left). Place names in Scotland with a Pictish element date from the 3rd-9th centuries AD, although many have a second Gaelic element, which may have been added in the 9th and 10th centuries, when many of the people living in these areas would have spoken both languages.

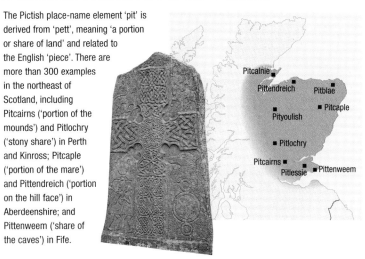

The Pictish place-name element 'pit' is derived from 'pett', meaning 'a portion or share of land' and related to the English 'piece'. There are more than 300 examples in the northeast of Scotland, including Pitcairns ('portion of the mounds') and Pitlochry ('stony share') in Perth and Kinross; Pitcaple ('portion of the mare') and Pittendreich ('portion on the hill face') in Aberdeenshire; and Pittenweem ('share of the caves') in Fife.

WELSH AND CORNISH NAMES

Welsh names can be found in English border counties such as Cheshire, Shropshire and Herefordshire, as well as in Wales. An example is Crewe, which means 'a ford' or 'stepping stones'. Nearly all Cornish place names have Celtic rather than Anglo-Saxon roots, because the English did not settle there until the 9th century.

WELSH

Aber 'mouth of a river', as in Aberdare ('mouth of the River Dar') in the Rhondda, and Abergavenny ('mouth of the River Gafenni') in Monmouthshire.

Caer 'fortress', as in Caernarfon ('fort in Arfin') in Gwynedd, and Cardiff ('fort on the river Taff').

Coed 'wood', as in Betws-y-coed ('chapel in the wood') in Conwy, and Coedpoeth ('burnt wood') in Wrexham.

Cwm 'valley', as in Cwmbrân ('valley of the River Bran') in Newport, and Cwmafan ('valley of the River Afan') in Neath.

Tre(f) 'farmstead', as in Trefeglwys ('farm by the church') in Powys and Tredegar ('Tegyr's farm') in Blaenau.

Llan 'churchyard', as in Llandudno ('church of St Tudno') in Conwy, and Llangollen ('church of St Collen') in Denbighshire.

Pen (see page 28, opposite)

Pont 'bridge', as in Pontypool ('bridge by the pool') in Torfaen, and Pontypridd ('bridge by the earthen house') in the Rhondda.

CORNISH

Pen (see page 28, opposite)

Porth 'harbour', as in Perranporth ('harbour of St Piran's parish') and Porthleven ('smooth harbour').

Tre 'hamlet' or 'farm', as in Tremaine ('hamlet of the stone') and Treneglos ('farm of the church').

The arrival of the 'English'

The Anglo-Saxons, whose language formed the basis of English, first came to Britain during the Roman occupation. But they did not put down roots until the 5th century AD – after rule by Rome had collapsed. As more of these migrants arrived, they gradually settled everywhere apart from Cornwall, Wales and most of Scotland, although you will spot some Anglo-Saxon place names, such as Hawick, Falkirk and Motherwell along Scotland's eastern border and in the Lothians.

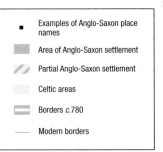

	Examples of Anglo-Saxon place names
	Area of Anglo-Saxon settlement
	Partial Anglo-Saxon settlement
	Celtic areas
	Borders c.780
	Modern borders

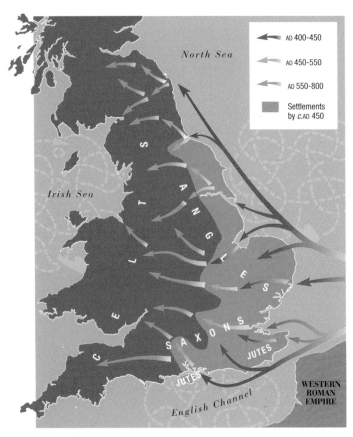

Anglo-Saxon migration Between AD 400 and 800, Britain was settled by various Germanic tribes. The Angles came from the Schleswig-Holstein peninsula, between modern-day Denmark and Germany, to settle in the east of England and what is now Northumberland, between the Humber and the Tees. Others came from farther south, from Saxony, settling first in southern England, then pushing across to the west.

THE FIRST ENGLISH NAMES

Most of the place names used in England today were coined by the Anglo-Saxons between the 5th and 11th centuries. Many include the name of a local lord. Alfreton in Derbyshire, for example, took its name from a man called Aelfhere, Brandeston in Suffolk from someone called Brant, and Menston in Yorkshire from a Mensa. But the majority of Anglo-Saxon place names describe landscape features such as hills, woods and valleys. Acton means 'a town set in oak woods' and 'Hooton', in the three south Yorkshire towns of Hooton Levitt, Hooton Pagnell and Hooton Roberts, means 'settlement on a spur of high ground'.

Ham 'homestead'. Examples include Amersham ('homestead of a man called Ealhmund') in Buckinghamshire, and Rotherham ('homestead on the River Rother') in Yorkshire.

Wic 'a Roman fort', from the Latin word *vicus*. Combined with 'ham' it means 'settlement alongside a Roman fort'. Examples include Wickham Market in Suffolk and Wykeham in Yorkshire.

Ing 'a group of people ruled by a tribal leader', from the Latin *ingas*. Examples of its use are Hastings ('Haest's people') in East Sussex, and Reading ('Reada's people') in Berkshire.

Ingham combines 'ingas' and 'ham' (see above), as in Birmingham ('estate of Beornmond's people') and Nottingham ('estate of Snot's people').

Barton 'outlying farm [where barley or corn is grown]' from the Old English *beretun*. Examples of its use include

Mulbarton ('outlying farm where milk is produced') in Norfolk, Surbiton ('south farm') in Surrey, and Steeple Barton ('steep farm') in Oxfordshire.

Brough, burgh and **bury** 'fortified site'. Examples include Brough in Derbyshire, Bury St Edmunds ('fortified site or town associated with St Edmond') in Suffolk, and Iron Age hill-fort sites such as Almondbury, near Huddersfield in Yorkshire, Battlesbury in Wiltshire, and Danebury in Hampshire.

Dun 'hill'. Examples include Clevedon ('hill of the cliffs') in Somerset, and Durham ('hill island' or 'promontory').

Field 'large area of open land in a wooded landscape'. Examples include Lichfield ('open land near Letocetum') in Staffordshire, and Wakefield ('open land where wakes are held') in Yorkshire.

Ford 'a ford'. Examples include Oxford ('ford used by oxen'), Stamford ('stony ford') in Lincolnshire, and Stratford ('ford on a Roman road') in East London and in Warwickshire.

Haigh and **hale** 'nook' or 'corner'. Examples include Edenhall ('nook of land by the River Eden') in Cumbria, and Haughton ('farmstead in or by a nook of land') in Shropshire and in Staffordshire.

Hurst 'wooded hill', as in Ewhurst ('yew-tree covered hill') in Hampshire, Chislehurst ('wooded hill with gravelly soil') in Kent, and Hurstwood ('wood on a hill') in Lancashire.

Ley 'woodland clearing'. It was often combined with someone's name as in Barnsley ('Beorn's woodland clearing'), Yorkshire, and Brackley ('Bracca's

ROMAN NAMES

In AD 43, four Roman legions and 20,000 auxiliaries landed on the Kent coast and defeated local British tribes in a series of skirmishes. It took more than 40 years for the Romans to establish their rule, and even then rebellious tribes in the north and west continued to put up strong resistance until the Romans left in the early 5th century. Somewhat surprisingly, this long occupation left little trace on English place names, as most Roman names were later replaced. The fact that the Celtic language survived throughout the occupation and for quite some time afterwards may also help explain this scarcity.

Evidence of a few Roman place names and settlements does remain. Some developed a more modern form, for example Lindum gradually became Lincoln and Isca became Exeter. The element 'caster', 'cester' or 'chester' in a name indicates the site of a Roman fort, as in Doncaster ('Roman fort on the River Don') and Chichester ('Cissa's Roman camp'). Also the Latin *portus*, meaning 'a port', finds its way into Anglo-Saxon names, such as Portsmouth.

North Sea

Irish Sea

English Channel

- Falkirk
- Prestwick
- Hawick
- Durham
- Edenhall
- Wykeham
- Skipton
- Menston
- Hurstwood
- Wakefield
- Whitley
- Almondsbury
- Barnsley
- Pilley
- Warmsworth
- Rotherham
- Hale
- Hale
- Brough
- Burton
- Staveley
- Wensley
- Cumberworth
- Mansfield
- Alfreton
- Nottingham
- Carlton
- Hale
- Dunton
- Haughton
- Lichfield
- Mulbarton
- Stamford
- Gillingham
- Wednesbury
- Nuneaton
- Breedon on the Hill
- Birmingham
- Bury St Edmunds
- Brandeston
- Stratford upon Avon
- Ashley
- Wickham Market
- Brackley
- Oakley
- Dunton
- Bletchley
- Steeple Barton
- The Rodings
- Oxford
- Clevedon
- Denchworth
- Rockley
- Amersham
- Finchley
- West Ham
- East Ham
- Reading
- Acton
- Whitley
- Surbiton
- Woking
- Chislehurst
- Battlesbury
- Burton
- Danebury
- Ewhurst
- Crawley
- Gillingham
- Stratford Tony
- Hastings
- Burton

STRATHCLYDE
NORTHUMBRIA
WALES
MERCIA
EAST ANGLIA
ESSEX
WESSEX
KENT
SUSSEX
WEST WALES

'Hill, hill on the hill' The way in which language gradually passes out of living memory is evident in the example of Breedon on the Hill in Leicestershire (above), where the church that succeeded an Anglo-Saxon monastery stands on the site of an Iron Age fort. The first part of the name, 'bree', is Celtic for 'hill'; the second part is a form of the Anglo-Saxon word 'dun', also 'hill'. The 'on the hill' must have been tagged on at the end when the meaning of 'dun' had also been forgotten.

The naming of England The Angles, who colonised the area now known as East Anglia, gave their name to their new homeland – England. They included the north-folk of Norfolk and the south-folk of Suffolk. Wessex was the territory of the west Saxons, Sussex the home of the south Saxons and Essex that of the east Saxons. Middlesex lay in between.

woodland clearing'), Northamptonshire. Sometimes the term is linked with the name of something found in the clearing, such as a type of tree, bird or implement. Examples of this usage are numerous and include Ashley ('clearing in an ash wood') in Cambridgeshire, Crawley ('woodland clearing where

crows live') in West Sussex, Finchley ('woodland clearing where finches live') in north London, Pilley in Yorkshire and Staveley in Derbyshire (both 'woodland clearing where poles or staves are found'), and Whitley ('clearing with trees that have white bark or blossom'), near Reading in Berkshire.

Ton or **tone** 'enclosure', 'village' or 'farmstead'. Examples of its use include Carlton ('village of the freemen') in Nottinghamshire, Nuneaton ('the nuns' farm on the river') in Warwickshire, and Skipton ('sheep farm') in Yorkshire.
Worth also 'enclosure' or 'farmstead'. It was frequently combined with a

personal name. Examples of this include Aldsworth ('enclosure of a man called Ald') in Gloucestershire, Denchworth ('enclosure of a man called Denic') in Oxfordshire, and Warmsworth ('enclosure of a man called Waermund') in Yorkshire. In southwest England, such place names often end in **-worthy**.

Raiders from the north

An attack in AD 793 by marauding Vikings on the monastery at Lindisfarne in Northumbria heralded a new era of conquest from across the North Sea. The Vikings were ruthless killers, but they were also farmers and traders who were keen to settle and make good use of the land they had seized. They were to dominate north England and parts of Scotland for nearly 300 years, but the Scandinavian place names they introduced have endured for far longer.

THE LEGACY OF VIKING SETTLERS

The Vikings left behind many traces of their occupation in the areas where they settled: Danes in north and east England, Norsemen in north and northwest Scotland and along the Welsh coast. Fragments of the various Scandinavian languages and dialects crop up frequently in place names in these areas. Many describe natural features in the landscape, such as 'beck', 'dale', 'fell' and 'foss' (see 'Did you know?', right), but, as a testimony to Viking agricultural expertise, there is also a generous scattering of terms relating to farms and farming. Some of the most common are 'ing' meaning 'meadow', 'garth' meaning 'a grassy enclosure' and 'laithe' meaning 'barn'.

H	The Five Boroughs of Danelaw
■	Examples of Scandinavian place names
	Area of Norse settlement
	Area of Danish settlement
	Ancient borders
	Border of Danelaw
	Modern borders

DID YOU KNOW?

You are probably more familiar with Viking words than you think. They can be spotted in the names of numerous sites and landscape features across Britain:

Fell 'mountain', as used in the name of the Yorkshire peak, Fountains Fell.

Dale (from *dalr* or *dael*) 'valley', as used in Langstrothdale, one of the Yorkshire Dales.

Gill 'ravine'. An example is Scargill ('ravine where merganser seabirds are seen'), a village in Co. Durham.

Foss 'waterfall', as used in Janet's Foss in Yorkshire.

Keld 'spring'. Examples include the Yorkshire villages of Keld and Keldholme ('island or river meadow near the spring').

Carr 'marsh', as used in Carcroft ('enclosure near the marsh'), a village in Yorkshire.

Holme 'island'. Among many examples of its use are several villages in Yorkshire, East Anglia and the East Midlands, as well as a Sandholme ('sandy island') in east Yorkshire.

Lund 'wood'. Examples of it use include the two Yorkshire villages of Lund.

Scar 'cliff' or 'rock', as used in Newberry Scar near Middleton, in Teesdale.

Ey 'island' as in Anglesey (Ongull's island) and Swansea (Sveinn's island).

Ness 'headland', as used in Thorpeness ('a village near the headland') in Suffolk.

Beck 'stream'. An example is Troutbeck ('place by a trout stream') in Cumbria.

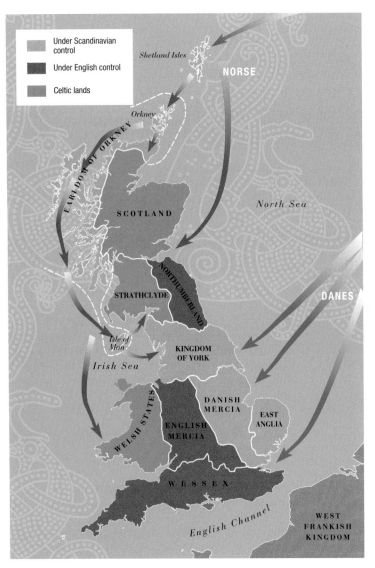

Viking attack Danish warriors plundered the east coast, while Norwegians raided the Orkneys, the Western Isles and Ireland, before settling in parts of northern England.

By 'farmstead' or 'village'. Examples include Coningsby ('king's village') in Lincolnshire, Ingleby ('village of the English') in Derbyshire, and Denaby ('Danes' village') and Selby ('village by willow trees'), both in Yorkshire.

Booth 'temporary shelter', often on a farmstead when combined with the ending 'by', as in Boothby ('farmstead with shelters') in Lincolnshire.

Kirk 'church', as in Romaldkirk ('church of St Rumwald') in Co. Durham, Kirby Bedon ('village with a church in the manor of the de Bidum family') in Norfolk, Kirkby Overblow ('village of the iron smelters with a church') in Yorkshire, and Kirton in Lindsey ('village with a church in Lindsey county') in Lincolnshire.

Scales 'a herdsman's hut'. Examples include several Scales in Cumbria, and Newton with Scales ('new village with a herdsman's hut') in Lancashire.

Thorpe 'outlying farmstead or hamlet'. Examples include Burythorpe ('hill hamlet') in Yorkshire, Grassthorpe ('grassy hamlet') in Nottinghamshire, and Gunthorpe ('Gunni's outlying farmstead') and Sculthorpe ('Skuli's outlying farmstead') both in Norfolk.

Thwaite 'clearing, 'meadow' or 'paddock'. Examples of its use include Armathwaite ('clearing of the hermit'), Braithwaite ('broad clearing'), and Seathwaite ('sedge clearing'), all in Cumbria.

Toft 'plot of land on which a homestead was built'. Examples of its use include Lowestoft ('Hlothver's homestead') in Suffolk, and Bratoft ('broad homestead') and Wigtoft ('homestead by a creek'), both in Lincolnshire.

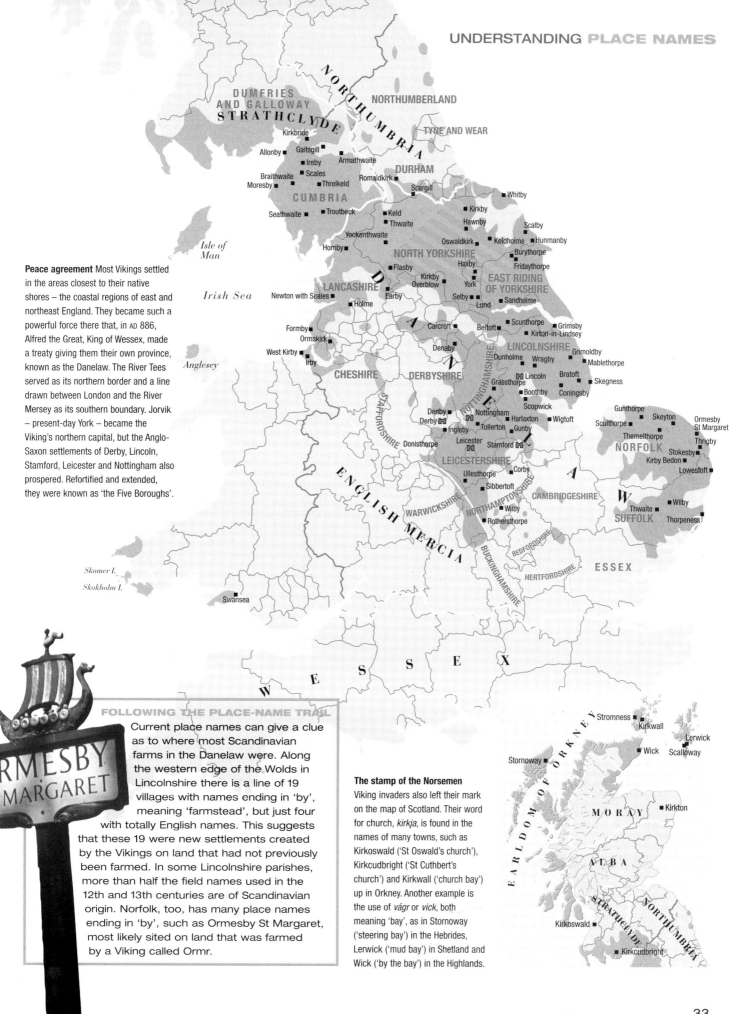

Peace agreement Most Vikings settled in the areas closest to their native shores – the coastal regions of east and northeast England. They became such a powerful force there that, in AD 886, Alfred the Great, King of Wessex, made a treaty giving them their own province, known as the Danelaw. The River Tees served as its northern border and a line drawn between London and the River Mersey as its southern boundary. Jorvik – present-day York – became the Viking's northern capital, but the Anglo-Saxon settlements of Derby, Lincoln, Stamford, Leicester and Nottingham also prospered. Refortified and extended, they were known as 'the Five Boroughs'.

FOLLOWING THE PLACE-NAME TRAIL

Current place names can give a clue as to where most Scandinavian farms in the Danelaw were. Along the western edge of the Wolds in Lincolnshire there is a line of 19 villages with names ending in 'by', meaning 'farmstead', but just four with totally English names. This suggests that these 19 were new settlements created by the Vikings on land that had not previously been farmed. In some Lincolnshire parishes, more than half the field names used in the 12th and 13th centuries are of Scandinavian origin. Norfolk, too, has many place names ending in 'by', such as Ormesby St Margaret, most likely sited on land that was farmed by a Viking called Ormr.

The stamp of the Norsemen

Viking invaders also left their mark on the map of Scotland. Their word for church, *kirkja*, is found in the names of many towns, such as Kirkoswald ('St Oswald's church'), Kirkcudbright ('St Cuthbert's church') and Kirkwall ('church bay') up in Orkney. Another example is the use of *vágr* or *vick*, both meaning 'bay', as in Stornoway ('steering bay') in the Hebrides, Lerwick ('mud bay') in Shetland and Wick ('by the bay') in the Highlands.

From the Normans to New Towns

The Norman invasion of England in 1066 added a liberal sprinkling of French words to the English language, but it hardly had any impact at all on place names. Later developments, such as the Industrial Revolution, were to be much more influential, although even from the Middle Ages onwards, a succession of new towns were being established, often taking their names from notable personalities and events of the time.

Gallic influence

The Normans brought a new social elite of nobles and church leaders to England's shores, extending into Scotland under David I a century later. Few settlers of more humble rank followed in their wake. The toilers and gatherers of society remained largely of Anglo-Saxon and Viking descent. So the Norman influence on place names was mainly confined to sites associated with the grand castles, cathedrals and monasteries that they built to help establish and defend their power. Towns with Norman French names, such as Beaumaris ('beautiful marsh') in Anglesey, Belper ('beautiful retreat') in Derbyshire, Devizes ('on the boundaries') in Wiltshire, Grosmont ('big hill') in Monmouthshire and Pontefract ('by a broken bridge') in Yorkshire grew up from the settlements centred around fortified Norman strongholds.

Double-barrelled place names in central and southern England are often Norman in origin too. They usually combined the old name of a manor with that of its new Norman owner. Examples include Kingston Bagpuize ('de Bagpuize's royal manor') in Oxfordshire, Wootton Bassett ('Basset's farmstead by a wood') in Wiltshire, and Thorpe Mandeville ('estate belonging to the de Mandeville family') in Northamptonshire.

Urban booms

Population increases in the 12th and 13th centuries led to the creation of many new towns in England and Wales, with a mass of Newports, Newtons and Newtowns appearing during this period. Flourishing commerce brought a flood of new market towns too, including Newmarket in Suffolk and Market Harborough in Leicestershire. More established places sometimes added the Old English word 'chipping', meaning 'market', to their original name to highlight their success. Among these are Chipping Norton in Oxfordshire and Chipping Ongar in Essex.

Industrialisation in the 18th and 19th centuries fuelled a further flush of urban expansion (see opposite), and in the 20th century, over-crowding and war damage triggered the creation of 28 planned new towns (see pages 186-187). Most simply took the name of a previous village or settlement on the same site. Milton Keynes in Buckinghamshire, for example, was first recorded in 1422 – Milton means 'farmstead' or 'estate' in Old English and Keynes refers to Lucas de Cahaignes, lord of the manor there in the 12th century.

The personal touch

In the 18th and 19th centuries, it became popular to name places after local landowners and captains of industy, as a mark of their importance or wealth. Arkwright Town in Derbyshire is named after the family of Sir Richard Arkwright, inventor of the

> **DID YOU KNOW?**
>
> Place names such as Blandford Forum, Lyme Regis and Chew Magna appear to have an obvious Latin derivation, but few actually date back as far as the Roman occupation. They were created in the Middle Ages, when Latin was the language used for administration by the Church and the educated classes. It became fashionable to use Latin words such as *forum*, meaning 'market', *magna*, meaning 'great', and *regis*, meaning 'king', to create the names for places that were considered to be of some importance.

Monastic influence French immigrants after the Norman conquest included Cistercian monks. Their wealth is evident even from the ruins of the magnificent abbeys they built, including Rievaulx (above). The name is a Normanisation of 'rye vallis' ('valley of the River Rye').

Beauly
Belses
Richmond
Jervaulx
Rievaulx
Pontefract
Beaumaris
Belper
Belvoir
Montgomery
Melton Mowbray
Stanton Lacy
Thorpe Mandeville
Grosmont
Kingston Bagpuize
Beaumont
Wootton Bassett
Devizes
Montacute
Beaulieu

spinning frame, and Raynes Park in Surrey stands on estates owned by the Rayne family in the 19th century. A touch of romance lies behind the naming of Maryport in Cumbria. 'Mary' was the wife of Humphrey Senhouse, who built the harbour there between 1750 and 1760.

Several 20th-century new towns were also named in honour of illustrious individuals. The engineer Thomas Telford gave his name to Telford in Shropshire, while Peterlee in Co. Durham commemorates the local miner's leader during the 1930s, Peter Lee.

THE INFLUENCE OF INDUSTRY

The Industrial Revolution brought a crop of new towns named after the raw materials that drove the developing local industries. Coalport and Ironbridge (below) in Shropshire, Coalville in Leicestershire and Ironville in Derbyshire are examples. Some industrial communities, such as New Brampton in Derbyshire and New Lanark in Strathclyde, took their names from existing settlements. Many built on former common land took the name of an earlier settlement, as at Baddeley Green, Staffordshire, and Silkstone Common, Yorkshire.

Some 19th-century industrialists built their workers villages close to their factories. Port Sunlight in Cheshire was founded by William Hesketh Lever and named after a brand of soap he manufactured there. The Cadburys built a town for their employees on the old Bournbrook estate near Birmingham, changing its name to the more French-sounding Bournville because of the high quality of chocolate made across the Channel.

A princely plot Places such as Princetown in Devon (above) owe their names to Royal connections. The village was named after the Prince of Wales (later George IV, right) who owned Dartmoor and gave the land on which it, along with its famous prison, was built.

FIND OUT MORE

- *Signposts to the Past*
(M. Gelling, Phillimore, 2nd ed., 1988)
- *English Place-Names*
(K. Cameron, Batsford, 1996)
- *The Landscape of Place Names*
(M. Gelling and A. Cole, Paul Watkins, 2000)
- *The Cambridge Dictionary of English Place-Names*
(V. Watts, CUP, 2004)
- *The Oxford Dictionary of British Place-Names*
(A.D. Mills, OUP, 2003)
- *The Penguin Dictionary of British Place Names*
(A. Room, Penguin Books, 2003)
- *A Popular Dictionary of Cornish Place-Names*
(ed. O.J. Padel, Alison Hodge, 1988)
- *Scottish Place-Names*
(W.F.H. Nicolaisen, Batsford, 1976)
- *Scotland's Place-Names*
(D. Dorward, Mercat Press, 1995)

LANDS

THE STORY OF LANDSCAPE

38-91

CAPE

EXPLORE YOUR LANDSCAPE

92-131

THE STORY OF LANDSCAPE

Britain is a small piece of land – less than 1000 miles from tip to toe – yet it has an extraordinarily varied landscape, both urban and rural. Geology has dictated the lie of the land, but man has moulded it by establishing settlements and roads, clearing woodland for cultivation and grazing, and exploiting natural resources for fuel, building and industry.

All the natural richness of our landscape owes its existence to what lies under the soil – the geology of Britain, the basic rock bones of the country laid down over the course of some 3000 million years. The oldest and highest land in Britain rises in the west and north. The mountains of the Scottish and Welsh highlands, the Lake District summits and the moors of the far southwest are all founded on ancient rock. Some of it – the igneous granite and basalt – is solidified volcanic lava and molten rock; some is the result of chemical changes under heat and pressure – the metamorphic schists and gneisses. Subterranean upheavals some 400 million years ago hoisted the cooled rocks high; then wind and weather ground them down. Life was difficult in the rugged highlands and moorlands with their poor soils, so they were always sparsely populated.

Middle-aged Midlands and the new east

Old red sandstone is the bedrock of much of the grazing land of southwest Scotland, the Welsh borders and Exmoor. But where the grass grows green and lush is where people naturally settle, and that is also true of the carboniferous limestone of the Pennine Hills and central England. The presence of coal brought the devastation of industry to some of these landscapes, although it also brough jobs and – for some – riches.

Lincolnshire, the east Midlands and the Cotswolds benefited from a 200 million-year-old band of golden oolitic limestone that grew grass ideal for sheep grazing and produced a beautiful building stone. Towards the

Chalking up the Downs The Seven Sisters cliffs in Sussex (below) mark the southern end of a wide band of chalk extending to North Norfolk. Neolithic farmers cleared the woodland covering the chalk downland to grow crops. As they exhausted the shallow soil, they left it to be grazed and moved on. It is this grazing, particularly by sheep over many hundreds of years, that has created the expansive downland grasslands.

DID YOU KNOW?

Foraminifera are tiny sea creatures, less than 1cm ($\frac{1}{2}$in) long, with shells rich in calcium. The chalk blanket that covered most of Britain 100 million years ago was built up at the rate of 1m ($3\frac{1}{4}$ft) every 100,000 years, from the shells of countless of these tiny foraminifera. Just how countless? Well, at its thickest the chalk layer is 500m (1640ft) deep.

SEDIMENTARY ROCKS

Clays and sandstones. Up to 65 million years old

Chalk, clays and sandstones. 65-140 million years old

Limestones and clays. 140-195 million years old

Marls, sand and conglomerates. 195-230 million years old

Magnesian limestones, marls and sandstones. 230-280 million years old

Limestones, sandstones, shales and coal. 280-345 million years old

Sandstones, shales, slates and limestone. 345-395 million years old

Shales, mudstones, greywacke. 395-445 million years old

Shales and mudstone. Limestone in Scotland. 445-510 million years old

Shales, slates and sandstones. 510-600 million years old

Mainly sandstones and siltstones. 600-1000 million years old

METAMORPHIC ROCKS

Schists and gneisses. 500-1000 million years old

Mainly gneisses. 1500-3000 million years old

IGNEOUS ROCKS

Mainly granite, gabbro and dolerite

Basalt, rhyolite, andesite and tuffs

Volcanic craggs The Quiraing mountains on the Isle of Skye, composed of igneous rock, are uninhabitable.

FOUNDATIONS OF THE LANDSCAPE

Ancient igneous rocks form the mountains of Scotland and Wales. Sedimentary deposits of coal, shale and slate lie through northern England and South Wales; chalk and younger clays are found in the southeast.

south it was chalk whose sweet turf fed the sheep – chalk laid down in a sea that covered most of northern Europe 100 million years ago.

Pieces have continued to be added to the geological jigsaw. In the southeast corner of Britain, only 10,000 years ago, the melting glaciers spread a carpet of tilth and clay across East Anglia at the end of the last Ice Age. This layer was thick and fertile enough to support a great sheep grazing industry, followed by an even greater arable one in our own time.

Lush pastures A belt of oolitic limestone underlies the open, rolling countryside, woodlands and pastures of the Cotswolds (above). This rock supported a landscape traditionally suited to the rearing of sheep, on which the region's prosperity was founded. While sheep farming has declined in recent times, agriculture remains dominant and settlements are few and far between.

FIND OUT MORE

• www.geologist.demon.co.uk The Geologists' Association website lists details of its publications and field guides.
• www.geologyshop.co.uk A comprehensive site with articles on various topics of geological interest and links to 1200 related websites, including those of geology museums.
• www.soton.ac.uk/~imw/Geology-Britain.htm Information and detailed maps on the geology of Britain.
• www.bgs.ac.uk/magazine/geology/ An interactive map from the British Geological Survey enables you to discover the geology of a particular area.
• www.aonb.org.uk The website of the National Association for Areas of Outstanding Natural Beauty (NAAONB) has regional information on Britain's geology and landscape.

Orkney Islands

Outer Hebrides

Aberdeen

Glasgow   Edinburgh

Newcastle upon Tyne

Liverpool   Manchester   Sheffield

Birmingham

Cardiff   London

How landscape has shaped where we liv

There are more types of landscape packed into Britain than anywhere of comparable size on Earth. Through the ages the characteristics of each one have dictated whether or not people choose to live there and how they do so. Settlements have been wedged into precipitous valleys to be close to a stream or natural harbour, grouped on high ground for defence, clustered around a coal pit, or spread out over fertile plains.

Water-power The supply of fresh water and the opportunity to harness the current's power for driving machinery, has always drawn settlers to Britain's many rivers and streams.

The most sought-after locations

The landscapes with the richest pickings were the ones that attracted the most people. London grew up at the most seaward point that the River Thames could be bridged, so benefited from trade and travellers by land and sea. East Anglia, with its rolling sheep-grazing landscape and its proximity to ports on the far side of the North Sea, became the most populous and prosperous part of medieval Britain. Handsome half-timbered towns were built by streams, thanks to a wool trade stimulated by immigrant Dutch and Flemish weavers.

Once the Industrial Revolution got under way some 250 years ago, towns and villages built of local stone sprang up in places where there was fast-flowing water to power mills and machines, such as at New Lanark near Glasgow and in the Ironbridge gorge on the River Severn. Later, hastily built terraces of red brick were rushed up

wherever coal, ore and other raw materials could be mined, such as in the south Wales and Durham coalfields, the Staffordshire Potteries and Teesside ironworks.

From harsh reality to easy choices

People are remarkably tenacious in forging a place to live, even in the most difficult landscapes. Polperro in Cornwall (see below) and Robin Hood's Bay in Yorkshire are both fishing villages that have been squeezed into the cliffs above inlets from which boats can readily be launched. Hebridean

A tight space to live A natural harbour was a magnet to early settlers, allowing access to the sea for fishing and a safe haven for boats. In the Cornish fishing village of Polperro (below), people packed homes into a small area of flat land behind the port. More recently houses have spread out along the cliffs.

DID YOU KNOW?

Landscapes are changeable things. The Forest of Dean on the borders of Gloucestershire and Monmouthshire is heavily wooded these days. But in the 17th century a local landowner, Sir John Winter, was felling trees at the rate of 100,000 a year; and by Victorian times, the charcoal burners and shipbuilders had almost stripped the forest bare.

Changing scenes The Warwickshire landscape is enormously varied. Hill and woodland at Ilmington (above) give way to large arable fields on the Felden plain. To the northwest lies Baddesley Clinton (right), in the heart of the Forest of Arden.

Where the woods stop, the grass and grain begin

crofting and fishing settlements cling to basalt ledges above scattered patches of cultivated land. Many of these, such as Innie Vae and Arin on Calgary Bay in the Isle of Mull, lie abandoned, defeated by the harshness of their landscapes and by the 'clearances' in the 19th century (see page 81).

Nowadays, with the decline or disappearance of old industries such as fishing and mining, it is all change. Cornishmen do not need to live in granite-built villages next to the sea or near the local tin mine, just as the people of south Wales do not have to inhabit red-brick pit villages, or Scottish islanders maintain a croft house. You are just as likely to find them living and working in London or Kent – or Australia – and their traditional dwellings occupied by a Dutch computer programmer, or a Surrey-born novelist.

The geological diversity that lies beneath Britain's soil can give rise to great differences of landscape within a relatively small area. William Shakespeare's Warwickshire has seen many changes since he was growing up and poaching deer there in Tudor times. But much of the county's old rural character has remained intact.

In the southern half of the county two distinctive landscapes meet around the wide valley of the River Avon. In an area of gently rolling countryside lie the scattered woods and grazing pastures that Shakespeare called the Forest of Arden. In medieval times this was wood-pasture, a landscape of widely spaced trees, their lower limbs pollarded or cut short to allow animals to graze the underlying grass and eat the fallen fruit. Among the trees – mostly oaks, of which some remain – were hamlets and farms built of red brick and forest timber, working a mosaic of small fields. A good deal of this Arden landscape can be seen today.

The Feldon landscape to the southeast, by contrast, is bedded on fertile clay. It was once a densely populated arable area, farmed on the medieval open-field system of big fields growing crops in rotation. The Black Death in the mid 14th century depopulated the region, and the open fields became sheep grazing land. After the wool trade went north in Tudor times, the Feldon fields were enclosed, producing a landscape of large arable fields, a little woodland and a few lonely farms set in open countryside that has changed little to this day .

Ancient settlement leaves its mark

The ground of Britain hides thousands of undreampt-of houses, villages, walled fields and religious sites that formed the background to the lives, work and worship of our distant ancestors. Even after thousands of years, many of our now-empty landscapes are etched with reminders of ancient ways of life.

Secret underworld The pockmarked landscape seen from the air (left) is a clue to the existence of Grimes Graves, the Neolithic flint mines in Norfolk. Miners' picks made from antlers have been found here.

Houses, tools and dreams of the Stone Age

Some prehistoric sites are easy to spot from aerial surveys or unusual features on the ground, but others can lie undetected for centuries. The neat little houses of Skara Brae lay under a sand dune on Orkney's Bay o'Skaill for the best part of 4500 years, unsuspected until storms uncovered them, complete with the sandstone beds, tables, chairs and store cupboards of the people who lived there. The houses even had cavity-wall heating, using the heat given off by the settlement's rubbish dump.

The flint mines at Grimes Graves in Norfolk – more than 300 shafts and a labyrinth of caverns mined some 3500-4000 years ago – were thought to be a burial site until a clergyman excavated them in 1868. At Avebury in Wiltshire, by contrast, the Stone Age religious monuments have always been easy to see – huge rugged boulders in two enormous circles that surround the modern village, with a ceremonial avenue of standing stones leading

The fabulous historical layer-cake of Jarlshof

The great archaeological site of Jarlshof lies at the southern tip of the Shetland Islands. No one suspected what lay beneath the old laird's house on the dunes until a storm in the late 19th century washed away the piled sand.

At the bottom of the archaeological layer-cake are the well-preserved remains of round, Bronze Age stone huts, one of them the work-place of a smith whose clay moulds, fashioned by him around 800 BC, are still to be seen. On top of these stand the ruins of an Iron Age broch, a defensive tower, along with four wheelhouses built with radiating stone walls between 600 and 400 BC.

In the next layer up are some longhouse ruins. The longhouse, where a family lived in one end and their animals in the other, was a typical dwelling of the Norse farmers and fishers who settled Shetland in the early centuries AD. Three later houses lie on top – an early medieval farmhouse, a larger 16th-century house, and finally the rather grand laird's mansion of about 1600 that stood in ruins on the site, apparently the only dwelling on the headland until that fateful storm.

away. But their meaning, and the dreams and purposes that inspired their placing, are impossible to know for certain.

Bronze Age work and worship

Some ancient landscapes have only recently come to light. Sacrificial religious ceremonies must have been behind the activities at Flag Fen, just east of Peterborough, where Bronze Age people around 1100 BC deliberately broke tools, weapons and ornaments before throwing them into a lake from a huge wooden platform the size of a modern sports stadium, only unearthed by accident in 1982. In the same era as the Flag Fen offerings were being made, out on the headland of the Great Orme in north Wales, copper miners were excavating an enormous complex of tunnels, whose extent – some five miles have been discovered to date – was not appreciated until recently.

The Bronze Age houses at Grimspound, on the other hand, have stood in plain sight on their Dartmoor slope since around 2000 BC. The round huts set in their walled

Fenland finds Archaeological discoveries among the Bronze Age timbers at Flag Fen in Cambridgeshire, including an early wheel and tools such as shears, are helping to create a picture of life in this ancient community.

compound were used as storage sheds by the shepherds on the moors until their archaeological significance was eventually recognised.

Farming and fighting in the Iron Age

At Butser Ancient Farm in Hampshire, experiments are carried out to show how Iron Age farmers lived – erecting round houses, keeping farm animals of the 300 BC era, building haystacks and chicken pens according to existing post-hole patterns. But it is the surviving constructions of the Iron Age people themselves that still form dominant features in our landscape – especially the rings of defensive earthworks that enclose enormous hill-forts such as Maiden Castle near Dorchester in Dorset.

FIND OUT MORE

● www.shetland-museum.org.uk; www.historic-scotland.gov.uk Both Shetland Museum and Historic Scotland provide detailed information about the Jarlshof site.
● www.english-heritage.org.uk See English Heritage's website for Grimes Graves and the shafts that can be visited.
● www.historic-scotland.gov.uk Historic Scotland provides information about the Skara Brae site.
● www.flagfen.com Flag Fen's website contains a description of the finds and their preservation.
● www.butser.org.uk Butser Ancient Farm, Waterlooville, Hampshire, offers courses on the Iron Age.
● www.ancientstones.co.uk A guide to the stone circles, standing stones and ancient hill-forts of Britain.
● Britain BC: Life in Britain and Ireland Before the Romans (Francis Pryor, HarperCollins, 2003) An authoritative account of the ancient Britons' way of life.
● The Handbook of British Archaeology (Lesley and Roy Adkins, Constable & Robinson, 1998) A helpful reference book for those with an interest in archaeology.

Peeling back history At Jarlshof, on Sumburgh Head, Shetland, medieval ruins sit above layers of dwellings from the Bronze and Iron Ages and Norse era. Excavations have revealed human habitation on the site going back 3000 years.

The orderly march of the Romans

When the first Roman war party arrived in 55 BC it was soon chased away by the locals. A century later the invaders from the Mediterranean peninsula returned, with every intention of staying. In the 400 years of their rule in Britain the Romans brought about profound changes. They introduced native Britons to city life and comforts, to an efficient nationwide communication system, and to a unified rule. Their monuments – Hadrian's Wall, the Fosse Way, the baths at Bath, the great walls of Silchester and Caerwent – still stand, while the civilising effect of their customs and laws continues to pervade life in Britain.

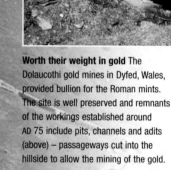

Worth their weight in gold The Dolaucothi gold mines in Dyfed, Wales, provided bullion for the Roman mints. The site is well preserved and remnants of the workings established around AD 75 include pits, channels and adits (above) – passageways cut into the hillside to allow the mining of the gold.

Signs of a town Grid lines in a field representing streets, and the surviving defensive walls up to 4m (13ft) high, are the visible clues to the site of Silchester, Hampshire (below). Typically, the Romans built the town at a major road junction and excavations show that it contained such essential facilities as an amphitheatre, baths and temples.

Border patrol Housesteads Fort was one of 16 forts strategically positioned along Hadrian's Wall around AD 122. The well-preserved site offers glimpses into the lives of the soldiers billeted here to guard the empire's most northerly frontier.

Britain's first townies

The Romans arrived in Britain in AD 43 as experienced urban dwellers. They planned and created large, powerful and efficient towns like London, York, Chester and Gloucester (see page 46), as well as taking over and rebuilding the few haphazardly developed towns of the Belgae Celtic tribe, such as Colchester and Winchester.

Settlements with Roman origins are easy to spot, thanks to the Romans' insistence on order and logic in everything they created. Where the towns still exist, they will certainly have spread hugely over the past 2000 years, but the basic shape will have remained: a rectangular walled settlement whose spine was a wide north-south road, lined with shops, crossed by a road running east-west at a central open square. Here the market hall and administration offices were situated. Grids of residential streets filled the rest of the town. The two main roads entered and left the town by fortified gates in the walls. The site of the abandoned town known as Calleva Atrebatum, at Silchester in north Hampshire, (see right) illustrates this typical Roman layout.

Under the Roman thumb

The Romans ran a tight ship, and that included keeping the turbulent natives under close scrutiny and control. They built forts at hundreds of locations, wherever there was a danger of insurrection. Generally, the larger forts followed a similar pattern to that of a town: a rectangular or square walled site with fortified gates, containing a central administration area, public buildings such as a temple and soldiers' latrines, barrack blocks and a commander's house.

Hadrian's Wall in Northumberland preserves a number of Roman fort layouts. The one at Vindolanda, near Bardon Mill, has reconstructions of houses, shops, a temple and a section of the wall. The nearby Vindolanda Roman Army Museum has everything you need to imagine yourself into the routine of a Roman soldier.

Country living, Roman-style

Away from the towns and the fortified strongholds, Romans who had been granted ownership of land (often retired military men) built themselves villas at the heart of their estates. These dwellings developed from simple structures in the early years of the occupation to elaborate complexes built of stone or brick, with many rooms grouped round a central courtyard, the interior walls painted with murals, the floors inlaid with fabulous pictorial mosaics.

The Roman villa in the thickly wooded valley at Chedworth in north Gloucestershire was excavated in 1864. It provides an insight into the structure and character of a grand and luxurious country house of the Roman era. The Chedworth villa developed over nearly 200 years of occupation into a lavish estate mansion with many bedrooms and day rooms, exquisite mosaic floors, two bathrooms and a lavatory with running water. The Romans always felt the chill of the British climate, and the house at Chedworth has underfloor heating in the form of a hypocaust – hot air from a furnace blown through a cavity over which the floors were raised.

Farming, the British way While many Britons joined the Romans in their towns, or rose to be rich enough to buy estates and build villas of their own, many more natives in the more remote places remained largely unaffected by the new regime. Most lived in thatched, wooden-framed round-houses with wattle-and-daub walls, but at Chysauster in west Cornwall (right) – an area with few trees – a short 'street' of eight stone-walled houses some 2000 years old has been preserved. As for the farming landscape worked by these natives, Romano-British fields tended to be small, rectangular and marked out by ditches or low banks. Look out in some of the more empty regions of England, such as inland Cornwall and Devon, for compact fields outlined by earth and stone banks that may have been farmed by native Britons up to and during the Roman occupation.

Decorative details Mosaic floors were particularly fashionable in Roman times. Wealthy villa owners would commission their own designs, while others would buy them 'off-the-shelf' from workshops in the town. They would place them in the main room in the villa so they could be admired by visitors. Popular themes included scenes from mythology or nature, such as the detail of 'Spring' (left) from the dining-room floor at Chedworth Roman Villa in Gloucestershire. Many floors have survived in almost perfect condition, such as at Fishbourne Palace in West Sussex. The Corinium Museum in Cirencester, Gloucestershire, contains some fine examples of Roman mosaics.

FIND OUT MORE

• *Roman Towns in Britain* (Guy de la Bédoyère, Oxbow Books, 2004) A study of the development and decline of Roman towns and the construction of public buildings.
• www.romans-in-britain.org.uk The history of Roman Britain.
• www.brims.co.uk An informative website for children.
• www.vindolanda.com A detailed description with photographs of the Vindolanda fort and Roman Army Museum on Hadrian's Wall.
• www.nationaltrust.org.uk The National Trust website carries information about Chedworth Roman Villa.
• www.english-heritage.org.uk English Heritage's website features Chysauster Ancient Village in Cornwall.
• www.romanbritain.freeserve.co.uk/villa.htm Detailed material, including photographs and illustrations, about Roman villas in Britain, written by Guy de la Bédoyère.

The Roman road-building programme

When the Romans arrived in Britain in AD 43, they found roads that were no better than trackways, poorly maintained, badly drained and so muddy as to become impassable in winter. The Romans scarcely gave them a glance; they simply started from scratch, and within a hundred years had built a network of some 10,000 miles of well-drained, paved, solidly founded and purposeful roads – a transport infrastructure that was not to be equalled for the next 1800 years.

Why did the Romans build their roads?

The Romans were invaders, and at first needed a means to get men and materials of war quickly from the coast to the forts they immediately set up at London and other strategic points. Then they had to establish a reliable infrastructure for their great push north and west into the heartlands of Britain.

Once the country was conquered – it took about 40 years – the warlike tribes had to be kept continually under the eye and thumb of the occupiers from strongholds built all over Britain. These forts (see pages 44-45), their garrison towns and the developing trading towns required an extensive, well-maintained road system to support them. Soldiers, civilians and animals, corn and trade goods, raw materials from mines and quarries, news, messages and orders all needed passage with a minimum of delay and danger.

From survey to thoroughfare

The Roman roads were built through a thickly forested land of hills and valleys. The puzzle of how to pick a true line in such a muddled terrain was solved with typical Roman efficiency. The surveyors used a groma, an instrument that was a cross between a sighting tool and a plumb line, to determine a straight course between landmarks. Then they had the surrounding forest strip cleared, and the route marked with poles. Small hills and marshy ground were no problem; the one could be cut through and the other crossed by building a brushwood

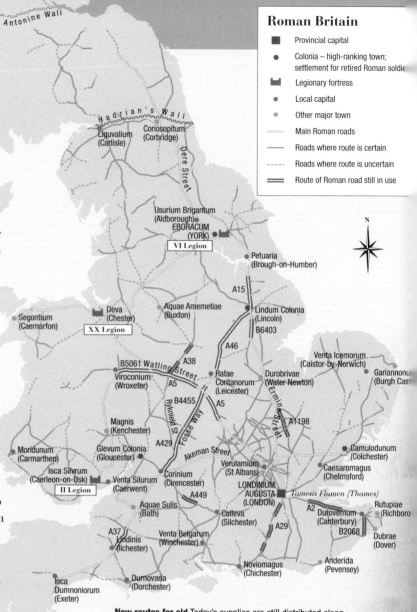

New routes for old Today's supplies are still distributed along routes such as the Fosse Way, Ermine Street and Watling Street, which were created by the Romans to move armies and equipment.

causeway or an earth embankment. The surveyors tried to lay as straight a line as possible – sometimes for dozens of miles at a stretch.

Imperial networking

The three major Roman roads on which the British transport network was built up were the Fosse Way, Ermine Street and Watling Street.

• The Fosse Way ran northeast from Exeter (Isca) via Bath (Aquae Sulis), Cirencester (Corinium) and Leicester (Ratae Coritanorum) to Lincoln (Lindum Colonia). This was the first important road built by the Romans, and it followed the line of the initial frontier they declared between the civilised Roman empire (everything south and east of the Fosse Way) and the barbarian world (everything beyond).

- Ermine Street (still used now, see left) was the route north from London via Lincoln to York (Eboracum).
- Watling Street headed northwest from London to Chester (Deva).

Other major roads included Akeman Street – London to the Fosse Way at Cirencester (Corinium); and Dere Street – York via Hadrian's Wall to the Antonine Wall on the Firth of Forth in Scotland.

Apart from the important arterial thoroughfares, there was a capillary network of minor roads. With these the Romans opened up hitherto inaccessible areas for industry and agriculture – for example, the Forest of Dean for timber, the Mendip Hills for lead, the Welsh hills for gold (see page 44), parts of the Fens for grain growing, and the Dorset coast for building stone.

End of the road

When the Romans left Britain around AD 410, they carried their skills and their organisational genius away with them. It took only a few years for the magnificent roads to start breaking up and flooding. Within two generations men had forgotten who had built them, and whispered that the old roads were the works of giants. Yet the hard core of the Romans' roads endured so effectively that today many of our major roads follow Roman routes and are built on Roman foundations. What a testimony to the skill of those imperial road-builders 2000 years ago.

You can spot the route of a Roman road on an Ordnance Survey (OS) map (see pages 26-27), even if it has since taken on different functions. At Shepton Mallet (above) the dead straight Roman line now incorporates a minor road, major road, town street, country lane and footpath.

A ROMAN ROAD IN CONSTRUCTION

Soldiers built the Roman roads of Britain, and evidence of their methodical work can still be seen. First, they cleared the ground, then they dug a trench along the line of the road and filled it in with a layer of large stones. A second layer of smaller stones was added, and a third layer of fine pebbles, broken brick fragments or gravel was spread on top. The soldiers shaped the surface to form a camber or domed top to allow water to run off, and sealed it with closely fitting paving stones. The road was then edged with upright stones to create a permanent verge and drainage channel. Some major roads were up to 27m (90ft) wide. A mile-long stretch of Roman road, complete with hardcore, an obvious camber and drainage ditches, has survived at Wheeldale in the North York Moors National Park.

The Saxons and Vikings work the fields

The Romans left Britain around AD 410. Soon after, Saxons, Angles and Jutes from Germany and Denmark invaded in waves of conquest that continued for the next two centuries. The incomers – Anglo-Saxons, as they came to be called – found a landscape of encroaching forests, native British and Romano-British settlements and towns, and the crumbling remains of the mighty works of the Romans.

The Anglo-Saxons make their mark

Soon after their arrival, the 5th-century Anglo-Saxon invaders began developing scattered settlements, individual dwellings and villages wherever they could clear the trees for new agricultural land. The most popular settlement locations were the gravel river valleys, such as the Thames, the Kennet and the Trent, where there was good grazing and plenty of wood, while the river provided fish, water for drinking and irrigation, and a means of transport.

From around the 8th century some Anglo-Saxon villagers began to farm the arable land using a system of three or more 'great fields', managed in rotation so that one field would be under grain, one under peas or beans, and one left fallow to regenerate. Each man held an allotment of land in each great field, and these holdings were ploughed by ox-teams (oxen and plough were

Cultivating the strips In the village of Midlem, near Selkirk in the Scottish Borders, the strip field patterns introduced by Angle farmers more than a thousand years ago can still be seen clearly, stretching beyond the houses and their back gardens.

shared between several owners) into long, thin strips separated by furrows. The ridge-and-furrow markings can still be clearly seen on the ground (see pages 104-105). In Northamptonshire, the patterns of open-fields are particularly well-displayed around Manor Farm at Stuchbury, and at The Leys near Woodford.

Summer on the tops

Vikings began to raid and settle in Britain from the end of the 8th century AD (see pages 32-33). Both Vikings and Anglo-Saxon herders relied on transhumance, the practice of taking sheep and cattle up to fresh pastures on the high ground in late spring and living up there all summer in temporary settlements. In the autumn many of the animals would be slaughtered, with only breeding stock kept over the winter. The herders' drove routes and the foundations of their circular sheepfolds and stone houses are still visible in a number of places, such as on Hadrian's Wall inside the old Roman camp of Brown Dikes, where Viking sheepfolds remain.

Life on an Anglo-Saxon farm The excavated and reconstructed village at West Stow, in the valley of the River Lark north of Bury St Edmunds in Suffolk, provides an insight into Anglo-Saxon rural life and craft (left, working wood on a pole lathe). Rectangular pits formed storage cellars, animal pens and the basements of wood-floored houses whose main structures stood above ground. Big wooden-walled halls housed communal activities such as feasting or indoor work. There were no boundaries between the properties, indicating that the householders were probably closely related. The land worked by the inhabitants appears to have amounted to about 50ha (125 acres). They grew crops such as oats and barley, and raised cattle on the river meadows and sheep on higher ground.

PIONEER CHURCHES

Christianity began to spread widely from the 7th century onwards. The first notable Christian buildings were the minster (monasterium) churches, centres from which roving missionaries went out to spread the Word. At Repton in Derbyshire, capital of the Anglo-Saxon kingdom of Mercia, St Wystan's Church has a minster crypt dating from c.AD 750. As parishes were established, more localised churches were built with the characteristic slit-like Saxon windows with peaked arches. You can see churches such as these at Brixworth, Brigstock and Earls Barton in Northamptonshire, and at Deerhurst in Gloucestershire, where the Saxons founded St Mary's Church and nearby Odda's Chapel, on the banks of the River Severn.

There are clues to the location of these pastures on Ordnance Survey (OS) maps (see below): the words 'hafod' in Wales and 'shieling' in Scotland and northern England denote summer settlements. In North Yorkshire, 'the shieling above Leyburn' has become 'Leyburn Shawl'. The shieling and hafod systems persisted into the 19th century in some more remote areas of Scotland and Wales, such as the Outer Hebrides and Snowdonia.

House of worship The Saxons of eastern England learned of Christianity from St Cedd, the Celtic missionary who built the Chapel of St Peter-on-the-Wall at Bradwell-on-Sea, Essex (above), in 654. He used stones from a ruined Roman fort.

You can spot sheep herders' upland summer settlements in north Wales (left) by looking for 'hafod' on an OS Landranger map (above, near Bala).

49

Medieval settlements emerge from the land

The Britain invaded by the Normans in 1066 probably already contained a well-developed network of towns and villages. But like those other conquerors from Rome 1000 years before, the Normans did not hesitate to impose order and discipline on their new territories, resulting in the genesis and growth of most of the towns we see in Britain today.

Up close to castle and monastery

After the Conquest in 1066, William I rewarded his supporters with grants of land. To defend themselves and subdue the locals, the Norman lords built castles – first of wood, and then huge, stone fortresses. In the shadow of these strongholds, towns soon sprang up.

Pontefract Castle in west Yorkshire was built by Ilbert de Lacy from 1080, and the town of Pontefract developed in the form of streets butted up against the castle walls. Although most of the castle was demolished at the end of the Civil War in 1649, the town had long outgrown its big brother and continued to thrive. In northwest Wales the medieval walls around the towns that grew next to the 13th-century castles of Conwy (below) and Caernarfon are still well preserved, while those at Beaumaris can be traced from fragments and on the town map.

The Norman monarchs and lords also initiated a grand programme of monastery-building. On the land they gave to the Church, towns such as Bury St Edmunds in Suffolk and Tewkesbury in Gloucestershire began to develop next door to the monasteries. Sometimes abbots grew to be as powerful as nobles in their localities and had a major impact on the development of the local economy. At St Albans successive abbots diverted the main road through the town, started up a market and obliged everyone to process their wool and grind their corn in the monastery's mills.

Early medieval abbots could be ruthless. The autocratic 10th-century abbots of St Albans decided that their prosperity was threatened by the success of the nearby town of Kingsbury. So one of them bought Kingsbury's fishpool from its owner, the king, and drained it; and then a successor bought the entire town and flattened it, effectively removing any possibility of competition.

Castle complex Conwy in north Wales is typical of a medieval town that developed around a castle. The fortress was built by Edward I between 1283 and 1289, and the formidable town walls, complete with 22 watchtowers, still stretch for nearly a mile around the settlement (below).

The shaping of the new towns

In the 200 years following the Norman Conquest some 130 new towns were created in England (nearly 70 in Wales), largely in response to a huge population growth (see pages 148-149). This created demands for more food and the conditions for a boom in trade. Most towns were built around a market square, where people could gather to exchange goods and news. Towns grew around these public places, and dwelling-houses with shops in their ground floors lined the market squares (see page 139). Sometimes these were literally square, as at Norwich, while in other places they could be irregular, such as the market place at Boston, Lincolnshire, which developed out of a cramped area near the church into a tapering shape.

One distinctive form of early medieval town planning is easy to spot on the map and on the ground – the layout in the form of a grid. At Salisbury in Wiltshire the bishop proved himself a canny speculator, laying out a grid of streets and then leasing building plots. Stratford-upon-Avon was another of these grid-patterned towns, laid out that way in 1196.

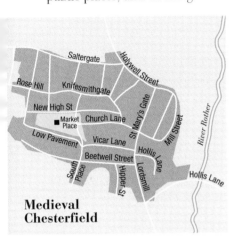

Medieval Chesterfield

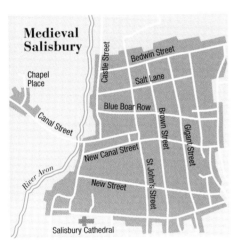

Medieval Salisbury

Planning insights The wedge shape of the market place in Chesterfield, Derbyshire, was typical of many medieval settlements that grew around this core of town life. Salisbury's grid pattern dates from 1220, when the town was moved from Old Sarum to a more fertile site.

Settlements beside the sea

Ports had their own privileges, tax concessions, perks and defence obligations thanks to their location as strongholds against seaborne invaders, and as gateways for goods and people leaving and entering the country. A port might be a place long established on a sheltered harbour, or it might have been developed in response to changed circumstances. Hull was newly built in the 13th century on a peninsula formed when the River Hull changed course and reached the River Humber via a new mouth.

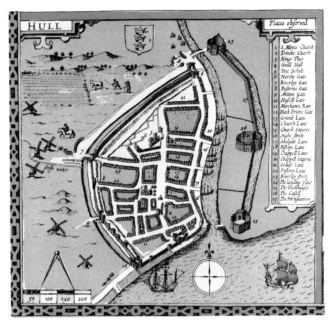

Birth of a port Old maps often provide clues to a town's origins. The map of Hull, on the banks of the Humber (above), shows that it was a significant port in medieval times. It was well-fortified, with a moat to the west – later to become the city's docks – and the original course of the River Hull to the east acting as a further defence.

Towns that never made it

New Winchelsea in East Sussex was a grid-patterned town laid out in 39 rectangular plots on a knoll after its seaward predecessor, 'old' Winchelsea, was destroyed in a great storm in 1287. Situated as it was, with the powerful and prosperous Cinque Ports of Hastings and New Romney as neighbours, the new town should have thrived. It depended on the sea for fishing and for its profitable wine trade with France (some of its fine cellars can be seen today). But it was built too far inland, so that its tidal harbour silted up. The Black Death devastated its population, and French raiders repeatedly attacked it. New Winchelsea shrank to the sleepy, forgotten and charming place it is today.

Gate to the town Remains of medieval settlements, such as town walls and gates, can often be seen on the ground or marked on maps. Built in the 13th century, New Gate (below) is one of the original entrances to New Winchelsea, East Sussex.

Ruling the country for God and man

Dotted all across the British landscape are the lumps and bumps, the ruins, ditches and banks, that show where the landowners lived and struggled to hold onto their estates in medieval times. Norman lords created great mounds on which to construct their castles, border farmers in the north of England built fortified towerhouses to provide havens from marauders for their families and stock, and abbots grew ever more rich and powerful through the vast and productive estates they commanded.

Castles fit for lords

After William I's conquest of Britain in 1066, Norman lords needed strongholds that would guarantee their safety and send a discouraging message to potential rebels. The pioneer Norman castle was built of wood on an artificial mound known as a motte. Adjacent to the motte stood a large, fenced enclosure, the bailey, which held the soldiery of the castle together with livestock and supplies. Fine examples of motte-and-bailey earthworks can be seen at Topcliffe in north Yorkshire, where the Percy family built a stronghold on land granted to William de Percy by William, and at Pleshey in Essex, where a 15m (50ft) high motte from the 12th century is enclosed by a deep ditch.

Some later stone-built castles were protected by a moat or water-filled ditch, a good deterrent to attackers. Not that moats were always defensive – often they were dug for other motives, such as drainage of the site, or as a status symbol, such as the one surrounding Ightham Mote, near Sevenoaks in Kent (above), begun in about 1330.

Water feature One of the few moated manor houses to be seen in Britain is the 14th-16th century Ightham Mote in Kent (above). Its name derives not from the surrounding moat, but from the medieval 'moot' or council, which is thought to have met here. The moat at Ightham would have served little defensive purpose – this was for show, a clear signal of the lord of the manor's status.

The earthly power of the monastic estate

Monasteries may have started as humble houses of prayer, but in early medieval times many of them became extremely rich and powerful landowners. This was especially true of the Cistercian houses; Cistercians were obliged by their rule to live in remote places, so they usually found themselves surrounded by tracts of wild land that had never been brought into cultivation. These 'wastelands' became huge monastic estates.

The Cistercian order's Rievaulx Abbey in Yorkshire was founded in 1131; neighbouring Fountains Abbey (right) the year after. Within a century they had become the most powerful landowners in the north, controlling lead mines, fisheries, quarries and extensive sheep grazing. The monasteries' far-flung agricultural estates were managed by monks from the mother house assisted by lay brothers who occupied separate quarters beside the monastery or lived in outlying farms known as granges. Not only did the lay brothers tend the flocks, they worked as stonemasons, blacksmiths, tanners and shoemakers. If you go to Fountains Abbey, you can see the remains of the outbuildings (right) that made up a typical monastic worshipping and working community.

The Black Death deprived the granges of their workforce. Overstretched resources and royal resentment of the wealth and privilege retained by the monasteries sowed the seeds of their downfall two centuries later (see pages 60-61).

Fountains Mill The 12th-century corn mill on the River Skell still survives.

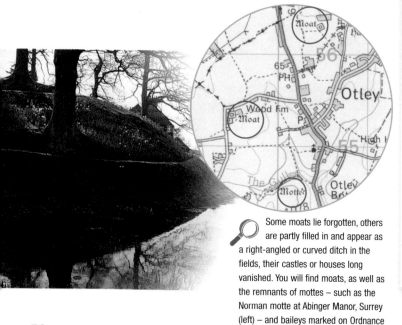

Some moats lie forgotten, others are partly filled in and appear as a right-angled or curved ditch in the fields, their castles or houses long vanished. You will find moats, as well as the remnants of mottes – such as the Norman motte at Abinger Manor, Surrey (left) – and baileys marked on Ordnance Survey (OS) maps (above).

Defending the wild border lands

Life was rough along the Scottish borders in early medieval times, especially after the punitive incursions into Scotland of Edward I at the end of the 13th century. Fearing attack from all sides, locals with enough labour and money built themselves pele towers. These were towers with three storeys – animals in the lowest storey, a kitchen and hall above, and bedrooms and living rooms at the top.

Bastles were later, slightly more domestic versions of the pele. They were fortified farmhouses with tiny windows and thick walls, built from around 1500 when border farmers were plagued by bloodthirsty stock rustlers known as reivers. Animals were kept safe in the lower floor of the bastle, and a ladder rose through the ceiling to give access to the family quarters above. Woodhouses Bastle near Rothbury, in the Cheviot Hills, gives a powerful idea of the austerity of such dwellings.

Home fortifications
The Vicar's Pele beside St Andrew's Church at Corbridge, Northumberland, is a well-preserved towerhouse. It was built c.1300 using stones carted from the former Roman camp of Corstopitum.

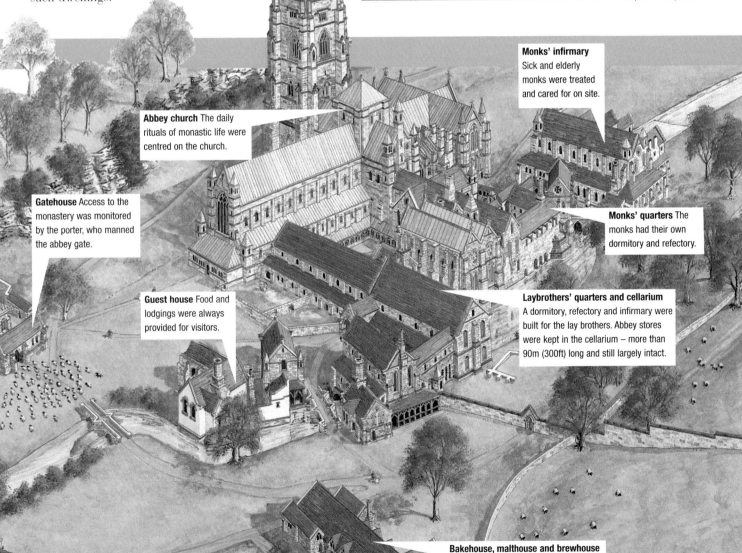

Monks' infirmary
Sick and elderly monks were treated and cared for on site.

Abbey church The daily rituals of monastic life were centred on the church.

Gatehouse Access to the monastery was monitored by the porter, who manned the abbey gate.

Monks' quarters The monks had their own dormitory and refectory.

Guest house Food and lodgings were always provided for visitors.

Laybrothers' quarters and cellarium
A dormitory, refectory and infirmary were built for the lay brothers. Abbey stores were kept in the cellarium – more than 90m (300ft) long and still largely intact.

Bakehouse, malthouse and brewhouse
A hive of activity, where the monks baked bread, and stored malt for brewing ale. Other activities may have taken place here, such as the preparation of wool.

The shaping of the medieval landscape

By the mid 14th century, just before the Black Death took its huge toll on the population, the feudal system had reached its height. This rural boom had changed the face of the land, with many new villages, millions of acres cleared for open-fields, grazing and pasture, and extensive hunting grounds. Evidence of this frenetic activity still fills the countryside today.

Uniform development Medieval landlords made their mark on the landscape by laying out new villages, such as Appleton-le-Moors, North Yorkshire (above). The houses and their plots of land (tofts), laid out in uniform rows either side of a village green, now occupied by front gardens and a road, are sure signs of a planned settlement.

Early village planning

Although some early medieval villages seem to have formed spontaneously out of individual dwellings in close proximity, others were certainly planned (see also pages 98-99). It was in the interests of landlords, such as barons and abbots, to have their tied workers living all in one place, so freeing the land for agriculture. Also, landlords were keen to have the peasants where they could keep an eye on them and control them more easily. At Appleton-le-Moors in North Yorkshire (left) the shapes of the tofts or plots of land laid out for the new village in the 12th-century can still be seen in the fields that border Appleton's back lanes.

The village green in former times was an important place for animals to graze and folk to meet. In the Norman era it was commonplace for villages to be laid out around greens. County Durham has many of the best examples. At Tudhoe, south of Durham, rows of houses flank the green, which is long and narrow and used to lead away into the common land of Spennymoor.

Ridge and furrow in the open fields

Out in the fields near the village, men, women and horses were ploughing their three great fields much as their Anglo-Saxon forebears had done. Strip-farming left its mark on the landscape in the shape of the characteristic ridge and furrow of the open-fields (see pages 104-105, 146-147). These

Forest sport Medieval kings could hunt for sport in numerous forests, such as the New Forest in Hampshire (left), chasing quarry spied and flushed out by the huntsmen (below). Many nobles wanted their own game preserves adjacent to a castle or house, and so large tracts of land all over Britain were enclosed into parks, surrounded by ditches and banks, often topped by hedges or fences. These boundaries can still be traced at places such as Croft Castle in Herefordshire.

sites still lie thick on the Midlands countryside, such as the fields around Ullenhall and Warmington near Stratford-upon-Avon in Warwickshire.

Clearing a space

Plenty of people did not live in village or town, but eked out livings in harsh environments which they had to adapt. Freelance coal miners set up on their own in places such as the Forest of Dean, near the Severn Estuary. In the Pennines farmers were still 'assarting' – clearing woodland to make isolated farms. In the Lincolnshire fens assarting took the form of enclosing the unworkable

wet fen a small piece at a time, draining the enclosure and putting it down to grazing.

The woodlands that survived the axe did so because they were useful to man – either as pollarded wood pasture for grazing, or as coppiced woodland where the regenerating stems could be harvested, allowed to grow and harvested again in a never-ending cycle. Remnants of ancient managed woodland can be spotted by the stumps of coppiced trees, boundary banks, an irregular outline and old ponds and trackways (see pages 116-119).

Communal cultivation The 365ha (900 acre) Mill Field at Laxton, in Nottinghamshire, is one of the last remaining open-field systems in Britain. Villagers farm the unenclosed strips using traditional crop rotation.

DID YOU KNOW?

Some forests are more traditional than others. In the Forest of Dean, Gloucestershire, the law is still technically enacted by a Court of Verderers, as it has been for a thousand years. Any Forest-born man still has the right to apply for a 'gale' or grant of Crown land and mine it himself under the title of Freeminer, provided he is over 21 years old and has already worked in a Forest coal mine for a year and a day.

The Black Death and a blighted land

The Black Death was the worst tragedy in the known history of Britain. There was no remedy for this cataclysmic virus that arrived in England from mainland Europe in 1348. By the time it burned itself out at the end of 1349, the disease had wiped out more than one-third of Britain's population. The plague profoundly changed the nature of the landscape. With more than half the country's workforce dead, and the surviving workers realising that their skills were now much more valuable, the death knell of the labour-intensive, crop-growing feudal system had sounded.

At death's door The catastrophic effects of the Black Death – as seen through the eyes of a 14th-century artist – reversed the fortunes of many a town and wiped more than 3000 villages off the map.

Upland farms lose out

The Black Death effectively emptied large parts of Britain's countryside – not as a direct result of flight from the plague itself, but because it made traditional farming uneconomic in the uplands. There were far too few hands to push ploughs, pull weeds and scatter seed. Hundreds of villages lay abandoned, their fields reverting to bog or scrub, as the inhabitants were ejected by the landowners to make way for sheep, which was the most economic way of farming a depopulated countryside.

The villages that died

You can still distinguish the outlines of abandoned medieval villages (right) by the rectangular banks and platforms that were the foundations of the houses, holloways that bypass or traverse the site, which were once village thoroughfares, and the proximity of water – either a well or a spring. To get the best possible view of an abandoned village, visit the site in strong sunshine shortly after sunrise. The low angle of the sun will help the hummocks and ridges stand out in strongly contrasted shadow and light. The effect is accentuated by dew or frost. Other clues to a lost settlement are churches of an earlier date than the Black Death that stand on their own in the fields (see pages 98-99). Around them you may spot the tell-tale banks and humps of a deserted village. In north Lincolnshire there is a splendid example at Gainsthorpe, southeast of Scunthorpe.

The shrinking town footprints

It was not only in the countryside that the Black Death ruined local economies. The medieval towns with their cramped lodgings, primitive hygiene and animals roaming the streets, were fertile breeding grounds for disease.

Mark of village life A hummocked field, criss-crossed with the hollows and platforms of village houses, gardens and central street, is all that remains of the once-thriving village of Wharram Percy (above), in the East Riding of Yorkshire. It is a vivid example of a medieval manor estate depopulated through the introduction of sheep farming after the Black Death. For a reconstruction of the village at its peak, see pages 146-147.

Worcester lost more than half its inhabitants to the Black Death, Norwich about one-third. Maps show how the built-up area of Winchester, like other towns, declined at this time (see page 149). Parish churches fell into disuse through the death of the clergy and greatly diminished congregations.

A long-term effect was the stagnation of many towns that had previously been on the rise (see pages 148-149). Of south Yorkshire towns before the Black Death, Tickhill was only second to Doncaster in prosperity. The town had a fine Norman castle and a handsome church to bear witness to its importance. Castle and church remain, but Tickhill these days is a sleepy market town. The economic devastation caused by the Black Death stunted the town's growth irreversibly.

Preparing for new troubles

The great phase of building new castles from scratch was over by the time of the Black Death. But the political strife and uncertainty in the decades leading up to the Wars of the Roses (see page 59) saw several new fortresses built, such as Lord Scrope's Castle Bolton near Leyburn in the Yorkshire Dales. Its massive 3m (9ft) thick walls were erected in the years leading up to 1399 and the usurping of the crown from Richard II by Henry Bolingbroke, later Henry IV.

From the more settled Tudor times onwards, fortifications gave way to comfort – although not along the Scottish border, where an Act of Parliament obliged anyone with land worth more than £100 to build a castle. Generally this meant a pele tower or a bastle (see page 53).

The port that crumbled into the sea

The Black Death was not the only phenomenon to cause a settlement to vanish. The Suffolk port of Dunwich was one of East Anglia's most prosperous towns, but it stood on an unprotected shore between crumbling cliffs. Nine churches, a hospital, two monasteries, a harbour and the houses of a population numbering 5000 were all taken by the sea between the 14th and 17th centuries. A fragment of the Franciscan Greyfriars Priory (right), and a lump of the lepers' hospital, along with a small village to the west of the original town, are all that can be seen today. The priory ruins are themselves only a short distance from the encroaching tides.

Fortunes rise and fall A violent storm in 1328 began the decline of Dunwich, partly cutting off its harbour and allowing Walberswick to take its trade.

Map labels: Walberswick, modern coastline, approximate ancient coastline, Dunwich Forest, Dunwich, North Sea, Dunwich Common, Position of 12th-century port

Conflict on the moor Culloden, in 1746, was the last battle to be fought on the British mainland. The defeated Jacobites were outnumbered 9000 to 6000 by the Duke of Cumberland's forces. His English had strong Scottish support and far superior reserves of artillery and cavalry.

A countryside stained with the blood of battle

Britain's meadows, moors and hills look peaceful, but down the centuries they have been the setting for bloody battles. Some, like the Battle of Hastings – fought on October 14, 1066 – are known by all, while other confrontations were small-scale skirmishes, now long forgotten. Many of the battlefields of the medieval age and the centuries of unrest that followed can be identified and explored.

The English versus the Celts

From the early 12th century border battles raged on and off as English kings sought to dominate Wales and Scotland. A Heritage Centre and a statue of Robert the Bruce mark the site of the Battle of Bannockburn (June 23-24, 1314), near Stirling, where 13,000 Scots defeated three times that number of English. Quarrels continued, with advances and retreats on both sides until, in 1503, Henry VII's daughter, Margaret, married James IV of Scotland. But this did not end the conflict, and on September 9, 1513, James was killed, with many of his lords – the 'Flowers of the Forest' – and up to 10,000 of his men at the Battle of Flodden Field, near Wooler in Northumberland.

The Welsh too were capable of giving the English a hard time. The names of the fields around Cadfan Farm near Llandeilo in the Tywi valley – Cae Tranc, the Field of Death; Congl y Waedd, the Place of Shouting; Cae Ochain, the Field of Groans – recall the scene at the Battle of Cadfan in 1257, when Prince Llewelyn the Last killed 2000 of Henry III's men. At the Battle of Bryn Glas

On the warpath Look out for statues of victors, such as that of Owain Glyndwr in Conwy (left), who led the Welsh to victory at the Battle of Bryn Glas. It is said that a small stand of towering Wellingtonia trees (right) marks a mass grave for the fallen of the battle.

(June 22, 1402), beside the River Lugg near Bleddfa in Powys, Prince Owain Glyndwr's Welshmen destroyed a force of 4000 Englishmen, killing a quarter of them. On the ground you can see four mounds where, some say, the dead were buried.

A year later, at the Battle of Shrewsbury (July 21, 1403), as William Shakespeare recounted in *Henry IV Part 1*, the Royalist army crushed Glyndwr and his allies Hotspur and Mortimer. The battlefield lies just north of Shrewsbury; there is a viewing mound, and a church built in 1406 as a memorial to the dead.

Titanic clash of two houses

The Wars of the Roses, the 30-year civil war that broke out in 1455, was a contest between the Houses of York (the white rose) and Lancaster (the red rose) for the crown of England. One of the bloodiest of many savage encounters was the Battle of Tewkesbury (May 4, 1471) in north Gloucestershire, at which Lancastrians who had fled the battlefield were dragged from sanctuary in Tewkesbury Abbey and slaughtered in the streets. Two modern sculptures in oak mark the battlefield, part of which is still called Bloody Meadow.

The House of Lancaster lost at Tewkesbury, but won the war at the Battle of Bosworth (August 22, 1485), near Nuneaton on the borders of Warwickshire and Leicestershire, where Richard III was killed and Henry Tudor took the crown as Henry VII. A Battlefield Centre stands on the site today.

Brother against brother, friend against friend

The English Civil War of 1642-6 produced a series of skirmishes and set-piece battles as Parliament under Oliver Cromwell disputed power with Charles I. Two well-preserved battlefields of this era are Marston Moor (July 2, 1644) in west Yorkshire, where a monument commemorates the defeat of the Royalists under Prince Rupert of the Rhine; and Naseby (June 14, 1645), just south of the A14 in Northamptonshire, at which Cromwell's disciplined New Model Army under Sir Thomas Fairfax heavily defeated the king's cavalry and footsoldiers, effectively winning the war for Parliament.

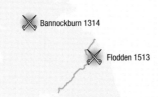

Scotland

Culloden 1746

Bannockburn 1314

Flodden 1513

Conflict and conquest From Hastings in the south to Culloden in the north, fierce battles have been played out across the countryside of Britain. The map shows some that were turning points in history. There are dozens of other sites, which can be spotted easily on Ordnance Survey (OS) maps by the crossed swords symbol.

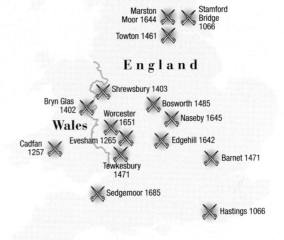

Marston Moor 1644
Stamford Bridge 1066
Towton 1461

England

Shrewsbury 1403
Bryn Glas 1402
Bosworth 1485
Worcester 1651
Naseby 1645
Wales
Cadfan 1257
Evesham 1265
Edgehill 1642
Barnet 1471
Tewkesbury 1471
Sedgemoor 1685
Hastings 1066

Lost causes and dreadful slaughter

Two battlefields are especially poignant for their tales of lost causes. The flat peatlands of the Somerset Levels were the setting for the Battle of Sedgemoor (July 6, 1685), where James II's troopers crushed an attempted coup by the Duke of Monmouth. In Scotland, the site of the Battle of Culloden (April 16, 1746), on Drummossie Moor near Inverness, has been preserved. The Battlefield Centre explains how George II's troops smashed the Scottish clans supporting Bonnie Prince Charlie, grandson of the exiled James II, in the uprising he hoped would gain him the throne. Both battles were followed by gruesome scenes as fleeing fugitives were massacred.

FIND OUT MORE

● www.battlefieldstrust.com The Battlefields Trust's website has a Resource Centre covering battles in Britain.
● www.english-heritage.org.uk English Heritage maintains a Register of Historic Battlefields.
● www.visitscotland.com/library/battlefields A visitor's guide to Scotland's battlefields.
● www.english-heritage.org.uk/battleabbey English Heritage guide to the Battle of Hastings site and Battle Abbey.
● www.braveheart.co.uk/macbrave/history/bruce/bannock.htm An account of the Battle of Bannockburn.
● www.bbc.co.uk/wales/southwest/sites/local_history/pages/cadfan.shtml A description of the Battle of Cadfan.

Mark of battle At Naseby (above), site of a decisive Civil War battle, a monument stands where the right flank of the Parliamentarian army was positioned.

The Church loses its grip on the land

If you look at modern Ordnance Survey (OS) maps, you will be able to spot places with a monastic connection from names such as Abbots Bromley, Grange Farm and Priory Farm (Staffordshire, right). In Wales, names with *llan* denote a church or monastery, *mynach* means monk and *mynachlog* a monastery.

The monasteries of Britain were past their peak of prosperity by the end of the 15th century. Yet in the 1520s they still owned a quarter of the productive land in Britain. It was a situation that would set Church and Crown on a collision course, transforming the way much of the countryside was managed.

Tippling monk Monasteries often had a large cellarium or storehouse where supplies for the monastic community were watched over by a cellerer (above).

The beginning of the end

Many monasteries had been in existence for the best part of 400 years, and during that time the biggest houses had acquired huge land holdings and vast resources (see pages 52-53). Such power and prosperity had turned the originally poor and humble abbots into plutocrats. So much wealth and authority in the hands of so few presented a tempting target for a king short of money and keen to extend the power of the Crown.

In the late 1520s Henry VIII wanted to divorce Catherine of Aragon so that he could remarry and try to beget a male heir. Pope Clement VII kept refusing Henry permission to divorce, so in 1536 the king broke off ties with the Roman Catholic Church and had himself declared Supreme Head of the Church of England. It was all the excuse he needed to sweep away the monasteries and grab their lands and riches.

The curtain falls

A commission of enquiry into the monasteries in 1535 played into Henry's hands by painting a picture of decaying buildings, drunken monks, pregnant nuns and grasping, lecherous abbots. The first wave of closures in 1536 affected the smaller and more decrepit monasteries, but by 1539 they were all being 'dissolved' – in other words, forcibly shut down. Their monks were expelled, their libraries and treasuries ransacked and their goods and lands confiscated.

Altogether some 850 male and female monastic houses were closed. The great abbey churches and the monastery buildings had the stained glass taken from their windows and the lead ripped from the roofs. In some cases the buildings were partially destroyed. Wind, rain and frost were left to complete the demolition job, assisted by local builders who 'quarried' the ruins over the ensuing centuries for ready-shaped stones and timber for the homes of the new landowners.

A new order of movers and shakers

Most of the monastic land was sold or given away. In prosperous mid-Tudor times there was no shortage of self-made men – wool merchants, graziers, men of business – keen to buy land, and there were always court favourites that had to be kept sweet with grants from the king. In some instances parts of the monastery were incorporated in a new house, as happened with the cloisters at Lacock in Wiltshire (below) and Combe near Coventry; while in others, such as the Abbey House at Malmesbury, a brand-new house was built on the site.

The far-flung estates of the monasteries were broken up and sold, and the monks were replaced as landlords by rich purchasers. Former agricultural land was give over to leisure purposes; landscaped parks were laid out around the new houses, and sporting woodland was planted. It was the start of the era of the great private estates, which dominated the landscape for the next four centuries.

Abbey conversion You can often spot remnants of former religious buildings in country houses. Look out for medieval arches, windows and doorways, or cloisters such as at Lacock Abbey, Wiltshire (above). Founded in 1232, the abbey was dissolved in 1539 and converted into a private house; it is now a National Trust property.

MONASTIC RUINS - SIX OF THE BEST

The monasteries of Britain have now lain in ruins for nearly 500 years – longer than they were operational. A remarkable number of monastic sites can still be explored. Here is a selection.

Holy place Inchcolm Abbey was founded on one of Scotland's early Christian sites.

Castle Acre Priory, near Swaffham, Norfolk (English Heritage). Founded 1089; Cluniac order. Extensive ruins include the towering west front of the abbey church. The prior's lodging is intact.

Fountains Abbey, near Ripon, North Yorkshire (National Trust). Founded 1132; Cistercian order. The remains of the abbey church with tower, vaulted undercroft, chapter house, warming room and kitchen give a good idea of life in a large monastic community (see pages 52-53).

Inchcolm Abbey, Inchcolm Island, Firth of Forth (Historic Scotland). Founded 1124; Augustinian order. The finest abbey remains in Scotland include the church, chapter house and cloisters in a solitary setting overlooking the Firth of Forth.

Lindisfarne Priory, Holy Island, near Berwick-on-Tweed (English Heritage). Founded c.635, re-established 1083; Benedictine order. Norman red sandstone arches, towers and monastic foundations are the remaining evidence of an isolated centre of Christian learning, frequently targeted by Viking raiders. The island is cut off from the mainland at high tide.

Llanthony Priory, Vale of Ewyas, near Abergavenny. Founded c.1100; Augustinian order. A large part of the north aisle arcade still stands. Original vaulting and parts of the towers can be seen. The Priory is located deep in the Black Mountains.

Mount Grace Priory, Osmotherley, North Yorkshire (National Trust and English Heritage). Founded 1398; Carthusian order. The best-preserved Carthusian monastery in Britain. The perpendicular church tower remains and it is possible to make out the cells where the monks lived as hermits, each with his own garden. One cell has been reconstructed.

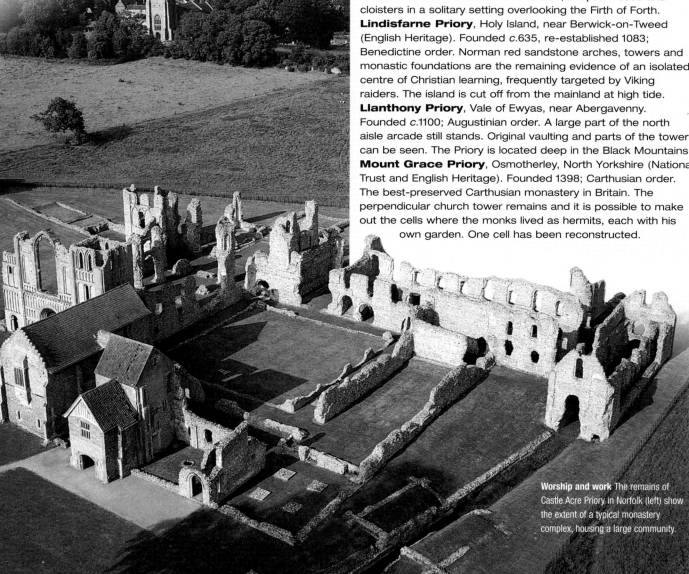

Worship and work The remains of Castle Acre Priory in Norfolk (left) show the extent of a typical monastery complex, housing a large community.

A revolution in the countryside

After the Dissolution of the Monasteries in the 1530s, 'new men' acquired the monastic estates. By the 18th century, agricultural reform had swept away the open-fields along with most woodland pasture and common grazing, and a neat, planned, productive and, above all, private countryside had come into being.

Fencing and improving the land

The new landlords of the monastic estates were not all noblemen; many were yeoman farmers, working on their own, some of them able to buy up land and rent it out themselves. But by the mid 18th century the farmers had mostly been ejected and employed as waged labourers by the rich landowners, who persuaded Parliament (a body made up largely of themselves and their friends) to allow them to buy up swathes of open-fields, commons and wood pastures. These were then 'enclosed' – parcelled up with hedges, fences or ditches into small private fields. Counties such as Essex lost their wood pasture, and Romney Marsh in Kent was drained for sheep grazing. During the reign of George III (1760-1820) some 2 million hectares (5 million acres), more than one-tenth of the available surface of Britain, were enclosed for the profit and pleasure of those who could afford to do the enclosing.

The new landholding era was also a time of invention, and agriculture felt its force. The soil of the enclosed land

Seeds of improvement New methods of cultivation were enthusiastically embraced by the big landowners of the 18th century. Jethro Tull's horse-drawn seed drill, invented in 1701 (above, with Tull), could drill and sow three rows at a time – a far more productive system than the traditional method of scattering seeds by hand.

was improved with marl and made more productive by drainage. Landowners such as Thomas Coke of Holkham in Norfolk and the Earl of Lichfield at Shugborough in Staffordshire put into practice what they learned from a new breed of agricultural improvers – Jethro Tull (1674-1741) and his innovative horse-drawn seed drill; Charles 'Turnip' Townshend (1674-1738), who showed how growing turnips and hay by his Norfolk Four-Course System could improve the soil for

Good breeding Robert Bakewell (left) revolutionised the quality of British livestock in Georgian times by introducing selective breeding. One result was the Lincoln sheep (below), still prized for its thick fleece.

more profitable wheat and barley; and Robert Bakewell (1725-95), who bred bigger and better cattle, sheep and horses by careful selection and methodical record-keeping. Some enlightened Georgian landowners created 'model farms' on their estates, where innovative agricultural and breeding techniques could be given full rein based in impressive new suites of buildings. Two fine examples, at Wimpole Hall in Cambridgeshire and Shugborough Hall in Staffordshire (both National Trust), have been refurbished and opened to the public with rare breeds of animals, working dairies and mills, and costumed guides.

The rise of the great estates

The possession of ever larger holdings of land by powerful private owners, and the convergence of interests between those owners through marriages, sporting connections and political relationships, fuelled the rise of the great estates all through Tudor, Stuart and Georgian times. Landowners such as the dukes of Devonshire (see pages 112-113), Buccleugh and Atholl controlled vast tracts of Britain. Owners walled off parkland, planted trees, laid out vistas and built themselves a huge country mansion, usually designed in Neo-Classical style, which acted as a centrepiece for the whole estate.

At Wentworth Woodhouse, near Sheffield in south Yorkshire, the Marquis of Rockingham engaged the celebrated architect Henry Flitcroft in the 1730s to add a gigantic east front more than 183m (600ft) long to his house. Follies were erected in the park – the Needle's Eye, a pyramid pierced by a Gothic archway; a 30m (100ft) high tower called the Hoober Stand; a column 35m (115ft) high; and a family mausoleum almost 30m (100ft) tall. Hills were removed and valleys created to improve the view. Such projects were in train all across Britain – the conspicuous expenditure of men who wanted to imprint their lineage on the land for eternity.

Dutch genius drains the Fens

Cornelius Vermuyden (1595-1683) was a Dutch engineer who worked in England on drainage projects for most of his long life. His greatest achievement was the drainage of the low-lying, marshy Fen country of Bedfordshire, Cambridgeshire and Norfolk. This project started in the 1630s with the cutting of the 20-mile Old Bedford River (named after the 4th Earl of Bedford who raised the capital for the venture) to carry flood waters to the sea. Twenty years later the New Bedford River (below, running to the right of the River Ouse at Downham Market) was cut in parallel, to divert sea surges away from the land into the flood reservoir between the two artificial waterways. When the scheme was finished, more than 200,000ha (500,000 acres) of prime land had been reclaimed for agriculture and the look of the Fenland landscape changed for ever.

A tidy landscape In the 18th century, wealthy landowners began to buy up huge areas of open land, which they enclosed to create a planned landscape of orderly fields, such as around Kersall in Nottinghamshire (background). To spot enclosures of this type, look out for a regular pattern of square or rectangular fields surrounded by hawthorn or blackthorn hedges. The roads are usually straight.

FIND OUT MORE

• The Rare Breeds Survival Trust Dedicated to conserving Britain's livestock heritage. www.rbst.org.uk
• Wimpole Hall, Home Farm The farm (National Trust) has many rare breeds of sheep, cattle, pigs, poultry, horses and goats rarely seen today. www.wimpole.org
• Shugborough Hall, Park Farm A working Georgian 'home farm' (National Trust). www.shugborough.org.uk
• www.bbc.co.uk/history/society_culture/industrialisation/agricultural_revolution_01.shtml The history of the agricultural Revolution in England 1500-1850.
• www.berkshirenclosure.org.uk The Berkshire Record Office provides detailed information on how to spot enclosures.

Nature tamed in the great gardens

Britain is rich with grand gardens laid out by landowners from the 16th century onwards. Some display the rigid formality loved by the Tudors and Stuarts, and inspired by Renaissance Europe. Many more offer the sweeping vistas, lakes and Classical monuments of the English landscape garden of the 18th century. Others reflect the mix of the formal and natural that delighted Victorians and Edwardians. All will tell you much about changing horticultural fashion and the aspirations of those who harnessed nature for their pleasure.

Tudor knots of symmetry

Gardeners of the 16th century took their ideas from the French, arbiters of all that was courtly and fashionable. It was the French who engendered the Tudor love affair with knot gardens, compact geometric compartments full of flowers or herbs, separated from each other by box hedges and narrow gravelled paths.

At first the hedges were waist-high, and each compartment bore no relation to any other. Then notions of symmetry came in; the little boxes began to echo each other's shapes, sometimes to the point of forming figurative designs such as Tudor roses, love hearts and amorously intertwined initials. They might be filled with sweet smelling herbs – chamomile, mallow, rosemary, marjoram, lemon balm, hyssop – or with flowers. But order was the ideal, as at the Tudor palaces of Hampton Court and Hatfield with their regimented lawns and hedges.

Pioneering plantsman John Tradescant the Elder introduced more than 90 new plants species to Britain, including lupins and cornflowers. He served royalty and nobility, and set up his own botanic garden in Lambeth, where he is buried in the churchyard of St Mary, now home to the Museum of Garden History.

A touch of the exotic

Orderly arrangements of knots (known to Stuart gardeners as 'parterres' – see right), rectangular lawns and fruit trees were still the fashion during the 17th century. But the world beyond the British shores was opening up, and a touch of exoticism crept in as ideas and plants came trickling back with returning adventurers. Chief among the agents of change were the Tradescant father (see above) and son, gardeners to royalty and the gentry, including Robert Cecil, 1st Lord Salisbury, Lord Buckingham and Queen Henrietta Maria. John the Elder (c.1570-1636) travelled through Europe, North Africa and Russia and brought back with him strange roses, fritillaries and mulberries for the gardens he laid out for Lord Salisbury at Hatfield House.

John the Younger (1608-62) succeeded his father as royal gardener, and returned from the Americas with exotics that included yuccas and tulip trees. Topiary became another symbol of nature under strict human control; the gardens at Levens Hall in Cumbria still retain the hedges first moulded into strange abstract and animal forms in the late 17th century.

Gardening in cinemascope

By the start of the Georgian era in the early 18th century many landowners had been on the Grand Tour, and they returned full of ideas for their gardens and parklands. They wanted the Classical and the Baroque, at first in their gardens in the form of statuary, but soon out in their parks in temples, grottoes, follies, Palladian bridges and serpentine lakes. Whole new vistas must be opened up, hillsides shifted, valleys created, villages abolished, so that the landowner on his terrace could enjoy that ideal, symbolic transition from formal gardens through a sweep of lawns and a curl of lake to the haphazardness of trees – from civilised order to 'untamed' wilderness.

Order is all The Privy Garden at Hampton Court, laid out for William III in 1702 with wide parterres and mathematically precise planting, is a high-point of the Stuart formal garden.

Came the hour and came the men, the new breed of landscape designers such as William Kent, James Gibbs, Humphry Repton and, most prolific of all, Lancelot 'Capability' Brown. Many outstanding examples of Georgian landscaping are still to be seen, among them Stourhead in Wiltshire, Aske Hall near Richmond in North Yorkshire, and Painshill Park in Surrey.

Victorian romantic rusticity

With the impact of the Industrial Revolution and the building over of so much British countryside, Victorian and Edwardian gardeners and landscapers tended to favour an escapist mixture of the romantic and the homely. At Attadale near Strathcarron in the Highlands the gardens, laid out in the late 19th century, are backed by superb wild vistas of moor, woods, water and islands.

The most influential gardener was Gertrude Jekyll (1843-1932), a fomer artist who, often working with the architect Edwin Lutyens, created deceptively informal gardens, using her painter's eye to compose patterns of seemingly random colour and texture. She designed some 350 gardens, including a walled garden at Lindisfarne Castle in Northumberland and many more modest works, often in her home county of Surrey (see page 163).

A new breed of landscaper

The high landscaping ambitions of Stuart and Georgian magnates have been resurrected at Alnwick, where in 1996 the Duchess of Northumberland began to transform 16ha (40 acres) of derelict land within the castle grounds into a public garden on the grandest scale. Its innovations include the Poison Garden and the spectacular centrepiece Grand Cascade, which contains 323m (1060ft) of weirs.

Improving nature The view over the Octagonal Lake to the Corinthian Arch at Stowe in Buckinghamshire looks natural but is man-made – part of 'Capability' Brown's first major commission. The 100ha (250 acre) gardens contain huge open spaces, ornamental lakes, wooded valleys, and 40 temples and monuments.

Up the garden path At the Manor House at Upton Grey in Hampshire (right) a striking Arts-and-Crafts mix of formal and wild gardens, rose lawns and walled terraces was achieved by Gertrude Jekyll (above, in a sketch by Edwin Lutyens). Her emphasis on herbaceous borders grouped in individual colours has remained influential in garden design as have the 13 books she wrote on horticulture, such as *Home and Garden* and *Children and Gardens*.

FIND OUT MORE

● Museum of Garden History In Lambeth, London, the story of gardening, including tools and re-created knot gardens. www.museumgardenhistory.org
● *A Little History of British Gardening* (Jenny Uglow, Chatto & Windus, 2004) A romp through British gardening from the Stone Age to today.
● www.gardenhistorysociety.org The Garden History Society website.
● www.bbc.co.uk/gardening/design/timeline_index.shtml Explore our rich horticultural past using an interactive gardening timeline.
● www.gardenvisit.com Garden design books and courses; garden finder maps and tours.

Return to Rome The architect John Wood the Elder (1704-54) devised a scheme for Bath that was to have a major influence on the ordered nature of Georgian town planning. Echoes of his unrealised dream to make Bath a Roman city can be see in the amphitheatre-like Circus (lower left), built in 1754. His son, John Wood the Younger (1728-81), built the Royal Crescent (upper left) in 1767-75, the first of many crescents in towns across Britain.

A golden age of town planning

The establishment of peace across the country with the end of the Wars of the Roses (see page 59) and the enthroning of the Tudor dynasty brought new urban prosperity to Britain. In the following centuries, as Britain gained an empire and began to industrialise, so the population rose and towns expanded – at first haphazardly, then during the 18th-century Age of Elegance with the order and symmetry imposed by Georgian planning.

The city that ate its neighbours

Tudor prosperity helped London develop from the 1540s onwards, although still chiefly within its medieval walled site, as rich men bought up and built on monastic property after the Dissolution (see pages 60-61). By 1580, when Elizabeth I called for controls on unregulated expansion, the city's population had reached 200,000. During the 17th century it doubled its size, sprawling out east and west along the River Thames,

especially in the rebuilding that followed the 1666 Great Fire of London (see page 150).

Expansion continued all through the Georgian era as the population soared past the million mark. The poorer classes tended to settle where there was work around the East End docks, which were kept busy by commerce with the burgeoning empire. The better-off, keen to get away from the poverty, stinks and diseases of the city, moved ever further west. Covent Garden's monastic site had been developed in the 1630s by the Earl of Bedford; Berkeley Square and Lincoln's Inn Fields followed, along with most of what is now known as London's West End. Villages, meadows, woods and commons were all swallowed up in the inexorable advance of the city's outskirts.

A happy alliance of speculation and elegance

The Palladian ideal of Classical symmetry and simplicity, adopted so enthusiastically by 18th-century landowners building their 'big houses', was echoed in the expansion of London and other favoured towns. Handsome squares, terraces and circuses of fine Georgian Neo-Classical design were built by architects such as Sir William Chambers (1723-96), Robert Adam (1728-92; see page 157) and his brothers John, William and James, and Sir John Soane (1753-1837). Many developments

Green-field development After the Great Fire in 1666, London began to develop westwards. Soho Square (below, 1754) was built on fields in formal Georgian style. The next street north was Tyburn Road, today's Oxford Street, and then open country as far as the villages of Hampstead and Highgate just visible on the horizon.

Aberaeron – Nash and the clergyman combine forces

Small town design The domestic scale of Aberaeron (below) was a departure for John Nash (left, on a wax medallion of around 1820). The late 18th and early 19th-century architect was better known for laying out Regent's Park and Regent Street in London.

In 1805 Susanna Jones of Tyglyn inherited £150,000 from her cousin Lewis Gwynne. Susanna's husband Alban Thomas Jones, a 54-year-old clergyman, changed his name to Gwynne, and enthusiastically set about spending his wife's money by dredging the mouth of the River Aeron on the west coast of Wales and building a new harbour there.

A complete Georgian town soon followed, laid out to a design by the era's leading architect, John Nash (1752-1835). Today, a quarter of the buildings in the little port of Aberaeron are of listed architectural importance. The terraced houses of Portland Place and the central Alban Square, some with porticos and pediments, are fine examples of early Regency design; their size was deliberately restricted so as not to look out of place in a coastal area of small buildings and intimate settings.

Fresh fruit for the forces You can still find evidence of the market gardens and orchards set up to supply Britain's armed forces. The shapes of soft fruit fields that once supplied the Royal Navy base at Plymouth in Devon can be seen on the south-facing slopes of the Tamar Valley (below), where cherry trees grow to this day.

Look out for rural names in what is now a city centre. Places such as St John's Wood and Lincoln's Inn Fields in London, Fallowfield in Manchester and Balsall Heath in Birmingham show how urban expansion ate up the countryside.

were not commissioned, but were built speculatively and sold piecemeal to the highest bidder.

In Edinburgh, the 'Athens of the North' (see page 157), in elegant spas such as Bath and prosperous country towns like Stamford in Lincolnshire, well-to-do people wanted a place of their own, and that required expanding the towns into the surrounding fields. Some local administrators made attempts to prevent green sites being overrun, but money generally talked loudly enough to silence them. With minimal planning controls, builders and speculators made profits hand over fist. The legacy of their opportunism is Britain's wealth of Georgian towns (see pages 151-157).

Feeding the urban tiger

The ever-increasing urban populations had to be fed. A rash of market gardens sprang up around the important towns and cities, especially London. The earliest market gardens, in Elizabeth I's reign, were cultivated by Protestant refugees from the Low Countries. Then, from the second half of the 17th century, market gardening spread to new areas as owners moved outwards in tandem with the expanding city limits. Vegetables were grown on the rich soils around Evesham in Worcestershire and in the Somerset Vale of Taunton Deane, on vacant plots in every town, and on farms close to urban markets or to military and naval bases. Some of these shanty towns gained permanence, such as Calstock near Plymouth, which supplied the Royal Navy.

The Industrial Revolution grows from the ground

By 1830, the Industrial Revolution was in full swing, changing Britain from a green and pleasant pastoral land to the world's first industrial economy. None of it would have happened without a stroke of geological good fortune or the inventiveness of pioneering Georgians.

Treasure under the earth

The mineral riches of Britain had been exploited long before the 18th century. Copper was worked by Bronze Age man in north Wales. The Romans mined lead in Derbyshire and Shropshire, the Mendip Hills in Somerset, and in Wales. Lead and coal mining were long established in the Yorkshire and Durham dales. Coal had been mined since medieval times in the northeast, likewise tin in Cornwall. But the mining industry was still small-scale.

The growth of industry from the 18th century transformed large areas of Britain that before had been open countryside. It was driven by the exploitation of mineral deposits, and it was in the mineral-rich regions that the industrial boom took place. Development in south Wales, west Yorkshire and northeast England was fired by coal

Mineral deposits

- Iron ore
- Coal
- Chalk
- Limestone
- Clay
- Brick clay
- Slate
- Lead

Scotland
Glasgow ■ ■ Edinburgh
Newcastle
Hull
Manchester ■
Sheffield ■
Peterborough
Corby
Wales · England
Swansea ■
LONDON ■
Dover ■
Poole
Portland
Plymouth

Lead weight As the demand for lead ore increased with the onset of the Industrial Revolution, lead mines spread across the north Pennine landscape (above, weighing lead ore in Northumberland in the early 19th century).

deposits; the Midlands, and Northamptonshire around Corby, by iron ore. The slate mines of Wales, limestone belts and brick clay deposits of southwest and central England were exploited for materials to satisfy the boom in mass building.

From home labour to steam power

At first the Industrial Revolution remained small-scale and local. Cottage industries – home-based production using members of the family – took root in isolated rural areas, typically among sheep or cattle farming families who had time to spare between their routine tasks. People in their own homes made lace, spun and carded wool, knitted and wove for local merchants. Canny Georgian inventors, such as John Kay with his Flying Shuttle (1733) and James Hargreaves with the Spinning Jenny (1764), made machines that allowed people to produce more work with less effort.

The Georgians also harnessed the power of water, but it was with the development of the immensely more effective power of steam that the revolution took off. Sites with a supply of water, coal and wood, not too far from the source of raw materials – iron, tin and lead, wool and cotton – were rapidly developed. In the rural gorge

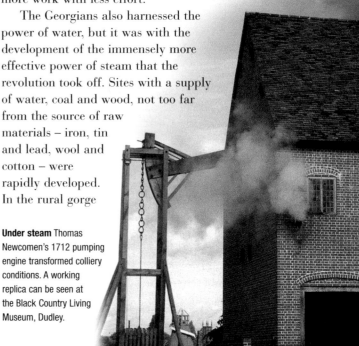

Under steam Thomas Newcomen's 1712 pumping engine transformed colliery conditions. A working replica can be seen at the Black Country Living Museum, Dudley.

of the River Severn at Coalbrookdale in Shropshire, Abraham Darby had all the water, coking coal and wood he needed to pioneer the cheap smelting of iron in 1709. Chain-makers around Cradley Heath in the west Midlands did not have to go far for coal and iron ore.

Underground workings, such as the tin mines of Cornwall, could be drained and expanded once Thomas Newcomen had shown the world how to pump water by steam in 1712 and James Watt further refined the steam engine in 1769. Meanwhile, the Lancashire spinners and weavers of cotton remained in their villages, because the air was damp enough to spin the fragile threads of the imported material.

Industry eats the landscape

Soon, technical advances were forcing the pace. It was more efficient to gather the cottage workers into manufactories – soon shortened to factories – to work as close as possible to the raw materials. New towns sprang up around these industrial centres (see pages 160-161), towns of cheap brick where workers pouring in from the countryside could be housed. Villages that were close

together simply amalgamated. The enormous expansion of towns such as Leeds, Manchester and Birmingham had dramatic consequences for the surrounding landscapes. Countryside disappeared under houses, factories, spoil heaps and industrial waste.

Before the Industrial Revolution, a network of small metal-working villages comprised the Black Country. But the countryside that separated these settlements was steadily swallowed up. New streets of workers' houses were built in Tipton, Dudley and Walsall; waste fouled rivers and wells. As more people arrived in search of work, outlying farms and market gardens were given over to the developers. Canals, which were vital for transporting raw materials and goods, and then the railways, soon devoured more green land.

Seeds of change Coal works changed the face of the rural landscape and villages soon sprang up to house miners. At Neath in south Wales (below, 1798), the small-scale extraction of coal for copper smelting was the start of what became a major coal-producing area.

FIND OUT MORE

• The Black Country Living Museum The Dudley museum brings the Industrial Revolution to life with historic buildings from the region, exhibitions and displays of traditional crafts. www.bclm.co.uk
• Killhope, the North of England Mining Museum Walk the Lead Mining Trail in County Durham. www.durham.gov.uk/killhope
• www.oxfordarch.co.uk Articles on industrial archaeology.

Transport shrinks the land

The roads of the Tudor and Stuart eras were winding, potholed and dangerous, all but impassable in winter. Goods could not be moved safely to ports or markets, and industry had to be based close to the source material. It was not until the advent of the canal system, and then properly surfaced roads, that the Industrial Revolution could take off.

Travelling by stages

Road travel in Tudor times was so slow and hazardous that anything small enough went by packhorse. Strings of laden animals would be led along roughly cobbled tracks that wound over the hills to market towns in the valleys. Flocks and herds on the move had their own system of drove roads (see pages 122-123). It was simply not possible to move large, heavy or fragile goods quickly

The business of roads John McAdam (1756-1836) made his name with his road surfacing system, for which he was paid £2000 by Parliament in 1825. His money-spinning technique was satirised in a contemporary cartoon, 'The Colossus of Roads'.

Clocking up the miles By the mid 18th century, the state of Britain's roads was improving – better surfacing methods and the introduction of turnpike trusts to attend to maintenance resulted in a faster, smoother journey for the mail and stage coach (above, 1792).

or safely overland in bulk. In the 1650s, stage wagons, stopping every few miles to change horses, took ten days to travel from London to Liverpool – in winter the journey could take two weeks or more.

During the 18th century, Parliament authorised turnpike trusts to charge tolls for the use of their section of road, which would be kept in decent repair with the proceeds. In the 1750s stage coaches could reach London from Manchester in four and a half days – 'however incredible it may appear', as the company's advertisement said. London to Cambridge took two days, London to Edinburgh a fortnight. At the start of the 19th century there was a dramatic improvement when Scottish engineer John McAdam promulgated the 'Macadamisation' of roads, which involved laying a hard core of broken stones and a surface of easily drained, fine-crushed material – similar to the method employed by the Romans 1700 years before.

In the first 30 years of the 19th century the stage coaches had their heyday. By 1820 you could leave London at ten in the morning and be in Cambridge at teatime, after a not uncomfortable journey. But the scream of the train whistle – the death knell of the coaches – was already beginning to be heard across the land.

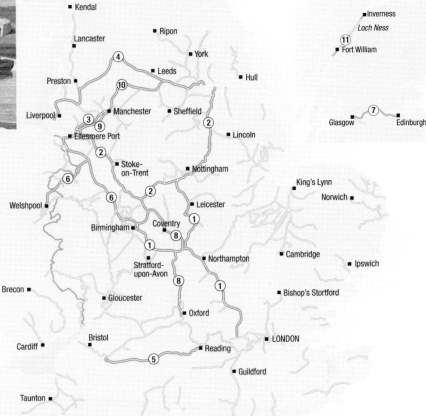

New routes by water Canals spread like tentacles across Britain, at first taking the easiest route around the contours rather than the most direct. By the early 19th century, short cuts were being carved through country and town. The Regent's Canal (above, at Paddington Basin) opened in 1820 to link the Paddington Canal, west of central London, to Limehouse and the docks in the east.

═══ Major canal
① Grand Union
② Trent & Mersey
③ Manchester Ship Canal
④ Leeds & Liverpool
⑤ Kennet & Avon
⑥ Shropshire Union
⑦ Forth & Clyde
⑧ Coventry & Oxford
⑨ Bridgewater
⑩ Calder & Hebble
⑪ Caledonian
─── Other canals and waterways

MARCHING WITH GENERAL WADE
Transport through the Scottish highlands was sparse until the arrival of General George Wade in 1724. His mission was to control the highlands, whose clans had easily evaded the military during various Jacobite rebellions. Over the next 12 years, Wade built a 250-mile road and bridge network extending as far as Inverness and Fort William, linking garrisons and complementing existing routes. His bridge over the Tay at Aberfeldy (above) is still in use.

Canals take the load

The spread of the canal network ensured the success of the Industrial Revolution, allowing heavy goods and raw materials to be transported in bulk the length and breadth of the country. Britain's first waterway purpose-built for the new idustrial age was the Bridgewater Canal from Worsley to Manchester, a distance of 7 miles, and then to the Mersey. It was designed by the engineer James Brindley, and completed in 1772. The success of the Duke of Bridgewater's investment, which carried coal from his mines to Manchester at ten times the weight per consignment as road transport, was the catalyst for a 'canal mania'. Canals were built all over the Midlands and the north in the 1780s and 90s.

Where the canals linked raw materials with manufacturing centres, such as the Bridgewater Canal, or cities with a sea port, like the Grand Trunk Canal, 1777, joining the Potteries district with Liverpool, they were a triumph. But many canals were built optimistically in remote or agricultural districts, and never showed a profit. From the 1830s, the advent of the railways progressively made the canals redundant.

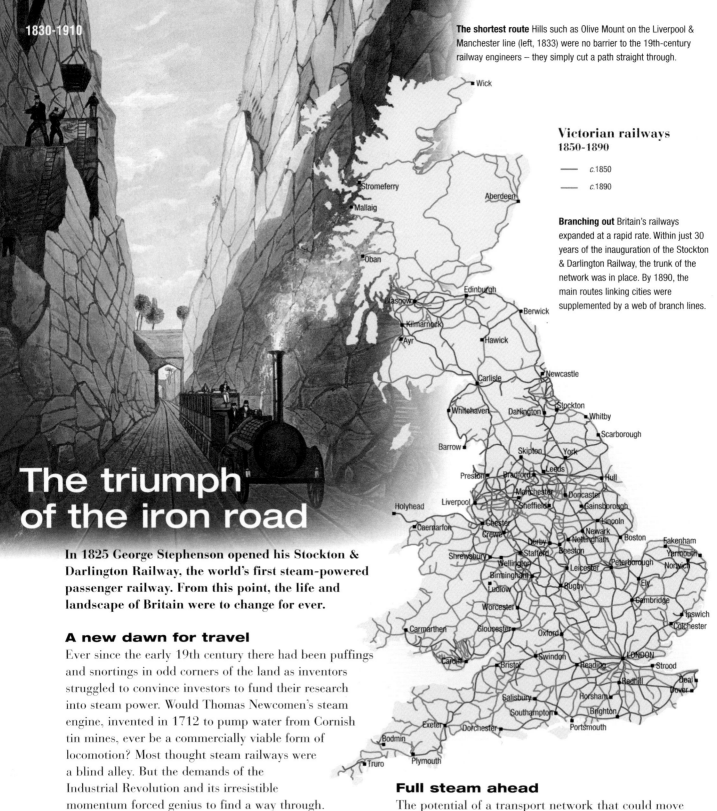

Victorian railways
1850-1890

—— *c.*1850
—— *c.*1890

Branching out Britain's railways expanded at a rapid rate. Within just 30 years of the inauguration of the Stockton & Darlington Railway, the trunk of the network was in place. By 1890, the main routes linking cities were supplemented by a web of branch lines.

The triumph of the iron road

In 1825 George Stephenson opened his Stockton & Darlington Railway, the world's first steam-powered passenger railway. From this point, the life and landscape of Britain were to change for ever.

A new dawn for travel

Ever since the early 19th century there had been puffings and snortings in odd corners of the land as inventors struggled to convince investors to fund their research into steam power. Would Thomas Newcomen's steam engine, invented in 1712 to pump water from Cornish tin mines, ever be a commercially viable form of locomotion? Most thought steam railways were a blind alley. But the demands of the Industrial Revolution and its irresistible momentum forced genius to find a way through.

When the Stockton & Darlington Railway opened there were just two working steam locomotives and 25 miles of passenger railway. No one had ever travelled faster than the speed of a galloping horse. The world – even the ambitious, mass-manufacturing world of the Industrial Revolution – moved at Bronze Age speed. The majority of people lived and died without travelling more than a few miles from their birthplace. The growth of the railways changed all that.

Full steam ahead

The potential of a transport network that could move people and goods ten times faster than ever before attracted the sharpest investors and the finest engineering brains of the day. The most important towns and cities were linked up, and the factories and textile mills of the industrial north were soon connected with every town and every port. A great upsurge in output saw Britain become the 'Workshop of the World'.

The social effect of the railways was profound. Journeys that once took a day or more now took hours –

THE FORGOTTEN HEROES WHO BUILT THE RAILWAYS

The army of rough and ragged men known as navigators (left, 1892) – usually shortened to 'navvies' – did the dangerous work of railway building in all weathers, in appalling living conditions, often drunk and underfed, cheated and neglected by their employers. They accomplished miracles of digging and mounding, blasting and hacking. Thousands died on the job. They blasted rock to form tunnels (Britain's longest is the 4.5-mile Severn Tunnel, built 1873-85) or open-topped cuttings through hills. They spanned valleys with mighty embankments or lofty viaducts, such as the 24-arch Ribblehead Viaduct on the Settle & Carlisle line.

Their ultimate memorial is perhaps the Forth Railway Bridge (below). It opened in 1890, having claimed the lives of 57 navvies.

Epitaph at Ely Cathedral on the tombstone of two navvies killed on Christmas Eve 1845:

THE SPIRITUAL RAILWAY
The line to Heaven by Christ was made
With heavenly truth the rails are laid

From Earth to Heaven the Line extends
To Life Eternal where it ends

God's love the Fire, His Truth the Steam
Which drives the Engine and the Train
All you who would to Glory ride
Must come to Christ, in Him abide

Come then poor Sinners, now's the time
At any Station on the Line
If you'll repent and turn from Sin
The train will stop and take you in

as the writer, and critic of the railways, John Ruskin said of the viaduct driven across Monsal Dale in Derbyshire, '… now every fool in Buxton can be in Bakewell in half-an-hour, and every fool in Bakewell at Buxton'. Steam railway travel was also a genuine liberator and horizon-widener, not just for the well-to-do but for anyone who could afford a few pence for the fare. The Duke of Wellington's fear that the railways would 'encourage the lower classes to move about' had come to pass.

The late 1840s witnessed 'railway mania', a period of frantic railway building, during which speculators such as George Hudson, the so-called 'Railway King', made and lost millions of pounds. By 1850, at the height of the mania, a quarter of a million navvies were busy building 3000 miles of new line to add to Britain's existing 10,000 miles. That mileage doubled in the second half of the 19th century, as the tree extended its branches to all corners of the land: by 1900 nearly every town and village had its branch line.

Height of bridge-building The Forth Railway Bridge was one of many engineering feats of the 19th century designed to carry railways across rivers. Three double cantilevers, each 110m (361ft) high, stride across the Forth estuary near Edinburgh like a great red dinosaur. It took 4000 navvies seven years to build the 2438m (8000ft) long structure, using 54,000 tons of steel and 6.5 million hot rivets.

FIND OUT MORE

• National Railway Museum Tells the story of the railways with locomotives, models and memorabilia. www.nrm.org.uk
• *The Railway Navvies* (Terry Coleman, Vintage/Ebury, 2000) An account of the men who built Britain's railways.
• www.railcentre.co.uk The history of the Stockton & Darlington Railway.

Cities spread in all directions

In the Victorian era Britain became the mightiest manufacturer of goods on earth. The effect on the landscape was astonishing: towns and cities sprawled across the countryside, industry polluted the land, and the coast was devoured by seaside resorts.

Elbow room for London

London experienced yet another upsurge in population, trebling in 50 years from around 950,000 in 1801 to 2.7 million in 1851. By 1901 nearly 7 million people lived in the capital. Under this internal pressure there was nowhere for the city to go but outwards. Green fields along the Thames east of the docks and northwards around Hackney Marshes were swallowed by wharves, warehouses, cheap housing and industrial building – the East End of Charles Dickens.

For those who could afford it, the movement was westwards, as it had been for the Georgians 100 years before. The suburban village of Chelsea and the areas around Pimlico, St John's Wood and Notting Hill were built up, gentrified and absorbed by the ever-expanding city, while to the north the city limits crept up towards Hampstead Heath and Highgate. The railways made it possible to commute into the city from country places such as Wimbledon, Sydenham and Enfield, which were soon swallowed in their turn.

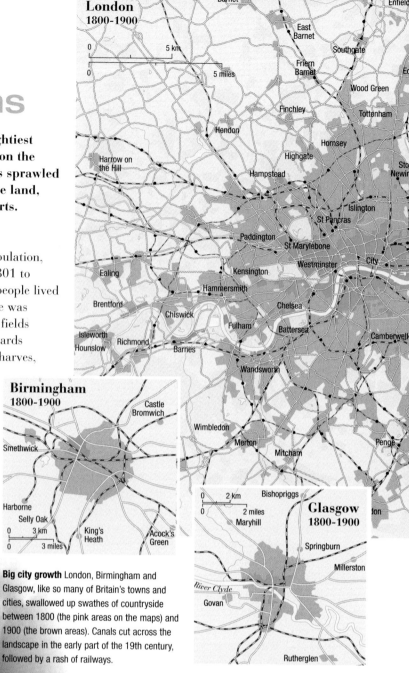

Big city growth London, Birmingham and Glasgow, like so many of Britain's towns and cities, swallowed up swathes of countryside between 1800 (the pink areas on the maps) and 1900 (the brown areas). Canals cut across the landscape in the early part of the 19th century, followed by a rash of railways.

The swelling industrial centres

All of Britain's major towns and cities gobbled up their neighbouring countryside, but some expanded more quickly than others. Glasgow, a modest town of 77,000 in 1801, grew through the tobacco trade with the Americas, the cotton industry, shipbuilding and heavy engineering. It had doubled in size by 1821, and doubled again in the following 20 years. By 1851 it had a population of 359,000; by 1901 it had ten times the number of inhabitants of 100 years before. Georgian streets reached out to Blythwood; Victorian villas and tenements to Partick, Kelvinside and Pollokshields.

In 1801 Middlesbrough consisted of four farms and about 25 people by the mouth of the River Tees. Within 30 years the railway had come and the area began to

Life in the back streets There was a price to pay for Britain's industrial expansion. Many of the inner-city poor, such as the residents of Glasgow's East End tenements (left, 1868), lived in crowded, dirty conditions.

Industrial pollution By the 1860s the Black Country night sky around Bilston – now part of Wolverhampton – was alight with fire and smoke pouring from chimneys. The area had become a centre for coal-making and iron manufacturing.

The tortured landscape

The New Englander Elihu Burritt, appointed US Consul at Birmingham by Abraham Lincoln, penned his powerful description of the hellish landscape of the Black Country in 1868:

'Nature has the under-hand, and from the crown of her head to the sole of her foot she is scourged with cat-o'-nine-tails of red-hot wire, and marred and scarred and fretted, and smoked half to death day and night, year and year, even on Sundays. Almost every square inch of her form is reddened, blackened, and distorted by the terrible tractoration of a hot blister. But all this cutaneous eruption is nothing compared with the internal violence and agonies she has to endure. Never was animal being subject to such merciless and ceaseless vivisection. The very sky and clouds above are moved to sympathy with her sufferings and shed black tears in token of their emotion.'

export coal; pig iron production followed in the 1840s. The town grew and spread over the fields and marshes as its population skyrocketed to 5462 in 1841 and 75,532 by 1891.

In 1801 Cardiff was a small coastal town of 15,000 people with a tradition of fishing and port trading. The Industrial Revolution brought heavy engineering to the coastal plain where the town lay; but more significantly it created a huge expansion in the docks. Dozens of coal mines opened in the south Wales valleys, and coal moved like a black river down the railways and canals to Cardiff and away by sea to markets all over the world. By 1901 the population had grown twentyfold to 228,638.

Birmingham was the industrial centre of the Midlands and by the 1850s had become known as the 'city of a thousand trades', producing pins, brassware, jewellery, guns, buttons, toys and many other items. The population grew from 85,753 in 1811 to 232,638 in 1841, after the arrival of the London to Birmingham railway. By the late 19th century the city had topped 840,000, absorbing places such as Balsall Heath and Edgbaston.

WORKERS' PLAYGROUNDS EAT UP THE COAST

By the start of the Victorian era the seaside craze was well under way (see pages 174-175). Fishing villages such as Brighthelmstone (Brighton) and Eastbourne in Sussex spread out along the cliffs to accommodate holidaymakers. Speculative estates like Regency Kemp Town, east of Brighton, pushed up land prices and tempted landowners to sell farmland for development. Long stretches of coastline gradually disappeared under bricks and mortar as cheap train travel put a seaside holiday within reach of factory workers: Lancashire mill workers went to Blackpool (below) and London's East Enders to Southend-on-Sea in Essex. Both places became sprawling pleasure resorts with piers and promenades, funfairs and gardens, and streets of inexpensive lodgings.

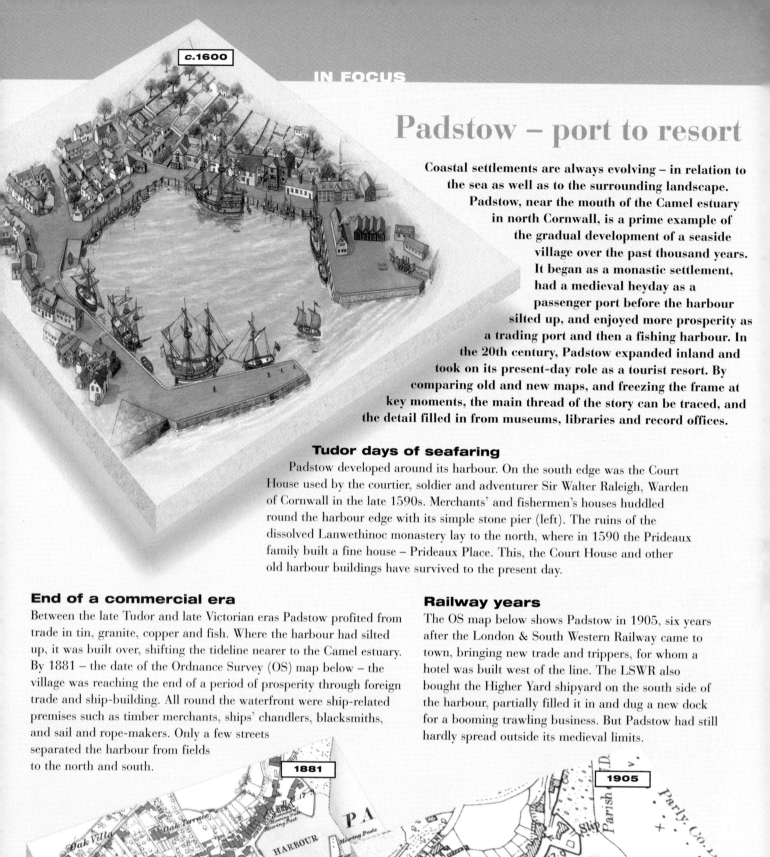

c.1600

Padstow – port to resort

Coastal settlements are always evolving – in relation to the sea as well as to the surrounding landscape. Padstow, near the mouth of the Camel estuary in north Cornwall, is a prime example of the gradual development of a seaside village over the past thousand years. It began as a monastic settlement, had a medieval heyday as a passenger port before the harbour silted up, and enjoyed more prosperity as a trading port and then a fishing harbour. In the 20th century, Padstow expanded inland and took on its present-day role as a tourist resort. By comparing old and new maps, and freezing the frame at key moments, the main thread of the story can be traced, and the detail filled in from museums, libraries and record offices.

Tudor days of seafaring

Padstow developed around its harbour. On the south edge was the Court House used by the courtier, soldier and adventurer Sir Walter Raleigh, Warden of Cornwall in the late 1590s. Merchants' and fishermen's houses huddled round the harbour edge with its simple stone pier (left). The ruins of the dissolved Lanwethinoc monastery lay to the north, where in 1590 the Prideaux family built a fine house – Prideaux Place. This, the Court House and other old harbour buildings have survived to the present day.

End of a commercial era

Between the late Tudor and late Victorian eras Padstow profited from trade in tin, granite, copper and fish. Where the harbour had silted up, it was built over, shifting the tideline nearer to the Camel estuary. By 1881 – the date of the Ordnance Survey (OS) map below – the village was reaching the end of a period of prosperity through foreign trade and ship-building. All round the waterfront were ship-related premises such as timber merchants, ships' chandlers, blacksmiths, and sail and rope-makers. Only a few streets separated the harbour from fields to the north and south.

Railway years

The OS map below shows Padstow in 1905, six years after the London & South Western Railway came to town, bringing new trade and trippers, for whom a hotel was built west of the line. The LSWR also bought the Higher Yard shipyard on the south side of the harbour, partially filled it in and dug a new dock for a booming trawling business. But Padstow had still hardly spread outside its medieval limits.

1881

1905

Today

Gateway to holidays This poster enticed families to Padstow in 1962 on the daily 11am Atlantic Coast Express from Waterloo. The service, which had run since 1907, closed in 1964, but the disused line found a new use as the route for the Camel Trail cycle path to Bodmin Moor.

Growing big on fish

A new jetty south of the harbour was built ten years after the railway arrived, with a north jetty added in the 1930s. But the most notable change in Padstow during the 20th century was its expansion south around the railway, and west around the improved roads, which is clear from today's OS map, above. By the time the railway closed, the town was one of Cornwall's most popular seaside resorts. In the 1970s chef Rick Stein opened a fish restaurant on the harbour, the start of a seafood empire that has brought a new age of prosperity for Padstow.

New industry and its workers fill the land

The 19th-century mass-manufacturing processes of the Industrial Revolution demanded manpower on an enormous scale. The building of housing and all its related services – shops, schools, churches and chapels, pubs, railway stations, streets, gasworks – caused new villages to spring up, others to grow into towns, and towns to swell into centres of industry.

New villages of the coalfields

As coal production leaped from 30 million tons a year in 1835 to 133 million tons in 1875, and on up to 287 million tons in 1913, new communities took root in the dust and dirt of the coalfields. The valleys of south Wales, one of Britain's prime coal-mining regions, saw huge upsurges in population. In 1851 fewer than 1000 people lived in Glamorgan's Rhondda Valley. Ten years later the population was 3000, and by 1911 that number had soared to 160,000 – the result of some 70 collieries opening in a few decades.

The effect on the Rhondda landscape, as on that of all industrial south Wales, was dramatic. The high moorland ridges that looked down into the Rhondda Valley remained almost untouched countryside; but along the valley floor the pit villages of Pontypridd, Porth, Tonypandy, Ystrad, Pentre, Treorchy and Treherbert, confined by the steep hillsides, elongated until they ran into one another, creating a continuous snake of terraced houses, pits and slag heaps some 12 miles long.

Landscapes of slate and coal

The buildings of the Industrial Revolution were roofed with Welsh slates, and the landscape of north Wales underwent enormous changes from the effects of slate quarrying. In 1801 Ffestiniog village had a population of 732. Slate was first discovered in the area in 1849. By the end of the century 4800 men worked in 14 quarries there. Much of the working was hidden inside the mountains,

At the foot of slate mountain In the late 1900s the booming slate industry at Blaenau Ffestiniog had a dramatic impact on both landscape and population. Massive quarry spoil heaps still dwarf the terraced houses of slateworkers (above, dressing slate in 1910).

Patterns of change When the last pits closed in 1992, the colliery at Trelewis in the Taff Bargoed Valley (above, photographed in 1979) employed 80 per cent of its community. The former colliery is one of three in the valley now landscaped into a community park, a growing trend in south Wales.

but huge waste tips proliferated along the Conwy Valley, as did industrial railways, dressing mills, reservoirs, engine houses, river quays and coastal harbours. By 1901 Blaenau Ffestiniog, known as 'The City of Slates', had become a sprawling quarry town of 11,433 inhabitants.

Similar dizzying growth occurred in northeast England. In 1801 the rural Easington district of coastal County Durham had some 2000 inhabitants. A century later, thanks to the development of coal mines along the county's seaboard, 50,000 lived in the area. The opening of a new pit required the rapid creation of the red-brick mining town of Easington Colliery. In 1902 the mine had 87 employees, but by 1914 there were 1896 pit workers. Spoil from the mine, tipped over the cliffs, blackened the beaches, and raw sewage from the village polluted the sea.

Market towns join the expansion

The coming of mechanised industry and the railway changed the sleepy market towns of Britain. A needle factory at Alcester in Warwickshire; carpet weaving in Bridgnorth, Shropshire; flannel mills at Newtown in Powys – these resulted in housing development outside the compact town centres that often dated back to medieval times. The railway was the catalyst for new building between station and town centre, and in many cases the prosperity generated by improved transport saw the town centres developed, too, with grand buildings such as a Corn Exchange (Hitchin, Hertfordshire) or a fine General Hospital (Saffron Walden, Essex).

FIND OUT MORE

• www.nmgw.ac.uk For information on Big Pit, the National Mining Museum of Wales, housed in a former colliery.
• www.llechwedd-slate-caverns.co.uk Details on the Llechwedd Slate Caverns museum, Blaenau Ffestiniog.
• www.saltaire.yorks.com For visitors to Saltaire.
• www.portsunlight.org.uk The history and architecture of Port Sunlight.

ENLIGHTENED PLANNING OF WORK AND HOME

Some philanthropic Victorian employers, appalled by the disease, dirt and darkness in which Britain's industrial workers lived and laboured, set about building exemplary factories with adjacent 'model villages' where their employees could live with dignity. Saltaire, near Bradford in Yorkshire, built between 1853 and 1876, was the brainchild of the wool magnate Sir Titus Salt (right), who ensured the mill was light and airy, and the village had neat cottages, an educational institute, a school, a library and sports ground. Port Sunlight on Merseyside, built from 1888 onwards by W.H. Lever, the creator of Sunlight soap, had hundreds of cottages, a swimming pool and a theatre; while in the 1890s the Quaker chocolate manufacturer George Cadbury built a green and spaciously laid out village for his workers at Bournville, then south of Birmingham.

Workers' paradise? Saltaire (below) was laid out by wool baron Sir Titus Salt (right) in close relation to the giant mill where most of the villagers worked. In its heyday the mill employed 3000 workers, whose well-built homes had piped water and outside lavatories. The village had health, education and sports facilities; along with two churches – but no public house.

Farming hits the high and low points

It is a romantic misconception to look back on the 19th century as a golden age of farming when every field was fruitful and every rural belly full. There were some boom times, but the story for Victorian farmers and farm labourers was often grim.

Depression grips the countryside

Agriculture tends to thrive in time of war, when cheap food imports dry up and there are plenty of hungry mouths to feed. That is what happened during the Napoleonic wars at the start of the 19th century; and with the manufacturing towns expanding and demanding ever more food and clothing, the prospects seemed set fair for agriculture. But after 1815 and victory over Napoleon, imports flowed again and the price of corn and wool dropped like a stone.

The government tried to protect the suffering farmers by introducing the Corn Laws in 1815, restricting foreign imports to keep up domestic corn prices. But this made bread much more expensive, and surpluses of domestic corn still forced grain prices down. Farmers went bankrupt, and farm labourers were thrown out of work to starve and beg. To make matters worse, new technology, such as threshing machines and seed drills, steadily replaced more and more men and women in the fields. There were riots, nocturnal machine-smashings and rick-burnings, and there could have been a full-scale rural

uprising. The government feared a popular revolution like the one in France only 40 years before, so when six farm labourers tried to form a trade union at Tolpuddle in Dorset a severe example was made of them. In March 1834 they were sentenced to deportation to Australia and seven years' hard labour. At Tolpuddle you can still see the stump of the sycamore tree where the 'Tolpuddle Martyrs' met, and visit the Tolpuddle Martyrs Museum.

From High Farming to lean times

The 1845 General Enclosure Act began to address the needs of the landless poor by providing allotments for them. By the mid 19th century a great revival in the fortunes of agriculture had begun, which became known as the era of High Farming. In this more peaceful agricultural revolution science and study combined to create heavier-yielding crops and livestock, more efficient use of organic fertiliser from potash to bird droppings, more advanced machines and tools, and improved drainage to make the most of the land. A long period of peace, only briefly broken by the 1854-6 Crimean War, and the insatiable appetite of the growing cities were the backdrop to this prosperity.

THE SWING RIOTS

In August 1830 agricultural labourers in east Kent began a series of attacks on the threshing machines they perceived as a threat to their livelihood. Over the following four months riots spread through southeast England, with protesters demanding higher wages and tithe reductions. Machines were smashed, and barns and hay-ricks burned. Farmers and landowners received threatening letters from a mythical 'Captain Swing', who attracted a bounty on his head (left). Some 700 rioters were imprisoned, 481 sentenced to transportation and 19 executed.

192

FIFTY POUNDS Reward.

Whereas, on Saturday last, Letters signed **"SWING"** were sent to Mr. Hawkings, and Mr. D. Symes, Farmers of Axmouth, threatening to destroy their premises by FIRE; whosoever will give information leading to the discovery and conviction of the writer,

SHALL RECEIVE A REWARD OF

50 POUNDS

All Communications to be addressed to the *Church Wardens and Overseers of Axmouth.*

N. B. The above Letters passed through the Colyton Post Office, & bear the Axminster post mark.

Dated December the 6th, 1830.

J. Hunt, Printer, Bookbinder, and Stationer, Lyme and Axminster.

High point of farming Cogges Manor Farm, near Whitney (left), in Oxfordshire, embodies the elements of a typical prosperous Victorian farm. The farm is now a working museum of Cotswolds rural life in the 19th century.

The end of High Farming came in the 1870s. A series of rainy summers ruined the harvests and brought disease to the fields and the stockyards, while cheap imports of North American wheat forced British farmers to sell their produce for next to nothing. There was a return to the post-Napoleonic cycle, with farmers selling up or leaving fields unsown and unreaped, and country folk leaving rural areas such as Swaledale in North Yorkshire and swathes of Exmoor. Parts of the hitherto meticulously cared-for countryside became wild and overgrown, and once more unemployed labourers were forced either to beg or to seek work in the manufacturing towns.

The Highlanders make way for sheep

If the plight of English labourers was wretched, so was that of the Scottish highlanders. The 1745 Rebellion under Bonnie Prince Charlie, crushed at the Battle of Culloden (see pages 58-59), had led to the dissolution of the traditional clan way of life. Clan chiefs sold off their land to rich 'foreigners' from England and lowland Scotland. Increasingly, the labourers were shifted onto small agricultural holdings known as crofts, where they worked for the landowners' kelp (seaweed) industry. From the early 19th century, as the market for kelp failed and landowners were eager to replace their unprofitable tenants with profitable sheep, the mass movements of the crofters, or 'clearances', followed. A year's notice was considered generous. Then the agent's men were called in, thatch and roof timbers were tumbled and burned, and families were turned out to do the best they could. Some were looked after by caring landowners, most were given poor land elsewhere or expected to remove themselves. Thousands did, leaving to start new lives in America, Canada or Australia. Others ended up in urban slums.

Clearance village sites (see pages 110-111) are sometimes marked by ruined houses, but more often by 'lazybeds' – lines of mounded ridges where crofters grew potatoes – which furrow the hillsides round the village sites. The Clearance villages seem especially poignant on the Scottish islands, often in locations of great beauty such as Lorgill in Skye, Mingulay in the Outer Hebrides, and the twin settlements of Innie Vae and Arin above Calgary Bay in Mull.

Highland clearance Soldiers read the riot act to crofters at Aignish Farm, near Stornaway, in 1888. Landowners' agents adopted brutal tactics to clear the land for sheep. For the largely destitute highlanders, emigration was the only remaining option, especially when famine followed potato blight in 1846.

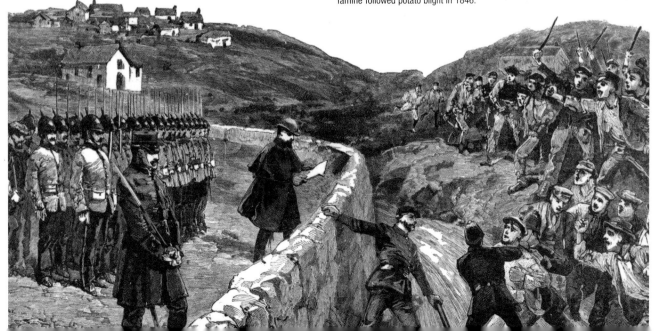

Suburbs and wartime eat away at the land

The confusion and slaughter of the First World War left city-dwellers hankering after the certainties of a more gentle rural age. A home in the country just outside the town seemed the remedy. This desire, and the spread of industry to city outskirts, fuelled an exodus into the green fringes of urban areas, especially London. War in 1939 brought this to a halt but left its own marks on the land.

Suburban sprawl Like many areas of Britain close to urban centres, Dartford in Kent was covered in private housing developments in the 1930s.

Green turns to grey

In the 1920s and 30s suburbs proliferated, absorbing old communities and countryside into the skirts of London, aided by the growth of the overground and Underground railways (see pages 190-191). Places such as Sidcup in Kent, Morden in Surrey, Edgware in Middlesex and Enfield in Hertfordshire were drawn into the urban sprawl of semi-detached houses (see pages 188-189) where once there was green breathing space.

The 1911 Greater Birmingham Extension Act spread that city's boundaries to include urban districts like Handsworth and villages such as King's Heath and Yardley. Between 1919 and 1939, 115,000 houses were built in Birmingham, including a rash of new housing estates, the largest at Kingstanding and Bordesley Green east of the city.

By the 1920s Glasgow was the most overcrowded city after London and in desperate need of land for housing. Between 1926 and 1938 it more than doubled in size, moving west

along the Clyde to take in the communities of Yoker and Scotstoun, and absorbing settlements around the city. Glasgow Corporation invested heavily in public housing, building estates in the 1920s at Knightswood, Mosspark, Hamiltonhill and Possilpark, higher-density tenements in the 1930s at Blackhill, Balornock and Haghill.

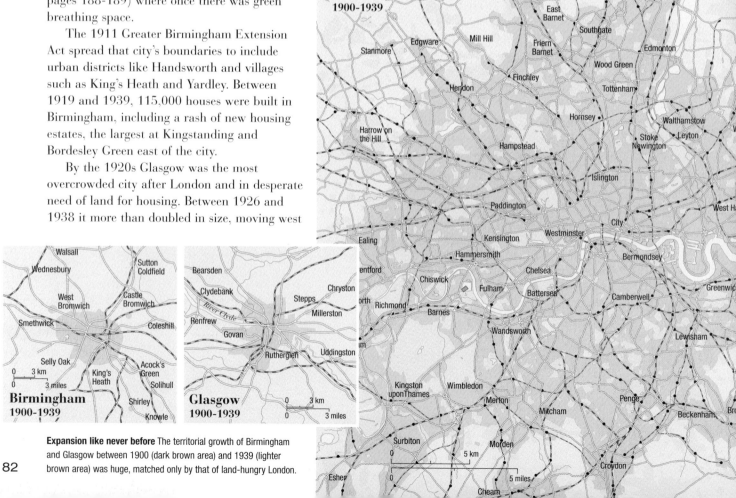

Expansion like never before The territorial growth of Birmingham and Glasgow between 1900 (dark brown area) and 1939 (lighter brown area) was huge, matched only by that of land-hungry London.

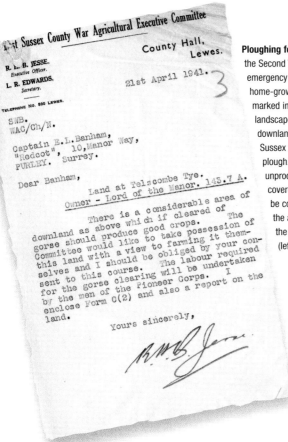

East Sussex County War Agricultural Executive Committee

County Hall,
Lewes.

R. B. JESSE.
Executive Officer.
L. R. EDWARDS.
Secretary.

21st April 1941.

TELEPHONE NO. 800 LEWES.

SWB.
WAC/Ch/N.

Captain E.L.Benham,
"Redcot", 10,Manor Way,
PURLEY, Surrey.

Dear Banham,

Land at Telscombe Tye.
Owner - Lord of the Manor. 145.7 A.

There is a considerable area of
downland as above which if cleared of
gorse should produce good crops. The
Committee would like to take possession of
this land with a view to farming it themselves and I should be obliged by your con-
sent to this course. The labour required
for the gorse clearing will be undertaken
by the men of the Pioneer Corps. I
enclose Form C(2) and also a report on the
land.

Yours sincerely,

Ploughing for victory During the Second World War emergency demands for home-grown food had a marked impact on the landscape, with swathes of downland in counties like Sussex brought under the plough. Even seemingly unproductive gorse-covered areas could be commandeered by the authorities at the stroke of a pen (left, 1941).

Farming boom and bust

The farming slump of the late Victorian and Edwardian era was halted by the outbreak of the First World War. German U-boats blockaded Britain, and self-sufficiency in food and clothing was the cry. But the end of the war brought an echo of events after the Napoleonic Wars a century before – farming slumped, the government failed to prop up domestic corn prices, farms and land went out of production, and cheap food imports flooded the market, rising to 70 per cent of national consumption by 1939. Swathes of arable land were turned into pasture or grass and many farm workers lost their jobs, and with them their homes. There was also a transformation of moor and hill country as the Forestry Commission, created in 1919, responded to the timber shortages caused by the First World War. Soon vast areas of East Anglia, northern England, Wales and Scotland began to disappear under fast-growing conifer plantations.

Modern farming had its first stirrings between the wars with the advent of primitive tractors, chemical fertilizers and artificial concentrates for feeding cattle, pigs and chickens. Even fewer farm workers were needed now. At the same time as hundreds of thousands of better-off city workers were setting up family homes in country towns and new estates outside London, Birmingham, Glasgow and other urban centres, many country people left the recession-hit land for better wages and employment prospects in the cities.

THE DEBRIS OF WAR
The Second World War brought many ruptures to the British landscape. The most obvious was the widespread ruin caused by the bombing of major cities such as London, Liverpool, Cardiff and Glasgow (see pages 196-197). But it was also in defence of the land and as a platform for attack that the countryside was pockmarked with hurried development.

Airfields for fighter and bomber squadrons were laid out on agricultural land, most in the flat fields of East Anglia which were closest to the target cities in Nazi-occupied Europe.

In the dark early days of the war Britain expected to be invaded at any moment. From 1939 to 1940 coastal defences such as searchlight batteries and gun emplacements were built, beaches were mined and barbed wired, and small concrete machine-gun posts called 'pillboxes' dotted the countryside. The guns have gone, but much of the concrete debris remains in fields and on the coasts, often clear to see, sometimes hidden in the undergrowth.

Defence of the skies The dome at Langham airfield, Norfolk, was built for training RAF anti-aircraft gunners.

Stopping the tanks The curious overgrown mounds beside the River Wey, at Waverley Abbey, Farnham, Surrey, are tank traps.

Machine-gun post A typical 'pillbox', south of Chelmsford in Essex.

Coastal barrier Chunks of concrete sea defences can still be seen littering the coast at Winterton-on-Sea, in Norfolk.

New transport paves over the landscape

At the start of the 20th century Britain's roads were still 'macadamised' (made of stones) and largely unclassified; the railways ruled the transport world. Air travel had not even been invented. Then the motor car changed the way we view transport, and a new kind of paved landscape emerged.

Taking to the road

By 1934 there were 1.5 million cars in Britain; by 1961, 10 million. Today it is 30 million and rising. Our enthusiasm for the car has been an extraordinary phenomenon, with major implications for the landscape.

The dusty, muddy surfaces of British roads, unsuitable for motor travel, were tarred from about 1910 onwards, the start of an enormous road-building programme that has been accelerating ever since. Britain's first full-length motorway, the M1, opened in 1959. Soon driver tiredness caused by the monotony of this new long-haul motoring, allied to unrestricted speed, started to claim lives. So Britain's first motorway service station was opened the following year at Newport Pagnell. Although the décor, services and food were all plain, the facility was a success. Nowadays there are nearly 70 motorway service stations, marooned self-contained settlements complete with shops and restaurants that owe their being to the car rather than a river or trade route.

There are now over 2000 miles of motorway, and many ring-roads and bypasses round once-congested towns. The effect of these new roads on the landscape has been far-reaching. Apart from the country lost to make way for roads, their ancillary buildings such as petrol stations and cafés bring urban architectural themes into rural surroundings. Strategic road intersections across Britain have spawned industrial and trading estates, shopping malls and giant supermarkets. Road traffic disturbs the natural as much as the human world with its intrusive sights, smells and sounds, and exhaust emissions are a long-term cause of concern.

Air travel takes off During the 1930s Britain's Imperial Airways, formed in 1924, began to develop and promote flights to the Continent in addition to its long-haul routes to India and Africa.

In the air

The first commercial air service began in 1919, but, like the car, air travel was at first the preserve of the well-off. This changed after the Second World War, especially in the 1970s with the arrival of cheap jet travel to holiday destinations. In the 30 years following the war, Heathrow, today the world's busiest airport, replaced a landscape of farmhouses, cottages, fields and market gardens with hangars, runways, terminal buildings, hotels, warehouses and ancillary roads. Terminal 3 stands on the site of the original hamlet of Heath Row.

Now London alone is served by five airports, while all major British cities have at least one. Pressure is always on to develop more airports. The environmental consequences are the same as for road building, although less of the countryside is concreted over.

A new journey begins A workman sweeps the carriageway before the 1959 opening of the M1 between London and the Midlands. The speed limit of 70mph was not imposed until 1965, as a temporary measure at first, and then permanently in 1967. Initially about 13,000 vehicles used the M1 daily, compared with today's figure of almost 100,000.

Under the sea to France

The notion of joining Britain to the rest of Europe via a road tunnel under the English Channel was mooted as far back as 1802, when the country was temporarily at peace with France. Napoleon was interested. But war broke out again in 1803, and the scheme was shelved.

The idea remained a dream until 1986. Then work on the tunnel started in earnest. The French and English teams of tunnellers broke through to each other in 1991, and in 1994 the 32-mile Channel Tunnel linking Folkestone and Calais opened. The three-tunnel rail connection carries 500 train crossings a day, and allows rail travellers to reach Paris from London in three hours. It has also spawned Britain's first new railway construction in 60 years. The high-speed Channel Tunnel Rail Link, crossing Kent from the coast to central London, and due to open in 2007, has turned the tide of closure begun by Dr Beeching 40 years ago.

Britain's lost railways As Chairman of the British Railways Board in the early 1960s Dr Richard Beeching transformed the rail network, closing 5000 miles of unprofitable track (shown in red below) and more than 2000 stations. In a shift of focus onto high-speed inter-city passenger trains, he scrapped hundreds of wayside goods depots and some 300,000 freight wagons – pushing more freight trucks onto the roads. Beeching's branch line closures saved only a quarter of the projected £30 million.

Tunnel overspill The Folkestone terminus has re-shaped the landscape at the foot of the North Downs chalk escarpment.

The Iron Road shrinks

Britain's railways lost out spectacularly to the car in the 20th century, particularly after the Second World War. In 1900 there were 22,000 miles of rail track (see pages 72-73). Everyone and everything went by rail. A century later, there are 10,000 miles of ageing railway, which is increasingly expensive to maintain and run.

The damage was done in the 1960s when Dr Richard Beeching, Chairman of the British Railways Board, wielded his 'Beeching Axe' (see left) to close thousands of miles of uneconomic branch lines, such as the Somerset & Dorset Railway from Bath to Bournemouth (1966), the Mid-Wales Railway (1962) and the Deeside Line from Aberdeen to Ballater (1966). Walkers and cyclists have benefited, as many disused lines have now been turned into footpaths and cycleways. But the branch line closures have forced more and more rural communities into reliance on the bus and car for transport.

The machinery of power puts down roots

Since the Second World War home and work life have been driven more and more by a dependence on machines and new technology. This demands huge amounts of power, so swathes of countryside are now dominated by the fuming chimneys and cooling towers of power stations, the whirling arms of wind farm generators, the vast geometry of oil refineries and the armies of giant steel pylons.

Tapping into water

The first large-scale attempts to harness naturally regenerating, sustainable energy to produce power used water. At first it was the ancient technology of water wheels to power mills; then in the late 19th century, after the discovery of electricity, hydro-electric schemes in which water was forced through turbines. Britain now has some 200 hydro schemes, the vast majority in Scotland, where there are plenty of remote glens to dam and mountain streams to trap. Lacking smoking towers and huge buildings, hydro schemes intrude on the landscape less than other forms of power station.

Power from under the ground

Until nuclear power came to Britain ten years after the Second World War it was fossil fuels – coal, gas and oil – that fired most of the power stations producing Britain's electricity. Invariably built on the grandest of scales, these vast temples of power dominate their landscapes and feature such striking structures as the gigantic, steaming cooling towers of Fiddlers Ferry near Warrington and Ferrybridge next to the A1 in Yorkshire. Also in Yorkshire, the 259m (850ft) chimney at Drax is matched

Beached monster Sizewell B power station (above) with its domed reactor contrasts starkly with the flat Suffolk coastline. Inside Hinkley Point A power station in Somerset (left) in 1965, fuel elements are loaded into a cradle. Hinkley A closed in 2000 and is now being decommissioned.

in scale by its cooling towers, each large enough to swallow St Paul's Cathedral.

The best known of the pre-nuclear power stations are the London twins: the Art Deco four-chimneyed hulk at Battersea (1937-80), and the plainer Bankside (1963-81), both designed by Sir Giles Gilbert Scott (1880-1960). Battersea is now a shell undergoing redevelopment, while Bankside glories in its reincarnation as the Tate Modern.

The nuclear option

Britain began building commercial nuclear power stations in the 1950s – Calder Hall on the Cumbrian coast, opened in 1956, was the first in the world. Within the next 20 years, 17 stations were built. There are now 14 in operation, although all are planned to close by 2035. The stations have a distinctive bulky look, with a plain box-like exterior, such as Trawsfynydd in Gwynedd, Wales, from which, in some cases, a strengthened containment dome rises, covering the reactor, as at Sizewell B in Suffolk, the last station to open in 1995.

The stations have an inevitably dramatic impact on the landscape as they always stand alone, sited away from centres of population in remote coastal or estuarine locations where there is unlimited coolant water.

Oiling the wheels

We also expect on demand the petrol and diesel to run our cars, trains and buses. Britain's first crude oil refinery

Vast steaming landmark The cooling towers of the coal-fired Fiddlers Ferry power station near Warrington can be seen for 30 miles.

opened in 1922 at Llandarcy near Neath. There are now 12 refineries in Britain, sited on or near the coast so as to receive their base material of crude oil as efficiently as possible – Grangemouth just west of Edinburgh by pipeline direct from the North Sea, the others by ship. At places such as Milford Haven in Pembrokeshire, and Coryton on the Essex shore of the Thames Estuary, the miles of contorted pipework, the vast distillation columns and the brilliant orange flares form a striking intrusion into the natural landscape.

Keeping it clean

An antidote to the pollution caused by fossil and nuclear power has been the harnessing of wind power. But a wind turbine farm – a cluster of white columns 80m (250ft) high, supporting huge 'propeller' rotor blades whirling as they harvest the wind's energy – still has an impact on the landscape. The first in Britain opened in 1991 at Delabole in Cornwall. Wales has dramatic examples at Llandinam (103 turbines) and Carno (56), both near Newtown in Powys. By 2010, 10 per cent of our electricity should come from wind turbines, but by then many will be offshore.

FIND OUT MORE

- www.energyinst.org.uk/education/coryton/page3.htm Oil refineries and the petroleum industry.
- www.dti.gov.uk/energy DTI website on all forms of energy.
- www.bwea.com/map/ Wind energy and other renewable sources.

Crazy mechanics of power The huge Grangemouth oil refinery lies west of Edinburgh on the Firth of Forth, receiving its crude oil by pipeline from the Forties Field in the North Sea. At night the unceasing work of the refining process creates a spectacular light show.

The great grid that powers our homes

We tend to take electricity for granted. The supply from the National Grid seems limitless, its delivery to our homes and workplaces as smooth as silk. And yet, the creation of this network took decades in the early 20th century, a huge engineering and technical feat that is still growing.

March of the pylons The visual impact of steel pylons carrying high-voltage overhead cables across the land is enormous. Installing the cables underground would preserve the view but also cost 20 times as much.

Bringing order to chaos

The National Grid has only been in existence in a complete state since 1935. Before then there was a chaotic scene across Britain. By the start of the First World War there were more than 600 separate electricity companies, most of them too small to operate economically, and all competing with each other. Some used an AC (Alternating Current) system, others DC (Direct Current). London alone had 50 kinds of supply, with 24 different voltages and 10 different frequencies. Each town had its own electricity generating station; the capacity of such stations was rarely more than 5000 horsepower. If one broke down, electric power throughout its region was shut off. The north of England produced more electricity than the south, but it was the south that consumed more. Rural areas had little or no supply, and in towns most lighting was still powered by gas.

The surge in the manufacturing of munitions during the First World War made demands that this fragmented network of electricity providers could not satisfy. Manufacturers and domestic consumers complained, and Parliament decided to take action. The Electricity Supply Act of 1919 established the Electricity Commissioners, with a brief to modernise Britain's supply of electricity. Six years later, the Glaswegian industrialist Lord Weir headed a government enquiry into the sorry state of the electricity industry – '... a failure', as he put it,

'the resultant loss to the country has been heavy, and becomes daily heavier'. The result was the Electricity Supply Act of 1926, the first move to co-ordinate a national supply of electricity.

Creating the 'grid'

The Central Electricity Board (CEB) was then created to replace the privately run power stations with a smaller number of bigger and better stations, with common levels of production and maintenance. Local networks of selected stations were linked in a publicly owned National Grid, using an AC high-tension mains transmission system to form the standard supply across Britain. By 1935 the National Grid was complete, with bulk electricity flowing across a high-voltage network to supply the places where it was in greatest demand – generally in the south of England.

That early National Grid operated at 132 kilovolts (132,000 volts), a high voltage for the era, but soon rising demand required an increase to 275kv. Much of today's National Grid – known as the 'supergrid' – operates at 400kv. The electricity flows through conductors (cables) made of bundles of aluminium alloy or aluminium with a steel

The cable men During the building of the National Grid in 1933 workmen at Mapledurham in Berkshire lay out 33,000-volt cables. They were then hoisted into position to run between pylons on either side of the Thames.

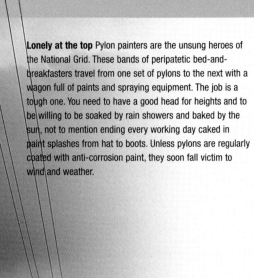

Lonely at the top Pylon painters are the unsung heroes of the National Grid. These bands of peripatetic bed-and-breakfasters travel from one set of pylons to the next with a wagon full of paints and spraying equipment. The job is a tough one. You need to have a good head for heights and to be willing to be soaked by rain showers and baked by the sun, not to mention ending every working day caked in paint splashes from hat to boots. Unless pylons are regularly coated with anti-corrosion paint, they soon fall victim to wind and weather.

core. Increasingly the cables are being buried underground, but most are still carried overhead on rows of steel pylons – the cheaper alternative – marching across our valleys, hills and fields. Some see the pylons as eyesores disfiguring the countryside, others as objects of engineering beauty. To most they are an established part of many rural views – an acceptable price to pay for the convenience of power.

TIMELINE OF POWER

Pre-1914 More than 600 private companies operate thousands of small, inefficient electricity generating stations all over Britain.

1919 Spurred by the shortcomings revealed during the First World War, Parliament passes the Electricity Supply Act and appoints the Electricity Commissioners to shake up Britain's electricity supply industry.

1926 After a government enquiry led by Lord Weir, Parliament passes another Electricity Supply Act. This leads to the creation of the Central Electricity Board (CEB), and the setting up of the National Grid of interlinked, publicly owned power stations.

1935 The National Grid is completed. The new network of efficient stations, operating to much improved standards, delivers bulk high-voltage electricity where demand is greatest.

1956 Calder Hall electricity generating station opens in Cumbria – the first commercial power station in the world to be fuelled by nuclear energy, and forerunner of many more in Britain (see page 86).

2003 After years of campaigning by the residents of Cwm Brefi, the mountain village near Lampeter in west Wales becomes the last community in Britain to be connected to the National Grid. The 11 households contribute £5000 each towards the cost of connection, which totals £300,000.

Machines in a featureless landscape In the Yorkshire Wolds huge combine harvesters march across prairie-like fields. From the 1950s, increased mechanisation of farming and the push for higher yields led to the removal of old field boundaries.

Transformation and conservation of the country

Changes in the British farming landscape between the feudal era and the first half of the 20th century were as nothing compared with what happened when intensive mechanised farming appeared after the Second World War. Some changes such as the destruction of hedges were highly visible. Others, like the effect on wildlife, took longer to register. When they did, the conservation movement hit back.

The rise of the mega-farms

Modern farming took hold in Britain after the war. Out went the farm horse; in came tractors and powerful machines operated by one person to do the same job that once required several agricultural labourers. Throughout the land, tall silos and outbuildings the size of warehouses rose above the farmhouses, and tarmacadamed roads and lanes replaced muddy cart tracks.

Wetlands were drained and ploughed, hedges removed and meadows artificially fertilised. Modern chemicals put paid to insect and weed pests, while nitrate and phosphate fertilisers forced huge yields of cereals and vegetables out of the prairie fields. Artificial insemination, concentrated feeds and intensive rearing boosted production of milk, meat and eggs.

There was a price to be paid for this intensity of cultivation. The chemicals and the hedge-ripping cut

> **DID YOU KNOW?**
>
> In the Midlands and the south of England during the 1960s, some 5000 miles of hedges were destroyed every year for intensive farming.

songbird, butterfly and wild flower numbers dramatically. In forestry, the huge conifer plantations of the Forestry Commission, such as Kielder Forest in Northumberland (see page 121), produced a blandly uniform upland landscape poor in wildlife. People started to realise that the health of the British countryside was rapidly deteriorating.

A green revolution

Small-scale organic farms dedicated to producing food using only natural means struggled to establish themselves in the late 20th century in a mass-producer's cheap food market, but in the 1990s they began slowly to gain ground. You are most likely to see an abundance of wildlife on such farms, and on farms open to the public that are managed along traditional lines, such as Kingcombe Farm near Maiden Newton in Dorset (below). In the early years of the 21st century reforms of the EU-wide Common Agricultural Policy (CAP) placed a new onus on British farmers to work their land in an environmentally friendly way in order to qualify for farm subsidies.

A new political will to conserve the 'best' parts of rural Britain emerged in the years immediately after the Second World War. In 1949 the National Parks and Access to the Countryside Act created the designations Site of Special Scientific Interest (SSSI) and Area of Outstanding Natural Beauty (AONB) to protect vulnerable areas. SSSIs now cover more than 7 per cent of England and Wales, and

Rich in flora and fauna A huge variety of plants thrives in the protected meadowland of Kingcombe Farm in Dorset. In turn they support a host of birds, small animals and insects such as the Marbled White butterfly (right), found mostly in southern England.

The big clean-up

Several projects stand as shining examples of how a landscape ruined by human activity can be restored – and even improved.

Reclaim the beach In the 1990s the Turning The Tide project managed a clean-up of County Durham's colliery-polluted coastline that many thought impossible. When the last of Durham's coastal pits closed in 1993 the beaches were fouled with mine waste and the sea was thick with sewage. But now the clifftop colliery sites have been landscaped, environmentally friendly sewage disposal installed, new footpaths established, and the sea is washing the beaches clean.
www.turningthetide.org.uk

Saving the Broads Agricultural fertiliser run-off, enriching the waters of the Norfolk Broads, had turned them into murky, sterile soups by 1970, their native plants and wildlife killed as burgeoning algae stole the oxygen and blocked the sunlight. The Broads Authority was set up in 1988 to remedy the problem. Working with local wildlife trusts and other conservation bodies, the Authority has overseen a programme of pumping out polluted sludge, replanting rare water plants and discouraging diesel boats. Slowly the broads are recovering.
www.broads-authority.gov.uk

More projects Other notable reclamation projects have seen gravel quarries become lakes, as at the Cotswold Water Park (see pages 128-129), coal-mine slag heaps turned into grassy forested hillocks, as at Ebbw Vale and Ashton-in-Makerfield (see page 128), and a belt of Community Forests established on derelict land in and around 12 major towns and cities.
www.communityforest.org.uk

A coast regenerated County Durham's Easington Colliery beach before (right) and after restoration. (below).The five-year, £10-million Turning the Tide project regenerated 12 miles of coastline despoiled and choked by a century of colliery waste tipping.

11 per cent of Scotland, while AONBs account for 14 per cent of England and Wales.

The 1949 Act also led to the establishment of the first ten National Parks: Brecon Beacons, Dartmoor, Exmoor, Lake District, North York Moors, Northumberland, Peak District, Pembrokeshire Coast, Snowdonia and Yorkshire Dales. Added to these later were the Norfolk and Suffolk broads and, in 2005, the New Forest, while in Scotland the Cairngorms and Loch Lomond and The Trossachs are now National Parks. Many organisations have also joined the fight to halt and reverse the post-war decline of the countryside. They include the National Trust, the Royal Society for the Protection of Birds (RSPB), English Nature, local Wildlife Trusts and the Woodlands Trust (see right). Reserves set up by these conservation bodies include the birdwatchers' haven of Titchwell Marsh on the north Norfolk coast (RSPB), the thrilling limestone cleft of Lathkill Dale National Nature Reserve in the Peak District (English Nature), and the ancient oak woods of Crinan Woods in Argyll, Scotland (Woodlands Trust).

FIND OUT MORE

● www.woodland-trust.org.uk How the Woodland Trust works to protect our native woodland.
● www.rspb.org.uk Website of the Royal Society for the Protection of Birds.
● www.english-nature.org.uk English Nature website, including school projects and details on SSSIs.
● www.wildlifetrusts.org All about the Wildlife Trusts.
● www.anpa.gov.uk The National Parks website.
● www.nationaltrust.org.uk/environment The National Trust's environment and conservation website.

EXPLORE YOUR LANDSCAPE

Trade, industry, transport of goods and essential supplies, field systems and enclosures – even the pursuit of wealth and power – all have left their mark on the layout of Britain's towns and countryside. Documents and maps can tell you much of the story, and may help to set you on the right track when you step out into the fresh air to explore your area on foot.

Making a start The countryside around you and the layout of your town or village may seem to be a stable backcloth to daily life, but it is likely to have undergone many dramatic changes over the centuries. Finding out when, how and why these occurred is both fascinating and fun.

- One of the quickest ways to get a good overall picture of how the landscape around you has developed is to consult maps of the area (see pages 26-27). Start with an up-to-date Ordnance Survey (OS) map, then compare it with earlier ones, which will probably be in your local reference library or record office (see pages 18-19). Make a note of the major changes that you spot.
- You can also find documents, such as planning applications and electoral rolls relating to features noted on maps you have consulted, in local reference libraries and record offices. Even a brief glance at these resources should help you to draw up a plan of action (see opposite).
- Keep a map, preferably a current OS one, with you as you walk around and make a note of what you discover. Also jot down any questions that arise, possibly to be answered by another search through the archives.
- Although focused just on England, a useful book that will help you to structure your exploration, no matter where you live, is *The Making of the English Landscape* (W.G. Hoskins, Penguin Books, 1991).

Field patterns Many of the stone walls that divide up the land in the Peak District follow boundaries laid down in medieval times.

Hidden past Signs of industry may be found even in the depths of the countryside. The long, grassed-over mound near the hamlet of White Coppice in Lancashire (above) is all that remains of an embankment constructed when quarrying was a major souce of income in the area.

Working out what you want to know

Before you set out on a journey of exploration, draw up a rough plan of action, including any questions you want answered. You may deviate from it as your knowledge expands, but it will give you a starting point.

Distinctive features Find out about special points of interest in your area, and focus your research, at least initially, on a particular topic. In the New Forest, you might try to identify the sites of cottages seen on a tithe-award map of the 1840s that were abandoned by the late 19th century. In northeast Scotland, you could survey the remains of the planned Victorian fishing settlement at Lybster. Every area will throw up something different.

Shape and size Why does the medieval parish church at Llandyfaelog in Carmarthenshire stand apart from the village inside a circular enclosure? Why do the central streets of Flint in north Wales form a grid pattern? Look at a current map of your town or village and see if anything stands out that you might investigate. Perhaps you live in open countryside. In that case, you could investigate if the present pattern of hamlets, cottages and scattered farmsteads is an ancient or fairly recent one by comparing it with what is featured on earlier maps.

Mysteries to solve What is the explanation for those curving ridge-and-furrow patterns in nearby pasture? Does an old map reveal a flourishing settlement or grand estate that has since completely disappeared? Attempting to answer such questions could lead you down an exciting path of discovery.

Some basic guidelines

Working through the material you gather in a methodical way will ensure you get the most from your research.
- Keep cross-checking visual and documentary evidence. If you spot the remains of a moated site, a search in local archives may reveal who constructed it and when.
- Your first interpretations may be wide of the mark. Be prepared to change them, as you uncover more clues.
- Comparisons with other places are essential to check how specific to your area a particular feature is. In rural Essex, you might check how many parish churches have a timber belfry or a Tudor brick porch.

FIND OUT MORE

- *Medieval England: An Aerial Survey* (M.W. Beresford and J.K.S. St Joseph, Cambridge University Press, 1979)
- *The History of the Countryside* (Oliver Rackham, Orion, 1986)
- *Rural England: An Illustrated History of the Landscape* (Joan Thirsk ed., Oxford University Press, 2002)
- *The Making of the English Village* (B.K. Roberts, Longman, 1987)
- *The Making of the Industrial Landscape* (Barrie Trinder, Sutton Publishing, 1988)
- *Trees and Woodland in the British Landscape* (Oliver Rackham, Orion, 2001)
- *The Harvest of the Hills: Rural Life in Northern England and the Scottish Borders, 1400-1700* (Angus Winchester, Edinburgh University Press, 2000)

Plotting the urban landscape

Until the Industrial Revolution of the mid 18th century, the countryside was still visible from most British town centres. Comparing maps down the ages will help you to discover how these green acres were swallowed up. Look for street names, such as The Meadows or Little Common, or for surviving pockets of woodland – all possible clues to a rural past.

How towns ate the land

Old maps enable you to get a good sense of the size and layout of your town or city at different points in time. By comparing them, you can see how and when the settlement grew beyond its medieval limits and, perhaps, how much the central street plan has changed, or to what extent property boundaries have altered. You will also notice how spaces have been filled and how paths across what were once fields and open countryside have evolved gradually into streets and alleyways.

The earliest town plans

At the beginning of the 17th century, John Speed (1552-1629) drew a series of county maps that he published in 1612 as the *Theatre of the Empire of Great Britaine*. Included were maps of the various county towns, many of which have been widely reproduced, particularly in the county histories that you are likely to find at your local reference library or record office (see pages 18-19).

• Note the position of the market place at the heart of the town and consider how its shape compares with today's.

• Look for the walls that enclosed most of the towns drawn by Speed and see if any of the streets were already spreading beyond them.

• Look for the names of the principal streets, then check to see how many of them survive.

Maps of the 18th century

English county maps of the second half of the 18th century (see pages 26-27), such as Hodskinson's 1783 map of Suffolk or Yates's 1786 map of Lancashire, sometimes have town maps as insets.

• The local record office or reference library will have copies of your county maps, including an 18th-century one. You should also ask whether it has been published, perhaps as a CD. Most English towns have at least one map from the 18th century, if not earlier, commissioned by the borough council or some other local body.

• Late 18th-century maps will show your town at the start of the Industrial Revolution, when it was beginning to grow rapidly. See how many ancient features are marked, such as remnants of town walls or castle ruins. Has the market place been encroached upon by shops and stalls? Have the livestock markets been removed from the central streets? Are there any planned developments of new streets beyond the ancient core?

Maps of the 19th century

Your local record office or library is also likely to keep maps of your town that were commissioned by the local borough council or printed by local firms during the early 19th century. Compare these with Ordnance Survey (OS) maps (see pages 26-27) of the later 19th and early 20th centuries to find out

Military outpost John Speed's map of Lancaster in 1611 shows a town dominated by its castle. Most other buildings sit along and around Market Street, with a few spreading out into the surrounding countryside along St Leonard's Gate and Penny Street.

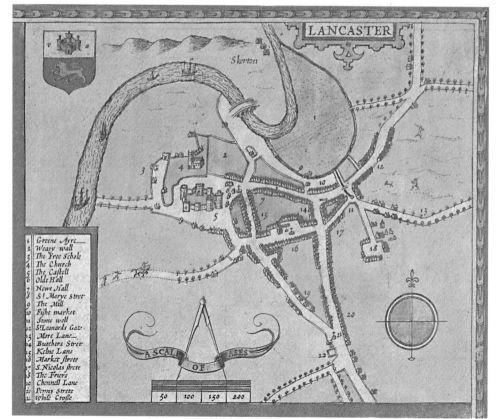

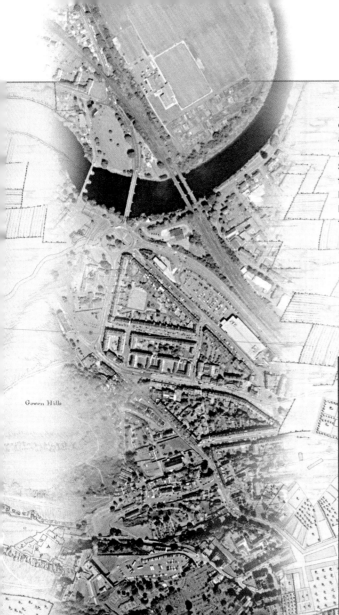

Gowen Hills

The first maps of most Scottish towns were made in the late 18th century, such as that of Renfrew in 1796 by John Ainslie. There were also military maps made in the period of the Jacobite rebellions, examples being Perth (1716) and Stirling (1725). The National Library of Scotland website **www.nls.uk/digitallibrary/map/** (below) includes maps of fortifications and also of whole towns in great detail. The website also has plans of Scottish towns published by the surveyor John Wood between 1818 and 1826. As well as being published individually, 48 of these plans were also published in Wood's *Town Atlas of Scotland*

Spread of urbanisation By superimposing a modern aerial photograph of Stirling over a military map of the town as it was in 1725 (left), you can see in an instant how the place has grown in the past two centuries. Much of the general layout remains the same, but more and more open land is vanishing as property developments creep ever inland and outwards from the escarpment and castle (bottom of map).

(1828). For many smaller Scottish towns these are the earliest plans that were created, and in addition to showing the town at a very large scale, they often also name land and property owners.

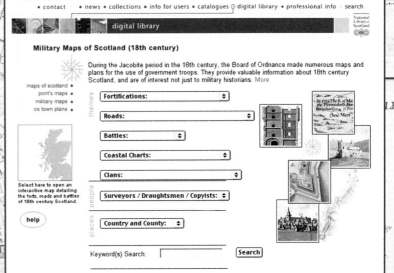

how your urban landscape developed in Victorian (1837-1901) and Edwardian (1901-10) times.

- Trace how the surrounding fields in the earlier maps became covered with streets, housing or industry.
- Note the names of new streets. They might suggest who the landowners or builders were, or help you to date them if they are named after a Prime Minister, such as Lord Palmerston (1855-8 and 1859-65) or a military victory, such as the Crimean War battle of Alma (1854).
- Look for the first appearance of churches, railway stations, sewage works and other public services.

Modern maps

Up-to-date town and OS maps are as valuable as older maps for understanding the story of urban growth in your area. Compare them with earlier maps and you will quickly spot the changes in layout and the evolving relationship with the surrounding landscape.

- See how much room is taken up by car parks, shopping precincts, industrial sites and other developments and ponder on when and why these sites were chosen.
- Notice the impact of ring roads and underpasses. Such developments have cut off the medieval castle at Carlisle in Cumbria and the parish church at Doncaster in Yorkshire from the historic core of these towns.
- Follow the growth of rail and road links with cities and other towns. Did these new routes of communication have an effect on the layout of your town?

FIND OUT MORE

- *The Cambridge Urban History of Britain* (P. Clark, M. Dauton and D.M. Palliser eds., 3 vols, Cambridge University Press, 2001)
- *The English Urban Landscape* (P. Waller ed., Oxford University Press, 2000)
- www3.getmapping.com Detailed aerial photographs and mapping services for any area in Britain. Images can be downloaded directly to your computer.

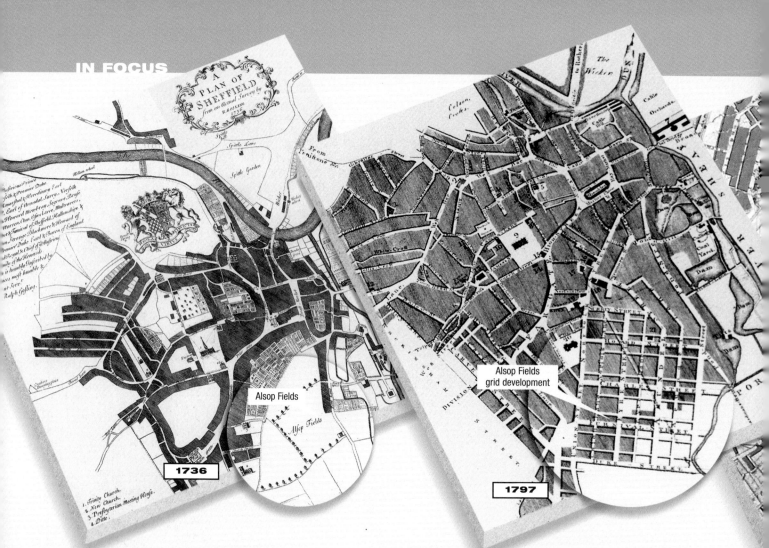

A PLAN OF SHEFFIELD from an Actual Survey by R. GOSLING

Alsop Fields

1736

Alsop Fields grid development

1797

The market town gets smoky

The oldest surviving map of Sheffield (above), drawn by Ralph Gosling in 1736, shows the town just starting to spread beyond its medieval limits. Part of the lord's deer park is now a farm, known as Alsop Fields. Market Place and Beast Market still lie at the centre and many street names, such as Far Gate and Snig Hill, date from the Middle Ages. The site of the castle, demolished in 1649, is marked by Castle Hill and Castle Fould. There are just a few more recent buildings, north of the River Don. But the march of industry had begun. In 1726, Daniel Defoe described Sheffield as 'very populous and large, the streets narrow, the houses dark and black' – probably due to smoke from the growing number of cutlers' forges.

The seams begin to burst

William Fairbank's map of Sheffield in 1797 (above) shows a grid of new streets covering Alsop Fields. More buildings have also appeared in the northwest suburbs, although the town is still largely contained by its two rivers, the Don and the Sheaf.

The invention of high-quality 'crucible' steel in 1742 by a local manufacturer, Benjamin Huntsman, and that of Old Sheffield Plate in 1743, helped to create new industries and boost the more traditional one of cutlery manufacture. Improved transport and the opening of the River Don Navigation in 1751 widened the market. Sheffield, by 1764, was 'a town of considerable note for its manufactures'.

Watch the 'Steel City' grow

Sheffield was once a small medieval market town, dominated by the lord's castle and its huge deer park. But during the Industrial Revolution of the 18th and 19th centuries it expanded rapidly, eventually becoming one of Britain's largest cities, noted for its steel industry. By examining a succession of maps and paintings of the landscape made over this period, you can follow this transformation. You can chart the march of change in your own area by using the same method.

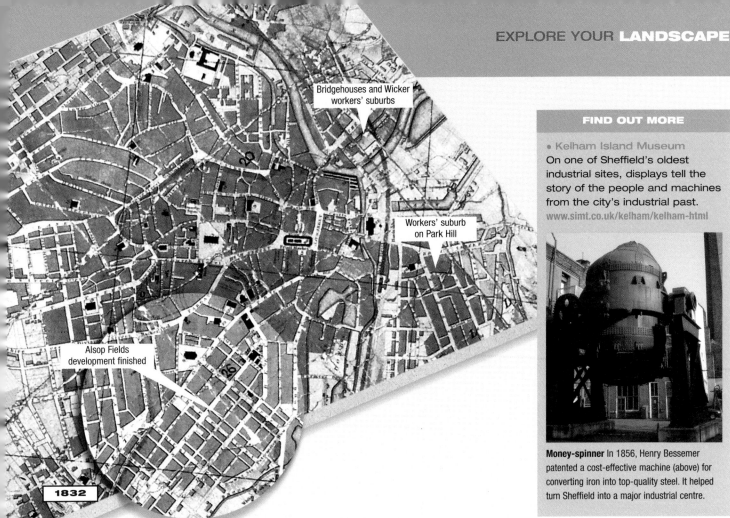

Bridgehouses and Wicker workers' suburbs

Workers' suburb on Park Hill

Alsop Fields development finished

1832

FIND OUT MORE

● **Kelham Island Museum**
On one of Sheffield's oldest industrial sites, displays tell the story of the people and machines from the city's industrial past.
www.simt.co.uk/kelham/kelham-html

Money-spinner In 1856, Henry Bessemer patented a cost-effective machine (above) for converting iron into top-quality steel. It helped turn Sheffield into a major industrial centre.

Expansion takes off

By 1801, the population of the parish of Sheffield was 45,755. Fifty years later it had reached 135,310 and the suburbs were spreading into the surrounding countryside. J. Tayler's 1832 map (above) shows buildings filling what were once the orchards, gardens and other open spaces of the old town. The Alsop Fields development is complete and a large estate for coal miners and other workers has risen on Park Hill, across the River Sheaf. Two other suburbs have evolved on former common land north of the Don: Bridgehouses and the Wicker, which are already starting to merge into one large enclave. Sheffield's social divide is becoming more marked as the middle classes move out into leafy suburbs along the new turnpike road to Manchester.

'Steel City' smothers the landscape

On early Victorian maps, Sheffield's suburbs gallop westwards, yet contemporary paintings show that the surrounding countryside could still be reached quickly on foot from the town centre. John McIntyre's view of Sheffield around 1850 (below), depicts a congested town, full of the new steelworks' chimneys, belching their smoke, but still framed by fields and moorland.

Over the next 50 years, as the population rose to over 400,000, 'Smoky Sheffield' grew into the 'Steel City', swallowing up great tracts of countryside. But amid all this expansion, the medieval pattern of its central streets remained constant at Sheffield's core.

c.1850

Understanding village shapes

No two villages are alike. Some are small, neat and tidy, dominated by the manor house and the medieval parish church; others are large and sprawling, with petrol stations, builders' yards and perhaps an industrial estate on the edge. Some have kept their basic plan, others have been transformed. What can you deduce from the shape of yours?

A pattern of life Landscape can dictate the shape of a village. Kettlewell, Yorkshire (right), grew where the Cam Beck flows into the River Wharfe, but the steep slopes of the valley have prevented it from sprawling. A church was founded in the 12th century and terraced fields provide evidence of farming in Anglo-Saxon times. Later, villagers turned to lead mining. A corn market and cattle fairs were still being held here in Victorian times.

Signs of regular shapes

To find out why your village is shaped the way it is first look around to see if it has a regular plan. See if the properties fronting the street or village green have equal widths and stretch in parallel lengths to a back lane.

- Property boundaries tend to remain fixed over very long periods of time. Some of the houses will have disappeared and new ones will have been squeezed in, but the general pattern will not have altered a great deal.
- Some villages were planned in the 18th or 19th centuries by landowners or industrial entrepreneurs. Others date back further. County Durham, in particular, has many villages that were planned in the Middle Ages (see pages 54-55).

Signs of irregular shapes

Planned villages are the exception. Many villages have an irregular shape and are often strung out along a street. If your village existed before the Industrial Revolution, its shape is likely to have developed since medieval times.

- Look for houses and cottages built in clusters. They may be gathered around the church or manor house.
- Early maps (see pages 214-215) may show the clusters more clearly. Have the gaps between been filled with new buildings?
- Follow the lines of the roads and lanes. What is now a long, curving street with houses might once have been broken up along smaller stretches. Or a road might twist and turn along the headlands of the blocks of strips in the former open fields. Look for clues in street names such as Westfield Lane or Longlands Avenue.

Learning from maps

Look at old maps (see pages 214-215) to find out whether the shape of your village has altered. Estate maps made in the 16th or 17th centuries show that many villages have kept the same shape over hundreds of years. Toddington, in Bedfordshire, expanded in the 20th century but is still recognisable as the village that was depicted on a map drawn by the Elizabethan map-maker Ralph Agas to accompany a survey in 1581.

If you look at maps made in the 18th or 19th century you can see the shape of your settlement before the ribbon development of modern times.

- If you live in a village rather than a district of scattered farmsteads, look for an enclosure or tithe award map.
- For tiny settlements, turn to the first edition, six-inch Ordnance Survey (OS) maps, made between the 1850s and the 1870s.

Deserted and shrunken villages

You might well find that your village had a larger population in the Middle Ages than it does now. Thousands of villages shrank or were completely deserted in the centuries after the Black Death (see pages 56-57). The history of one village can be very different from that of its neighbour. At Foston, in Leicestershire, only the isolated church and Hall Farm survive, but across the parish boundary lies Wigston Magna, the largest village in the county.

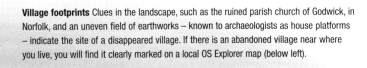

Village footprints Clues in the landscape, such as the ruined parish church of Godwick, in Norfolk, and an uneven field of earthworks – known to archaeologists as house platforms – indicate the site of a disappeared village. If there is an abandoned village near where you live, you will find it clearly marked on a local OS Explorer map (below left).

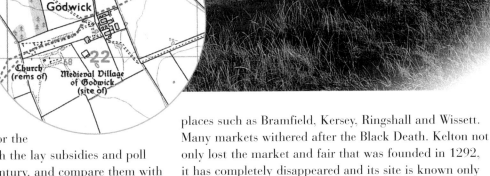

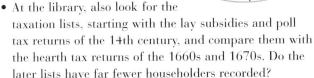

- Look for rectangular-shaped grassy mounds, where buildings once stood, above the sunken tracks of former streets and lanes. They show up on aerial photographs, so check whether your local reference library has any.

- At the library, also look for the taxation lists, starting with the lay subsidies and poll tax returns of the 14th century, and compare them with the hearth tax returns of the 1660s and 1670s. Do the later lists have far fewer householders recorded?

- At your local record office look for any manorial or parish records, such as registers of baptisms, that may provide clues that the population level fell.

Abandoned markets

A large number of villages and towns acquired the right to hold a weekly market and an annual fair in the Middle Ages. Suffolk had more than 90 markets, including small places such as Bramfield, Kersey, Ringshall and Wissett. Many markets withered after the Black Death. Kelton not only lost the market and fair that was founded in 1292, it has completely disappeared and its site is known only from Joseph Hodskinson's 1783 map of Suffolk.

- Look out for a regularly shaped village green. It might have been a medieval market place.

- Notice any names that refer to former markets. In Norfolk, the village of Thorpe Market has a triangular space where a market was held in the 13th century.

Villages in the 19th century

Many villages, especially those controlled by a squire, were smaller at the end of the 19th century than they were at the start, because country people moved to the towns to find work in the new industries (see pages 80-81, 162-163). You can tell whether your village grew or shrank in Victorian times by looking at the population figures recorded in census returns (see pages 218-219).

Market days Look out for remnants of a market cross, perhaps on a village green, such as the 13th-century stump at Bolton-by-Bowland, Lancashire (left). The presence of a market in days gone by indicates that this was once a place of some significance. Many markets were abandoned after the Black Death.

FIND OUT MORE

- *Victoria County History*
An ongoing project to create an encyclopedic history of each county of England. If your area has been covered, there will be a record of whether a royal charter was granted to the local lord of the manor for a market.
www.englandpast.net

- www.mdr.nationalarchives.gov.uk/mdr/
Contains details of the Manorial Documents Register. At present, records for Wales, Hampshire, Middlesex, Norfolk, Surrey and Yorkshire are on-line. They include court rolls, surveys, maps and documents relating to boundaries and customs.

Tracing the bounds of your parish

You may be only vaguely aware of the boundaries of your parish, but this old administrative unit is a key to the story of your landscape. Such knowledge was once vitally important for local communities who were dependent on their commons and wastes – the parish lands where they could graze livestock or dig peat for winter fuel. From the 16th to the 19th centuries parishes were also responsible for the poor, the highways, and petty law and order, so parish officers had to be certain which houses and cottages lay within their jurisdiction.

Parish shapes and sizes

Most rural parishes were formed by 1200. In much of lowland England their boundaries were usually the same as those of the manors of the local lords who had founded the church, but in some regions, such as Lincolnshire and Nottinghamshire, parishes were often formed from more than one manor.

The considerable variation in size and shape of parishes was dictated particularly by the quality of the soil, as well as by natural barriers such as woods and rivers and even ancient disputes with other parishes. In Lincolnshire, the compact parishes on the Wolds are very different from those that extend in narrow strips into the neighbouring Fens. The parishes of the Vale of Pickering stretch for miles onto the North York Moors. Some Welsh parishes were so large that they had to be divided into smaller units called townships, and then again into hamlets or quarters. This was also true of some lowland parishes in northern England, such as the parish of Great Budworth in Cheshire, which covered 35 townships. In south and west England the equivalent unit to the township was known as the tithing.

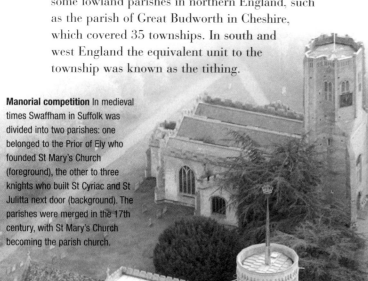

Manorial competition In medieval times Swaffham in Suffolk was divided into two parishes: one belonged to the Prior of Ely who founded St Mary's Church (foreground), the other to three knights who built St Cyriac and St Julitta next door (background). The parishes were merged in the 17th century, with St Mary's Church becoming the parish church.

See how the land lies Your parish boundary will be marked on an OS Explorer map. A black dotted line along the road running north-south (above) shows the boundary for Ugley, Essex. The letters BS near the top indicate a boundary stone.

Boundaries on maps

It is easy to trace your present parish boundary – marked as a thin dotted line – on Ordnance Survey (OS) Explorer maps (see above). You can also spot minor place names that were derived from words for a boundary, such as Merebrook ('boundary stream') and Shirebrook ('county boundary stream'). Threap, meaning a dispute, occurs in names such as Threapland in Cumbria.

- At your county record office, follow the boundaries that were marked on the first-edition OS maps. These are the ancient boundaries before the changes of late Victorian times. Look for 'detached portions' that were tidied up by an Act of Parliament in 1894, when Urban and Rural District Councils took over many parish responsibilities. In Scotland there were similar local government changes, with elected county councils beginning in 1890.
- Tithe and enclosure award maps (see pages 26–27) are arranged by parish and bounded by parish limits. Estate maps often mark prominent boundary points, such as crosses or poles.

Consulting the records

Your local record office will hold a range of records that can tell you more about the size and shape of the ancient parishes around where you live. Start by looking

Inspecting the line Parish boundaries often run along the edge of fields, such as at Slaidburn, Lancashire (above). Boundary stones are clearly marked on OS Explorer maps, but may take some searching for if they have become hidden in undergrowth.

for names and descriptions of parishes in 19th-century directories (see pages 216-217).

- As the parish dictated the administration and work of the lives of most people, it was essential that they were reminded regularly of its boundaries. In estate papers and, less commonly, manor court rolls, you may find a written account from the 16th to the 18th centuries of a 'perambulation of the bounds' of your parish, when large crowds of parishioners walked all the way round

the parish boundary at Rogationtide in early summer, with the minister leading the way and saying prayers at various points, such as a prominent tree – the Gospel Oak. Boundary landmarks were impressed on the villagers, such as a stream or a ditch, up to high points marked by a tree or a rock, or in featureless areas specially erected stones or poles marked with a cross and the initial letter of the parish.

- At your local library, look at the relevant volumes of the *Victoria County History* (www.englandpast.net see page 99), to see if they contain information on the parish boundaries for your area.

Boundary stones

On an OS Explorer map, you can pinpoint the markers used to denote your parish boundary and then search for them on the ground.

- Boundary stones come in all shapes and sizes and might be found tucked half-hidden into the side of a country lane or rising plainly from the middle of open moorland.
- Stones that were shaped as a cross were often damaged during the Reformation in the 16th century.
- Chamfered edges to a base indicate that the stone is probably medieval.
- If you spot a date cut into a stone, it could be an inscription made during a Rogationtide perambulation rather than the year the stone was erected.
- If there is a stone with a particular name near where you live, such as White Cross or Lady Cross, you may find it mentioned as a boundary point in medieval charters or deeds kept at your local record office.

Parish perimeter If you spot a township boundary plaque, such as for Hopton and Coton (above), it denotes a subdivision of a large parish, usually in northern England.

Markers on the moors Boundary stones stand out clearly on moorland, where they often have a dual function as waymarkers, such as this stone on the route of the Cleveland Way and Lyke Wake Walk across the North York Moors.

Basic shelter A far cry from the dairy parlours of today, early cowsheds, like this bank barn in Patterdale, Cumbria, were simple constructions, made from local materials.

Buildings of the working countryside

In spite of the mechanisation of farming and the decline in traditional crafts, there are many centuries-old farm buildings to see beside modern replacements. They range from cowsheds and stables to windmills and maltings, many still in use.

The farmer's home and farmyard

Until Tudor times most farmhouses were thatched, with walls made of timber frames infilled with rubble, brick, or straw-and-mud 'daub' slapped onto a latticework of wattles. They were larger versions of the cottages of the farm's peasant labourers (see pages 270-271). In parts of Britain without local sources of building stone, such as East Anglia, this style persisted into Georgian times. In places like the Cotswolds, Yorkshire and the Scottish borders, the farmhouse was made from the locally plentiful stone, with a roof of stone or clay tiles. Such local styles using local materials persisted until the coming of canals and railways allowed cheap bricks and slates to appear on buildings all over Britain (see pages 268-269).

Next to the farmhouse is usually a large open working space, or farmyard (see pages 80-81), surrounded by the outbuildings, which may date back to the 19th or 18th

centuries. Most farmyard buildings are still set fairly close together, for the farmer's convenience.

Farmyards dating from the 17th and 18th centuries might incorporate a dovecote, like the gabled and half-timbered example at Luntley Court in Herefordshire. A dovecote will often pre-date the farmhouse because it would have been built first to provide food while the more lengthy project of the house was underway.

Stables for farm horses have now become redundant. Many are riding stables, but they also have been converted into rural workshops and sales outlets, such as at Castle Ashby in Northamptonshire.

Look out for less glamorous modern structures like the silage clamp, often banged together out of disused railway sleepers and covered in old tyres, and the slurry lagoon, a big storage tank for farmyard manure and other effluent.

The late medieval introduction of root crops and reliable hay storage meant that farm animals did not have to be slaughtered at the onset of winter, but could be kept alive until spring. They were generally housed on or near the farmyard in byres (cattle and sheep), sties (pigs) and coops (hens). Intensive animal farming has seen the spread of long, low buildings containing battery cages for hens, often forming enclaves away from the farmhouse and yard.

Roomy birdhouse The Luntley Court dovecote was built in 1673, a year before the house it served.

Cathedrals of the harvest

Barns for storing the harvested produce – mostly grain, hay and straw – were generally thatched wattle-and-daub constructions until medieval times, when the buildings became larger and more substantially built. Three superb examples in Essex are the 12th-century Grange Barn at Coggeshall and the 13th-century Wheat and Barley Barns at Cressing Temple nearby. Monasteries built huge tithe barns of stone to store their tribute and among the most impressive are the barns at Abbotsbury in Dorset,

Storage on a grand scale Coggeshall Grange barn in Essex, built for a Cistercian monastery around 1140, is one of Europe's oldest timber-framed barns.

Ashleworth in Gloucestershire and Bredon in Worcestershire. Open-sided barns are a feature of many farms today, as are tall cylindrical silos for storing grain.

Other buildings to look for

Every village had a forge, and some will survive, perhaps as a house or pub, or even in working order, as at Branscombe in Devon. Big glass greenhouses dot the landscape in horticultural areas such as the Vale of Evesham and around Wisbech in Cambridgeshire, and the great pagoda-roofed hulks of maltings rise over barley country such as Suffolk and the lowlands of Fife.

FIND OUT MORE

Fine collections of historic agricultural buildings can be seen at locations across Britain.
- Auchindrain Township Open Air Museum Inveraray, Argyll. www.auchindrainmuseum.org.uk
- Avoncroft Museum of Historic Buildings Bromsgrove, Worcestershire. http://ourworld.compuserve.com/homepages/avoncroft1
- Museum of Welsh Life St Fagan's, Cardiff. www.nmgw.ac.uk/www.php/mwl
- Museum of East Anglian Life Stowmarket, Suffolk. www.eastanglianlife.org.uk
- Chiltern Open Air Museum Chalfont St Giles, Buckinghamshire. www.coam.org.uk
- North of England Open Air Museum Beamish, County Durham. www.beamish.org.uk
- Ryedale Folk Museum Hutton-le-Hole, Yorkshire. www.ryedalefolkmuseum.co.uk
- Weald and Downland Open Air Museum Singleton, West Sussex. www.wealddown.co.uk

LOOKING AT MILLS

Away from the farm, the tall towers and crossed sails of windmills are highly visible features of the landscape. Look carefully and you will see that there are three basic types: tower, smock and post (see below). A good example of a tower mill, built in 1860, is the five-storey Billingford Mill in Norfolk, while Cranbrook Mill in Kent, built in 1814, is a fine smock mill. Outwood Mill in Surrey is the oldest working post mill in Britain and dates from 1665.

Faced with more efficient mechanical methods of milling flour, windmills ceased commercial production by the 1950s. Many were pulled down or converted into houses (see page 300); but some still grind flour, such as the mill at Wilton, near Marlborough, in Wiltshire.

Many watermills have also been converted for residential use, their huge wheels now still and merely for show. But some are open to the public, including Cotehele mill (National Trust) near Saltash in Cornwall, which continues to grind flour.

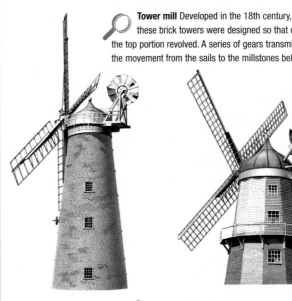

Tower mill Developed in the 18th century, these brick towers were designed so that only the top portion revolved. A series of gears transmits the movement from the sails to the millstones below.

Smock mill These 12-sided buildings were half brick and half timber. Like the tower mill, only the cap rotates with the sail. The miller could reach the sails from a gallery.

Post mill This is the oldest type of windmill, dating back to the 11th century. Massive oak beams support a large central post on which the whole mill rotates.

Water mill An undershot mill-wheel (above), where water flows through the vanes at the bottom, is less efficient than an overshot mill-wheel, where water strikes from the top, as it requires four times as much water volume to produce the same power.

Following the fields

The shape and name of every field tells a story. Fields with straight hawthorn hedges or stone walls were created when most communal open-fields and commons were enclosed by private Acts of Parliament, between 1750 and 1850. Small fields with irregular boundaries, twisting and turning up a hillside or around a wood, are likely to have been cleared of trees and rocks by medieval peasants or by their Elizabethan and Stuart successors. Field names will hold clues to how the land might have been used or to what crops it yielded.

Patterns in the landscape

The neatly planned appearance of swathes of the English countryside, stretching in a broad band south from the River Tees in the northeast to Dorset in the southwest, contrasts with the randomly shaped fields of areas such as the Welsh Borders and the Weald of Kent (see page 144).

In many parts of medieval England, the land of a parish was farmed in large communal open-fields. Much of this land has long since been converted to pasture, but the curving patterns of ridge-and-furrow (see main picture, above) can often be seen, providing evidence of ploughing. Large areas of ridge-and-furrow were obliterated in the 20th century by deep ploughing, but there are survivors, many of the best in Leicestershire and Warwickshire. Ridge-and-furrow patterns are much rarer in wooded, moorland or fenland parishes, which had only small open-fields.

Spotting ridge-and-furrow fields Look out for long, curving strips. They were shaped like an elongated 'S' to enable the plough-team of oxen to turn as they reached the end of the strip.

- Notice how the strip patterns follow the lie of the land, and blocks of strips, known in manor court rolls or deeds as furlongs or flatts, go off in different directions.
- See how the hawthorn hedges that define the present fields, created by the Enclosure Acts in the 18th or 19th centuries (see pages 62-63), often ignore the older pattern of ridge-and-furrow beneath. You may be able to follow the older patterns across several fields.

Medieval farmers make a mark In some areas, such as near Tissington in the Peak District National Park, the medieval ridge-and-furrow pattern can still be seen clearly. You may find that the furrows often appear greener than the ridges. This is because they were used not just to divide the strips, but also for drainage. In winter they might be marked by settled snow or water, in spring by buttercups.

- If hedges or walls bound the earlier curving outlines of strips, they will be the result of enclosure by private agreements among farmers between 1500 and 1700.
- From medieval times up to the Parliamentary enclosure, farmers called their strips 'lands', a name that will be found in manor court rolls. At the end of a block of strips was the 'headland', allowing access and space for the plough-team to turn. Headlands were not ploughed and became raised by the accumulation of soil. Look for straight raised banks running across the landscape.
- Notice the deep boundary ditches that were dug to separate the open-fields from the commons or woods. Even if they have been partly filled in, you might be able to follow the boundary line (see pages 116-117).
- Not all ridge-and-furrow is medieval and associated with the strip system. New land that was taken in from the parish commons and wastes by the Enclosure Acts was often ploughed with straight narrow patterns of ridge-and-furrow to drain it. See how these patterns do not extend beyond the enclosing hedges or walls. They are common in hilly areas such as the Pennines.

Investigating field records

You can trace the history of local fields at your county record office. Look for old maps, mid 19th-century tithe awards and, to delve further back, manorial documents.

- Estate maps from the 16th to 18th centuries (see below) and enclosure award maps (see pages 26-27) show how open fields were divided into strips. There is often a precise match between the shape and sizing of the strips on a map and the ridge-and-furrow patterns on the ground (or seen in an aerial photograph).

- Tithe awards (see pages 26-27) in local record offices or the National Archives (see DIRECTORY), note whether fields were arable, meadow or pasture. From these you can see how land use has changed.

- Read the records of manor courts, which managed the open-fields (see page 146). The jurors or 'homagers' of the court recorded 'paines', the penalties for breaking regulations. They were local men who made decisions on the best ways to farm, such as when to sow crops.

Old-time practices Manor courts appointed a pinder to put stray animals into a pinfold, or pound, until a fine had been paid. Has your village still got a pinfold, such as the one in Dalton-in-Furness, Cumbria (above), or perhaps a Pinfold Lane that might help you to identify the site?

What's in a name? Field names will tell you how the land was once used. 'Wongs' were meadows, 'stubbings' were fields cleared from woods or scrubland, 'longlands' strips of arable crops in the open-fields. Other fields were named after the crops that were grown.

- You can collect all the field names of your parish from the Middle Ages to the present day by using manor court rolls, estate maps, tithe award and enclosure award maps, and any other documents that record field names incidentally. Those names that are noted in the latest county volumes of the English Place-Name Society (available in libraries and record offices) are a useful starting point. In some parishes modern field names differ from the old, but on the whole the names have remained remarkably consistent.

- You will probably come across examples of strange names such as 'catsbrain', meaning a soil where clay is mixed with pebbles. Welsh fields include both English and Welsh names and Scottish names may be in Gaelic, Scots or English. Names such as West Field, Town Field and Hall Flatt stem from the open-field system. Many meanings are straightforward, but be aware how names can be corrupted over time. For example, Sufferlong, recorded in Kibworth Harcourt (Leicestershire) in 1652, is probably a corruption of 'south furlong'.

Charting the boundaries Old maps, such as the 1744 Blaen-Sawdde estate map, Carmarthenshire (above), show ancient field patterns and list field names and sizes. You may find some of these names repeated on later Ordnance Survey (OS) maps.

FIND OUT MORE

- *A History of English Field Names* (John Field, Longman, 1993) Describes how field names came to be, and how even a modern street name can be traced to its rural roots.
- *Fields in the English Landscape* (Christopher Taylor, Sutton Publishing, 2000) Uses what can be seen in the landscape today to explore the history of the field.

Up among the hills and moors

Romantic writers and artists 200 years ago found inspiration in the aesthetic qualities of mountains and hills, yet earlier visitors described these landscapes as dismal and gloomy, and manorial surveys dismissed them as 'barren' and 'waste'. Meanwhile, farmers worked on regardless – grazing cattle and sheep, digging turf for fuel, using bracken for animal bedding and cutting heather to thatch roofs. Signs of their robust lives are all around.

Pattern of moorland life The grazing of sheep is typical of upland areas such as Ugborough Moor, Devon. Straight hedges mark the boundaries of enclosed pastures, cleared long ago from the moor, and small farmsteads dot the landscape.

The story of hamlets and farmsteads

In an upland area, you will see many more hamlets and scattered farmsteads than in the lowlands, where villages cluster around a church and manor house, surrounded by arable fields. In Wales, where about 60 per cent of the land is more than 152m (500ft) above sea level, isolated farmsteads are even more common than hamlets. In Scotland, farmsteads also abound, although pre-18th-century 'farmtouns' (see page 110) that once dominated the landscape can be traced by the suffix 'ton' in names such as Milton, Kirkton and Muirton.

Hamlets and farmsteads were the earliest forms of settlement, pre-dating the first Saxon and Viking villages. They are rarely recorded before the mid 13th century, when manor court rolls began to be kept (see page 147). By this time the population was expanding rapidly and many new farms – the ones most likely to appear in the records – were being cleared from the moors and woods.

Tracing settlements You can find out about hamlets and farmsteads and how old they are by comparing old maps with new and tracing the names of the farms and their occupants through manorial records at your county record office. Many of the names will have changed over time, such as the Pennine farm known now as Belle Clive. It was recorded as Billeclif between 1208 and 1211 and means 'Billa's bank' from an Old English personal name.

- At your local reference library or record office ask whether the English Place-Name Society has published volumes for your county. These will show the earliest spellings of place names and explain their meaning. Some of the surnames recorded in manor court rolls and the poll tax returns of 1377-81 may derive from local

Family enterprises Most of the farms that were cleared from Dartmoor in medieval times were grouped in hamlets, perhaps as joint ventures by energetic young men. Some isolated farmsteads developed into hamlets when the sons of the first farmers built houses for themselves and their livestock. The foundations of a group of longhouses belonging to such a hamlet have been excavated at Hound Tor, at about 305m (1000ft) above sea level on the east side of Dartmoor (below). They appear to have been abandoned after the Black Death, when land was no longer scarce.

The unchanging face of upland farming

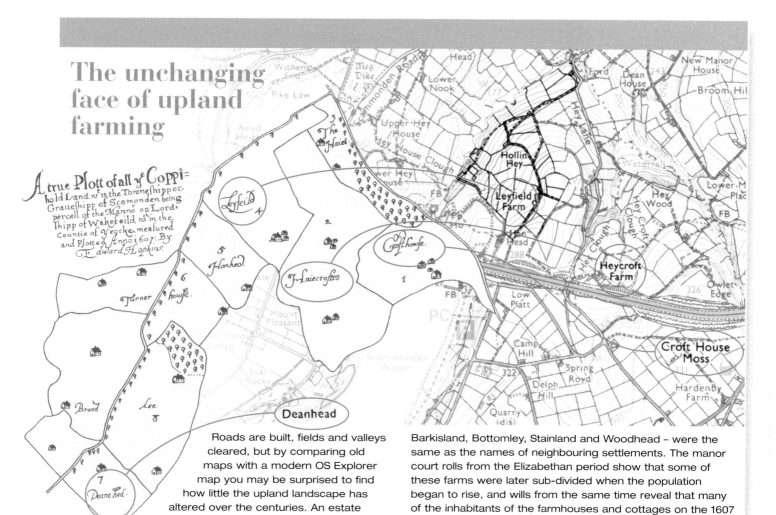

Roads are built, fields and valleys cleared, but by comparing old maps with a modern OS Explorer map you may be surprised to find how little the upland landscape has altered over the centuries. An estate map of 1607 of Scammonden, west of Huddersfield, Yorkshire (above left), records the farms in the township. Their names can be traced through references to them in manor court rolls, all the way back to the families who opened up this Pennine valley by clearing woods and moorland in the first half of the 14th century. They had not moved far as their surnames –

Barkisland, Bottomley, Stainland and Woodhead – were the same as the names of neighbouring settlements. The manor court rolls from the Elizabethan period show that some of these farms were later sub-divided when the population began to rise, and wills from the same time reveal that many of the inhabitants of the farmhouses and cottages on the 1607 map were weavers as well as farmers.

Fast-forward 400 years to an OS Explorer map of today (above right) and there is still much to recognise in the landscape. Although the M62 motorway slices through Scammonden and a swathe of land has been swallowed by a reservoir, the farms still have much the same names and many of the old field boundaries can still be followed.

farmsteads – such as Broadbent, from a farmstead of the same name in the Lancashire Pennines.

- Ask to see transcriptions of any medieval charters, deeds and manorial records. Look for early references to farmsteads and hamlets and the clearing of new land from the woods and moors near where you live. These clearances will be named as 'assarts', 'intakes' and 'stubbings', or perhaps by dialect words such as the West Yorkshire 'royd'. Often, these words will be attached to a person's name, so you can tell that Gilroyd was 'Gilbert's clearance'. Typically, only one or two acres were cleared at a time, because the work was hard, and when the population increased rapidly in the late 13th century even smaller parcels of land were taken in from the parish wastes. After the Black Death (see pages 56-57) the demand for new land ceased.

From hamlet to village Compare the pattern of settlement on 18th-century county maps and first-edition Ordnance Survey (OS) maps (see pages 26-27) to spot the many hamlets that did not appear until the 19th century, after the parliamentary enclosures of commons and wastes (see pages 62-63). Some of these places have industrial origins and grew into villages, such as the lead-mining community at Allenheads, Northumberland.

FIND OUT MORE

• *The Harvest of the Hills: Rural Life in Northern England and the Scottish Borders, 1400-1700* (Angus J.L. Winchester, Edinburgh University Press, 2000). A description of the relationship between people and the land, and the culture of rural communities.

Setting the boundaries of the land

From the earliest days farmers have looked for ways to prevent their animals straying, and to separate one type of crop from another. As notions of private property took hold it became important to separate roads from fields, and to distinguish a landowner's domain from his neighbour's. There are many kinds of boundary, from wire fences and earth banks to the water-filled ditches of wetland fields, but the most common are hedges and drystone walls.

Thin green lines

Hedges have existed since before the Romans. At first they were a line of portable hurdles that could be installed or removed at will. Some were strips of undergrowth left in place deliberately and then nurtured when a forest was cleared; others were newly planted. There were surges of hedge-planting when the Anglo-Saxons cleared forests and wildwoods for agricultural land, and during the enclosure of fields in the 18th and 19th centuries (see page 62).

In the 1950s Britain had about half a million miles of hedges. Then landowners began to rip them out because they were too expensive and time-consuming to maintain, and hindered large modern farm machinery. Up to half the total mileage of hedges was destroyed in just 40 years, before people began to appreciate the ecological and environmental value of hedgerows. Today more hedges are planted (see left) than removed.

The traditional way to keep a hedge thick and in good shape is to trim, prune and cut it back by hand. The quicker way is to use a slashing machine. This leaves a splintered surface and also reduces the efficiency of the hedge, because unless the stems are regularly realigned horizontally they tend to grow vertically, destroying the inner framework and gradually reducing its effectiveness as a barrier.

A reviving art Hedge-laying is an ancient method of maintaining hedges. The stems are allowed to grow, then cut half-way through near the ground and bent over at right-angles or diagonally. Vertical stakes rammed into the ground between the stems make a latticework frame, around which are woven the trailing twigs and shoots of the still-growing stems.

Dating hedges

A rough-and-ready method for dating hedges is to take a 30m (100ft) stretch and count the number of tree and shrub species in it – discounting elder and bramble, which can appear and disappear quickly. Multiply that number by 100, and that is the age of the hedge in years. A more accurate method is to sample three stretches of the hedge and take an average. For example:

• Stretch A – oak, ash, hawthorn, blackthorn, rowan, holly = 6 species
• Stretch B – oak, ash, willow, dogwood, rowan = 5 species
• Stretch C – oak, ash, willow, hawthorn, holly, hazel, sycamore = 7 species

Average number of species = 6
$6 \times 100 = 600$
Rough age of hedge = 600 years.

Barriers of water In the reclaimed wetlands of the Somerset Levels, man-made drainage ditches called rhynes demarcate the landscape

Hedging and walling in action
When walking through dairy or sheep-farming areas you may be lucky enough to see a hedger or waller (below) in action. Demonstrations take place at various open-air museums around Britain. The National Hedgelaying Society and the Dry Stone Walling Association (see 'Find out more' below) are dedicated to the preservation and maintenance of hedges and walls. If you want to have a go yourself, contact the British Trust for Conservation Volunteers (see 'Find out more' below).

The old stone wall

Drystone walls have been built for more than 2000 years, mostly in upland areas where stone is plentiful. At first they were crudely constructed, of stones cleared from the land by hand. More sophisticated techniques evolved later (see right), as monasteries built them to enclose sheep pastures on far-flung fells. Walls around fields on lower-lying land tend to be older; they gradually crept further up the contours as higher, wilder common land was enclosed during the 18th and 19th centuries.

The walls are built on a foundation of small stones laid in a trench. The waller builds up the wall in layers, filling the centre with rubble. The whole structure is solidified by inserting a layer of through-stones half-way up the wall – these are large, shaped stones, laid across the grain of the wall. A layer of vertical or slanting stones tops the wall off.

Dating walls

Drystone walls are more difficult to date than hedges. The basic building method has never changed and so a recent wall can look as though it has been there for centuries. Manorial records (see pages 147, 322), estate records (see pages 113, 318-319) and enclosure awards (see pages 27, 215) may mention the putting up of walls between fields and so reveal when they were built. The following characteristics may also point to a wall built long ago:
• it surrounds small, irregular fields near a farmstead
• it separates the site of former Anglo-Saxon and Danish open fields from wetland or wasteland
• it is of irregular construction with some big boulders, with no through-stones or top stones
• if it does not change direction to avoid an obstacle, the chances are that it was built before the obstacle.

Patchy distribution Remnants of haphazard, irregular ancient field boundaries still exist in parts of Britain, including south Wales (pictured). But in the 25 years following the Second World War more than 150,000 miles of hedgerow were lost.

FIND OUT MORE

• www.hedgelayer.freeserve.co.uk
Information about hedgelaying.
• www.britainexpress.com/History/
english-hedges.htm The history of
English hedges.
• www.hedgelaying.org.uk Website of
the National Hedgelaying Society.
• www.britainexpress.com/History/
drystone.htm Information on
drystone walls in England.
• www.dswa.org.uk Website of the
Dry Stone Walling Association.
• www.btcv.org Website of the
British Trust for Conservation
Volunteers.

On the trail of the lost highland and island folk

In the late 18th and 19th centuries entire working families in the north and west of Scotland, and its islands, eked out a living from a small agricultural holding known as a croft, supplemented by the cutting, collecting, drying and burning of seaweed ('kelp'). Evidence of these communities remains in many abandoned crofthouses, while unusual furrows and ridges in the landscape indicate earlier farming settlements. Records flesh out the lives of these hard-working people.

The changing scene

Life is very different today for the remaining 18,000 or so crofters of the highlands and islands, who have security of tenure, government grants and the right to buy their crofts. Before the Crofters' Holdings (Scotland) Act of 1886, tenants had few rights and landlords ruthlessly evicted thousands of crofters during the Highland Clearances (see pages 80-81). Visit the region's libraries and museums, and explore the abandoned settlements (see 'Find out more', opposite), and you can discover much about the crofting tradition.

The earliest settlements

Before the introduction of crofting in the 18th century, most people in the highlands and islands lived close together in communally run townships, or farmtouns. Small areas of arable land around the farmtoun were cultivated in strips in a common-field system known as 'runrig'. Each tenant or subtenant had grazing rights on the surrounding rougher land and on the shielings (see page 49), the cattle's summer grazings, that lay beyond the township.

- Look for strip patterns, which can be seen as ridges and furrows, used to allow the land to drain. The ridges could be 1.8m (6ft) high and 6m (20ft) wide. Notice the thin grass boundaries between the strips.
- Visit the Auchindrain Township Open Air Museum (see opposite) to see a surviving old settlement.

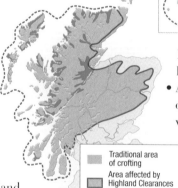

Crofters' territory You can find evidence of crofting from its heyday throughout the modern crofting areas of Orkney, Shetland, Ross, Caithness, Sutherland, Inverness, Argyll and the Hebrides. The effects of the Clearances were different in each region.

Shetland Islands

Orkney Islands

Traditional area of crofting

Area affected by Highland Clearances 1763-1886

Crofting today

Understanding the life of crofters

When new industry and agricultural methods were introduced in the 18th century, highland and island tenants were shifted to the coasts and given crofts, or smallholdings. Here they had to learn to fish and provide the workforce for the kelp industry, as well as working what was often the poorest of land.

- Visit crofters' houses (see opposite). Note the use of local stone and clay for walls, and turf and heather for thatched roofs. The houses were single-storey and open to the rafters. Livestock was kept at the lower end of the house and wells were dug to supply water.
- At your local library look for collections of old photographs (see pages 212-213), which show crofters and their wives working side by side on their land. Notice how men used foot-ploughs to dig the rows for planting potatoes, while the women spread seaweed from the shore as fertiliser, which they carried in large wicker baskets on their backs. The women also used these baskets for carrying the peat that the men had dug for winter fuel.
- On the ground, look for 'lazybeds'. These were the small plots where crofters grew their crops of potatoes.

Lost way of life An abandoned crofting settlement near Lochgilphead on the west coast of Scotland is a poignant reminder of the people forced to leave Scotland during the Clearances.

Signs of the Clearances

The decline of the feudal clan system, which began in the 1730s, culminated after the battle of Culloden Moor in 1746 (see pages 80-81). Many estates changed hands and the new landowners saw sheep farming, which required little labour, as the only profitable business. A trickle of emigrants that began around 1730 escalated after 1763, spurred on by generous land grants abroad. Between 1765 and 1777 about 20,000 people left the highlands and islands, followed by a further 15,000 in the next 30 years.

By the 1820s, most labour was surplus to requirements, and when, in 1846, potato famine came, most landowners saw eviction as the way forward. The later 19th-century clearances saw thousands shipped to Canada, New Zealand and Australia.

- On the ground, search for ruined walls enclosing abandoned fields and the foundations of derelict houses (see 'Find out more'), which show the scale of the Clearances.
- At the National Archives of Scotland (see DIRECTORY), see the Department of Agriculture and Fisheries records (AF 50/7 and AF 50/8). Each county volume for 1883 is arranged alphabetically by estate. The returns name the crofts, the tenants and the number of people living on each croft.

FIND OUT MORE

There are several sites on the Isle of Skye, on remote headlands or close to the sea, where the remains of crofts are visible. You can see the 12 dry-stone houses and outbuildings in the deserted village of Boreraig that were cleared for sheep farming by Lord MacDonald in 1853 and replaced by one shepherd's house. Lazybeds (see opposite) can be traced near Galtrigill.
- The Isle of Skye Museum of Island Life Housed in an atmospheric group of thatched crofthouses illustrating the crofter's daily life. www.skyemuseum.co.uk
- Auchindrain Township Open Air Museum An original highland township that survived the Clearances. www.auchindrainmuseum.org.uk

Harvest of the sea Crofters had to exploit what they could to boost their subsistence economy. Kelp gathered from beaches helped to fertilise their crops, but it was the landowners who benefited most, using the seaweed to produce potash for the manufacture of glass and soap.

Cutting Seaware, Skye

Viewing a great estate

The estates that Britain's biggest landowners built up from the late 17th to the 19th century still dominate many local landscapes. Even if your village did not form part of one, you may know villages nearby that did, and you rarely have to travel very far to come across grand houses and rolling parkland, dotted with temples, mausoleums, towers and other eye-catching follies.

CHATSWORTH IN 1870

The house and park at Chatsworth, Derbyshire, the home of the dukes of Devonshire, reached the height of their development in the late 19th century. It was one of many country estates that evolved with changes in landscape fashions and the fortunes of Britain's landed classes over three centuries. Characteristics such as 18th-19th century refashioning of the house, the splendid gardens with grand water features, the landscaped park and the discreetly sited workers' village are likely to feature on any great estate near to where you live.

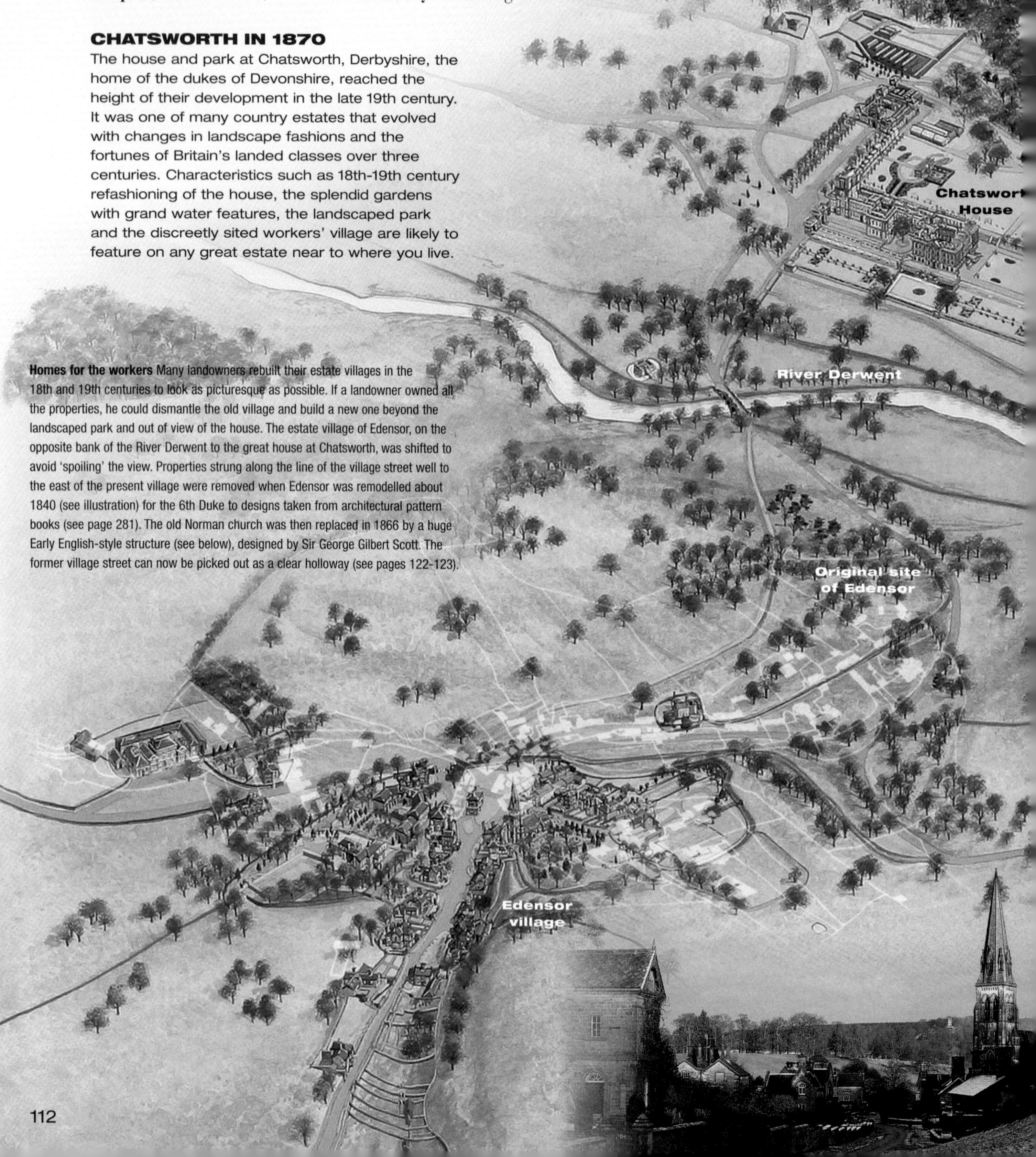

Homes for the workers Many landowners rebuilt their estate villages in the 18th and 19th centuries to look as picturesque as possible. If a landowner owned all the properties, he could dismantle the old village and build a new one beyond the landscaped park and out of view of the house. The estate village of Edensor, on the opposite bank of the River Derwent to the great house at Chatsworth, was shifted to avoid 'spoiling' the view. Properties strung along the line of the village street well to the east of the present village were removed when Edensor was remodelled about 1840 (see illustration) for the 6th Duke to designs taken from architectural pattern books (see page 281). The old Norman church was then replaced in 1866 by a huge Early English-style structure (see below), designed by Sir George Gilbert Scott. The former village street can now be picked out as a clear holloway (see pages 122-123).

Chatsworth House

River Derwent

Original site of Edensor

Edensor village

The changing house Like many great houses, Chatsworth, first built between 1687 and 1707 in grand Baroque style, replaced an earlier Tudor building. Its formal French-style gardens were then transformed by 'Capability' Brown, who completely re-moulded the immediate landscape, as he did at more than 200 other estates. Something of the formality of those earlier days was then restored with the glasshouses, including the majestic Great Stove, and spectacular water features of the Victorian gardener and engineer, Joseph Paxton (right), who was appointed head gardener in 1826.

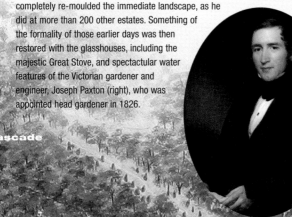

Cascade

Great Stove

Wandering the parks The fashion that began in the 1720s for rolling parkland, clumps of trees and stretches of water extending into the distance made an enormous impact on the landscape. At Chatsworth, the damming of lakes 122m (400ft) above the house provided the water to power the spectacular Cascade (above). Parks were also adorned with temples, obelisks and bridges to give the impression that the landowners were the enlightened successors of the ancient Greeks and Romans. Few of these follies served any purpose other than that of a summerhouse or perhaps a mausoleum. Look out for inscriptions on follies and monuments that may explain their use and give a date. You can use maps and prints at your local record office to trace what a park looked like at various times, then explore on the ground to see what features survive from each period.

Big house records

Architectural fashions changed over the centuries and you have to peel away several layers to discover how the styling of a house and its surroundings may have evolved.

- At your local library, look for descriptions of houses, their gardens and parks made by travellers such as Celia Fiennes (1690s), Daniel Defoe (1720s) and John Byng, Viscount Torrington (1780s and 1790s).
- Also at your local library, look for prints of houses, including those that have been demolished. To see houses and their formal gardens before they were remodelled into landscaped parks, look for the bird's-eye views drawn by Leonard Knyff and Jan Kip in *Brittania Illustrata* (1707).
- Look for 16th-19th century estate papers at the National Archives (see DIRECTORY) or your county record office. You may find plans of a house near where you live, changes made to the design during its construction, financial accounts, names of the craftsmen and masons, and the origins of the building materials.

The signs of estate villages

- You can spot estate villages by the uniformity of the house design. Many were built in Tudor or Jacobean styles, using traditional local materials for their walls and roofs. Others were given Gothic-style gables or Arts and Crafts bargeboards and decorative brick chimneys.

Moving houses It was not uncommon for landowners to shift entire estate villages to improve the view from the big house. At Milton Abbas, Dorset, Viscount Milton demolished the village in the 1770s, and built rows of identical cottages (above) well away from his house. The earthworks of the old properties are still visible.

- Look for inscriptions on houses, such as the landowner's initials, and datestones that share similar dates. See whether any almshouses bear the name of the landowner.
- The neat, tidy cottages in estate villages were often of a higher standard than those in the sprawling villages that had no paternal landlord. Nonconformist chapels were allowed only if the squire was a Dissenter himself. If a pub was provided it usually bore the name of the family that owned the land.
- Look for surveys, maps, leases and annual accounts among collections of estate papers at county record offices. These may tell you tenants' names, the size of their farms and the rent they paid. Notice when farmhouses, cottages and barns were built, what types of livestock were kept, what crops were grown, and perhaps what new industrial enterprises were tried.

Rediscovering rural life in old photographs

The rural landscape from the Victorian era up to the end of the Second World War is captured in countless old photographs, giving a vivid picture of life through the seasons in country communities of the time. They show a far more populated countryside than today, with men, women and children labouring in the fields at tasks that have now become mechanised. These images are readily available, often at your local library, museum or record office (see pages 212-213).

Don't believe everything you see

The paintings that hang in art galleries and country houses tend to show idealised landscapes, that reflect the standing and aspirations of the wealthy landowners who commissioned them. Their estate workers are usually out of sight or represented by mere dots in the background. Photography allowed for the creation of more realistic images, but take care when interpreting the scenes recorded in early photographs. Many were staged and often the photographer was trying to record working practices or fashions in dress that were disappearing at the time. If you look at a photograph of a shepherd wearing a smock or a team of oxen pulling a plough, do not assume that this was normal practice when the picture was taken.

Division of labour Some photographs may have been posed, but they still give a good idea of rural life. Women and girls had their own responsibilities, whether for farm produce (left, 1855) or looking after the poultry.

Tools of the trade The horse-drawn hay cart is a common sight in old photographs, but you may also spot unusual farming implements such as the long-bladed scythe with a swivel end (right, 1910), used for cutting meadow hay. Scythes usually had a fixed end.

Who did what?

Large numbers of people were employed on the land and you will see a wide range of tasks represented in old photographs.

- Look out for who was doing what. In Suffolk the most prestigious job was being in charge of the horses, especially the magnificent Suffolk Punches, but in East Yorkshire teenage boys who were hired as farm servants looked after the horses and did the ploughing, harrowing, muck spreading and harvesting with a binder.
- Note the specialist tasks being undertaken, such as hedging or shepherding, and the range of hand tools, including scythes, sickles, bill hooks and flails.
- Observe how the women played a full part in the running of a family farm. They can be seen milking the shorthorn cows and, wearing headscarves or bonnets and full-length dresses to keep out the sun, binding the sheaves of corn that stood among the stubble and earning a little extra by gleaning grains of ungathered

corn at harvest time. Photographs from the Second World War show land girls driving tractors and doing jobs usually performed by men.

- At harvest time everyone was expected to help. Notice that the landscape was full of children, either at work or at play.

Interpreting the images

Look out for photographs of the first tractors (see below). If they are dated they will help you to decide when the horse-and-cart era came to an end in your part of the countryside. On some farms it lasted until the 1950s or even later.

- Barns, stables and cowsheds still survive on many farms (see pages 102-103). Old photographs of them may help to show you how they were used and why they were designed as they were. They might help you to understand why such buildings are often ill-suited to modern farming, which could be the reason why so many have been demolished or neglected.
- You might find surviving sheep folds and the places where sheep were dipped to kill parasites or where their fleeces were washed. Some old photographs of rural life portray groups of men shearing sheep, driving flocks along a village street, or chopping turnips for winter feed. They may also show the importance of the family pig and the annual killing.
- Notice how the countryside was remarkably free of traffic before the advent of the car. Old photographs show that waggons, carts and sleds were used for transporting crops and manure. The isolation of rural farmsteads until the bicycle became widespread can be imagined from photographs of donkey carts, horse-drawn traps and buggies on unsurfaced lanes and roads.

Crafts of the countryside

The blacksmith or saddler often appear in photographs. They were focal points in village life. Look also for specialist crafts such as basket-weaving or the making

Local brew Each region had its specialist activities. Kent was renowned for growing hops, which are used to flavour beer, and a huge number of London's Eastenders traditionally came to help pick them in late summer (above, mid 20th century).

of hurdles. If you see a saw pit, timber yard or corn mill, you might be able to find the site on a first edition Ordnance Survey (OS) map (see pages 26-27), and identify the owners in directories (see pages 216-217) and census returns (see pages 218-219).

FIND OUT MORE

- *The Museum of English Rural Life* At the University of Reading in Berkshire, the museum houses a comprehensive collection of artefacts, photographs, films and books that record the changing face of farming and the countryside. www.ruralhistory.org/index.html
- *The National Library of Wales* (see DIRECTORY) Holds a collection of 750,000 images from the early days of photography to the present, many of life in rural areas. www.llgc.org.uk
- *Museum of Scottish Country Life* Old photographs in the museum's archive help to tell the story of Scottish country life from *c*.1750. www.nms.ac.uk/countrylife/index.asp

Modern methods The latest innovations were a popular topic for photographers. You may find images, such as harvesting by motor on a Lincolnshire farm (left, 1907), that record the gradual mechanisation of farming, although at first it did not appear to cause a reduction in the work force.

How ancient woods reveal their age

Britain's woodlands have been worked and nurtured for thousands of years, and have filled our imaginations with folk characters such as the Green Man and Robin Hood. By following a series of signs, you may well discover that there are remnants of ancient woodland closer to home than you think.

The remains of a landscape of trees

After the scouring of the last Ice Age, Britain grew thick with wildwood – trees such as oak, elm and lime have flourished here from around 7500 BC. Woodland was first deliberately planted about 400 years ago; any woods that predate 1600 are known as 'ancient woodland'. In spite of constant cutting and clearing throughout the centuries, much remains, such as the old beeches of the Savernake Forest in Wiltshire and the hornbeams of Epping Forest in Essex.

You can quickly learn to spot ancient woodland by studying Ordnance Survey (OS) maps and following clues on the ground. The irregular outlines, the boundary banks and the slopes and streams – look for these and other indicators to uncover ancient woodland.

Finding signs on a map

Although it is best to check out clues to ancient woodland by visiting the wood itself (see below), you do not necessarily have to. On a map, the outline of a wood, its name, the angle of the ground on which it lies, the presence or absence of a stream or a bank, even the shapes and names of the countryside round about, all present vital information as to whether that wood is a piece of ancient woodland or not.

The best maps to use are the OS Explorer series (see pages 26-27), which show field boundaries and plenty of other close-up detail, as in the example of Hagg Wood (right).

Other map indicators are the proximity of heath or common land, and the presence of a parish boundary (see pages 100-101) – parishes were created in medieval times or earlier, and their boundaries were often formed by woodland.

FOLLOW THE CLUES TO ANCIENT WOODLAND

Telltale plants Plants such as bluebells (below), dog's mercury, cuckoo pint, ferns, wood sorrel, marsh hellebore, enchanter's nightshade and meadowsweet are characteristic of ancient woods, where they have established themselves over hundreds of years.

Working the wood Coppicing, the harvesting of poles from coppice stools (the butts of trees, such as hazel, ash and beech, from which the poles grow), helps to maintain the wood and provide material for furniture making and other woodland crafts (see pages 118-119).

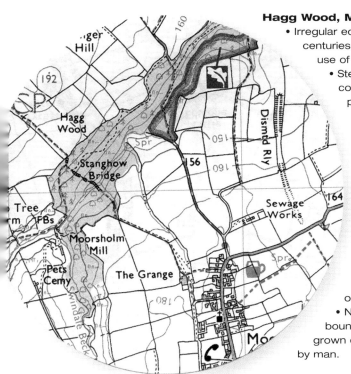

Hagg Wood, Moorsholm, Cleveland
- Irregular edge of the wood – caused by centuries of change in ownership and use of surrounding land.
- Steep slopes (look for bunched contour lines) – hard to farm in pre-mechanisation days, so often left under their natural woodland.
- Wood follows a winding stream or river – ground beside running water was often too boggy to farm.
- Boundary shape does not fit the pattern of the adjacent field shapes – suggests the wood already existed when the surrounding land was enclosed for fields.
- Ancient name – 'hagg' is an old local name for coppice.
- No internal man-made boundaries – the wood has not grown on land previously shaped by man.

DID YOU KNOW?

Look at the name of a wood – it can be a clue to whether it is a piece of ancient woodland.
- Grove, lea, copse, thorns, hagg, hanger – old names for different types of woodland.
- Kiln Wood, Brick Copse, Tanner's Spinney – former industries that harvested the wood.
- Assington Thicks, Priory Grove, Grange Wood – names that reflect a nearby settlement.
- Ash Grove, Oak Spinney, Elm Hag, Beech Hanger, Hazel Copse, Maple Lea – names of long-established native tree species.

Lie of the land Stand back and take a look at a wood from a distance. An irregular edge, a steep slope and a stream gully are three good signs of ancient woodland.

Evidence of grazing Ancient woods will often have pollarded trees (below) at their edges. Pollarding the big boundary trees (cutting off their boughs several feet above ground height) allowed animals to graze common land right up to the edge of the wood.

Woodland limits Low, winding ditches and banks often mark the boundaries of ancient woodland. They were dug to prevent grazing cattle from entering the wood and damaging young coppices.

In search of woodland craft and industry

You are never far from woods in Britain: peaceful places, perfect for a quiet walk or nature ramble. Once they were hives of activity, worked for their supplies of wood and bark. Many woods have been cleared in recent years, but the remnants show signs of past industry, and old woodland skills are being revived.

The importance of woods

Woods looked very different to our ancestors of a hundred or more years ago. Some trees were allowed to grow to full height before they were felled for timber, but most of the trees were coppiced (see pages 116-117) to provide wood for essential objects such as fences, hurdles, poles, gates, ladders, handles and furniture. Wood of only a few years' growth was cut into logs and faggots for industrial and domestic fires, and the twigs (known in the Midlands as 'rammell') were used for kindling. The bark was stripped and taken away by tanners to provide the tannin, or tannic acid, essential to the tanning process.

Charcoal – the all-purpose fuel

The ancient woods of Britain were once filled with the smoke rising from charcoal burners' kilns. Charcoal, made by burning the young wood of carefully managed

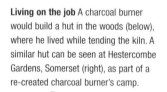

Living on the job A charcoal burner would build a hut in the woods (below), where he lived while tending the kiln. A similar hut can be seen at Hestercombe Gardens, Somerset (right), as part of a re-created charcoal burner's camp.

Hidden hearths White coal pits, such as those in Holmesfield Park Wood in Derbyshire (above), can be spotted by the blackened earth beneath the foliage. They were used repeatedly to burn stacks of wood for days at a time to create white coal.

coppices, was used for many different purposes. In particular, it was the main source of fuel for the water-powered blast furnaces of the 16th to 18th centuries.

- During the several days that the 'colliers' were making charcoal, they lived in temporary huts made of poles and covered with turf sods. A good example is preserved at the Weald and Downland Open Air Museum in Sussex (see DIRECTORY), or you can spot them in old rural photographs (see pages 114-115). Notice the coppiced wood stacked in hearths and covered with sods to exclude the air, so that the wood was charred slowly until all the moisture was lost.
- Former hearths, or platforms, in woods are often overgrown (see above). You can spot them by looking for blackened soft soils forming rough circles about 4.6m (15ft) in diameter. Rabbits tend to make burrows in them because of their softness. Elsewhere, you may see charcoal platforms forming terraces in a hillside.
- Lead smelters used a fuel known as white coal, which was charred to a lower temperature than charcoal. Hundreds of the white-coal pits or kilns, once covered with turf or bracken, survive in woods near old lead-smelting mills, particularly in Derbyshire and the Yorkshire Dales (see page 127).

Woodland signs in the records

Most woods were privately owned. Manor court rolls and estate papers held in county records will mention woods and their management. You may find accounts of illegal fellings and the obligations of tenants to fence a wood to prevent the grazing of young shoots by livestock. The customs of some manors allowed tenants to graze cattle, horses and pigs at certain times of the year or to pollard trees (see pages 116-117) by lopping branches 2-5m (7-18ft) above ground.

- Look in the catalogues of estate papers for leases that allowed the 'coaling' of coppiced wood between the 16th and 18th centuries, the heyday of most coppiced woods when the iron and lead smelters paid high prices for charcoal. In 1653, George Sitwell of Renishaw Hall, a leading Derbyshire ironmaster, was allowed to fell 700 cords, or bundles, of oaks in the parish of Beighton and 'to convert the same to charcoal'.
- You may find references in estate accounts and leases to the transportation of charcoal and white coal by wheeled vehicles as well as packhorses.

Decline and recovery

The decline of Britain's woodlands began in the late 18th century with the replacement of charcoal by coke, derived from coal, in iron and lead smelting. The demand for charcoal fell and it became more profitable to convert coppice woods to timber growing, often with new species introduced, such as larch or sweet chestnut.

In 1919 the Forestry Commission was created and the change to conifer plantations was rapid. Between 1946 and 1976 about 30 per cent of Britain's ancient broad-leaved woods were destroyed by agricultural expansion or by replacement with conifers. But the tide has now turned, and the Woodland Trust, among others, is committed to preserving many old woods. Coppicing is undergoing a revival, particularly in southeast England.

- Spot the woods, or sections of woods, where the trees are different from those mentioned in leases and other records from earlier centuries. In woods in the north of England in the 19th century, beech trees – native in the south of England – were widely introduced.
- At your county record office, look at Victorian estate papers for 'woodwards' accounts' of what sort of trees were planted and felled. To date any changes, look at leases and bills of sale and old photographs.
- County reports known as *General Views of Agriculture*,

Permission to work Estate accounts often hold leases concerning woodland activity. In 1682, the Duke of Newcastle granted a lease (below) in Derbyshire, which allowed two tenants, Thomas Starky and John Rogers, to make pits and kilns to convert wood into white coal and charcoal, to burn rammell (twigs), erect workmen's cabins and have free passage for oxen, horses, wains and carts to the nearest highways.

Practising an old skill A woodsman in Lancashire continues the tradition of coppicing, cutting trees to the ground for wood and to encourage new growth.

from the 1790s and early 19th century, such as *General View of the Agriculture of Devonshire* by C. Vancouver (1808), have long sections on woods written at the time when many were undergoing change.

- If your local wood does not have any of the new species, and if the trees are mostly tall and thin, and competing for light, it may be that the old trees have not been coppiced since charcoal went out of fashion. Many old coppice woods have not been managed since the First World War.
- Compare the current Ordnance Survey (OS) Explorer map (see pages 214-215) of your district with first-edition OS maps to spot any changes. See how many woods preserve their original shape, even if the tree species are different. Notice whether any woods have been reduced in size or have disappeared altogether.

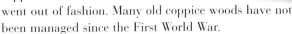

FIND OUT MORE

For further information about Britain's woodlands and ways in which you can become involved, contact the following organisations.

- www.woodland-trust.org.uk Find out where your nearest woodlands are located by looking at the Woodland Trust's on-line Directory of Woods. The Trust organises local talks, guided walks and volunteer work parties.
- www.smallwoods.org.uk The Small Woods Association aims to encourage the care and enjoyment of small woodlands and supports woodland crafts.
- www.greenwoodtrust.org.uk The Green Wood Trust works to regenerate broad-leaved woodlands by teaching traditional skills such as coppicing. It runs courses and offers opportunities for volunteer work.

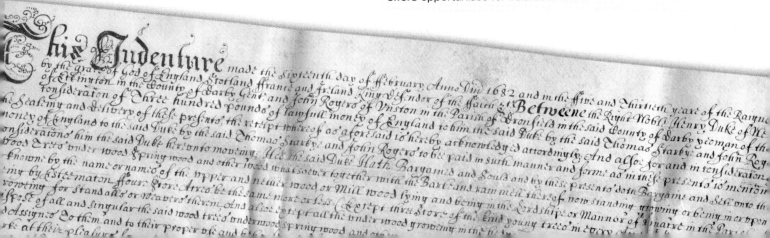

A nationwide view of England's trees

From 1924 to 2000 the Forestry Commission has regularly carried out county-by-county surveys of England to determine the extent and type of woodland cover. The fieldwork has resulted in the National Inventory of Woodland and Trees (NIWT), a rich resource of maps and statistics. Wherever you live in England, the inventory will give you a clear picture of the changing state of your county's woods and forests through time.

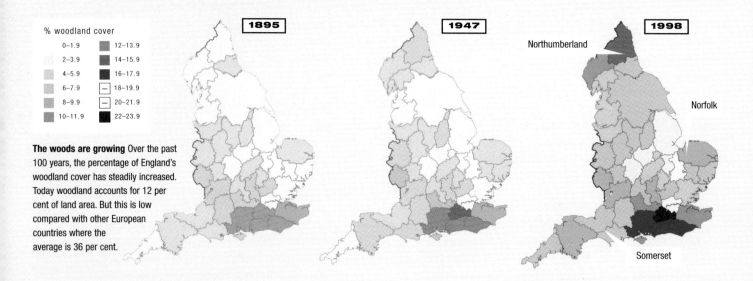

% woodland cover

0–1.9		12–13.9	
2–3.9		14–15.9	
4–5.9		16–17.9	
6–7.9		18–19.9	
8–9.9		20–21.9	
10–11.9		22–23.9	

The woods are growing Over the past 100 years, the percentage of England's woodland cover has steadily increased. Today woodland accounts for 12 per cent of land area. But this is low compared with other European countries where the average is 36 per cent.

Somerset – land of oak and ash

The patterns of woodland change from county to county, shaped by each area's history. This is reflected in the NIWT, which has catalogued not only every swathe of woodland but also every lone tree. The 2002 survey shows Somerset to be a county with a surprisingly meagre covering of trees – about 7 per cent of the land area. In 1980 there was even less woodland – only 5.6 per cent. There are 1286 sizeable woods of 2ha (5 acres) or more, with an average area of 18ha (44 acres), and twice as many small pieces of woodland averaging just under half a hectare (1.25 acres).

As for the type of tree cover in Somerset, slightly more than half the woodlands are broadleaved, with oak and ash predominating. Conifers account for about a quarter of the woodland: most of them (17.5 per cent) are larch.

Norfolk – copses, clumps and pine plantations

In spite of its arable landscape, Norfolk has more tree cover, at 9.8 per cent, than Somerset, with 2191 woods of more than 2ha (5 acres). The woods' average area is 20.3ha (50 acres), which is comparable with that of the larger woodlands of Somerset.

Norfolk possesses a vastly greater number of small pieces of woodland – more than 16,000 compared with Somerset's 2478. This reflects Norfolk's historic status as a shooting county, where any landowner worth his salt planted copses to shelter game. The county is also low-lying and windswept, so every farm needed a sheltering clump of trees. Such windbreaks are more numerous than in Somerset – Norfolk has 42,900 narrow rows of trees and about 3000 classified as 'wide' (which are also useful as game cover). Norfolk has fewer free-standing trees than Somerset, numbering just under 4 million.

The proportion of broadleaved to coniferous woodlands in Norfolk and Somerset is roughly the same, with oak accounting for around a quarter of broadleaved trees in both counties. But Norfolk shows an overwhelming imbalance of species in its coniferous woodlands: four out of every five trees in these woods is a pine. This

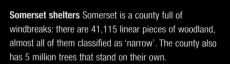

Somerset shelters Somerset is a county full of windbreaks: there are 41,115 linear pieces of woodland, almost all of them classified as 'narrow'. The county also has 5 million trees that stand on their own.

Norfolk plantings The Corsican pines at Holkham were planted on the dunes in the 19th century as a shelter belt. Pine trees dominate Norfolk's coniferous woodland – many were planted after the Second World War as sustainable sources of timber.

reflects the massive Forestry Commission plantings after the Second World War on the sandy Breckland heaths in the southwest of the county, where Thetford Forest covers around 21,000ha (51,900 acres).

Northumberland – the march of coniferous armies

An initial impression of Northumberland might be one of a county of treeless coasts and moors, but the NIWT tells a different story. In fact, Northumberland has more than twice as much land under trees (16 per cent of the county's total area) as Somerset (7 per cent).

Northumberland's trees are grouped differently from those of Somerset and Norfolk. The two southern counties both possess more small woods than Northumberland. Norfolk has more large woods, too; but the difference is that the Northumbrian woods, although fewer in number, are almost twice the average size – 38.1ha (94 acres) – of the East Anglian ones. The northern sportsmen and farmers seem to be able to do without windbreaks, since there are fewer than 2000 linear woodland features in the whole county. As for trees standing out on their own – blustery Northumberland with its cool temperatures can show fewer than a quarter of a million.

The biggest contrast between north and south is in the proportion of coniferous to broadleaved woodlands.

SPECIES OF TREES

Trees can be classified as native, naturalised or newcomers. Native trees have been here since before the last Ice Age, and include oak, ash, beech, birch, hazel, Scot's pine and elm. Trees that were introduced hundreds of years ago are said to have naturalised (sycamore, horse chestnut and Norway spruce). Newcomers have been introduced recently, mainly to produce timber (pine, larch, poplar and Douglas fir).

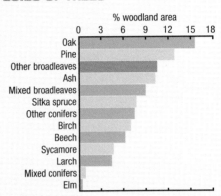

% woodland area
0 3 6 9 12 15 18
- Oak
- Pine
- Other broadleaves
- Ash
- Mixed broadleaves
- Sitka spruce
- Other conifers
- Birch
- Beech
- Sycamore
- Larch
- Mixed conifers
- Elm

Mighty oak, tragic elm Long a symbol of England, the oak is still the dominant tree species (16.1 per cent). Pine is second due to large commercial forests, mainly in the north. The tiny presence of elm (0.4 per cent) reflects the devastation caused from the 1970s by Dutch elm disease, which killed some 80 per cent of mature trees.

Only 13.3 per cent of Northumberland's woods are broadleaved; the most numerous species (20 per cent) is birch, an early coloniser of post-Ice Age Britain. Three-quarters of the woods are coniferous, with sitka spruce – an introduced commercial forestry tree – representing 68 per cent of the species. That indicates just how important the Forestry Commission's presence is in Northumberland, another county that was high on the list for post-war commercial planting.

Northumberland conifers Broadleaved species like silver birch (right) are outnumbered by huge expanses of conifer forests in Northumberland. The enormous Kielder Forest (below) is England's largest and most productive forest. It is owned by the Forestry Commission and consists of around 150 million trees, mostly Sitka spruce.

FIND OUT MORE

- *The Forestry Commission's National Inventory of Woodland and Trees* Available from Forestry Commission Publications, PO Box 25, Wetherby, West Yorkshire LS23 7EW
- www.forestry.gov.uk/forestry/ hcou-54pg9u To access the inventory information on-line.

Travel on the rural highways and byways

Take a look at the road signs in your local area. You may spot some intriguing names, such as Salterway, Hollowgate or Packman Lane, which will set you wondering about their meaning. The roads, country lanes, footpaths and bridges in your area all have a story to tell about the local people, packmen and drovers who used them years ago. You can find plenty of clues that will explain their origins.

Routing for old names

In the 18th and early 19th centuries, the most important highways became turnpike roads (see pages 124-125), and country lanes were widened when the commons were enclosed. But many of the old names have survived.

- At your county record office, note the names on the 19th-century first edition six-inch Ordnance Survey (OS) maps, tithe award and enclosure maps, and any other local maps that are available (see pages 26-27). Then visit your local library and consult the county volumes published by the English Place-Name Society (see DIRECTORY). Look for the earliest references to these names and you may find explanations of their meanings.

- The word 'road' was rarely used before the late 17th century. The Anglo-Saxons used the term 'ways' and the Vikings 'gates'. Look for names such as

Watering holes Pub names, such as the Woolpack in Slad, Gloucestershire (above), the Packhorse or the Drovers' Arms, give clues to their history.

Drovers' network Look out for the old droving routes (above) – now often local walking trails – along which cattle, sheep, pigs and geese were driven across Britain to supply London and other fast-expanding cities from the end of the 16th century.

Bradway ('the broad way') or Ridgeway, and Sandygate or Kirkgate ('the route to church'). In upland districts spot the Corpse Ways, which were the traditional burial routes from remote hamlets to the parish churchyard.

- 'Lane' had the same meaning as today, but dialect words such as 'sty' or 'rake' were also used for minor tracks or paths. Oxton Rakes in the Peak District commemorates the route by which oxen were driven to summer pastures.

- Find out what sort of traders might have used your local roads. The routes taken by packmen transporting salt from the Cheshire saltworks to Midland market towns can be followed on maps by looking for names such as Salters' Ford, Salters' Hill and Saltergate. The Salters' Closes provided overnight grazing.

Following ancient tracks

See if you can find the old routes on the ground. Many of our roads have developed from the well-trodden paths of days gone by, but you may notice that some appear sunken with very steep banks.

Holloways The deep holloways or hollowgates (see right) were formed by the wear of wheeled traffic. In moorland areas, where tracks did not have to follow a definite line, notice how they fan out across the landscape

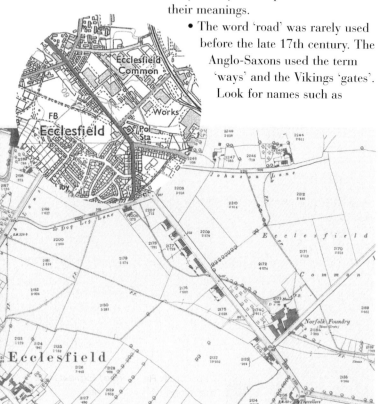

Changes on the ground Compare maps such as the first edition Ordnance Survey (OS) map from 1892 of Ecclesfield, Yorkshire (above), with a modern-day OS Explorer map (inset) and you will be able to see how lanes have developed into roads, where footpaths led to, and perhaps uncover the origins of a mysterious road or place name.

to form a group of shallow holloways. The age of a holloway cannot be estimated from its depth because a sunken track could be produced in a few seasons of heavy traffic, but there may be other clues to help you to date them. For example, you might find deeply worn tracks leading to the site of a forge or furnace that was built in the 17th century and abandoned a hundred years later.

Bridges Look for sturdy medieval bridges with pointed arches, such as the bridge over the River Wye in Bakewell. These were wide enough to take wheeled traffic.

- At the county record office you can read the quarter sessions records from the 17th and 18th centuries to find out when bridges were repaired or enlarged by order of the Justices of the Peace (JPs).
- Check whether bridges near where you live were marked on the earliest county maps by Saxton or Speed (see pages 26-27).
- You may find a narrow packhorse bridge in your area, just wide enough to take a loaded horse. These bridges are most likely to be seen in upland districts, such as the Pennines, on routes that were never made into turnpike roads or widened for wheeled traffic. They date from about 1650-1750, when they often replaced wooden bridges. Their simple design should not mislead you into thinking that they are much older.

Local footpath features

Flagstones Look for lines of flagstones, known as 'causeys' or 'causeways', that were put down as footpaths or bridleways by parish authorities or landowners. Most surviving examples date from the 17th to the 19th centuries. Many are now overgrown or have been covered by modern surfaces.

Guide stoops If you live in Derbyshire, or the West and North Ridings of Yorkshire, look for early 18th-century waymarkers known as guide stoops (left). They helped to guide travellers across remote and featureless moorland, pointing the way to the nearest market towns and sometimes local villages and hamlets.

Finger posts Do any 'finger posts' made of cast iron (below), point directions in your parish? They date from the late 19th and early 20th centuries.

Stiles Are the stiles in your area all of the same design? The Peak District 'squeezers' (below) are two upright stones, splayed at the top to allow you to squeeze through. Also look out for any standing or recumbent stones with holes in them that once supported a gate hinge.

Making a deep impression You might find a sunken lane near where you live. Some of these byways can be more than 4.5m (15ft) deep, such as the aptly named Hollow Lane (left), leading from Montacute towards Ham Hill in Somerset. They became deeper as wheeled traffic gradually replaced packhorses between the 16th and 18th centuries.

FIND OUT MORE

- *Welsh Cattle Drovers* (Richard Moore-Colyer, Landmark Publishing, 1976). An account of the old droving routes.
- *A Dictionary of British Place Names* (A.D. Mills, Oxford Paperback Reference) Explains the meanings of place names.
- www.st-andrews.ac.uk/institutes/sassi/spns The Scottish Place-Name Society provides help on tracing the origins of names.

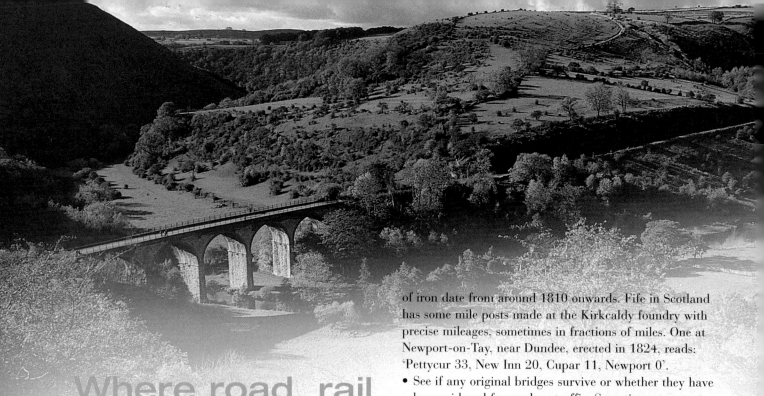

of iron date from around 1810 onwards. Fife in Scotland has some mile posts made at the Kirkcaldy foundry with precise mileages, sometimes in fractions of miles. One at Newport-on-Tay, near Dundee, erected in 1824, reads: 'Pettycur 33, New Inn 20, Cupar 11, Newport 0'.

- See if any original bridges survive or whether they have been widened for modern traffic. Sometimes, you can tell only by looking under the bridge for where the two structures were joined. Look for the dates or name of the turnpike trust on the bridges.

- At road junctions, look at the buildings to see if any were toll-keepers' cottages. Many are only one storey high and have large windows at both the front and sides to allow the toll-keeper to spot oncoming traffic.

- You may find a stretch of early turnpike road that was abandoned when a steep hill was by-passed. It will now be a grassy track, but will feature on early Ordnance Survey (OS) and county maps (see pages 26-27).

Where road, rail and canal cross the land

Turnpike roads, canals and railways revolutionised the transport system in the 18th and 19th centuries at a time when Britain's population and industries were booming. They made a huge impact on the local landscape, leaving a trail of evidence that you can follow on the ground and in records.

Looking for signs of turnpike roads

Britain's roads were in such a poor state by the late 17th century that Parliament introduced turnpike trusts (see pages 70-71) to fund improvements and make the roads suitable for wheeled traffic. Many signs of the old turnpikes still exist, such as toll-keepers' cottages, milestones and bridges, trust records and surveyors' reports.

Pay as you go A toll-house (1824) on the cross-Pennine turnpike, now the A6033.

Tracing turnpikes Look along roadside verges for turnpike milestones and water troughs for the horses. Most early to mid 18th-century milestones are simple stone slabs with the mileage recorded on the side facing the road. Cast-iron plates were added in the second half of the 18th century, and milestones made entirely

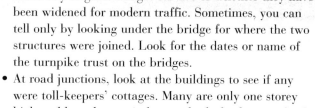

Counting the miles A wide variety of milestones can be spotted: some mark just one destination; others, such as at Alston (left), at a crossing point on the Pennine moors, list several destinations. Wedge-shaped versions, like the one near Southport (above right), allowed the traveller to see the distance from afar. Some turnpike trusts had their own styles, including cylindrical designs, such as the cast-iron milestone at Ashford-in-the-Water, Derbyshire (above left).

The high route Look out for disused railway tracks that have become walking routes. The Monsal Trail in Derbyshire crosses the old Midland Railway viaduct (left), built in 1863.

Turnpikes in the records At your local record office, look for turnpike trust minute books and for surveyors' reports and correspondence. Search early directories and local newspapers (see pages 216-217) for coaching and waggon services. Look for the principal stopping places, the names of inns that may still exist (see page 262) and the many service providers, such as the Breconshire Trust.

• Trace the course of early turnpike roads on late-18th-century county maps and compare with those seen on enclosure maps and first-edition six-inch OS maps (see pages 214-215). Make a note of any changes.

• Acts of Parliament setting up turnpike trusts are available from the House of Lords Record Office (see DIRECTORY). They give details of the type of traffic that used the road, the location of toll gates and the charges levied.

Navigating the canals

The canal system (see page 71) played a key role in transporting heavy goods such as building materials in the 18th and 19th centuries. You can follow disused stretches of canals along towpaths and under the bow-shaped bridges which allowed the horses towing the boats to cross to the other side. Spot the canal company's name on plaques on bridges.

• Look out for engineering feats, such as flights of locks, tunnels and aqueducts. You may still find signs of a lock-keeper's cottage or boatmen's pub beside a lock or at a canal junction (see page 249).

Canals in the records At your local county record office, you can identify the type of goods carried on a canal by looking at old photographs (see pages 212-213) and documents, such as the private Acts of Parliament that authorised the construction of canals.

• The 18th-century county maps (see pages 26-27) mark early canals,

Country halt Look for signs of disused stations, such as Hatton, near Lancaster (below). Platforms often remain, but the buildings may have been converted to another use. Some former steam train lines have been restored by local groups of enthusiasts, and both these societies and railway museums often hold excellent collections of railway memorabilia, including timetables such as for the Lancashire and Yorkshire Railway, 1910 (above).

such as the pioneering Duke of Bridgewater Canal (completed in 1772) on Burdett's 1777 map of Cheshire. Compare these with the first-edition six-inch OS maps, which show the completed system.

• Look for prints and paintings of the waterways in your local record office or museum.

On the track of railways

Evidence of Britain's extensive railway network – before it was severely pruned in the mid 20th century – can be seen across the countryside (see pages 72-73). If there is a disused line near where you live, note how bridges, viaducts, cuttings, embankments, tunnels, sidings and signal boxes have made an impact on the landscape. If you find a bridge over a wide grassy track, see whether it matches up with a 'dismantled railway line' marked on the current OS map. Some lines have been converted into footpaths and cycle tracks.

Railways in the records At your county record office, look at large-scale OS maps from the mid-Victorian period onwards to see how the railway system developed and to spot branch lines that have since been abandoned.

• Images of steam locomotives have been captured in many books of old photographs (see pages 212-213).

• Records of former railway companies, including maps and plans, staff records, reports and accounts are held at the National Archives in Kew and Edinburgh, and the House of Lords Record Office.

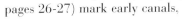
FIND OUT MORE

• *National Railway Museum* Vast collection of rolling stock and historic documents (see pages 252-253). www.nrm.org.uk

• *Nicholson Guides to the Waterways* (OS-Nicholson, 2000-2003) A comprehensive series of guides to the canal network.

• www.canalroutes.org A detailed exploration of the history of Britain's inland waterways.

Looking for signs of rural industry

The story of where you live might begin with an iron works, a mine or a slate quarry that was set up deep in the countryside. For centuries, rural people have earned their living from many industries, not just farming. You will find signs of these activities on moorland, in woods, on the coast and beside rivers.

Monuments to tin The ruins of the once lucrative tin-mining industry litter the Cornish landscape, such as the pumping engine house at Wheal Coates, St Agnes, built in 1872. Workings extended deep under the sea.

Uncovering the evidence

The countryside has hummed with industrial activity since prehistoric times. There are signs of ancient flint mines at Grimes Graves in Norfolk and copper mines at Llandudno in North Wales (see pages 42-43). But the greatest surge in rural industry took place in the 18th century (see pages 68-69).

To find out about the industries in your area, talk to older members of your community, such as former tin miners. At your local library and record office, search for old illustrations and photographs (see pages 212-213) of industrial landscapes, and look for documentary and map evidence. You might find a lease for a coal mine among estate papers or see that a quarry was still being worked at the time of an early Ordnance Survey (OS) map (see pages 26-27). These might explain physical features in the landscape such as overgrown workings or derelict dams.

Countryside clues First-edition OS maps often mark the sites of former industries, such as Rainstorth Colliery, near Sheffield (1892, left). Visit the area now, and you might spot some remains.

Following an industry

Many industries were specific to certain areas. The local geology often played a key role in their location (see page 68).

The early iron industry Mining for iron ore took place across much of Britain from the Weald in Kent through the Midlands and south Wales, north to Yorkshire. You can spot the sites by looking for the abandoned bell pits of the ironstone miners. They often appear in woodland as water-filled depressions up to 2m (6ft) in diameter and 6m (20ft) deep. Look for traces of charcoal blast furnaces and forges, wheel pits and the outlines of dams.

- You can identify old iron-working sites through names such as Cinder Hill or Smithies on OS maps. At your local reference library or record office, consult the volumes of the English Place-Name Society or the *Victoria County History* (see 'Find out more', page 99) for any mention of them in charters and leases. Many sites were worked by monks and are mentioned in the ecclesiastical records.
- At your reference library, refer to British Geological Survey maps, which mark outcrops of ironstone and coal. Then, at your record office, turn to 18th-century county maps to spot the 'fire engines' that pumped the water out of mines. Landowners were keen to exploit mineral deposits – look for evidence in estate papers.

Cornish tin mines Tin was mined in Cornwall from prehistoric times. The greatest period of activity was in the late 18th and 19th centuries, when beam engines were

Walking into history Even on a family walk in local countryside, you might come across signs of an industrial past. A millstone lying in open moorland at White Coppice in Lancashire (above) provides a clue to past activities in the area.

used for pumping and winding, and for crushing ores. Mineral railways took the tin from smelting works to the ports on the coast. Foreign competition brought most of the industry to an end in the Victorian period.

- Look for the remains of engine houses, chimney stacks, wheel pits and winding gear. Many mines, such as those at Botallack, near Land's End, are perched precariously on steep cliffs overlooking the sea.
- At your county record office and library look for old photographs of mines and mining villages. Note their layout on first-edition, large-scale OS maps. Search surviving company records for maps, reports, accounts and correspondence.

Millstone-making The entrances to the Peak District National Park are marked by a distinctive sign in the shape of a millstone. Hundreds of millstones, in various stages of manufacture, litter former quarries on the park's gritstone edges and on adjacent stretches of moorland. The heyday of this ancient industry was from the 16th to the 19th century.

- Abandoned millstones that were intended for corn-milling have a flat side for grinding, a convex top, and narrow, rounded edges. They

commonly had a diameter of 152-178cm (60-70in). Most of the remaining stones were used for pulping wood into paper or for grinding paint. They come in different sizes, are flat on both sides, and have sharp, right-angled edges.

- Look for the levelled tracks and holloways (see pages 122-123) leading from the quarries. The millstones were moved along these on sledges.
- At your local record office, search for millstone hewers in the census returns and for the names of quarry owners in trade directories (see pages 217, 218-219). Information on the running of the industry may be found in account books, leases and correspondence. Early editions of OS maps will show you which quarries were in production and when.

Swaledale lead mining Lead mines were associated with limestone districts, such as the Yorkshire Dales, the White Peak of Derbyshire and the Mendips in Somerset. The industry goes back at least to Roman times and flourished until the late 19th century. When the lead mines of Swaledale in the Pennines became exhausted, the local population fell by 50 per cent between 1871 and 1891.

- On the ground, look for deep grooves in the hillsides, known as 'hushes', which were made by damming a stream to uncover the veins of lead. Search for the drainage channels of the deeper mines, which appear as stone-built tunnels in the hillsides. Find the ruins of former smelting mills, such as Old Gang Smelt Mill, near Reeth, whose chimneys and ruined buildings are surrounded by heaps of debris.
- At your local record office, spot the mines and smelting mills on early OS maps and in old photographs. Search for the leases and business records of mining companies.

Explosive material An accident at the Chilworth gunpowder works (left), which killed six men, is recorded in a 1901 edition of the *Surrey Advertiser*. Old newspaper reports (see pages 216-217) such as this can highlight former industries where you live.

FIND OUT MORE

- *The Making of the Industrial Landscape* (Barrie Trinder, Weidenfeld & Nicolson, 1997) Describes rural industry in the 18th and 19th centuries.
- Great Orme Mines Llandudno, north Wales. Explore the tunnels of a copper mine that dates back to the time of the Bronze Age. www.greatorme.freeserve.co.uk
- Geevor Tin Mine Pendeen, Cornwall. Work ceased at Geevor in 1990 and the mine is now open to the public. www.geevor.com

Rips and repairs in the landscape

For better or for worse, the stamp of heavy industry on the landscape can be jaw-droppingly spectacular. Even in places where the effects seemed irreversible, ingenuity, energy and money have helped to remedy the deepest scars.

Before and after The three huge slag heaps (top) left by Garswood Hall Colliery in Ashton-in-Makerfield, Lancashire, used to be known as The Three Sisters. Today the spoil heaps have been transformed into the Three Sisters Recreation Area, set among ponds, woodland and open fields.

Mining heaps

Perhaps the most spectacularly visible industrial devastation of the landscape took place in the 19th and 20th centuries as a result of coal mining in south Wales, Lancashire, Yorkshire, County Durham, Lanarkshire and Lothian. Ugly pithead winding gear and mine buildings dotted the landscape, while red-brick colliery villages sprawled over the once-green countryside. Towering menacingly over the scene were the great black spoil tips or slag heaps.

But this is not the story today in the former coal-mining towns. Most of the industry has gone and the landscape is being transformed. Nearly all the colliery heaps have been reclaimed. Seeded with grass and trees, the scenic hillocks, such as those at Ebbw Vale in south Wales, look as though they have always been there. Many are now incorporated into parkland, the heavy industry of the past giving way to a new industry of leisure, as in the Three Sisters Recreation Area in Lancashire (above).

Big holes in the ground

Industry did not make these huge spoil heaps without creating equally large holes. Perhaps the best-known post-industrial hole is the 60m (200ft) deep pit at Bodelva near St Austell, where china clay had been dug since 1830. It was acquired by the Eden Trust in 1998 and turned into the Eden Project botanical garden.

Digging for gravel across central and southeast England to help fuel the post-war boom in road and house building has produced many wide, shallow holes. When the gravel is exhausted, the problem of what to do with the pits has often been solved by turning them into watersports and leisure parks. Cotswold Water Park in Gloucestershire consists of 133 lakes that have formed from the extraction of the rich gravel deposits of the Upper Thames Valley. The park, covering an area 50 per cent larger than the Norfolk Broads, has metamorphosed into a haven for wildlife such as otters and the rare water vole, as well as hosting 20,000 wintering wildfowl such as pochard, gadwall and tufted duck.

Flooded pits are also a feature of abandoned quarry workings, and many have become fishing lakes and diving centres. Stoney Cove's granite works in Leicestershire

From industry to fun The flooding of more than 100 gravel pits over an area of 40 square miles has created an ideal watersports venue at the Cotswold Water Park. With gravel extraction still going on in the area it is still set to expand.

Man-made peaks The processing of china clay at St Austell is Cornwall's largest industry. It has produced huge waste heaps, white and grey mini mountains of spoil known locally as the 'Cornish Alps'.

Live and let live In spite of the chemical works that dominate the horizon at Seal Sands, Teesmouth, the extensive mud flats form part of a National Nature Reserve, renowned for its waterfowl and seal species.

were active in the first half of the 20th century, but when work stopped in 1958, the quarry filled with natural spring water. With its terraced depths of 6m (20ft), 20m (66ft) and 35m (115ft), it is an ideal setting for the sport of diving.

Where quarries are still active, the holes remain. Whatley Quarry in the Mendip Hills of Somerset, worked for its limestone, ground up for the building industry, has produced a hole 1 mile long, 91m (300ft) deep and still growing. The Delabole slate quarry in Cornwall, active since at least the early 17th century, plunges 130m (425ft) below ground level, and has a circumference of 1½ miles. The Delabole Slate Company continues to remove 120 tons of slate block per day, but modern mining techniques have improved quarrying efficiency, ensuring that waste mountains are a thing of the past.

Dealing with the muck of industry

Although heaps and holes are immediately apparent, in some places the mark left by industry has been more insidious, the damage done in the days when there was nothing to stop the poisoning and polluting of the land. County Durham's coastal coalmining communities devastated their cliffs, beaches and sea by tipping colliery waste and raw sewage. But the beaches have been cleaned (see page 91), and the coal tips cleared and landscaped.

Particularly badly hit was the lower Swansea Valley, one of the largest areas of industrial dereliction in Europe, crowded with industrial plants that processed coal, zinc, tin, lead, steel and copper. In the 1960s a project was initiated to clean up the valley, and 20 years on the derelict buildings had gone and the soil cleaned of pollutants so that trees could be planted. Today the site is transformed – a landscaped mix of light industry, shopping centres and outdoor recreational facilities.

(see page 91)

FIND OUT MORE

• *How Green Was My Valley* (Richard Llewellyn, Penguin Books, 1939).
• Dinton Pastures Country Park Gravel pits near Windsor turned into lakes and islands. www.greenlink-berkshire.org.uk/ Dinton_Pastures.htm
• Stoney Cove National Diving Centre Story of the granite works and details of diving activities. www.stoneycove.com
• Cotswold Water Park Information on leisure activities and wildlife. www.waterpark.org
• Delabole Slate Quarry Information on the quarry and its products. www.delaboleslate.co.uk
• Durham Heritage Coast Story of the coast's clean-up. www.turning-the-tide.org.uk
• Lower Swansea Valley Story of post-industrial transformation. www.swanseaheritage.net/themes/ industry/index.asp

Seeing how the modern countryside has changed

If you were to travel back only about 70 years, much of the countryside would appear very different. You would see more hedges, more meadows and more people. The results of two remarkable surveys will help you to create a vivid picture of what rural life was like before intensive farming transformed the British landscape.

The National Farm Survey

A good way to capture the old pattern of farming before the days of mechanisation is to consult the National Farming Survey of 1941-3 (see also page 304). The wartime government, concerned to ensure the efficient production of food, investigated every farm of more than five acres – nearly 300,000 in all. Each farm was graded A, B or C, according to the competence of the farmer. You can find the records of this extensive survey at the National Archives at Kew and Edinburgh (see DIRECTORY).

- Look at the forms completed by the farmers, recording the size of the farm, the number of tractors, working horses and full-time staff, including land girls, the acreages devoted to cereals, root crops and grassland. By studying all the returns for your village or parish you can obtain a clear picture of local farming practices and management at the time.
- By reading the answers on the forms you

will be able to see who had a water supply to the farmhouse, farm buildings and fields, whether electricity had been installed, and whether the farm was infested with rabbits, rats and mice, or wood pigeons.

- Look at the maps, based on the Ordnance Survey (OS), which were colour-washed to show the extent of each farm and its field boundaries. These will enable you to check for change or continuity with the present day.

The Valuation Office surveys

After the 1910 Finance Act, the Inland Revenue carried out surveys and valuations of all the land and property in Britain (see also page 310). Records for England and Wales are held at the National Archives at Kew (series IR 58, IR 121, IR 124-35). Those for Scotland are in the

Top marks Answers on National Farm Survey questionnaires tell you who owned and worked a farm and how well it was run. At Abbey Farm in Muchelney, Somerset, the tennant farmer in 1942, a Mr Cridland, apparently did an excellent job (see left). The farm can be identified from its code number on the accompanying field map (below).

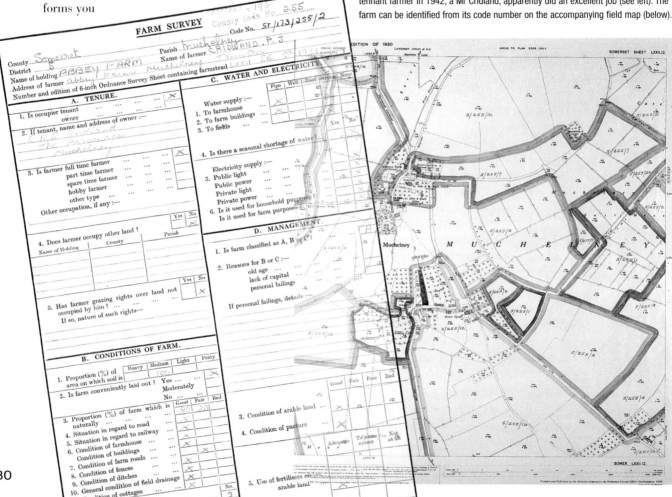

National Archives at Edinburgh (RS 51-88, IR 101-33). Local records may survive at your county record office.

- The records include the surveyors' field books and forms that were filled in by property owners. Farms and other properties referred to in the field books are identified on accompanying OS maps.
- Compare both 20th-century surveys with the tithe awards and maps of the 1830s and 40s (see pages 26-27) to see whether farms changed size and shape. Compare the amount of arable, meadow and pasture in the 1910s and 1940s with the same figures recorded a century earlier.

The look of farming today

Farming has altered radically since the Second World War. Food production has increased, yet fewer people are employed on the land – one person on a tractor can do the job of many agricultural labourers. Yet the rural landscape still hums with life that you can discover.

- Look out for newspaper reports about diversification, such as the growing of coriander in the Pennines for the Asian market in west Yorkshire, the construction of trout farms, the rearing of pheasants, or the setting up of farmers' markets for local food producers.
- At your local library or record office search for newspaper reports (see pages 216-217) and the archives of conservation bodies, such as the Council for the Protection of Rural England (see DIRECTORY).
- Look at how the countryside today is catering for leisure pursuits and tourism. Has rambling, climbing and cycling affected the local economy and the appearance of the landscape, with campsites, signposted paths, or farmhouse bed-and-breakfast and self-catering facilities? These are all part of the continuing evolution of our countryside.

Charting changes Notice how old farmhouses, outbuildings and field walls were constructed of local materials that blend into the landscape (see pages 102-103). Contrast these with the large modern farm buildings (above) that often look out of place. What has happened to the old outbuildings? Were some converted into housing? Talking to farmers and farmworkers is a good way of finding out about the huge changes that took place in the 20th century. You might discover why hedges were destroyed and what effect it had on bird and mammal populations; when silos replaced traditional haystacks; and what happened to the stables when horses were replaced by tractors.

Shot into shape If you live in an upland area of Britain, you may notice the distinctive patchwork appearance of local moors. This is because they are used for shooting grouse, and every 10-12 years stretches are burned to ensure a fresh supply of heather for the birds. Grouse moors in Britain (marked as squares on the map above) are shot less intensively than in their late-Victorian and Edwardian heyday (above right). Look for old or ruined shooting butts and cabins. At your county record office, search for enclosure awards and maps, and estate papers (see pages 26-27), which may reveal when a grouse-shooting moor came into being and how many birds were shot in a season.

COMM

THE
STORY OF
COMMUNITIES

134-209

UNITY

EXPLORE YOUR COMMUNITY

210-265

THE STORY OF COMMUNITIES

You may live in a busy town or city, or in a sleepy village, or even in an isolated cottage miles from your nearest neighbours, but no matter where you call home, you are part of a community. By uncovering the story of where you live, you will learn how it has grown and changed over time, and meet the various people who played a key role in events.

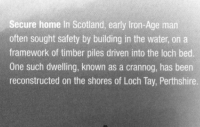

Secure home In Scotland, early Iron-Age man often sought safety by building in the water, on a framework of timber piles driven into the loch bed. One such dwelling, known as a crannog, has been reconstructed on the shores of Loch Tay, Perthshire.

Ice and stone Archaeological evidence suggests that primitive communities of hunters were living in Britain about a quarter of a million years ago, at the end of the first of the world's great Ice Ages. Life must have been extremely tough for those early settlers. We know they huddled round camp fires to eat the animals they killed, for stone tools, bones and charcoal from the fires themselves have been unearthed. Modern humans probably arrived from the Continent after 40,000 BC, but life did not change much – it was still all about hunting and gathering to stay alive. A flock of birds and a plump horned ibex engraved on a Derbyshire cave wall at the end of the last Ice Age, some 12,000 years ago, hint at the preoccupations of these early Britons.

Gradually life became more sophisticated, so that by the late Stone Age, around 5000 years ago, animals were being domesticated and reared for food, the forests that had succeeded the ice were being felled, and fields of wheat and barley were being cultivated. But arable farming was still run on the 'slash-and-burn' principle, requiring farmers to move on and fell more forest once the old land was exhausted. People still lived a more or less nomadic existence, just like their hunter-gatherer ancestors, rather than in permanently settled communities.

Men of metal

Around 2000 BC new immigrants made their appearance on the British scene. Over several hundred years, they came across from Spain and from the lands around the Rhine, and with them came skill in making bronze. These newcomers produced efficient, hard-edged

Cutting edge Sharp, bronze tools such as those from Flag Fen, near Peterborough, helped transform society.

metal tools and weapons as well as ornaments and household goods. They soon dominated the southern part of Britain, where they built settlements of round huts and used their bronze tools to cut down swathes of wild forest, creating walled and ditched fields which they then worked with light ox-drawn ploughs.

The next wave of innovators, the Celts, arrived from France around 600 BC, bringing with them skills in manufacturing iron. Farming implements, including ploughs, could now be forged from this metal, which is harder, sharper and more durable than bronze. It became easier to work the land, and in many areas of Britain cereal production took over from animal husbandry as the principal form of agriculture. Soon permanent farming communities were established and people started to regard the land on which they had settled as 'theirs'.

cities of today. In the countryside, most Britons still lived in round houses with wattle walls and thatched roofs; but many of these rural communities were centred on a handsome villa of stone or brick, the home of a Roman landowner and his family – the squirearchy of the day.

Dawn of medieval feudalism

The Romans left Britain around AD 410. Their exit was followed by the arrival of waves of Saxons, then Norsemen and Danes (see pages 48-49). Each set of newcomers at first fought and then farmed their way into the landscape. Villages grew up, with houses straddling riverbanks or grouped round a central green. The surrounding land was cultivated, using a seasonal three-field system of rotating crops. Law and order was imposed through community meetings and councils.

Many communities grew up on the fertile soils of river valleys, where the stiff clays had become workable once the Gauls had arrived with their notion of attaching wheels to a plough. Some people were still housed in wattle-and-daub huts; others, depending on their terrain, built with stone. For protection, settlements were sited on hilltops, surrounded by huge ramparts of mounded earth, or on man-made islands in the marshes.

Ruled by Rome

In AD 43 the Romans invaded Britain and stayed for the best part of 400 years, changing the structure of day-to-day life beyond recognition (see pages 44-47). They drove long straight roads through the dense native forests, drained the marshes and set up huge farming enterprises. But above all they established a number of large towns, such as Colchester and St Albans, which became social and economic centres. Firm national laws and codes of behaviour governed these highly organised communities.

Thousands were drawn into these towns, creating new communities of people who had no tribal, social or blood ties with each other, but were living together for reasons of economic advantage and convenience – much like the

Quick build Using forced labour, a Norman lord could build a castle, around which a new community would grow, in just a few weeks. William the Conqueror constructed about 20 such fortresses across England during his reign (1066-87), including one at Berkhamstead, Hertfordshire (above, in 1086).

When the Normans invaded England in 1066, they found that settled community life was beginning to flourish. Like the Romans a millennium earlier, these sophisticated incomers enforced their rule from the top downwards. They also built to last, in stone – castles, cathedrals, churches and city gates and walls. Under the protection of these great structures, new cities, towns and villages were established and grew rapidly.

The Norman feudal system of government placed nearly all power in the hands of the nobles and barons, whose inter-family struggles were a frequent threat to social stability. But the laws of the Normans were to offer a strong, workable code of conduct under which community life in Britain began to flourish during the early Middle Ages.

Major medieval centres

In the Middle Ages, most towns were tiny by modern standards, distinguished from villages often only by their weekly markets and annual fairs. But a few larger settlements were starting to emerge, most notably the capital London, former Roman military bases such as Exeter and York and thriving trading centres set up by the Anglo-Saxons and Vikings, such as Norwich.

London – international city

By the height of the Middle Ages, in the mid 14th century, London had grown into a bustling cosmopolitan centre, recognised as one of Europe's major cities. It had replaced Winchester as England's seat of government and was enjoying commercial success as Britain's major port.

In 1300, almost 100,000 people lived in and around London, and, like today, most were youthful. Many were only in their late teens and early twenties, having arrived in the city as servants or apprentices, and stayed just a few years, before moving on or returning home.

The attractions and opportunites of the 14th-century capital drew in people from all over Britain and the Continent. But sometimes this constant flow of visitors and immigrants was only just enough to sustain, let alone swell, the population. As was the case in many large medieval cities, living conditions in London were cramped and unsanitary. Disease was rife, and it was not uncommon for the death rate to be well in excess of the birth rate.

The emergence of provincial centres

The importance of provincial towns in medieval Britain was not only defined by their economic status but also by military might and links with the Church and nobility.

York, Exeter, Lincoln and Colchester had originated as Roman garrison towns and were important before the Norman Conquest. Military considerations led William the Conqueror to build a new castle (Newcastle) on the north bank of the Tyne and the Scottish kings to develop Edinburgh along a volcanic ridge that made for the perfect defensive site. Both castles attracted flourishing communities around them.

Towns with a major royal castle and cathedral cities, such as Durham and Lincoln, needed markets, shops and manufacturers to feed, clothe and service large groups of people. Such settlements grew rapidly in the 12th and 13th centuries. Steady population growth across Western Europe in the early Middle Ages (see pages 148-149) encouraged international trade, boosting the size of ports such as Bristol, where merchants were busily exporting their wool, cloth and grain. At the peak of their prosperity in the early 14th century, the leading provincial towns served as regional capitals and were crucial to Britain's position of power in medieval Europe.

THE MEDIEVAL METROPOLIS

When Domesday Book was being compiled in 1086, London was already by far Britain's largest settlement. It must have been very crowded, as early maps show that most of its expanding population still lived in houses within city walls that followed the line of those built by the Romans almost a thousand years before (see below). A single bridge crossed the Thames to Southwark on the south shore. The royal court and parliament were in the suburb of Westminster.

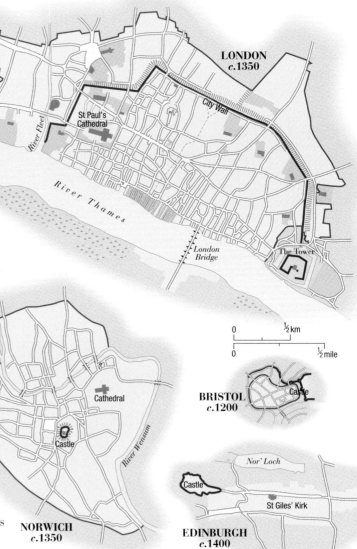

Expansion of influence Although by comparison with London, the great provincial centres of medieval Britain remained small, they too were on the move. Royal and ecclesiastical links, then the wool trade, boosted Norwich's growth, Bristol became a major port and Edinburgh's role as the capital of Scotland attracted trade via its port of Leith, giving it an edge over the other east coast burghs of Dundee and Aberdeen.

Norwich – the second city

During the Middle Ages, Norwich grew to become the largest and most important provincial city in Britain. It started as a Saxon settlement, where two old Roman roads crossed the navigable River Wensum at its lowest bridging point. At the time of the Conquest in 1066, when most English towns had barely 200 inhabitants, at least 5000 people called Norwich home, and by 1075 the Normans had built a formidable royal castle there. Domesday Book (1086) records 125 French merchants and craftsmen living and working in the New Borough that had been laid out to the west of the castle. The large market place there is still the city's commercial heart. Then, in 1096, Bishop Herbert de Losinga tore down a large part of the pre-Norman town to create a lavish precinct around the new cathedral that he was already building to serve the whole of East Anglia.

Norwich continued to prosper and expand, mainly through the growth of its textile industry and the trading skills of its merchants. This success attracted newcomers and by 1300 the population had risen to nearly 25,000. The stone walls, erected around the city between 1297 and 1370, were just over 2 miles long and enclosed an area of 1 square mile, the same as then covered by the city of London.

The Black Death in 1348-9 (see pages 148-149), followed by a prolonged depression in the cloth-trade, cut the city's population down to well under half its peak level by the early 16th century. But, despite such setbacks, Norwich continued as Britain's second city right up to the dawn of the Industrial Revolution in the late 18th century.

Status symbol Norwich's importance in medieval England is reflected in the magnificence of its Norman cathedral. The Romanesque tower soars heavenward and is visible for miles across the local landscape. The grand cloisters, added in the 13th century, are the second largest in Britain.

March of prosperity Commercial success triggered the spread of street after street of tightly packed houses, such as in Elm Hill (right), over the surrounding meadows (see 1559 woodcut, above). Elm Hill has some of the oldest surviving domestic dwellings in Norwich, dating from the early 16th century.

The spread of medieval towns

Many of today's towns and cities date back to the Middle Ages, and evidence of their history is still recognisable. You can follow the medieval street pattern at St Andrews in Fife, walk along the fortified walls of Conwy in north Wales, and around the Norman market place at Devizes in Wiltshire. Even in the great Victorian cities, you can find street and area names, such as the Bull Ring in Birmingham, Blackfriars Street in Manchester, and Briggate and Headrow in Leeds, that speak of a medieval past.

Royal favour The Borough of Doncaster holds 13 royal charters, dating from 1194 to 1836. The sixth (above) of 1532 set the final seal on the town's independent status.

Boom time for boroughs

Between the arrival of the Normans in 1066 and the Black Death in 1348, the population of the British Isles grew at a rapid rate. This stimulated new markets and fairs, and with them new towns. More than 130 were founded in England and at least 66 in Wales between 1100 and 1300, most based around a market place. Some developed from an existing village, but many grew on a totally new site, such as at Market Harborough in Leicestershire.

Over a hundred places are described as boroughs in Domesday Book. These were towns that had received a royal charter, a formal document by which the king granted them some rights to self-government. Richard I (1189-1199) and his brother John (1199-1216), both constantly at war and needing to raise money for their armies, sold many places this entitlement, often with permission to hold a market or fair. It is common to find that a town has several royal charters (see left), later ones often just confirming old privileges when a new monarch came to the throne, although sometimes new rights were added.

Records of Scottish boroughs or 'burghs' date back to the reign of David I (1124-1153), although archaeological evidence suggests that there were several before this date. By 1210, there were 40 of them, many of which were still small. Thirty of these were on the east coast, trading locally and with the Netherlands and Baltic ports. By the 14th century, Aberdeen, Perth, Edinburgh and Dundee had become the leading burghs.

Taking care of business

Most of the boroughs that flourished progressed to self-government under a mayor and a 'corporation' of up to 24 leading townsmen, usually senior members of the merchant and craft guilds (see pages 140-141). They even chose their own Members of Parliament. In the port of Kingston upon Hull, the leading merchants who controlled the export of wool and other goods from there dominated the town's affairs, as an inner council of 12 aldermen, who were elected for life. They would progress through the ranks, taking turns to act as chamberlain (treasurer), bailiff (steward) and ultimately mayor. It was generally accepted that the rich were the ones who ruled.

The hub of the town

The market place lay at the heart of all medieval towns. Both food and livestock were sold there, with the abattoirs nearby, although the stink of the tanneries (where hides were converted to leather) was usually banished to the edge of town. Specialist markets might be held in side-streets off the central area, and were often given names such as Meal Lane to indicate what was sold there.

Smaller towns of less than a thousand inhabitants, such as Ashbourne and Bolsover in Derbyshire, held a market on just one day a week and an annual fair usually celebrated on 'the eve, day and morrow' of the feast day of the saint to whom the parish church was dedicated. Larger towns had more market days and numerous fairs. Scarborough Fair, established in 1253, was exceptional in lasting 45 days from the Assumption of the Blessed Virgin Mary (15 August) to Michaelmas (29 September).

Business centre The grand architecture of inns such as the 15th-century George at Glastonbury (above) reflect their commercial importance.

A DRINK AND A DEAL AT THE INN

Market day was not just for buying and selling, but for meeting people and making new business contacts. Inns and taverns were sited close to the market place and many smaller ale houses were dotted along nearby back streets. In all of these, private deals were made, especially in the corn, wool and cloth trades. Collectors of the tolls paid by market traders were constantly trying to limit trade to the market place and to the times signalled by the ringing of the market bell, but were generally unsuccessful. Among the largest late-medieval inns were the George at Glastonbury, the Angel at Grantham and the Chequers at Canterbury, which had a hundred beds and stretched the full length of Mercer Lane.

Hot properties Shopkeepers and specialist craftsmen sought prime positions in town centres. Some had stalls in the market place which, over time, became part of a row of houses. Others had 'shops', which were both workshops and retail outlets, with either stalls projecting onto the streets on market days, such as those still largely intact in Church Street, Tewkesbury, Gloucestershire (below), or with upper storeys above an arcade. They were 'open all hours'.

Finding burgage plots Properties fronting the market place were highly desirable. Competition for space meant such buildings were tall and narrow at the front, but had long gardens with outbuildings stretching to a 'Back Street' in parallel strips called burgage plots – owned by 'burgesses' or leading citizens. Some of these are evident today, and are often best seen on old maps, such as the 19th-century one of Sherston, Wiltshire (below), showing that by then many burgesses had gained a second property, opening on to Back Street.

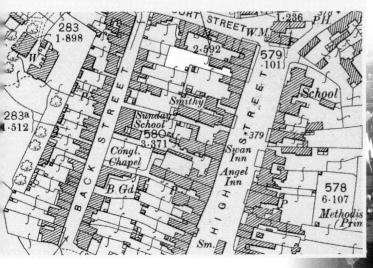

Lording it over the town Many medieval towns never achieved full independence and remained dominated by their lord, who controlled the market and kept law and order through his manor court. Most towns of around 1000 to 2000 people, such as Ludlow in Shropshire (below) or Skipton in Yorkshire, nestled under the shadow of the lord's castle, and the first Welsh towns, including Cardiff, Newport and Swansea, were centred on Norman fortifications. Others, such as Glastonbury in Somerset and St Albans in Hertfordshire, were dominated by an abbey or cathedral, rarely gaining their independence until after the Reformation in the mid 16th century.

Trade and craft take control

The commercial success of merchants and craftsmen was the driving force behind the independence of towns during the Middle Ages. Their increasing wealth helped to fund the purchase of rights and privileges from feudal landlords and the collective strength of their trade associations, or guilds, allowed them to grasp the reins of power.

The business of the guilds

As early as the 10th century, merchants were banding together for mutual support and to protect their rights. By the 12th century, increasing specialisation had driven skilled artisans to form similar groupings, or guilds. These also served to ensure high standards of practice, and by the 15th century were so powerful that it was impossible to carry out any trade or craft without serving a long apprenticeship with a guild master. Satisfactory completion led to the rank of freeman, the first step to possibly becoming a guild official and even a town councillor. By controlling entry into a trade, guilds were most people's only route to status and prosperity.

Coat of arms of York's Company of Merchant Adventurers

Social and charity work

From the start, the guilds sought prestige within the community by donating labour and funds for construction and maintenance of public buildings and the city walls and other defences. They also sought links with the Church, and carried out charitable work on behalf of the poor, sick and needy. In some cathedrals and parish churches, chapels or windows were funded by local guilds.

As their civic powers grew, various guilds took turns to police the streets and even arranged processions and feasts to mark special dates. In Coventry, one of the wealthiest cities in England by the 14th century, the prestigious Corpus Christi Guild organised a lavish annual procession at Corpus Christi, a moveable feast that fell between May 23 and June 24, celebrating the sacrament of consuming bread and wine in Christ's memory at Holy Communion.

Continuing the tradition

A few guilds retain something of their importance to this day. The London Livery Companies (so-called because of the distinctive dress worn by senior officers) are still highly influential in the City of London. They elect the capital's Lord Mayor, often from among their own number, and hold gatherings of the rich and powerful in their magnificent halls.

Statement of importance By the mid 14th century, the growing wealth and power of the merchant and trade guilds had led to their grand meeting halls becoming a prominent feature of many of Britain's major towns and cities, such as King's Lynn, Coventry and York, where four such guildhalls survive. The oldest of these is the stately timber-framed Merchant Adventurers' Hall, built from 1357 to 1361. A chapel and hospital occupied the ground floor, and the first floor served as a meeting hall (above). The Company of Merchant Adventurers who built it had begun as a religious fraternity devoted to charitable works, but evolved to become a trade association for textile dealers. They eventually became the wealthiest merchants in the city with total control over York's foreign trade.

A taste of medieval street life

What is largely lost to us today is the workaday atmosphere of medieval towns. Much of what remains is on the grand scale, such as the stately castles of Welsh borders and the cathedral precincts found in Lincoln, Norwich, Wells and Canterbury. But some places do contain vivid reminders of that crushed and chaotic scene where merchants and craftsmen lived and worked in the same streets as others in their trade, little different from a Middle Eastern bazaar.

The noise and stink of trade

In York, the narrow 15th-century street known as The Shambles is crammed with timber-framed houses, where the ground floors once served as butchers' shops and opened out directly on to the narrow street. Many a town had a similar area known as The Shambles, where fishmongers (below) or butchers sold their wares. Given the nature of these trades, the general conditions there must have been smelly and unsanitary – and we still say 'what a shambles' as an expression for a mess.

Although they were refashioned in Victorian times, The Rows, still a thriving shopping area in Chester, also give you an excellent sense of what walking down a medieval street must have felt like. There the tightly packed layout of buildings dates back to the 13th century, when merchants and craftsmen conducted their business from open-fronted shops and warehouses, both at street level and on an upper gallery, supported by balustrades and reached via a flight of rough wooden steps.

Preserving the past Frome in Somerset dates back to AD 685 and was once the centre of a thriving cloth trade. Luckily, it has escaped extensive redevelopment. More than 350 listed buildings remain, along with parts of the original medieval street plan, which includes Cheap Street (above), just off the main market place. Tudor buildings line this narrow, cobbled walkway and an open stream still runs along it, much as it did to carry away waste in the Middle Ages.

DID YOU KNOW?

Sewage in medieval towns was often just thrown into a nearby stream or dumped on the street. The earliest reference to the family of William Shakespeare in Stratford-upon-Avon is an order of 1552 fining his father for blocking the way with a midden (dung or refuse) heap, instead of using the 'common muckhill'.

THE MYSTERY PLAYS

One way guilds sought to gain prestige was by putting on parades and pageants. These included the mystery plays (the term derives from the fact that each guild was responsible for the 'mastery' – or 'mystery' – of its trade or craft), which were made up of cycles of up to 56 scenes or short plays, portraying the history of the world from the Creation to the Last Judgment. By the 14th century the plays were being performed regularly as an extension to the traditional Corpus Christi Day parades, with each guild responsible for acting out one of the scenes. They were performed either on a fixed stage or, more often, on wagons as they were wheeled through the streets. It became common for trade fairs to be held on the same day to take advantage of the crowds the plays drew.

Reviving the past Only four complete mystery-play texts survive. One, dating from 1378, originated in York, and has been performed there – both on wagons and a fixed set – regularly since 1951.

Medieval wool trade By the 14th century extensive wool trading routes had become established throughout England, and over the sea to Europe. Although no new roads were built until the 17th century, existing Roman roads and navigable rivers enabled the trade to thrive. The wealth generated is still visible in the buildings of wool towns such as Stow-on-the-Wold (above, left).

Towns that grew fat on sheep

From early medieval times English wool was renowned throughout Europe as the best there was. With growing populations demanding woollen clothing both at home and abroad, the wool trade boomed. The riches accumulated by the wool merchants can be seen today in an architectural legacy of handsome town houses, proud market squares and improbably huge parish churches.

The wool towns of Old England

Throughout the Middle Ages, East Anglia was the most populous and prosperous part of Britain. This affluence peaked in the 14th and 15th centuries when the region's extensive sheep pastures and strong links to the Continent allowed it to capitalise on the production and export of wool and cloth, medieval England's money-spinner.

In the early 14th century Edward III had encouraged Flemish master weavers to set up their businesses in England. The skilled artisans were pleased to come as the raw materials were cheap. They brought with them the techniques of fine weaving, dyeing and 'fulling' – a process that gave the cloth a superior finish. The high-quality cloth was much sought after and brought wealth to the towns associated with the industry, such as Hadleigh, Nayland and Lavenham in Suffolk, Halstead and Coggeshall in Essex, and Worstead in Norfolk. In the

Cotswolds, where the wool of the native sheep was longer and finer than that of East Anglian breeds, towns such as Chipping Camden, Cirencester, Tetbury and Stow-on-the-Wold enjoyed much prosperity, too.

Today the illustrious past of the wool towns can be seen in a rich legacy of buildings. At the centre of town there is often a large guildhall, which would have housed the guild in charge of the production and sale of wool and woollen textiles, and a wool hall, where purchasers conducted their business. Most striking of all are the 14th-15th century churches, whose soaring dimensions and ornamental grandeur seem out of proportion to the size of the towns.

The woolmaster's house

You can spot the houses of well-to-do merchants simply because they were as handsome as money could make them. Look particularly for fine carvings and decoration

Showing off the wealth Paycocke's, a house in Coggeshall, Essex, was built in the 16th century by the wool merchant John Paycocke as a wedding present for his son. The merchant spent lavishly on the woodcarvings that decorate the exterior beams and internal panelling.

around doorways and windows (left). A wool merchant had to keep up appearances – trade relied on it, and pride insisted on it. A wonderful example of a medieval wool merchant's house is that of William Grevel – 'flower of the wool merchants of all England', as his memorial brass styles him – in the Cotswold wool town of Chipping Camden. The house, built in about 1380 of the local gold oolitic limestone, is exquisitely detailed, from the decorative oriel window to the arches, doorways and gables.

If he could afford it, a wool merchant would not only lavish money on his own house, he would build a church or beautify an existing one. This had the dual purpose of improving his chances of a place in Heaven and letting his neighbours and rivals know how well he was doing. The church of St Peter and St Paul at Northleach, Gloucestershire, is an exceptional 'wool church'. It has an aisled and arcaded nave (paid for by local merchant John Fortey in the 1430s) that would grace a cathedral, and a soaring two-storey porch with 15th-century glass. Its glittering display of medieval brasses (many incised with woolpacks and guild symbols) are a memorial to the town's prosperous woolmen and their wives.

The wool market slumps

By the middle of the 17th century the powerful clothiers of London had gained a stranglehold on the woollen cloth trade, and the business was concentrated in a few East Anglian and Cotswold towns. When clothmakers in the West Riding of Yorkshire began to exploit the power of fast-running streams, and later steam, to power mechanical production, the southern producers were left hopelessly behind. The coming of the cotton industry administered the final blow, and by the end of the 18th century the once supreme wool towns of the south had seen their trade all but vanish.

Lavenham – frozen in time

When taxes, Continental wars and cheaper competition drove the clothing business out of Lavenham in Tudor times, the town stagnated. There was no money for rebuilding, so Lavenham stayed exactly as it was. Today it is as though it has been frozen in time, allowing a fascinating insight into a medieval wool town.

The streets are lined with crooked, bent and bowed timber-framed houses, while the 15th-century church of St Peter and St Paul is one of East Anglia's most harmonious and striking wool churches. In the market square stands the guildhall of Corpus Christi, a masterpiece of timber framing completed around 1530, just before the Reformation destroyed the old guilds. Down the street the 14th-century Swan Inn is a fine collection of buildings that incorporates Lavenham's former Wool Hall. Like the houses all around Lavenham, every part of the Swan creaks and is out of true, but it has defied the odds to survive.

Corporate sponsors The ostentatious style of St Peter and St Paul in Lavenham reflects the tastes of its 15th-century benefactors, particularly the wool barons John De Vere and Thomas Spring I, II, and III.

Calling time on wool The Swan Inn is one of 300 listed buildings in Lavenham. No other wool town has survived in such an intact state.

Looking for patterns in rural communities

A church, manor house and cottages clustered around a green – you may think of this as the classic rural settlement, but in much of Britain people live in tiny hamlets and scattered farmsteads. The pattern of these settlements is closely linked to their medieval origins. Look at a modern map and you can still get a good idea of how your area was settled centuries ago.

What the patterns reveal

The type and pattern of settlement in your area is dictated by the landscape and how the land was used in medieval times. Over a large swathe of England stretching up from mid-Somerset to Northumberland, manor estates surrounded by arable fields cultivated on the open-field system of farming were common (see pages 146-147). Many of today's compact villages have developed from these manors. In the southeast of England, East Anglia and along the Welsh border, the medieval landscape was dominated by hamlets and scattered farms as fields were smaller and often bounded by woods. But in highland and moorland areas, most people lived in isolated homesteads, eeking out a living from the barren land.

Even within counties, patterns could vary. In Kent, small farms dotted across the wooded rolling hills of the Weald were linked to ancient seasonal pastures used for grazing pigs, while in Romney Marsh scattered hamlets grew up as the marshes were gradually reclaimed.

If you look at Ordnance Survey (OS) Landranger maps (see pages 26-27) even today the differences in settlement patterns are striking. Each pattern provides clues to the history of rural communities.

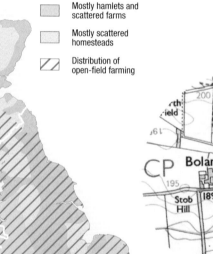

The clutter of border country Look at a map of west Herefordshire and the mass of detail is striking: a web of small lanes wind through woods, past isolated farms and numerous hamlets, with hardly a village in sight. The medieval open-fields here were smaller because the area was sparsely populated.

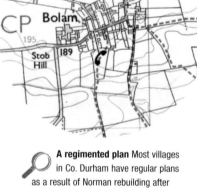

- ▨ Mostly villages
- ▨ Mostly hamlets and scattered farms
- ▨ Mostly scattered homesteads
- ▨ Distribution of open-field farming

A regimented plan Most villages in Co. Durham have regular plans as a result of Norman rebuilding after they were razed to the ground by William the Conqueror. Bolam's layout is typical of Norman planned villages: two rows of houses face each other across the village street, with plots of land of equal size behind each row.

Strung out along a valley
You can easily spot a distinct settlement pattern on maps of the Lake District: elongated hamlets extend along the valley floors below the high fells, where there are fertile pastures for grazing. Borrowdale (below and right) has no villages, but note how hamlets and farms, such as Rosthwaite and Stonethwaite, often take the Viking place-name element 'thwaite' (see pages 32-33), meaning a clearing. These names are an indication of the influence of the landscape on their location.

FIND OUT MORE

Take a good look around your village or hamlet and its surrounding area for any signs of what the land may once have been used for, such as the ridge and furrow plough marks of medieval open-fields (see pages 54-55). Then study some early maps of the area, which often reveal the shape of villages before many of them were transformed by industry or by the car. (For more information on all the maps mentioned here, see pages 26-27 and 214-215.)

• **Ordnance Survey (OS) Explorer maps** These maps allow you to zoom in for more detail on your local area. For a closer look at your own parish, find the first edition of the OS maps that were made in Victorian times. These are available at local libraries and on-line at: www.ordnancesurvey.co.uk
• **Tithe Awards** Dating from the late 1830s and 40s, these records list the owners and occupiers of every piece of land in the parish. Each field, garden or orchard is numbered and shown on the accompanying map. The records are kept in local record offices, the National Archives at Kew (see DIRECTORY) and at the National Library of Wales at Aberystwyth (see DIRECTORY).
• **Enclosure Award maps** A good source of reference for parishes that were farmed on the medieval open-field system until they were enclosed in the 18th or early 19th century. Compare these maps with the present-day landscape of the area they cover and you can often still detect the pattern of ancient fields and roads on the land.

Not much in between Study a map of south Leicestershire and you will immediately notice the large spaces between compact villages – the landscape would have been even more empty in medieval times as isolated farmsteads were not built until the open-fields were enclosed in the 18th and 19th centuries. Some of the gaps in the landscape have been created by deserted medieval villages (see pages 56-57). Look out on the map for signs of a deserted village, such as 'Church (Remains of)' and 'Fish Ponds' at Knaptoft. Landscapes such as this have only a few lanes, connecting neighbouring villages and providing access to fields. Note the right-angled bends in some lanes – these skirt around the old blocks of ploughland strips and slope in different directions according to the lie of the land.

The manor – the heart of village life

The basic layout of almost every modern village dates back more than 500 years to the days when life revolved around the needs of the manor and the seasonal struggle for subsistence. The manor was the most important institution in the Middle Ages; it defined the social hierachy of the community and established the laws by which the villagers lived. The manorial system was based on economic ties between the lord of the manor and the peasants who lived on his land and farmed his fields.

Toiling the manor fields

Some manors were worked as a 'home farm' that provided food for the lord's household and a surplus for sale. Others were owned by absentee landlords and leased to a tenant for an annual rent. The peasants of the manor had to work on the lord's land for most of the year, ploughing, harrowing, sowing, weeding and harvesting. In return they could work their own plots of land and keep just enough produce to eek out a frugal life for themselves. Life was harsh – poverty and hardship, famine and disease stalked daily existence.

A lord of the manor also owned the right to mine coal, iron and other minerals on his manor. The manorial records for Lord Furnival's estate in Sheffield reveal that in 1268 he had 'smithies' for working iron that had been mined in his park.

Along with these rights came luxuries that only the very privileged were allowed such as a rabbit warren, dovecote and fish ponds. These were a valuable source of food for the lord and his household.

The local court of law

Each manor held a court to resolve disputes between tenants, punish those who had broken the local rules and decide on farming practices. The court was presided over by the lord's steward or bailiff but run by 12 jurors, or 'homagers', chosen by the tenants. These jurors made decisions on matters such as whether to restrict the number of cattle that could be grazed, how much to fine someone who had not muzzled his dog, or what to do about blocked drains. They also elected the officers for the coming year, such as the constable (who enforced law and order), the pinder (who rounded up stray animals) and the ale-taster (who tested the strength of a brew).

Manor courts continued to flourish well into the 16th and 17th centuries and some, such as the manor court of Laxton in Nottinghamshire, still operate today.

Parish church The church was the hub of village life. The parish priest, appointed by the lord, held daily services attended by all villagers at least once a week. The church also acted as a village hall and meeting-place, where the manor courts were held, tenants paid their rents and villagers gathered to watch plays or take part in festivities.

Fields The manor was surrounded by three open-fields, each one divided into one-acre narrow strips for cultivating crops such as wheat, barley, oats, rye, peas and beans. There was also common land for grazing cattle and gathering wood.

Peasant houses Peasants lived in rough thatched cottages, each with a small yard around it, called a toft. A long rectangular plot behind the house (the croft) provided grazing for cattle and allowed peasants to grow fruit trees and cabbages, onions, parsley and herbs.

Peasant houses

A MEDIEVAL MANOR AND ITS VILLAGE

The medieval village of Wharram Percy was deserted at the end of the 15th century but excavations of surviving earthworks have made it possible to reconstruct what the village looked like in the 13th century (see pages 56-57 for a photograph of the site today). Untouched by modernisation, its compact layout is a perfect example of a medieval manor estate: two parallel rows of cottages flanking a central street, while at either end of the village are the manor house and parish church.

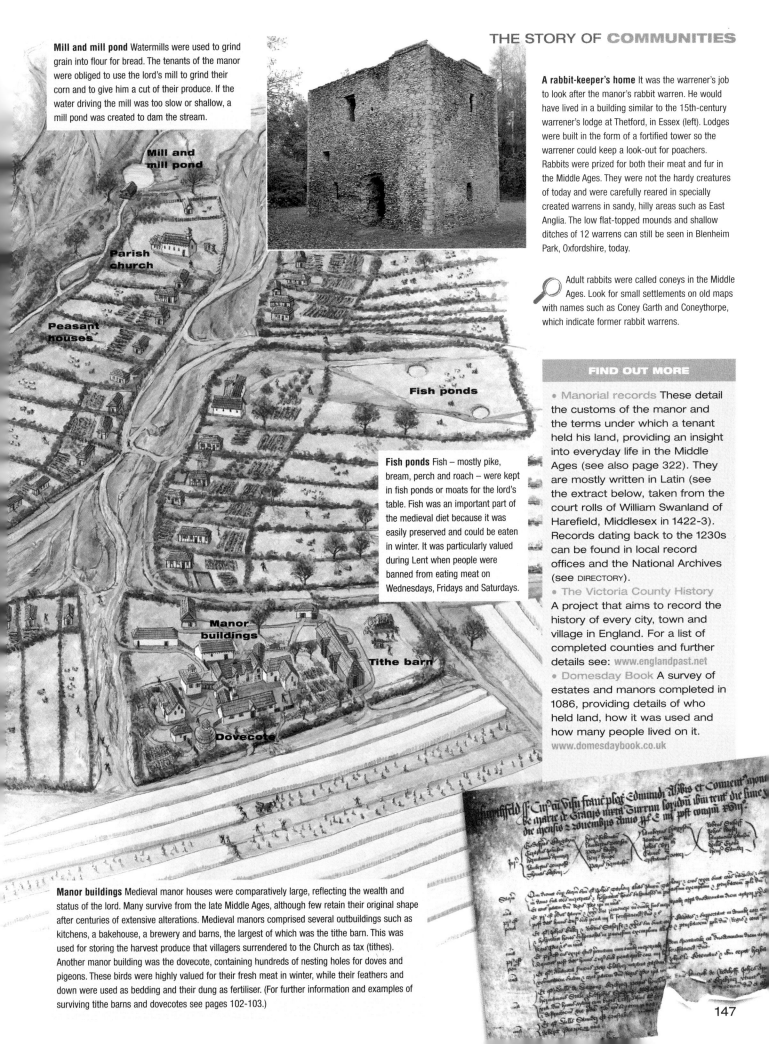

Mill and mill pond Watermills were used to grind grain into flour for bread. The tenants of the manor were obliged to use the lord's mill to grind their corn and to give him a cut of their produce. If the water driving the mill was too slow or shallow, a mill pond was created to dam the stream.

Mill and mill pond

Parish church

Peasant houses

Fish ponds

A rabbit-keeper's home It was the warrener's job to look after the manor's rabbit warren. He would have lived in a building similar to the 15th-century warrener's lodge at Thetford, in Essex (left). Lodges were built in the form of a fortified tower so the warrener could keep a look-out for poachers. Rabbits were prized for both their meat and fur in the Middle Ages. They were not the hardy creatures of today and were carefully reared in specially created warrens in sandy, hilly areas such as East Anglia. The low flat-topped mounds and shallow ditches of 12 warrens can still be seen in Blenheim Park, Oxfordshire, today.

Adult rabbits were called coneys in the Middle Ages. Look for small settlements on old maps with names such as Coney Garth and Coneythorpe, which indicate former rabbit warrens.

Fish ponds Fish – mostly pike, bream, perch and roach – were kept in fish ponds or moats for the lord's table. Fish was an important part of the medieval diet because it was easily preserved and could be eaten in winter. It was particularly valued during Lent when people were banned from eating meat on Wednesdays, Fridays and Saturdays.

FIND OUT MORE

• **Manorial records** These detail the customs of the manor and the terms under which a tenant held his land, providing an insight into everyday life in the Middle Ages (see also page 322). They are mostly written in Latin (see the extract below, taken from the court rolls of William Swanland of Harefield, Middlesex in 1422-3). Records dating back to the 1230s can be found in local record offices and the National Archives (see DIRECTORY).
• **The Victoria County History** A project that aims to record the history of every city, town and village in England. For a list of completed counties and further details see: www.englandpast.net
• **Domesday Book** A survey of estates and manors completed in 1086, providing details of who held land, how it was used and how many people lived on it. www.domesdaybook.co.uk

Manor buildings

Tithe barn

Dovecote

Manor buildings Medieval manor houses were comparatively large, reflecting the wealth and status of the lord. Many survive from the late Middle Ages, although few retain their original shape after centuries of extensive alterations. Medieval manors comprised several outbuildings such as kitchens, a bakehouse, a brewery and barns, the largest of which was the tithe barn. This was used for storing the harvest produce that villagers surrendered to the Church as tax (tithes). Another manor building was the dovecote, containing hundreds of nesting holes for doves and pigeons. These birds were highly valued for their fresh meat in winter, while their feathers and down were used as bedding and their dung as fertiliser. (For further information and examples of surviving tithe barns and dovecotes see pages 102-103.)

The ups and downs of the medieval population

From the Norman conquest to the mid 14th century, Britain enjoyed a period of stability and growing prosperity. The population climbed steadily and many towns and villages expanded. But in 1348, the arrival of the Black Death triggered a rapid decline that was to last for more than 150 years.

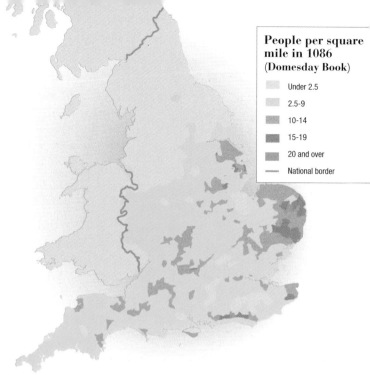

People per square mile in 1086 (Domesday Book)

- Under 2.5
- 2.5-9
- 10-14
- 15-19
- 20 and over
- — National border

Following the fluctuating numbers

There were no census returns in the Middle Ages, but fortunately by referring to the Domesday Book, compiled in 1086, it is possible to make a reasonable estimate of England's population at the time (see map, right). It must have varied between 1.5 million and 2.25 million, and is known to have risen steadily throughout the 12th and 13th centuries to around 5 to 6 million by 1300.

Then, in 1348, the Black Death reached British shores. By the time it had finally burned itself out in late 1349, almost 40 per cent of the population had died. Further epidemics followed, so that within a single generation England had barely 3 million inhabitants; by the 1460s, there were only around 2 million. Trade fell off, markets were abandoned and towns shrank. Coventry and York

Brought to book In December 1085, William the Conquerer ordered a survey of the land and resources held by his subjects, in order to work out what taxes he could levy. It was largely completed by the autumn of 1086 and the information recorded in two huge volumes. Some major cities, such as Winchester and London, are omitted and most people included are not named, but it still gives some idea of population levels in England at the time, showing that Lincolnshire, East Anglia and East Kent were the most settled regions, with 10 people per square mile on average.

were among the many once bustling centres of commerce (see pages 140-141) that by the mid 15th century were complaining of 'decay'.

Recovery was slow: by 1500, England's population was still only half of what it had been 200 years before. The largest provincial cities – Norwich, Bristol, York and

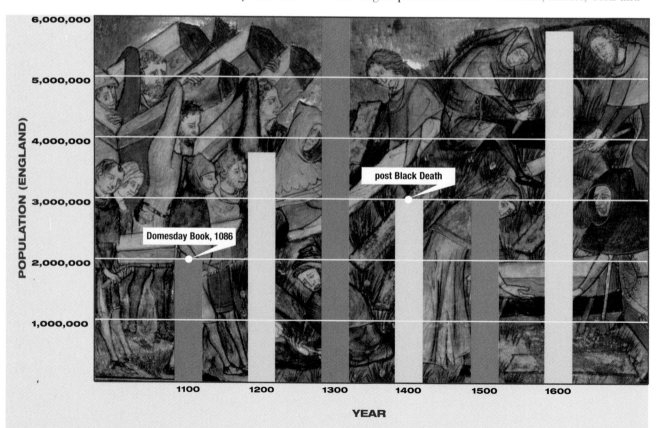

Domesday Book, 1086

post Black Death

POPULATION (ENGLAND)

YEAR

Exeter – held just 8000 or so inhabitants. Smaller cathedral cities, such as Durham or Lincoln, had a mere few thousand and the average market town averaged around 1500 citizens.

Scotland seems to have experienced similar shifts in its population to England during the Middle Ages, but there is little evidence from which to estimate numbers before the late 17th century, when about 1 million people lived there. Medieval Wales was small and largely rural. In 1500, its population was probably no more than 200,000.

Winchester – the shrinking city

At the dawn of the Middle Ages, Winchester was one of England's major cities – a centre of prosperity and seat of government. The castle was a royal residence; the grand cathedral, along with the Bishop's Palace and St Mary's Abbey, dominated the southeast corner of the city; weekly markets attracted visitors from across Europe; and by 1100 there were more than 50 parish churches and about 1300 private houses. By the start of the 14th century, the population of Winchester was around 11,600 – more than one-tenth that of London.

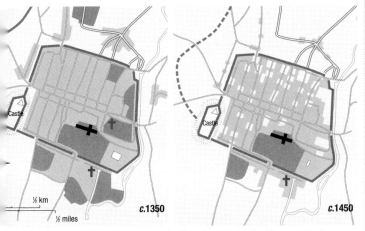

c.1350   c.1450
½ km
½ miles

■ Church property
■ Built-up areas

A disastrous fire in the castle in 1302 was a turning point, forcing out the royal family and their entourage. Then the Black Death raged with devastating effect from 1348 to 1349. Half the clergymen in the diocese perished. In February 1352, a royal grant spoke of the 'waste and depression in the city from the time when the deadly pestilence last prevailed'. Plague returned in 1361 and regularly thereafter.

In 1450, petitions from the city to the government in London referred to 997 empty houses. By 1524, Winchester had just 595 households. There was some recovery in Elizabethan times, but the city never regained the pre-eminence of its medieval heyday.

WHERE TO PLACE DISTINCTIVE FAMILY NAMES

Regional differences were far more marked in medieval Britain than they are today. This was true not only of customs and speech patterns, but also of family names.

In the Middle Ages, people generally stayed in one place for generations and, if they did move, seldom went far. Most of the population remained within what they called their 'country', an area that did not stretch beyond the nearest market town, rarely more than 20 miles away from where they were born. Every corner of Britain had its 'core families', and identifying them from factors like the distribution of common surnames is a crucial part of unravelling the story of where you live.

The most distinctive names are those derived from small hamlets and farmsteads, such as Akehurst in Sussex, Dungworth in Yorkshire and Heathcote in Derbyshire. These often originate from a single family.

Many surnames are still mainly concentrated in the areas where they originated during the Middle Ages. Most Eardleys are found in the Potteries, the Sowerbuttses in north Lancashire and the Dafts in Nottinghamshire. Round is most common in the Black Country around Dudley, and nearly everyone with the surname Arkwright (maker of 'arks' – a storage cabinet shaped like a Noah's ark) lives in Lancashire.

The link between a name and a particular place is also true of Scotland. Home is a common surname across Berwickshire and Hamiltons still abound near the town they take their name from – Hamilton in South Lanarkshire.

The few medieval people that did wander far from home often acquired names linking them to their place of origin. Those who drifted away from Wales can usually be identified when surnames such as Welshman, Walsh or Wallis crop up in the records.

The British 19th Century Surname Atlas (CD from www.archersoftware.co.uk) is a useful tool for researching the origin and spread of British family names. It generates maps (see right) for every surname recorded in the 1881 census for England, Scotland and Wales.

Akehurst

Arkwright

Hamilton

Welshman

KEY TO SURNAME MAPS
Colours indicate incidence of the surname by county.

lowest → highest

Growth in the face of fire and plague

By the mid 16th century, towns were beginning to prosper with an upturn in trade. Catastrophes such as fires and the plague became less frequent, and enthusiastic Georgian planners set to work, transforming market towns and county capitals.

People per square mile
- 300-399
- 200-299
- 50-199
- 0-49

c.1650

c.1801

Who lived where and when There was a marked shift in population density between 1650 and 1801. The Industrial Revolution, which began in the mid-18th century, drew migrants to the manufacturing areas of the northwest of England and around Edinburgh and Glasgow in Scotland, while London took time to recover from the ravages of plague and fire. The population of England and Wales almost doubled from about 5 million in 1650 to 9 million at the time of the 1801 census, while Scotland's population increased from 900,000 to 1.6 million over the same period.

The capital bursts at the seams

London experienced a population explosion in the 16th and 17th centuries: the number of inhabitants rose from 60,000 in the 1520s to nearly 500,000 – 10 per cent of the English population – in 1700. By 1750 it was the largest city in Europe, and by 1800, with a population of 960,000, it was well on the way to becoming the first to reach one million.

And yet far more people died in London than were born there. The shortfall was more than made up for by immigrants. In the 1580s a London clergyman commented that every 12 years or so 'the most part of the parish changeth, as I by experience know, some going and some coming'. Every year between 1650 and 1750 at least 8000 people from different parts of Britain, in addition to Huguenot refugees and others from abroad,

contributed to the capital's expanding population. Many young migrants walked to London, others came by carriers' carts. In 1637, when John Taylor published a list of the arrival and departure times of carriers in London, the city was linked to all parts of Britain by weekly services.

London's growth would have been more rapid had it not been for frequent outbreaks of plague. The city suffered four great plagues – in 1563, 1593, 1603 and 1625 – before the last, and worst, in 1665, when at least 70,000 inhabitants died. 'Lord,' wrote the diarist Samuel Pepys, 'how everybody's looks and discourse in the street, is of death.'

Razed to the ground

The following year, London was devastated by a great fire. It started in Pudding Lane in the early hours of September 2, 1666, and continued burning for four days. Five-sixths of the city within the walls was destroyed. Yet the ruins provided an almost blank canvas for the rebuilding of the City, and London was soon born again.

Fires were a major hazard throughout Britain, in towns where the houses were timber-framed and the roofs thatched. Nearly every town suffered at least one major fire between 1500 and 1700, and for some the damage was so extensive that it provided the opportunity for wholesale rebuilding. To comply with new regulations introduced in the 18th century, traditional timber and thatch was replaced by less inflammable materials such as stone, brick and tiles, completely changing the character of many towns. Warwick was largely rebuilt after a devastating fire in 1694, and little of the Dorset county

London ablaze Nearly 200,000 people were made homeless by the Great Fire of London in 1666; 13,200 houses and 89 parish churches, including the medieval St Paul's Cathedral, were destroyed. According to the diarist John Evelyn, London's night sky was like the top of a burning oven that could be seen from 40 miles away.

A Georgian phoenix Of all the towns that rose from the ashes of fire, Blandford Forum in Dorset (left) is one of the most complete. Four fires broke out here between 1579 and 1731, after which the market town was completely rebuilt in tile and brick of various colours by the brothers John and William Bastard. They designed and built the parish church, the Town Hall in the market place, and most of the houses. The designs were strictly hierarchical: the houses of the merchants and professional people who lived on the outskirts of the town were given a symmetrical design, with an ornate central doorway; the shopkeepers in the town centre were provided with smaller homes with an entrance to one side; and the houses of the workers were built in pairs, sharing an entrance door and passage.

Fire marks Look out for the badges of fire insurance companies, which were attached to insured buildings from about 1710. Records are kept at the Guildhall Library, London (see DIRECTORY).

town of Dorchester predates 1613, when 300 houses were burned to the ground. A further four fires between 1622 and 1775 wreaked even more destruction.

The new townscape

In the late 17th and 18th centuries trade increased, both within Britain and overseas. Coinciding with the beginnings of the industrial age, the expanding economy created a wave of national prosperity that transformed the urban landscape. The most ambitious towns became more than just market places as they encouraged the gentry from outlying rural areas to build town houses so that they could enjoy the new social distractions: assembly rooms, theatres, concert halls, walks and gardens, and racecourses, complete with grandstands. The Georgians made their mark as town planners demolished buildings to

make way for elegant squares, terraces and crescents, and removed congested livestock markets from central streets. New churches and chapels were built in classical styles, with pillars and porticoes, as architects turned for their inspiration to the temples of Rome and Greece.

Designed to impress

Towns flaunted their new-found sense of importance by replacing old buildings with bigger and grander edifices. At Abingdon in Berkshire, the market hall was swept away in favour of the new County Hall, built between 1678 and 1682 for the meetings of the Berkshire assizes. Sometimes, old timber-framed buildings were simply hidden behind new facades, as at Ludlow in Shropshire and Totnes in Devon. The prosperous medieval centre of Stamford, in Lincolnshire, was transformed into an elegant Georgian town, with fine houses and grand public buildings. Like other booming provincial towns, its pride in its modernity was expressed by the commissioning of maps and prints, and by the founding of its own newspaper, the *Stamford Mercury*.

Read all about it Towns were eager to extol their virtues, and newspapers, such as this edition of the *Newcastle Courant*, provide an illuminating picture of the development of the Georgian town, its trades and sources of wealth, and the views of its inhabitants.

Towns built for work or play

During the 17th and 18th centuries, specialist towns developed of a kind that had never been seen before. Some were ports or industrial centres, others flourished as fashionable spas and bathing resorts. By the late 18th century, old cathedral cities such as York and Canterbury had been far outstripped by new industrial towns, with Manchester leading the way.

Industrial giants arise

By 1700 England had at least a dozen towns where most of the workforce was employed in industry. Some old-established provincial centres, such as Norwich, found prosperity from the newly mechanised textile industry in the 17th and 18th centuries, but industrial towns such as Leeds and Manchester grew much quicker than the traditional market centres and became the boom towns of the Industrial Revolution.

Some towns developed a particular industry that was to become their defining feature. Sheffield was the leading centre for cutlery manufacture. Three out of every five men were involved in the trade. It was a smoky place, full of the sound of hammering. Between 1616 and 1736 its population rose from 2207 to 10,121.

Leeds was a centre for the woollen trade and its imposing civic buildings, elegant houses and two large Dissenters' meeting houses reflected the town's wealth. Dissenters – who refused to accept the doctrines of the Church of England – were numerous and influential in the industrial towns; they were people of independent spirit who had often risen from humble backgrounds.

Between 1700 and 1771 the population of Leeds expanded from 6000 to 16,380. In what soon became a feature of industrial towns, thousands of poor people were crammed into small cottages and workshops close to the factories and only a stone's throw away from the splendid mansions and gardens of the rich merchants.

Launch pad HMS *Buckingham* sits on the launching stocks at Deptford in 1752. The dockyard on the Thames was set up by Henry VIII in 1513 to build warships and grew in importance as demand for new ships increased.

New docks for sea adventures

The discovery of new lands across the seas in the 17th and 18th centuries, a burgeoning foreign trade and the threat of war with the Dutch and French led to a rapid expansion in Britain's ports and dockyard towns. Portsmouth, the site of Henry VIII's royal naval dockyard, grew rapidly during the wars with France in the 1690s, and dockyard towns such as Deptford and Greenwich developed along the Thames. Chatham dockyard on the River Medway – well situated for access to the North Sea – played a key role in supporting the Royal Navy in Georgian times. As the dockyard flourished so the town's population rose from less than 1000 in 1600 to more than 5000 a century later.

Cotton rich Mills such as the Union Street Cotton Mills (left) were a common sight in industrial Manchester in late Georgian times. Steam-powered mills produced fabrics for garments such as the sack-jacket (above), dating from 1775-85. Manchester's population soared from 40,000 in the 1780s to 142,000 in 1831 as labourers flocked in from the surrounding countryside to find work in the mills.

Whitehaven – built from scratch

In 1566 Whitehaven, on the Cumbrian coast, consisted of just six fishermen's cottages. By 1730 it had become a flourishing Georgian port with a population of more than 3000. Whitehaven is unusual in that it was carefully planned and built from scratch. Sir Christopher Lowther, a member of a long-established Cumbrian landowning family, founded the port in the 1630s to export coal. Fifty years later, Sir John Lowther planned a new town in a grid pattern, providing good-quality housing for its inhabitants; several well-preserved Georgian houses still survive in Lowther Street.

Successive Lowthers spent large sums acquiring land around Whitehaven to secure mining rights and to provide access to the coast. Sir John wrote: 'Where there are ships the whole world is the market.' By the late 17th century he had almost a monopoly of the trade in Cumbrian coal across the Irish Sea to Dublin and to Europe. His extensive collieries stretched for miles beneath the seabed. Sir John was succeeded by Sir James Lowther, who obtained a substantial share of the Virginian trade in tobacco – imported from America through Whitehaven – and developed his collieries on a large scale. The 270 houses he built in 1736 at Ginns, near Whitehaven, survive as three rows set into the hillside.

On the quayside Georgian buildings line the harbour (above) where coal ships have given way to pleasure boats and 21st-century tourists come to admire the scene.

From nought to port Whitehaven's neat grid of streets laid out in the 17th century (left) was inspired by Christopher Wren's designs for the rebuilding of London after the Great Fire. The port was the first planned town since the Middle Ages.

A passion for water

The fashion for spas came to Britain from Europe in the 17th century. The wealthy flocked to spa resorts, staying for weeks to bathe in and drink from the springs in the hope of benefiting from their supposed healing properties. Other social pleasures grew up around the spas such as plays, concerts and dancing. The best architects were commissioned to build pump rooms and baths, promenades, crescents and squares. In Buxton, The Crescent was designed by Carr of York about 1780, and in Leamington, The Parade was laid out in 1815-33. The most successful spa was Bath, renowned for its springs since Roman times. During the 18th century it became a watering place for the aristocratic and fashionable, and its population grew from 2000 to 28,000.

Similarly, a passion for sea-bathing led to the creation of fashionable coastal resorts such as Scarborough, Brighton, Margate and Eastbourne. Dedicated to relaxation and entertainment, and patronised by royalty, these towns maintained an air of exclusivity far removed from the burgeoning industrial cities and ports.

Taking the waters A plethora of elegant spa towns sprang up in Britain during the Georgian era. One of the first spas – named after the Belgian health resort of Spa – was Tunbridge Wells, where The Pantiles was laid out in 1638. Like Epsom, it flourished because of its proximity to London. At Harrogate's mineral springs visitors stayed in lodging houses that offered bathing in heated sulphur water and, as elsewhere, a new town began to grow around the springs.

Strathpeffer

Harrogate
Boston Spa
Buxton
Woodhall Spa
Matlock Bath

Llandrindod Wells
Droitwich
Royal Leamington Spa
Malvern
Cheltenham
Bath
Epsom
Royal Tunbridge Wells

Liverpool – from medieval fishing village to Victorian trading powerhouse

In the Middle Ages Liverpool was a small village on a tidal creek, or 'pool', that flowed into the Mersey – 'liver' referred to its thick or sluggish water. It provided a haven for fishing vessels and in 1207 King John made it a port, founding a new borough with a simple plan of seven streets. A great stone castle was completed by 1235, and the church built at the other end of the town was dedicated to St Nicholas, the patron saint of seafarers. More than 500 years later, as trade with the New World took off, Liverpool was transformed into a thriving commercial centre. By the early Victorian period it had become one of the world's major international trading ports.

A growing market town

Liverpool was a small town in Tudor times. Farmers sold their produce at market and local craftsmen traded their wares in the street, but the town still relied heavily on fishing. It suffered a terrible outbreak of plague in 1558, which killed about a third of the population, and the port was badly damaged during the Civil Wars of 1642-51, when Liverpool was a garrison town, changing hands three times between Royalists and Parliamentarians.

Liverpool's fortunes changed in 1666 when the *Antelope* set sail from its port carrying a £200 cargo of linen cloth across the Atlantic to Barbados. Nearly a year later the gallant vessel returned loaded with sugar cane to a rapturous reception. By the end of the century Liverpool was trading with all the English colonies in the New World.

The 'pool' realises its potential At the turn of the 17th century, Liverpool's natural harbour in the Mersey estuary (right) was a small but busy haven for fishing vessels. By the time the century drew to a close, Liverpool had become a wealthy market town with a rapidly growing shipping trade. Celia Fiennes on her visit to Liverpool in 1698 remarked on 'the houses of brick and stone built high and even' and the 'abundance of persons well dress'd and of good fashion'. As it prospered the town expanded to include 24 streets, and a fine new town hall was built in 1674. The crumbling castle – damaged in the Civil War – dominated the waterfront until it was demolished in 1726.

c.1600

The making of a great port

The old pool could no longer cope with the increasing volume of trade and this posed a new problem: how to load and unload cargoes in the difficult tidal waters of the Mersey. In 1708 the townsmen accepted the advice of the engineer Thomas Steers, who suggested that they drain and replace the pool with a great stone dock – 183m (200 yards) long and nearly 92m (100 yards) wide, with massive floodgates to hold back the tide. The scheme was completed in 1721 and almost immediately proved to be a great success.

Liverpool's trade expanded rapidly as large amounts of tobacco and sugar, and later cotton, were imported from America and the West Indies. Atlantic trade was the mainstay of Liverpool's prosperity but the port's coastal trade also doubled between 1689 and 1737, the town's position making it the main supply port for Lancashire's developing industries. Liverpool prospered on the profits from trade. When Daniel Defoe visited in the early 1720s, he remarked 'Liverpool is one of the wonders of Britain ... there is no town in England, London excepted, that can equal Liverpool for the fineness of its streets and the beauty of its buildings'.

1765

c.1680

Lime Street

New Quay   St Nicholas' Church

Customs House (on the site of the Old Dock)

Albert Dock

1847

Old Dock

A city reaches the peak of its trading days

Under Jesse Hartley, chief engineer to the port from 1824 to 1860, Liverpool's waterfront was transformed again into a vast area of enclosed docks (left). His legacy included the Albert Dock of 1845, a masterpiece of design, built entirely of cast iron, brick and stone.

A new Customs House was erected on the site of the Old Dock and St Nicholas' Church, a grander version of the chapel that had long dominated the waterfront, was now tucked behind the New Quay. Lime Street became the bustling thoroughfare it is today after Lime Street Station was opened in 1851.

Trading legacy You can still see reminders on some of Liverpool's commercial buildings of its lucrative trading links with Africa and all corners of the globe in the 18th and 19th centuries. Part of the town's growing wealth came from the slave trade. Ships set sail from Liverpool on a triangular passage to Africa and the West Indies. Goods were exchanged for slaves in Africa, who were transported to the West Indies and traded for rum, tobacco and sugar. These were then shipped back to Liverpool's merchants.

GEORGIAN CIVIC PRIDE

Liverpool's population soared in the 18th century as money poured in from the docks into its banks; in 1720 it was estimated at 10,000 and in 1770 at 30,000.

As Liverpool's merchants prospered, so they lavished money on grand public buildings, some of which survive today. A splendid new Town Hall and Exchange by John Wood of Bath opened in 1754 and was rebuilt by James Wyatt after a fire in 1795. Designed in Classical style, it had an impressive Corinithian portico and a large dome topped by a statue of the Greek goddess Minerva. The Theatre Royal was another grand Georgian building, constructed in 1772 by Sir William Chambers and eventually demolished in 1965. It attracted large audiences by drawing all the top performers of the day.

Symbols of wealth The profits from trade enabled Liverpool's wealthiest families to build elegant brick houses such as 62 Rodney Street – one of Georgian Liverpool's most sought-after addresses and the birthplace in 1809 of Prime Minister W. E. Gladstone. His father, John Gladstone, was a prosperous shipping merchant who made his money through sugar and coffee plantations in Jamaica.

155

The urban flowering of Scotland

The 1707 Act of Union, which joined England and Scotland to create the kingdom of Great Britain, sparked a huge growth in Scottish towns. As the feudal chiefs began moving to the power centres of Edinburgh and London, the old clan system broke down and the rural population gravitated towards the towns to find work in the burgeoning new industries.

The burghs of Scotland come of age

In the early 18th century, the urban population in Scotland was much smaller than it was in England. Most Scottish burghs – boroughs that had been granted a charter to trade in the Middle Ages – were little more than villages and few had more than a thousand inhabitants. Life revolved around the bustling market places, where traders jostled for attention among the milling crowds.

A few burghs were more sizeable: in 1707 Edinburgh was a thriving city with 30,000 people – although still relatively small in comparison with London's population of 500,000. Glasgow was half the size of Edinburgh, but growing rapidly as trade with the New World took off. Aberdeen and Dundee, both with long-established textile and fishing industries, had populations of 10,000.

On the move

The union of the Scottish and English crowns was not universally popular north of the border. The Jacobites made repeated unsuccessful attempts to restore a Stuart to the British throne but all hopes were finally dashed with the defeat of Bonnie Prince Charlie's rebellion at Culloden

CULROSS – AN INDUSTRIALIST'S VISION
One small Scottish burgh that flourished in the early 17th century was Culross, on the north shore of the Firth of Forth. The merchant and early industrialist Sir George Bruce, a member of one of Scotland's oldest landowning families, owned salt pans and coal mines near the burgh. As early as 1575, his drainage and ventilation schemes enabled coal to be mined to a depth of 73m (240ft), which vastly increased output and brought prosperity to the burgh. He developed the Jacobean merchant's house in Culross, now known as 'The Palace', and created the Lower Town, where the houses were designed in a Scottish vernacular style with crow-stepped gables and red pantiled roofs. Many of the buildings have been restored by the National Trust for Scotland and some of the shops and cottages still show signs of the former trades of their inhabitants.

Preserved tolbooth The Town House in Culross towers over its market place. Built in 1626, it later served as both a prison and a meeting hall.

Moor in 1746 (see pages 58-59). Attracted by the possibility of new ventures elsewhere, many of Scotland's feudal overlords abandoned the Highlands, leaving their agents to clear the tenants from their estates and use the land for the more profitable business of grazing sheep.

Many people emigrated – from 1763 to 1775 about 20,000 departed for America and Canada – while others moved to towns in the Lowlands in search of work. This mass migration, combined with a natural

A town on the verge of greatness In the early 18th century Glasgow was Scotland's second largest burgh but had a relatively small population of 15,000. The burgh grew up on a ford of the river Clyde, a location which proved to be its ticket to success when it was granted commerce with the New World after the Act of Union in 1707. Glasgow was ideally placed for the lucrative transatlantic trade and grew rapidly.

increase in population, turned the narrow belt of the Lowlands into one of Europe's most densely populated areas. Sixty per cent of Scots living in towns in 1801 were to be found in Edinburgh and Glasgow, but many smaller burghs grew rapidly during the second half of the 18th century with the onset of the Industrial Revolution.

The Carron Ironworks near Falkirk (see pages 160-161) opened in 1759 and the town's population grew from 3900 in 1750 to 11,500 in 1830. Paisley's population also tripled over the same years as its weaving industry flourished. Greenock, at the mouth of the River Clyde, became the centre for exports and imports via Glasgow to other parts of Britain and across the Atlantic. Its population soared: in 1707 it had 2000 inhabitants but by the time of the first national census in 1801 the number had increased to 17,500. This tremendous urban growth was to continue into the 20th century, as industrialisation transformed Scotland.

Edinburgh – classical wonder of the north

After the Act of Union, Edinburgh kept its status as the Scottish capital, partly because the Church of Scotland and the Scottish legal system remained separate from those of England and Wales. This political union eventually brought a period of stability and prosperity for Edinburgh and a spate of building ensued. Many classically styled public buildings were erected, such as the Register House, designed by Robert Adam in 1774, the Royal High School, built by Thomas Hamilton in 1825-9 and the National Gallery of Scotland, erected by William Playfair in 1790-1857. Combining Gothic and Greek architectural features, these buildings earned Edinburgh its nickname: the Athens of the North.

The most elegant new town of them all

By the mid 18th century Edinburgh's crowded medieval Old Town could no longer accommodate the city's growing population. Sanitation and drainage were poor and disease was rife. In 1766 a competition was held to plan a New Town to the north of the castle, running east towards the Palace of Holyroodhouse. The scheme of a young architect called James Craig was chosen. Craig designed a grid of three parallel streets – Princes Street, George Street and Queen Street – each half a mile long, with spacious garden squares at either end.

The New Town took a couple of generations to complete. At one end, St Andrew Square was built between 1766 and 1785 by the architect James Brown; at the other, Charlotte Square was begun in 1791 to a design by Robert Adam. Princes Street was completed in 1805, and from 1800 more squares and crescents were laid out to the north of the New Town. These were named after local aristocratic families, such as Moray Place, which was developed for the Earl of Moray in 1822-30.

Robert Adam

Townscape mastermind Charlotte Square (left) in Edinburgh's New Town (above) was the inspiration of the architect Robert Adam (1728-92). The square's elegant terraces were laid out in a uniform style, with a grand pedimented central block giving the impression of an urban palace. Adam became renowned not only for his distinctive designs, but also, unusually for the time, for his attention to every interior detail, down to fire grates and light fittings. For a glimpse of life behind the doors in Charlotte Square, visit The Georgian House at No. 7, owned by the National Trust for Scotland.

Rural settlements recover and diversify

Britain's villages took more than a century to get over the ravages of the Black Death (see pages 56-57). It was only during the relative stability of the Tudor and Stuart ages (1485-1714) that there was a steady increase in the rural population and life in the countryside began to recover. But the growth that brought prosperity to some was to drive many others off the land – to find either a piecemeal trade at home, or to seek an income in the factories of nearby towns.

Where the old ways continued

In much of lowland England, particularly on the heavy clay soils of Midland counties such as Leicestershire and Northamptonshire, most rural parishes continued to be farmed under the medieval open-field system well into the 18th century. They were usually dominated by their squires, or by a few rich farmers, and most inhabitants lived off the land. The centre of England was full of smallholders who worked their family farms, passing them on from father to son.

In other parts of England, such as on the uplands of Devon and in the wooded areas around Shropshire, settlements tended to be smaller and tiny hamlets and isolated farmsteads were typical. Here the focus was on rearing beef and dairy cattle, rather than on growing cereals, so farms consisted mainly of pastures and meadows, with the right to graze their animals on the commons being crucially important to those who only had small parcels of land. Although a large number of open fields were enclosed during the Tudor and Stuart periods (see pages 62-63), farming remained the chief occupation in most communities, and again it was not uncommon for a single family to have lived and worked on the same patch of land for generations.

Picture of a rural idyll In the late 18th century paintings of idealised country scenes were fashionable, a taste that made a fortune for the artist George Morland (1763-1804). Despite the sentimental nature of his work, such as his portrait of pea-sellers (above), he did create a record of work and play in the farming communities of the day.

Generating wealth The success of dairy farming in 18th-century Cheshire did not just benefit those with fertile acres to farm. Jobs were also created in industries that were processing milk, butter and cheese for a national market.

The seeds of change

The recovery of the national population from the 1530s onwards was the principal cause of change in village life. By the time of the Civil War (1642-6), there were as many people living in Britain as before the Black Death (see page 148). Greater demand encouraged the growth of trade, allowing some farmers to specialise. Market gardeners flourished around London and dairy farms near urban areas thrived, selling their milk to the growing number of townspeople. By the close of the 17th century, many farmers who worked the lush pastures of Cheshire were able to concentrate on making cheese, which they exported as far as London and the south coast ports. Instead of growing cereals for themselves, they used their profits from dairy produce to buy any bread, corn and malt they needed from the local market towns.

But in some parishes, while peace and population growth brought wider opportunities and an overall increase in prosperity, they also helped to drive a deeper wedge between rich and poor. An estate map of 1597 of the small parish of Terling in Essex shows most of the houses as simple, single-storeyed dwellings. Maps drawn a generation or two later show a scattering of new houses, some two or three storeys high, with large rooms and chimneys, revealing that the general living standard of farmers in the area had improved considerably.

Those that grew richer could afford to buy more land, leaving less for others. This pushed up its price, often well out of the reach of the poorest. As the population grew, so did the numbers of those forced to pay high rates to farm their tiny smallholding or to labour for a pittance in someone else's fields. When the people of Terling were assessed for a tax on their hearths in 1671, the squire had 20 hearths, about one-third of the farmers had three or more, but around half of the householders had just one.

The life of a Shropshire parish preserved in print

Despite the general increases in the population from the 16th century onwards, the wooded counties bordering England and Wales remained relatively uncrowded. There was still enough space to allow poorer families to erect the odd cottage and to clear a few acres of parish wasteland on which to grow crops. Myddle, a Shropshire parish of hamlets and scattered farmsteads, was typical of this region. The clearance of around 405ha (1000 acres) of workable land between the late 15th and the early 17th centuries gave many cottagers small pockets of land to farm.

We know all about life in Myddle in the late 17th century thanks to a local man, Richard Gough, who wrote its history around 1700-6. He distinguished the 12 larger farms of the parish from the 48 middle-sized 'tenements' and the growing number of cottages and their smallholdings. The social structure of the parish was formalised by the arrangement of the seating in the church. The gentry sat in the front pews, ordinary farmers and better-off craftsmen occupied the middle seats, while the cottagers were squeezed in along the south wall and at the back.

Parish study Gough's history of Myddle is a vivid insight into the lives of Stuart country people.

Working from home

In many rural districts, families increasingly had to earn their living from local industry as well as from farming. Having a dual occupation as a blacksmith-farmer or a weaver-farmer became increasingly common during the 18th century. As the population rose further, younger sons often found that there was no land for them to farm and so had to earn their living from crafts and labouring. In Leicestershire, growing numbers turned to framework

knitting for their income (see page 247). In the Yorkshire Dales, smallholders and cottagers earned extra from the hand-knitting of socks and hosiery or from employment in the lead mines.

Long before the Industrial Revolution, some rural parishes had become industrial settlements. The parish of Whickham in Gateshead, Northumbria, was transformed into a coal-mining community in the reign of Elizabeth I. A diocesan census in 1563 counted 93 households in Whickham; by 1666 the householders recorded in a hearth tax return had risen to 367. At the end of the 16th century, the population of the Peak District soared as poor immigrants moved from other parts of Derbyshire and neighbouring counties to seek employment in what had become the most important lead field in Europe. Most of them had no land and were dependent on their earnings from the mines.

When Britain's population reached the unprecedented level of more than 10 million by the end of the 18th century, those with neither land nor craft had little choice but to move into town. London was the destination of many young people, but most rarely ventured further than 20 or so miles from where they were born.

THE SCOTTISH LINEN MAKERS

The most widespread cottage industry in Scotland before the Industrial Revolution was the manufacture of linen goods, such as sheets, tablecloths, sailcloth and clothing. Planned villages such as Huntly near Aberdeen and Ormiston in East Lothian were set up by landowners to encourage the industry and house the workers. In the early 18th century pedlars from lowland Scotland hawked cheap linen goods in many parts of England, and linen was also exported to the colonies for use as slave clothing. As late as the 1830s, two-thirds of Scotland's handloom weavers in the linen, cotton and woollen trades still lived in villages or small market towns in eastern Scotland.

Hive of industry When Queen Victoria's reign began in 1837, around 900 hand-looms were busy weaving cloth in the sturdy stone cottages of Kilbarchan, Renfrewshire. Weaving was the mainstay of the area's economy, few villagers having any farming links.

Places forged out of industry

The great surge of industrial activity across Britain in the late 18th century caused the almost spontaneous sprouting of working settlements. The people who flocked to such new settlements – coal miners, quarrymen, and workers in textile mills and iron foundries – often formed close-knit communities in their new surroundings. Today the industries may have declined, but the towns endure.

THE POETRY OF POLLUTION

In the 18th century Coalbrookdale grew so ugly and polluted that genteel visitors were often moved to declamatory verse. In 1785 Anna Seward described the smoke and glare of the furnaces:

... red the countless fires,
With umber'd flames, bicker on all thy hills,
Dark'ning the Summer's sun with columns large
Of thick, sulphureous smoke, which spread, like palls,
That screen the dead, upon the sylvan robe
Of thy aspiring rocks; pollute thy gales,
And stain thy glassy waters.

A Shropshire powerhouse

Abraham Darby formed the Coalbrookdale Company in 1709, when in a side valley of the River Severn gorge he smelted iron for the first time with coke, a by-product of coal, rather than charcoal. That pioneering act allowed Britain's vast deposits of coal to be used for ironmaking rather than trees, which were a dwindling and slow-growing resource. It set in train the Industrial Revolution.

Coalbrookdale was hardly a leafy rustic paradise before Darby arrived; there had been industry around the Shropshire coalfield for centuries, since the area was not only rich in coal deposits but also iron, clay and limestone. But with Darby and his family's innovations the Severn gorge soon filled with ironworks and potteries, fed by coal brought in by canal, river and tramway from the Coalbrookdale mines. Communities such as Madeley, Dawley and Lawley, Oakengates and Broseley swelled as miners and other industrial workers moved

into the region. A sprawling area of workers' cottages, tramways, ironworks and collieries, claypits and potteries came into being.

The Cromford mills

Set in the steep valley of the River Derwent, Cromford was a small community of farmers and lead miners up to the mid 18th century. But its east Derbyshire location, with its fast-flowing Bonsall Brook and Cromford Sough watercourses, was just what the cotton mill pioneer Richard Arkwright was looking for in 1771. By December of that year he had built the first water-powered mechanical yarn-spinning mill there. The five-storey building employed 200 workers and cottages were built to house them and their families.

By 1801 there were more than 1100 people in Cromford, living in the little purpose-built town. It was well served by neat rows of three-storey houses, each

inhabited by a single family. There were looms on the top floors so that the yarn produced at the mills could readily be turned into cotton fabric.

Amenities included the 300-seater St Mary's Church, a school, a village lock-up, shops and a hotel for visiting businessmen, as well as a weekly market. The Arkwright family looked down on their creation from their newly built mansion, Willersley Castle.

Scotland's great community of iron

Carron Ironworks was founded in 1759 between Larbert and Grangemouth on the Firth of Forth. It was an excellent position with raw materials close at hand and the rushing waters of the Carron to power the four blast furnaces and hammers. It was the first works in Scotland to use coke instead of charcoal for fuel. The ironworks turned out a huge array of goods, most famously lightweight cannons for use on ships. The guns were named 'carronades' after the company, and between 1778 and 1882 the Carron Company produced thousands of them. They were taken on board all of Lord Nelson's ships, including HMS *Victory*.

The ironworks also produced ploughs, water wheels, spades and even the first steam engine designed by James Watt. When the Forth & Clyde Canal opened in 1790,

The cotton king The portrait shows Richard Arkwright at the height of his wealth and glory, having changed the face of Cromford in just 20 years. As well as the mills, he had built rows and rows of gritstone three-storey cottages to house his mill workers and their families. It was the first planned industrial housing in Britain.

providing direct links to both the east and west coasts, Carron was able to expand even further. By 1814 it was the biggest ironworks in Europe, employing 1000 men and thousands more in ancillary trades. The workers were housed in terraces of red sandstone cottages which swelled nearby villages such as Larbert and Stenhousemuir.

Penrhyn, a town built on slate

When Lord Pennant bought out his lessees and personally took over his family's small and uneconomic slate quarries in the Ogwen Valley near Bethesda in 1782, he initiated a massive expansion of the north Wales slate industry. In the 1730s the quarries had been yielding about 2000 tons a year, earning the Pennant family less than £100; by the 1830s they were producing 75,000 tons a year at a profit of more than £62,000. The delighted owners were able to build a fabulous castle – Penrhyn Castle – on the coast, with a slate four-poster bed that weighed a ton.

The 2000 Penrhyn quarrymen lived in far simpler style. They lodged week by week in grim slate-built 'barracks' as part of an industrial township of quarry offices, railroad tracks, slate-splitting sheds, sawmills and spoil heaps that spread along the valley.

Before the boom Painted in 1790, workers' villages sit in rural isolation as a plume of smoke rises from Carron Ironworks in the distance. In time, as the industry took off, the area would become a sprawling industrial township.

FIND OUT MORE

Look at these websites to find out more on industrial towns.
• www.ironbridge.org.uk Ironbridge Gorge Museums, including the Coalbrookdale area.
• www.pandyweb.freeserve.co.uk/ crom_his.html Information about the history of Cromford.
• www.falkirk-wheel.com/wheel/falkirk/ information/ironage.htm Information about Falkirk district and Carron Ironworks.

Victorian countryfolk move to the towns

The Industrial Revolution was a time of upheaval for rural communities. Cottage industries could not compete with mechanised factories and for rural folk the pull towards the cities and the promise of job security were irresistible.

Village life changes for ever

Britain's largest social transformation was triggered by new technology. Work that had once been done on handlooms in rural Lancashire, for example, could now be carried out in large factory sheds. The sheds were sited in burgeoning towns such as Manchester. They took jobs away from the cottage-workers, creating economic depression in the provinces. An income gap grew between people employed in the cities and the rural jobless, so country folk began to leave their villages and head for the cities.

At the start of the 19th century, such a change in lifestyle would have been a huge undertaking. But trains had now made it easy for people to move their lives wholesale to the towns. People began to flow along the railway lines and into the urban pool like stormwater down a gutter.

The railways also spread news, ensuring that people heard talk and read of the riches to be had in the industrial cities of the north and in the capital. A wealth of better-paid jobs, real or imagined, drew migrants from the provinces to London, which, for those who failed to find work, also offered systems of charity or rich pickings for criminal activity.

The rural population drain

The population increase in the towns was mirrored by creeping depopulation of the country. Britons congregated in one long swathe of territory that ran like a sash from the left shoulder of England in the northwest, through the Midlands and down to the right hip in the southeast. Likewise, north of the border much of the population gathered in a belt across Scotland's pinched-in waist from Greenock in the west to Edinburgh in the east.

Once migration to the city began, it became self-perpetuating. Those who stayed behind were prey to new rounds of economic strife, because fewer people were making or spending money. With each rural slump, more people left the villages where their families had lived for generations to find work in the factories of Birmingham or Nottingham, the shipyards of Cardiff or the Clyde.

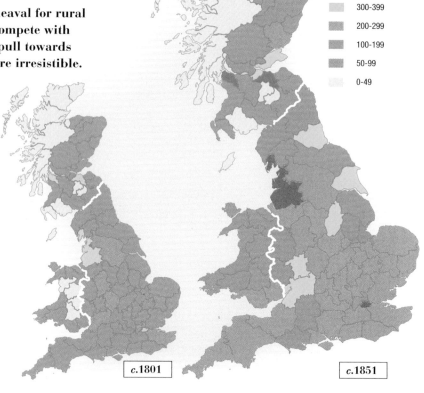

People per square mile
- 1000 and over
- 600-999
- 400-599
- 300-399
- 200-299
- 100-199
- 50-99
- 0-49

*c.*1801

*c.*1851

A population in transit In 1801, there were 16.5 million people in Britain. London was the only city with more than 100,000 inhabitants, so most of the rest of the British population lived in the countryside. Just 50 years later the population had doubled, and about two-thirds of British people lived in towns. Rustics, farmers and cottage craftsmen saw their grandchildren grow up to be factory workers, chimney sweeps and grimy townsmen. The two generations had effectively become foreigners to each other.

ROME IN THE BLACK COUNTRY

Throughout the 19th century there was a tidal ebb and flow of Irish agricultural workers in and out of England. They followed the harvest from one place and one crop to the next, then returned home for the winter. But after the Irish Potato Famines of 1845 to 1851, the influx of rural Irish poor became greater, and this time they did not go back to their blighted country. One of the places the Irish settled in large numbers was Wolverhampton. Many of them occupied the established slum known as Caribee Island. There were so many Irish Catholics in Wolverhampton that the town became known jokingly as Little Rome. The census of 1851 showed that one in eight of the town's population was Irish or of Irish descent. They built a church for themselves – Saints Mary and John – and every day on the streets of Wolverhampton people could be heard speaking in the ancient Gaelic tongue.

A countryside lost to the stockbroker belt

While country people were filing into the city, the city was expanding into the countryside. At the end of the 19th century, Gertrude Jekyll, the writer and horticulturalist (see page 65), noticed how much her native Surrey had changed in the course of her own lifetime, how the entire county was becoming urbanised.

'When I was a child,' she wrote, 'all this tract of country was undiscovered; now, alas! it is overrun... One cannot but regret that the fact of its being now thickly populated and much built over has necessarily robbed it of its older charms. In the older days, London might have been at a distance of two hundred miles. Now one can never forget that it is at little more than an hour's journey.'

She knew she could not stop the process, so she set out to make a written and photographic record of her beloved county. That record was published under the title of *Old West Surrey*, and it reads like a long lament for a lost landscape.

It was not just the physical city that Jekyll saw encroaching on the countryside – it was modern urban life with all its slapdash, time-is-money methods.

'The strain and throng and unceasing restlessness that have been induced by all kinds of competition and by ease of communication have invaded this quiet corner of the land.'

On page after page, amid her evocative photographs of ancient cottages and of farm workers in white corduroy, she rails against the use of modern two-and-a-half inch bricks to mend old chimneys, cheap and easy ridge tiles where local hiptiles would be right, Swedish pine instead of English oak. What she was witnessing and describing for posterity was the birth of the stockbroker belt. And she loathed it.

Those were the days... In her 1904 book, *Old West Surrey*, Gertrude Jekyll was describing more than just the urbanisation of her beloved county. The very fabric of society was changing as cottage industries gave way to new technology. Godalming's 16th-century White Hart Inn (above) is still standing, but the type of customer propping up the bar is likely to be a City worker back from a hard day at the office. The days of a rustic carter in a smock frock (right) downing a pint at his local are long gone.

The great Victorian suburban adventure

The expansion of the suburbs in the mid-Victorian era was one of the most remarkable events of the age. Aided by buses and trams, and particularly ever-expanding rail networks, people poured out of town and city centres to set up home in more spacious outlying districts, only to travel back to those centres to work. It established the living pattern that most Britons share today.

Building boom In the late 19th century houses were packed into 'tunnel-back' terraces (above, in London), with front doors onto the street and adjoining back gardens. They were put up by an army of different builders, which explains the subtle variations in style on many Victorian suburban streets.

A transformation in living

The creation of suburbs was an astonishing feat of engineering. In Camberwell, south London, 5670 houses were constructed in two years (1878-80) by 416 self-employed builders. But it was also a startling social phenomenon. The character of whole districts was changed for ever; the new geography of towns forced people to conduct their lives differently. When people moved out to the suburbs they left behind the 'inner city', a troubled urban core that was then, as it often is now, the domain of the poor and dispossessed.

There is a discernible and regular pattern to the formation of Victorian suburbs: new arrivals settle first in the centre, and they migrate outwards in ripples as they better themselves. This happened in Birmingham. The first ring of working-class suburbia comprised central places such as Yardley. The next ring, the bailiwick of the new bourgeoisie, took in the 'carriage-trade' areas such as Edgbaston – the commuter zone.

The same process can be seen in London, where new migrants (or immigrants such as the East European Jews who arrived at the end of the 19th century) would

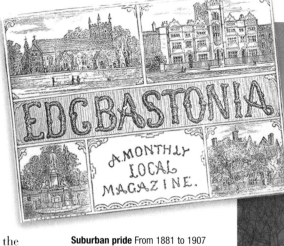

Suburban pride From 1881 to 1907 Edgbaston had its own monthly magazine entitled *Edgbastonia*. The first issue boasted that 'Edgbaston is unquestionably the fashionable suburb of Birmingham'. Such well-to-do communities required an impressive church, something big and imposing that underlined the respectability of the neighbourhood. These Victorian churches, such as St Augustine's (right), are monuments to bourgeois propriety rather than to Anglican piety.

Almost as soon as they were built the suburbs attracted the scorn of snobbish writers. Mrs C.S. Peel, author of *The New Home*, wrote in 1898 that 'the suburbs of any large town appear to me detestable'. She added haughtily that they were for 'people who yearn for the pleasures of the country and who find their diversions in golf, tennis, bicycling, boating or gardening, and whom cruel fate prevents from living in the real country'. And Sir Walter Besant, writing in the same year, described the urban expanse of south London with towering contempt as 'a city without a municipality, without a centre, without a civic history; it has no university; it has no intellectual, artistic, scientific, musical, literary centre – unless the Crystal Palace can be considered as a centre; its residents have no local patriotism or enthusiasm; it has no clubs, it has no public buildings, it has no West End.'

Mr Pooter comes to town Suburban pretensions were more gently teased by George and Weedon Grossmith, first in the pages of *Punch* and then as a book, *The Diary of a Nobody* (right). The 'nobody' was Mr Pooter, a City worker who, despite the best efforts of his friends and family, tried to live out the ideal suburban life. 'My dear wife Carrie and I have just been a week in our new house, "The Laurels", Brickfield Terrace, Holloway – a nice, six-roomed residence, not counting basement, with a front breakfast-parlour…We have a nice little back garden which runs down to the railway. We were rather afraid of the noise of the trains at first, but the landlord said we should not notice them after a bit, and took 2 pounds off the rent.'

The Diary of a Nobody

Written by George and Weedon Grossmith
With 29 Illustrations by Weedon Grossmith
and an Introduction by J. C. Squire

" The Laurels," Brickfield Terrace, Holloway.

live first in the East End. Better paid working men would move into formerly bourgeois neighbourhoods surrounding the centre, while the middle-class people would move further out still, adding ten minutes or so to their commute. To take a train out of a British town is to go on a ride up the social scale.

A nationwide phenomenon

In Liverpool, large houses were built along the banks of the Mersey – 'thousands are scattered over the sea-shore from Southport to Hoylake', wrote one contemporary historian. The less well-off middle-classes followed the rich cotton merchants out of town, and they did not always wait for the railway to make it easy for them. In the middle of the century, 20 years before the Cheshire Line came to their rescue, suburbanites colonised a great arching halo of land some miles away from central Liverpool, swallowing up the villages of Walton, Knowsley, Huyton, Wavertree, Childwall and Woolton.

In Glasgow the drift into suburbia was not just fuelled by increased prosperity, but also by the need to go where the work was. The city's main factories, including its shipyards, had always been outside town, along the banks of the Clyde, closer to the ports and supplies of coal, iron and other raw materials. Some workers' houses were built more or less on site, such as those at Hallside, erected in 1873 by The Steel Company of Scotland.

Revolution by rail

The trains were the key to the growth of the suburbs. As was to happen in the next century with the London Underground (see pages 190-191), lines were built speculatively in the confidence that the station and the spruce new Railway Hotel next door would swiftly bring even newer houses and paying commuters. The expansion of the railways was thought to be a force for social good. Indeed, trains were the very symbol of progress to the Victorian mind.

The railway network would not be nationalised until 1948. But the Railway Act of 1844 forced the handful of private rail companies to provide cheap travel at a penny a mile, heralding an increase in third-class travel. For some this measure was not enough. Charles Pearson MP argued passionately for more lines and more steam engines. 'It is only within the last few years that persons of my condition of life have been satisfied to live out of town,' he declared in 1846. 'We were crammed and jammed together in the city and believed that it was essential to our convenience and happiness. Now sixpence takes us by an omnibus backwards and forwards; the poor man has not sixpence to give.' Horse-drawn buses are all well and good, Pearson was saying, but the true social and moral advantages will come with cheap new railways to allow the skilled working classes to live and breathe the soot-free air of the suburbs.

New ways to travel to work

As cities grew, people began to live further than just a walk from their workplace. London, by far the largest city in Britain, was the first to see the phenomenon of daily commuting. Train services connected the new suburbs with the city centre, and by the middle of the 1850s, 27,000 people were travelling in and out of the capital every day.

The mobile workforce

Most Victorian train-commuters were middle-class professionals. Artisans and labourers usually walked to their jobs, or took the horse-drawn omnibus. But the passing of a Cheap Trains Act in 1883 obliged the train companies to run affordable 'workmen's trains'.

One company, the Great Eastern, had been voluntarily running such a service since the 1860s, at a penny a ride. As a result, more cheap terraced housing was built to the northeast of London in the areas served by the Great Eastern – Tottenham, Walthamstow and Leyton – than in the south and west of the city. Railway stations were constructed around the financial district of the City to serve the burgeoning numbers of commuters. Fenchurch Street Station was opened in 1854 and was followed by Blackfriars, Canon Street and Liverpool Street. Office workers arriving at termini further from the City, such as Paddington, continued their journey by horse-drawn omnibus.

Morning rush hour The introduction of the workmen's 'penny train' in the 1880s enabled Londoners to live in the suburbs and travel to work via stations such as Victoria (above).

Catching the first tube

By the 1850s buses had completely clogged the heart of London. The answer was to build a new kind of railway that would carry passengers beneath the streets. In 1854, the Metropolitan Railway Company was granted the right to build a short stretch of underground railway from Paddington to Farringdon. This 'cut-and-cover trench', which opened in 1863, was the world's first stretch of underground railway, and it functions to this day.

The trains were the same smoke-belching steam variety as used on the rest of Britain's railways, so to ride an underground train was a profoundly unpleasant

DID YOU KNOW?

The name of the Metropolitan Railway Company was adopted by many European languages as the generic word for an underground railway: both the French *métropolitain* and the Russian *myetro* are derived from it.

Hiding the line When the tenants of Leinster Gardens complained about the building of Bayswater Station (left) in 1868, a false house was put up between numbers 23 and 24 to fill the space and disguise the tracks.

The power of the horse

On the streets of Victorian Britain horses were the force that kept public transport moving. Between the 1820s and 1870s, the streets of the larger cities filled up with horse buses and horse trams; their clip-clop became the distinctive sound – and their manure the characteristic smell – of the Victorian city centre.

The first regular bus service in Britain began in 1824 between Pendleton in Salford and Manchester. The idea was brought to London by George Shillibeer, who borrowed the word 'omnibus' from an entrepreneur doing the same thing in Paris. Shillibeer's omnibuses plied a route between Paddington Green (near where the trains terminated) and the Bank of England. They were a great success, and other companies soon set up on different routes. By 1856 there were 800 omnibuses in London, each one drawn by three horses abreast.

Over time the buses grew familiar to the point where ladies could respectably use them. They were not very comfortable, especially in winter. 'At this wet and dirty season of the year,' wrote *Punch* in 1861, 'Men sitting in an omnibus frequently sustain some little inconvenience, in having every now and then their knees brushed by a lady who gets into the vehicle with her enormous skirts, on which she has swept up a lot of mud in the streets, and necessarily wipes it off upon their trousers.'

The first horse-drawn tram service opened in London in the 1860s, but it was in provincial towns that the tram was most enthusiastically adopted. In the 1870s, tracks were laid in Liverpool, Bolton, Leeds, Plymouth and Hull. In 1885 Blackpool became the first city in Britain to use electric trams, and other cities, such as Bradford, soon followed. Blackpool's tramway is still in operation today between Fleetwood and Blackpool Pleasure Beach.

Making tracks The citizens of Glasgow, like those of other British cities, had an innovative form of public transport in Victorian times – horse-drawn buses. Tram tracks were laid in Glasgow in the early 1870s and by 1896 (below) the city owned 3000 horses to pull the cars. Electric trams were introduced in 1898.

experience for the commuter. The suffocating atmosphere left one passenger who travelled on the first day 'coughing like a boy with his first cigar'. And the artist and thinker William Morris described the new railway as 'that vapour-bath of hurried and discontented humanity'. Such complaints continued until trains were electrified in 1905 (see pages 190-191).

London's underground expands

The underground system grew rapidly in the latter half of the 19th century. The Metropolitan company built surface lines that reached out west to Hammersmith, north to Harrow, and east to Whitechapel and New Cross. The company bought land next to the railway and encouraged property developers to do the same. London grew along the routes laid down by the railway companies.

By the end of the century there were six underground railway companies, all contributing to the cat's cradle of tunnels beneath London. The Metropolitan District Railway opened a stretch of line from Westminster to South Kensington, then used the building of the Thames Embankment (see pages 180-181) to extend the line along the river to the Tower. At the same time, the company made a speculative push west and south to Ealing, Wimbledon and Richmond. A relic of the Metropolitan District Railway Company is preserved in the present-day name of that line: the District.

FIND OUT MORE

• London's Transport Museum The collection, housed at Covent Garden Piazza, includes Victorian horse-drawn buses and trams. The website gives information on the history of Victorian transport. www.ltmuseum.co.uk
• Glasgow Museum of Transport Displays of vintage vehicles, including horse-drawn buses and early trams, can be seen at this museum in Kelvin Hall, Glasgow. www.glasgowmuseums.com
• www.victorianlondon.org Descriptions of omnibuses and trams in Victorian times.

Monuments to civic pride

Victorian and Edwardian businessmen, manufacturers and civic dignitaries enjoyed displaying their wealth and success by erecting magnificent buildings at the heart of their burgeoning cities. No matter how proud a visitor might be, these buildings should serve to humble and overawe him. No matter how modest the means of the native citizens who passed or entered the town hall, warehouse or railway station, they should be uplifted and flushed with civic pride.

A testament to power Glasgow City Chambers (left) was built to reflect Glasgow's status as the 'second city of the Empire'. Its entrance echoes Rome's 3rd-century Arch of Constantine; the three-storey staircase (above) is of the finest Carerra marble.

Pride of the town

Grand town halls were designed to exhibit pomp and circumstance to all comers. Glasgow's City Chambers (1882-90) is a huge turreted and towered palace with a loggia whose vaulted ceiling is composed of 1.5 million Venetian mosaic pieces. Birmingham's Town Hall (1834) emulates the temples of Rome, surrounded by pillars and bookended with mighty pediments. Many smaller towns, not to be outdone, made even greater efforts with their town halls – Rochdale (1866-71) has a clock tower almost 60m (200ft) tall; Bolton (1873) a tremendous classical portico and an imposing Great Hall. Ipswich (1868) is Italianate in three colours: yellow Bath oolitic limestone, red Mansfield sandstone and white Portland stone.

By Edwardian times there was a trend towards reflecting civic pride in the composition of an area of the city, rather than just a single building. In Cardiff, the Civic Centre in Cathays Park is a dignified and expansive collection of buildings in white Portland stone. The centre comprises a City Hall (1905) with a 60m (200ft) dome topped by a Welsh dragon, the Law Courts (1906), the west wing of the University of Wales College (1903-9), and the splendid National Museum of Wales, which was not formally opened until 1927.

Liverpool's Edwardian Pier Head, by contrast, trumpeted a message of commercial rather than political consequence with its 'Three Graces' – the domed Port of

Liverpool Building (1907) and the soaring clock towers of the Royal Liver Building (1911) flanking the elegant palazzo-style Cunard Building (1914-18).

Cathedrals of steam

In the early days of rail travel, railway companies needed to reassure nervous travellers, so tended to choose familiar and homely architectural styles for their stations (see pages 250-251). But once everyone knew about railways the companies let themselves go and exhibited as much grandeur as any town corporation.

A traveller felt confident of being served by a mighty organisation when contemplating the curved train shed and mock-cathedral façade of Bristol Temple Meads station (1871-8); the balustraded roofline of Bath Green Park (1874), in keeping with the town's Palladian architecture; and above all the extraordinary opulence of London's St Pancras station (1864-8). The palatial exterior of St Pancras led to a vast train shed of cast iron and glass almost 30m (100ft) high and straddling the platforms in a single breathtaking span of 74m (243ft).

Muck and brass

Factories and warehouses reflected the wealth of the Victorian owners, generally self-made men who wanted to trumpet their success. The Watts Warehouse in Manchester's Portland Street, built as a splendid showroom in 1851-6 for the brash drapery king James Watts, is a fabulous confection six storeys high. Each floor has its own architectural style, including Tudor, Italianate, Flemish and Palladian, topped by a turreted parapet.

The mills in which the textiles were produced, though in less central and poorer districts than the civic showpieces, were often made to look

Arriving in style The elaborate Gothic-style Temple Meads station in Bristol was designed by Matthew Digby Wyatt for the Great Western Railway.

enormously imposing. William Holland's Victoria Mill (1867-73) in Miles Platting (a suburb of Manchester) is a huge six-storey 'Palace of Labour' with a giant chimney rising from the centre of its façade. Also in Manchester, Redhill Street Mill (1818) is eight storeys high and was the tallest iron-framed building in the world in its day.

Knowledge for all

Self-improvement through education was a Victorian ideal; and here, too, grand aspirations were matched by fine architecture. The Victoria & Albert Museum, the Science Museum and the Natural History Museum were all built in South Kensington in the decades following the Great Exhibition of 1851. The Natural History Museum (1880) was based on a design by Captain Francis Fowkes, who intended it as an Italian-Renaissance style cathedral to science. Alfred Waterhouse made many practical adjustments and the result is a striking Romanesque building, faced in terracotta and adorned with exquisite figures of animals and plants.

Libraries were temples of learning, too. Dunfermline-born but US-reared Andrew Carnegie (1835-1919) became the richest man in the world through iron and steel interests. He endowed more than 3000 public libraries, including 660 in Britain. The designs of the Scottish Carnegie Libraries exhibit every style from Scots Baronial (Stirling, 1904) and French Renaissance-cum-Scottish domestic (Kelso, 1906) to Neo-Classical (Dumbarton, 1910) and dignified Scots Palladian (Kirkwall, 1909).

Highest aspirations The Tower Works on Globe Road, Leeds, which made pins and combs for the textile industry, displays two fanciful 'classical' chimneys. The one on the right (1864) was modelled on Verona's Lamberti Tower and the other ventilation-shaft-in-disguise (1899) shares its proportions with Giotto's campanile in Florence.

Play time Schools opened their doors for after-hours activities, such as the Children's Happy Evening Association learn-to-play session in 1906 at Victoria School in London's Bethnal Green. The school still exists today.

the industrial centres of the north and isolated communities in areas such as Cornwall, in particular, were poorly catered for. In 1858 the Newcastle Commission was set up to investigate elementary education in England and Wales. The report revealed that less than half of all children aged 5-10 attended school and of those only 10 per cent were educated to an adequate standard.

Free schooling for every child

Schools in early 19th-century England and Wales failed to meet the demands of a booming population, often charging fees or catering solely for the gentry. But this changed with the 1870 Education Act, which set up a system for free schooling nationwide.

The dawn of a new era

In the mid 19th century there was a growing demand for education as the population rose sharply and social thinking began to change. Many believed that universal education would reduce crime and immorality, and industry needed workers who could read, if only so that they could follow written instructions.

Until then, schooling had mostly been geared towards the middle classes: 'charity schools' run by clergymen were funded by subscriptions; grammar schools educated the sons of wealthy merchants and farmers; and public schools catered for the sons of the gentry (see right). The education system in Scotland was far more advanced and by the beginning of the 18th century most parishes in the Scottish Lowlands had a school, funded by ecclesiastical groups, charitable foundations or a local landowner.

Between 1811 and 1837 two religious societies, the Church of England National Society and the British and Foreign Schools Society, set up 3500 elementary schools for children from poor families but they could not meet the growing demand. An 1851 education census pointed to huge disparities in education provision across Britain:

Opportunities for all

After increasing pressure from social reformers, Parliament introduced the 1870 Education Act. The ground-breaking new law stated that a school must be provided wherever there was no voluntary school, and

RUGBY SCHOOL LEADS THE WAY

There was a huge surge in the establishment of public schools in the Victorian era. The new middle-classes, who had made their money from industry, saw these schools as a way of moving their children up the social ladder. A main aim of public schools was to mould pupils into gentlemen. They were then fed into the upper echelons of the civil service, military and Church.

Rugby was the most influential public school of the 19th century, due in large part to the pioneering approach of Thomas Arnold (1795-1842), who was headmaster from 1828 to 1842. To his mind, the aim of education was '1st, religious and moral principle; 2ndly, gentlemanly conduct; and 3rdly, intellectual ability'. In other words, the most important goal of a school was to turn out principled and well-rounded members of society.

Model master A portrait of Thomas Arnold in 1839.

Arnold changed the course of public school education in Britain by employing assistant masters who went on to found or lead other public schools according to his methods: boys divided into houses, each with a master; prefects with responsibility for discipline; and a wide curriculum with an emphasis on classics. Aspects of Arnold's pattern of education continue to influence secondary schooling today.

Schools for paupers

The so-called 'ragged schools' are believed to have originated with a Portsmouth shoemaker named John Pounds. In 1818 he set up the first of these free schools, which were for poor children who were often excluded from other schools because of their tattered clothing and appearance. Lord Shaftesbury helped form the Ragged School Union in 1844, which raised funds and recruited voluntary teachers. Within 30 years there were more than 200 such schools. The largest in London was located in three former warehouses next to the Regent's Canal in the East End. It was administered by Dr Barnardo, and is now the Ragged School Museum (right).

Disciplinary measures Teachers had various methods of keeping order, such as the dunce's cap and finger cuffs (left). To stop fidgeting, the child's fingers were placed in the holes in the cuffs and then the two parts were tied behind the fidget's back. This prevented the pupil from working, but, like standing in a corner with a dunce's cap, it gave the child time to reflect on the wrongdoing, which was considered beneficial.

that the new schools would be administered by local school boards. Both the voluntary schools and the board schools were to be funded by government.

In 1880, once enough board schools had been built, education for children up to the age of ten was made compulsory. In 1890 fees for primary education were abolished; in 1899 the school leaving age was raised to 12 (then to 14 in 1918); and in 1902 school boards were replaced by local education authorities directly responsible to the government.

In Scotland a further-reaching Act of 1872 set up school boards to regulate education provision. Schooling became compulsory for children aged 5 to 13 (14 from 1883). Schools were funded partly by local rates, partly by fees until 1892 when free education became the norm.

The rise of the new universities

Until the 19th century, Oxford and Cambridge were the only English institutions allowed to award degrees, although the Scottish universities St Andrews, Edinburgh, Glasgow and Aberdeen had been doing so since the 15th

and 16th centuries. As the Victorians grew in wealth and confidence, so did their quest for learning. The ancient university foundations could no longer cope with the growing economic and intellectual needs of Britain's new industrial society. Influential reformers were also campaigning for the wider provision of further education. One of these men, the radical reformer Jeremy Bentham, was instrumental in founding the University of London in 1828, which later became University College London. Durham University was founded soon after, in 1832, followed by Manchester, Liverpool, Leeds, Birmingham and Aberystwyth. By 1900 universities had been established in most major urban centres.

FIND OUT MORE

• The Ragged School Museum At 46-50 Copperfield Road in London, the museum tells how poor children were offered an education. www.raggedschoolmuseum.org.uk
• The British Schools Museum Displays on elementary education from 1810 to 1945 are shown at this museum in Hitchin, Hertfordshire. www.hitchinbritishschools.org.uk

Height of fashion The modern shopping mall has its roots in the splendid arcades of the 19th century. Many survive today, including the restored County Arcade in Leeds.

Michael Marks

A retailing revolution hits the high street

At the start of the Victorian era most shops were privately owned, the proprietor and his family living above the business that proudly bore his name. Many towns still had open markets, dating back to medieval times, and itinerant tinkers offered services such as knife sharpening door-to-door. But rapid urban expansion soon led to greater demand for goods and services: markets grew – some going under cover in ornate arcades – shops opened new branches and the department store was born.

Shopping on the town

Rapid urban expansion in the 19th century brought many changes to the established retail structure. Unlike older settlements, which had always had a commercial link with local farms, many of the new industrial towns had no open space for a weekly market. They had to invent one: Liverpool, for example, built a covered market hall in the city centre, the first town to do so. Other towns across the north of England, where the climate sometimes made open markets uncomfortable, followed Liverpool's lead.

The market halls evolved rapidly into covered shopping precincts, which became known as 'arcades'. Each one housed a parade of individual shops, and they gave the growing middle classes a place to shop away from the cold, dirt and stench of the open streets. The buildings were funded by speculators, and some were designed by celebrated architects of the day such as Frank Matcham,

best known for his theatres (see page 177). Often the arcades were highly ornate structures made of glass and cast iron, similar to the Crystal Palace in London.

The first and most fashionable was Burlington Arcade in London's Piccadilly in 1819, but equally impressive arcades were built in northern towns such as Leeds and Halifax, and also in Cardiff. There is a fine Edwardian arcade on the seafront at Bognor, West Sussex.

The birth of the supermarket

The growth of the middle classes stimulated other changes in the retail trade. A few entrepreneurs found that they had the skill and the capital to run more than one shop. One such man was Michael Marks, a Jewish refugee from Poland who began in 1884 with an all-for-a-penny stall on Kirkgate, Leeds. He then moved to Manchester where he joined forces with Tom Spencer, an ambitious cashier.

Chain-store success The story of Marks & Spencer began in 1884 with Michael Marks's Penny Bazaar at Kirkgate Market, Leeds (above). Marks soon joined forces with Tom Spencer and laid the foundations for what has become one of Britain's best-known high-street retailers.

Tom Spencer

Growing business In 1882, John Sainsbury opened the first of his four stores in Islington's Chapel Street: two sold provisions, one specialised in dairy produce and the other in poultry and game – a luxury in what was then a working-class area. Today, Sainsbury's has more than 700 stores and employs some 150,000 people.

They grew their business on Derby Street, and then in 1904 transplanted it back to Leeds, setting up in Cross Arcade. It was by now a powerful retail business, but people in the north continued to refer to Marks & Spencer as a penny bazaar up to the 1930s.

The seeds of supermarkets were sown a decade or two before Marks and Spencer got together. In 1869, John Sainsbury opened his first shop at 173 Drury Lane, London. He was one of the first to make use of 'railway milk': he brought his produce in from the countryside rather than keep a cow at his shop, which was common practice at the time. He built a business on the claim that his butter was 'the best in the world'. As he grew more successful he opened branches in Stepney, Chapel Market in Islington, Croydon and Balham.

Everything in store

Some of these empire-building Victorian grocers took another route to riches. A generation before Sainsbury set up shop, another retailer had moved out to the then rural village of Brompton to avoid the blight of cholera. His name was Charles Henry Harrod, a merchant specialising in tea. When the expansion of London reached his village, Harrod unexpectedly found himself perfectly placed to provide retail services to the wealthy new urban incomers.

In 1883, the Harrod family took the opportunity of a fire in the properties adjoining their shops to expand their premises along Knightsbridge. The *Chelsea Herald*, reporting on the newer, bigger Harrods, was breathless: 'Stretching for a long way into the distance is the tea and grocery counter, where pyramids of tea and sugar and mountains of coffee are mixed up with tins of biscuits, breeches' paste, blancmange, glycerine, lobsters, plate powder, sugar candy, boot-top powder, wax vestas, salt prawns, phosphor paste, oysters, milk, knife polish, house flannel, dog biscuits, mustard, and a thousand and one other articles.'

HIGH STREET SPOTTING

If you want to know what kind of shops used to be in your local high street, start by looking up above today's shopfronts: you may spot the relics of older businesses (see pages 238-239). In Stoke Newington in London, above a shop named London Pride, you can see the old sign for Marks & Spencer. There is also a sign advertising Dyson's the grocer above the Post Office, although that business is long gone. Butchers' shops leave the most obvious evidence of the past. Many had tiled floors for hygiene reasons, and often these are still in place. There is a bookshop in Lewes, East Sussex, which still has a mosaic depicting farm animals on its floor; and a Chinese take-away in Pembroke Dock in Wales has a frieze showing cows in a field.

Oh, they did like to be beside the seaside

The idea that sea air and sea bathing were healthy had been around for some time before the Victorian era. Places such as Brighton, Scarborough and Eastbourne were already regular bolt-holes for the wealthy. But for most of the British population the pleasures of a maritime resort were as distant and mysterious as the moon. That would soon change with the coming of the railways.

A trip to the coast

As railway lines began to criss-cross Britain in the mid 19th century, seaside resorts could be visited by people of all social classes. And with their cargoes of urbanites in search of fresh air, the railways turned dozens of fishing villages and spas into seaside boom towns. Brighton was one of the first beneficiaries.

The town had been fashionable while it was patronised by the extravagant George IV, but after his death in 1830 Brighton began to ail. The railway came in 1841 like a life-giving transfusion of blood. Suddenly it was easy for Londoners to get some sea air – and almost at a whim. They did so in their thousands. During one hot week in 1859, 73,000 people – about 5 per cent of the population of London – took the train from Victoria to Brighton. The town itself put on a rapid growth spurt to accommodate its legions of visitors: Brighton's population doubled in the 30 years after the railway arrived.

A different class of visitor

The holidaymakers of the 1840s and 50s were mostly well-to-do and middle-class. Their idea of a refreshing break was to walk by the sea, indulge in some amateur botany or shell-collecting, and perhaps take a dip with the help of a bathing machine. The character of seaside resorts changed after the introduction of the Bank

FELIXSTOWE
IT'S QUICKER BY RAIL
FREE ILLUSTRATED GUIDE FROM ANY L.N.E.R. OFFICE OR AGENCY, OR INFORMATION BUREAU, FELIXSTOWE

Fast track to the beach The coming of the railways brought seaside towns like Felixstowe in Suffolk within easy reach of urban day-trippers.

Holidays Act in 1871. This piece of legislation guaranteed time off for all workers at Christmas, Whitsun, Easter and the beginning of August. As a result teeming masses of clerks and shop assistants from London flocked to the coast. The effect of this seasonal emancipation of the office boys was to drive out the decorous bourgeoisie. They either stuck to the more salubrious parts of town (abandoning Brighton for Hove) or moved on to resorts that guaranteed a certain exclusivity. Bournemouth was one such: the town council made a point of resisting the railway, and banned donkeys on the seafront.

The newspapers, meanwhile, comforted their middle-class readers by heaping scorn on the hoi polloi. In Hastings the local rag lamented the profusion of 'excursionists of a certain office-frequenting, ledger-keeping cast of countenance'; and *Punch* sneered at the Margate crowds as 'the very flower of the flock of Brixton Rise, or the crème de la crème of Peckham Rye'.

The growing tide of popularity

But the urban working classes were good for business. In Blackpool in 1896 the town clerk counted 316 stallholders on the foreshore, all there to extract a penny or two from the daytrippers and weekenders from the mills of Lancashire. The town was at the height of its popularity. In 1861 some 135,000 people passed though its railway stations; in 1901 it was nearly 3 million. The August bank holiday trip to the seaside was now as fixed a festivity as

Taking a dip Children paddle in the sea at Tenby, Wales, in 1890. The bathing machines spared the modesty of Victorian ladies, who would change into their full-length bathing costumes inside the carts and descend gracefully down the steps and into the water.

Crammed in like sardines Stoic day-trippers stake their claim to a tiny bit of Blackpool sands in 1947, but not a bathing costume in sight. A trip to the seaside on August bank holiday became almost compulsory for city-dwellers.

Christmas Day or Guy Fawkes Night. Only the destinations varied: from the East Midlands holidaymakers flowed into Skegness and Great Yarmouth; Londoners went on their joyful annual pilgrimage to Margate and Southend.

They continued to do so throughout the first half of the 20th century and well into the 1960s. By that time, package holidays abroad and flexible leave provided other, more exotic ways of taking the annual break. Today towns such as Bournemouth, Brighton, Scarborough and Harrogate rely heavily on the conference trade – and expense accounts – to populate the grand Edwardian hotels that line the seafronts. We do still like to be beside the seaside, but we are as likely as not to be working when we are there.

All decked out Piers like the one at Brighton, complete with jolly amusement arcades and stalls, were part of the seaside experience along with stripy deckchairs and ice cream.

A peculiarly British amusement

The pleasure pier is a very British building. No other country has them; only in Britain do the seaside towns dip a long architectural toe in the chilly sea. The first piers were built at the beginning of the 19th century as jetties for loading and unloading boats, but almost immediately they became places to promenade and to be seen. There were riots in Victorian Margate when the local authorities began to charge a penny for access to the jetty.

The first pier to install amusements for visitors was the old chain pier at Brighton, opened in 1823. At its height it accommodated a souvenir shop, a camera obscura and a wine shop. The pier was demolished by a storm in 1896, but by then there were two other piers in Brighton. Indeed, the coastline of Britain positively bristled with piers – a couple of dozen were constructed in the 1860s alone in towns such as Great Yarmouth, Scarborough, Hastings, Worthing, Southsea, Morecambe, Douglas and Rhyl. Many of these piers were built with the subscriptions of local businesses, suggesting that they were seen locally as an important

means of attracting money-spending visitors to the coast. The piers had no attractions at first. They were a perpendicular extension of the seafront, a typically Victorian way of going out to sea without the risk of seasickness or the vexation of getting in and out of a boat. That genteel purpose changed as the seaside resorts sought the business of the more boisterous working classes: towards the end of the century the piers acquired the punch-and-judy shows and the comical turns; later came the dodgems and the doughnut stands.

But the heyday of the pier was by then long past. In 1940, all of them suffered the indignity of having a large hole blown in their decks, lest they be used as landing stages by invading Nazis. Some came by even greater misfortune: Brighton's West Pier, the only Grade 1 listed pier in Britain, was closed as an unsafe structure in the 1970s. A quarter of a century later, when it was about to be restored, it had two fires and two catastrophic collapses in the space of a year. Its charred skeleton is now a roost for birds.

New time for leisure

Crowd puller Around 38,000 spectators came to see England (above) play Scotland in Liverpool for the British Championship in April 1911. The match ended in a 1:1 draw.

There was almost no such thing as free time for the working classes in the early 19th century. In the factories, men, women and children toiled for 12 hours or more a day, six days a week. Sundays were for religious observance and not regarded as leisure time. But the 1850 Factories Act granted all workers one free afternoon a week, on Saturdays. Soon new entertainments appeared to fill those precious hours.

Going to the game

The Victorians invented spectator sports as we now know them. They took long-established games, such as football and cricket, and, with their passion for organisation, they codified the rules, arranged tournaments and persuaded the public to part with a few pennies to watch.

Within a generation, professional sport had become a major money-spinner, and across Britain stadiums were built or enlarged to maximise the potential profit. Football grounds especially became a feature of every sizeable town. With the introduction of the FA Cup tournament in the 1871-2 season, the game moved from being a public school activity to a competition of national standing. It became particularly popular in working-class districts of the Midlands and northern England, where it was fiercely competitive. Games started at 3pm – as most still do – because the half-day holiday began at 2pm, giving workers an hour to get to the ground.

Factory owners encouraged the interest in football, because it helped to foster feelings of solidarity among the workforce. Many now famous clubs began as works teams. West Ham was formed at the Thames Iron Works in 1895, and Newton Heath (now Manchester United)

was founded in 1878 by workers from the Lancashire and Yorkshire Railway Company. Arsenal Football Club started life in 1886 as the team of Woolwich Armaments in south London, moving north to Highbury in 1915 to take advantage of better transport links and a bigger local population.

Rugby – from school to clubs

Another sport that started at school was rugby. It began life as a variant of football at Rugby School (see page 170), from which it took its name. Pupils who moved on to Oxford and Cambridge encouraged others there to play it. By 1871, these converts had formed an association with written rules, and a new sport was born.

What began as a middle-class activity started to gain popularity with working-class communities in south Wales and the north of England as leisure time increased. In the Welsh coalfields, a boisterous and self-confident immigrant community who had moved here to find work in the collieries, welcomed the opportunity for collective expression in the sport. Northern clubs were often formed around workplaces, churches and pubs. They played a faster-moving version of the game than their southern counterparts, drawing large crowds.

Professional rugby started at Huddersfield in 1895 with the formation of the Northern Rugby Football Union; in 1922 the name was changed to the Rugby Football League.

Sport for gentlemen

The origins of cricket are obscure, but the first recorded match took place in Kent in 1646. It was played mainly by aristocrats, and the development of cricket grounds was at first motivated by a desire to keep the common folk out, rather than make money by letting them in.

In the late 18th century, there were regular matches at White Conduit Fields in Islington, north London, but rowdy crowds regularly disrupted the game. To remedy this, one player, Thomas Lord, leased a ground on Dorset Fields in Marylebone. But this site, known as Lord's, attracted noisy spectators, too. So the players moved again – finally settling in St John's Wood. Despite the location of the new Lord's, the Dorset Fields players kept their old name: the Marylebone Cricket Club, or MCC.

But cricket was not confined to London and the southern counties. In Yorkshire and Lancashire it became a highly competitive spectator sport, where towns were pitted against their neighbours.

Pedal power The cheap bicycles that became available in the 1890s were taken up enthusiastically by men and women of all classes. In the days when roads were still uncongested and unpolluted, cyling was a healthy and sociable way to fill your leisure time. Cycling clubs that met for weekly outings (below) sprang up all over Britain. By the early 1900s, London alone had 274 such clubs.

Curtain up

The form taken by theatrical entertainment in Victorian Britain, and the shape of the theatres themselves, were determined by the Theatres Act of 1843. The law stated that smoking and drinking were forbidden in playhouses. This ban, combined with the legal definition of a theatre as a place where dialogue was performed, led to the proliferation of alternative venues where the entertainment consisted of sentimental or bawdy songs, the air was thick with smoke and the tables crowded with beer mugs – the music halls.

But soon legislation was brought in to regulate music halls too. From 1878, they were required to have a Certificate of Suitability. Since most were profoundly unsuitable for almost any purpose, many of the more rowdy, pub-like halls closed. In their place arose well-appointed and frequently luxurious variety theatres. Top performers in these new entertainment 'palaces' often became major celebrities, revered by all levels of society. When Dan Leno (above), the great pantomine dame, died in 1904, his funeral was a focus of national mourning.

Many of the variety halls were designed and built by the prolific Frank Matcham (1854-1920). He had no architectural training, but was blessed with a talent for squeezing capacious buildings into small, awkward pieces of land. Among his surviving gems are the Tower Ballroom, Blackpool; the King's Theatre, Glasgow; the Gaiety Theatre, Isle of Man; and the Shepherd's Bush Empire and Hackney Empire (below), both in London.

Where the workers had to live

The 1851 census recorded, for the first time, that more people lived in the towns than in the country. For two generations, there had been a drift into the cities. As the growing mass of workers pressed into the cheapest, most run-down areas of manufacturing towns such as Liverpool, Manchester, Nottingham and Leeds, a new word was coined for the cramped, fetid buildings they inhabited – 'slums'.

The misery of the urban slums

The slums of Victorian Britain are hard for a modern mind to imagine. They were filthy, dark and airless, and they were ridden with crime and disease. But most of all, they were monstrously overcrowded. Sometimes a family of ten would occupy a single room, and every room in a street or a block would be just as densely populated.

Pressure on housing often helped turn neighbourhoods into slums. As the better off moved out to less crowded areas, landlords subdivided their once smart homes into as many separate dwellings as they could to maximise profits. This was the fate of districts such as Glasgow's Saltmarket. It had started out as a fashionable Georgian suburb but was a teeming slum by the late 19th century. Some of London's worst slums also developed in this way.

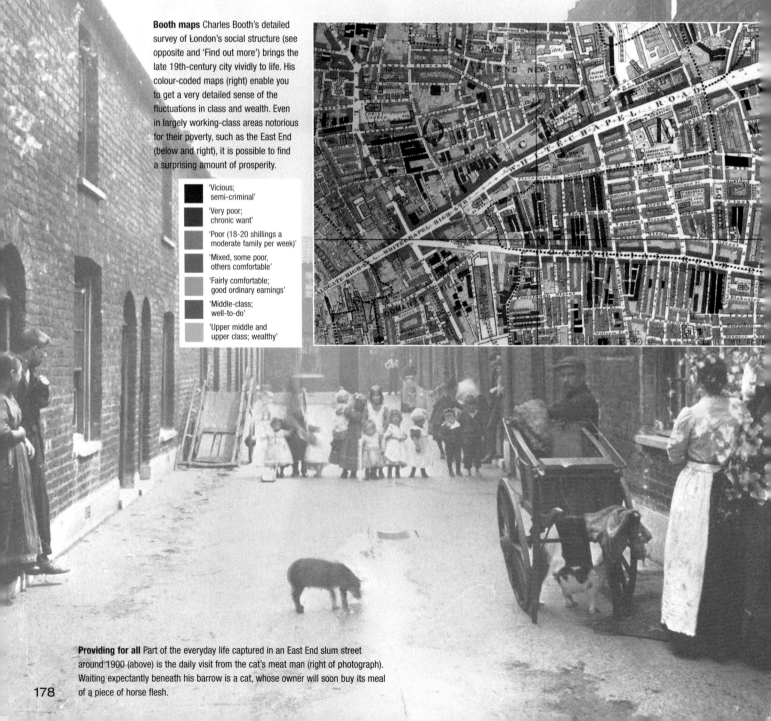

Booth maps Charles Booth's detailed survey of London's social structure (see opposite and 'Find out more') brings the late 19th-century city vividly to life. His colour-coded maps (right) enable you to get a very detailed sense of the fluctuations in class and wealth. Even in largely working-class areas notorious for their poverty, such as the East End (below and right), it is possible to find a surprising amount of prosperity.

- 'Vicious; semi-criminal'
- 'Very poor; chronic want'
- 'Poor (18-20 shillings a moderate family per week)'
- 'Mixed, some poor, others comfortable'
- 'Fairly comfortable; good ordinary earnings'
- 'Middle-class; well-to-do'
- 'Upper middle and upper class; wealthy'

Providing for all Part of the everyday life captured in an East End slum street around 1900 (above) is the daily visit from the cat's meat man (right of photograph). Waiting expectantly beneath his barrow is a cat, whose owner will soon buy its meal of a piece of horse flesh.

Courts of squalor and filth

Property developers also saw opportunites to make money from the teeming masses. Jerry-built estates known as 'courts' or 'court-houses' sprang up to house the swelling numbers in the industrial centres. In Nottingham and Leeds (see pages 278-279), where the burgesses refused to allow new building on the fringe of the city, the poor were effectively corralled into courts in the town centre. These courts were seen at their worst in Liverpool, where the working classes were vastly augmented after 1846 by refugees from the potato famine in Ireland.

The appalling inner-city conditions inspired Charles Booth to make a detailed investigation of working life in London. His *Life and Labour of the People in London (1892-97)* includes maps (see opposite), with the streets coloured according to their social class and character.

The other side of the coin

A few philanthropic industrialists did try to improve living conditions, at least for their own workers. Sir Titus Salt built the model village of Saltaire in Yorkshire (see pages 78-79) in the 1850s to provide living space for employees at his mills. As well as houses, there was a school, shops, a laundry and chapels. The Cadbury family built a similar estate for their staff at Bournville, near Birmingham, but such innovations did nothing to help most slum-dwellers.

The man who struck a real blow for change was the banking millionaire George Peabody. He endowed many good causes including a housing trust, set up in 1862 'to ameliorate the condition of the poor and needy'. The nominal rents charged by the Peabody Trust were still beyond the reach of the poorest, but it marked a step in the right direction. What Friedrich Engels labelled as the 'filth, ruin and uninhabitableness' of much working-class housing survived well into the 20th century, but the slums' days were numbered.

Social experiment In 1888, William Hesketh Lever (left) founded the workers' town of Port Sunlight, Cheshire (above), named after his most popular product – Sunlight soap. Styled as a scaled-down version of a middle-class suburb, it offered a quality of life unimaginable to most 19th-century industrial workers.

Living hell Southwell Workhouse is now a museum (see 'Find out more', below), a grim reminder of a time when many were forced to trade-in freedom for a roof over their head.

INTO THE WORKHOUSE

Workhouses were the last resort of the poor and destitute. They came about as a result of the Poor Law Amendment Act of 1834. Previously parishes had provided for the poor, but the growth of the urban population and the poverty that came with the Industrial Revolution meant they could no longer cope. The new law enabled them to club together to build places where the homeless could be housed and put to work.

Southwell Workhouse in Nottinghamshire was grimly typical. It functioned on a regime far stricter than most modern prisons. Men were separated from women, and children from parents. Inmates were then sub-divided into groups that represented their moral standing in the eyes of the authorities – the most contemptible category were the 'idle and profligate', that is, able-bodied but unemployed. All inmates were set to work. Women and children washed and sewed; men grew vegetables or, like convicts, broke stones for road-building. In return they were fed, clothed and housed. No-one could leave without a formal discharge. Being sent to the workhouse was, in effect, a prison sentence for the crime of being poor.

Workhouses finally closed their doors only in 1948, when changes in the social security system made them redundant.

FIND OUT MORE

• Thackray Museum, Beckett Street, Leeds. Displays show how improvements in public health and medicine have changed people's lives since the 1850s. Contains reconstructions of the Victorian slums in Leeds.
www.thackraymuseum.org
• The Workhouse An exploration of the day-to-day life of the poor, sick and destitute, situated in the former workhouse at Southwell, Nottinghamshire.
www.nationaltrust.org.uk/places/theworkhouse
• www.workhouses.org An on-line survey of the history, culture and background of the workhouse.
• booth.lse.ac.uk On-line archive of Charles Booth's survey into life and labour in late 19th-century London, including maps and original reports.

Fighting the great Victorian stink

Few of the thousands of people who stroll along the Victoria Embankment in central London each day are aware that they are walking over one of the great triumphs of Victorian engineering: the main trunk sewer for north London, part of the world's first fully co-ordinated, citywide sewage disposal system.

The Victorian cesspit crisis

By the mid 19th century, Britain's rapidly growing cities were in the grip of an unprecedented sanitation problem. Most had no real sewers at all; they relied on cesspits. Some houses had such pits in their basements. As they filled up, they saturated the brickwork, rotted the wood of the foundations, and sometimes seeped into the living space. The stench filled even well-to-do homes, and there were cases of entire families being asphyxiated in their sleep because of noxious gases in the air.

The carting of 'night soil' out into the countryside to fertilise the earth had almost ceased: urban sprawl had rendered farmland too far from town, and in any case farmers could now buy cheap, top-quality seabird manure, or *guano*, imported from South America. So domestic cesspits were often sluiced out onto the street, or emptied by hand a bucket at a time – a dreadful job frequently given to small children. All this left many large urban centres literally overflowing with human waste.

Joseph Bazalgette

During the hot summer of 1858, thousands of people fled London to escape 'the great stench'. Inside the House of Commons, right on the banks of the putrid River Thames, Members of Parliament debated the crisis, while sacks soaked in chloride of lime were hung from the windows to disinfect the suffocating air. The reek was so powerful that it almost became necessary to suspend Parliament. But the honourable Members did manage to come up with a solution by nominating the engineer Joseph Bazalgette to solve the problem.

The stink tsar's solution

Bazalgette was appointed the chief engineer to the Metropolitan Commission for Sewers – today we might call him a 'stink tsar'. He built two massive underground sewers – one for the north of London, one for the south. These 82 miles of pipework connected to all the hundreds of sewers that had previously discharged straight into the Thames. They also collected waste from the increasingly widespread 'water closets', pioneered by Thomas Crapper.

Construction of the main pipes took until 1865, causing a brick shortage that pushed up the price by a half. But when finished, Bazalgette's great tunnels were like two highways, carrying the city's effluent to twin pumping stations on either side of the river – at Abbey

THE "SILENT HIGHWAY"-MAN.
"Your MONEY or your LIFE!"

River of death In London, before the modern sewerage system was built, human and animal waste simply flowed down gutters or covered sewers into the Thames. The river itself became an open sewer, described by *Punch* magazine as a 'foul sludge and foetid stream', yet this was the main source of drinking water for London's poor.

Mills, near Stratford in east London, on the north side of the Thames, and at Crossness, near Abbey Wood, on the south. The Crossness reservoir held 27 million gallons of raw effluent, which was released twice a day at high tide into the ebbing water and carried far out to sea.

A masterpiece of design

The centrepieces of Bazalgette's project were the two central London embankments: Victoria on the north bank of the Thames and Albert on the south bank, named in honour of the Queen and her consort. They concealed the trunk sewers that served the two halves of the city, and also boxed in the river itself, which now could no longer wash up its filth on to the muddy foreshore. In a manner typical of Victorian efficiency, Victoria Embankment was also designed to accommodate tunnelling for London Underground's District Line, which was being built at the same time.

Bazalgette's success in the capital was to serve as a template for solving the sewage problems of a number of provincial cities. Over the next 30 years, similar projects were undertaken in Newcastle, Liverpool, Manchester and Bristol. Their salutory effect was dramatic: in the last big cholera outbreak of the 1840s, deaths across England from the disease reached a total of around 60,000; in 1893, just 135 were recorded.

Romanesque splendour Crossness Pumping Station may have been built to carry raw sewage as far from the streets of south London as possible, but the ornate iron-work in the Engine House (above) is more in keeping with a medieval palace. As well as this visual feast, visitors can marvel at the enormous size and intricacy of the four original engines, each one capable of pumping 6 tons of effluent with every stroke.

Multi-tasking By running his main sewers through embankments bordering the Thames (below), Bazalgette avoided digging up vast areas of the city to house them. He also created a site for new roads, walkways, gardens and even track for the growing underground railway (see tunnel '1' in a contemporary engraving below).

FIND OUT MORE

Look at these websites to find out more about Victorian solutions to sewage, along with design details of a wide variety of pumping stations and their engines.

● www.crossness.org.uk Covers the history and layout of Bazalgette's Crossness Pumping Station and the machinery that ran it, together with details of opening hours and notice of special events.
● www.leevalley-online.co.uk Has information on pumping stations along the Lee Valley Navigation Scheme, including the north Thames site Bazalgette built at Abbey Mills in east London.
● www.museumoftechnology.com Cambridge Museum of Technology – now housed in the town's old sewage pumping station – offers a clear, layman's guide to the developing technology that allowed the Victorians to revolutionise urban water supply and sewage disposal.
● www.leicestermuseums.ac.uk Serving as a general guide to Leicester's museums, the site includes details of the city's Abbey Pumping Station Museum, home to the 'Flushed with Pride' exhibition. This covers topics such as the history of plumbing, sewage control, laundry and the water supply from Roman times up to the present.
● www.claymills.org.uk The on-line tour of Claymills Pumping Station in Staffordshire feels almost as good as actually going there. Opening hours are also given.

Bringing power to the people

Public utilities were transformed in the course of the 19th century. Networks for street-lighting, gas and electricity supply, and long-distance communications were swiftly and seamlessly woven into the urban fabric. Together with the provision of a clean water supply, these innovations amounted to an almost miraculous improvement in the quality of town life.

Lighting the streets

Gas lamps were the first step towards lifting the murk of urban life. They had an immediately beneficial effect on crime because mugging and robbery became harder to commit once cities became much brighter at night. The first gas lamps were installed in Westminster in 1814. They were such a curiosity that crowds followed the lamplighters on their rounds. The lamplighters themselves were less enthusiastic, and at first refused to light the lamps for fear of explosions. But the fear and the novelty soon wore off, and within ten years gas-fuelled streetlights were commonplace: in 1823 there were 40,000 lamps in London, lighting 213 streets.

The first London lamps were powered by a gasworks built with private money. Other cities rushed to copy this business model, and gas companies sprang up in most substantial towns across Britain. Derby was typical: the first gas lamp in the town was lit on February 19, 1821, at the centre of the Market Place. It was described at the time as 'a beautiful column or rather candelabrum supporting a very handsome lantern'. The gas-producing works of the original Derby Gas Light and Coke Company were on Cavendish Street. Three small arches in front of the Derwent Housing Association are all that remain of that building, although the company's late-Victorian offices can still be seen on Friar Gate. Here, the company name is wrought high in the brickwork, and there is a clue in the name of the bar at street level: The Gaslight.

The long decline of the gas lamp began in the 1880s, when safer and more efficient electric lamps came into use. The obsolescent gas lamps, many of them highly ornate, were

Daily chore The lamplighter was a common sight in Victorian Britain. Despite the introduction of electricity, gas lamps were still in use on some city streets as late as the 1970s.

Driving force Power stations were erected throughout Britain to generate electricity for both industrial and domestic use. Lots Road power station (above) was built to supply London's District tube line with electricity in 1905. When it closed in 2002, the station still provided some 75 per cent of the power for the whole Underground network.

PICKING UP THE PHONE

The telephone, like the telegraph, was pioneered in the City of London, where the swift traffic of information was most highly prized. Britain's first telephone exchange opened at 36 Coleman Street in 1879: it had seven subscribers. Later in the year two more exchanges opened – at 101 Leadenhall Street and 3 Palace Chambers, Westminster – and the number of subscribers rose to 200.

This was the start of a telephonic 'Big Bang'. That same year, 1879, exchanges opened in Glasgow, Manchester, Liverpool, Sheffield, Edinburgh, Birmingham and Bristol. In 1880, the first trunk line was laid between Leeds and Bradford: now it was possible to make inter-city calls. London's first trunk link was with Brighton: it came into service in 1884.

In 1912, the Post Office installed the first automatic telephone exchange at 24 Station Road (now Upper High Street) in Epsom. The equipment was bought second-hand from Chicago, and was automatic in the sense that operators (always young women) were no longer required to make the connection with the recipient's phone.

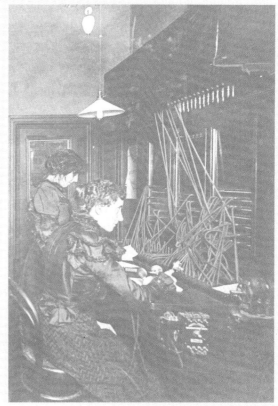

New connections The first General Post Office manual exchange opened in London in 1902; demand was so heavy that a second opened just a few months later. Female telephonists (right, 1905) operated the switchboard.

gradually replaced or converted to electricity. Some have been kept for decorative purposes, for example on the gates of Buckingham Palace in London.

The dawn of electricity

The 20th century was to be electric, and this superior form of energy required its own infrastructure. Electricity-generating power stations were built across the land, just as gas stations had been constructed a lifetime before.

The best surviving example of an early power station is Lots Road, on the Thames at Chelsea. It was built in 1902-5 to supply power to the newly electrified underground railway, and at the time was said to be the largest power plant in the world. Its generator hall was so enormous it was likened to the interior of a cathedral. Coal was delivered by barge to wharves where the chic Chelsea Harbour development now stands. Lots Road supplied electricity continuously for nearly a century. It was coal-fired until the 1960s when it was converted to oil and more recently to gas. At the time of its closure in 2002, it was the oldest – if no longer the largest – power station in the world.

FIND OUT MORE

• **Science Museum** The South Kensington, London, museum has galleries devoted to both telecommunications and power, with many exhibits relating to the advances made in the late 19th and early 20th centuries. www.sciencemuseum.org.uk
• **Milton Keynes Museum** The home of the Telephone Museum, featuring telephones, switchboards, exchanges and kiosks. www.mkmuseum.org.uk
• **Connected Earth** An on-line museum, founded by British Telecom, which tells the history of communication. www.connected-earth.com
• www.hampsteadscience.ac.uk/ article_Lots_Rd.htm Includes information on Lots Road power station in London.

Cities make way for the dead

You will find at least one municipal cemetery in any large British city. Most of them were founded in the 1850s in response to a serious civic crisis: the massive population explosion among the dead.

The first public cemeteries

Under common law, all citizens had a right to be buried in the churchyard of their home parish. But by the dawn of the Victorian era, far more people lived – and so were dying – in urban parishes, and churchyards were becoming seriously overcrowded.

The accumulation of dead bodies had serious consequences for the living: putrefaction in the earth was seeping out into the water supply. This led to frequent outbreaks of cholera, generating more deaths and yet more graves. Public cemeteries were established to deal with the overflow. One of the earliest urban cemeteries was built in Edinburgh at Calton Hill in the 1770s, but the first public cemetery was The Rosary in Norwich, which opened in 1819. Others soon followed in London, including Kensal Green (1827), Norwood (1837) and Highgate (1839).

The new cemeteries were commercial enterprises. Typically, a joint-stock company would be set up and the sale of shares would generate capital to buy land. The profit and the shareholders' dividend would come from the sale of plots to individuals, hard-pressed parish authorities and private organisations such as city guilds.

By the middle of the century the government had accepted that the ancient right to a church burial had to be rescinded. The Burial Act of 1852 enforced the closure of urban churchyards and opened the way to municipal cemeteries, which were neither the responsibility of the established church nor profit-making organisations.

A dignified resting place for the dead

The state-run necropolises suited those who thought it distasteful for a company to turn a profit on death. They also appealed to the growing numbers of middle-class dissenters from the Anglican faith, who had been burying their dead in non-church grounds. Many municipal cemeteries, such as Brookwood near Woking (see below), had two chapels: one for Anglicans and, at a distance, another for non-conformists. Some cemeteries set aside areas for Catholics. Jews usually conducted their death rites in cemeteries of their own, although West Ham cemetery has a walled Jewish section, housing a Rothschild family mausoleum.

The design of urban cemeteries owed much to the work of John Claudius Loudon. He was editor of *Gardeners' Magazine*, and in 1843 he published an influential book, *On the Laying Out, Planting and Managing of Cemeteries*. He greatly admired Père-Lachaise, in Paris, where the cemetery is landscaped and planted to create secluded

ALL ABOARD FOR THE ONE-WAY RIDE TO THE HEREAFTER

Most municipal cemeteries were built on the edge of town, but Brookwood Cemetery, near Woking in Surrey, is an immense and glorious exception. It was conceived in 1850 as the public cemetery for London. Two thousand acres of land were purchased – enough, it was thought, to accommodate all London's dead for ever after. The cemetery opened in November, 1854. At the time it was the largest in the world. The only convenient way to reach it was by rail. A special service ran from a Necropolis terminus next to Waterloo (the building still stands, at 121 Westminster Bridge Road). There were two stations inside Brookwood Cemetery, one serving the Anglican plots and the other the non-conformist. The train had a hearse carriage, as the deceased, the mourners and the undertakers all travelled together. The service ran until 1941, when the London platform was destroyed by bombing. But the cemetery survives, so large that it feels more like a tract of open country than a burial ground.

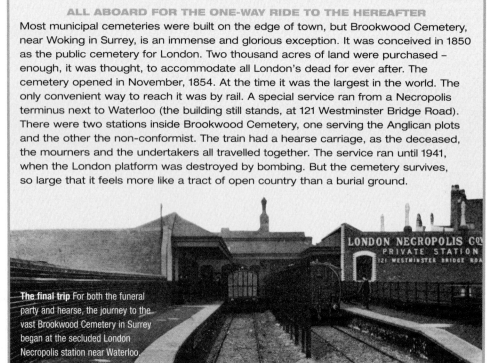

The final trip For both the funeral party and hearse, the journey to the vast Brookwood Cemetery in Surrey began at the secluded London Necropolis station near Waterloo.

DID YOU KNOW?

The overcrowding of graves in churchyards required that dead were piled upon dead in the same plot, with the result that the ground level rose like an incoming tide. This is why many ancient churches appear to be sited in a hollow at the centre of their churchyard.

ASHES TO ASHES

There was a growing interest in the ancient practice of cremation in the 19th century, partly because of the practical concern for public health: many cemeteries were located in congested urban areas close to sources of drinking water, which led to frequent outbreaks of cholera. Cremation was legalised in 1885 and the first official service was that of Mrs Jeanette C. Pickersgill in Woking, Surrey, in the same year. In the 1890s crematoria were built in Liverpool, Manchester and Glasgow, but one of the grandest is that at Golders Green in London, built in 1902.

A mark of respect The magnificent Necropolis in Glasgow, established in 1833, contains monuments which tended to the abstract and the classical and away from the Christian symbolism common in churchyards. Often the best architects of the age were commissioned to design an edifice that reflected the deceased's position in society.

corners and inspiring vistas. Loudon was also concerned with the sanitary aspects of design. He recommended that cemeteries be sited on the south slopes of hills (as is the case with the Glasgow Necropolis – see right) so that the ground could be dried by the sun. Water-loving trees such as weeping willows were to be avoided, as were deciduous trees that cast wide shadows and kept the ground damp. Yews, cypresses and evergreens would, he felt, serve the interests both of solemnity and of hygiene.

The new cemeteries chimed with the aspirational spirit of the age: they provided the space and the opportunity for the Victorians to express their social status, even in death. They exactly reflected the hierarchy and organisation of a living city: the most prestigious and expensive plots were near to the central chapel or the main highways, where the bigger the monument, the greater the man. In the 'suburbs' were the 'guinea graves' paid for by families who could scrape together the 21 shillings for a plot and a name plaque. On the outer edges were the 'slums': mass graves where the anonymous poor were buried 30 at a time.

A grand way to go Boy hero Albert Habwell's funeral procession in 1914 was typical of the era's penchant for solemnity and ostentatious display of wealth in the manner of the 19th-century Victorians. You may be able to find old photographs showing how funerals were conducted in your community.

FIND OUT MORE

● www.cemeteryfriends.fsnet.co.uk
The National Federation of Cemetery Friends offers information on Victorian cemeteries.
● www.mausolea-monuments.org.uk
The Mausolea and Monuments Trust provides details of selected monuments.
● www2.jewishgen.org/cemetery
A comprehensive list of Jewish cemeteries in Britain.

A vision of green cities

By the late 19th century, cities were growing at an unprecedented rate, their people deprived of the benefits of contact with the countryside. The problem of over-blown urban centres became a focus for reformers. One, Ebenezer Howard, offered a solution that was to have a lasting effect on British town planning.

An urban utopia

Unlike proposals put forward by many of his fellow reformers, Ebenezer Howard's plans for reuniting workers with England's 'green and pleasant land' were highly practical. In 1898, he published a book – optimistically entitled *Tomorrow* – which was a blueprint for creating small, self-sufficient urban communities.

These 'garden cities', as he called them, would be no more than a mile wide, with inhabitants able to walk out of town into the surrounding country, and also to their place of work. As well as being economically self-sufficient, such towns would provide a market place for rural communities round and about. The town would benefit from being set in the country, and the country would benefit from the town.

Howard had rich, influential friends, and in 1903 he was given the chance to put his ideas into practice when he founded the garden city of Letchworth in Hertfordshire. It was an almost immediate success. People queued up to go and live there and manufacturers, such as the Spirella Corset Company, were persuaded to set up new

factories on an industrial estate – a novelty at the time – and so provide work for the inhabitants. Letchworth Garden City took root and flourished.

The garden-suburb experiment

Letchworth's success led to the garden-city concept being adapted to an established urban setting. Land north of Hampstead Heath in London was bought by the philanthropist Henrietta Barnett and it was there, from 1907, that the architects Raymond Unwin and Barry Parker built Hampstead Garden Suburb. Inhabitants could get to work in central London on the new underground trains, so it was never designed to be self-sufficient. But it was a model suburb. Unwin is credited with inventing the cul-de-sac: a road that goes nowhere.

The garden-cities movement continued between the wars. A new community was founded at Welwyn in 1920. But the Second World War halted its growth, and afterwards the idea of building ideal towns from scratch re-emerged in a more down-to-earth and less rustic form: new towns.

The birth of new towns

In 1946, the government authorised the planting of a series of satellite towns around London, sited at Basildon, Bracknell, Crawley, Harlow, Hatfield, Hemel Hempstead and Stevenage. Like the garden cities, they were to be small, self-contained and surrounded by green fields. But their immediate aim was to replace

LETCHWORTH HOUSING EXHIBITION 1907
COTTAGES – TYPES 1 no 3   H. CLAPHAM LANDER.
A.R.I.B.A. – ARCHITECT
LONDON & LETCHWORTH

Town meets rural idyll The houses built in 1913 around the village green-like Norton Common in Letchworth reflect an idealised vision of country life. The original design brief was to provide workers with quality homes in a healthy setting at an affordable price. Although styled as 'cottages', their interior layouts (see plans for a typical dwelling, above) owe little to the similarly labelled houses of most country folk of the time, and their £200-plus price tags were better matched to the more middle-class pocket.

LETCHWORTH'S HIPPY TRAIL

The first inhabitants of the pioneering garden city of Letchworth were as idealistic as Howard himself. Many were enthusiastic supporters of the Arts and Crafts Movement: what one might call Edwardian hippies. The town had the feel of a commune and was the butt of many jokes as a result. People came on day-trips from London to snigger at the teetotal pub, the smock-wearing potters, the pipe-smoking feminists and the open-air theosophical school.

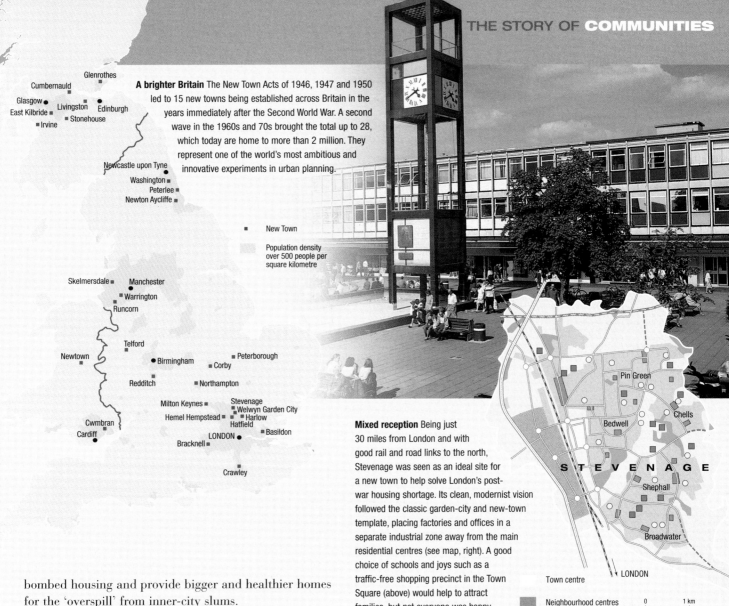

A brighter Britain The New Town Acts of 1946, 1947 and 1950 led to 15 new towns being established across Britain in the years immediately after the Second World War. A second wave in the 1960s and 70s brought the total up to 28, which today are home to more than 2 million. They represent one of the world's most ambitious and innovative experiments in urban planning.

- New Town

Population density over 500 people per square kilometre

Mixed reception Being just 30 miles from London and with good rail and road links to the north, Stevenage was seen as an ideal site for a new town to help solve London's post-war housing shortage. Its clean, modernist vision followed the classic garden-city and new-town template, placing factories and offices in a separate industrial zone away from the main residential centres (see map, right). A good choice of schools and joys such as a traffic-free shopping precinct in the Town Square (above) would help to attract families, but not everyone was happy. Some old-town residents were strongly opposed to the redevelopment. They even appealed to the House of Lords to try to stop it from going ahead.

Town centre

Neighbourhood centres

Residential areas

Industrial areas ○ Primary schools

Woodland areas ■ Secondary schools

0   1 km
0   1 mile

bombed housing and provide bigger and healthier homes for the 'overspill' from inner-city slums.

At first the new towns were highly popular and generally regarded as a huge success. More were built in the Midlands and the north of England: at Corby, to house steelworkers, and at Telford, Runcorn, Washington and Warrington. But as people became used to their comfort and convenience, many came to be seen as soulless places, lacking any sense of history, and full of drab, characterless housing. Yet the new towns were a source of many innovations. They pioneered pedestrianised city centres and cycle paths – not because the planners were ecologically minded, but because they grossly underestimated the growth in use of the motor car.

Continuing the vision

A second wave of new towns, built in the 1960s and 70s, were conceived to preserve Howard's vision. At Cumbernauld near Glasgow homes were set on slopes to give every citizen a view of the hills beyond. But at Milton Keynes, Buckinghamshire, the striving for connection with the countryside took on a form that provoked much mirth and even derision: lifelike glass fibre cows in the fields.

A fresh start A family, probably in search of an escape from the war-torn inner city, inspects the first batch of houses built at Crawley in Sussex (below), the only new town to be constructed south of London. Work began there in 1947.

A brave new world of suburban homes

After the devastating experience of the First World War, the government committed itself to creating 'homes fit for heroes', offering basic amenities such as baths, indoor toilets and gardens. You can see the results in the sprawling public housing estates of the inter-war years, and their middle-class cousins, the semi-detached 'Tudorbethan' houses and wide leafy avenues that surround so many of Britain's towns and cities today.

On the home front Town planning, mortgages and the problems of slums were hot topics after the First World War, and formed the subject of a book by Richard Reiss, *The Home I Want* (1919). People were encouraged to buy their own property, which became a reality for many thanks to the mortgage loans provided by building societies such as Abbey Road (left). In 1944 Abbey Road merged with the National to become Abbey National.

Better, cheaper, sunnier

At the end of the First World War, a committee was set up under Sir Tudor Walters to consider what a home fit for a hero might look like. His report recommended that these homes be as different from the slums and tenements of the late-Victorian era as possible: there were to be no more than 12 houses to an acre of land; they all must have a bath, an indoor toilet, a larder and a coal store.

In addition to the legal requirements, there were budgetary constraints set by the builders. The homes had to be two storeys high, because bungalows were wasteful of space and three-storey houses were inconvenient in a world without domestic servants.

Terraces were out of fashion – too close together, too urban – but, on the other hand, detached houses were too expensive to build and to buy. The ubiquitous compromise was the semi-detached house. It was economical for the builder; it afforded a reasonable amount of privacy to each house; and it allowed tradesmen easy access to the coal bunker in the back garden. Both local authorities and speculators, encouraged by a series of Housing Acts, set about building entire suburbs to these specifications. There was also a requirement – laid down in a government document of 1919 entitled

the *Housing Manual* – that the streets be wide enough for the sun to penetrate the lower windows even in winter. Given the average height of a two-storey home, and the angle of the sun at noon on Christmas Day, a road would have to be 21m (70ft) wide to keep the sitting-room windows on one side of the street out of the shadow of the house opposite. Accordingly, wherever semis were built, the streets were always 70ft wide – no more, no less.

Green and pleasant streets

The pavement and carriageway in these suburbs were designed to suggest a rustic idyll. Everybody wanted to live in a tree-lined avenue, but English forest species were too large to line a suburban street – they would block out all that carefully engineered daylight, and eventually undermine the foundations. So planners took advantage of the work of Victorian botanists and planted trees such as Japanese flowering cherries. These were manageably small, and they looked striking in springtime.

The suburban trees were sited in strips of green that ran between the grey pavements and the grey roadway like piping on a bandsman's trousers. The providers of electric and telephone cables soon realised that it was much easier to dig up grass than paving

> **DID YOU KNOW?**
>
> There were about 13 million homes in Britain at the outbreak of the Second World War. Of these, 35 per cent – 4.5 million – had been built in the preceding 20 years.

The largest housing estate in the world

Many of the new interwar houses in Britain were built by local authorities for working-class families. The most ambitious of these schemes was the Becontree Estate built by the London County Council at Dagenham, near Ilford in Essex. It was called a 'cottage estate', a euphemistic way of saying that the houses were smaller and less upmarket than the speculative 'Tudorbethan' suburbs. But the estate as a whole was, and is, vast.

Between 1921 and 1932, 25,000 homes were built on land compulsorily purchased from Essex farmers. The estate was in effect an entire town of more than 100,000 people. All the homes had front and back gardens, and were provided with gas and electricity. In return for a home in this redbrick paradise, residents were expected to obey the council's rules on keeping their gardens tidy and their pets and children under control.

The Becontree experiment was repeated in other cities. Notable examples include the Wollaton Park Estate in Nottingham which, in a fanciful touch, was laid out like a huge cartwheel with a little park at the hub.

Going upmarket More than half a million homes were built in the ten years after the First World War. The typically tidy terraces on the Becontree Estate (above, Valence Circus, 1945, and right, 2004) offered all mod cons for working-class families.

There was also Wythenshawe, a kind of dormitory town for the workers of Manchester; and there was Speke, which performed the same function for Liverpool. But none of the provincial projects compared in scale to Becontree. It is now an Essex borough in its own right, and remains the largest housing estate in Britain – indeed in the whole world.

stones, and their workmen made good use of the green verge. Consequently, over the decades, verges tended to grow wider while pavements narrowed.

New Tudor England

The design of the houses themselves came from builders' pattern books which were published in regular editions, like magazines. The prevailing fashion was for houses that had a whiff of Olde England about them, homes that harked back to an idealised age where horrors such as the Somme were unknown. This nostalgic impulse led to the familiar 'Tudorbethan' villa (see page 286). The mock-Tudor, half-timbered effect was simple to achieve. All it took was for the builder to nail black-painted floorboards to the gable ends of the finished house. Some builders were inventive enough to nail a different pattern of boards on conjoining houses, just to give them a dash of individuality. This kind of touch was important to the potential purchasers: middle-class family men who commuted to an office in the city and read the novels of Walter Scott in the train on the way home. In the building boom of the 1920s, hundreds of thousands of houses were built to suit that particular taste. They were, in fact, homes fit for bank managers to live in.

The growth of the London Underground

Around the turn of the 20th century, the lines of the London Underground were electrified one by one. Electric trains were quieter than steam trains and could accelerate and come to a stop much more quickly, so they could zip between stations, loading and unloading their human freight with the minimum of delay. They were the perfect means of transport for busy Londoners in a hurry.

Digging deep

The electrification of London's underground railway system coincided with the invention of new tunnelling technology. There were now machines that could burrow at a deep level through the heavy clay of the London Basin, north of the Thames. Such advances led to a renewed round of speculative railway construction. The Northern Line pushed on as far as Edgware, where, in 1924, a station was planted in the virgin meadowland. The expansion of the network triggered the growth of suburbia, with rows of houses and shops rapidly springing up along the creeping tendrils of new track. Most of the growth was confined to the north of the river, as nearly all of south London sits on a vast water-logged aquifer unsuitable for tunnelling.

The wonders of Metroland

The Metropolitan Line, like the Northern, spread briskly outwards. It, more than any other line, opened up access between central London and its suburbs, helping to establish the daily ritual of the commute into town. The high priest of this rite was the poet John Betjeman. He sang the praises of the trains, the people who used them and the places where they lived, calling this genteel world Metroland:

Gaily into Ruislip Gardens
Runs the red electric train,
With a thousand Ta's and Pardon's
Daintily alights Elaine;
Hurries down the concrete station
With a frown of concentration,
Out into the outskirt's edges
Where a few surviving hedges
Keep alive our lost Elysium – rural Middlesex again.

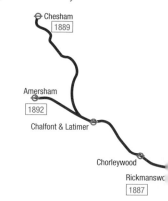

Chesham 1889
Amersham 1892
Chalfont & Latimer
Chorleywood
Rickmansworth 1887
Uxbridge 1904

ART DECO FLIGHTS OF FANCY

During the era of rapid expansion of the network, the directors of the London Underground went to great lengths to ensure that new stations and ticket halls were objects of architectural worth. In the 1920s, Charles Holden was commissioned to design all the stations at the northern extremity of the Piccadilly Line. He created a series of astonishing Art Deco fantasies. The ticket hall of Arnos Grove (below) looks like a Martian mothership from a Flash Gordon serial, while Southgate, one stop up the line, features an exuberant Deco lampost outside and a stunning row of elegant chrome uplighters within, running alongside the escalators.

There was also a plan to give the trains a gleaming Art-Deco look as well. Three sharp-nosed, streamlined vehicles were built, but they were expensive and soon dropped in favour of the familiar flat-faced cabs introduced in 1938.

UNDERGROUND

Ruislip Village and all around lie the quiet fields and lanes

BOOK TO RUISLIP

Cheap Return Tickets on Sundays

Route to a healthier life The extension of London's underground railway into the leafy suburbs and beyond in the early part of the 20th century made it possible for people to work in the heart of the City yet live in a cleaner, greener setting. It also offered to those stuck in the overcrowded inner-city cheap, easy access to the countryside, as was trumpeted by contemporary posters (left).

▬▬	Bakerloo Line
▬▬	Central Line
▬▬	Circle Line
▬▬	District Line
▬▬	Hammersmith & City Line
▬▬	Jubilee Line
▬▬	Metropolitan Line
▬▬	Northern Line
▬▬	Piccadilly Line
▬▬	Victoria Line

Pioneer commuters The world's first deep-level 'tube' railway opened in 1890 to ferry workers from Stockwell in south London to its City terminus at King William Street (left). The station closed in 1900, when the line was extended to a more accessible site at Moorgate Street.

Bomb shelters

The Second World War brought work on the Underground to a halt. But during the war years the network was put to novel uses. Deep stations such as Elephant and Castle were often turned into underground dormitories where people could shelter from the bombs. Empty stations were used as command centres (see 'Forgotten stations', right) and a new stretch of tunnel between Redbridge and Gants Hill, on the Central Line, was even transformed into an aircraft factory.

A new phase of expansion began once the post-war reconstruction of Britain was complete. The first section of the Victoria Line, cutting a swathe across the network from northeast to southwest, was opened in 1969. The Jubilee Line entered into service in 1979 and, in the 1990s, was extended into the rejuvenated dockland area of East London. The centrepiece of this grand project is Canary Wharf station. Its cavernous hall was built on an immense barge, floated into position and then deliberately scuppered – the latest in a long tradition of engineering feats to have shaped London's subterranean railway.

Forgotten stations

There are more than 40 abandoned stations on London's underground rail network. The different lines were once run by rival companies that built competing stations close together. Consolidation of the system, from around 1907, led to one or other becoming redundant.

Evidence of these stations is everywhere. Just north of King's Cross you can still see the familiar arches and red tiling of York Road station, which closed in 1932. If you look out of the window between Tottenham Court Road and Holborn on the Central Line, you will spot a ghost station called British Museum, where no-one has alighted for 70 years. Near Hyde Park Corner there is an abandoned station called Down Street, which served as a secret bunker for Winston Churchill and his Cabinet during the Second World War. Close by is the former entrance to Knightsbridge station, now incorporated into the front of the Pizza-on-the-Park restaurant (above, right). And around the corner from Harrods lies another defunct station with a distinguished wartime record: Brompton Road was used as an anti-aircraft control centre.

FIND OUT MORE

For more information on the London Underground, visit London's Transport Museum, Covent Garden Piazza, London WC2E 7BB (Tel. 020 7565 7299) or log on to:
• www.fact-index.com/l/lo/london_underground.html
Websites on abandoned stations include:
• www.starfury.demon.co.uk/uground
• www.pendar.pwp.blueyonder.co.uk/Tube

Mapping out commuterland As the underground railway pushed farther out into the suburbs, clear mapping of the system became crucial. Attempts based on real positions and distances (below) could be confusing. But in 1931, engineer Harry Beck offered a more practical solution: the now familiar 'circuit diagram' map based on what travellers really needed to know – how lines and stations link up.

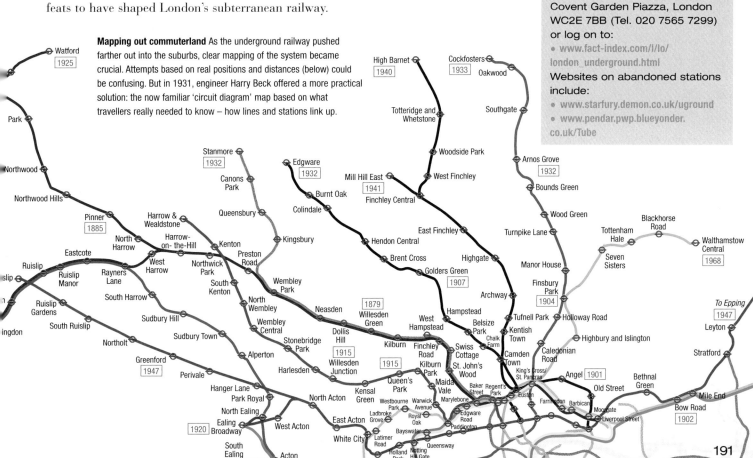

The march of the moving image

Since its arrival in the late 19th century, the medium of cinema has managed to keep pace with myriad changes in taste and fashion. 'Picture palaces' from each decade survive as evidence of the rise, fall and rise again of a characteristic 20th-century night out. Those of the 1920s and 30s can still make heads turn with their exotic Art Deco designs, inside and out.

Entertainment for the price of a sandwich

The first moving pictures to be seen in Britain were shown at the end of the 19th century in music halls or the upstairs room of camera shops. The nitrate film stock was highly flammable, and there were several fatal fires during film shows, which led to the passing of the Cinematograph Act in 1909. This law required that these new-fangled entertainments be shown in buildings specially constructed for the purpose.

You can spot a former cinema from the detailing, such as the Egyptian-style motifs on the Carlton in Essex Road, Islington, north London, built in 1930. It is now a bingo hall.

The first known purpose-built cinema in Britain predates the 1909 law. It is believed to have been the Central Hall at Colne in Lancashire, now long gone. Many picture houses were built in the years up to 1914. Most had a capacity of just 200-300 seats. But in the hedonistic 1920s, picture houses evolved into vast, opulent buildings. They were themed to look like Roman villas (The Ambassador, Salford), or Egyptian pyramids (The Empress, Miles Platting, Manchester). The show was equally sumptuous: cartoons, comedy shorts and newsreels, interspersed with orchestral performances, dancing girls and levitating Wurlitzers – 'all for the price of a sandwich', as one cinema advertisement proclaimed.

Decline and fall

The heyday of the 'supers' came to an end in the 1930s. Films were becoming more sophisticated and interesting in their own right – due largely to the advent of 'talkies' – so the extra entertainments became redundant. The new cinemas adapted accordingly. Art Deco cinemas built in

Visual impact Many a 1920s' and 30s' Art Deco cinema grace Britain's towns and cities. You can spot them by the ship-like styling, and bold geometric shapes. They were brightly illuminated with neon lights. The Odeon Cinema in London Road, Isleworth, west London (above), was designed by the architect George Coles in 1935. Today, its tower and façade front a modern development of flats, shops and offices.

New for old Even small country towns had at least one cinema. Many have been converted: the 1935 Regal in Wells, Somerset (above), is now a nightclub.

the 1930s, such as the striking Roxy in Stretford, Manchester, were once again quite small affairs. They slotted comfortably into high streets. The fact that these latest cinemas were in prime retail territory led in the end to their demise. In the 1960s and 70s, when television took away their audiences, many of the high-street cinemas were converted into shops or bingo halls, or were left to rot.

Forgotten picture houses

When the bingo craze faded, these buildings were sold to developers and pub chains. The Coronation Cinema House in Surbiton, Surrey, is one such example. It opened in 1911, on the day George V was crowned. It closed in 1966, became a bingo hall and, for a while, looked as if it might house a naturists' club. When it was bought by the pub chain J D Wetherspoons, it was given something like its original name: The Coronation Hall. The Roman-themed Grosvenor Picture Palace in Manchester went

through a similar set of changes: closure in the 1960s, then bingo hall and pub. It was taken on by the Firkin chain, which has the tradition of giving every pub an apt name beginning with the letter F, and so it is now known as the Footage and Firkin.

A fresh start

At the start of the 1980s it appeared that television was about to kill off cinema completely. A ticket to see a film cost far more than the nightly rate for hiring a video, and converted 'multi-screen' venues were not attracting audiences.

But the cinema was saved by technology, and by the films themselves. Blockbusters such as *Star Wars*, which hit the screens in 1977, were better seen on a huge screen with mighty speakers in every corner to swamp the senses. New cinemas, such as the iMax in London, were built to make the most of audio and special effects techniques – and of the digital technology that came on its heels – to thrill, excite and scare the daylights out of the audience.

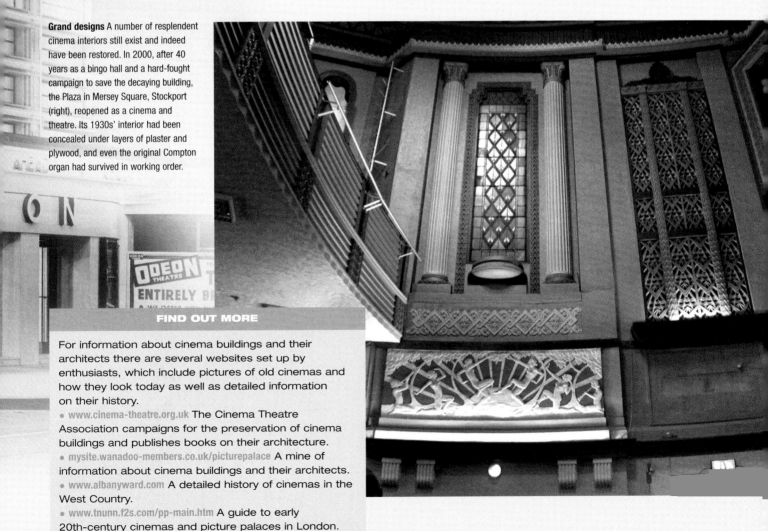

Grand designs A number of resplendent cinema interiors still exist and indeed have been restored. In 2000, after 40 years as a bingo hall and a hard-fought campaign to save the decaying building, the Plaza in Mersey Square, Stockport (right), reopened as a cinema and theatre. Its 1930s' interior had been concealed under layers of plaster and plywood, and even the original Compton organ had survived in working order.

FIND OUT MORE

For information about cinema buildings and their architects there are several websites set up by enthusiasts, which include pictures of old cinemas and how they look today as well as detailed information on their history.
• www.cinema-theatre.org.uk The Cinema Theatre Association campaigns for the preservation of cinema buildings and publishes books on their architecture.
• mysite.wanadoo-members.co.uk/picturepalace A mine of information about cinema buildings and their architects.
• www.albanyward.com A detailed history of cinemas in the West Country.
• www.tnunn.f2s.com/pp-main.htm A guide to early 20th-century cinemas and picture palaces in London.

Communities adapt to the loss of heavy industry

By the outbreak of the First World War, Britain's workhorse industries – coal, steel and shipbuilding – were as wheezy and weary as ageing pit ponies. The story of the nation's colliery towns, shipyards and foundries in the 20th century is a sorry one – a tale of long and sometimes painful decline.

Depression hits hard

Early in the 1920s, after a brief post-war boom, Britain descended into a deep economic slump. At Christmas 1920 more than a million men – most of them ex-servicemen – were unemployed. Many workers in the biggest industries were given extended Christmas holidays and never asked back.

Industry recovered from this wasting disease, but only temporarily: the Great Depression of the 1930s was a serious relapse. The effect of these convulsions was devastating. In many parts of industrial Britain, whole towns depended on the local factory for employment, and in the valleys of south Wales, almost all villages had a colliery (see pages 78-79). If it closed, every wage earner was put out of work at once. For whole communities, there was suddenly no money coming in, and no prospect of any money ever coming in again.

Faced with this hopeless future, thousands of families abandoned their homes and moved south. About half a million people quit Wales and the northeast of England in the 1930s, and many of them were drawn into the gravitational pull of London.

Protest march In 1936, 200 men from the northeast town of Jarrow caused a stir when they walked the length of England to present a petition to Parliament. Their shipyard had been closed down and they wanted the government to reopen it. Although their demands were not met, the Jarrow men raised public awareness and sympathy for their plight.

Coming up with the goods From Plymouth to Edinburgh in the first half of the 20th century, a web of heavy manufacturing industry could be traced across Britain. Some centres of activity survive, such as car making in the Midlands, but much has disappeared, changing the face of many communities for good.

A new approach

To stem this population drain, the government planted new factories in depressed areas. They were called 'trading estates', and they were designed to provide work in the newer, lighter manufacturing industries. Where once men had poured steel, they would now crank out pots and pans.

The first state-run trading estates were the Team Valley Estate near Gateshead in Tyne & Wear, the Hillington Estate in Glasgow, and the Treforest Estate near Pontypridd. They were the start of the move away from heavy industry and towards light and service industry that continues today.

Prime location American investors in Britain wanted to base their operations near London, the greatest market of all. In the 1930s the dollar financed the industrial development of the Great West Road out of London, including the Gillette Factory (left), with its impressive clock tower. Once the line of communication was established, light industry continued westwards, peeling out along the M4 in a kind of ribbon development towards Reading and then on to Swindon.

once the war and the reconstruction were over, the debilitating decline set in once more. It was becoming increasingly costly to get coal out of the ground even though, in 1962, it was estimated that there were enough reserves in the British Isles to last for 750 years.

Coal production was concentrated in the deeper coal fields of Yorkshire, Derbyshire, Nottinghamshire and Durham, a sentence of death for the pits of south Wales. The valley collieries closed one by one, and now they are nearly all gone. The shafts have been filled and the pitheads cleared away. Many of the slagheaps have been levelled, and the ones that remain have been grassed over so that they look like green pyramids or barrows in the landscape. The same fate befell the English mines after the strike of the 1980s. There were more than a million miners in Britain at the end of the Second World War; now there are about 25,000.

The decline of the shipbuilding industry was equally spectacular. On the eve of the First World War, Britain produced more ships than the whole of the rest of the world – by 1980 its market share was 1 per cent. The war took its toll on the industry's resources, followed by the devastation of the 1930s economic recession. Then after the Second World War a lack of investment and modernisation allowed developing countries such as South Korea, with their cheaper labour, more advanced technology and bigger dry docks, to take much of the business. In the 1950s it became clear that the shipyards of the Clyde could not survive. There were two big spates of closures, one in the 1960s and another in the 80s. The 23 shipyards operating at the end of the Second World War are now reduced to three.

Much of Britain's heavy industry was hamstrung by a dependence on an infrastructure set up by the Victorians. They had become dinosaurs, and for many of them, when their time came, there was nothing for it but to die out.

Echoes of an industrial past Redundant cranes, once employed in the Clyde shipbuilding industry, form an imposing backdrop to a flotilla of yachts taking part in the 2003 Fife Regatta race around Cumbrae Island in the Clyde river estuary.

But trading estates were not a government idea. The first empty factory shells had been built by speculators in the 1920s, just as houses were at that time. The speculators knew that manufacturers would be happy to buy space on an estate near to the markets of a big city. And the establishment of the National Grid (see pages 88-89) meant that these industries were 'footloose', that is, they could be placed anywhere. You did not have to site your business close to a coalfield when electricity was now brought right to your door.

End of the line for heavy industry

The Second World War temporarily halted the erosion of heavy industry: while Britain was under siege, it had to turn to its own resources to make guns and warships. But

The scars of two world wars

Of all the forces that have changed Britain's cities, none has been less predictable and more radical than the bombs dropped by German aircraft. Most damage was caused by the bombardments of the Second World War but the first air-raids on Britain took place in the Great War of 1914-18.

Terror from the skies

As early as 1915, Zeppelin airships bombed King's Lynn and Great Yarmouth on the Norfolk coast. Other places soon followed, including London, Gravesend, Sunderland and Edinburgh. By 1917, Germany was using the faster, more deadly Gotha G-V planes for airstrikes. In May, 95 people were killed in an attack on Folkestone, but the capital remained the prime target. During the summer of 1917, around 150 Londoners were killed and about 400 injured by bombs dropped from planes. Such random attacks on non-military targets were seen in Britain as utterly barbaric. You may spot the odd plaque, such as that on 61 Farringdon Road, opposite Smithfield Market in the City of London, marking the destruction caused by this new and terrifying method of waging war.

Blitzed to oblivion

Bomb damage in the Second World War was far too widespread to be commemorated on individual buildings. Nearly every town and city, particularly the major ports and industrial centres such as Manchester, Liverpool, Birmingham, Bristol, Coventry (see below), Glasgow, Cardiff and Swansea, has its own tale of destruction to tell. During the 'Christmas raids' of 1940, railway arches being used as a shelter in central Liverpool took a direct hit, killing 42. A three-night blitz on Swansea in February 1941 obliterated the town centre, leaving more than 500 dead or injured. A marked lack of pre-war housing in your town may indicate that it too was reduced to rubble.

Striking at the nation's heart

From September 1940 to May 1941, London was the enemy's main target. Germany's aim was to crush national morale and hence hasten surrender. A total of 13,000 tons of explosives and one million tons of incendiaries was dropped, causing damage so extensive that it took more than 50 years to repair. The distinguishing feature of Aldersgate Street in the 1950s was a mountain of debris brought from bombed-out spots around the City and dumped there. As late as the 1970s, office workers parked their cars in exposed cellars, overgrown with willow herb.

A heritage erased Before the Second World War, Bristol and Coventry had many fine buildings, some dating back to medieval times. Both were also centres for the aircraft industry, making them prime targets for enemy bombardment. In November 1940, the historic heart of each city was almost totally obliterated. A map of modern-day Bristol showing where bombs fell (below) gives a clear picture of the level of destruction, as do contemporary photographs of Coventry's war-torn streets (right).

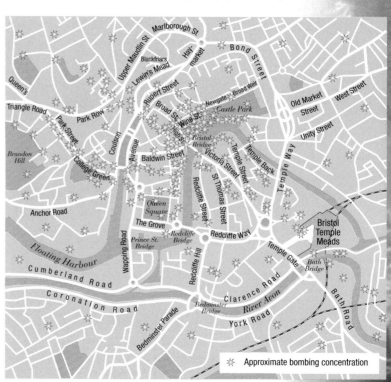

✳ Approximate bombing concentration

Public warning In 1915, posters were issued to help British civilians distinguish between their own and enemy aircraft from the ground. But the success of such measures was to prove limited, as Germany retaliated by mainly flying under the cover of darkness. By 1918, more than 830 people had been reported killed in air raids and around 1990 injured.

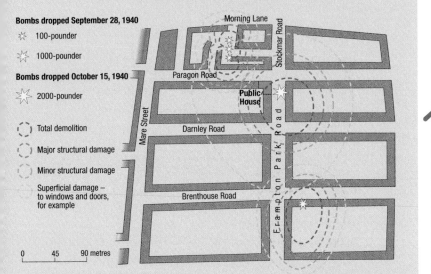

Bombs dropped September 28, 1940

☼ 100-pounder

☼ 1000-pounder

Bombs dropped October 15, 1940

☆ 2000-pounder

◌ Total demolition

◌ Major structural damage

◌ Minor structural damage

Superficial damage –
to windows and doors,
for example

0   45   90 metres

Morning Lane

Stockmar Road

Paragon Road

Public House

Mare Street

Frampton Park Road

Darnley Road

Brenthouse Road

East End bombardment When the Second World War broke out, the streets shown above in Hackney, east London, were lined with substantially built, Victorian terraced houses. During the night of September 28, 1940, a stack of three 100-pounder bombs and a single 1000-pounder fell on the area. A larger bomb, a single 2000-pounder ('land mine'), was dropped on the night of October 15. The circles of destruction shown on the map indicate the damage caused. Thirteen people died as a result of these two actions and around 2000 were made homeless.

Tell-tale signs of war Most bombsites may now have been built over, but there are still many other visible relics of enemy air-raids.

🔍 **A row of 1960s houses,** probably just two or three, looking utterly incongruous between terraces of Victorian dwellings, is likely to be an indication of wartime bomb damage. The original homes on the site were probably destroyed by enemy action, their replacements being part of the process of post-war regeneration that took place right across Britain.

🔍 **Defensive pillboxes** can be seen in many places: the narrow gun slits on their exteriors are a clear clue as to their original purpose. Built in a hurry when a German invasion was expected, many are positioned in clusters around strategic points such as railways and airfields. Any RAF base that was functional in the war years is likely to have some nearby. A clutch of them lies on the approach to RAF Mildenhall in Suffolk. And a set of five keeps a beady eye on the train track near Newmarket, just south of RAF Snailwell.

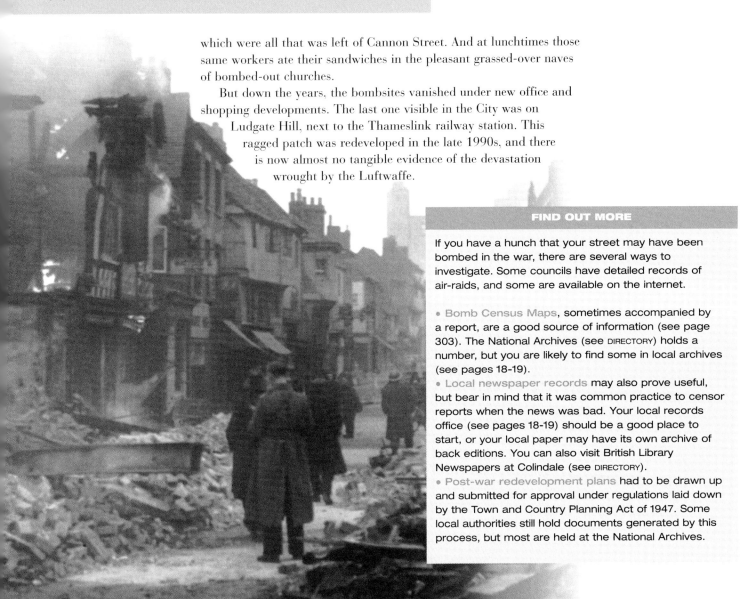

which were all that was left of Cannon Street. And at lunchtimes those same workers ate their sandwiches in the pleasant grassed-over naves of bombed-out churches.

But down the years, the bombsites vanished under new office and shopping developments. The last one visible in the City was on Ludgate Hill, next to the Thameslink railway station. This ragged patch was redeveloped in the late 1990s, and there is now almost no tangible evidence of the devastation wrought by the Luftwaffe.

FIND OUT MORE

If you have a hunch that your street may have been bombed in the war, there are several ways to investigate. Some councils have detailed records of air-raids, and some are available on the internet.

● **Bomb Census Maps**, sometimes accompanied by a report, are a good source of information (see page 303). The National Archives (see DIRECTORY) holds a number, but you are likely to find some in local archives (see pages 18-19).

● **Local newspaper records** may also prove useful, but bear in mind that it was common practice to censor reports when the news was bad. Your local records office (see pages 18-19) should be a good place to start, or your local paper may have its own archive of back editions. You can also visit British Library Newspapers at Colindale (see DIRECTORY).

● **Post-war redevelopment plans** had to be drawn up and submitted for approval under regulations laid down by the Town and Country Planning Act of 1947. Some local authorities still hold documents generated by this process, but most are held at the National Archives.

Building homes for a brave new world

Enemy bombing in the Second World War destroyed around 200,000 homes in Britain and rendered another quarter of a million uninhabitable. Many of these were in run-down inner city areas, so unintentionally the bombers speeded up the job of slum clearance. But come the peace, planners were faced with an accute shortage of housing: about 750,000 new homes were needed, and fast.

Hi-rise experiments The soaring 31-storey blocks of the Red Road Flats were erected by the Corporation of Glasgow at Petershill in the 1960s. At the time, they were the tallest residential buildings in Europe. Almost from the start, they were beset with problems caused by cost-cutting and bad planning, which led to a poor sense of community, lack of necessary services and a high incidence of vandalism. By the 1980s, two of the blocks had been declared unfit to live in.

Housing the masses

It was the responsibility of local councils to find answers to Britain's housing shortage after the Second World War. A temporary solution was the 'pre-fab' (see page 287), but for a more permanent one, some planners pinned their hopes on the 'new towns' (see page 186), while others looked to the Continent, where blocks of flats had long met the need for mass urban housing. Many low-rise buildings were put up in the 1950s, adding greatly to Britain's stock of council housing. But most were cramped and poorly built and often not much of an improvement on the terraces and tenements they replaced.

Homes in the sky

At the start of the 1960s, a new solution for inner-city housing was found. It was the high-rise tower block, an idea adapted from the revolutionary vision for city living conceived by the modernist architect Le Corbusier. Such 'progressive' buildings were becoming fashionable, but from the planners' point of view their prime attraction was that they allowed a large number of new homes to be built on a relatively small plot of land, and they could be put up quickly using modern materials such as steel and concrete. It was also, at least in theory, possible to surround the blocks with landscaping, creating an oasis of peaceful parkland, where city folk could relax and play in green, leafy surroundings right on their own doorstep.

Tower blocks sprang up across Britain in the 1960s and 70s, but many proved to be unsatisfactory. Rather than remaining boldly white, their concrete render tended to turn rapidly to a depressing grey; the surrounding green spaces rarely materialised; and for families with children, as well as for the elderly, the frequently broken lifts and endless flights of stairs were simply impractical.

Quick fix 'Pre-fabs' were the temporary solution to the housing shortage that stemmed from the destruction of wartime air-raids. These little pre-fabricated houses could be put up in four hours, and thousands were planted on cleared bombsites, such as at Stroud in Gloucestershire (below). They were not meant to last more than ten years, but many remained occupied well into the 1960s and a handful still stand, 60 years on.

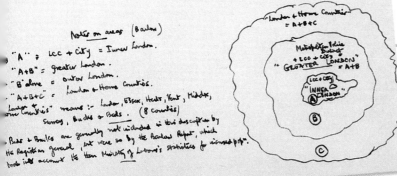

Notes on areas (Barlow)
"A" = LCC + City = Inner London.
"A+B" = Greater London.
"B" alone = outer London.
A+B+C = London + Home Counties.
"Home Counties" means :- London, Essex, Herts, Kent, Middx, Surrey, Bucks & Beds. (8 counties)
Bucks & Berks are generally not included in this description by the Registrar general, but were so by the Barlow Report, which took into account the then Ministry of Labour's statistics for insured pop.

City limits His studies of the capital's population (left) led Sir Patrick Abercrombie to define the desirable area of 'green belt' to encircle the city in his *Greater London Plan* of 1944. The idea proved so successful that it has been adopted in many of Britain's urban areas (see map, right).

Green belt
Urban area

Aberdeen
Dundee
Glasgow · Falkirk · Edinburgh
Ayr
Newcastle
Leeds
Liverpool · Manchester
Stoke-on-Trent · Nottingham
Burton-upon-Trent
Birmingham
Cambridge
Cheltenham
Gloucester
Oxford
Bristol · London
Bournemouth · Southampton

THE GREEN BELT

One of the great planners of the post-war era was Patrick Abercrombie. He rebuilt Plymouth's devastated city centre, and was asked by the government to come up with recommendations for the future of London. Abercrombie saw that the physical growth of the capital, which had been going on for 2000 years, had reached a point where many citizens were losing contact with the surrounding countryside. He concluded that the outer limits of London should not be allowed to go further than its 1939 boundary. Beyond that there should be a 'green belt' of countryside surrounding the city like a girdle and crossed by a network of connecting routes. The population overflow should be siphoned off to satellite towns, from which people could commute into London for work. Abercrombie's ideas were first implemented in the Town and Country Planning Act 1947, and preservation of the green belt has been a priority of politicians ever since.

New schools for a new age

The modernist, multi-storey approach that produced the tower blocks was more successful when it came to planning new schools. Britain needed an extra 5 million school places in the 30 years after the war. This was due in part to the huge population explosion – the baby boom. But it was also a consequence of the raising of the school leaving age, first to 15 in 1947, and then to 16 in 1973.

The new schools built to accommodate this vast increase in pupil numbers could hardly have been more different from the many dark, heavy, imposing Victorian structures that sprang up after the 1870 Education Act (see page 170). Accepted wisdom now dictated that places of learning should be bright and airy, so as not to intimidate the pupils. Although multi-storey to create the necessary space, it was decided that they should not be too high and should be arranged on a campus principle, with special blocks for specific activities. Children would walk in orderly files under covered walkways from the music block to the assembly block to the woodwork block, getting plenty of fresh air along the way.

Rapidly constructed in reinforced steel and pre-cast concrete, the new buildings were not always as durable as they should have been. The favoured flat roofs may have looked uncomplicated and modern, but in the wet British climate they had a tendency to spring leaks. Pupils grew used to having lessons in rooms where the wastepaper basket was used to catch the incessant drip-drip-drip of water from the ceiling. But in general the modernist principle worked for schools, where the community was young, lively, flexible and not permanently in residence.

A brighter outlook The flexible layout of modern schools allowed them to be fitted more easily into awkwardly shaped sites and readily expanded to accommodate the high student numbers that resulted from the introduction of comprehensive education in the 1960s. Most boroughs achieved this transition by closing smaller schools and channelling pupils into one giant establishment with enough facilities to serve all, as at Holland Park School in London (above).

FIND OUT MORE

• www.tcpa.org.uk Website of The Town and Country Planning Association, with up-to-date information and commentary on planning initiatives, past and present, across Britain.
• www.englishpartnerships.co.uk/newtowns.htm Background history and brief profiles of all new towns built between 1946 and 1970.
• *Cities of Tomorrow* (Peter Hall, Blackwell Publishers, 2002) A concise history of 20th century urban planning.

The triumph of the car

More than any other innovation, the car has transformed the way people conduct their day-to-day lives. It has changed how we shop, work and play, and thanks to car parks, shopping centres, one-way systems and the whole paraphernalia of driving, altered for ever the look of our towns.

Family day out Weekend outings took on a new meaning in the 1960s (left) as cars became affordable. No longer did people have to rely on public transport – they could go where they wanted, when they wanted.

Time's up A car is booked for outstaying its welcome at one of Britain's first parking meters in London in 1958. Today there are around 4000 traffic wardens in Britain enforcing a host of parking restrictions.

The car becomes king

A government report in 1964, entitled *Traffic in Towns*, described the motor car as a 'Trojan horse', and said that it was proving 'more brutally destructive in some of its consequences than any that emerged from the original Wooden Horse upon an unsuspecting population'. The report laid out a strategy for coping with the ever-increasing number of motor vehicles hurtling down major roads and parked in endless rows on minor ones. But in many ways it was already too late: in city centres and in the suburbs the car was already beginning to dominate.

In 1924, the industrialist William Morris, founder of Morris Motors, had hopefully looked forward to the day when 'the worker goes to his factory by car'. Now that vision had come to pass, and it was changing the nature of the spaces in which people lived. A car made it possible for people to make their homes much further away from the factory – or indeed the office – and so they moved out of the already depopulated city centres. This centrifugal effect created the phenomenon known as 'urban sprawl'.

At the same time, developers were buying land from farmers who owned the fields alongside upgraded roads between large towns. If the road was on a bus route, there

was money to be made from cheap housing for people who could use the bus to commute. Collections of bungalows and shops, dubbed 'ribbon developments' in the 1930s, spread rapidly out along the highways. They cut off the countryside from the road, but provided none of the benefits of a nearby town to the rural economy, and not many of the benefits of a rustic lifestyle to the townfolk who moved into them. The same 1964 report described ribbon development as 'perhaps the greatest disaster the long-suffering face of our country has had to endure'.

Giving towns over to traffic

Something had to be done to contain the motor car, and the solution was a kind of appeasement. In the post-war years, by-passes and ring roads were built around many cities to keep these four-wheeled locusts out of historic centres. Radial routes took the cars out to the concentric ring-roads, resulting in the characteristic spider's web of traffic that was superimposed on many towns.

If the historic centre of a city had been bombed flat, then it was often reconstructed as a pedestrian shopping area. In Coventry, this haven of walk-and-shop was called

DID YOU KNOW?

There are thought to be around 24 million cars on the road in Britain today. According to the 2001 Census, seven out of ten households now have a car compared to three out of ten in 1961, and 28 per cent of households own two or more cars compared to just 2 per cent in 1961. The Census also revealed that in 1999-2001, if the main driver in a household was a woman, on average she made 1290 trips in the year; if a man was the main driver, he made only 1190 trips.

The evolution of the petrol station

For some time after the car was invented, there was no such thing as a petrol station. Drivers bought their petrol in two-gallon cans from shops and poured it into the tank using a big funnel. The first petrol pump was installed at Aldermaston in 1920, on the road from London to Bath. The Automobile Association sponsored this pump, and a chain of others across the countryside.

These early petrol stations stood at the kerbside like bus-stops, or were an incidental adjunct to roadside shops. Later, as cars became more common, the selling of fuel became a viable retail business in its own right. They dropped the shop, and sold nothing much besides petrol. The first self-service pump came to Britain in 1960. It then became clear that once drivers had to get out of their cars to fill the tank and pay, they could be sold other items as well. Petrol stations acquired little general stores, just as little general stores had once acquired petrol pumps. Petrol retailers also took to providing other motoring services such as a carwash, or were attached to full-scale car dealerships.

Today, 'non-petroleum sales', as they are called in the business, are at least as important commercially as the profit that flows from the pump. A partnership between supermarkets and oil companies has arisen, leading to a new style of petrol station. Bright and as visible as lighthouses, they have become an oasis on the road, where drivers and passengers, as well as their cars, can be restocked and refuelled.

On the forecourt Colyford filling station in east Devon (above) dates back to 1928 and was typical of the stations in many villages across Britain. In 1952, its Hammond hand-operated pumps were replaced by electrically operated Avery Hardoll pumps. These were in use until the station closed in 1999. It is now preserved as part of the Motoring Memories museum.

Parking places The bomb damage of the Second World War gave planners the opportunity to develop new shopping centres with mass car ownership in mind. Coventry's Precinct (left, 1961) was one of many such centres, designed for pedestrians only, but with a vast multi-storey car park attached.

by the medieval name 'The Precinct', and this name was subsequently adopted for any car-free retail zone.

Naturally, workers and shoppers still wanted to bring their cars into town. When they did so, they were shooed off the streets by traffic wardens (a profession invented in 1960, although the first parking meters in Britain were installed outside the American embassy on Grosvenor Square in London in 1958), and coralled into multi-storey car parks. Other containment measures included one-way streets and no-right-turns.

Ownership continues to rise

None of these measures were enough to prevent the tidal encroachment of the motor car. They were just too cheap not to buy, and too convenient not to drive. The number of car owners in Britain doubled in the course of the 1960s – from about six million to almost 12 million. No amount of legislation or urban planning could stop it, and the tide continued to rise for the rest of the 20th century, regardless of environmentalists' pleas to call a halt.

The words on the streets

The demands of the car have profoundly altered Britain's roads. A visitor from 100 years ago would stand agog at the variegated jungle of signposts that line Britain's thoroughfares, the garish stripes and dashes on the carriageway, the flashing lights and beacons signalling stops and starts, the blizzard of written information about what lies ahead, and the roaring surge of traffic that moves through it all. So how did all these signs evolve?

M1
The NORTH
Sheffield 32
Leeds 59

Sign language In the 1960s Britain's new motorways needed signs that could be read at speed. White-on-blue colouring using Jock Kinneir's Transport typeface in upper and lower-case letters was chosen for legibility.

Designs of the times A new road sign is painted at the Royal Label Factory, Stratford-upon-Avon, 1935.

Making sense of the signs

Most people barely even register the mass of 'street furniture' that has been erected around our roads. Street signs seem ordinary to the point of invisibility because they are almost completely uniform. The typeface, the symbols and pictograms, and the shapes and colours of the boards, are the same right across Britain's road network. But this was not always so. Until the Second World War there was a chaotic mix of signs giving vital information such as speed limits, and many were practically unreadable by a driver in a moving vehicle.

It fell to the government's Road Research Unit to impose some order. There was a series of experiments with signage in the 1950s, and in 1963 the government commissioned the typographer Jock Kinneir to create a typeface that would be visible and legible from a car travelling at speed. The typeface he created, known as Transport, was conceived in such a way that words could be compiled in tiles containing individual letters, like old-fashioned type, so that non-experts could make up the signs. At the same time, new signs were produced with diagrammatic representations of roundabouts and sliproad turn-offs. They were tested in Slough, and on the Preston by-pass – Britain's first genuine stretch of motorway.

Once the new signage designs were made public, there was heated debate as to whether capitals might not be better than Kinneir's mix of upper and lower-case letters. Articles in *The Times* argued that capitals were more legible and imposing. Kinneir's scheme won through and has stood the test of time. The white upper and lower-case letters on a blue background are still in use, and the Transport font has been adopted by countries around the world for their own road signs.

Saying it with shapes and pictures

At the same time as the typeface was under discussion, decisions were taken about conventions such as speed limit signs. It was decided they should be round with a red border and that the figure representing the speed limit should be at the centre of the circle – rather than on a plate beneath, as was often the case before the Second World War. Pictograms were created for instructions such

Where next? A profusion of signs such as those on the A3 at New Malden, Surrey, show how street furniture has proliferated on Britain's roads.

as No Overtaking. The convention that hazards were shown in a triangle with a red border, which had existed in a hit-and-miss way since 1904, was now made official.

Most of the famous pictograms that feature on the triangular 'hazard' signs were created in 1964 by the designer Margaret Calvert – the little girl featured on her Children Crossing sign (left) is a kind of stylised self-portrait.

The new signs made it possible to drive without having to read wordy instructions – indeed without needing to understand English at all apart from the universal imperative 'STOP' (which replaced the equally laconic, but rather haughty exhortation to 'HALT'). There have been a few minor tweaks to the system since the 1960s. Some new hazard signs have been invented, and there are now brown signs for tourist attractions. The red stop sign, once a circle, is now an unequivocal and instantly recognisable octagon.

Spot the difference The girl on Margaret Calvert's original Children Crossing sign had a ponytail. This has since been removed.

The fact that so little has changed in 40 years is a testament to the success of the system. Britain's road signage is now seen as a masterpiece of Modernist design – on a par with Harry Beck's renowned schematic map of the London Underground. It has even come to be known as 'the handwriting of Britain'.

Forward thinking Many of the basic pictograms from the mid 20th century are still in use today, such as the No Overtaking sign (left), which still shows 1960s-style cars. Animal signs, including the cow and the running stag, were drawn using details gleaned from the photographic studies of movement that were carried out in the 19th century by Eadweard Muybridge.

DID YOU KNOW?

Oxfordshire County Council, alone among all the local authorities in Britain, decided not to adopt the new road signs conventions introduced after the Second World War. In Oxfordshire the signs were white-on-black rather than white-on-blue, and in a different typeface from everywhere else in Britain. Some of these maverick signs survived until the 1990s.

THE LINE IN THE ROAD

The painted markings that adorn every urban road have evolved over time. Single white lines were introduced in 1927 to keep ever speedier cars to their own side of the carriageway and so reduce the number of head-on collisions. The ingeniously simple cat's eyes (below), which perform the same function at night, were first installed in 1934 in west Yorkshire, the home of Percy Shaw who invented them. Cat's eyes spread throughout Britain after 1947, on the orders of Jim Callaghan, then Junior Transport Minister. Zebra crossings appeared in 1951 (although the orange glow of Belisha beacons had been a feature of pedestrian crossings since 1935). Box junctions marked with yellow cross-hatching put a splash of colour on the road surface in 1964, and the zebras acquired their zig-zag lines in 1971. Mini-roundabouts appeared in 1976, and road-humps – graphically dubbed 'sleeping policemen' – were first mooted in 1983, since spreading like acne over suburban roads. Speed cameras added to the forest of poles on the roads in 1992.

Shopping and leisure drift out of town

Chain-strore veteran Woolworths was one of the first high-street chain stores. There were over 80 branches in Britain by the 1920s (below) and 768 by 1939. It is still going strong, and there are few shopping centres without a 'Woolies'.

In the course of the 20th century, the march of motorised transport turned many of Britain's city centres into congested and often awkward places to shop. But town planners were busy devising remedies – first inner-city, pedestrianised precincts and then huge out-of-town retail malls.

Change on the high street

The traditional Victorian high street, full of shops owned by individual butchers, bakers, grocers, ironmongers and outfitters, survived intact well into the 20th century. Most small towns also kept their market where the produce from local farms was sold. As late as the 1940s, cattle were being driven to market every week through the streets of Redhill in Surrey. But by the 1920s there were signs of change. The process now known as 'homogenisation' – whereby every town has the same selection of chain stores from Starbucks to Gap – had its beginnings just after the First World War, when improvements in transport and communications made it increasingly viable to move goods around the country.

Car-free consumer havens

It was in the aftermath of the Second World War that shopping habits were truly transformed. The commercial centres of many towns and cities, such as Plymouth, Bristol and Coventry, had been obliterated by bombing (see pages 196-197). Once the rubble had been cleared, planners were presented with a blank slate. They decided to separate motorised transport from pedestrians, and so the bomb-damaged cities became the focus of experiments in car-free shopping. The idea soon spread to the new towns, such as Harlow, Hemel Hempstead, Crawley and Stevenage, that were then under construction (see pages 186-187).

Coventry also pioneered the concept of 'leisure shopping', the idea that you could have fun spending time as well as money at the shops. One of the main attractions of the city's new precinct (see pages 200-201) was

Lady Godiva's Café – a big glass drum set on a concrete stalk from which you could observe the life below.

The new shopping centres became a craze in the 1950s, and could soon be found even in towns that had not been badly damaged in the Blitz. Many Victorian shops disappeared as their century-old leases ran out and local authorities rushed to modernise.

Shopping at the motorway mall

By the early 1960s, with car-ownership on the increase, city centres were becoming clogged with traffic. Soon the idea took root that the solution lay in an American concept – the out-of-town shopping mall. But planning permission for the first British one, at Haydock, between Liverpool and Manchester, was refused, and it was not until

Revolution in urban planning In May 1964, the Bull Ring, the largest car-free shopping centre outside North America, opened in Birmingham city centre. Built around the site of the city's ancient market, its shops were reached via a network of walkways and ring roads.

the middle of the 1980s that giant supermarkets and hangar-sized factory outlets began to appear, always sited conveniently close to a motorway, no more than half-an-hour's easy drive from a residential area. Their proliferation was phenomenal: in 1985, there were none; by 1997, there were 457. Each contained several million square metres of retail space – much of it under cover – designed to keep people dry, comfortable and spending happily for the entire day.

The effect of out-of-town shopping malls was not altogether good for community life. The draw of the keenly priced, well-stocked hyperstores, coupled with parking restrictions, helped to starve many local shops of customers. Thousands of the smaller businesses, often central to the character of an area, were forced to close. In 1961, there were more than 116,000 independent grocers across Britain; by 2001, only around 24,000 remained. And where neighbourhood stores were viable, the supermarkets started to open mini-versions of themselves – to mop up the commuters who just wanted to grab a sandwich for lunch or a ready-meal for dinner.

BLUEWATER: THE STORY OF A RETAIL CITY

Bluewater in Kent is the grandiose conclusion of the trend towards out-of-town shopping. It is not so much a retail centre as a retail city – a covered conurbation filled with shops and other 'leisure opportunities', including a cinema, health spa and 20ha (50 acres) of landscaping with boating and fishing lakes, cycle paths and a golf course. It opened in 1999, strategically sited on the M25 just outside London to bring the maximum number of potential customers within its orbit. Ten million

people live within an hour's drive (the developers invested £30 million towards the upgrading of roads), and the centre draws in nearly 27 million visitors every year. Shops are arranged in tiers – just as in the first experiment in leisure-shopping in Coventry in the late 1940s (see opposite). And as in Coventry, there is provision for shoppers to rest and grab a bite between sprees – enough restaurants, cafés and bars to seat 5000 at a time.

Sport moves to the edge

It is not just shops that have been moving away from the over-crowded urban centres: sports stadiums have also been leaving town. As the property market in Britain boomed in the 1980s and 90s, inner-city grounds became valuable development sites. At the same time football clubs were trying to transform themselves into profit-making businesses. By selling an old Victorian ground and building one elsewhere, they could make money and equip themselves with a facility fit for lucrative European competitions. The strategy worked best in the north, where former industrial land – brownfield sites – were plentiful and cheap. In 1995, Middlesbrough FC abandoned Ayresome Park for the 30,000-seater Riverside Stadium (below), built to the east of the city on the banks of the River Tees. If the move came with a sponsorship deal, so much the better: Bolton Wanderers went from Burnden Park to the Reebok Stadium; Huddersfield Town from Leeds Road to the Alfred McAlpine Stadium; Hull City from Boothferry Park to the Kingston Communications Stadium.

The rural scene transformed

At the start of the 20th century, many parts of Britain remained deeply rustic. They were not entirely untouched by progress, but the rhythms of life – the fairs, the sowing and harvesting, the lore and ritual, the very shape of the fields – were much as they had been for 400 years. By the end of the century, the people and ways of village life had changed utterly.

The horse leaves the picture

On the eve of the First World War, there were just over a million men and about the same number of horses working the land in Britain. So there was plenty of work for blacksmiths, and most villages still had a forge at their heart. Farmers would bring horses to the smith for the workaday business of shoeing, but the whole community would have jobs that required the blacksmith's skills: he was the man to mend a cracked frying pan, to fashion a decorative wrought-iron gate for the squire's house, to make a new tooth for a gear wheel or repair a plough.

Other country professions depended on the horse's indispensability to just as great an extent as did the smith. Wheelwrights and carters were skilled craftsmen, and their work was highly valued. Well into the 20th century, farmers in the Midlands resisted the encroaching tractor, saying that a well-made cart was longer-lasting and – if it did break down – easier to repair. It was held that iron-rimmed cartwheels gripped better on hills than a tractor's rubber tyres, and were less inclined to stick in heavy ground.

Nevertheless, agricultural workhorses were becoming obsolete; so consequently were the skills of the men who worked with them. The number of working horses in Britain halved between the First and Second World Wars, and the smithies closed at about the same rate. Two decades later, the spread of mechanised intensive farming methods (see page 90) meant that the number of farmhorses had dwindled almost to nothing, and the hot orange fire in the forge had gone out. A number of other country livelihoods dwindled towards extinction at roughly the same time. Among them were tanner, shepherd, thatcher, roper and miller – all professions that would have been familiar to a medieval yeoman, but were now doomed.

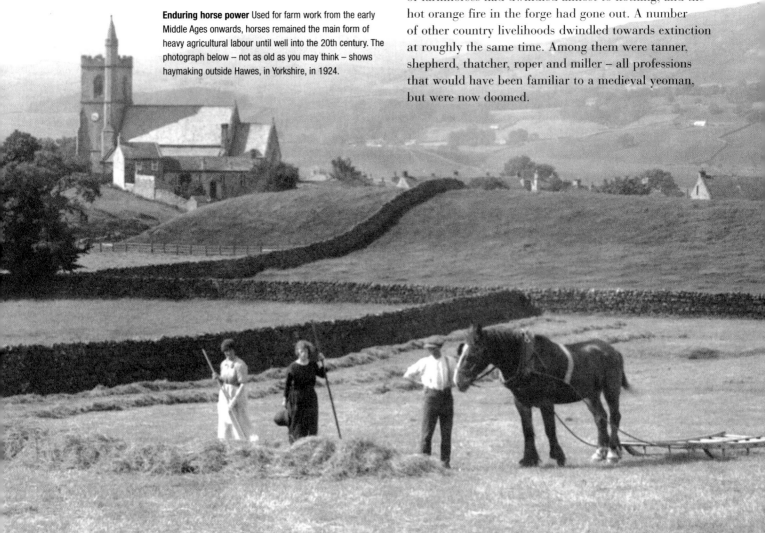

Enduring horse power Used for farm work from the early Middle Ages onwards, horses remained the main form of heavy agricultural labour until well into the 20th century. The photograph below – not as old as you may think – shows haymaking outside Hawes, in Yorkshire, in 1924.

The labour drains from the country

The mechanised turmoil of the Second World War somehow contributed to the demise of country ways and rural crafts. Men who had learnt modern skills driving tanks or flying bombers were not inclined to go back to making wattle-hurdles or cutting coppices. So the war hastened a process that had already begun: the drift of young men and women to the technological bustle of the city – and with it, the gradual emptying-out of the countryside.

This change was noted, and deplored, as it was happening. In 1953, Robert Trow-Smith wrote in his book *Society and the Land* that 'many villages today are moribund, lifeless and out-of-date units in the British scene, and there seems to be nothing that can really be done about it. Society has outgrown them and left them behind. Rural culture has had its day; but it died so recently that its heir is not yet apparent.'

A seismic shift in village life

The future of country communities became apparent soon enough. They were to evolve into the playground of the cities. A quarter of a million people left the land in the 1960s, but in the following two decades there was a marked flow in the other direction. Well-off citydwellers began to venture beyond the suburbs and into the countryside. These urban newcomers were people who bought second homes in pretty villages; or who moved their home to the country but carried on commuting; or who retired from an urban profession to live somewhere quiet (where they might take on the local store or open an antiques shop). For whatever reason, there were more city people living in the country, and they inevitably changed its culture.

The urban influx was sometimes resented by local people – especially in Wales, where for a while Welsh nationalists took to burning down the holiday homes of English incomers. But in fact it was the countryfolk themselves who encouraged the citydwellers to come. Since fewer and fewer of them were making a living from the land – by the 1980s only 2 per cent of the working population were in agriculture – they turned to the other great resource of the countryside: its tourist potential. Farmers (or more often, farmers' wives) supplemented their income by converting barns and cowsheds into cottages, or setting up caravan sites on fallow fields.

At the same time, new communications technology made it possible to run a business from any location.

New rural pursuits Digital age flexibility has prompted many a business to set up in an old rural building. The Popperfoto photo library (above) relocated from London's Fleet Street to a converted mill at Overstone Farm in Northamptonshire.

Farming in the community A popular trend among farmers seeking to diversify is the farm shop, such as the one at Abbey Home Farm near Cirencester (left), in Gloucestershire. Here home-grown organic produce is sold direct to local customers.

In the digital age, a small publishing house, a design consultancy or a wine importer can function perfectly well from a restored oast house or a decommissioned rural post office. The people who work in such businesses may be supplying services to customers in the city, but they earn and spend their money in the country, and so are as much a part of the rural economy as the seasonal strawberry picker, the veterinary surgeon or (until he goes the way of the basket-maker) the master of hounds.

These changes all add up to a remarkable turnaround. At the start of the 20th century the life of a citydweller could be so different from that of a far-flung villager that they would be almost alien to each other. A hundred years later, you could stand a modern dairy farmer next to the successful IT consultant living in the same village, and there would be no way of knowing which was which.

Dining in splendour The Café Royal in London's Piccadilly (left, 1912) was typical of the opulent dining rooms of the late 19th century. It was set up in 1865 by a Parisian wine merchant and continues to operate today, its Victorian decor reinstated.

servant. Soon restaurants began opening as independent businesses. One was Kettners, on Romilly Street in London's Soho, founded in 1867 by Auguste Kettner, who had previously been chef to Emperor Napoleon III. At the end of the century it was a favourite haunt of the Prince of Wales (the future Edward VIII), and of Oscar Wilde, who drank champagne here with his louche friends.

Tea at Betty's

Not everybody could afford to eat in the company of royalty. In the first years of the 20th century, a new kind of restaurant was born. These were places that preserved a certain gentility and sense of occasion, but catered to the tastes and pockets of the growing middle classes.

Betty's Tea Room in Harrogate was one such institution. It was the brainchild of Frederick Belmont, a Swiss confectioner, who arrived in England in 1907. He had intended to set up business on the south coast, but boarded the wrong train and found himself in Yorkshire. There he stayed, opening his first tea room in 1919. It served the same mixture of Swiss and Yorkshire specialities (*rösti* and curd tarts) that can be had there to this day. In the 1920s and 30s Belmont opened three more branches – at York, Ilkley and Northallerton.

The Corner House experience

Meanwhile, the Lyons company was providing the same kind of fare, but on a much larger scale, for the bourgeoisie of London. The first of the Lyons Corner Houses opened on the junction of Coventry Street and Rupert Street in 1909. The second was on The Strand and the third at Tottenham Court Road. The Corner Houses were more than just a large restaurant; they were an entire day out. Customers could have their hair done, make a telephone call or book tickets for the theatre. Then they could buy flowers and whole hams to take home.

Eating out becomes a social occasion

Going out to dine was popularised by the wealthy in the 19th century. But it was not long before less lavish establishments opened for all, fish'n'chip shops started the takeaway trend and ethnic cuisines arrived. Today, eating out is an accepted part of life.

Dining on the town

Restaurants as we know them are a Victorian idea. Before the 19th century, the only eating-houses were inns and taverns; the well-to-do tended to dine at home.

The first public dining rooms – where eating out was seen as a social engagement – were attached to grand urban hotels. At the Ritz in London a French chef, Georges-Auguste Escoffier (1847-1935), single-handedly invented the restaurant culture that we still recognise: menus (in French) offering a limited choice of dishes for each course, a formal setting, and waiters wearing the uniform and affecting the deference of a rich man's

Yorkshire fare A meal out came within reach of the middle classes with the opening of places such as Betty's Tea Room in Harrogate.

First fast-food joints

The Corner House experience became a nostalgic memory during the hungry years of the Second World War and food rationing. In the 1950s, Lyons was one of the first caterers in Britain to experiment with fast food. The company opened 11 specialised restaurants, such as the 'Grill and Cheese' and the 'Bacon and Egg'. But the most successful new idea came from the USA. It was a hamburger restaurant named after a cartoon character, Wimpy.

The Wimpy restaurants were so successful that they devoured the Lyons brand. The Corner Houses closed in the 1970s and were converted to burger bars. Eating habits were changing, and more and more ethnic eateries began to appear: in the 1960s and 70s, Indian and Chinese; then in the 1980s and 90s, Thai, Tex-Mex and Japanese.

PIZZA EXPRESS

Easy eating Pizza has become one of Britain's favourite dishes, with more than 10,000 restaurants dedicated to it.

The story of pizza in Britain

Perhaps the most successful cuisine in the second half of the 20th century came from closer to home. Pizza – that versatile and family-friendly Italian import – was pioneered in Britain by Peter Boizot, who had eaten it in Florence after the war. He opened his first restaurant, called Pizza Express, on Wardour Street in London. The second was opened on Coptic Street, next to the British Museum, in 1967, and now there are more than 300 across Britain. The jewel in the crown is the original Victorian Kettner's, where theatre-goers and Saturday-nighters can enjoy an economical meal in a room haunted by poets and kings.

GOING FOR AN INDIAN

Indian food has a long pedigree in Britain. As early as 1809, there was an establishment known as the Hindostanee Coffee House on George Street in London. But the first modern curry house was the Salut e Hind, which opened on Holborn in 1911. This was followed by The Shafi in Gerrard Street, which was staffed by lascars – former sailors from East Bengal. These early restaurants were patronised mostly by Asians; the first Indian to become fashionable with native Britons was Veeraswamy, which opened on Regent Street in 1927 and is still trading.

Spicing it up The British rapidly found a taste for Indian cuisine, eating out at restaurants such as Gaylord in Mortimer Street, London W1 (above, 1971).

Nearly all the pioneers of Indian cuisine were Bengali, but in the 1950s there was an influx of Punjabis into Southall, London, and into Glasgow. They established their own distinctive cuisine. In 1960 there were around 500 Indian restaurants in Britain; now there are more than 8000. In Bradford, the first Indian restaurant – The Kashmir – opened on Morley Street in 1958. That city might now claim to be the capital of Indian cuisine in Britain. Or perhaps the title belongs to Leicester, with its 'golden mile' of Indian restaurants. At any rate, the onion bhaji and chicken Madras have become an inalienable part of British cuisine.

EXPLORE YOUR COMMUNITY

The people, the streets, the churches, the workplaces, the shops and the public buildings – there are so many aspects to your village, town or city to explore. You can take to the open air, walk the pavements and look at the many clues all around you. Then search your local archives, where the many layers of your neighbourhood's story lie waiting to be discovered.

Where to begin

A visit to your local reference library or county record office should be the start of a richly rewarding journey. Somewhere in their files you are likely to find everything that has ever been published about where you live, along with hundreds, if not thousands, of original documents.

- You could start by unearthing all you can about eminent local people, the sort that the Victorians would have called 'local worthies'. For details of those who achieved national fame, you should also look in *The Dictionary of National Biography* (60 vols, OUP, 2004; and on-line by subscription – see **www.oup.com/oxforddnb/info/**).

- Or you might be more interested in an infamous person like Spence Broughton, the highwayman whose gibbet stood in what is now Broughton Lane, Sheffield, for 35 years after he was hanged there, as a ghastly warning to wrongdoers. Local newspapers, prison records and court records will reveal those who strayed on to the wrong side of the law.

Doing some groundwork Before you tackle the reference libraries and record offices, see what you can find out about your area by walking around it and looking for clues to its history. Strolling through ancient streets, or around a market place or beside a canal, can often give you a better sense of the place than hours of pouring over documents.

Building up clues

Look closely at the architecture of your town or village. The design of a building and the material used to construct it can usually tell you much about its age and original use.

Easy dating Remember that many buildings have a datestone, possibly over the front door or up in the gable.
Mixed styles Buildings have often been altered or modified at different times. That smart Georgian front may be covering up an older timber-framed structure.
Names House names can hold clues to age. The Red House is likely to be an early brick building, and houses in Alma Street probably date back to around the time of the Crimean War battle of that name, fought in 1854.
Change of use Many buildings no longer serve their original purpose. A worn inscription might tell you that a house was once a school or the bingo hall was a cinema.

The working life

Some places have, or had, links with a particular trade. Look for any signs of this, which you could use along with old records to unravel the story of local industry.

What to ask Set out the questions you want answered before you start. When and why did an industry or activity begin? When was its heyday? When were factories or other work places abandoned?

Finding key features

A good way to start your research is to focus on an aspect of your town or area that gives it a distinctive identity. This could be a town square, a church or a river crossing.

What to ask Which is the oldest part of the town? Did the town grow continuously or were there periods of decline, followed by renewed growth? Are there landmarks to see, or documents to discover, that will provide clues to the town's early history?

Working backwards

To discover the origins of the place where you live, it is often easiest to begin with the well-documented 20th and 19th centuries and work backwards.

Easy start Be realistic and begin with topics that are the most likely to yield information quickly. Key records, such as census returns, tithe award maps and manor court rolls, are usually easily accessible at your local reference library or county record office (see pages 18-19).
Visual approach Old newspapers and parish magazines may contain photographs of significant events. A street party celebrating VE Day in 1945, or perhaps the opening of a factory or sinking of a mine shaft, could have been captured on camera. Local newspapers often have their own archives, but you could also look in the local library or British Library Newspapers (see DIRECTORY).

Window on to the past Old photographs can help you to step backwards in time. You may have family albums lurking in the attic, or you could search the archives of local newspapers, which are bound to have recorded major events, such as the procession in Wandsworth, London (below), to mark Edward VII's coronation in 1902.

FIND OUT MORE

• *Researching and Writing History* (David Dymond, British Association for Local History, 1999)
• *English Local History, An Introduction* (Kate Tiller, Sutton, 2002)
• *The Oxford Companion to Local and Family History* (David Hey ed., OUP, 1998)
• *The English Town* (Mark Girouard, Yale University Press, 1990)

Old photographs and oral history

Old photographs grab our attention and help us to pose questions that will unravel the past. Who are these people and what are they wearing? Where exactly was that building? Some answers may lie in local archives, and you might find that talking to an elderly relative or neighbour helps too.

People and places caught in time

The new art of photography developed quickly in the early years of Queen Victoria's reign. Enthusiasts began to use the new medium in the 1840s and 50s to create a visual record of where they lived. You might well find a photo of the parish church before the graveyard was tidied up or extended, or a view of labourers digging a railway cutting, or a shot of that new form of public transport: the horse-drawn omnibus.

Ordinary people, who could not afford painted portraits, were now able to have an accurate likeness recorded cheaply at the photographer's studio. The Victorians often appear so serious in those early shots, but that is often just the result of holding a smile for the long

Civic pride Judging by the horse-drawn cab to the left of the picture and the fashions worn by the light scattering of people shown, the picture-postcard of Hereford High Street (above) was probably taken just before the First World War.

exposures required – usually several minutes – while a clamp was used to keep the head still. Spontaneous family 'snaps' only started to appear with the arrival of the Kodak Box Brownie camera, around 1900.

Picture-postcards The heyday of the picture-postcard was between 1900 and 1920, when cuts to working hours gave people more time to go on holiday or visit friends, and the speed of the railways meant the swift delivery of posted messages. People took pride in sending friends and family an image of their town square or parish church.

The Postcard Traders Association on **www.postcard.co.uk** can help you to find and date picture-postcards, and many are included in the books and archives given below.

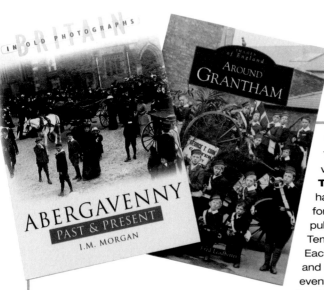

WHERE TO FIND OLD PHOTOGRAPHS

The invention of photography has bequeathed to us a detailed visual record of the years from the mid-19th century onward.

The local bookshop Towns and villages throughout Britain have been chronicled in books of old photographs. These often form part of a series, such as 'Britain in Old Photographs', published by Sutton (far left) or 'Images of England', published by Tempus (left) perhaps in co-operation with a local history society. Each book serves as a complete pictorial 'essay' on a community, and will include street and workplace scenes, records of special events such as coronation celebrations, Whitsuntide processions, Sunday School outings, annual fairs and weekly markets, and snaps of football teams, brass bands and church choirs. The best have informative captions.

Libraries and museums Most public reference libraries and some museums have large collections of local photographs. Some of these images are now available on-line (see page 25).

The National Archives at Kew (see DIRECTORY) An extensive collection, dating from 1842 to 1912, is catalogued at the National Archives in a series known as COPY 1. Other important collections are in the National Museums of Scotland and the National Library of Wales, Aberystwyth (see DIRECTORY).

The Rural History Centre Around 750,000 images of all aspects of rural life (particularly in the south of England), from the mid-19th century to the present, is stored in the Centre's archives, which are housed at the University of Reading in Berkshire (see DIRECTORY). See also 'Rediscovering rural life in old photographs' on pages 114-115.

Using oral history

Valuable information about the lives of ordinary citizens in the past was rarely written down and can be recovered only from talking to old people. George Ewart Evans was the first person to use this 'oral history' technique in a systematic way. He wrote a series of books, starting with *Ask the Fellows Who Cut the Hay* (Faber, 1956), which he based on the memories of men and women who were born in the last quarter of the 19th century and had lived and worked most of their lives in the Suffolk village of Blaxhall. His final book, *Spoken History* (Faber, 1987), is a summary of his work.

Evans showed that what had previously been dismissed as 'mere hearsay' was an invaluable, detailed explanation of a former way of life that was hardly mentioned in documentary sources. Oral history can give a realistic account of daily life, household arrangements and working practices. This is often the only way to learn how, for instance, hand-tools were used or meals were cooked.

• Record your own memories first. This will alert you to what questions to ask and may be useful to others.

• When you first visit someone whose memories you want to record, take along some old photographs to get them talking.

• *Oral History for Local Historians* (Stephen Caunce, Longman, 1994) is packed with good advice on interviewing techniques.

A way of life preserved One of the most widely acclaimed of the early photographers was Frank Meadow Sutcliffe. He moved to Whitby on the north Yorkshire coast in 1870 and over the next 40 years took hundreds of vivid and detailed photographs of the port and its people, leaving to posterity a unique record of the fishermen and their families.

Reading the images Few old photographs have names or dates on them, so you may have to learn to spot the visual clues they hold. Postcards can be easier to place, because there is often a dated message on the back. The following pointers should help guide you on your way:

• Look at buildings in the background that can be dated.

• Look at hairstyles and dress, which may also suggest a date.

• Ask why a photograph may have been taken, and by whom.

• Be aware that any customs, crafts or activities recorded may have been curious survivals rather than typical of the time.

• *Family Photographs 1860-1945* (Robert Pols, The National Archives, 2002) is a useful guide to interpreting old images.

FIND OUT MORE

Many books of personal memoirs give accounts of local communities in the fairly recent past. Some fine examples are:

• *Lark Rise to Candleford* (Flora Thompson, OUP, 1945) Rural life in 19th-century Oxfordshire.
• *Speak for England* (Melvyn Bragg, Secker & Warburg, 1976) Reminiscences of people in Wigton, Cumbria.
• *A Woman's Place: An Oral History of Working Class Women, 1890-1940* (Elizabeth Roberts, Blackwell, 1995).
• *Yorkshire Fisherfolk* (Peter Frank, Phillimore, 2002) Illustrated by numerous old photographs.
• *A Local Habitation: Life and Times, 1918-1940* (Richard Hoggart, OUP, 1989) A working-class childhood in early 20th-century Leeds.
• *The Road to Nab End* (William Woodruff, Abacus, 2002). Growing up in a Lancashire cotton-mill town just after the First World War.

A selection of good on-line sources of old photographs (including picture-postcards) is given on pages 24-25 in the 'Getting started' section.

Maps and plans

Unfold a map of your district and you immediately start to ask questions. Why is my village no more than a church, a farm and a few cottages, when its neighbour is large and sprawling? Why is the railway so far out of town? Why do some areas, such as the parish of Sandal Magna in Wakefield, Yorkshire, have such ancient-sounding names, while districts close-by have more modern names? A map can give you a feel for the distinctive character of a place.

Mapping out the past

Old maps can provide snapshots of an area at various points in its history. Compare them with modern aerial photographs to see if medieval features, such as moats and castle mounds, can still be identified on the ground and to judge how a place has grown, or perhaps shrunk. Look at other records from about the same date as your maps. There should be a census return (see pages 218-219) recording the inhabitants of your town or village at about the time the first Ordnance Survey map (see below) of the area was drawn up, or a directory (see pages 216-217) listing the various types of tradesmen. Try placing these people in the houses shown on your map.

Ordnance Survey maps

One of the best starting points for exploring the history of your community is an Ordnance Survey (OS) map. They are readily available, cover the whole of Britain and take

Forward thinking Make the most of any archive by phoning ahead to explain the purpose of your visit and, if possible, to enlist some expert help. You will be amazed at how much information you gather in a short space of time with such assistance.

you back quickly and easily from the present day to well into the 19th century (see page 26). Comparing OS maps of Barlow in Derbyshire (below) shows how they can provide a broad framework of developments in a community over the last two centuries, raising questions, possibly about changes in employment or the origin of place names, that can be answered by looking elsewhere.

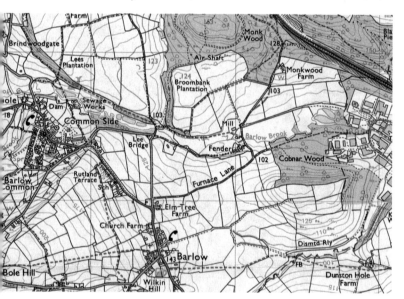

The here and now The up-to-date OS Explorer series map (see page 26) shows that the parish of Barlow has the small village of Barlow at its centre with a larger settlement, Common Side (likely to be the site of former common land), half a mile to the north. A row of houses called Rutland Terrace stands in between, and there are numerous scattered farms and extensive woods, including Monk Wood (bisected by the A61 trunk road) and Cobnar Wood, which is encroached upon by a trading estate.

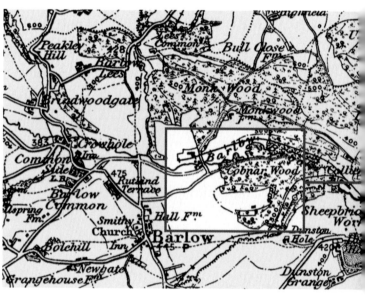

Looking back On the 1-inch OS map, published in 1907, no trunk road or trading estate is present, but a railway line passes through the lower part of Cobnar Wood towards a coal mine and an ironworks (Sheepbridge Works). Rutland Terrace is marked and Common Side is smaller than today. An earlier first edition 1-inch OS map of the area, based on a survey of 1837-9, shows no Rutland Terrace and few houses at Common Side, but the same underlying pattern of farms, fields and woods.

Tithe-award maps

You might be able to follow your community farther back in time using a tithe award and its map from your local archives (see page 27). These were drawn up between 1836 and 1852 for 11,395 parishes, listing all the properties in each area, which were plotted on the map and numbered. The size and use of each property is given, along with owners' and tenants' names.

- A tithe-award map, drawn on a large but not uniform scale, is often the earliest detailed map available of your parish or township. Compare it with a first edition six-inch OS map (see page 26) of the area, which is likely to have been drawn several decades later. Check whether features such as a railway or an industrial site marked on the OS map were there at the time of the tithe award.

- See if you can match families recorded in the 1841 and 1851 census returns (see pages 218-219) for your area to names of owners and tenants listed in the tithe award and to the farms and cottages on the map.

Enclosure-award maps

Many English and Welsh parishes have a parliamentary enclosure award (see page 62) with a map attached, usually dating from between 1750 and 1850. Altogether, 5341 awards were granted for England and 229 for Wales. Enclosures in Scotland were mostly private and few maps survive.

Dividing up the community Beedon in Berkshire was granted its first enclosure award in 1843 (inset), which lists the distribution of parcels of land around the village, including those given to Queen's College, shown on the attached map (above).

You can view enclosure awards and their maps at the National Archives (see DIRECTORY), or you could try your local record offices (see pages 18-19).

- Note how the land was distributed by an enclosure award: how much was allotted to the local lord, the church or the poor, or perhaps as a quarry or gravel pit for maintaining the highways (see pages 124-125).

- Look for the letter 'T' next to a field boundary. It tells you that the owner of the land on which it is marked is responsible for maintaining the wall or fencing along that boundary. Awards also set out rights of way along footpaths and mark public roads and watercourses.

Estate maps

You may strike lucky and find that your area appears on a map, or 'platt', that accompanied a survey of a manor or estate dating as far back as the late 16th or 17th centuries. These estate maps (see page 27) are mainly concerned with establishing boundaries and ownership, field names and, in a few cases, land-use. You will find them at both national and local record offices, mostly dating from the 18th and 19th centuries. Some of the earliest ones, including around 60 maps of the Duchy of Lancaster from before 1603, survive in the National Archives (see DIRECTORY).

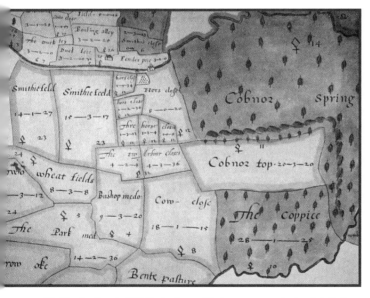

Marking territory In 1630, the land around Barlow was mapped out on behalf of the Cavendish family, who held estates there until 1813, when they passed to the Dukes of Rutland (note Rutland Terrace on the OS maps, left). These maps tell you that by this date only one cottage had been erected at Common Side and that Cobnar (spelt 'Cobnor') Wood had much the same shape as it does today. The present pattern of farmsteads, fields and woodland appears to have been well established.

FIND OUT MORE

- Current OS maps can be found on www.ordnancesurvey.co.uk
- *Reproductions of the First Edition One-inch OS Maps of England and Wales* (J.B. Harley ed., David and Charles, 1969-71)
- The Godfrey Edition, a series of reprints of more than 1700 old maps. www.alangodfrey.co.uk
- The complete collection of six-inch OS maps, 1846-99 can be viewed on www.old-maps.co.uk

Newspapers and directories

You can learn all sorts about your neighbourhood and its former inhabitants from old copies of local newspapers. They are crammed with information: announcements of births, marriages and deaths; lengthy obituaries of prominent local people; advertised businesses and sales; court cases and bankruptcies; sporting and social events. Consulting gazetteers or trade directories should fill in many of the gaps and answer questions raised by your research, helping you to forge a vivid impression of your community's past.

Where to find newspapers

Most local reference libraries hold old copies of local newspapers, and sometimes local record offices (see pages 18-19) keep them too. They are usually available only on microfilm, because they tear easily. The following places are also good sources.

- British Library Newspapers (see DIRECTORY), in Colindale, north London, houses back copies of every British newspaper, national and local. A catalogue and details of opening hours and facilities can be viewed on **www.bl.uk/collections/newspapers.html**
- The National Library of Wales (see DIRECTORY) and the Bodleian Library, Oxford (see DIRECTORY), also hold large newspaper collections. Many Scottish newspapers are held on microfilm at county record offices.
- *Local Newspapers, 1750-1920* (J. Gibson, B. Langston and B.W. Smith, 2nd ed., Federation of Family History Societies, 2002) tells you which local newspapers are kept where, throughout Britain.

Using newspapers Although your search is likely to require a long session at a microfilm reader, your efforts should be well rewarded. You may also find that the newspapers you want to look at have been indexed.

- Allow yourself time to become familiar with the format of a newspaper. You will soon get to know which sections to look at carefully and which to skip.
- Read the advertisements – they can be as informative as any news article, telling you about local business and what was for sale. You may learn when gas burners were first installed in local kitchens or when new fashions caught on in your area.
- If you are interested in entertainment and sport, newspapers are one of the richest sources of information, from details of weekly whist drives to the achievements of the local football and cricket teams.

Gazetteers

During the 19th century, several dictionaries of British places, or gazetteers, were published. The following are most likely to offer information on your area.

- Samuel Lewis's 'Topographical Dictionaries' for England, Wales and Scotland, with an atlas, appeared between 1831 and 1849. They contain brief histories of towns and villages with population figures and notes on businesses and local institutions. Copies are available at large reference libraries and at the British Library (see **www.bl.uk/collections/map_gazetteers.html** for details). A CD of them can be ordered from **www.genealogy.com**
- J. M. Wilson's *The Imperial Gazetteer of England and Wales* (1870) and *The Imperial Gazetteer of Scotland* (1882) give more detailed information. Again large reference libraries usually hold copies.

A step into history
Reading a wartime newspaper (right) can be one of the best ways of understanding the details of day-to-day life at the time. D-Day was less than six weeks away when this Brighton paper was published.

Community 'portraits' The earliest trade directories appeared in the late 17th century, listing useful addresses for merchants and businessmen, but the more detailed ones, likely to be of most value to you, date from the 19th and early 20th centuries. The first national series was published by James Pigot between 1814 and 1853. William White was another notable mid-19th-century directory publisher, but the best-known is Frederic Kelly, whose first directories appeared in 1845. Kelly's directories dominated the market right up to the early 1970s, when they finally ceased publication, superseded by the Telephone Directory and Yellow Pages.

Trade and commercial directories

The sense of what a town or district was like to live in at a particular time is often captured in its trade directories. They identify the main property owners ('principal inhabitants'), name the shopkeepers, and list the various tradesmen who helped to give a place its unique character.

Some cities, such as Birmingham and Sheffield, have directories dating from the late 18th century. Soon after, smaller towns were being covered and by the 1830s the first county directories appeared. Within a decade, trade directories for all parts of Britain were being issued every couple of years.

Who was who A Victorian trade directory, like the one for Bala, north Wales (right), may offer more than just information about the structure of your community at the time. You might discover something new about an ancestor or a local notable.

Where to find directories Reference libraries and record offices have large collections of local directories on their shelves. Pages can usually be photocopied.

- The Family Records Centre (see DIRECTORY) has several hundred English and Welsh directories on computer.
- The London Metropolitan Archives (see DIRECTORY) has a set of London directories on microfilm, but the largest London collection, as well as a major national one, is housed at the Guildhall Library (see DIRECTORY).
- Directories for many counties have been published on CD. A full list is available on www.genealogysupplies.com

What you will find in directories Most directories from the mid 19th century onwards will contain the following:

1 A long (though often unreliable) account of the history, topography and economy of the county or district.

2 A list of important towns, followed by their surrounding villages. Some late Victorian directories divide the entries for towns into street sections, which are accompanied by detailed pull-out maps.

3 Local administrative units, such as parishes, townships and manors, are named and described, giving an insight into how your community was organised in the past.

4 An introduction to each group of settlements, covering local history, land ownership and tenures, and the nature of the economy. The population figure from the most recent census is also noted.

5 Names, addresses and occupations of 'principal inhabitants' and classified entries for various tradesmen, arranged alphabetically.

6 Details of railways, coaches and other transport services.

WATCH OUT
Do not expect a directory to list everyone living in an area at the date given. It will not record those of humble status, such as servants and labourers.

FIND OUT MORE
- www.archivecdbooks.org A range of reproduction copies and CDs of old British journals and newspapers can be ordered from the on-line catalogue.
- www.historicaldirectories.org An on-line library of English and Welsh trade directories, dating from 1750 to 1919.

Census returns

The census books for 1801 to 1901 provide a decade-by-decade review of Britain in a century of unprecedented change. Find out the names of the people who once lived in your street or village, how they earned a living, and even where they were born. By working through the returns you can build a clear picture of how your community has evolved.

What the census can tell you

The first census was taken in 1801, but the enumerators' returns, which give personal details, do not survive before the census of 1841. With each census the returns gave more information, recording age, gender, birthplace and occupation. Census surveys are closed for 100 years, so the most recent survey that you can access is the 1901 census. Start your research here and work backwards to piece together the story of your community.

The 1901 returns These are the easiest records to access and use. They are available on-line (see below) and are fully indexed so you can search by street. Simply type

A glimpse into the past An 1891 census return for Zetland Road in Bristol shows a street of villas inhabited by the families of middle class tradesmen, including a commercial traveller and sugar broker. The households were small and each had one or two servants.

Address details can reveal which houses existed in your street – although house numbers were often omitted

in your address to find out who was living in your street in 1901.

The 1891 and 1881 returns An on-line service provides access to the 1891 and 1881 census records via the National Archives' website (see below). Although designed primarily for family history research, you can browse the records to find your street. Records are grouped by county, then by parish and then by enumeration district – the area that a census worker, or enumerator, could cover in a day. Click on the links next to the district numbers to see descriptions of the areas covered. When you have located your street, click on the link for the relevant district number to see the record. You can also view census returns at your local records office or the Family Records Centre in London (see below), who will give advice on how to use them.

WHERE TO FIND CENSUS RECORDS
The easiest way to access the returns is on the internet but they are also available at many record offices.

FOR ENGLAND AND WALES
On-line records for the 1901 census are available on a pay-per-view basis at www.1901census.nationalarchives.gov.uk (see right). The 1881 and 1891 census records can also be viewed on-line at www.nationalarchives.gov.uk/census/ There is a charge for using the 1881 and 1891 on-line service although there are plans to make this free when the site is accessed from the National Archives in Kew or Family Records Centre (see below).
Local record offices and city reference libraries normally have copies of census returns on microfilm or microfiche for the relevant county.
The Family Records Centre (see DIRECTORY) holds census records for 1841 to 1891 on microfilm and the 1901 returns are stored on microfiche.
The National Archives (see DIRECTORY) has microfiche copies of the 1901 census returns.
The National Library at Aberystwyth (see DIRECTORY) has copies of all Welsh records and those for the border counties of Cheshire, Shropshire and Herefordshire.
Census CDs have been published by the Mormon Church containing transcriptions of the 1881 returns. They are available from the LDS Distribution Centre, Birmingham (see DIRECTORY).

FOR SCOTLAND
Libraries and county record offices hold copies of local returns.
The National Archives of Scotland (see DIRECTORY) holds returns for 1841-1901 on microfilm or microfiche.
On-line returns for 1881, 1891 and 1901 can be accessed on-line at www.scotlandspeople.gov.uk

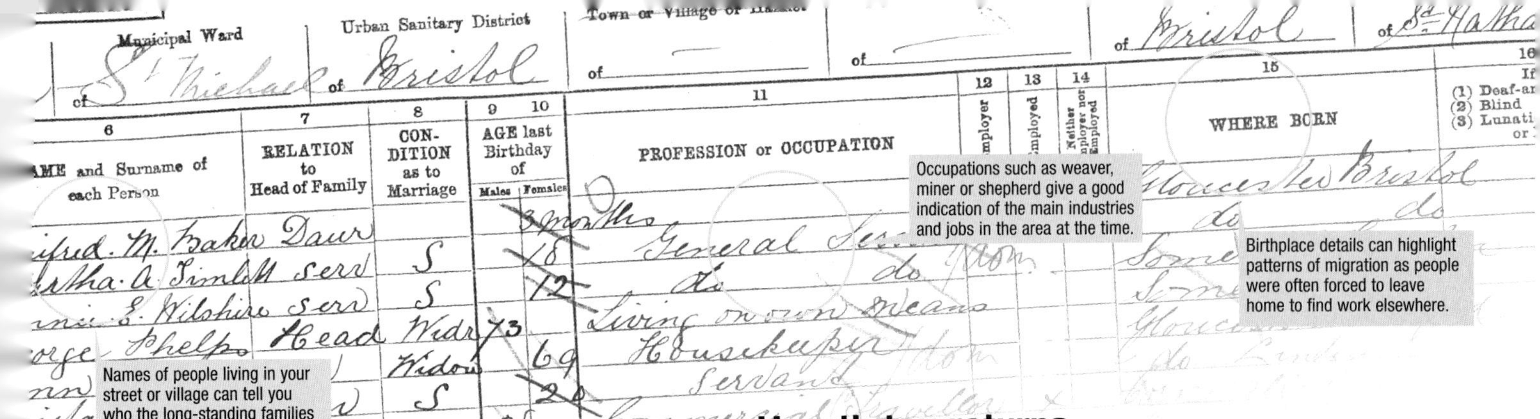

6	7	8	9 10	11	12	13	14	15	16
NAME and Surname of each Person	RELATION to Head of Family	CON-DITION as to Marriage	AGE last Birthday of Males / Females	PROFESSION or OCCUPATION	ployer	ployed	Neither ployer nor Employed	WHERE BORN	(1) Deaf-ar (2) Blind (3) Lunati or

Municipal Ward of St Michael *Urban Sanitary District* of Bristol *Town or Village of ...* of Bristol of St Mathia

Occupations such as weaver, miner or shepherd give a good indication of the main industries and jobs in the area at the time.

Birthplace details can highlight patterns of migration as people were often forced to leave home to find work elsewhere.

Names of people living in your street or village can tell you who the long-standing families in the local community were.

(handwritten census entries, partially legible:)
...fred M. Baker Daur ... S ... 3 months ... General Ser... Gloucester Bristol
...tha A. Timlett serv ... S ... 15 ... do ... do ... Some...
...nie E. Wilshire serv ... S ... 12 ... Living on own Means ... I...
...ge ... Phelps Head Widr 73 ... Housekeeping ... Glouce...
...nn ... S ... 20 ... Servant
...rieta ... head M 38 ... Commerc...
...mes S ... Wife M 34
...len S. do daur 2 months
...ldine R. do daur S 21 Gener...
...ssie Mc Williams serv S
...rles Harding Head M 75 Su...
...ne I. do Wife M 71
...to ... daur S 24

Returns from 1841 to 1871

The more recent the returns the more informative they are. The earliest survey to include personal details was the 1841 census but the information is less detailed than in subsequent returns.

- Relationships between household members are not given.
- The returns record the ages of children under 15 but round all other ages down to the nearest 5.
- Birthplaces are not recorded. People were simply asked if they were born in the county of their current address.

The census pitfalls

Census records are a mine of useful information but there are certain drawbacks that you should bear in mind.

- The reliability of the information depends on the statements given by householders and the accuracy of the copies that were made.
- There are sometimes discrepancies in details such as age and place of birth from one census to the next.
- Entries for occupations may appear to be inconsistent. A man might have been recorded as a weaver when he also had a small farm. Agricultural labourers often took on other jobs, especially during the winter.

FIND OUT MORE

These sources offer helpful information on finding and using census records.

- *Making Use of the Census* (Susan Lumas, PRO Publications, 2002)
- *Using Census Returns: A Pocket Guide to Family History* (PRO Publications, 2002)
- www.originsnetwork.com Access by subscription to the indexed 1871 census returns for various counties, and transcriptions of the 1861 and 1871 Scottish returns.
- www.genuki.org.uk/big/census_place.html A searchable database of places in the 1891 census.
- www.nationalarchives.gov.uk/pathways/census/ An on-line exhibition shows how the 1901 census records have helped to reconstruct the history of four communities.

Hearth tax returns

To build up a picture of the people who lived in your community before the 19th century, consult the 17th-century hearth tax returns. These list the heads of households who were liable to pay a tax on chimneys and provide information on their occupations. The tax was collected twice yearly between 1662 and 1688 in England and Wales, and returns survive for the years 1662-6 and 1669-74. Hearths in Scotland were taxed between 1691 and 1695.

- The number of hearths on which tax was paid reflects the size and comfort of the house and can give a good idea of the owner's social standing in a community.
- They also show the distribution of surnames: many distinctive names were still confined to the places where they originated.

WHERE TO FIND HEARTH TAX RETURNS

- The original returns are stored at the National Archives in Kew and the National Archives of Scotland (see DIRECTORY).
- Returns survive for half of the English counties and Glamorganshire. Enquire at your record office if anything has been published for your county.
- A project based at the Roehampton University (see DIRECTORY) aims to make available microfilm and printed editions of returns for all counties.

A wealth of hearths A tax return for Pudding Lane, London, in 1666 – just before the Great Fire broke out there – reveals not only the number of hearths in each property but the occupations of the tradesmen, including a fishmonger and a draper.

219

The records of Scotland

Before 1603, when James VI of Scotland also became James I of England, the Scots had a history that was totally separate from that of England and Wales. Even after that date, despite the union of the two parliaments in 1707, they followed a path of their own in many respects, particularly in relation to law, education and religion. You will therefore come across many records that are unique to Scotland.

A local start

As in the rest of Britain, the best place to begin your search is likely to be on home ground – at your local history centre or reference library. Many will hold treasure troves of material on your town or village, including old maps, indexes of newspapers and census records. You usually have to visit to find out exactly what is available, as few have catalogues on-line. Look in the phone directory for addresses and other contact details.

A fragmented Church

Before the Reformation of the late 16th century, Scotland was a Roman Catholic country. Episcopalianism then became the dominant form of Protestantism until 1690, when Presbyterianism was embraced by the Church of Scotland. In the 19th century, many more expressions of faith emerged including the foundation of the Free Church of Scotland in 1843.

This history manifests itself in the abundance of ecclesiastical buildings seen in most Scottish towns and cities, even in small settlements (see pages 232-233). It was common for competing ministries to build churches next to each other, each of which would keep its own records (kirk session minutes). The earliest date from 1553, later than in England and Wales, where it became mandatory to keep records in 1538.

Education and law

In 1696, laws were passed that led to the establishment of a national education system for Scotland. Provision was patchy at first, but by the early 18th century, every parish had its own school, offering a basic education, though usually only for boys.

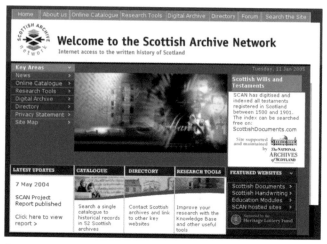

Scotland on-line The Scottish Archive Network (SCAN) is a useful tool for researching the story of almost any locality in Scotland. The website at **www.scan.org.uk** gives details of what is held in all of the country's archives, along with their addresses, phone numbers and opening hours.

It was not compulsory and it was not free, but it was cheap and of a high standard. Records on schooling in Scotland (see page 235) therefore relate to nearly all social classes in a community from a much earlier date than similar documents covering England and Wales.

Scotland has its own separate legal system, which will particularly affect any research you do into property transactions. Details of such dealing in Scotland have been recorded since 1617 in the Registers of Sasines (see page 318). They can be seen at the National Archives of Scotland (see DIRECTORY). Use of sasine registers is gradually being replaced by the Land Register, set up in 1979. It can be consulted on-line at **www.ros.gov.uk**

Aberdeen's churches
Like most Scottish towns in the past, Aberdeen offered its citizens a wide choice when it came to places of worship. Competition for supporters led to many churches being built almost side by side. The Belmont Relief Chapel (below, left), later known as the South Parish Church, was built within yards of the medieval Kirk of St Nicholas (right) in the 18th century.

Other useful legal records are those of the Dean of Guild Courts, containing information about buildings in the various burghs (see page 138); sheriff court records, which provide evidence of disputes and criminal cases; and Justice of the Peace records, which reveal instances of minor local misdemeanours. All of these documents are held by the National Archives of Scotland (see DIRECTORY).

Government in action

Parliamentary Papers will include specific 'Scotland' reports, which have much information about particular parishes. One, dated 1844, on the 'Poor Law Inquiry, Scotland', reveals that in Prestonpans parish, East Lothian, there were 144 paupers; women and children earned 8d a day for field labour; 19 pubs sold spirits and 11 shops sold alcohol. Parliamentary Papers are held by the legal deposit libraries, which include the National Library of Scotland (see DIRECTORY), the British Library (see DIRECTORY) and the National Library of Wales (see DIRECTORY), and by many university libraries, which usually charge a consultation fee.

Statistical accounts

Scotland is also fortunate to have reports giving detailed statistics on its various communities and their inhabitants, dating back to the late 18th century. Contents vary from place to place, but generally the topics covered include geography and geology, industry, agriculture, markets, populations, incomes, prices of goods, curiosities and antiquities, eminent citizens, churches and schools.

The two earliest sets of reports can be viewed at **edina.ac.uk/stat-acc-scot** You will also find the *Third Statistical Accounts* for some places giving information up to the mid 20th century, and there are accounts for Midlothian and East Lothian up to 2000, which are usually available at local reference libraries (a CD of the Midlothian report can be bought from **www.midlothian.gov.uk/Library/Publicat.htm**).

Maps

Much of the National Library of Scotland's map collection can be seen on-line at **www.nls.uk/digitallibrary/map/index.html** It includes the first detailed maps of Scotland, created by Timothy Pont (*c*.1565-1614). He travelled the country during the 1580s and 90s, surveying and making copious notes. The maps he drew formed the basis of the first atlas of Scotland, published in 1654 by Joan Blaeu as part of a monumental world atlas, the *Atlas Novus*.

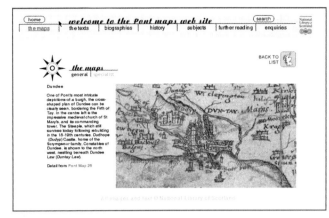

Pont maps The 77 surviving maps created by Timothy Pont (see below) are a rich source of information on life in 16th-century Scotland. Some focus on individual places, such as Dundee (above), while others cover swathes of countryside.

Burgh Surveys More than 70 Burgh Surveys have been produced and published by Historic Scotland (see DIRECTORY). These reports bring together current archaeological and historical research to provide a wide-ranging picture of the past. Each one includes a description of the geography and physical setting of a particular burgh together with a review of its history from prehistoric times to the present day.

FIND OUT MORE

• *Scottish Local History: an introductory guide* (D. Moody, Batsford, 1986)
• *Exploring Scottish History* (M. Cox, ed., Scottish Library Association, Scottish Local History Forum and The Scottish Record Association, 1999)
• *Tracing Scottish Local History* (C.J. Sinclair, National Archives of Scotland, HMSO 1994)
• *Tracing Your Scottish Ancestors: the Official Guide* (National Archives of Scotland, HMSO, 2003)
• *East Lothian Fourth Statistical Account 1945-2000, Vol. 1* (S. Baker, ed., East Lothian Council Library Service, 2003)
• *The Nation Survey'd: essays on late sixteenth century Scotland as depicted by Timothy Pont* (I.C. Cunningham, ed., Tuckwell Press/National Library of Scotland, 2001)

Meet the people of your street

Do you ever wonder who lived in your street before you, how large their families were and what they did for a living? A few visits to your local city or county archives should bring you the answers to these questions, and some of your neighbours can probably give a lively account of all the comings and goings.

Ask the neighbours

The best way to start your research on the people of your street is to talk to long-term residents. People usually love talking about their family history. Start by asking them how long have they been there. Where did the family come from? Why did they choose to move to your town or village? And why this house in this street? If you ask everyone the same questions, you will quickly get a broad overview of the lives unfolding around you.

Soon you will need to flesh out the information you have gathered with a visit to your local reference library and then, perhaps, to the city or county record office to track down any documents about your street. Always work back in time from what you already know.

Electoral registers and directories

Your local record office (see pages 18-19) will have a collection of electoral registers, giving the names and addresses of everyone who was entitled to vote in national and local elections from 1832 to the present day. Trade and commercial directories (see page 217) may take you back further. But neither source will give a complete picture, as universal suffrage for men was not granted until 1918 and for women until 1928, and the directories only list leading tradesmen and the better-off citizens.

Be alert to the fact that a street name or the house numbering may have been changed. Houses in many streets were not given numbers until well into the latter half of the 19th century.

High society Mention of your street in a 19th-century electoral register (left) will tell you that it was home to some of the area's leading citizens. For much of the century the right to vote was restricted to a moneyed, mostly male, elite. Qualification for the franchise – usually property ownership – is stated.

Face-to-face A street directory for Smethwick (right) tells you much about the prosperity of the area, but snaps, such as that of a street party held for George V's Silver Jubilee in 1935 (below) breathe life into such lists.

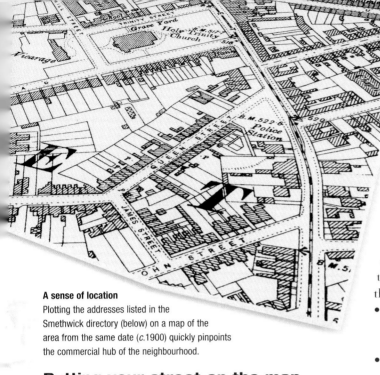

A sense of location
Plotting the addresses listed in the
Smethwick directory (below) on a map of the
area from the same date (*c.*1900) quickly pinpoints
the commercial hub of the neighbourhood.

Putting your street on the map

Reference libraries usually keep local maps, including
larger-scale Ordnance Survey (OS) ones (see page 26). It
might be useful to look at a map from the same period as
any directory or electoral register you have been searching
through. See how many houses, shops and other buildings
listed in the directory or register you can locate. This may
provide you with a useful framework of information for
when you turn your attention to census returns.

What the census reveals

Your library or record office will have a complete
set of census returns for your district from 1841
to 1901. Most will also have a catalogue to guide
you to your street, but be prepared to search in
more than one place. Be aware that the boundary
of a census enumerator's district might go down the
middle of a street, or swing round a corner, so that
your street might be in more than one district (see
also 'Census returns' on pages 218-219).

At first glance census returns can appear to contain
an overwhelmingly large amount of information, but
these guidelines should help you to work your way
through it all.

- Begin by looking at the census return for a period that
you have already done some research on, perhaps by
looking at a trade directory or map.
- Start by noting down all the families who were living in
your street in a particular year, then check how many
were there in earlier and later census returns. This will
give you an idea of who the 'core families' that stayed
put were and who came and went within a few years.
- From the 1851 census onward, the birthplace of each
person was noted. Although this information is not
always accurate, you could still use it to work out a
general pattern of migration from around Britain.
- Look especially at the birthplaces of the children within
one family. If they are different, they may indicate the
approximate dates of the movements of a family before
they arrived in your street. On the whole, people moved
within the neighbourhood with which they were
familiar, but the rapid growth of industry in many
towns during the 19th century attracted people from
further afield in search of work.
- Census returns can give an indication of the economic
status of a community by revealing how people earned
their living. Look first at the work done by the men,
noting the occupations of all the heads of households,
then those of the young men and boys. Next turn to the
women, but remember that many of them did jobs that
were part-time and not usually recorded.

Searching earlier records

The further back in time you go, the more difficult it is
to find detailed documentation. But the familiarity with
your local archives that you will gain by searching
through the more recent first, should prove useful when
hunting for the older, more obscure material. Look for
any mention of your street or district in the catalogues
of manorial and parish records (see pages 147 and 227),
for any references to old maps – especially tithe-award
ones (see page 27) – that you are able to examine, and
enquire about published sources of information, such as
hearth-tax returns (see page 219).

The naming of our streets

Most of us live on a street and in a community full of streets, with names that we probably take for granted. But there is a reason for every road name, and many are associated with intriguing stories. The word 'street' itself originates from the Anglo-Saxon 'strete', which refers to a paved road as constructed by the Romans.

Pathways into the past

Some of Britain's roads have their origins as ancient trackways used by travellers and tradesmen long before cars were invented. These old roads usually retain the word 'way' in their names. The Harrow Way is the oldest road in Britain, and it keeps its name for much of its route from Folkestone to Stonehenge. The old trackways are often sunk into the landscape, with high banks on either side, or they may follow a natural ridge. Names like Holloway Lane and Ridge Street reflect this.

Roman roads such as the Fosse Way and Watling Street (see pages 46-47) tend to keep their names as they pass through towns. They are typically straight, joining two places by the most direct route. Latin elements in some street names can still be made out through the fog of two millennia. Chesterton Lane in Cambridge dates back to the remains of the castrum or Roman camp ('Chester') to which the lane led, noted by the Saxon farmer who established his tun or farmstead there ('-ton').

Danish street names are common in the north of England, especially 'gate'. The Danish 'gata' and Anglo-Saxon 'geat' both meant a thoroughfare, not an opening in a wall. Once you understand this, the York street names of Castlegate, Coppergate, Fossgate and Stonegate make more sense – they are ways through the city that do not necessarily pass through any gates.

A meaning lost in time The shortest street in York has the longest name: Whip-ma-whop-ma-gate. It has changed over the years from the medieval 'Whitnourwhatnourgate', meaning 'what a street' – a street that is so short it can scarcely be called one. The new name seems to reflect an association with beating or whipping. But was that, as some claim, the siting of a whipping post nearby for chastising beggars and rogues, or was it the more esoteric practice of whipping dogs called whappets there on St Luke's Day? The question continues to baffle historians.

Medieval markets and mysteries

Street names can reveal the medieval origin of a town layout, and even who was selling what and where. In Salisbury in Wiltshire streets around the centrally placed Poultry Cross (right) have names such as Butcher Row, Fish Row and Salt Lane. Other names may not be as obvious. York's famous street of leaning old houses called The Shambles was the butchers' quarter in medieval times and takes its name from the 'shammels' – the shelves that butchers used to display their meat.

Medieval market square The medieval layout of Salisbury can be seen in the old market square's central Poultry Cross and appropriately named streets nearby such as Butcher Row and Fish Row.

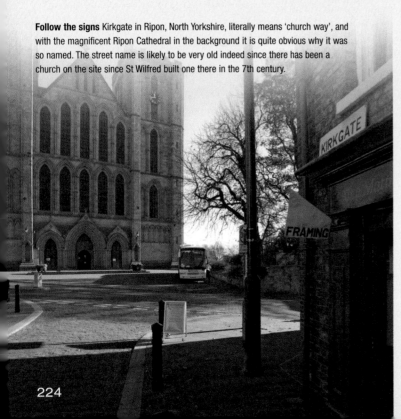

Follow the signs Kirkgate in Ripon, North Yorkshire, literally means 'church way', and with the magnificent Ripon Cathedral in the background it is quite obvious why it was so named. The street name is likely to be very old indeed since there has been a church on the site since St Wilfred built one there in the 7th century.

SEBASTOPOL ROAD

Military victories Sebastopol Road in Aldershot (top) is one of many throughout Britain, all likely to have been built in the mid 19th century and named after the great siege in the Crimean War (1853-6).

Pride of the Empire

In the 19th century huge movements of people from the country into the towns and from town centres outwards led to the creation of numerous suburbs to accommodate them (see pages 164-165). Thousands of new roads had to be named. Fortunately the street namers were not short of material. Britain was full of her own importance as an imperial power and so many of the names had a colonial flavour – Bombay Street, Jamaica Street, Tobago Street – or commemorated battles and martial heroes – Waterloo Road, Wellington Parade, Havelock Road.

If a town had particular associations, it generally wanted to draw attention to them when naming its streets. In an army garrison town such as Aldershot, it is no surprise to find mention of Crimean War commanders and battles – Alma Close, Raglan Close, Redan Gardens, Sebastopol Road – or Nelson Road, Victory Stadium and Trafalgar Place in Portsmouth, home of the Royal Navy.

Local heroes

Some streets are named after famous people from the locality. In Hereford there is a Gwynne Street where Nell Gwynne, mistress to Charles II, was reputedly born. It would be astonishing if Liverpool had not honoured the Beatles by naming Paul McCartney Way, George Harrison Close, John Lennon Drive and Ringo Starr Drive after its very own Fab Four.

Other names commemorate people held in high regard by the community but unknown outside it. In Ammanford, south Wales, a 1970s estate road is called Stewart Drive. It is named in honour of local doctor Donald Stewart, a much-respected Scotsman who came to Ammanford as a young practitioner in 1909 and served the town for the rest of his working life.

Always remembered Street names can be a lasting record of a local celebrity. Harry Lauder may not be as famous as he was in his music-hall heyday, but the singer's name lives on (above) in his native district of Portobello in Edinburgh.

FIND OUT MORE

• *The Street Names Of England* (Adrian Room, Paul Watkins Publishing, 1992)
• www.thepotteries.org/focus/002.htm Street names in The Potteries.
• members.aol.com/WHall95037/london.html The Lost London Index: an index of London street name changes and those that are no longer in existence or shown on maps.

Getting to know the people of your whole community

Once you know your street, you can see how it fits into the community as a whole. Again look closely at directories, maps, electoral rolls and census returns. What similarities and differences are there between your street and others close by? Are more people moving into or out of the area? What job do they do and how has this changed over time? Perhaps you will discover where someone famous, or infamous, lived.

Finding the local celebrities

Wherever you live, some son or daughter of the place will have made their mark on society.

Wall plaques Look out for a blue English Heritage or similar plaque on the walls of houses, commemorating an illustrious member of your community.

Street names Walk around and check on maps to see if any streets or public buildings are named after a local worthy.

STAN LAUREL WAS BORN IN THIS HOUSE 16th JUNE 1890

Famous son Signs of celebrity may be anywhere. A tiny terraced house in Ulverston, Cumbria, similar to the others crammed around it, is marked out as the birthplace of Stan Laurel (above), while his statue (left) graces a corner of North Shields where he lived as a child.

Local newspapers At your local record office (see pages 18-19) you will find a mine of information in old editions of local newspapers (see pages 216-217). Events such as royal visits and the openings of major public buildings were probably attended by the local celebrities of the time. Their political actions and business affairs will also have been extensively reported, and there are likely to be lengthy obituaries of most leading inhabitants.

Older local histories Ask at your local reference library if they keep copies of any older, published local histories. These frequently contain biographies of notable members of the community, which are often accompanied by photographs. Some, with such splendid titles as 'Accrington Captains of Industry' or 'Hallamshire Worthies', deal exclusively with the illustrious.

Uncovering the bad apples

Criminals are just as likely to be well recorded as the great and the good. Some areas may even have had a reputation for crime and disorder, especially at certain times of the year, such as when annual fairs like the Nottingham Goose Fair were held.

- Court cases were reported at length in local newspapers and the more sensational crimes frequently became part of local folklore.

- Prisoners are well documented from 1877, when the Home Office took over responsibility for prisons. Prison registers going back a hundred years and sometimes more are held at the National Archives at Kew (see DIRECTORY). These note the age of a convict, his or her physical appearance (accompanied by a photograph), place of birth, marital status and occupation.

- The inmates of prisons are listed in census returns (see pages 218-219), although in some cases they are recorded only by their initials.

- From the 16th century onwards Justices of the Peace tried many offences at meetings known as quarter sessions. Their records are kept in the archives of county record offices (see pages 18-19).

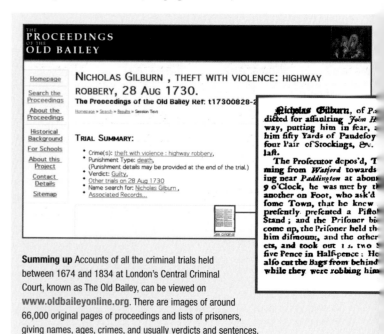

THE PROCEEDINGS OF THE OLD BAILEY

Homepage	NICHOLAS GILBURN , THEFT WITH VIOLENCE: HIGHWAY ROBBERY, 28 AUG 1730.
Search the Proceedings	The Proceedings of the Old Bailey Ref: t17300828-2
About the Proceedings	Homepage » Search » Results » Session Text
Historical Background	**TRIAL SUMMARY:**
For Schools	
About this Project	• Crime(s): theft with violence : highway robbery, • Punishment Type: death, (Punishment details may be provided at the end of the trial.)
Contact Details	• Verdict: Guilty, • Other trials on 28 Aug 1730
Sitemap	• Name search for: Nicholas Gilburn , • Associated Records...

Summing up Accounts of all the criminal trials held between 1674 and 1834 at London's Central Criminal Court, known as The Old Bailey, can be viewed on www.oldbaileyonline.org. There are images of around 66,000 original pages of proceedings and lists of prisoners, giving names, ages, crimes, and usually verdicts and sentences.

The all-encompassing parish

Records of key events in parishioners' lives were once kept in the parish chest inside a church, but are now housed in local record offices. They deal not only with spiritual concerns, but also with secular matters. From the 16th to the 19th century, the parish was responsible for appointing constables to enforce law and order, for maintaining the highways (see page 248), and for looking after the poor and needy.

Reading the registers Among notes on parish business and accounting, you will find details of baptisms, marriages and burials in your community possibly going back as far as 1538, when each church was ordered to record such rites of passage.

- Use the information to get an idea of how long some families have been in the area. Adding up the annual totals of baptisms and burials will show you whether the population was rising or falling at different periods of time. A sudden increase in burials might indicate a visitation of the plague or other deadly epidemic.

- Some parish registers note a man's occupation, (although they are rarely consistent in this before 1813), which will give you some sense of what the people in your community did for a living. Compare this with occupations noted on census returns from 1841 onwards.

Poor relief From the beginning of the 17th century, parishes levied local rates to provide money for the 'deserving poor'. Parish archives will also contain a record of this work.

- Money, clothes and shoes were doled out on a regular basis. The names of recipients are often recorded.

- Fathers of 'bastards' were identified and their names listed, with the sum they were required to pay for their child's upkeep recorded.

- Paupers originally from another parish were frequently sent back there, so as not to be a burden on their adopted community. 'Settlement papers' recording disputes taken before a Justice of the Peace give brief accounts of the movements and distress of abandoned wives and children, the infirm and the disreputable.

- Some parishes built poor houses to look after the most needy and provide work for the able. The workhouses erected after the Poor Law Amendment Act (1834) were the result of a new national system of unions of parishes (see page 179). Any surviving workhouse records, such as admittance registers, will be found at county record offices, and the inmates are listed in the census returns of 1841-1901.

Brief lives Early parish registers can be light on detail. Christenings recorded at St Mary's Church, Worsbrough, South Yorkshire, for 1774 (below), make no mention of the child's mother. Errors due to lapses of memory were also common, as many vicars made their records some time after the event.

FIND OUT MORE
- www.english-heritage.org.uk Information on Blue Plaques.
- www.familyhistoryonline.net Pay-per-view database of county records for England and Wales.
- www.familysearch.org Access to indexes of parish records worldwide, compiled by the Mormon Church.
- www.gendocs.demon.co.uk/institute.html List of Victorian public institutions in London, including workhouses.
- www.workhouses.org Detailed site on the Poor Laws and workhouses, including inmates.

Looking at your parish church

Your parish church is possibly your neighbourhood's oldest building, for centuries the focal point of local life. A close look at it, starting with the churchyard and exterior of the building, will reveal not only its history, but also much about your community, its times of feast and famine and the identity of important local families. Rich and poor alike will have taken pride in maintaining, enlarging and embellishing the church, and it is not difficult to unearth the evidence from what you see and from the parish records.

Clues in the churchyard

Before you go inside a church, look around the churchyard. The present appearance, with lych gate, paths and trees, probably dates from the Victorian period, but you will reach further back in time by studying the gravestones. You may find some graves from the 17th century; before then, they were marked with a simple wooden cross.

Who lies where? Look near the main door on the south side of the church for the earliest gravestones. Until the 18th or 19th century, the north side was regarded as the devil's side, where excommunicates, the unbaptised and suicides were buried. Churchyards are normally larger on the south side than the north, although later additions to their land may have obscured this arrangement.

Spot the names Only the better-off families in the 17th century erected gravestones, but by the 18th century the fashion had spread to most households. The poorest people might not have had gravestones even in the Victorian period, when some of the richer locals were commemorating their dead with elaborate memorials.

- Look for groups of gravestones with the same surname. These are likely to belong to long-resident families of your community. You may find their names appearing again in parish and census records (see pages 222–223).
- If the local stone has weathered badly and the wording is unreadable, check at the local record office to see if a family history society has made a 'monumental inscriptions' survey to record all the details.

Outer appearances

Stand back from your local church and observe the way in which it has been built. You may be surprised at the number of contrasting styles. This is partly because in the Middle Ages the rector, in return for receiving tithes from the parishioners, was responsible for building and maintaining only his part of the church, which included the chancel at the east end where the high altar is sited (see pages 230-231). The parishioners looked after the nave, aisles and tower, and often restyled their part of the church, while the rector's end remained untouched. Architectural variety also came about when parishes could not afford to rebuild, but just added a few features in a new style. This piecemeal work makes parish

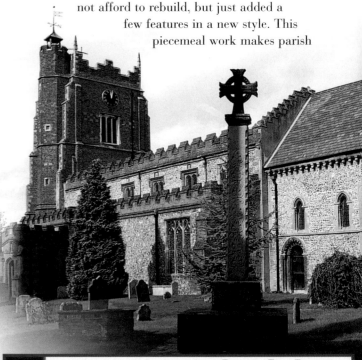

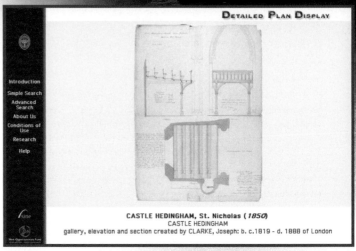

DETAILED PLAN DISPLAY

Introduction
Simple Search
Advanced Search
About Us
Conditions of Use
Research
Help

CASTLE HEDINGHAM, St. Nicholas (*1850*)
CASTLE HEDINGHAM
gallery, elevation and section created by CLARKE, Joseph: b. c.1819 - d. 1888 of London

churches all the more interesting to examine. Even if they appear to be of one era from the outside, it is often possible to find earlier work inside (see pages 230-231).

Style pointers Try to fit the architectural styles of the church to booms and slumps in the local economy. The tower at East Bergholt, Suffolk, was not completed because of the collapse of the woollen cloth trade in the 1520s.

• Look for private chapels, known as chantries, built by parishioners or local guilds (see pages 140-141). The most convenient space for them was beside the chancel.

• Churches were dependent on fund-raising events, such as the May games. You may see an inscription like the one at Long Melford, Suffolk, praising the contributions of 'all the well-disposed men of this town'.

The story in the stones

Look at the materials that were used to build your church for clues about how it was constructed and even paid for.

Recycled materials Early medieval masons used whatever local materials were at hand, including bricks and stones from Roman forts or boulders and pebbles from the fields.

• Humble materials could also be used to construct very fine buildings. In East Anglia the great churches that were built out of the profits of the cloth trade (see pages 142-143), such as Southwold and Stoke-by-Nayland, were constructed of rubble, with a veneer of knapped flints. A clue to the expense lavished on these churches is the imported limestone used for the corner stones and window frames.

• A church built entirely of the finest imported stone will suggest a parish that had become wealthy in the later Middle Ages. Such places are often on the coast or a river, where the stone could be easily landed.

Extending through the ages St Nicholas Church at Castle Hedingham in Essex (above) has, like many English churches, been restyled and added to over time, perfectly encapsulating the history of the area. The Norman 'wheel' window in the chancel dates from the 12th century; the tower is 17th-century, but was built with reused bricks from the nearby castle; and work on a gallery was carried out from 1850 (see plans, left). You may be able to trace alterations and restoration work to your church – www.churchplansonline.org gives on-line access to the Incorporated Church Building Society's archive of plans for new and existing churches from 1818 to 1982.

WHEN WAS YOUR CHURCH BUILT?
You can often date your church from architectural details, such as the shape of the tower or the size and decoration of the windows.

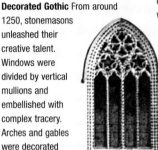

Norman Following their conquest of England in 1066, Norman barons built numerous small stone churches. They were planned in the shape of a cross and featured a central tower, round arches and small windows.

Early English The Gothic style, characterised by steeples, pointed arches and rib vaults, came to England via France around 1175. The design was more elegant than the Norman churches, with thinner walls and larger windows.

Decorated Gothic From around 1250, stonemasons unleashed their creative talent. Windows were divided by vertical mullions and embellished with complex tracery. Arches and gables were decorated with stylised leaves.

Perpendicular Gothic From 1350 to the Reformation in the mid-16th century, churches were built in a late-Gothic or Perpendicular style, named after the perpendicular lines of the mullions. These larger windows were filled with stained glass, often used to tell Biblical stories. Other features included flat lead roofs hidden behind battlements and pinnacles, carved wooden ceilings, long ranges of windows and fan vaulting. The sturdy towers are the glory of these churches.

English Baroque After the great fire of 1666, London acquired new churches, many designed by Christopher Wren and his pupil Nicholas Hawksmoor in the classical English Baroque style. Porticoes, graceful spires and internal galleries were among the features, such as at Hawksmoor's Christ Church, Spitalfields. In the 18th century the parishioners of expanding towns and rural landowners built churches in a more restrained classical style.

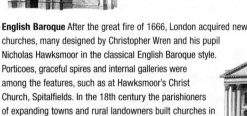

FIND OUT MORE
• www.church-search.com A database of Church of England parish churches.
• www.genuki.org.uk/big/parloc/search.html A database giving locations for parish churches.
• www.visitchurches.org.uk The website of The Churches Conservation Trust.
• www.britainexpress.com/History/english-parish-churches.htm The history of English churches.
• www.newadvent.org/cathen/15653b.htm 'Windows in Church Architecture' (from the Catholic Encyclopedia).
• *England's Thousand Best Churches* (Simon Jenkins, 2000, Penguin Books)

Inside your parish church

Your parish church is a time capsule of local history. Inside you will find effigies, monuments and brasses, sculptures and portraits, gravestones and plaques dedicated to past members of the community. If you trawl through the parish records at your county record office, you may find churchwardens' accounts going back hundreds of years detailing day-to-day transactions, who cleaned the church and when alterations took place.

Memorials to local worthies

To find out who were the movers and shakers of your parish, step inside your church and you will see a range of memorials to local people, from medieval effigies to lists of those who died in the First and Second World Wars. Some names will provide links to other local families who you may encounter elsewhere in your research.

Effigies, monuments and brasses Look at the inscriptions to discover who was important and why.

- If you see a stone carving of a man in a reclining position, clad in armour, often with his feet resting on an animal, and perhaps with his wife at his side, it is probably a local lord dating from the 13th to the early 16th centuries.
- Elizabethan and Stuart effigies were in Italian Renaissance style and made of polished alabaster. They often show a man and his wife kneeling or seated in prayer. In the later 17th and early 18th centuries, effigies became grander and more Baroque in style and featured family groups. Also popular at the time were lifelike classical busts or full figures, carved in marble.
- Look out for memorial brasses. They were popular from the 14th to the late 16th century, and again in Victorian times, but were not intended to be accurate portraits.
- If you study the gravestones inside the church and wall-mounted memorials, you will discover the names of the better-off parishioners.
- You may see charity boards, which recorded any charitable endowments to the church.

THE ANATOMY OF A CHURCH

However much your parish church has been altered and whatever its size, you will still be able to identify the most common features, such as the chancel, nave, pulpit and font. The Georgian box pews may have been removed by the Victorians, and the rood screen might be missing, but you may find an old painting or photograph in the church showing how it once looked.

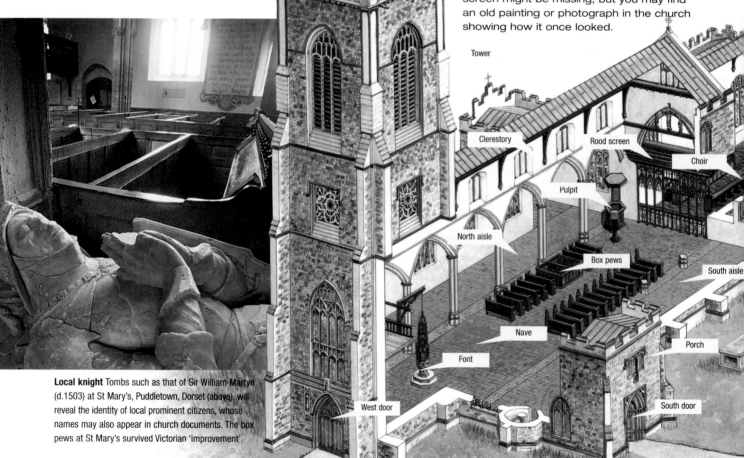

Pinnacle

Tower

Clerestory

Rood screen

Choir

Pulpit

North aisle

Box pews

South aisle

Nave

Porch

Font

West door

South door

Local knight Tombs such as that of Sir William Martyn (d.1503) at St Mary's, Puddletown, Dorset (above), will reveal the identity of local prominent citizens, whose names may also appear in church documents. The box pews at St Mary's survived Victorian 'improvement'.

Symbolic clues Parish churches were a riot of colour in medieval times before they were whitewashed during the Reformation in the 16th century. But you will still find them adorned with carvings of Christian symbols. The eagle is the symbol of St John the Evangelist and is commonly found on the lectern from where the Gospels are read. Look for the symbol of the saint to whom the church is dedicated, such as the lion of St Mark. You may see a fish, the early Christians' symbol of Christ from the story of the feeding of the five thousand; a dove represents the Holy Spirit; a lamb, the Redeemer; wheat heads, the 'bread of life'.

What to find in the records

The parish records in your county record office will record key changes and the day-to-day life of your local church.

Medieval wills These may contain bequests to finance new work in your local church, such as the insertion of windows, the heightening of the tower, or the addition of a chantry chapel.

Diocesan archives Look for licences, known as faculties, granted by a local bishop in the 19th and 20th centuries to authorise your church to make structural changes to the building.

Churchwardens' accounts Look out for details of expenditure on maintenance, cleaning and decoration. Some accounts survive from the Reformation and often provide information about alterations made to churches. An account for a York parish reveals that in 1547 a labourer was paid twopence for removing dirt from St Michael's, Spurriergate, at the time 'the seyntts [saints] was takyn down'. The accounts will say when the church-wardens paid the bell-ringers for celebrating major events, such as a coronation, and when parishioners were paid to shoot birds and vermin.

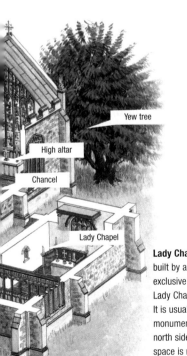

Yew tree

High altar

Chancel

Lady Chapel

Lych gate

Chancel The east part of the church, known as the chancel, belonged to the rector. The high altar could be seen dimly through the rood screen that divided the nave, and the parishioners, from the chancel. Look out for slots in the walls, where the screen was once fixed, and for a blocked staircase that once led to the large crucifix and the carved figures of the Virgin Mary and St John on top of the screen. Outside in the churchyard you may see a yew tree, a symbol of immortality.

Lady Chapel Today, the former chantry chapel, built by a wealthy parishioner or guild for their exclusive use (see page 229), is often known as the Lady Chapel, regardless of its original dedication. It is usually open for private prayer. Look for a monument or plaque to its original benefactor. If the north side of the church had a chantry chapel, the space is now sometimes occupied by the organ.

Nave The main body of the church is known as the nave. This was the parishioners' part of the church, where, during services, the congregation stood. If your church has a stone bench around the wall, it was intended for the old and infirm, hence the expression 'the weak to the wall'. In the Middle Ages the nave was also used as a village hall and meeting place. Pews may bear the names of wealthy local families.

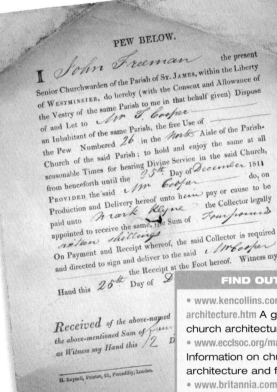

Pews for rent Well-to-do parishioners used to rent private pews by the year. Among your parish records at the county record office you might come across a document such as this pew rent receipt dated 1810 for St James's, Westminster.

FIND OUT MORE

• www.kencollins.com/glossary/architecture.htm A glossary of church architecture.
• www.ecclsoc.org/main.html Information on church architecture and furnishings.
• www.britannia.com/church/studies/index.html Historical articles on many parish churches.
• *Buildings of England* (Nikolaus Pevsner, Penguin Books). Accounts of many parish churches by the acclaimed architectural historian.

Recognising other houses of God

Walk around your town or village and you may find a variety of places of worship, not just the parish church. A town will probably have Baptist or Presbyterian chapels, a Catholic church, a Quaker meeting house and perhaps a synagogue, mosque or Hindu temple. Even a small village may have a Methodist chapel. These places of worship all hold clues to the character of your community.

Nonconformist churches

A Nonconformist or Dissenter was someone who refused to conform to the Church of England as it was re-established after the restoration of Charles II in 1660. Baptists, Congregationalists, Presbyterians and Quakers were the main groups to emerge in the 17th century, although at this period Nonconformists numbered only 4 per cent of the English and Welsh population. One of the largest groups were the Methodists, whose first national conference was held in 1744.

The first Nonconformist meeting houses were built by Puritan landowners in the 17th century. They were known as chapels, because they were similar in style and simplicity to chapels erected in the Middle Ages in remote places far from the parish church.

Where to look

If you live in a town, venture down the side-streets to look for chapels. The main streets were often too full to build on, or congregations could only afford these poorer sites. You will find that chapels are usually simple buildings, made from local materials and designed to blend in with the surrounding houses.

Revealing facts Look at the inscriptions: the foundation stone for Heptonstall Methodist Chapel at Hebden Bridge, Yorkshire, was laid by John Wesley, the founder of Methodism, in 1764. Gravestones will give you clues about the early worshippers.

Identifying marks An inscription over the entrance will provide the name and denomination of the chapel and the date of the building. Some, especially Welsh chapels, have names taken from the Bible, such as Bethesda, Bethel, Mount Zion or Pisgah.

- On entering you will find an interior focused on the pulpit, in a prominent position. There is little on the walls to distract the congregation's attention.
- The plainest meeting houses are likely to belong to the Quakers, founded as the Society of Friends by George Fox, who began preaching in 1647. Some, such as Briggflatts, near Sedbergh in Yorkshire, and Jordans, near Chalfont St Peter in Buckinghamshire, survive from the late 17th and early 18th centuries.

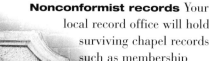

Date and denomination A plaque may tell you when the chapel was built and for whom. The Primitive Methodists split from the main body in 1810.

Nonconformist records Your local record office will hold surviving chapel records, such as membership lists, photographs of Whitsuntide Sunday School processions, and programmes of events.

The National Archives (see DIRECTORY) has a large collection of Nonconformist registers for births, marriages and burials, although in the 17th and 18th centuries Nonconformists generally used the Church of England for their baptism, marriage and burial services.

Scottish churches

If you live in Scotland, your town may have more than one large ecclesiastical building. This is because for a hundred years after the Reformation, Scottish Protestants dithered between Presbyterianism and Episcopalianism. Finally, in 1690, the official Church of Scotland chose Presbyterianism. Many existing churches, such as St Giles in Edinburgh, were converted from Catholic to Presbyterian places of worship. New churches built from 1700 to 1850 can be identified by galleries and a pulpit sited along a side wall facing a half-circle of pews.

- Subsequent schisms resulted in The Free Church of Scotland in 1843 and the United Presbyterian Church in 1847. Both have plain, sparsely furnished churches of local stone.
- You will find records, such as kirk (church) session minutes, in the National Archives of Scotland (see DIRECTORY).

Catholic churches

The earliest Catholic chapels date from 1790. You may find one in your town that was built after 1829, when the Catholic Emancipation Act finally removed most of the restrictions and penalties imposed on Roman Catholics in Britain.

- The Victorian Catholic churches and cathedrals in the large industrial towns, such as Manchester or Middlesbrough, were built in Gothic style.
- Strikingly modern churches were built in the expanding suburbs in the 1960s and 70s. The outstanding example is Liverpool's Metropolitan Cathedral of Christ the King, designed by Sir Frederick Gibberd in 1960.

About Catholic records The best way to find the records of individual churches is to consult *Catholic Missions and Registers, 1700-1880* (M. Gandy, 6 vols, 1993). Few congregations kept registers before the mid 18th century for fear of persecution.

Synagogues

William the Conqueror invited the first Jewish settlers to Britain in the 11th century. The earliest communities were Sephardic Jews, who came from Portugal and around the Mediterranean. Many were wealthy traders and money lenders. Poor Ashkenazic Jews from Russia, Poland and Lithuania arrived in Britain in their thousands in Victorian times to escape persecution. They settled mainly in the East End of London, Manchester and Leeds.

Worship on a grand scale Old illustrations or photographs may reveal a place of worship which no longer exists, but which once had a significant role in your community. The Great Synagogue in Dukes Place, London EC3, was destroyed by bombing in 1941. In its heyday in the 19th century (above), it served the large Jewish community in the East End and was the seat of the Chief Rabbi.

Jewish records Britain has about 400 synagogues. You will find them listed in the *Jewish Year Book*, published by the *Jewish Chronicle* (see DIRECTORY). Copies of the *Jewish Chronicle* (founded 1841) are available at British Library Newspapers (see DIRECTORY). Visit your local record office to see synagogue records, including registers, minute books and details of benefactors.

Mosques and temples

In the second half of the 20th century, Asian and African immigrants settled in Britain, forming large communities in areas such as Leicester and Bradford. There may be a mosque or temple where you live. Some are purpose-built, but others occupy converted chapels and former schools and factories. You will find them marked on large-scale modern maps at your library.

FIND OUT MORE

- http://rylibweb.man.ac.uk/ data1/dg/text/method.html The Methodist Archives and Research Centre.
- www.catholic-library.org. uk The Catholic Central Library houses records dating back to 1694.
- www.catholic-history.org. uk/crs The Catholic Record Society lists published records.
- www.catholic-heritage. net/sca/ The Scottish Catholic Archive holds church manuscripts.
- www.jewishgen.org A comprehensive website of Jewish records.

Back to local schooldays

Schools lie at the heart of any community. You may have been a pupil at the local primary or secondary school, as perhaps your parents or grandparents were before you. A close look at the buildings will provide clues about the school's history, while the distant voices of those who have filled its classrooms come closer through the photographs and log books in your local library and record office.

Early primary schools

The Victorians were the first major builders of schools in Britain. From 1870 the State began providing primary schools and in 1880 attendance was made compulsory (see pages 170-171). In some towns these schools are among the finest surviving Victorian buildings.

Sign of a school Many old school buildings have other uses today, but you will be able to identify them from their separate entrances for boys and girls.

School clues You may find a primary school in your area that dates back to this period.

- Look for steeply sloping roofs, mullioned windows and a bell turret in the Gothic style favoured by the Victorians.
- The school name and the date of its opening will be carved on the front.
- Look for a date stone and inscription on a building near a church or chapel. It may denote a Sunday school, which most children attended before 1880 to learn the 3Rs – reading, writing and arithmetic – as well as religious education.
- Some primary schools today are much older foundations, where children of all ages were taught. An inscription at Burnsall School, in the Yorkshire Dales, reads that it was founded in 1602 by Sir William Craven, a native of the parish who became Lord Mayor of London.

CHARITY SCHOOLS

The Society for the Promotion of Christian Knowledge (SPCK), founded in 1698, established charity schools in many areas of Britain, including remote parts of Wales and Scotland. Look out for small buildings, often bearing an inscription. You may find a charity school in your community, set up in the 19th century either by the National Society (Church of England) or the British and Foreign Schools Society (Nonconformists). They were often attached to churches or chapels and some may still have inscriptions saying who built them and when.

Skipping school School log books provide a fascinating picture of local life. In rural districts, assisting with farm work often took precedence over going to school, such as at Rhydygorlan 'Cwm' School in Merionethshire, when for the week ending October 28, 1904, the teacher noted that some children were not present because the 'thrashing machine' was in the district. Posing for the school photograph, such as at Carno School, Wales, in 1890, was an annual event. Look for captions listing the pupils' names, some of which may crop up elsewhere in your research.

Finding the paperwork

In your local record office you may find school log books (daily records kept by head teachers) dating from the 1840s and also admission registers, which had to be kept from 1870. Some log books are still held by schools.

- Look in your local library and record office for class photographs, magazines, reports, examination certificates and leaving certificates. Books of old photographs (see pages 212–213) often contain class groups.
- Parliamentary papers, such as the reports of the Charity Commission (1839-40, 1896-1907) and the Newcastle Commission (1857), provide information about elementary education, such as the types of school building, size of classes and what was taught. They can be seen at public reference libraries.
- For the 20th century, look in your local or county record office for the annual reports of the local education authority's education committee. They note class sizes and attendance, and the building of new schools.

Something old, something new Your local state secondary school may have a longer history than you think. Look for clues, such as old buildings on the present site. The Tudor red-brick range at the core of Boston Grammar School in Lincolnshire (above) was erected in 1567, using materials from a former Franciscan friary. It remained like this for 300 years before being extended. Today, Boston Grammar is a state secondary, and the Tudor building is the school library, surrounded by modern blocks (left).

Looking at secondary schools

You may find several different types of secondary schools in your area, including grammar and public schools (see pages 170-171). Although the oldest public schools, such as Eton and Winchester, have medieval or Tudor buildings at their core, most are Victorian Gothic in style and set in spacious grounds. These schools may have published an account of their history, which you can buy from the school, or you may find a copy at your local library.

History in the making Admissions registers, school magazines and class photographs may have been deposited at your local record office or kept at the school. Look out for printed histories that were produced to mark anniversaries or for the Millennium. Schools often provide an account of their history on their websites.

- Schoolmasters in the 17th and 18th centuries had to conform to the Established Church and their licences can be found among ecclesiastical court records at your county record office. Volumes of the *Victoria County History*, kept at your local public reference library, include information taken from documentary and printed sources on schools since the Middle Ages for some areas. The *Victoria County History* is an ongoing project to create a comprehensive history of each county of England. The website www.englandpast.net has details.
- Trade directories (see pages 216-217) will include the addresses of schools that have since been closed, but records are unlikely to have survived.
- In old copies of your local newspaper (see pages 216-217), you may find advertisements for the numerous 'dame-schools' that existed before 1870. They were run by older women in their homes.
- Before 1872, Scotland had burgh and parish schools. Records are held in the Burgh, Heritors' and Kirk Session records at the National Archives. Later records are also held there, in the Scottish Office Education Department archive.

FIND OUT MORE

- www.scit.wlv.ac.uk/ukinfo A website with links to universities and colleges of further education.
- www.applebymagna.org.uk Local history site covering education.
- www.gober.net/victorian/reports/schools.html Information on the Victorian education system.

Uncovering two hundred years of a seaside school

All villages, towns and cities have their primary schools – places where, often for more than a hundred years, the youngest community members have been nurtured in their earliest days of education. In central Brighton is a modern-looking primary school that disguises a rich history revealed in a search through local records.

The old school A rare photograph shows Middle Street before it was demolished in the 1970s. The tall windows and imposing façade were typical of Victorian schools.

Starting out

Middle Street Primary School in Brighton is a boxy 1970s building, shoehorned into a corner plot in the heart of the medieval part of the town. How did it come to be in such an unlikely spot?

The first place to start looking into the school's past is the local history centre. At the Brighton centre a card index lists all the town's schools under 'Education'. Middle Street was one of many board schools formed after the Education Act of 1870 (see pages 170-171), but the local archivist suggests there will be more to find at the county archive.

The catalogue of East Sussex County Archive is accessible on-line via the Access to Archives (A2A) website **www.a2a.org.uk** (see page 24). Initial results for Middle Street School look disappointing: a log book, some registers, title deeds

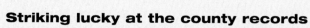

and a few photographs, a blueprint from 1946, and a letter from the clerk to the Brighton & Preston School Board dated 1897. The registers appear to go back to the 1820s, so the school existed long before it became a board school later in the century.

Striking lucky at the county records

A visit to the county archive produces a fuller list of its holdings. A brief history states that Brighton Middle Street School began as the Union Charity School, founded and maintained by subscription and by payment of a penny a week from scholars. The school became a board school in 1875, and a new building was erected. The Boys' and Girls' Junior Schools were combined as a Junior Mixed school in July 1930; and in 1935 this was amalgamated with the Infants' school. It was rebuilt on the same site in 1974.

The documents from the stacks put flesh onto these bare historical

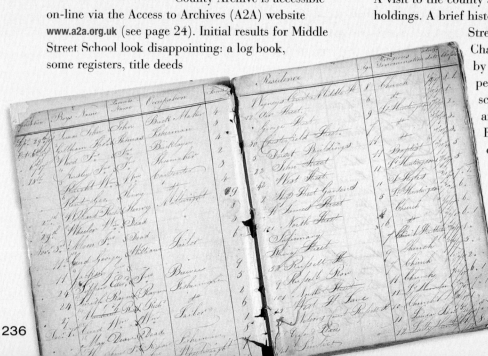

First day at school In an admissions register of 1817, the father of each new pupil is named and his occupation given, as well as the address and religious denomination of each child. The occupations include fisherman, millwright, shoemaker, tailor and brickmaker.

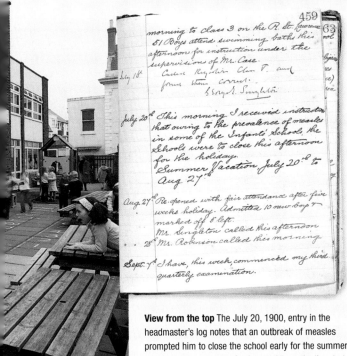

View from the top The July 20, 1900, entry in the headmaster's log notes that an outbreak of measles prompted him to close the school early for the summer holidays (the next entry, for August 27, marks the start of the new term). The kindly nature of the man shines through the log, and many of the themes would be familiar to teachers at Middle Street School today (left).

bones. There are admissions registers dating from 1817, and the single log book turns out to be fascinating. The heavy metal clasp is now broken, but it is still an imposing volume, an almost day-by-day account of the life of the school as seen from the top. What emerges are the broad themes and the seasonal rhythms of life in a Victorian board school. The head constantly laments that boys come to him from the infants' not knowing their letters, and visits from inspectors are noted.

The title deeds, sheets of vellum with wax seals and dense calligraphic writing, show that some of the land on which the school now stands was acquired by compulsory purchase in 1875, when the school was taken on by the board. Presumably, compulsory education meant more children so more space was needed: the Brighthelmstone Dispensary at No. 29 Middle Street had to make way.

Getting under the skin of the school
The plan of the school from 1946 gives an indication of what the Victorian building was like. The head's office looked down from the upper floor onto the playground and onto the street: the perfect headmasterly eyrie. And

there are far more photographs than the on-line listings suggested: a snap of the Christmas pantomime from 1938, and of Empire Day celebrations; group portraits of sports teams and of evacuees in the school yard before they were sent away to the safety of rural Yorkshire.

The press cuttings are especially useful as they point to highlights in the school's history and draw on sources lost to present-day researchers. One cutting reports the school centenary dinner in 1905. Speeches are recorded verbatim, with men describing in detail the life and layout of the school they attended in their youth – before the Victorian rebuild. This cutting also states that in the first weeks of the school's existence, the pupils were marched to the sea front to see the passing cortege of the dead hero Nelson. This explains why the school badge, in the years when pupils wore uniform, depicted a warship in full sail.

Going back to school
A visit to the school, with the headmistress's permission, turns up more material still. A teacher and a parent who works in the Brighton history centre are preparing an exhibition for the school's bicentenary in 2005. They have most of the missing log books and registers, which the school had kept, and – at last – photographs of the Victorian building demolished in the 1970s. These show an engraved stone plaque set over the entrance to the old building that recorded the school's history from charity institution in 1805 to board school. It turns out that this one scrap was salvaged after the demolition, and is now set in a corner of the playground. Illegible in places, and slightly mossy, it is a testament to this little school's 200 years of history.

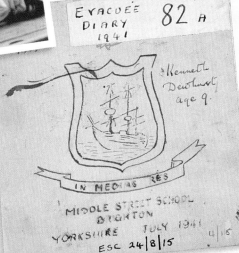

Forties memorabilia The front cover of a wartime evacuee's diary dated 1941 (right) shows the Middle Street badge depicting Nelson's warship. A press cutting found in the country records shed light on the origin of the motif in 1805. After the war, it was back to school as usual – with daily rations of free milk for pupils (above, in 1948).

Down at the local shops

Before the arrival of chain stores in the 20th century, the great variety of shops gave a place its distinctive character. Look carefully at your local shopping street or market place and the shops will reveal clues to their age and past uses.

What to spot in old towns

The shape of the buildings, design of the shop fronts and even faded signs give a feel for what shops were once like.

Shop frontages It is possible that the buildings you see today follow a line along the street that is hundreds of years old. If a shop breaks the line by projecting forwards, it could once have been a timber-framed building with upstairs rooms overhanging the road. The space below, where the shopkeeper displayed his goods on the pavement, may have been filled in.

Sales pitch In towns founded in the Middle Ages, the width of the shop might be the same as one or more old burgage plots of a medieval merchant or tradesman (see pages 138-139). You can sometimes spot these by looking at the earliest maps in your local record office for a regular series of plots leading back to an access lane.

Upwards glance Many a Georgian high street has handsome residential buildings above the shops where the shopkeepers lived. Look for sash windows and elegant stonework. In Victorian times, stores often filled the entire building and shopkeepers began to move to the suburbs.

Dating shop fronts

Look at the design of a shop front for clues to its date and what it used to sell.

Bow windows These were a feature of Georgian, Victorian and Edwardian shops. If the windows are original there will be imperfections in the glass. Also look for wrought ironwork, blinds that can be pulled down at an angle, and perhaps steps up to the entrance.

Old name plates Look for old shop names or the faint remains of advertisements on gable ends. If you spot a shop name, you may find it listed in old trade directories (see pages 216–217).

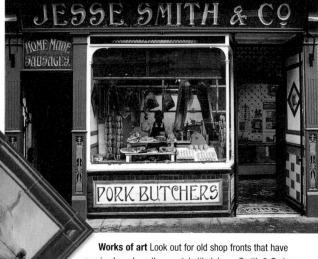

Works of art Look out for old shop fronts that have survived, such as the ornately tiled Jesse Smith & Co in Cirencester (above), complete with its picture of a contented pig (left). Some may still be in business, like Jesse Smith; others, such as fishmongers or dairies, may have changed use, but you might find that the original tilework has been preserved and restored by the new owners.

Captured on film If you visit your local studies library (see pages 18-19) or look at books about your community (see pages 212-213), you will find old photographs such as that of Well Hall Parade, Eltham (below), taken in 1915, which show local shops in different eras. Produce was often piled high on the pavement and the owner and his assistants, dressed in their aprons, would stand in the doorway or in front of the bow windows for the picture to be taken. Instead of brands such as Next, Boots or Dixons, photographs from the past show the names of local families that are distinctive to your neighbourhood.

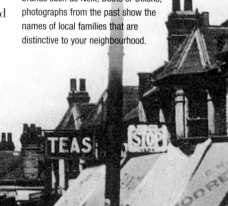

Thompson Robert Fawcett, coach builder, 27 Thorngate
Thompson Samuel, Cricketers' Arms P.H.48 & 50 Galgate
Thompson Thomas, butcher, 32 Galgate
Thompson Wm. cattle dlr. Barnley, Barnard Castle moor
Tilburn John Edward, grocer, 6 Market place
Todd Mary & Maggie (Misses), confectnrs. 23b, Bank
Turnbull James (Mrs.), farmer, Stone cross, Marwood
Ullathorne & Co. twine & shoe thread manufacturers
Urquhart Frederick, shopkeeper, 36 Bridgegate
Victoria Hall (Tom Borrowdale, proprietor), off Newgate
Waine Henry, hair dresser, 14 Bank
Walker Brothers, chimney sweepers. Bank
Walker Edwin, hair dresser, 8 Galgate
Walker Henry. saddler. 27 Horse market
Walker John, marine store dealer. 48 Bank
Walker John Wm. painter & decorator, 7 Marshall street
Wall George, insurance agent, 2 Ware street
Wallis William P. estate agent, Market place
Walton Mary (Mrs.) & Mark, graziers, Barnard Castle
    Moor head
Walton J. & Son, tailors, 29 Horse market
Walton John, grazier, Moor head, Marwood
Walton John Henry, insurance agent, Harmire
Walton Thomas, farmer, Marwood green
Ward Harry, printer & stationer, 21 Horse market
Ward John, Raby hotel, Market place
Water Works (Harry Ewbank Raine, manager),
    Pleasant
Watson, Watson & Wells, solicitors & commiss
    oaths, Newgate
Watson Bernard Norman, solicitor, see Watson
    & Wells
Watson Ernest, cycle dealer, Galgate
Watson George, Oddfellows' Arms P.H.
Watson Harry Crawford, solicitor &
    (firm, Watson, Watson & Wells
    Castle & Staindrop &
    registrar & high

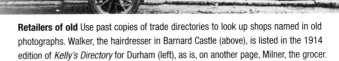

Retailers of old Use past copies of trade directories to look up shops named in old photographs. Walker, the hairdresser in Barnard Castle (above), is listed in the 1914 edition of *Kelly's Directory* for Durham (left), as is, on another page, Milner, the grocer.

Old newspapers and directories

To get a glimpse into the working lives of the people in your community look at advertisements and directories.

- Visit your record office and look in the archives of local newspapers (see pages 216-217) for advertisements from shopkeepers and tradesmen. These give an idea of the range of goods that were once on offer in your town.
- You can trace individual businesses in your town or village back through trade directories (see pages 216-217). Families often ran shops for many generations. By looking at successive directories you can get an idea of when an enterprise started and spot any changes, such as a draper becoming a grocer. You could even map out the whole of your high street at a given time in the past.

Who's minding the shop?

You can find who worked in your local shops and their trades by reading census returns (see pages 218-219). From 1841 onwards, everybody's occupation was recorded.

- Following census returns for all the shops in an area will give you a feel for the range of trades and crafts that were being pursued.
- Family members may have had the same occupation as the father. They might be described as 'assistant shopkeeper'.
- Successive census returns for shopping districts will reveal which businesses lasted and which failed.

Other records of business

Local record offices and museums hold a wealth of documents that reveal how people were once employed.

- Look in your record office for records of local businesses. They might include deeds to the property, account books and old catalogues.
- To learn more about 17th and 18th-century shopkeepers and tradesmen, look for probate inventories in your county record office. These were attached to wills and tell you much about the goods that were offered for sale. Even if they described themselves as grocers or drapers, shopkeepers sold everything they could. When John Lee, a Sheffield ironmonger, died in 1696 his goods included groceries, haberdashery, pigments, medicines and stationery. His neighbour, Samuel Staniforth, was a 'pinner' but, as well as pins and haberdashery, he sold stationery, books, medicines, groceries and ironmongery.
- Some local museums have collections of tokens issued during the 17th and 18th centuries by tradesmen and shopkeepers when coins were hard to come by. The names and places stamped on them can reveal the number and type of shops that existed in your village.
- For information on the tradespeople of Scotland in the 18th and 19th centuries, burgh records often include burgess lists. The Registers of Sasines (see pages 220, 318) show property transactions from 1617 onwards. These records are held at the National Archives of Scotland (see DIRECTORY).

Learning about big industry

Your town or city might owe its existence to a large industry such as cotton and textiles, coal mining, iron and steel production or car-making. You can find out how it influenced your community by visiting some of Britain's outstanding industrial museums. Your local record office or public library can also help you to build up a picture of industrial life in your area.

From heyday to today

Although many industries, such as cotton manufacture and coal-mining, have disappeared or shrunk out of all recognition, local societies and museums take great interest in preserving signs in the landscape and investigating the past. Many mill towns, pit villages and manufacturing centres have been in existence for less than four generations, which makes it easy to track their history back to their origins. By visiting museums and record offices, you can trace the stories of working communities as they flourished, declined and then slowly transformed again into the places we know today.

Every picture tells a story Visual records, such as the photograph of workers leaving the Jaguar Foleshill car plant in Coventry (top) in the late 1940s, and the advertisement for the British Motor Show (above) from *Punch* magazine, 1958, give an idea of what goods were produced in your area and the people employed in these industries. Study the buildings; you may recognise some that have other uses today.

Picturing the industrial life

Old photographs (see pages 212-213) are a good starting point for learning about the industries that made your community. To see a new ship rising above a row of terraced houses at the end of a street in Sunderland, or on the banks of the Clyde, is to grasp how an entire community depended on the fluctuating fortunes of shipbuilding.
- Look for illustrations of factory buildings and workers' houses that have been demolished. You will find these

places if you work back through Ordnance Survey (OS) maps (see pages 214-215) at your local record office.

- Note the distinctive dress of some workers, such as the shawls and clogs of the Lancashire cotton mill girls or the lamps, helmets and knee pads of the miners.
- Look for photographs of social events, such as galas, when trade unionists marched behind banners, led by a brass band. Churches, musical groups and sports teams also played a key role in the lives of workers.

Getting involved

Support local efforts to preserve the remains of the past by joining an industrial history or archaeological society.

- Ask at your library for details of any local society's activities, such as its programme of events and the membership secretary's contact details.
- Take part in projects to restore industrial premises. Local societies have restored many old mills and forges, such as the Chedleston flint mill in Staffordshire and Wortley Top Forge in Yorkshire.
- Join members of a society who are researching the documentary history of a local industry. Ask at your record office for information.

Talking to people

Recording the memories of former workers is an important way of preserving the past. Once an industry goes, the skills and dialects of the workforce gradually become forgotten.

- Ask former workers the purpose of tools that you have seen in a museum or photograph. How were they used?
- Ask about the words that were used in a craft or industry. What did a miner mean by a 'motty'? In the cutlery industry, what exactly is 'hollow ware'?

Powerful images Today, one of the few places where you can experience the sounds and smells of a working steam mill engine is in an industrial museum, such as the Museum of Science and Industry in Manchester. Steam power played a key role in the city's industrial development as a centre of the cotton trade (see page 152). Other local industries, such as locomotive building (Beyer, Peacock & Co, 1854-1966) and early car manufacture (Rolls-Royce and Ford), are also represented here.

Tracking down company records

The companies involved in each industry will have kept records about their operations, workforces and buildings.

- Search the catalogues at your local record office for company records. Look for board minutes, accounts, annual reports, catalogues and correspondence, which detail the running of the business, the number of employees, what was made and who the customers were.
- Search the internet or ask at the local record office for the whereabouts of special collections, such as the archives of the British motor industry at the Heritage Motor Centre (see below).
- For information about local trade union activity, visit your record office or contact the Modern Records Centre at the University of Warwick (see DIRECTORY). For Scottish records, try the Department of Manuscripts at the National Library of Scotland (see DIRECTORY).
- The Guildhall Library, London (see DIRECTORY), has a collection of fire insurance records, starting with the Sun Fire Office in 1710. The registers include names of owners of industrial sites and descriptions of buildings.

FIND OUT MORE

The following museums, some housed on the sites of old mills, mines and docks, can tell you much about the industries and the communities that grew up around them.

- Derwent Valley Mills World Heritage Site Look round the water-powered cotton mills and factories that Sir Richard Arkwright built in the valley from 1771 onwards (see also pages 160-161). You can explore the village of Cromford that Arkwright built for his workers and get a feel for the community that once lived here. www.derbyshire-thepeakdistrict.co.uk; www.cromfordmill.co.uk
- Beamish, The North of England Open Air Museum Experience life in the north of England in the 19th and early 20th century. You can go down a coal mine, ride on a tram and visit a re-created colliery village at this museum outside Newcastle upon Tyne. www.beamish.org.uk
- Museum of Science and Industry, Manchester Find out about Britain's first industrial city. Based in an 1830s railway station complex, the museum has an impressive collection of working steam mill engines (see left). www.msim.org.uk
- Museum in Docklands, London Historic boats, a Georgian warehouse of artefacts, and recorded interviews with dock-workers recall a time when this was a bustling port. www.museumindocklands.org.uk
- Heritage Motor Centre All the records of the British motor industry, including a collection of cars and photographs, tell the story of the car-producing communities at this museum in Gaydon, Warwickshire. www.heritage-motor-centre.co.uk

Tasting the life of industrial Britain

Every one of Britain's traditional heavy industries, from coal mining and slate quarrying to iron and steel working, shipbuilding, heavy engineering and textile manufacture, declined in the late 20th century (see pages 194-195). Now, after decades of demolition and scrapping, their relics and remnants are being preserved and converted into hands-on museums, where you can gain a sense of what it was like to hew coal, quarry slate, operate a loom or shape white-hot metal.

King Coal

The heavy industry that, more than any other, epitomises Britain's days as an industrial powerhouse is coal mining. The combination of hard, heavy work in dangerous, difficult conditions, allied to the legendary close-knit character of mining communities, gives coal miners a special place in the hearts of people who would shudder at the thought of going underground.

Several mining museums trace the story of King Coal from its 19th-century peak to the present day. At preserved mines such as the Big Pit National Mining Museum of Wales (Blaenavon, south Wales) and the National Coal Mining Museum for England at Caphouse Colliery (Wakefield, west Yorkshire) you can take a tour through the underground workings. In the dark, dank, claustrophobic tunnels you can see the narrow seams where men dug coal lying on their sides in puddles of water. The guides, ex-miners themselves, know exactly how to set the scene with tales both grim and inspiring.

Places to visit
• National Coal Mining Museum for England, Caphouse Colliery. www.ncm.org.uk
• Scottish Mining Museum, Lady Victoria Colliery. www.scottishminingmuseum.com
• Big Pit National Mining Museum of Wales. www.nmgw.ac.uk/www.php/bigpit

Illuminating story Underground tours bring the history of coal mining to life. Here a guide from the National Coal Mining Museum demonstrates a Davy lamp. It was invented by Sir Humphry Davy in 1815 to give miners a safe form of lighting, and the basic design has not changed since.

Digging for metal and rock

Coal miners were not the only men to work long hours under the earth. The extraction of iron, lead and tin ore demanded the same qualities of strength and endurance, and led to the establishment of the same kinds of exclusive industrial settlements – as did the quarrying of Welsh slate (see pages 78-79).

There are subterranean workings to explore, as well as the surface plant where the metal was separated from the rock, in museums dedicated to each of these industries: iron ore in the spooky Clearwell Caves in Gloucestershire's Forest of Dean; lead in the museums at Wanlockhead in the Lowther Hills south of Lanark and at Killhope in Upper Weardale, County Durham; and tin in Geevor mine at Pendeen in far west Cornwall. As for slate, there are several quarry workings open to the public in north Wales, notably the Welsh Slate Museum at Llanberis and the vast underground caverns at Llechwedd.

Close encounter A wander down the 1.25m (4ft) wide, 2.25m (7ft) high passages of Locknell Mine in Wanlockhead, Scotland, gives a sense of the cramped conditions in which miners worked.

Places to visit
• Clearwell Caves Ancient Iron Mines. www.clearwellcaves.com
• Scotland's Museum of Lead Mining, Wanlockhead. www.leadminingmuseum.co.uk
• North of England Lead Mining Museum, Killhope. www.durham.gov.uk/killhope
• Geevor Tin Mine. www.geevor.com
• Welsh Slate Museum, Llanberis. www.nmgw.ac.uk/www.php/wsm
• Llechwedd Slate Caverns. www.llechwedd-slate-caverns.co.uk

A working mill At Quarry Bank Mill you can see the machinery in action, including the 500-spool mule (above). The Lancashire looms are still powered by waterwheel and weave cloth that is sold in the museum's shop. The steam room tells how steam power was added in 1810 as a power back-up in the event of water shortages.

Working the metal

The processes of metal working with their fire, steam and clangorous tools and machinery are brought vividly to life at Ironbridge in Shropshire, cradle of the Industrial Revolution, with tours of the huge blast furnaces at Blists Hill set in a re-creation of a Victorian working town. At Abbeydale Industrial Hamlet in Sheffield you can see how craftsmen used great tilt hammers and grinding wheels to make steel scythe blades and other sharp-edged items. At Blaenavon in south Wales vast ironworks buildings from the late 18th century have been preserved, including furnaces, cast houses, kilns and workers' cottages.

Places to visit
- Ironbridge Gorge Museums. www.ironbridge.org.uk
- Abbeydale Industrial Hamlet. www.tilthammer.com/hamlet/index.html
- Blaenavon Ironworks Museum. www.btinternet.com/~blaenavon.ironworks/Pages/ironworks.htm

Moulding the clay

The pottery business dominated its landscape (chiefly the Midlands) with deep clay extraction holes, spoil heaps and the smoking chimneys of the conical kilns. At Gladstone Pottery Museum at Longton, Stoke-on-Trent, in the heart of the Potteries district of Staffordshire, you can experience pottery throwing, bone china flower making and pottery painting. The Etruscan Bone & Flint Mill at the nearby Etruria Industrial Museum gives an insight into what else besides clay went into pottery.

Places to visit
- Gladstone Pottery Museum. www.stoke.gov.uk/navigation/category.jsp?categoryID=33353
- Etruria Industrial Museum. www.stoke.gov.uk/navigation/category.jsp?categoryID=407544

Cotton and wool

Along with coal mining and metal-working, it was the textile trade that underpinned the Industrial Revolution. The mills with their gaunt silhouettes, towering chimneys and many rows of windows still stand in many towns and cities; some still work, but most are now redundant, killed off by competition. You can get an excellent idea of the noise, exhaustion and camaraderie of cotton mill work in Quarry Bank Mill at Styal in Cheshire with its steam engines, clattering looms and ex-millworker guides; while for wool mill history there is Coldharbour Mill at Uffculme in east Devon, where you can see carding and spinning operations as well as more fine steam engines.

Places to visit
- Quarry Bank Mill, Styal. www.quarrybankmill.org.uk
- Coldharbour Mill Working Wool Museum. www.coldharbourmill.org.uk

Turning clay into gold To walk across the cobbled yard of the Gladstone Pottery Museum is like walking back in time. The old workshops and coal-fired bottle kilns go back to Victorian times, when the factory was manufacturing the world's finest bone china.

Town hives of small industry

Wherever you live, there will be signs to spot and records to follow of the numerous small industries, such as malting, brewing, milling, printing and textile spinning, that once supported the needs of the population and gave them employment. You will not have to go back far in history to find your town buzzing with a variety of activities that have since disappeared.

Looking for the signs of industry

A walk round your town may provide clues, such as water channels, lime kilns, the remnants of a furnace hearth or simply street names, which will help you to spot the signs of former thriving industries. Many buildings will survive, perhaps turned into a garage, shops or even a restaurant. Looking at old Ordnance Survey (OS) maps (see pages 214-215) first will give you leads on where to search.

- To identify a corn mill site, look for the banks of the former dam, the head leat (or goit in north England) that brings water along a channel from the river to the dam, the foundations of the water wheel, and the tail leat that takes the water back to the river.
- Maltings, dating from the late 18th and 19th centuries, produced the malted barley essential for brewing. Many have survived, to be turned into shops or housing. Look out for their distinctive conical chimneys, the vast floors where barley was dried and grain germinated, and for the tank used for steeping the barley. Close by will be the river or canal that supplied the water and the means of transporting the grain.
- The charcoal blast furnaces of the 17th and 18th centuries were water-powered. Look for the dam and the channel that brought the water to the bellows. The hearth, or its former position, will be close to the bellows site, where the molten iron was tapped.
- Lime kilns for making quicklime were worked in a similar fashion. They may have been built into a limestone or chalk hillside or close to a canal terminus for transporting goods and materials. You can judge the scale of the enterprise from the size of the kilns.
- Windmills were used not just for corn-milling, but for drainage. If you live near a windmill, look at the design. Post mills, such as the one at Mountnessing, Essex, have a central post and the sails can be turned to face the wind. The tower mill at Holbeach, Lincolnshire, has its sails fixed to a rotating cap on the top of the tower. Cranbrook in Kent has a smock mill, so-called because it resembles a man dressed in a smock. If a windmill has gone, look for the circular mound on which it stood.

Looking at the records

The local record office will hold a wide range of records to help you to build up a picture of industrial life in your locality.

Census returns Explore the census returns for your community from 1841 onwards (see pages 218-219) and note the occupations that are recorded for the population. Your search will give you a good idea of all the businesses and industries and who worked in them.

- Look at people's places of birth to see if they came from long-resident families or if they were newcomers.
- See whether they lived close together, perhaps in specially built rows of houses.
- The occupations column might tell you how many women and girls were employed in small factories or as outworkers in their own homes. Find out how old they were by looking at the age column.

Cracking a local riverside nut

Follow a waterway in any town and you will soon find clues to activities that kept its people in employment years ago. The ancient market town of Kingston upon Thames in Surrey is known today more for its shopping centre and university than for any industry. But if you track its little fast-flowing Thames tributary, the Hogsmill river, you soon find a waterside university hall of residence called Middle Mill and a narrow road, Mill Street, lined with workers' cottages – clear evidence of former milling activity. But what did the mill produce, and could the exotically named local pub, The Cocoanut, provide a clue?

Trade names Look out for street signs, such as Mill Street, pub signs, or the names of new buildings that may indicate a long-gone industry in your neighbourhood. You might find the enterprise marked on an old map.

Directories You can trace small businesses by looking at entries in trade directories from the 19th and early 20th centuries (see pages 216-217) and, more recently, telephone directories, which can be found at the British Telecom Archives (see DIRECTORY).

Newspapers Look at old newspapers (see pages 216-217) for business advertisements.

Old photographs Books of old photographs (see pages 212-213) or collections in local libraries will often show the premises of light industries in the background or groups of workers posed at their tasks.

Maps Spot the sites of small industries on OS, tithe award and town maps (see pages 214-215). They will show places such as brickworks, mills and brewhouses. Street names, such as Windmill Close, also give clues.

Delving further back in time

Parish and other records might help you to follow local industries beyond the 19th century.

Parish records At your local record office, look at parish registers of baptisms, marriages and burials – some of them give the men's trades or occupations (see page 227).

Probate inventories These documents, attached to wills and kept at county record offices, show a deceased's personal estate, which might include the tools of his trade.

Title deeds By looking at title deeds in your local record office, you might be able to pinpoint the origins of a business and the names of any partners. The deeds are often accompanied by small maps of the site.

Apprenticeship indentures The National Archives at Kew (see DIRECTORY) has registers of apprentices for 1710-1811, which record the name, place of residence and trade of the master, and the name of the apprentice. These may give you a further insight into local industries.

Company and guild records Records of an old industry may be held locally by a long-established company or trade guild. The Cutlers' Hall, Sheffield, founded in 1624, holds registers of apprentices and freemen.

Peeling away the years An OS map of 1898 for Kingston upon Thames shows Middle Mill as a 'Printing Works', surrounded by streets of houses; but a map of 1865 reveals something altogether different – a 'Cocoa Fibre Works' and, apart from Mill Street, nothing but fields and orchards. So the pub (left) is a reminder of a shortlived 19th-century local industry – turning cocoa fibre into brushes and matting. A look at the 1871 census return for Mill Street confirms that it housed many of the fibre workers.

Cottage and village industry

Farming was not the only occupation in the countryside. The blacksmith, the carpenter and the village cobbler were familiar figures who served essential local needs and in some villages there were far more people working at a craft than working the land. Many rural communities were semi-industrial, often having a long-held association with a particular product or craft, such as hand-knitting or scythemaking.

Signs of village industry

Numerous small workshops were once dotted across rural Britain. Even in what are now sleepy villages, there is still ample evidence of these once bustling activities.

- Look for houses or pubs called 'The Old Forge', 'The Old Smithy' or any other name that suggests a craft formerly practised there.
- Keep an eye open for traces of faded advertisements for a trade above doorways or on gable ends of buildings.
- In wool-weaving areas (see pages 142-143), look for a row of large windows in the top storey of a house, allowing in extra light for a weaver to work by.
- Observe any outbuildings close to a house, especially those with chimneys. An old metalworker's workshop, for instance, might still have its hearth.

What the records reveal

You are unlikely to have to go far to uncover a mass of documentary evidence on rural industries in your area.

Old photographs and maps The practice of crafts, such as lacemaking or thatching, was a popular subject with Victorian photographers. But do check against other local records to make sure that such scenes were typical of when they were captured. You may also be able to site former local businesses by examining collections of old photographs (see page 212), perhaps with the help of an old OS map (see pages 214-215). You could discover that your local garage started life as a blacksmith's forge.

Directories Search through the old trade directories (see page 217) in your local reference library, being aware that a craftsman may have done much more varied work than his brief description suggests. Carpenters and joiners often acted as undertakers, while most blacksmiths were happy to forge anything in metal that a customer asked for.

Parish registers At your local record office look through the parish registers of baptisms, marriages and burials (see page 227) from the 16th to the 19th centuries. After 1813 a man's occupation was always recorded, and some earlier records include it too.

Census returns By searching the returns (see pages 218-219) for a village from 1841 to 1901, you can build up the story of its trade and industry during that time and follow family businesses through successive generations.

Militia returns Your local record office may have a militia return from the late 18th or early 19th century, when men aged between 18 and 45 were trained for military service in case Britain was invaded. These lists

Back in action Many former country workplaces have been restored (see 'Rural museums', opposite). At Marsh Mill, near Blackpool in Lancashire, you can see the machinery in action, producing flour as it did for the village of Thornton from 1794 to 1922.

Sign of industry Naming a local pub the 'Hammer & Pincers' suggests that it might once have been the home and workshop of the local blacksmith.

The framework knitters of Leicestershire

The framework-knitting trade of the East Midlands grew quickly from the late 17th century, so that by 1800 knitters were found in at least 118 Leicestershire villages and hamlets. Socks, shirts, gloves, cravats and various fabrics were knitted on a frame in cottages, long after workshops using powered knitting machines were introduced during the mid 19th century. Much of the story of this small but essential industry can be followed through the records.

- Local parish registers often noted the occupation in the abbreviated form 'FWK'. Between January 1, 1813, and December 31, 1817, the register of Countesthorpe parish in Leicestershire recorded 51 framework-knitters, nearly 70 per cent of the workforce.
- Directories (see page 217) list the middlemen, known as 'bag hosiers', and the owners of workshops.
- Large volumes known as Parliamentary Papers, kept at local reference libraries, cover many enquiries into 19th-century trades and industries. Felkin's Enquiry of 1845 into the hosiery trade included interviews with framework knitters and employers.
- Wills and inventories (see pages 324-325) for the area show that the earliest knitters were usually part-time farmers as well.

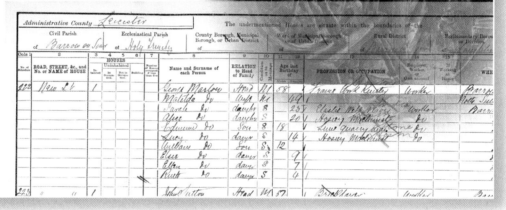

Family affair A 1901 census return (right) for the village of Barton upon Soar, near Loughborough, shows that the framework-knitting cottage industry still persisted into the 20th century. At the top of the return is 58-year-old George Marlow, his occupation 'frame work knitter', while three of his eight children are either weavers or machinists.

record each man's occupation. The Northamptonshire return for 1777 includes 94 men from the village of Raunds. Most were farmers, labourers or servants, but there were also several shoemakers, tailors, butchers, blacksmiths, carpenters, stonemasons, flax-dressers and lacemakers, plus a weaver, a miller and a baker.

Wills and inventories In the archives of your local record office, you will find the probate inventories that were attached to wills (see pages 324-325). These list the personal possessions of the deceased, including any tools or goods he might have manufactured.

The decline of rural crafts

By the late 19th century, cottage industries, faced with competition from factories and foreign imports, were no longer making a significant contribution to the household economy. In 1871, more than 20,000 Bedfordshire women plaited straw bonnets for a living – within 30 years their number had dropped to below 500. Meanwhile, the great agricultural depression (see pages 80-81) cut the number of jobs for farm labourers, leading to a sharp fall in the rural population as people left to find work in the cities.

RURAL MUSEUMS

A number of museums give you a taste of what it was like to live and work as a cottage labourer (see DIRECTORY for addresses).

- Museum of English Rural Life Exhibition and demonstrations of old machinery and tools, and a large archive that includes books, old photographs, films and sound recordings. www.ruralhistory.org
- Museum of Scottish Country Life Displays of machinery and tools and a hands-on learning centre for children, all based in a Georgian farmhouse. www.nms.ac.uk/countrylife
- Museum of Welsh Life Exhibitions and workshops with demonstrations of rural crafts. www.nmgw.ac.uk
- Black Country Living Museum Reconstructions of former workshops and demonstrations of traditional local crafts, including glass-cutting, metalwork and sweet-making. www.bclm.co.uk
- Weald and Downland Open Air Museum A working smithy, watermill, windpump and brick-drying shed are among the 50 reconstructed village buildings, dating from the 13th century to Victorian times. www.wealddown.co.uk

Keeping things moving Trams proved an effective solution to Bristol's growing transport needs in the early 20th century. By the 1930s, they offered one of the cheapest and quickest ways of getting large numbers of people around the city.

From A to B by road, water and rail

Until fairly recently, the way most people got around was on foot or on horseback, and many public paths and bridleways in your area will be centuries old. But from the late 18th century onward, the growth of industry and urban expansion made swifter transport essential. Across Britain you can still spot traces of the rail, tram and canal systems that emerged during the later 18th and 19th centuries.

Following the highways and byways

The industrial boom of the 19th century led to many new rights of way, making it more convenient for people to get to work before buses, trams and trains were widespread.

- Compare the footpaths and bridleways in your village or town on a modern Ordnance Survey (OS) map with those on a first edition six-inch OS map drawn up in the 1850s or 60s (see pages 26-27). Were there more paths 150 years ago, and where did they lead to?
- At your local record office (see pages 18-19) look for enclosure awards and their maps (see page 215), setting out which lanes and highways in your local area were granted general public access.

Down your street

A stroll around your neighbourhood should help raise a host of questions about local streets that can then be answered by a visit to your city or county archives.

- The name of a street may contain clues to its age and to any former purpose or use. It is likely that a street named after a battle will date back to the time that it was fought. One named after an eminent person may suggest local links with that person (see pages 224-225). Look out also for the use of local names for alleyways or narrow passages, such as 'gennell', 'snicket' or 'wynd'.
- Note the names of roads leading to neighbouring towns, then check at the county record office to see if they were turnpike roads (see pages 124-125) in the 18th and 19th centuries. Glossop Road, Sheffield, was a new turnpike road in 1821 that soon attracted a middle-class suburb around it.
- A road that curves and bends in an irregular fashion may have grown up along old field or woodland boundaries. Find out by looking at old OS, tithe or enclosure maps (see pages 214-215).
- A straight road will have been planned. Look to see where such new roads were built to meet up with an old one as suburbs expanded in the late 19th century.
- Look for old photographs at your local record office of streets you know. Was the shape different a hundred years or so ago, and can you see what was there before the suburban houses or new shops were built?

Buses and trams

By the 1870s, the efficient new way to travel around many of Britain's towns and cities was by horse-drawn bus or tram. London had a network of 860 such vehicles in the 1890s. Electricity began to take over from horse-power around the turn of the 20th century, and motorised buses made their debut just before the First World War.

- Look at old photographs of your town (see pages 212-213) taken over the past 150 years, and see how much transport has changed during that time.
- Search through the records of bus and tram companies at your local record office or at the Guildhall Library in London (see DIRECTORY). Note which routes served your community, and who worked on them.

Community tax Under an Act of 1555, the parish was responsible for the maintenance of local highways, and could levy a tax to pay for the work. Every able-bodied householder was also obliged to work on the roads for up to six days a year. Documents relating to this, including details of the frequent disputes that arose, can be seen along with other parish records at county record offices.

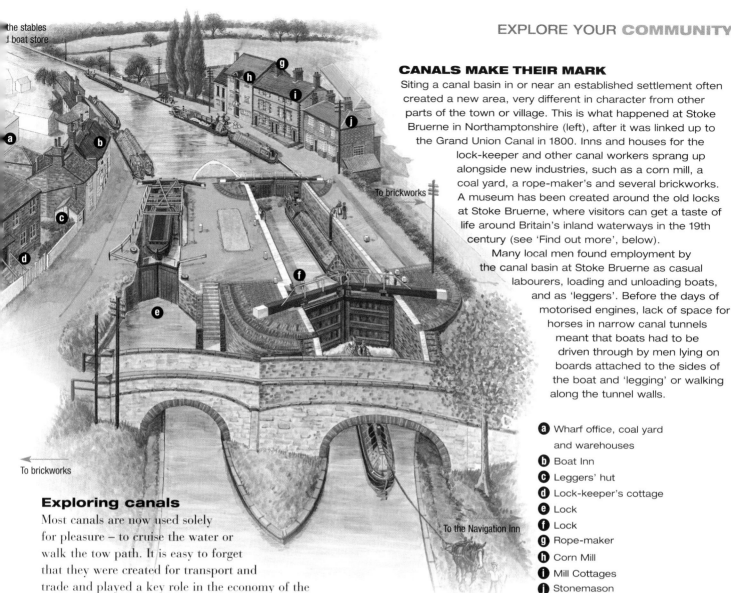

the stables
l boat store

To brickworks

To brickworks

To the Navigation Inn

CANALS MAKE THEIR MARK

Siting a canal basin in or near an established settlement often created a new area, very different in character from other parts of the town or village. This is what happened at Stoke Bruerne in Northamptonshire (left), after it was linked up to the Grand Union Canal in 1800. Inns and houses for the lock-keeper and other canal workers sprang up alongside new industries, such as a corn mill, a coal yard, a rope-maker's and several brickworks. A museum has been created around the old locks at Stoke Bruerne, where visitors can get a taste of life around Britain's inland waterways in the 19th century (see 'Find out more', below).

Many local men found employment by the canal basin at Stoke Bruerne as casual labourers, loading and unloading boats, and as 'leggers'. Before the days of motorised engines, lack of space for horses in narrow canal tunnels meant that boats had to be driven through by men lying on boards attached to the sides of the boat and 'legging' or walking along the tunnel walls.

a Wharf office, coal yard and warehouses
b Boat Inn
c Leggers' hut
d Lock-keeper's cottage
e Lock
f Lock
g Rope-maker
h Corn Mill
i Mill Cottages
j Stonemason

Exploring canals

Most canals are now used solely for pleasure – to cruise the water or walk the tow path. It is easy to forget that they were created for transport and trade and played a key role in the economy of the communities they served. Canals were responsible for the rapid growth of ports such as Runcorn in Cheshire and for the character of the small settlements that formed around junctions, such as Shardlow in Derbyshire.

- At your local reference library you may find information on your local canal in the printed volumes of Parliamentary Papers, especially in the 12-volume *Report of the Royal Commission on Canals* (1906-11) and its accompanying maps. They are indexed by place name, so you can quickly find any local material.
- Search for records of canal companies at your local record office. Read through their accounts, minute books, correspondence, and engineers' reports on the everyday running and maintenance of the waterways.
- Look at local census returns (see pages 218-219) and try to identify boat people. They were often included as part of the community they were in on census day.

The railway comes to town

Railways that were constructed during the Victorian age (see pages 72-73) have left their mark on most towns.
- Look for rows of railwaymen's houses near the station (see pages 250-251) – usually with names such as Station Road – and for pubs called the Railway Tavern.
- Search through your local census returns for people who worked on the railway – ticket collectors, firemen, porters and stokers.
- Records of many former railway companies survive, either in the National Archives at Kew, the National Archives of Scotland or the House of Lords Record Office (see DIRECTORY). Look for company reports, accounts, staff records, maps and plans, and even collections of old photographs. Staff records sometimes give complete service histories of the various workers.

FIND OUT MORE

- *The Railways of Britain: A Journey Through History* (Jack Simmons, Sheldrake Press, 1991)
- *Francis Frith's Trains and Buses* (Francis Frith, Frith Book Company, 2003)
- www.nwn.org.uk The National Waterways Museum's site includes details of canal history, along with numerous links to the websites of canal museums throughout Britain, including the one at Stoke Bruerne (see above).

Local station clues

The station that you pass through every day is worth a closer look, especially if it is one of the thousands built in the 19th century: the golden age of the train. See if you can spot the features that once made it the pride and joy of its community. Ornate wrought-iron footbridges, former coal yards and segregated waiting rooms are just some of the clues you may find that give a glimpse into your station's past.

The heyday of the railway station

In the hectic decades of the 19th century, railway companies joined in a competitive rush that sent lines first through every major town and then to far-flung corners of Britain, bringing travel within the reach of the poorest citizen. Stations sprang up everywhere. Many of these have today been stripped of their embellishments, and satellite buildings and yards sold off or put to other purposes. But some – like Settle in the main picture, which opened in 1876 – are remarkably well preserved.

As there were no railway stations before we started building them in Britain, the architects based the structures on familiar models such as estate cottages or suburban villas, each echoing the corporate style of the company that owned the line. Passengers had their comfort and convenience catered for with a refreshment room, waiting rooms, lavatories and a bridge connecting the platforms.

Spotting the signs of your station's Victorian heritage

Take a look at the layout of your station and see if you can work out how this has changed since its heyday (see right). The Victorian station typically comprised a central block of platforms with waiting rooms and a ticket office, which have often survived unscathed.

Nearby lay the goods yard, coal yard and sidings. When the railways lost out to road haulage, many goods yards closed, as did coal yards once the steam train was phased out in the 1960s. Look around your station and you may find that the car park occupies the old coal yard, the house over the road was the stationmaster's, and the shabby hut down the line was the original signal box. Near the station you may also spot terraces of houses in a similar style, which were built for workers by the railway company (see page 277).

Station clock Take a look at the clock in your station – the Victorian original still takes pride of place in many stations, as at Great Malvern (left). Station clocks transformed the way people thought about time. Until the railways arrived, London and other cities kept different times – there was no need to do otherwise. But an efficient train service demanded a standard time – Greenwich Mean Time – and co-ordinated timetables. Every guard had a watch, and when a train pulled into a station, he would pass the correct time on to station staff, who would then sychronise the clock.

Waiting room Your station may still have a single waiting room, but once there were probably at least two, segregated into 'Ladies' and 'Gentlemen', with lavatories attached. A coal fire in winter, a solid table and horsehair-stuffed benches would have added home comforts.

Refreshment room Few trains in Victorian times carried their own stock of food and drink. Passengers changing trains would make for the station refreshment room to order something from a menu that might range from 'Breakfast with Cold Meat & Marmalade' for 2 shillings to sherry, port and champagne for 5 to 8 shillings a bottle.

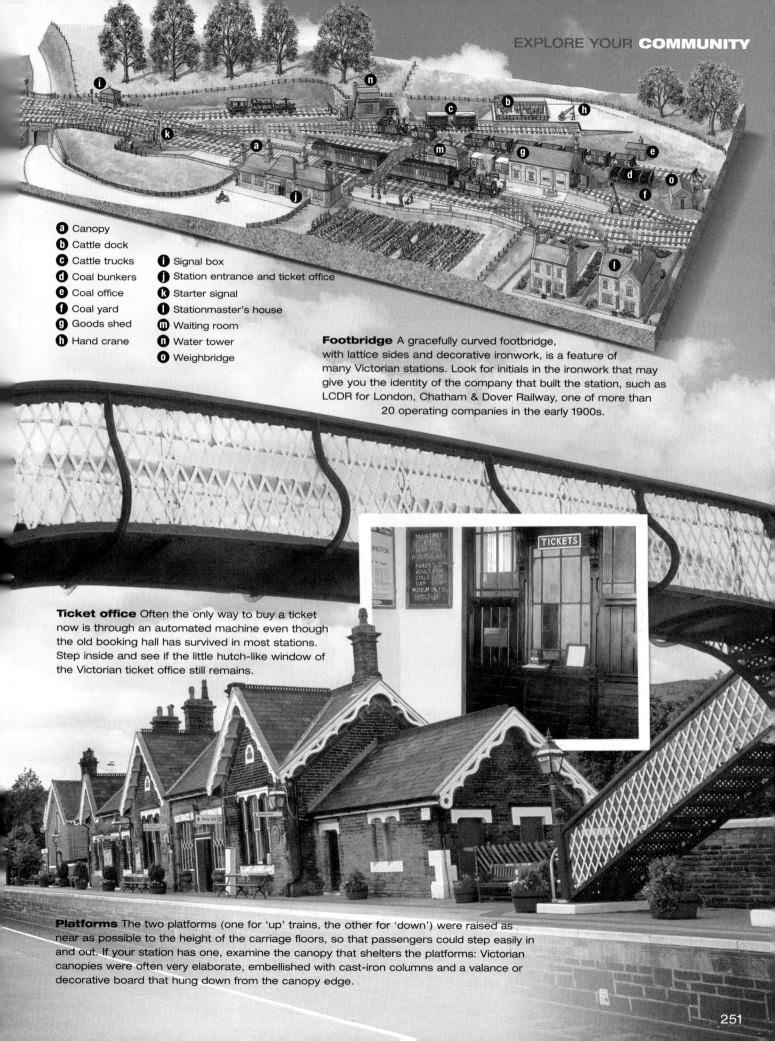

- **a** Canopy
- **b** Cattle dock
- **c** Cattle trucks
- **d** Coal bunkers
- **e** Coal office
- **f** Coal yard
- **g** Goods shed
- **h** Hand crane
- **i** Signal box
- **j** Station entrance and ticket office
- **k** Starter signal
- **l** Stationmaster's house
- **m** Waiting room
- **n** Water tower
- **o** Weighbridge

Footbridge A gracefully curved footbridge, with lattice sides and decorative ironwork, is a feature of many Victorian stations. Look for initials in the ironwork that may give you the identity of the company that built the station, such as LCDR for London, Chatham & Dover Railway, one of more than 20 operating companies in the early 1900s.

Ticket office Often the only way to buy a ticket now is through an automated machine even though the old booking hall has survived in most stations. Step inside and see if the little hutch-like window of the Victorian ticket office still remains.

Platforms The two platforms (one for 'up' trains, the other for 'down') were raised as near as possible to the height of the carriage floors, so that passengers could step easily in and out. If your station has one, examine the canopy that shelters the platforms: Victorian canopies were often very elaborate, embellished with cast-iron columns and a valance or decorative board that hung down from the canopy edge.

Transports of delight

Britain, as a pioneer of trains, bicycles, passenger jets and many other forms of conveyance, has some of the best transport museums in the world. Visit them to see the story of travel in your community come alive.

Freedom of the road

More than 100 years of British motoring is represented at the Heritage Motor Centre at Gaydon in Warwickshire. Here you can see the first cars to cause a flurry of excitement on Britain's streets, such as the 1896 Wolseley, and a walk along the museum's Time Road will give you an idea of how cars developed during the 20th century. The centre also holds the archives for Britain's car industry.

Motorbike fanatics get all the oil and leather smells, the buffed paintwork and engine intricacies they desire at the National Motorcycle Museum, Solihull. The collection includes more than 650 models.

The quieter, slower art of pushbiking is explored at the National Cycle Collection, Llandrindod Wells, Powys. Here you can see 250 machines, starting with an 1819 Hobby Horse and continuing with Boneshakers, Penny Farthings up to bicycles of today.

London's Transport Museum in Covent Garden tells the story of how people have got around the crowded capital. Exhibits include trams, horse-drawn buses, underground trains, trolleybuses and the celebrated London taxi. More vehicles can be seen at the Museum Depot in Acton Town, where uniforms, engineering drawings and poster artwork are on show. Tube and bus drivers can be heard reminiscing about the 'old days' as part of the museum's oral history project.

In Derbyshire, the National Tramway Museum at Crich has a collection of superbly maintained trams from around Britain, many of them offering rides (see above).

Places to visit

- Heritage Motor Centre, Gaydon.
www.heritage-motor-centre.co.uk
- National Motorcycle Museum, Solihull.
www.nationalmotorcyclemuseum.co.uk
- National Cycle Collection, Llandrindod Wells.
www.cyclemuseum.org.uk
- London's Transport Museum, Covent Garden, London.
www.ltmuseum.co.uk
- National Tramway Museum, Crich. www.tramway.co.uk
- National Motoring Museum, Beaulieu. www.beaulieu.co.uk

Out for a ride You can catch a tram, such as the Southampton tram car of 1903 (above) – or drive one – at the National Tramway Museum in Crich, as well as journey back in time, passing the historic buildings of the Tramway Village. Vehicles of all kinds belong to the National Motoring Museum collection at Beaulieu, Hampshire, including the sporty 1956 Austin Healey 100M (left), a 1933 Morris Mobile Grocery Shop and mass-market saloons like the 1960s' Ford Cortina.

On the water

As a seafaring nation Britain has many maritime museums – around 300 in all. Our coastal and sea trade, and defence, are explored in the displays and exhibits at the National Maritime Museum at Greenwich, and its sister at Falmouth, Cornwall, which holds the Small Boat Collection. All things maritime are covered, from slaving to passenger liners, naval warfare to international trade. Paintings, photographs and oral accounts show how seafaring communities were shaped.

Life and commerce on the canals (see pages 71, 249) and rivers is the topic at the National Waterways Museum in Gloucester Docks and the Boat Museum at Ellesmere Port in Cheshire, with their displays and collections of narrowboats, barges and tugs. You can climb aboard some of the vessels to get a taste of the living conditions.

Places to visit

- National Maritime Museum, Greenwich. www.nmm.ac.uk
- National Maritime Museum, Falmouth. www.nmmc.co.uk
- National Waterways Museum, Gloucester. www.nwm.org.uk
- The Boat Museum, Ellesmere Port.
www.canaljunction.com/mustbm.htm

On the rails

The National Railway Museum at York is a train-lover's dream – steam, diesel and electric locomotives, dining cars and Royal Saloons, snow ploughs and parcel vans. Other

Record breaker The *Mallard* (above), now at York's National Railway Museum, set a new world speed record for steam locomotives when it reached 126mph between Grantham and Peterborough in 1938.

attractions at the museum include railway story-telling, train rides, and thousands of items of train paraphernalia, including original posters. A fine collection of photographs and ephemera, signal boxes and equipment, as well as more than 20 steam locomotives, can be seen at the Didcot Railway Centre, while more gleaming locomotives take pride of place at STEAM, the museum of the Great Western Railway in Swindon's former railway works, established by Isambard Kingdom Brunel.

Places to visit
- National Railway Museum, York. www.nrm.org.uk
- Didcot Railway Centre. www.didcotrailwaycentre.org.uk
- STEAM, Museum of the Great Western Railway, Swindon. www.steam-museum.org.uk

In the air

Air travel has developed more dramatically during its short life than any other form of transport. The collections at the Royal Air Force Museums at Hendon in London and Cosford, Shropshire, range from the pioneer 'stringbag' planes of the early 20th-century to the modern Eurofighter. Civil aircraft include a BOAC Bristol Britannia 312, which operated on the London-New York route in the 1950s, and a 1960s' Vickers VC10. Among the Imperial War Museum's vast collection of military aircraft at Duxford, Cambridgeshire, you can see a de Havilland Comet 4, which in 1958 made history as the first jet to cross the Atlantic carrying fare-paying passengers. Twenty years later, Concorde was transporting people across the Atlantic at twice the speed of sound – a prototype is on display.

The Shuttleworth Collection at Biggleswade, Bedfordshire, features a notable collection of restored aeroplanes, including the scarlet de Havilland Comet which won the 1934 England-Australia race, and a 1941 Hawker Sea Hurricane designed for landing on aircraft carriers.

Places to visit
- Royal Air Force Museums, London and Cosford. www.rafmuseum.org.uk
- Imperial War Museum, Duxford. http://duxford.iwm.org.uk/
- Shuttleworth Collection, Biggleswade. www.shuttleworth.org

OTHER MUSEUMS TO VISIT

- Scottish Vintage Bus Museum, Lathalmond, Dunfermline. www.busweb.co.uk/svbm
- National Museums and Galleries of Wales (Maritime and Transport), Cardiff. www.nmgw.ac.uk/www.php/200/
- C.M. Booth Collection of Historic Vehicles, Rolvenden, Kent. www.motorsnippets.com/news_item_museums.asp?articleid=391
- Trolleybus Museum, Sandtoft. www.sandtoft.org.uk
- Benson Veteran Cycle Museum, Wallingford, Oxfordshire (open by appointment only, April-August, Tel. 01491 83841)
- The Canal Museum, Stoke Bruerne, Northamptonshire. www.canaljunction.com/mussbcm.htm
- Windermere Steamboats Museum, Cumbria. www.steamboat.co.uk
- Museum of Flight, East Lothian. www.nms.ac.uk/flight/index.asp

Up and away British Airways advertised its first flights to Europe from the new Gatwick Airport in 1936.

The public face of prosperity

If you stroll around your town and look at the street layout, the style of the public buildings and any parks and walks, you will uncover all kinds of clues about the character of the place. Was it shaped by the profits of medieval wool traders, fashionable Georgians or Victorian industrialists? What did people think of the new town hall design all those years ago? A visit to your local record office may uncover the answers.

Pride of the town
Take a close look at your local guildhall or town hall. It may reveal important clues to when and why it was built.

Prime location If you live in a town with a 16th or 17th-century centre, it may have a timber-framed hall raised on columns above an open arcade. The design provided shelter for traders at street level. The room or rooms above often served as a market hall and meeting place for the manorial court, as well as a school or cloth hall. Some public halls stood alone in the middle of the market place, at the heart of the town's commercial district. Today many, such as the 18th-century market hall at Dursley in Gloucestershire, are marooned by traffic.

Perhaps your town has a guildhall that projects into the main street, like those of Plympton and South Molton in Devon. It would have been built this way because it required more space than the houses and shops around it.

Working under cover The local cutlers met upstairs in the 14th-century guildhall in Thaxted, Essex, while traders worked in the arcade at street level.

Proud landmark If your town hall is in a striking classical design, with columns and a portico, it was probably built in the late 17th or 18th century to enhance the town's prestige.

The Victorians erected large town halls to accommodate splendid reception and dining rooms, chambers for meetings and offices for staff. Trading activities were moved out to new market halls and corn exchanges. The public buildings of the period share a grandeur imbued with civic pride (see pages 168-169). Manchester has a huge Gothic-style building, with arches, gables, spires and a tall clock tower; neighbouring Bolton favoured a classical style, with a flight of steps rising to six columns and a pediment, and a pair of lions framing the entrance.

Modern aspirations Even if your town hall was built in the 20th century, it could be an imposing classical-style structure, such as Barnsley (1932), or a part-Modernist, part-classical design, such as Waltham Forest (1938).

A sense of space
Walk around your town and look for the elegant parades and promenades, squares and crescents that were features of Georgian town planning (see pages 66-67, 150-153). You may discover public walks, which were especially popular at this time in spa towns such as Bath and Epsom, and seaside resorts like Brighton and Scarborough. New promenades were built in many towns in the 18th century, such as Leicester's New Walk, originally called

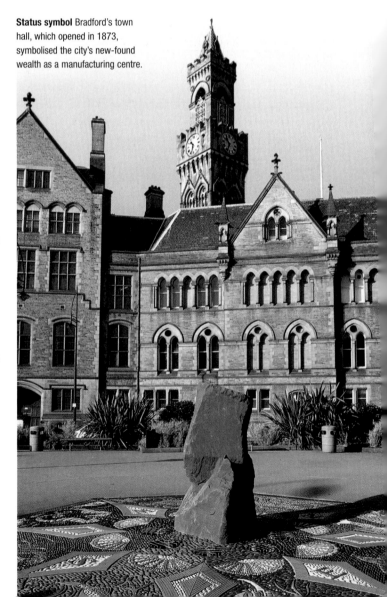

Status symbol Bradford's town hall, which opened in 1873, symbolised the city's new-found wealth as a manufacturing centre.

FOLLOW THE BANDSTANDS

The public parks that became a popular feature in the larger Victorian and Edwardian towns retain much of their original character. At the city or county record office, look for local authority plans and accounts, old maps and prints to find out when landmarks such as fountains or bandstands were built.

Spot the position Bandstands needed to be slightly elevated and have plenty of space around them to accommodate seated audiences for Sunday concerts.
• Look for an inscription on the bandstand – it might give you a clue about why it was built or who paid for it.
• Study an old town map (see pages 214-215) to see if a bandstand might once have stood in your park.
• Bandstands such as the one in Magdalen Green, Dundee (below), were designed to be decorative, often with elaborate ironwork, because they were focal points even when not in use.

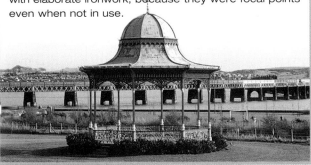

Queen's Walk, which was built in 1785 as a pedestrian link between the town and the racecourse. Old town walls sometimes became walkways, as at York, and Dorchester's Roman fortifications were turned into public walks and planted with lime, sycamore and chestnut trees.

Your public park may be the setting for a museum or art gallery. Many were built during the reign of Queen Victoria and, like town halls, the styles could be either Gothic or classical.

Research tips

Find out how your town developed by looking at plans, prints and documents in your local library or record office.
• Look for old prints of your town, known as 'prospects'. Samuel and Nathaniel Buck drew many prospects for local authorities in the mid 18th century.
• 'Proposed new developments' may be marked on old maps, and often completed by the time of the next map.
• Trace the story of a civic building by looking for plans, contracts, accounts and correspondence.
• In the late 19th century, streets had to be widened for electric trams. You will find the revelant private Act of Parliament at your local record office.
• Georgian towns had to move the livestock markets from the centres to improve public health and ease traffic congestion. Look for street names, such as Beast Market, which reveal where the old markets were held.

Newcastle gets a new look

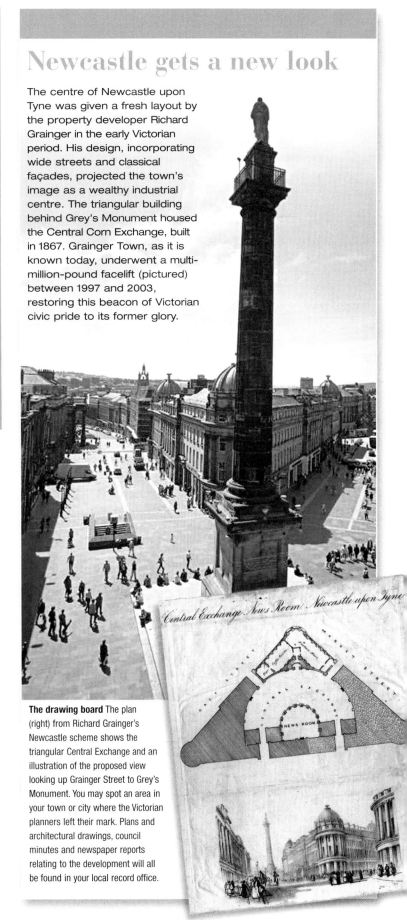

The centre of Newcastle upon Tyne was given a fresh layout by the property developer Richard Grainger in the early Victorian period. His design, incorporating wide streets and classical façades, projected the town's image as a wealthy industrial centre. The triangular building behind Grey's Monument housed the Central Corn Exchange, built in 1867. Grainger Town, as it is known today, underwent a multi-million-pound facelift (pictured) between 1997 and 2003, restoring this beacon of Victorian civic pride to its former glory.

The drawing board The plan (right) from Richard Grainger's Newcastle scheme shows the triangular Central Exchange and an illustration of the proposed view looking up Grainger Street to Grey's Monument. You may spot an area in your town or city where the Victorian planners left their mark. Plans and architectural drawings, council minutes and newspaper reports relating to the development will all be found in your local record office.

Monuments and memorials

Every community remembers its dead, in cemeteries and on war memorials and other monuments. Take a look at the stones and statues, read the inscriptions, and you will discover another chapter in the story of where you live.

War memorials

When you walk around your neighbourhood, look for street names commemorating a British military or naval victory, such as the battles of Trafalgar (1805) or Waterloo (1815). The first public war memorials to list the names of the dead were erected in the 1850s after the Crimean War, but it was only after the First World War (1914-18) that monuments were put up by public subscription in a mass act of remembrance. There are now some 54,000 war memorials throughout Britain.

Where to look Memorials were placed in prominent positions at crossroads, beside churchyards, or in parks, market places and public gardens.

- Look for memorials on plaques and boards in churches, chapels and community halls.
- The names of those who died in the Second World War are normally inscribed on the same memorial as the fallen of the First World War.
- At your local record office, search for newspaper reports and photographs of annual parades to the memorials on the nearest Sunday to Armistice Day, November 11; or look for the original unveiling of a monument.

In lasting memory The Imperial War Museum estimates that there are 1.5 million names on Britain's war memorials. You will find them not just on public monuments, but on plaques in places of worship, memorial parks, sports fields, schools and hospitals. A remarkable initiative by the museum, involving 500 volunteers and local history and veterans' societies, has produced the UK National Inventory of War Memorials. To find out how you can access the database and obtain a copy of the *War Memorials Handbook*, go to the museum's website, **collections.iwm.org.uk**.

Public cemeteries

The overcrowding of churchyards in the mid 19th century, caused by a huge growth in population, forced local authorities to build public cemeteries in most towns (see pages 184-185). Nowadays, some of the largest of these have fallen into disrepair, but their grand memorials in Gothic designs vividly capture the Victorian age.

Out of town Cemeteries were usually sited in areas that were on the outskirts of town at the time, such as Highgate, founded on London's northern extremity in 1839.

- Look at how the grounds were landscaped and divided into sections so that graves would be easier to find.
- Check to see if a plan of the cemetery is on display. It will give an overview of the layout of the whole cemetery.
- You may see an imposing entrance and drive, leading to separate chapels for Anglicans, Nonconformists and Catholics. Some cemeteries have areas for Jewish burials.

Cemetery records If a cemetery is still open, its records may be kept at the office on the site. Otherwise, you may find them at your local record office. The records, arranged chronologically, usually provide the name, address, age and occupation of the deceased person and the date of death and burial. Each burial plot was given a number which will enable you to find the grave on the plan of the cemetery.

- The National Archives of Scotland (see DIRECTORY) has cemetery records for 1900-75, under the code DOD 7/6.
- Cremation was ruled legal in 1885. Memorials include books of remembrance at the crematorium, and sometimes plaques, benches and trees in the grounds.

Reading monuments Study the memorials in your local cemetery to find out about former prominent members of your town. Inscriptions can reveal their standing in the local community and even their view of their own importance.

Sculpture on the street

The Victorians injected their sense of occasion and love of decoration into all areas of day-to-day street life. If you look around your town centre, you may still find examples of their functional street 'furniture'.

- Among the most striking items are the ornamental fountains built at the junctions of main streets or in public parks. They were erected by the local authority or benefactors wishing to improve the town's facilities.
- Look for boundary posts that name the old townships before the Urban District Council was created in 1894. They will be marked on Ordnance Survey (OS) maps (see pages 214-215).

Every statue tells a story

The Victorians, in particular, were fond of statues. Many still stand in public squares while others have been removed to a secluded spot in a park.

- Most towns have a statue of Queen Victoria. Some commemorate a royal visit, in which case photographs and a full report would have appeared in your local newspaper. You may find these at your record office.
- Look for statues of earlier monarchs, such as those of William III in Bristol and Hull, which celebrate the Glorious Revolution of 1688. Statues of Queen Anne, such as the one beside St Paul's Cathedral in London, are often mistaken for Victoria.
- Local aristocrats or Members of Parliament might have a statue, perhaps set on a column like that of Earl Grey in Newcastle upon Tyne (see page 255).
- Local worthies often merit statues: Lichfield in Staffordshire has one to the writer Dr Johnson (1709-84) and another to Commander Edward J. Smith, captain of the *Titanic*.

Drinks on the house The Victorians, concerned by the poor quality of the water supply, founded London's Metropolitan Drinking Fountain and Cattle Trough Association in 1859 to provide fresh water for all. Wealthy benefactors also paid for drinking fountains. Look out for their names in the inscriptions; one at Low Bradfield, Yorkshire, says: 'In memory of Mary Ann Smith: God's gift to man'.

- Read the inscription on a statue. It may praise the person's achievements and enable you to see why he or she was held in such high esteem by contemporaries. It may also tell you who was responsible for putting up the statue. Armed with this information, you can find out more about the person's role in your community from your local library or record office.

Life history Take a close look at statues for clues about their origin. A memorial in Lister Park, Bradford (right), honours the inventor Samuel Lister (1815-1906), who gave the park to the city. Panels around the base of the statue (above) illustrate his innovations in the field of textile machinery.

FIND OUT MORE

- *The English Town* (Mark Girouard, Yale University Press, 1990). An excellent guide on what to look out for in urban areas.
- www.bereavement-services.org A directory of Britain's cemeteries, crematoria and burial sites, with maps, contact details and links to related websites.
- www.tchevalier.com/fallingangels/bckgrnd/cemeteries/ A guide to Victorian cemeteries and funerary monuments.
- www.vintageviews.org/vv-tl/pages/Cem_Symbolism.htm A helpful glossary for interpreting Victorian cemetery symbolism.

Following the essential supplies

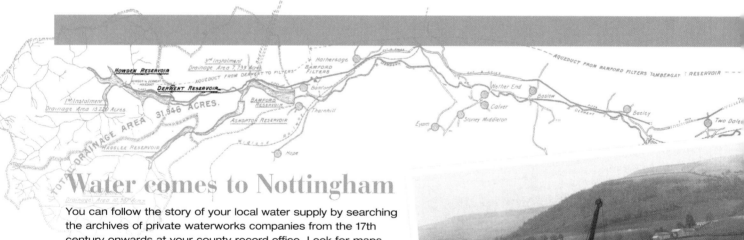

Find out where your water, gas and electricity come from, how and when your city, town or village was provided with these services, and when the postal and telephone services began. Each one of these improvements would have been momentous events in the story of your community.

Drawing up the water

Look around your neighbourhood for clues to how your local water was supplied in the past.
• Street names can indicate the location of public wells. Barker's Pool in Sheffield was a major source of water for the city from the 15th to 18th centuries. Today, only its name marks the site.
  • Wells are marked on early editions of large-scale Ordnance Survey (OS) maps (see pages 214-215).
  • Search through manor court rolls (see pages 146-147 and 322) in your county record office for references to wells in Tudor and Stuart times. In 1608 the manor court at Ecclesfield, Yorkshire, ordered that clothes must not be washed at drinking wells.

Hidden assets Look for wells that were enhanced with stone structures or converted into cast-iron pumps in the 19th-century. Some are inscribed with their date of construction, which may indicate when improvements were made to the local water supply.

Dealing with waste

Three Public Health Acts in the 19th century gave local authorities the power to improve sanitation and generated many records.
• Search the archives of the local authority at your record office for council minutes, surveys and reports, maps and plans of public works.
• Government inspections were carried out between 1848 and 1857. Ask your library if they hold a copy of a local sanitation report and its accompanying plans.

Gas and electricity

It is hard to imagine life without gas or electricity. But it took the inventive skill of our 19th-century forebears to harness them. You can still see signs of their ingenuity.
• Look out for any surviving gasometers, or at least their frames. To find out when they first appeared study the large-scale 19th-century OS maps in your record office.

Water comes to Nottingham

You can follow the story of your local water supply by searching the archives of private waterworks companies from the 17th century onwards at your county record office. Look for maps and plans of reservoirs, conduits and pipelines to trace the route by which water reached your city, town or village. In the case of Nottingham, the records of the Derwent Valley Water Board reveal how water was supplied to the city and its neighbours, Derby, Leicester and Sheffield, in the early 20th century. The Derwent Valley Water Act of 1901 signalled the construction of three dams across the Derwent and Ashop valleys high in the Peak District. An old photograph reveals that the building of the Derwent Dam was marked with the laying of a record stone (right) on June 21, 1907. Old plans (above) show how water was transported from the Derwent and Howden reservoirs through an aqueduct to Ambergate Reservoir in the east. From here pipes branched off to Nottingham in the north and Leicester and Derby in the east. In Nottingham, the water flowed into a further reservoir pumped by the Papplewick station before it joined the city's system.

- See if you can spot an electric power station in your area on an early 20th-century OS map. Bradford was the first town to have one, in 1889, but electricity did not replace gas to light houses until the 1920s. You can find today's power stations by following the lines of pylons marked on modern OS maps.
- Electric street lamps were first used in the 1860s and 1870s. Look for any surviving Victorian cast-iron lamps. Old photographs (see pages 212-213) of dimly lit streets may give you clues for where to search.
- Look also for advertisements in old newspapers (see pages 216-217) from the 1860s, when gas burners were first used for heating and cooking.
- Before pipelines brought gas from the North Sea in the 1960s, gas was produced from coal. If you live near a former coalfield, look for the coke-ovens that created gas as a by-product of the coal distillation process.
- You may find the records of early 19th-century supply companies at your county record office. These include maps, plans, architects' drawings and accounts.

Postal services

A feature that links every town in the land is the red post box, another Victorian innovation. You may also find evidence of early mail services carried by coach and horse.

What's in a post box? Look at the post boxes in the streets where you live; they might offer you a clue about when the surrounding houses were built. You can identify the ages of your local boxes by their royal ciphers: clockwise, from top left, Edward VII (1901-10), George V (1910-36), Edward VIII (1936), George VI (1936-52) and Elizabeth II (reigned since 1952). The design of the box can also be revealing. A post box in Dudley, Worcestershire (left), was built in neighbouring Birmingham in 1866 in the distinctive design of J.W. Penfold, known as the Penfold Hexagonal. It carries the cipher VR, for Queen Victoria, the monarch from 1837 to 1901.

- At your local record office or library, look for paintings of mail coaches, which were used from 1784 until they were replaced by the railways. Old directories (see pages 216-217) carry details of these postal services.
- See if the Post Office Archives and Records Centre (see DIRECTORY) has records or photographs for your post office.
- Is your local post office the original one? Check its present appearance against old photographs.
- Members of the Postal History Society have written local histories of the postal service. Ask if there are any at your library.

Telephone services

The first telephone exchange opened in 1879 at 36 Coleman Street, London. Check to see if your town has one. Some are housed in elegant 1930s or 50s buildings.

- The first public telephone boxes date from 1921. You may still have one of the cast-iron dome-topped boxes in your neighbourhood designed by Sir Giles Gilbert Scott in 1924. They feature the monarch's crown over the door and are painted in the same red colour as post boxes.
- Old photographs show telephone wires criss-crossing urban streets. To find out when they disappeared underground, ask at your local record office or the British Telecom Archives (see DIRECTORY). Among its records are telephone directories dating from 1880.

Water feature Look around your area for a Victorian pumping station like the splendid station at Papplewick, Nottingham, built in the 1880s. Still in working order, it was restored in 2004 and is open to the public.

In search of fun and games

By the mid 19th century, working people had more free time and began to look for entertainment. Impresarios and developers were quick to take advantage of new audiences and you may find that your town acquired a theatre and music hall at this time. Spectator sports were also popular, especially as even the professional football teams recruited their players from the local community, which helped to give a place a strong sense of identity.

Pantomime palace The lavishly appointed Alhambra Theatre in Bradford was built in 1914 by the impresario Francis Laidler to stage large-scale productions for the city's increasingly prosperous population. It was – and still is – renowned for its pantomimes.

Theatres of dreams

Many of Britain's towns have a long theatrical tradition. This may have begun with medieval mystery plays, and developed through the flowerings of Elizabethan and Restoration drama to the farces, musicals and 'angry young men' of the 20th century. Some Georgian and many Victorian and Edwardian auditoriums survive, but not always as theatres.

Most towns had a theatre or playhouse by the 18th century. You can spot any survivors by their plain, classical exteriors. They may be sited away from the central streets, such as the small Georgian theatres at Richmond in Yorkshire and Bury St Edmunds in Suffolk. Look in your library at the earliest town maps (see pages 214-215) and photographs (see pages 212-213) to see if there was a theatre in your town.

- Early Victorian theatres were much larger than their Georgian predecessors. They still used classical features, such as columns supporting a pediment over the entrance, as at the Theatre Royal, Newcastle, which opened in 1837.
- Look for the exuberant carvings decorating the late-Victorian or early 20th-century theatres: their auditoriums were embellished with cherubs, chandeliers and carved woodwork. They were often given exotic names, such as the Adelphi, Alhambra or Lyceum.

Music hall entertainment

Music halls and variety theatres started as extensions to pubs before they flourished in their own right in the second half of the 19th century, serving up a diet of song, dance and comedy to city working classes (see page 177). The best-preserved is the City Varieties Music Hall, Leeds, which developed from the White Swan pub and in 1865 became the City Palace of Varieties.

By 1875 London had more than 375 music halls or variety theatres. Wilton's Music Hall (opened 1858) was one of the most successful in the East End of London. It has been restored to its original condition and use, and is lit by a gas-burning chandelier of 27,000 cut crystals.

- The theatre history website **www.peopleplayuk.org.uk** has a 'guided tour' of the story of the music hall.

Show stopper Look out for ephemera, such as a theatre programme (left, 1894), to discover what was staged locally.

Come on, you Owls!

Sheffield Wednesday is one of the oldest football clubs in Britain. It was formed in 1867 and joined the Football League First Division in 1892 (defeating Notts County in its first game). You can follow its history, as you can with many clubs, through newspaper reports, census returns and other records, along with ephemera such as match programmes and old photographs.

- You might want to find out how your football team got its name. Sheffield Wednesday started as a cricket club that played mid-week from 1820. In 1867 it formed a football team to keep members together during the winter months. But by 1883 the football team had become so successful that it separated from the cricketers and formed its own club, turning professional in 1887.
- Clubs often moved once or twice before a permanent home was found at a new site in a working-class district or on the edge of town. You can spot these earlier sites on first-edition, large-scale Ordnance Survey (OS) maps (see pages 214-215).
- Wednesday's first permanent ground was at Olive Grove, on the southeast edge of the city. It is marked on first-edition OS maps. In 1899 the club moved across town to its present ground at Hillsborough, near Owlerton, hence the team's nickname The Owls.

WELCOME TO THE
SHEFFIELD WEDNESDAY
OFFICIAL CLUB WEBSITE

WEDNESDAY **WORLD**
CLICK HERE TO ENTER
MY ACCOUNT
HOME
▼ NEWS
▼ MATCH
▼ SQUAD
▼ TICKETS
▼ FANS
▼ CLUB
▼ HISTORY
▼ INTERACT
BETTING
MOBILE

Name:	Derek Dooley
DOB:	1929
Position:	Attacker
Clubs:	Wednesday
International Honours:	None

Sheffield-born Dooley joined the Owls in 1947 after beginning his career as an amateur with Lincoln City. Having earned a reputation as a goalscorer in the SWFC reserve side, he was given an opportunity at first team level.
He failed to impress on his first two outings, but a brace against ...ay in October 1951 prompted a scoring streak of 20 goal in 11 ... was a formidable opponent for defenders with his power and ...iasm, attributes which brought a total of 47 goals during the ...on season of 1951/52.
...that campaign Dooley struck five goals against Notts County, ...ainst Everton and Hull City and hat-tricks against Brentford

OPENING MATCH at Olive Grove,

MONDAY, SEPTEMBER 12th, 1887.

THE WEDNESDAY v. BLACKBURN ROVERS

BLACKBURN TEAM.

Right Wing. Goal. *Left Wing.*

H. Arthur.

Jos. Beverley. A. Chadwick.

Jos. Heyes. John Barton. Jas. H. Forrest.

S. Douglas. N. Walton. R. Rushton. L. H. Heyes. J. Berisford.

WEDNESDAY TEAM.

J. Smith.

F. Thompson. J. Hudson.

E. Brayshaw. W. Betts. A. Beckett.

H. Winterbottom. G. Waller. T. E. B. Wilson. T. Cawley. W. Mosforth.

Sporting success Most football league clubs have official and unofficial websites that often contain complete club histories. The official Sheffield Wednesday site is at **www.swfc.co.uk** It can tell you that the club won the Football League championship in 1902-3 and 1903-4, and again in 1928-9 and 1929-30, and added the FA Cup to this in 1896, 1907 and 1935.

Marking time Your local club may have a collection of memorabilia, such as Wednesday's team sheet (left) for its first match at its Olive Grove ground in 1887, just after the club had turned professional.

- Inside music halls or variety theatres, or at your local library or record office, look for posters, programmes, photographs and newspaper cuttings. These are likely to survive if the leading performers were star attractions.

Sport for all

Look at the ways in which the people of your community actively participated in sports (see page 176). League and cup competitions for amateur football and cricket teams flourished from the mid-Victorian period onwards.

- Search past editions of your local newspapers (see pages 216-217) for reports of games played by local teams and photographs of competition winners.
- At your record office, look for the documents of local branches of the Football Association, including minutes of meetings, results and presentations to winners.

Football crazy Britain's national game is part of the fabric of most towns, from school and amateur teams'

pitches to the stadiums that rise above city centres. Your local team might have published an official history. Also search the catalogues at your library or record office for match programmes, newspaper cuttings and photographs of former teams or star players. Many footballers would have lived in houses near a ground and you may find out more about them in census returns (see pages 218-219).

FIND OUT MORE

- **www.cinema-theatre.org.uk** The Cinema Theatre Association campaigns for the preservation of cinemas, theatres and music halls, publishes books about the buildings, and holds an archive for use by its members.
- **www.thefa.com** The Football Association's official website contains a directory of clubs and contact links. For details of Scottish teams, go to **www.scottishfa.co.uk**
- **www.rfu.com** The Rugby Football Union's official website contains a list of clubs and contact links as well as details of its Museum of Rugby at Twickenham.

Going down to your local pub

For centuries, places where people gathered to chat over a drink have served as the social heart of the community. Wherever you live, you will spot such establishments, from traditional inns to 1960s and 70s estate pubs, and a search through any records relating to them is likely to uncover a mine of information about the history of your neighbourhood.

The earliest 'pubs'

The term 'public house' came into use only gradually during the 18th century. Before then, alcohol was served in licensed alehouses or inns. Many did not last long and some were merely a room in a private house, where ale was brewed and served to provide useful extra income.

Tracing alehouse records Some communities had an amazing number of premises licensed to serve alcohol. Derby had 120 alehouses to just 684 domestic dwellings in 1693, and the Scottish town of Dunbar in East Lothian supported 46 in the 1790s, compared with just ten today.

- Search through quarter-sessions records at your county record office for details of brewster sessions, when town and parish constables had to present a list of all the licensed inn and alehouse keepers in their areas.
- Probate inventories attached to wills, which are kept at local record offices and the National Archives (see DIRECTORY), often record brewhouses and stocks of ale stored in their cellars (see also pages 324-325).
- Burgh records held at the National Archives of Scotland (see DIRECTORY) sometimes include applications for alehouse licences.

One for the road

Growth in trade during the Middle Ages led to a marked increase in the traffic on the roads. Travellers needed somewhere to stop for refreshment and rest.

- Look for pub signs, such as the Travellers' Rest, the Packhorse, or the Coach and Horses along main roads, especially on those that were once packhorse or drovers' routes (see page 122) or one of the coaching routes (see page 70) that criss-crossed Britain.
- Many former coaching inns have retained their Georgian appearance – look for sash or bow windows arranged symmetrically around a central doorway, perhaps

Coach stop Many of Britain's high streets still have Georgian hotels that started life as coaching inns. The Angel, Guildford, Surrey (above), was one of several such hostelries in the town. Details of coach services running from it are given in Kelly's 1855 directory for Surrey (right).

framed by a pediment and pillars. A large, arched entrance at the side that allowed coaches and waggons to pass through into a courtyard will be a clue to a building's use as an inn.

- See if you can spot any old mounting blocks in front of an inn or in its courtyard. These were to help customers clamber back up on to their horses.

Documentary evidence As well as looking around you, a search at your local record office (see pages 18-19) should yield information about any local coaching inns.

- Inns that were boarding points for coaches may be listed in early trade directories (see page 217).
- Look at old newspapers (see page 216) for any mention of an inn as the venue for social events.
- Inns often feature in old photographs (see pages 212-213).

Service station The facilities on offer for horses at the Commercial Inn, Fressingfield, Suffolk, in the early 1900s were as important as those for the coach passengers.

Country pubs

In the countryside, the pub was often the only alternative social centre to the church or chapel.

- Many a country pub started as a farmhouse-cum-alehouse with just one room for drinking. You might recognise the original part of a pub that has been extended to serve food and to provide games rooms.
- Some pubs were attached to the workshop of a craftsman, such as a blacksmith or a wheelwright. Look for pub names in fading paint on the walls of village shops and houses.
- Many rural pubs bear the name of a local landowner. On the Duke of Rutland's estates in Derbyshire, there are several Rutland Arms as well as a few pubs called the Peacock, after the emblem on the duke's coat-of-arms.

Country pub records Again, start by searching in local archives, such as your record office or reference library.

- Many pub names have changed over time. The old names can be traced by following a pub back through trade directories (see page 217).
- Look for innkeepers and publicans identified in census returns (see pages 218-219) and electoral registers.
- Ask individual breweries if you can see the title deeds to pubs they own. These give every change of ownership.

Town pubs

In England and Wales alone, there were more than 102,000 pubs in 1900, mostly in urban areas. They were generally comfortable places, full of colourful tiling and etched glass, reflecting the improved living standards of their largely working-class customers. Today there are only around 60,000, a good number of 'locals' having simply disappeared or been turned into something else.

Sign of the times The elaborate glass and tiled panels featured in numerous 19th and early 20th century pubs have often remained in place long after the buildings they adorned ceased to serve food, drink and a warm welcome. Some are more than just decorative: they carry information about ownership and the arrangement of rooms (right and below).

- In the late 18th and 19th centuries, many towns had large 'common breweries' that served the local pubs. Try and find them on first-edition, six-inch Ordnance Survey (OS) maps (see pages 26-27), then go and see what survives today on the same site.
- Some pubs had an offsales counter. Look for evidence in words like 'Jug & Bottle', 'Family Department' or 'Outdoor', etched on glass panels above the bar.
- In the 1920s and 30s, the popularity of the car and buses encouraged the building of roadhouses, large pubs catering for day-trippers. They had plenty of parking space, rooms big enough for a busload of people, and overnight accommodation. Note any near your town, usually by roundabouts and A-road intersections.

FIND OUT MORE

- *Licensed to Sell: The History and Heritage of the Public House* (G. Brandwood, English Heritage Publications, 2004)
- www.pubs.com/history.htm A lively account of the evolution of the public house in Britain from the alehouse to the gin palace.
- www.pubhistory.freeserve.co.uk Website of the Pub History Society, giving details of special events, useful links and advice on carrying out research.
- www.camra.org.uk Campaign for Real Ale (CAMRA) site. Includes a national inventory of pubs with interiors of outstanding interest.
- www.archives.gla.ac.uk/sba/ Scottish Brewing Archive, which collects and preserves the records of the Scottish brewing industry.

A home from home The plush, softly lit Victorian interiors of many city pubs have been well preserved, as at the Anglesey in London (right). Old photographs of the local area, which may help you with your research, are a popular way of creating a sense of the past.

The stories behind pub signs and names

Looking at the pub signs in your area and then trying to discover what lies behind the names and images on them can reveal a great deal about the history of where you live. Some of the names are popular in most parts of Britain and may relate to national and even international events, but many focus on local heroes and their deeds.

MARQUIS OF GRANBY
Devenish

The Granby connection In the 18th-century the Marquis of Granby set up many of his retired army officers as innkeepers – who gratefully named their pubs after him.

Romans, the Church and royalty

It all began with the Romans, whose symbol to identify a public house to an illiterate population was a trail of vine leaves. The British took up the idea but, more appropriately for a colder climate, displayed a bush instead. In 1393, a law was passed making it compulsory for every pub and hostelry to show a symbol on a signboard, and the names of the symbols soon became associated with the establishments themselves.

At first many of these images and names were of a religious nature, such as the Cross Keys (of St Peter) and the Sun (a symbol of Christ). But after the Reformation in the late 16th century, many publicans thought it wiser to choose secular names, especially those with royal overtones – the Rose and Crown, or the King's or Queen's Head.

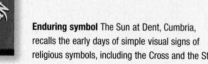

Enduring symbol The Sun at Dent, Cumbria, recalls the early days of simple visual signs of religious symbols, including the Cross and the Star.

Some refer to romantic royal adventures. The Royal Oak (left, at York) is the third most common pub name and commemorates where the future Charles II hid from his enemies after his defeat at the Battle of Worcester in 1651. Having a long reign seems to be the key to a king or queen having a pub named after them: the commonest royal pub names are the George (after George III, 1760-1820) and the Queen Victoria (1837-1901). The latter can be given a modern twist: the woman depicted on the sign outside Bristol's Queen Victoria pub is not the long-serving monarch but Victoria Beckham, Posh Spice.

The good, the bad and the plug-ugly

Drinkers have always enjoyed raising a glass to their heroes, and many publicans have immortalised the great, the good and the bad by naming their establishments after them. Pubs might be named after powerful local landowners as an act of flattery – the Waldegrave Arms in Chewton Mendip, Somerset, and the Raby Arms in Barnard Castle, County Durham. Widely commemorated wartime heroes include the dukes of Marlborough and Wellington, Admiral Nelson and Winston Churchill; also that much-honoured 18th-century general, the Marquis of Granby.

Very popular are sporting heroes such as boxing champions – the Bendigo in Nottingham (taking the professional name of local 19th-century champion, William Thompson), and the Tom Cribb (see right) and the Henry Cooper in London. In some cases, the signs might display likenesses of sportsmen, such as Ian Botham (at the Cricketers in Blackhall, County Durham) and Lester Piggott (at the Jockey in Baughton,

---

WHEN IS A CAT NOT A CAT?

The Cat Head at Chiselborough in Somerset shows a cat on its signboard, but the 'cat head' referred to is the name for the beam in a sailing ship to which the anchor is secured. Maybe a past landlord had been a sailor and had found this snug berth after leaving the sea. And the 'cat' of the Cat and Bagpipes at Northallerton in Yorkshire is actually a short form of 'catphractes', a Roman term for troopers in body armour, and recalls the Scottish border raiders in their iron breastplates who terrified the northern English throughout the late Middle Ages and beyond.

Worcestershire). Folk villains take their place, too, with romantic baddies such as the pirate Captain Kidd having a pub in Wapping named after him and the highwayman Dick Turpin being commemorated by one in York. Generally the named figure has some connection with the location of the establishment – Kidd was hanged in Wapping and Turpin in York.

Birds and bees

Nature has been an inspiration to the namers of pubs. The Birch Tree, the Blackbird, the Honey Bee and the Spotted Dog were probably chosen for connotations that were particularly pleasant to their choosers. But there are plenty of clues to stories behind some pretty names. The Rose and Daffodil near Swansea in south Wales hints at harmony between two neighbouring and often antagonistic countries, as does the Rose and Thistle at Alwinton near the Scottish border in Northumberland; while the Pheasant, the Stag, the Fox and Hounds and the Leaping Salmon tell you about field sports that have

BUCKET of BLOOD

Bloody memories The Bucket of Blood at Phillack, Cornwall, was so-called after a murder victim was found in the pub's well. The Lamb and Flag in London's Covent Garden once had the same gory name – in this case because of the bare-knuckle prize fights that took place there.

traditionally been popular locally. Local insects (the Red Admiral or the Grasshopper) are commonly recalled, although the Ladybird is relatively rare.

Blazing Donkeys and Buckets of Blood

Best of all, perhaps, are the pub names that have you scratching your head for an explanation. The Blazing Donkey (Ramsgate, Kent) refers to a fire in the 1780s that gutted the stables. But what are we to make of Portsmouth's Sociable Plover, or the Bucket of Blood at Phillack in Cornwall (see above)? One of the strangest, the Shrew Beshrewed at Hersden, Kent, refers to the custom of punishing a scolding woman by tying her to a chair and ducking her in the river – the phrase 'Beshrew thee' meant 'Devil take thee'. The perversely named Nobody Inn at Doddiscomsleigh, near Exeter, Devon, came by its present name after a former owner took it into his head to refuse entry to customers.

Boxing champion Londoner Tom Cribb, commemorated in a Panton Street pub, fought and won the first international prize fight on 28 September, 1811, against American Tom Molyneux (inset). Cribb won £2600 and a cup valued at 80 guineas.

FIND OUT MORE

● www.bjcurtis.force9.co.uk The Inn Sign Society's informative website.
● www.fatbadgers.co.uk An independent pub and hotel guide that lists common and strange pub names.
● www.camra.org.uk Campaign for Real Ale (CAMRA) website lists pubs of outstanding historical interest.

HOME

THE STORY OF HOMES

268-293

EXPLORE YOUR HOME

294-331

THE STORY OF HOMES

The way homes are built and embellished can tell you a great deal about the history of your area, including changes in local fashion and taste as well as the occupations and lifestyles of earlier inhabitants. Even the design of a modern house may be influenced by traditional styling, and it might be possible to trace records about previous buildings on the same site, and about the families who lived there.

Granite
Limestone
Sandstone
Slate

Before the Industrial Revolution brought mass-production and better transport, builders generally had to use materials that were close to hand. Stone for walls was hauled from the nearest quarry; clay for bricks, tiles and plaster was dug up on site; timber for framing cut from local woods; and straw for thatch gathered at harvest time. Building methods and designs were largely determined by whatever was readily available locally (see 'Regional building styles', opposite).

The look of a building may also tell you about former residents. Weavers' cottages in parts of the north of England and the Midlands tend to have unusually big windows, to let in extra light to work by. A row of identical, single-storey cottages is likely to have been almshouses.

Remember also that the original structure of a building might be hidden behind 'skins' of plaster, weatherboard or brick, perhaps added to keep out the wind and rain or simply to ape fashion. Signs of such alterations are mixed styles, irregularly positioned windows and changes to the roofline and pattern of brick or stonework.

Patterns in stone Stone is one of the most durable building materials. Many of the oldest surviving houses are constructed from it and generally reflect local geology – from the slates of Wales and Cornwall to the dark granites and sandstones of northern England and Scotland and the honeyed limestones of the Cotswolds (see map, right). Skilled craftsmen often carved fine details into stone, creating rich, lasting decoration such as the moulded window mullions and roof finials seen across much of Gloucestershire.

Stone-wall construction would vary according to the status of a building, fashion and local tradition. Blocks of neatly cut, dressed stone (ashlar), laid in random or even courses, might form the walls of better-quality homes, while simple cottages were built using rough, untreated, irregular stones (rubblework).

 Rubblework

 Random ashlar

REGIONAL BUILDING STYLES

Dependence on local materials and techniques for the construction of the earliest buildings resulted in a wide range of distinctive regional house styles, still much in evidence right across Britain.

Earth walling Turf and mud, plastered over for strength, provide the cheapest walling, and were therefore popular with poor Scottish crofters. Solid unbaked clay, known as 'cob', helped created the rounded walls seen in many Devon cottages (above). In East Anglia, clay is moulded into bricks or 'lumps'.

Pargetting In Essex, Suffolk and the southeast of England, a protective plaster coating, based on the abundant supply of local chalk, was often applied to timber-frame houses. This would be moulded to form patterns and ornate details, particularly in the second half of the 17th century.

Harling Up until the 19th century, a rough-cast, protective finish on walls of shingle or gravel mixed in a lime-based mortar was popular in the north of England and in Scotland. It was semi-porous, allowing any build-up of moisture to evaporate quickly.

Cladding Tiles and slates were used as a protective covering in coastal areas. By the 18th century, cheap softwood imports had also made timber weatherboarding (below) popular in the southeast of England.

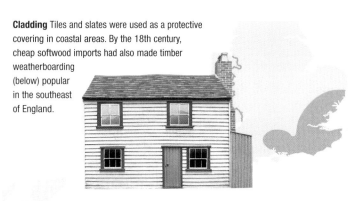

Pantiles Imported from Holland in the 17th century, S-shaped pantiles became popular for roofing along the east coast of both England and Scotland. They are rare in western counties, probably because of the greater distance from the Continent.

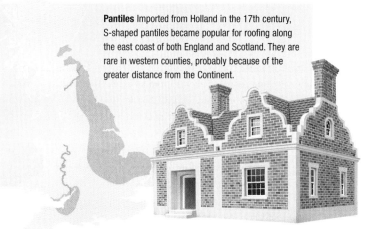

TIMBER FRAMING

The simplest form of structural wooden framing was the cruck frame (right), where pairs of long timbers, known as crucks, curve inward to join at the ridge of the roof. It was relatively quick and simple to construct, which may explain its widespread use. Only in the wealthier southeast of England was the more flexible box frame of vertical posts linked by horizontal tie beams (above) preferred. This allowed for two or three full storeys, as well as the addition of extra wings.

Flint and pebbles In the east and southeast of England, the local flint offered an economic, durable material for walls. The egg-shaped nodules were split to provide a flat outer surface with a dark lustrous quality. Pebbles, often rendered or tarred, were also used.

From wattle and daub to bricks and mortar

Most people in the Middle Ages built themselves a flimsy thatched hut by interlacing branches (wattle) to form a framework of wall panels, on to which they smeared a plaster made of mud, straw and animal dung (daub). Such simple dwellings quickly disintegrated, so few have survived to this day. The medieval houses that remain are mostly the grander, more substantial homes of merchants, landowners and farmers. It was only with the introduction of brick that a more lasting record was created.

Life in the manor hall

The manor house of the local lord would be rather more elaborate than other properties in a village. Most of the sturdy, timber-framed building was taken up by a large hall with a hearth at its centre, from which the smoke of the fire curled up and escaped through gaps in the roof. This was the focal point of the household, where estate workers and servants slept, ate and lived out their lives in the grime and gloom – windows were small and, before the use of glass, wooden shutters kept out the wind and rain.

The lord's table stood on a dais at one end of the hall. At the opposite end, a cross passage – with exterior doors to either side – divided off service rooms or livestock. If a kitchen existed, it was generally detached to safeguard against fire. There might also be outbuildings – barns, stables and brewhouses – frequently arranged around a central courtyard.

During the 15th century, the manor house became larger and more elaborate in its layout and build, sometimes including both inner and outer courtyards.

Wealden houses

In parts of the Weald of Kent and Sussex, a boom in trade during the 15th century led many prosperous yeoman farmers to enlarge their properties by adding an upper level. They still consisted largely of one central hall that was open to the roof, but at each end upper chambers were incorporated that 'jettied', or projected, over the lower walls. The earliest of these houses were built around a box frame (see page 269) with an infill of wattle and daub covered in lime plaster, although the use of stone and later brick gradually crept in.

Lordly style In medieval times, even the wealthy lived mainly in one large room – the hall, where meals were cooked over an open fire. The solar, or sleeping quarters, were above the small, curtained-off parlour. An oak frame formed the main support structure and increasingly stone was used as infill or even as a base, as at Minworth Greaves, in Warwickshire (left).

SAFE AS HOUSES

In parts of Wales and along the Scottish border fortified farmhouses and tower houses provided the occupants with protection during the turbulent years of the late Middle Ages. The most common tower house was a rectangular stone building providing accommodation for cattle or storage in the vaulted ground floor and living quarters for the family on the floors above. A classic example is the 15th-century Smailholm Tower (left), a few miles outside the Scottish border town of Kelso.

Moving up To maximise living space in the cramped streets, many medieval townhouses were built up to three storeys high, each successive level 'jettying' out to overhang the one below, as in The Shambles, York (left). Merchants and craftsmen often sold their wares from a shop at ground level and lived on the upper floors.

A lasting legacy

Stone was expensive in the Middle Ages and on the whole was used to build castles and churches, although by the 14th century it was becoming increasingly used by the nobility to create houses like Penshurst Place in Kent, with its imposing baronial hall. Some simpler houses were built from stone in areas close to quarries, particularly in Scotland, but these were usually roughly constructed and tended not to survive.

By the 15th century, in areas such as Yorkshire and the Cotswolds where stone was readily available and there was a long tradition of high quality masonry, the growing prosperity brought by the wool trade (see pages 142-143) led to a proliferation of many fine smaller stone houses. In the Cotswolds, local stone is still a common feature in window mullions, roofing slates and walls.

The brick revolution

The material that radically altered the architecture of the Middle Ages was brick. First introduced by the Romans, it made a huge comeback once the Tudors had perfected its manufacture. Bricks made it possible to build safer, more effective chimneys and so to move the fire away from the centre of the hall. The layout of homes could then be radically altered, allowing for the easier and more flexible addition of upper floors, and for rooms to become smaller. At the same time, interiors were made lighter and warmer through the wider use of glass.

These developments led to the modernisation or rebuilding of many old timber manor houses by the introduction of brick outer walls, mullioned windows and richer detailing. On some timber-framed building, brick replaced wattle and daub as infill.

No expense spared The few who could afford brick made extensive use of it in the 16th century. At Spain's Hall, in Finchingfield, Essex (below), its flexibility has been exploited to create ornate gable-ends and chimney stacks.

INNOVATIONS FOR THE HOME

1000

NORMAN
1066-1189

Early Middle Ages (medieval)

1100

GOTHIC
1189-1485

1200

c.1150
Saltford Manor near Bristol marks the start of a growing trend among the minor gentry and merchant class for building more substantial homes from stone. Possibly the oldest surviving stone town house is the late 12th-century Jew's House in Lincoln.

c.1300
Aydon Castle, a late 13th-century fortified manor house in Northumberland, installs one of the latest innovations, a wall fireplace, vented via a chimney built along an outer wall.

1300

Later Middle Ages (medieval)

1400

c.1450
Glass windows, though expensive, become increasingly popular in domestic buildings, such as the merchants' houses along Church Street in Tewkesbury, Gloucestershire (see page 139).

TUDOR
1485-1558

1500

Tudor

ELIZABETHAN
1558-1603

1590s
Hardwick Hall, in Derbyshire, highlights the Tudors' growing mastery of building with brick and glass.

1600

271

Putting the roof over your head

Roofs and chimneys are well worth an upward glance, since they can tell you much about the age, status and quality of a home. A roofscape might be an impressive arrangement of ridges and valleys, created from lead, clay, stone or slate, or just a simple upturned 'V' covered with thatch. Chimneys can range from little more that a piece of piping poking through the roof tiles to bold blocks of masonry set against an outside wall and complex displays of intricately crafted artistry, rising majestically against the skyline.

CREATING A FRAMEWORK

One of the biggest challenges faced by early builders was to provide sufficient support for the required roof span without filling a major part of the living space below with supporting posts. During the late Middle Ages and the Tudor period, several standard methods of roof construction evolved.

In the queen-post roof, the rafters were simply carried by paired uprights and in the king-post roof, a row of single uprights propped up the ridge piece – the main timber running along the apex of the roof. After 1350, these styles were joined by the more complex crown-post roof (above, right), where sturdy braces at the top of each upright carried the main horizontal support for the rafters, known as the collar purlin.

By the end of the 16th century, butt-purlin roofs were taking over. Here sturdy principal rafters, jointed to the tie beam, formed a truss that carried the main horizontal supports for the common rafters, the butt purlins.

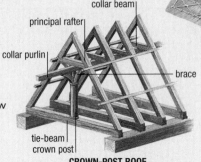

CROWN-POST ROOF

collar beam
principal rafter
collar purlin
brace
tie-beam
crown post

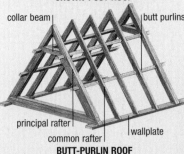

BUTT-PURLIN ROOF

collar beam
butt purlins
principal rafter
common rafter
wallplate

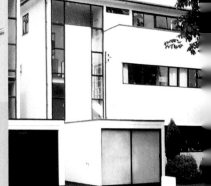

Thatch, made from straw, reed or heather, depending on availability, was used for centuries because it was light and reasonably rain and wind-proof. But it was also a fire risk and was banned on new houses in London from 1212.

CHANGING ROOF FASHIONS

Roofs are generally built in two main styles that date back to medieval times: hipped (below, left) or gabled (below, right). A common variation is the mansard roof – introduced in the 17th century – with two different pitches on each slope, the lower part being steeper than the upper and often fitted with windows to create extra living space.

Modern and functional Flat roofs, which are cheap and easy to install, became a distinctive feature of late 20th-century housing.

In general, the older a roof is, the steeper its pitch. A steep pitch helps rain and snow to run off quicker, which is useful with thatch. The introduction of more reliably watertight tiling made this less important.

Houses built in medieval times have plain, overhanging eaves without gutters or downpipes. Georgian roofs tend to be shallow, often hidden behind a balustrade or parapet. The Victorians revived the steeper medieval-style roof, adding decorative tiles along the ridge and trimming the 'V' of the gable end with ornately carved wooden bargeboards. Other medieval features re-emerged in the late 19th century, including turrets with conical roofs, which became popular in Scotland.

Twentieth-century technology brought greater design flexibility. Flat, single-slope and asymmetric roofs are now commonplace on the modern skyline.

SEALING OUT THE ELEMENTS

The earliest roofing material, thatch, is still used across Britain. But by the late 19th century improvements in production and transport had made the more durable slate and tiles cheap and readily available. Choice of roof cover has expanded still further in the past 100 years to include concrete, plastic, tarred felt and corrugated iron.

Stone tiles were used from the 14th century in areas where the local stone could be split thin enough for roofing. Limestone was generally used on steeply pitched roofs and sandstone on shallower pitches.

Clay tiles first appeared around 1500, but were rare in the north and west of Britain until the late 17th century. The earliest were handmade and irregular in shape. The Victorians introduced scallop-shaped tiles and often created patterns by mixing different colours.

Slate was used from late medieval times on better-class properties in Cornwall, Wales and the Lake District, where it was quarried. But by the mid 19th century, it had penetrated to all parts of the British Isles and was widely used for working-class terraced homes.

Picturesque detail The Tudors made an art out of brickwork, a skill clearly displayed in their chimney pieces, such as those at Trent Park in Middlesex (left). The style enjoyed a revival in the 19th century, but poorer quality workmanship usually betrays the chimney's real age.

Up on the rooftops M-shaped slate covered roofs were typical of the Georgian period. The attics were the living quarters of servants, often hidden behind parapets. Lines of chimney pots stand proud on the rooftops. These were introduced in the second half of the 18th century to solve the problem of smoking fires by increasing the updraught.

FROM A HOLE IN THE ROOF TO ART

The open central hearth was a key feature of homes in the Middle Ages. But it was smoky and by the end of the Tudor era demand for upstairs chambers had made it impractical.

The earliest form of chimney was the smoke bay, or fire hood, built from lath and plaster. Later, bricks were used, but it was not until the 16th century, when they were more widely available, that the chimney became a common feature in homes. Early

Stack of brick The earliest chimney pieces, such as the one shown here, were massive and generally very plain in design. If they protrude from the outer face of a wall, this is a sign that they were a later addition to an older house.

chimneys were generally built on the gable-end wall of a building, initially projecting from the outer face, but later incorporated into the plane of the wall.

Often a second fireplace would be installed on the first floor, which joined the chimney stack before it emerged from the roof. By the middle of the 16th century, four or more flues were being incorporated within one stack so that clusters of chimneys started to appear on the rooftops.

In all shapes and sizes

Stone, brick and even cob were used to build chimneys. At first, they tended to be large and functional, with little or no ornamentation. But by the turn of the 17th century, builders were creating chimneys in a range of styles – square, rectangular or round in lavishly embellished stone and brick. As Tudor technology made bricks cheaper and more available, their flexibility was exploited to fill the rooftops with increasingly complex designs – intricate moulding, coloured patterning and recessed panels.

Stone chimneys were nearly always built from smooth ashlar, but some were of rubblework (see page 268) or even a combination of stone and brick with the top castellated or styled like a classical column.

A compact solution for town living

From the 17th century, houses became more sophisticated as builder's pattern books introduced new styles from the Continent. The opulence of the Baroque period was tempered by the Classical symmetry and proportion of the newly adopted Palladian style from Italy. An explosion of speculative building produced a mass of terraced houses for the middle classes as Britain stood at the dawn of a new age – the Georgian period.

THE EARLY GEORGIAN TOWN HOUSE

The tall narrow front and floor plan stretching back from the road of the early Georgian town house provided plenty of living space. The ground floor had an entrance hall, where visitors were received. The principal living rooms were on the first floor, or piano nobile, with a drawing room for formal entertainment and a more intimate back parlour for the family. The second floor contained bedrooms, and the servants' living quarters were in the attic.

Windows Sash windows, flush to the brickwork, formed mostly with six panes over six, were sometimes topped by classical lintels. The windows became progressively smaller further up the building, reflecting the hierarchy of the floors.

Doors A flat door-hood, supported by finely moulded or carved brackets, was found even on the more modest homes. On grander houses, the door was sometimes emphasised with a more ornate hood or canopy.

Basement This was the servants' world, where food was cooked and the clothes washed and ironed. The basement also contained the coal cellar, into which coal was deposited via a coal hole in the pavement outside.

Roof An M-shaped roof with two gables often covered the double span of the Georgian town house. The mansard roof, with two pitches (see page 272), was also popular, as it allowed for more spacious living quarters in the attic.

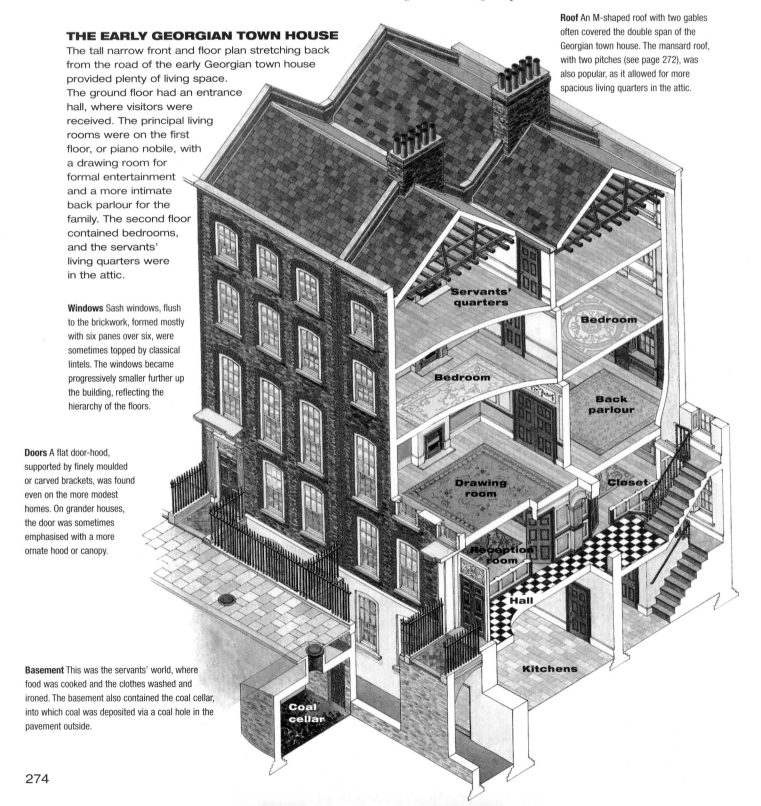

Servants' quarters

Bedroom

Bedroom

Back parlour

Drawing room

Closet

Reception room

Hall

Kitchens

Coal cellar

Classic styles from abroad

In the 1600s, architects increasingly looked to Continental Europe, and Italy in particular, for inspiration. The style known as Palladian was introduced in Britain by the court architect Inigo Jones in the 17th century and followed the rules of classical architecture as expounded by the Italian architect Andrea Palladio (1508-80). Governed by symmetry and strict classical principles of proportion, Palladianism soon became a dominant influence and can be seen in great country houses such as Holkham Hall in Norfolk, city terraces such as Queen's Square in Bath and even modest homes.

There was a change in the choice of building materials. Brick began to be used widely even for modest houses, replacing timber framing in areas where stone was not available. Where timber framing was still popular, it was usually covered with plaster, weatherboarding or tiles. Some brick buildings were fronted in Portland stone to make them look grander; others were finished with stucco, a plaster made from a mixture of lime and sand (see page 276). The stucco was often incised with lines and painted cream to give the appearance of fine stonework. Many terraces in London's more fashionable areas are faced in this way.

Terraced homes

The ever-growing population stimulated speculative development in urban areas (see pages 66-67, 150-157). Rows of elegant, classically fronted terraces appeared. The finest terraces, such as those in London's Mayfair and Robert Adam's Charlotte Square in Edinburgh (see page 157), were influenced by the Palladian style and resembled Italian Renaissance palaces. To avoid the monotony of long straight streets, many Georgian town planners introduced crescents and circuses.

Not all development was so grand. Large, three-storey tenement buildings were a common feature in Scotland, particularly in Edinburgh

Dutch flair Continental styles, such as the crow-stepped gables at Denham Village in Buckinghamshire (right), were a popular feature on homes in the 17th century. The gables originated from Holland.

and Glasgow, and eventually became notorious for their insanitary and overcrowded conditions.

Taxing regulations

After the Great Fire of London in 1666, a series of building acts had been introduced to reduce the risk of fire. These prohibited the use of wood to decorate façades, and door canopies could no longer project. Window frames had to be recessed and parapets had to stand above the roof line.

A brick tax from 1784 to 1850 led to an increase in the size of bricks. The window tax from 1696 to 1851 imposed a charge of two shillings a year on each house, and a further sum if the dwelling had more than ten windows, causing owners to block some up.

In rural areas, agricultural innovations (see pages 62-63) led to an increase in prosperity. Rich farmers built farmhouses along classical lines, and some landowners constructed estate cottages and model villages, such as Milton Abbas in Dorset, for their workers (see pages 112-113).

FIND OUT MORE

• Dennis Severs' House A perfectly restored Georgian house in Spitalfields, London, is a museum telling the story of a family of Huguenot weavers. www.dennissevershouse.co.uk
• Building of Bath Museum Exhibits on the architecture and history of Bath and the people who have lived there. www.bath-preservation-trust.org.uk
• The Georgian Group A charity dedicated to the preservation of Georgian buildings. www.georgiangroup.org.uk
• The Georgian House A fine preserved house in Charlotte Square, Edinburgh. www.nts.org.uk

INNOVATIONS FOR THE HOME

1616
The architect Inigo Jones introduced Palladian style to Britain when he began the Queen's House in Greenwich. The style did not become widespread until a hundred years later.

c.1670
Sash windows started to appear. Early sliding sashes were held in place by pegs and generally had wide glazing bars.

1720s
Glazed fanlights were introduced above doors to provide natural light for the dark hallways. Their name derives from their semi-circular shape.

1775
The first water closet was patented by a watchmaker named Alexander Cummings, but Joseph Bramah produced a more reliable model three years later.

JACOBEAN 1603-1625
BAROQUE 1625-1715
PALLADIAN 1715-50
NEO-CLASSICAL 1750-1830

1600
1650
1700
1750
1800

Jacobean
Restoration
William-and-Mary/Queen Anne
Early Georgian
Mid Georgian
Late Georgian

Mass production meets Regency elegance

During the first half of the 19th century, the demand for urban housing intensified as people moved from the countryside to seek work in the towns and cities. The wealthy lived in elegant terraces while the poorest were crammed into squalid back-to-backs. The mass production of building materials allowed cheap and fashionable ornamentation to be used to adorn even modest homes.

The hallmarks of Regency homes

The large Regency house was taller than its Georgian equivalent (see pages 274-275) with more storeys and a half basement replacing the full basement. In style it was a less rigid interpretation of the principles of Classicism. Stucco (see below, left) was used extensively on ground floor walls and for decorative architraves and cornices. Doorways were flanked by dignified columns; many front walls were formed into shallow curved bays and bow windows were typical. French doors often replaced large sash windows and led onto balconies or verandas.

Domestic innovations, such as the kitchen range (see opposite), were beginning to make an impact. The range had been introduced in the late 18th century, making it possible for the first time to bake, roast, simmer or boil rapidly using one source of heat. Closed ranges, where the fire was completely enclosed, were not produced until the 1840s. Wooden water pipes were being replaced with iron ones that leaked less and could sustain higher pressure, and larger houses now had piped water to a single tap in the kitchen close to a shallow stone or lead sink. Water for cooking and washing was heated in a copper. In poorer areas a single water pump often served many households.

Service areas could be found at the back of all houses. Behind the grand terraces there were mews buildings with large doors for the horses and carriages. Above were the haylofts and accommodation for grooms and coachmen.

A fashion for ironwork

Elegant, lightly executed ironwork gave Regency homes a distinctive look. Railings, gateways, porches, balconies and verandas, often decorated in motifs of vines, scrolls and flowers, were frequently finished in a green paint mixed with powdered copper to create an antiqued bronze effect. The larger-scale production of cast iron enabled elaborate patterns to be produced at lower prices. Cast iron replaced wood for rainwater gutters, hopper heads and downpipes, which were now standard on new housing.

FACTORY-MADE BUILDING MATERIALS

The construction of the canal network in the 18th century and the railway system in the 19th provided an easy and cost-effective means of transporting goods. Mass-produced materials began to appear in places as far apart as Sussex in southern England and Ayrshire in Scotland, and buildings began to take on a uniform style in towns across Britain.

Brick Many areas of Britain produced bricks. There was an abundant supply of excellent 'brick-earth' in the Thames Valley.

Glass The area around Newcastle-upon-Tyne was producing more than 650,300m² (7,000,000sq ft) of crown window glass annually in the 1830s. This type of glass was used to glaze sash windows.

Ironwork Cast and wrought iron were manufactured in the Midlands.

Slate Slate is lighter than other roofing materials and allows a shallower pitch of roof. Quarried particularly in Wales, it was distributed throughout Britain.

Stucco An external plaster rendering made from different materials, of which the most common was Parker's Roman Cement. This was manufactured by burning nodules of clay. The principal centre of the industry was Harwich in Essex.

Wood Pine was imported in great quantities from the Baltic and Scandinavia and it was invariably painted.

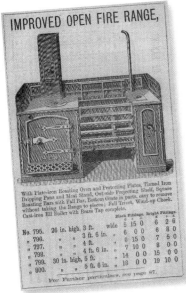

IMPROVED OPEN FIRE RANGE,

Home improvements The 19th-century range was one of many innovations that transformed domestic life.

Housing the workforce Brick-built cottages began to make an appearance in the 19th century. At this time, railway companies built terraces of small two-up-two-down homes in a uniform style for their workers, such as the row of cottages in Railway Village, Swindon, Wiltshire (below).

Planning town expansion

The architect John Nash (1752-1835) brought order and style to London. In 1811 he began work to lay out Regent's Park and Regent Street and build the surrounding grand stucco-fronted houses and terraces. Characteristic terrace schemes were constructed in the spa towns of Cheltenham and Tunbridge Wells and the seaside resorts of Hove, Hastings, St Leonards and Brighton, where Nash's Royal Pavilion reflects Regency flamboyance and fun. Other architects and speculative builders also adapted the classic style and proportions of the Georgian house, incorporating elements such as pediments, ornate fanlights and stucco detailing.

Genteel residential districts sprang up in the still largely rural areas around cities such as Liverpool, Bristol and Edinburgh. In these suburbs fashionable villas were often built as semi-detached pairs.

The building of middle-class suburbia began in earnest in the 1840s and the terraces spread outwards, across what up to then had been countryside. These suburban houses pandered to the middle classes' desire to emulate their social superiors. Ornamental exterior details, based either on the Italianate style or the Gothic Revival, proved particularly attractive to the average clerk and his family.

Cottages for the workers

Most rural cottages were originally humble abodes, made of mud, timber and thatch. In the Regency era, a growing number of enlightened landowners were demolishing these unsightly hovels and building new cottages for workers on their estates (see also page 113). Among the best known are those at Blaise Hamlet, near Bristol, designed by Nash. They were created following a consciously Picturesque style and came to be known as *cottages ornés*. Usually a rustic cottage of romantic design, they were invariably topped by a thatched roof, featuring a riot of gables, elaborate barge boards, dormers and ornamental chimneys. The idea of the cottage was appropriated by the middle classes in the 19th century and introduced into suburbia.

FIND OUT MORE

• Sir John Soane's Museum The London home of the Regency architect Sir John Soane, built by himself in 1824 in Lincoln's Inn Fields and now a museum that houses his collection of art and antiques.
www.soane.org

INNOVATIONS FOR THE HOME

1814
Gas first used for public street lighting (see page 182).

1818
John Nash used cast iron in the construction of the Royal Pavilion at Brighton.

1820s
Cast iron water pipes began to replace wooden pipes.

1832
The method of manufacturing sheet glass was discovered. It was much thinner and cheaper than crown or plate glass.

1840s
Kitchen ranges, featuring a completely enclosed fire, began to be produced.

GOTHIC REVIVAL 1745-1920 | THE PICTURESQUE 1745-1830

JACOBETHAN AND CLASSICAL REVIVAL 1830-90

Regency

Early Victorian

1810

1820

1830

1840

1850

Living back-to-back

By the turn of the 19th century, vast areas of densely packed 'back-to-back' housing were being built to accommodate the thousands pouring into Britain's expanding industrial cities to find work in the mills and factories. The aroma of food, the stench of the earth closets, the cries of infants and the clatter of work noise filled these 'rookeries'.

At home in the 'courts'

In industrial cities such as Birmingham, Nottingham, Leeds and Glasgow, shrewd landowners and speculative builders were trying to pack as many people as possible into every available piece of land. They developed a style of back-to-back housing, mostly consisting of poorly built terraces crammed around a small courtyard. There was no overall plan and little thought was given to the provision of sanitation, ventilation or natural light.

From the street a row of back-to-backs looked much like any other terrace. The difference was that each home was only one room deep and shared a back wall with another row of houses facing onto an inner courtyard or 'court'. The only access to these closed courts was often through a narrow tunnel or alley, making waste and ash removal extremely difficult. In the days before sanitary reform, these yards would be piled high with human waste. Some courts were inhabited by livestock, since people coming to work in the towns from the surrounding countryside often set up pigsties and hen roosts. The result was a gloomy, rancid, disease-ridden enclave, where crime was rife and life generally short.

Community spirit

The back-to-backs may have offered little in the way of home comforts, but they were comparatively cheap to rent, were usually close to a source of work, and fostered a close, supportive sense of community. Some people worked from their homes within the court, even running workshops that employed others. The small metal goods and toy trades of Birmingham were particularly suited to home-working. It was possible to earn a living, while keeping an eye on the children as they played at skipping games or hopscotch in the courtyard.

The slums of Victorian Leeds

In late 18th and early 19th-century Leeds, blind-backs – with no rear windows and their fronts facing each other across a small yard – were the solution to housing the swelling masses. But growing demand soon led to more properties being erected on the backs of these, creating back-to-backs, and it was not long before houses were deliberately built as such. Many included a cellar to accommodate the poorest labourers. There was often just one privy for everyone living around a single courtyard.

The cramped, insanitary conditions of the Leeds back-to-backs aided the spread of disease, such as the cholera epidemic of 1832, and in 1866 legislation was introduced to control the quality of any new dwellings being built. The construction of back-to-backs was not outlawed, but now the streets on which they stood had to be at least 36 feet wide with each block limited to a maximum of eight houses separated by a yard, which contained a row of privies. These improved back-to-backs had a living room opening directly off the pavement and a scullery/kitchen on the ground floor, two bedrooms on the first floor and a single attic room.

FIND OUT MORE

- **Birmingham Back-to-Backs** Visits to the restored houses at Court 15, Inge Street, are by pre-booked, guided tours only. For information on opening hours call 0121 666 7671. www.nationaltrust.org.uk
- **Thackray Museum** Exhibits include a reconstruction of a Leeds back-to-back slum. www.thackraymuseum.org
- **Leeds Civic Trust** Information on the Leeds back-to-backs. www.leedscivictrust.org.uk/backs.htm

---

A Birmingham 'rookery' Court 15 (circled, right, and main picture) was built between 1802 and 1831, one of thousands of courts put up in Birmingham. Eight small houses fronted on to Inge Street and Hurst Street, with a further three facing inwards. Each was occupied by up to 16 people, with just a single-brick-thick wall dividing one house from its neighbour. The building of back-to-backs was banned in Birmingham in 1876, but the last tenants did not leave Court 15 until 1966.

Daily ablutions A central paved courtyard (left) usually contained two wash houses. Inside was a 'copper', where water was heated for washing and the family bath. Clothes were hung out to dry on numerous lines that criss-crossed the courtyard. There were four shared privies within Court 15 – these simple 'earth closets' were emptied periodically by 'night soil' men. Flushing toilets, connected to mains drainage, were not installed until the 20th century.

INGE STREET

HURST STREET

House
House
Shop
House
House
House
House
Shop
Shop
House
Shop
Shop

Court 15
(c.1896)

Ash-pits | Store | Wash house | Privies | Shop

Court 15

STREET

CITY FISH BAR

Working court The inhabitants of Court 15 had a wide variety of skills and trades, from carpenters, wire-drawers and watchmakers to glass-workers and bedstead makers. Some worked at home and one family of lock-makers rented a workshop in the court. By 1896, all the houses fronting Hurst Street had become shops (right). In 1900, there was a cycle shop, hairdressers and herbalist, and ten years later a sweet shop, bakers, newsagents and fish-and-chip shop.

279

The golden age of the suburban villa

The Victorians had a taste for the flamboyant and the decorative. Embellishments such as turrets, castellated parapets and porches supported by classical columns topped with leafy capitals appeared on even quite humble homes. By incorporating details formerly reserved for grander dwellings, the clutches of smart 'villas' that were built around Britain's cities reflected the aspirations of the families who flocked to live in them.

THE VICTORIAN VILLA

The arrival of the railways in the mid 19th century allowed many people to live further away from the often crowded, smokey city centres in which they worked. Densely packed suburbs of medium-sized houses soon sprang up along the leafy lanes that stretched out into the surrounding countryside.

These houses were generally well constructed and embellished with decorative moulding and colourful brickwork. Grander homes were often approached via a flight of steps beneath a portico over the front door. A rear extension was added in place of the basement to house a kitchen, scullery and sometimes a WC. Public and private areas were distinctly divided by passages and stairs, making the plan of the house more complicated. Privacy was important to the Victorians, so balconies overlooking the street were abandoned and it became desirable to have a back and often a front garden.

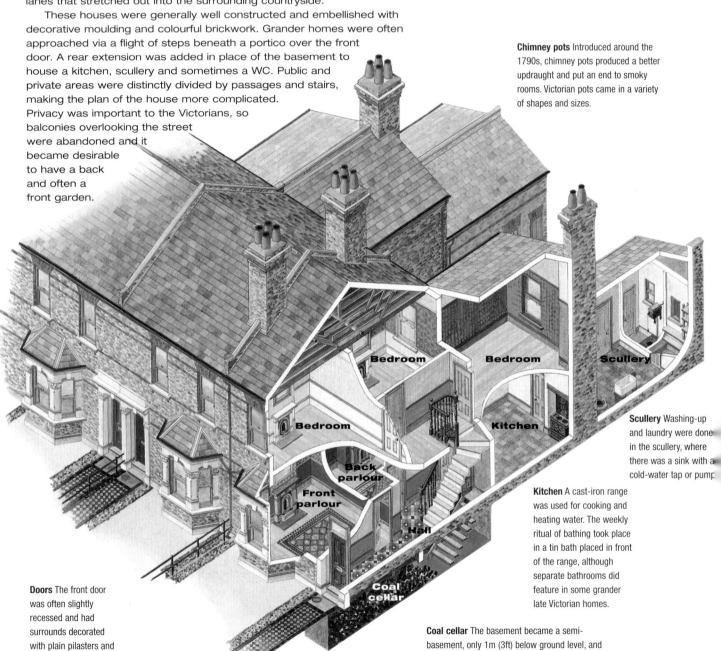

Chimney pots Introduced around the 1790s, chimney pots produced a better updraught and put an end to smoky rooms. Victorian pots came in a variety of shapes and sizes.

Scullery Washing-up and laundry were done in the scullery, where there was a sink with a cold-water tap or pump

Kitchen A cast-iron range was used for cooking and heating water. The weekly ritual of bathing took place in a tin bath placed in front of the range, although separate bathrooms did feature in some grander late Victorian homes.

Coal cellar The basement became a semi-basement, only 1m (3ft) below ground level, and was normally used for storing coal.

Doors The front door was often slightly recessed and had surrounds decorated with plain pilasters and leafy capitals.

Windows The bay window increased the size of the front room and improved its lighting. Decorative mouldings and coloured brickwork were often incorporated as dressings to add interest around the plain windows.

Mixing and matching

Victorian builders drew heavily on the past for their ideas and borrowed liberally from many designs traditions, including the Gothic, Greek Revival, Tudor, Elizabethan, Italianate and Classical. They were fond of incorporating several different styles into the same building.

By 1860 the mock-Gothic had become the most popular style – probably a reaction against the plainness and restraint of the Georgian. Based on the pointed arch and featuring carved ornamentation, high roofs and steep gables, it echoed the church architecture of medieval times. Mock-Gothic features could be found on both low-cost and expensive homes and left their mark on entire suburbs, such as those of north Oxford.

By combining a variety of materials, including terracotta and coloured bricks, marble and stone, decorative features were created and used as dressings. These added interest around the plainer, large-paned windows of the period. In addition, the use of multi-coloured brickwork, incorporating patterns of yellow, red and black bricks as an integral part of the structure, was soon employed in all types of housing from villas to farm-workers' cottages. The face bricks used for the side and back of homes were usually inferior to those on the front.

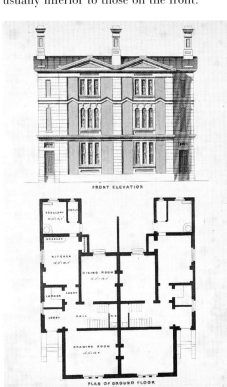

Pattern-book design The most popular Victorian styles spread quickly through widely published pattern books.

Noble airs In an age of keen social pretensions, the Victorians often gave their houses names that hinted at aristocratic connections, such as The Grange. An ancient heritage might be suggested by medievalisms such as Monkhall and Castlefield, and importance conveyed by using the name of a national hero, such as Nelson, or a military victory, such as Sebastopol. Numerous suburban workers' terraces were dubbed 'villas' (see above), conjuring up visions of rustic gentility.

Seeing the light

The bay window was originally a status symbol, but was eventually installed in homes of all types. It extended the floor area of the front room and featured big single-paned windows that let in more light. New technology had made it possible to produce large areas of glass relatively cheaply, and the repeal of the window tax in 1851 had encouraged architects to include more glazing in their designs.

The conservatory was another desirable Victorian home feature, made possible by the arrival of larger, stronger and cheaper glass sheeting. Great pride was taken in the exotic plants that could be cultivated in them, and they were often lavishly decorated and furnished. Fine rugs would be strewn across the richly patterned tile flooring, and iron tracery along with stained and etched glass were popular.

FIND OUT MORE

• www.victorian-society.org.uk The Victorian Society campaigns to protect Victorian buildings, publishes a wide range of material and organises visits and talks.
• www.vam.ac.uk Victoria & Albert Museum, London, mounts exhibitions and events on the Victorian era.

INNOVATIONS FOR THE HOME

1851
At the Great Exhibition, plate glass and many other new materials and inventions for the home were exhibited for the first time.

1850s
New brick-making machines dramatically increased the number of bricks that could be produced, and prices began to fall.

1850s
Damp-proof courses were introduced, which prevented moisture rising up the walls of homes.

1860s
Gas lighting became common in homes.

1869
Gas-powered geysers began to offer an economical and convenient means of heating water.

MIXED STYLES INCLUDING: GOTHIC REVIVAL 1745-1920 | JACOBETHAN AND CLASSICAL AND ITALIANATE REVIVAL 1830-90

Mid Victorian

1850

1855

1860

1865

1870

1875

Revivals, new visions and the Edwardian age

Late-Victorian architects looked for a new style to bring housing into the 20th century and once again they found inspiration in the past. Blending Old English and Queen Anne features, they created suburbs of spacious red-brick houses surrounded by large gardens. Many can still be seen, handsomely restored, in places such as Hampstead Garden Suburb and Bedford Park in London.

Suburban idealism Built between 1875 and 1886, Bedford Park in west London was the first garden suburb (below, 1882), offering generously spaced homes, all with gardens, set in leafy streets for middle-class families of moderate means. Houses were built in the Queen Anne Revival style by architects such as Norman Shaw, and were characterised by a predominance of red brick and clay-tiled roofs with ornate gables, dormer windows and tall chimney stacks.

Changing plan of terraced houses

The late-Victorian and Edwardian period spawned a mass of semi-detached red-brick, slate-roofed houses in the many new suburban developments around Britain's towns and cities. These new homes were better constructed than in the past and each was provided with a WC or earth closet, ashbin and coal shed.

Middle and upper-class families were tending to have fewer children, and fewer servants were being employed, so, with less accommodation needed, two-storey houses became popular. The interior layout was simpler and one or two inside toilets were regarded as a necessity.

In the Edwardian era, plots became wider and the houses less tall. The layouts changed: kitchens and service rooms were now included as part of the main body of the house rather than in an extension at the back, and reception rooms were placed on either side of the hall instead of one room behind another. The rear garden was an essential element and was reached via French doors.

Looking back to an idyllic past

By the late 19th century, wide use of mass-produced materials had led to uniformity in architectural finishes, lacking the craftsmanship of earlier times. But some architects, influenced by the Arts and Crafts Movement's idealised vision of a medieval world where the craftsman was respected, were making a mark on housing design. Inspired by local traditions, they focused on simplicity, in contrast to the ornate style of the late Victorians.

The typical Arts-and-Crafts house is long, low and highly irregular, with casement windows often opening onto a cottage-like garden. This style strongly influenced the design of the

---

THE BIRTH OF THE COUNCIL ESTATE

The first council houses, in London, Liverpool, Manchester and Sheffield, were constructed as a result of the 1890 Housing of the Working Classes Act. To ease congestion in inner-city areas, local authorities were granted land outside the cities where it was cheap to build. Known as 'byelaw terraces', the housing developments conformed to the provisions of the Public Health Act of 1875, which insisted on good drainage and sanitation. All council houses had an indoor WC, although it would sometimes still be housed in a rear extension.

first garden city at Letchworth (see page 186) and the garden surburb at Hampstead, north London. It was also copied in suburban homes across Britain, reflected in features such as leaded lights and inglenooks.

Living in flats

While families tended to live in the suburbs, single people and couples were increasingly attracted by the new mansion blocks being built near city centres. Albert Hall Mansions in London was typical of these late-Victorian and Edwardian flats. Designed by Norman Shaw in 1880, it stood six storeys high and had lifts, bathrooms and wine cellars, all fronted by a suitably grand entrance.

The late 19th century also saw the birth of the maisonette. Originally the term was used to describe a purpose-built single house split horizontally into flats, but later came to mean a flat that extended over more than one floor with its own entrance at ground level. The only external evidence of this layout today is that there are two front doors onto the street.

Stylish accommodation Edwardian mansion blocks were embellished with decorative brick, stone and ironwork. They had smart entrances with wide panelled doors and impressive pediments. Many of these blocks, such as Editha Mansions (above), have been carefully renovated.

Housing Scotland's workers The late 19th and early 20th-century four-storey sandstone tenements in Glasgow's West End (below) are a distinctive feature of the city's architecture. Tenements, occupied by all classes on different levels, were common in densely populated urban centres long before the concept of flats was adopted south of the border. Some of Scotland's tenements were built to high standards and had the external appearance of the more luxurious terraced houses, while others, designed for artisans and their families, were more utilitarian in style and offered poor-quality, cramped living quarters.

FIND OUT MORE

• www.bedfordpark.org The Bedford Park Society website contains a comprehensive history of the area.
• www.hgs.org.uk Take a virtual tour of Hampstead Garden Suburb and its architectural highlights.
• www.letchworthgardencity.net Take a virtual tour of Letchworth Garden City, the first garden city.
• www.morrissociety.org The William Morris Society is devoted to one of the founders of the Arts and Crafts Movement. It organises lectures, tours and museum visits.
• www.nationaltrust.org.uk Cragside House, Morpeth, Northumberland, and William Morris's Red House, Bexleyheath, southeast London, are both Arts and Crafts properties in the care of the National Trust.
• http://pike.colloquium.co.uk/~glasgow west/home.htm Glasgow Conservation Trust West works to preserve the character of Glasgow's tenements.

INNOVATIONS FOR THE HOME

December 1878
Joseph Swan gives the first public demonstration of an electric light bulb, with a thin carbon filament in a vacuum. On October 21, 1879, Thomas Edison lit his prototype incandescent bulb, which lasted for 150 hours.

1879
First telephone exchange opened in London.

1881
Lord Kelvin lit his Glasgow home with electric light, and Sir William Armstrong's Cragside House in Northumbria became the first home in the world to be lit by hydroelectricity.

1885
Invention of the more efficient incandescent gas mantle resulted in gas lighting becoming generally popular as the quality of the light was improved.

1890s
Gaslight was brought within reach of the working class with the introduction of penny slot meters. Gas was piped to homes which had attachments for wall fittings, chandeliers and table lamps.

1910
Electricity was installed in most new houses.

MIXED STYLES INCLUDING: GOTHIC REVIVAL 1745-1920 | QUEEN ANNE REVIVAL 1870-1890 | ARTS AND CRAFTS 1880-1925

Late Victorian

Edwardian

1875
1880
1885
1890
1895
1900
1905
1910
1915

The changing styles of doors and windows

Many clues to the status of a building and the people who live there, as well as to its age, can be gleaned from the appearance of the doors and windows. The front entrance, as the first focus of any visitor's attention, has increasingly been designed to impress.

Making a grand entrance

Early medieval doors were made from vertical planks of wood, usually oak, and shaped to a point at the top. The planks were fixed to horizontal timber 'ledges' or another layer of planks with nails or wooden pegs, often arranged in an eye-catching pattern on the surface. Iron hinges were made by a blacksmith and hung on sturdy iron pins.

By the 17th century, the arrangement of rough planks had given way to more sophisticated wooden panelling, and a favourite form of over-door embellishment was a semi-circular hood supported on carved brackets; by the 18th century, this had taken on a flattened classical-style (see page 274). Elaborate door-surrounds had largely disappeared by the Victorian age, when, despite the diversity of styles, doors were often simpler in design, with four rather than six panels.

Porches were added to cut out draughts and provide shelter for people waiting to enter a house. They ranged from simple thatched, timber structures to multi-storey gabled extensions that were a significant feature of 16th-century buildings. In 20th-century suburbia, they helped add a touch of individuality to row-upon-row of near identical houses.

Lighting up the hallway

By the mid 19th century, large strong sheets of glass could be produced fairly cheaply and sizeable fanlights made from a single pane became a popular feature over the front door. Glazed door panels followed and sidelights were also frequently introduced on one or both sides of the entrance. By the 1950s, front doors made almost entirely of glass – held within a slim wooden or metal framework – had become the height of modernity.

The earliest windows

Unglazed, shuttered openings served as windows in most medieval buildings, and little changed until the Tudor Age (1485-1603), when developments in glass-making started to have an impact (see opposite). From the 16th century onwards, as glass became more readily available, window frames were adapted to accept small panes or 'quarries' of glass that were set in lead 'cames', creating what are known today as leaded lights.

Classical statement The Georgian door, framed by an elegant stone or wooden doorcase and sometimes reached by a short flight of stone steps, was designed to impress. The imposing example (left), typically has six panels and a decorative 'pattern-book' fanlight, allowing light to stream through, brightening the hallway.

Copying the past Many doors that appear to be medieval are actually Victorian. The styling of past centuries appealed greatly to 19th-century taste, and pointed Gothic Revival-style doors (above) became highly fashionable.

Delivery time Letter plates appeared on doors after the introduction of the Penny Post in 1840. You may spot the early versions, which were small and vertical. Before 1700, door furniture was made of wrought iron. It was replaced by cast iron in Georgian times and usually painted matt black; polished brass was reserved for the wealthy. House numbers became mandatory in London in 1805.

Natural ventilation Windows that opened were a rarity before the appearance of glazed casements, such as the mid-16th-century window at Athelhampton, Dorset (above). Casements had stone mullions, iron or wood frames, stained-glass insets and ornate ironwork handles. In the 1720s, property advertisements were describing them as 'common windows' since, by then, the sash had become fashionable.

New look Technical restrictions on the size of glass meant that the first sashes tended to have more panes per frame than the usual six of Georgian windows.

The arrival of the sash window

Around 1670, a new style of window began to feature in British buildings – the sash. Its revolutionary opening mechanism, with one frame gliding smoothly over the other, helped to create a crisp look that was perfectly suited to the clean lines of the Classical architecture of the time.

Early sash windows were set flush with the façade, but a building act of 1709 stipulated that the window frame should be set back to stop fire spreading. In 1774, the act was strengthened, so that it became mandatory to have the sash box not only set back, but also recessed behind the brickwork.

The glazing bars of early sash windows were often thick, but as the 18th century progressed they became narrower and delicately moulded, while the panes of glass grew larger. Later still, glazing bars were sometimes made from brass or iron. Larger panes of glass were in use in Victorian times and by the 1880s a wide variety of window styles and types were common.

The Regency bow In the early 19th century, windows lengthened and bow windows appeared on terraced homes, such as in Brighton (right), to lighten rooms. Coloured glass was sometimes included at the edge of the frame.

'Crown glass' (see page 276)

GLASS INNOVATIONS

For centuries, sheet glass could only be formed by blowing a cylinder of molten glass, cutting this in half, then repeatedly reheating and beating each piece to flatten it. This delicate process generally produced only small pieces, which were expensive and rarely used outside stately buildings and the homes of nobility.

'Crown glass' (see page 276), first manufactured in Britain in 1678, allowed for larger panes, and was in general use by the mid 18th century. It was made by blowing a globe of glass which was then spun on a rod or 'pontil', so that the glass flared out into a flat circular plate, about 122-137cm (48-54in) in diameter.

But panes remained relatively small until methods of drawing out molten glass into sheets were introduced in the mid 19th century. An excise duty from 1746 to 1845 also placed restrictions on size and weight.

Light relief Look out for the use of decorative coloured glass in windows and doors in Victorian houses, such as those in The Chase, Clapham, London (left). It was a common feature by the 1870s, using naturalistic themes such as flowers, plants and birds.

Modern outlook Mass-produced metal-framed windows began to appear on houses in the 1920s. Houses built in the late 1950s and early 1960s (above) are characterised by large window panes set into metal frames, creating a light, airy feel.

Ideal homes for a modern age

From 1919 to 1939 more than 4 million houses were built in Britain. The majority of these were semi-detached – you can see avenues of them in most towns. They were bought by the newly affluent middle classes with the aid of mortgages. Architects rarely played a part in the design; instead the developers simply adopted familiar styles that would appeal to potential buyers.

Bow windows A glazed double bay at the front allowed the maximum amount of light in, as well as providing a view up and down the road. The wooden-framed casement windows had coloured glass and sometimes leading in the top lights.

Coal and gas fires Most rooms had an open fireplace, with either a traditional oak or tiled surround. Gas taps were installed next to fireplaces to allow for gas fires.

Bathrooms and WCs Hot and cold running water was piped directly into the bathroom. The indoor WC, usually in a separate room, was still a novelty for most people. Tiling on the walls and floors was common in both areas.

Façades Half-timbering, especially on the gables, and tile-cladding over red brickwork were widely used to create a traditional look.

Front gardens Most suburban semis had a sizeable area at the front, usually laid out formally, with neat flower beds around a patch of lawn. Crazy paving and privet hedges were popular (see pages 288-289).

Labels on illustration: Bedroom, Bedroom, Bathroom, Bedroom, WC, Drawing Room, Hall, Kitchen

THE 'TUDORBETHAN' SEMI-DETACHED

The design of many of the suburban homes built by speculative developers during the 1920s and 1930s was influenced by the Arts and Crafts style (see pages 282-283). Purchasers were drawn by the traditional values reflected in the 'Tudorbethan' half-timbering and other features, such as leaded windows, stained glass and gabled porches. Despite this idealised cottage look, the internal layout was spacious and designed to meet the needs of the 20th-century, urban middle classes. There were usually at least three bedrooms, including a box room for a baby or small child squeezed in over the hallway. A general increase in leisure time was making gardens an important feature, and many people were enjoying them for the first time.

Front door A sizeable porch sheltered the area around the front entrance. Light streamed into the hallway through the glazed upper half of the door and the adjacent window, in which stained glass often featured.

Kitchen Fewer or no servants meant that the hard-pressed housewife was now turning to the growing number of labour-saving devices, such as electric cookers and washing machines, that were beginning to appear on the market. Surfaces were enamelled or tiled to make them easier to clean.

The appeal of the semi

The concept of the semi-detached home first became popular in the early 19th century, as a way of making smaller houses look like larger villas. After the First World War, the 'semi' became the template for suburban developments as it required a smaller plot than a detached house and could be priced more cheaply. The semi also offered much prized space and privacy compared with the terraced houses in which so many people had grown up.

In the 1930s the need to provide the working classes with affordable accommodation near their workplaces led many inner city councils to construct blocks of flats in the neo-Georgian style. Better-off tenants might choose to live in 'serviced' accommodation and enjoy the services of a porter. The flats had open-plan interiors that could be divided by retractable partitions. The rooms were heated by electric fires or underfloor heating.

'A machine for living in'

After the First World War, a number of young architects began experimenting with new ways of building houses. The Modern Movement envisaged the home as a 'machine' designed for ease and efficiency. It was characterised by buildings with flat roofs, metal windows, sheer white walls and light, open-plan interiors – a dramatic contrast to the cluttered look of the previous decades. All this involved the liberal use of glass and reinforced concrete.

Bomb-damage in the Second World War created a desperate need for cheap, speedily constructed housing. Prefabricated elements and modern building methods were swiftly brought together and, in 1944, 150,000 'pre-fabs' were constructed by local authorities to help replenish pre-war housing stock. Known as 'homes for heroes', they were made from steel, timber, concrete and asbestos sheeting, and paved the way for the wider use of prefabricated elements in building. Most had up-to-the-minute conveniences such as built-in cookers and refrigerators and for many inhabitants delivered a previously undreamt-of standard of living.

AN ELECTRIC HOME IS HEALTHY, CLEAN AND COMFORTABLE
USE
Hotpoint
REGD. TRADE MARK
ELECTRIC APPLIANCES
in **YOUR** home
MADE IN ENGLAND

The Electric Cooker

The Electric Cleaner

The Electric Washer

The Hotpoint Electric Appliance Co. Ltd.
24 NEWMAN STREET, LONDON, W.1

Domestic breakthroughs New electric appliances (above) became all the rage in the 1920s, transforming home life.

FIND OUT MORE

• Geffrye Museum The museum, in Shoreditch, London, has settings of English domestic interiors, including those of the 1920s and 30s.
www.geffrye-museum.org.uk
• The Twentieth Century Society Campaigns to protect buildings dating from 1914 to 1999.
www.c20society.org.uk
• 2 Willow Road, Hampstead, London The house – one of the outstanding examples of Modernist architecture in Britain – was designed and built in 1939 by the architect Ernö Goldfinger as his family home. It is filled with furniture, also designed by Goldfinger.
www.nationaltrust.org.uk

Modernist villas By the late 1930s suburban housing (left) began to take on the streamlined look of the Modern Movement. Smooth white-painted rendering appeared over brickwork, and metal window frames often extended round the bay in 'suntrap' style. These windows were glazed with curved panes of glass designed to allow as much sunlight as possible to reach the front rooms of the house.

INNOVATIONS FOR THE HOME

1920s
Metal windows, often mass-produced, began to be used on houses. These were large, sometimes from floor to ceiling, to let more light into the house.

Late 1920s and 1930s
Many homes were being equipped with electricity, gas, and hot and cold running water. This boosted the use of labour-saving domestic appliances such as electric fires, stoves, and washing machines.

1936
The BBC started regular television broadcasts, although many homes did not acquire a TV set until the second half of the 1950s or early 1960s.

Late 1940s
Fully fitted kitchens appeared in the post-war years with continuous worktops, stainless steel sinks and surfaces covered in Formica – a wipe-clean, heatproof material.

MIXED STYLES INCLUDING: **NEO-GEORGIAN** 1890–1950 | **INTERNATIONAL** 1920–1950 | **ART DECO** 1925–1935

Modernist

1915
1920
1925
1930
1935
1940
1945
1950

Suburban pride and joy

Making a statement and keeping up with the Joneses has long been part of suburban life. From flying duck wall plaques and stylised sunflower motifs on windows to crazy paving and the monkey puzzle tree, a desire for the latest fashion in home or garden accessories over the decades has left its mark on great swathes of suburbia.

Taking flight In the 1930s and 40s flying duck pottery wall plaques were hung on living-room walls in suburban homes across Britain. They were a distant echo of the Art Deco taste for representing movement.

The 'little people' of suburbia

Garden gnomes were originally carried by German miners as good luck tokens, underlining their role in folklore as protectors of nature. It is said that they were brought from Germany to Britain in the 1840s by Sir Charles Isham, the 10th Baronet of Lamport Hall in Northamptonshire.

Gnomes were popular with the Victorians, but they found their true home in the gardens of suburban houses in the 1920s and 30s. Embraced as symbols of goodwill, hope and luck, they became a common sight alongside concrete fishing wells and other features which formed 'magical' rockery gardens fit for fairies and elves, echoing the fantasy world conjured up by the 'Tudorbethan' style of the houses (see page 286).

They were less common after the Second World War, but gnomes again became popular in the 1960s when plastic versions began to appear, adding to those made of ceramic, terracotta, earthenware and concrete.

A crazy fashion for paving

Victorian gardeners economised in the creation of paths and patios by using irregular fragments of stone. This 'crazy' paving was adopted across suburbia but, rather than using real stone, the paths were frequently composed of broken concrete paving stones. Paths were also formed of poured concrete and, in the early 1900s, grit and gravel were rolled into the surface before it set. In the 1930s coloured dyes were mixed with the concrete which, after an initial garish phase, faded in the sunlight. Sometimes patterns were scribed into the wet surface to emulate crazy paving.

Since the 1960s the accommodation of the family car has dictated how a plot is covered. Ever more intricate paving or brickwork patterns have

Garden makeovers Suburban homeowners lavished attention on their gardens, keeping them well-manicured and adding summerhouses (above right, 1930s). The gnome was a beloved accessory, often arranged in a fantastical group, such as the 1930s scene at Blackgang Chine on the Isle of Wight (left). Crazy paving (below) was also popular in the early 20th century, creating an ornamental look by making use of broken concrete paving stones, dyed with bright colours.

HUMOROUS NEIGHBOUR (to Amateur Gardener "Crazy" paving his garden)—
"Hullo, Browne, Gone Jig-saw Crazy?"

Imitating the past

Modern Georgian-style windows often feature panes of so-called bottle-glass. Originally these 'bull's eyes', formed where the rod, or 'pontil', was attached during the blowing process in the manufacture of crown glass (see pages 276 and 285), were discarded for their poor quality or used only in inconspicuous windows. From the 19th century on, manufacturers produced such panes deliberately as a decorative feature that, as well as providing a Georgian look, increased privacy by obscuring the view through the window. The mock-Georgian style was also the influence behind built-in fanlights. DIY stores have sold thousands of 'Georgian' front doors that have a 'fanlight' set into their upper half. They bear no relationship to the doors of Georgian times when the fanlight was always a separate unit set above the door (see page 284).

A splash of suburban Art Deco

Geometric forms, zigzags, sunbursts and chevrons in abstract patterns and rendered in brilliant colours are the principal distinguishing features of the Art Deco style of the 1920s and 30s. This style of architecture and design, reflecting energy, optimism, texture and light, has left its mark on suburban houses.

Of all the Art Deco motifs, the one most commonly seen in suburbia is the rising sun. It appears everywhere from garage doors to gable ends and, most popularly, on front gates. Its origins are disputed. The influence may have come from the ancient cultures of Egypt and Central America, but the more likely explanation is that the 1920s was the period when sunbathing became fashionable and people looked to the sun for health and well-being.

A passion for colour A 1930s glass roundel of a yacht at a seaside bungalow at Selsey, Sussex (above), is typical of the fashion for coloured glass. Stylised flowers, the rising sun and country cottages all appeared as leaded light panes. Look out for a galleon in full sail, a popular image that provided reassurance through its depiction of a golden seafaring era when Britain was a rising power.

become the symbol of suburban prosperity as garden after garden has been adapted or even obliterated to provide driveways and parking.

A modern version of crazy paving is timber decking. It has appeared in back gardens across Britain, bought in kit form from DIY stores. Historically, decking has been used to create railway platforms, piers and jetties, and in its modern guise is an uncovered version of the verandas typical of houses in the tropics, where open-air living is part of the lifestyle. In suburban back gardens it often forms a simple raised square area, but the more adventurous schemes include screens, pergolas, pools, Jacuzzis and barbecues.

Bull's eye window Bottle-glass was commonly used for window panes to give a Georgian-style look.

Post-war housing dreams

After the bombing of the Second World War, new housing was urgently needed. Shortages of materials and trained craftsmen led to designs that were quick and easy to erect, with components often prefabricated then put together on-site. Building styles were generally uniform across Britain, with little use of elaborate decorative finishing touches and often little reference to the past.

Building styles Houses were designed to have a clean, functional look, with very little or no ornamentation. Built of brick, they were sometimes covered in render, or clad with clay or concrete tiles, white timber or plastic weatherboards. Roofs generally had a shallow pitch and chimneys became a rarity as cental heating gradually made fireplaces redundant.

Windows and doors The large sheets of glass, housed in mass-produced metal frames, let in plenty of light through both windows and doors. Flat-topped porches supported by steel tubing were common.

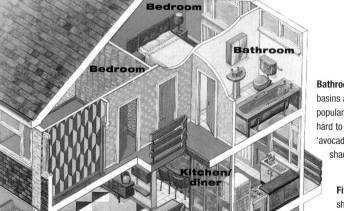

Bathroom suites Coloured baths, basins and toilets were hugely popular. By the 1970s, it was often hard to find a plain white suite, 'avocado' being the fashionable shade (see page 306).

Fitted kitchens Fixed cupboard and shelving units, with appliances such as a cooker and fridge built into them, created a streamlined, functional work area. Pressed steel or enamel sinks became common and often a separate utility room housed a washing machine, dryer and freezer.

Tower-block estates

In the 1950s and 60s, high-rise blocks of flats were seen as a solution to the pressing need for housing within industrial towns and cities, where building land was in short supply. They made it possible to construct a large number of homes within a relatively small area. Local councils across Britain were rushing to erect the new tower-block 'villages', exploiting the most up-to-date building materials and techniques to speed up the building process.

A scheme built at Roehampton by the London County Council between 1952 and 1958 helped set the high-rise trend in Britain. It included large quantities of steel, and reinforced and pre-cast concrete, delivering modern living spaces that were enclosed by walls of almost continuous windows. These allowed the maximum amount of sunlight to penetrate the rooms and offered spectacular views of the surrounding area.

But for such an industrialised approach to be financially viable, the new tower-block estates had to be organised on a large scale. This led to taller buildings crammed with large numbers of flats and maisonettes, which often made for a rather soulless environment.

THE 1960s TOWN HOUSE Although semi-detached homes remained popular, by the mid 1960s a new type of terraced house was beginning to feature in urban and suburban areas – the 'town house'. These were two or three-storeys high with an integral garage at ground level and living rooms generally on the first floor. Emphasis was on open-plan living, and to achieve this the hallway was abandoned and an open-tread staircase was incorporated into what was usually an L-shaped living room. Instead of a separate dining room, kitchens were enlarged to create a distinct area for eating in.

Copious storage space was also provided, with built-in cupboards and wardrobes. By the late 1960s, central heating was an essential feature of every new home, and it became rarer to have fireplaces installed.

Success story Trellick Tower in west London, finished in 1972, is proof that tower blocks, if well designed and built, can make desirable homes. Large balconies and picture windows offer spectacular views and let light stream into the sizeable rooms.

Converting the past

There was a growing realisation during the 1970s that it might be better, and possibly cheaper, to meet the demand for more homes by refurbishing some of the older housing stock, rather than clearing and replacing it. This view, coupled with a general trend towards smaller families and a lack of domestic servants, led to many large, run-down Georgian, Victorian and Edwardian houses being 'developed' and split into flats or bedsits.

The mood of the time was also for modernisation. Original fireplaces, their purpose made redundant by central heating, were stripped out; walls were knocked down to create large open-plan living spaces; and panelled doors and ornately carved banisters were covered over with hardboard to create the smooth, uncluttered look that was in vogue.

Soon every conceivable type of building was being seen as a potential home. City apartments, or 'lofts', were being created in former office buildings and warehouses. They became synonymous with stylish, urban living and helped to establish new ways of thinking about light and space, unashamedly using the sometimes rough, industrial materials of the original interior to create a fresh 'look'.

A new kind of estate

By the 1980s, some housebuilders were again looking to the past for inspiration. Replicas of Tudor or Georgian styles were becoming popular for the new estates of luxury 'executive' homes, that appealed to the aspirations of the professional couple with their young family. Such homes were rarely designed by architects, but the draughtsmen who created them used great skill to formulate styles that reflected quality and a sense of tradition, and had modern, practical and spacious interiors. Their job was made easier by the use of factory-assembled trussed roofs and timber framing and steel supporting beams, all of which allowed the creation of a box, the inside of which could simply be divided up with plasterboard, rather than with solid, load-bearing brick walls.

The end of the 1980s saw further rejection of post-war modernism. Even the Prince of Wales joined the debate, going as far as building a new 'traditional' village, Poundbury, on his estates in Dorset.

AN 'IDEAL' HOME

In 1954, the government lifted post-war restrictions on the development of private housing. This fuelled a boom in house building and a number of developers rose up to satisfy people's growing desire for what Lawrie Barratt – who founded Barratt Homes in 1958 – dubbed 'their own little castle'. Barratt, along with other firms such as Wimpey and McLean, almost reinvented the house-building industry, putting together packages that included fully fitted kitchens and bathrooms, furniture packs and special purchase schemes. Although choice of house styles was limited, the interiors made good use of space and offered a high degree of comfort. Most properties had gardens and garages.

Affordable housing Builders like Wimpey helped to make home-ownership a reality for many in the 1950s and 60s.

INNOVATIONS FOR THE HOME

1949
Britain's first high-rise block of flats, a ten-storey building in Holborn, central London, is built. From the early 1950s to the early 90s, about 6500 tower blocks were erected.

Early 1960s
MFI pioneers the sale of self-assembly, flat-pack furniture by mail order.

1964
Stylish, affordable, modern furniture hits the high street with the opening of Terence Conran's first Habitat store on Fulham Road in London.

1972
Architect Tony Goddard creates the first 'loft' apartments in Britain by converting a derelict Victorian warehouse at Oliver's Wharf, Wapping, in London's Docklands.

1979
Government boosts trend towards home ownership by giving council tenants who have lived in their homes for more than three years the right to buy them at a discounted price.

1987
IKEA opens its first British store at Warrington, near Manchester. Its low-cost, flat-pack furniture follows the lead taken by MFI and Habitat for making good design affordable.

Late 1990s
Private companies, such as the Manhattan Loft Corporation, set a trend for revitalising the inner-cities with their conversions of former industrial buildings into homes. Spurred on by this, many city councils, such as Birmingham, Manchester and Liverpool, initiate the regeneration of their run-down centres.

1950
1960
1970
1980
1990
2000

Future living today

In the 21st century, concerns about the impact of new building on the environment have started to influence house design. Some architects and planners hope to create urban 'villages' – integrated communities of housing, businesses, shops, schools and leisure and sports facilities that will attract a broad mix of people. While builders are looking for ways to speed up construction, priority is still being put on quality, the use of recycled materials and the inclusion of energy-saving features.

Modern construction methods

Rather than using numerous individual components that require skilled labour to put together on site, more homes are being built from larger prefabricated units. This allows them to go up much faster, usually with less wastage of materials and with fewer unforeseen delays because of bad weather.

The mid 1980s saw the beginnings of a revolution in timber-frame construction, involving the use of factory-made, precision-engineered systems that included floors and structural wall panels, already fitted with external doors, windows and conduits for the supply of services such as water and electricity. Such modular methods of building even allow individual rooms, including fully equipped bathrooms and kitchens, to be built in a factory as a complete box. They are then transported to the site by lorry and lifted into position by crane.

Increasingly, lightweight steel beams are being used to provide the basic structural support, particularly in roofs and floors. Aircrete (aereated concrete) blocks, which are partially made from recycled waste such as ash, are taking over from more traditional bricks for foundations and walls. As well as being light and strong, they provide excellent insulation, helping a building to retain heat in winter and to stay cooler in summer.

Eco-friendly living

There is a growing emphasis on creating homes that are better insulated and need less fuel to heat and run them. Several projects have been constructed with these aims in mind, including BedZED (the Beddington Zero Energy Development) at Beddington in Sutton, Surrey, developed by the Peabody Trust. It is a mix of housing and work space. One of its aims is to show that an ecologically friendly lifestyle can be both attractive and affordable.

A number of key features make BedZED special. It was built almost entirely using natural, recycled or renewable materials that were available from within a 35-mile radius of the site. A special energy-generating unit was installed that is able to produce all the heating and power needed by the development using recycled tree waste. The community also has a water-saving policy, which includes making use of rainwater and recycled water whenever possible. The creators of BedZED claim it to be the first large scale, 'carbon neutral' community –

'Green' living BedZED homes (below) are designed to be as energy-efficient as possible. The houses face south to make the most of the heat from the sun, windows are triple-glazed and all materials used have been selected for their excellent insulation properties. A transport plan includes a car pool and aims to reduce the need for travel by providing facilities for work and leisure on site.

one that does not add in any way to the levels of carbon dioxide gas in the atmosphere.

The addition of workshop and office space on site helps to boost the local economy and conserves energy that might have been used for commuting by some of the BedZED population. Unlike most modern developments, the properties are offered at both the going market price and on special subsidised schemes to attract people on a wide range of incomes.

Sustainable hi-tech At Abode, a community of futuristic housing near Harlow in Essex, buildings are positioned to make the most of solar heating. While the overall look of the buildings is thoroughly modern, some traditional building materials, such as thatch, weatherboarding, coloured render, slates and tiles have been used. Many of the 82 homes are wired so that telephone, audio and computer signals can be routed to any room. Some of these installations can be programmed to carry out functions automatically: curtains can be set to open and close and lighting to go on and off at pre-set times; and home owners can use their mobile phone to switch on the heating, a cooker or washing machine while they are out.

Housing for the new millennium

The Millennium Communities Programme was set up to bring together new ways of planning, designing and constructing housing schemes to promote a 'greener' way of living. The first Millennium Community to be developed is Greenwich Millennium Village (GMV), built on industrial wasteland on the south bank of the Thames in London. Work began in 1999 to regenerate this neglected patch of land, with the aim of creating more than 12,000 homes by 2015, along with schools, a shopping centre and recreational areas, including an 'Ecological Park'.

The extensive use of factory-finished, prefabricated parts has allowed the buildings to go up relatively quickly. Recyclable materials are being used wherever possible, and any waste generated is also being recycled.

The aim at Greenwich Millennium Village is for energy consumption to be around 80 per cent lower than average for a community of its size. Individual homes are not fitted with boilers; instead their hot water comes from centralised 'energy centres', designed to limit the emission of carbon dioxide and other waste products into the atmosphere. All the properties are equipped with 'water-efficient' domestic appliances and water-saving taps.

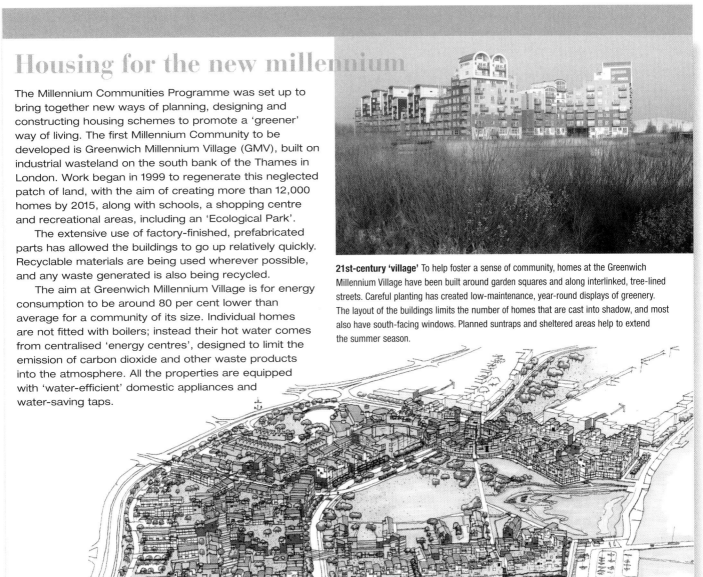

21st-century 'village' To help foster a sense of community, homes at the Greenwich Millennium Village have been built around garden squares and along interlinked, tree-lined streets. Careful planting has created low-maintenance, year-round displays of greenery. The layout of the buildings limits the number of homes that are cast into shadow, and most also have south-facing windows. Planned suntraps and sheltered areas help to extend the summer season.

EXPLORE YOUR HOME

Have you ever wondered when your home was built, who used to live there and what events have taken place within its walls? You may even wish to find out what was there before it was built. By looking for clues, talking to neighbours and exploring records, local and national, you can start to work back and piece together the story of your home, inside and out.

Where to begin Before you start researching the story of your home, ask yourself what you want to achieve. There are three paths to follow – you can find out when a property was built, discover the people who lived there or uncover what was on the land before your home existed. You may find that you have to switch between the goals, depending on how the trail unfolds, and no two homes will follow the same path. The following tips should make the research process easier.

- Find out to which administrative district your home belongs. It will help to know the parliamentary ward, civil or church parish, census registration district, historic estate or manor. Your local record office (see pages 18-19) should have this information. Remember that the boundaries sometimes change (for example, many counties changed in 1974), so as your search takes you back in time, you will need to refer to contemporary maps and records.

- Work backwards in time, moving from clue to clue. Start with recent records such as electoral registers (see pages 326-327) or title deeds (see page 302) and use the information to look for other sources such as wills (see pages 324-325) and census returns (see pages 218-219, 328-329).

- Sometimes researching properties next to your home can yield useful information. If you obtain names of past neighbours, they may lead to documents (such as title deeds) that refer to your property.

Know your boundaries A map dating from 1885 shows the parliamentary boundaries for North East Lancashire. It is important to have a clear idea of the administrative districts your home falls in so you can easily locate it on older maps or records grouped by district.

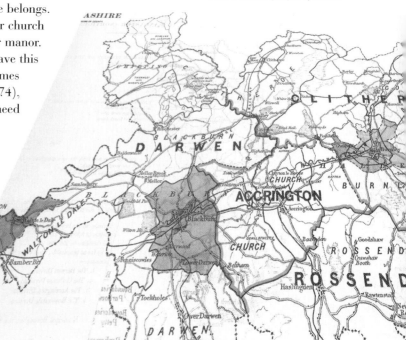

Key research sources

The following resources are all potentially helpful in your research, but the order in which you use them will depend on the information you discover as you progress.

- title deeds (see pages 302, 310, 318, 329)
- maps such as tithe and estate maps (see pages 26-27)
- sale catalogues (see pages 304-305)
- estate records (see pages 318-319, 322, 329)
- rate books (see page 327)
- census returns (see pages 218-219, 328-329)
- tax records (see pages 219, 310, 330-331)
- wills (see pages 324-325, 331)
- street directories (see pages 217, 305, 315, 327)
- photographs (see pages 212-213)
- newspapers (see page 216).

The hunt begins

The records you will need are stored in local study centres, record offices or specialist archives, and you will almost certainly need to visit more than one of these places. Start locally and then explore further afield: local sources may hold the information you need and so save you a longer trip. See 'Getting started', pages 18-21.

Local study centres These hold records, newspapers and photographs linked to the local area. If you live in a large town or city, you should also keep an eye open for city record offices. Most are listed in the 'Directory of sources' (see pages 332-339).

County record offices Look here for material relating to the administration of the county, plus privately deposited documents such as title deeds. All county record offices are listed in the 'Directory of sources' (see pages 332-339).

National archives Government surveys and records are held here. These include the National Archives, the National Archives of Scotland, the National Monuments Record Centre, the British Library, the National Library of Wales, the National Library of Scotland and the General Register Office for Scotland (see DIRECTORY).

FIND OUT MORE

- www.nationalarchives.gov.uk/househistory/guide/ A National Archives guide to using records to research the history of your home.
- www.nas.gov.uk/miniframe/fact_sheet/ buildings.pdf National Archives of Scotland factsheet giving a general introduction to useful records for researching the history of your house in Scotland.
- www.bricksandbrass.co.uk/houseage/ ageform.htm A comprehensive questionnaire that helps you to work out the date that your house was built with lots of information and pictures showing period styles and furnishings.

Visiting the archives

If you have never used an archive before, the following tips should help (see 'Getting started', pages 18-19).

- Make contact in advance to ensure you are looking in the right place. Ask about opening times, the location of the archive and entry requirements – for example, most record offices require you to register as a user, which means you may have to bring some form of identification.
- Rules and regulations are fairly strict – you will not be allowed to bring certain items into the reading area, such as pens, erasers, pencil sharpeners, food or drink, as they could harm the documents.
- Always seek advice when you arrive. Most archives employ staff to help get you started, and can usually provide leaflets or guidebooks that explain in more detail how to undertake specific lines of research.

Time to search The information held in county or city record offices in your region may date back to the Middle Ages. To make the most of your visit you should check beforehand whether the office holds the documents you are looking for. Allow yourself plenty of time with the records – you may find they reveal some unexpected information that can broaden your search.

REFERE
Boundaries of pro
Parliamentary
Boundaries of
Petty Sessional Divisions
Parliamentary Boroughs

Cliffe High Street today The flat at No. 8A, above the third shop from the left, was gutted by a fire in 1996 (inset) – a disaster that led to remarkable discoveries about the building's past

The fire that uncovered a flat's hidden secrets

Even the most ordinary-seeming homes may have a story that stretches further back than anyone would imagine. A flat above a shop in Lewes, East Sussex, surprised the owner when a seemingly disastrous fire revealed its history.

Appearances can deceive

No. 8A Cliffe High Street is at first glance an entirely unremarkable home. It is a flat above a row of shops at the end of the main shopping street in Lewes. There are four shops in the row, and the tiled façade of the shop at the far end looks old. But the frontage of the shop next door at No. 7 is fairly modern: 1930s at the latest. It is hard to say whether the building is genuinely old or not.

Paul Manners has lived above No. 8 for decades. His father bought the whole block, and in the 1950s ran a café called The Polar Bear in the shop below his son's present home. But it was not until 1996, when a fire gutted the building, that its true history was revealed.

The truth rises from the flames

The fire swept through the open roof cavity of the block and destroyed Paul Manners' home. It consumed furniture, plasterboard dividing walls, as well as some of the much older lath-and-plaster, and left the roof open

to the sky. But Paul's domestic misfortune was an archaeological godsend, because it revealed the ancient oak beams of the original building. The fire had also caused considerable damage to the listed buildings of the Harvey's brewery, 100 yards away, so a professional historical surveyor was on the site soon after the flames were doused. The surveyor looked at the exposed and blackened oak beams in the flat at No. 8, which over the centuries had become as hard and impervious to flame as steel. His hunch, based on the configuration of the beams, was that Paul's building was around 350 years old.

The sophisticated construction led the surveyor to surmise that the building had been put up by London craftsmen and was a home of some importance. This fitted with the fact that Lewes was a fashionable place to live from the mid 17th century, as it became increasingly an administrative centre for Sussex. Paul, meanwhile, had noted other oddities. There was an original window frame close to the floor of his upper rooms, and the floor of the first storey ran through the centre of a very old door jamb. He guessed that the ceiling below must have been raised in the 19th century, after the building was converted into a row of shops. The remains of a Victorian awning, entombed behind a later street-side wall, made this theory seem more plausible.

Backed up by the records

While Paul set about the long task of rebuilding his home, the surveyor did some digging in the county archives. He found that the whole row was once known as the Great House, and that in 1685 the owner was a widow called

Ancient workmanship The fire uncovered an original window frame near the floor of the present-day flat, suggesting a change in floor height, and two vertical beams joined together by a beautifully crafted metal strap, pointed out by the owner (inset).

The evidence uncovered by the surveyor sent Paul back to his own files. He has the deeds of the building, with maps, plans and indenture documents, all passed down from his father. These papers fill in other details in the house's history. They show that in Victorian times the owner of the shop below was Mr Tickner, who sold clothes, boots and shoes at No. 7 and china at No. 8. Tickner wanted a showroom for his china on the first floor (where Paul's sitting room is now). Perhaps it was the ambitious Mr Tickner who also raised the ceiling below, to make his ground-floor shop more commodious for his customers.

A lasting legacy

It took Paul almost a year to restore his home. It is now a bright modern flat, but in every room there is evidence of its long past. A great beam runs like a dark stripe across the white walls of his sitting room. It is blacker at the streetward end – a visible reminder of the 1996 fire. In the kitchen a supporting beam runs vertically from floor to high ceiling. It is in fact two huge pieces of wood, held together by a finely crafted metal strap at the height of the kitchen table. This strap has probably been in the same spot for centuries, despite the changes and traumas the building has endured – a pleasing thought for the homeowner each time he sits down next to that ancient, functional piece of workmanship.

Judith Stevenson. She had inherited the house from her father, Samuel Towers of Cliffe (who also owned the Ann of Cleves house, still a tourist attraction in the town). The Great House and its attendant buildings are described in one 17th-century document as comprising 'messuage, barns, stables, warehouse, dyehouse and shoppes'. The need for more than one stable points to the main building having served as lodgings for several gentry families, and the jumble of other buildings suggests that they were all involved in commerce. In the early 1700s the building was divided into four homes. Each was then altered in its own higgledy-piggledy way: staircases, chimneys and outhouses were added in subsequent decades. The line of one chimney is still discernible in Paul's study, and a diagonal sawmark in one timber suggests it was made in connection with a now-forgotten banister.

Documentary evidence A lease (right) dated 1896 for 8 Cliffe High Street includes a plan of the premises and names Frederick Thomas Tickner, boot, shoe and china dealer, as the owner. A deed dated 1650 (below) between Samuel Towers of Cliffe and his wife Elizabeth confirms 'the several occupancy' of the main Great House building by six other gentry families at the time.

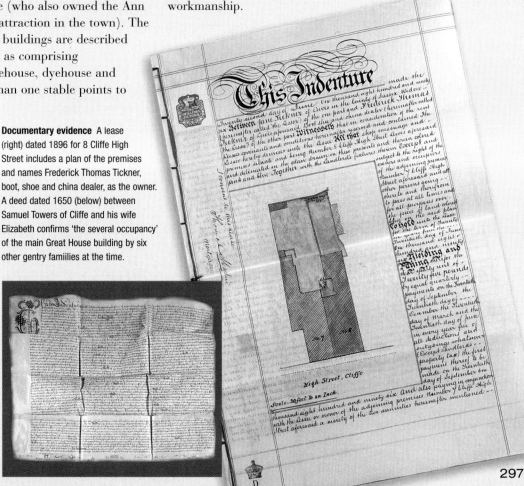

Looking out for visual clues

Before you even begin to explore the archives, look around closer to home. You can find clues to the age of your property from the local neighbourhood and even inside your own four walls. Architectural features might indicate a rough construction date, while house or street names can provide further clues. Even boxes of 'rubbish' in an attic may contain useful documents.

Building up a picture

An initial information-gathering process will help you to place your house in the context of your road or street, making it easier to establish when it was built.

A question of style Ask yourself whether the style of house that you live in is similar to those around it – which would suggest they were built at the same time, or designed by the same architect – or whether it is markedly different. Is your house more modern or more old-fashioned than the rest?

Clues in the location Where is your house situated? Houses nearer the centre of a town or village are likely to be older than those on the outskirts, which could have been added during the 19th-century population explosion or as part of the mass expansion of town and city suburbs in the 1920s and 30s. You can search for these patterns of development on old maps and plans held in local and national archives (see pages 26-27).

Ask the neighbours Talk to local residents, especially those who have lived in the area the longest. They should be able to tell you about former occupants of your house, how the street has changed, or if there are any interesting anecdotes that can be followed up during your research.

Period features

The architectural style of your home can offer key clues about when it was constructed (see pages 268-293). By taking account of building materials, the shape and style of the home and its roof, the size and position of windows, the number of chimney stacks and even door furniture, you can begin to assign a rough date to when your property was built.

Walls and windows Building materials and styles have changed over the years and can help you to date your home.

• Patterns of wooden beams and the wall materials used can indicate the age of the building. Irregularly sized bricks laid on a thick bed of mortar (see left) date from the 17th century. From the mid 19th century onwards, even-sized, manufactured bricks were used.

• Windows have changed perhaps more than any other feature. Different styles, such as casement, sash, metal-framed or stained glass (see pages 284-285), all provide pointers to the age of a home.

What's in a name? House names such as 'The Old Bakery' (above) and 'Miller's Cottage' can provide clues about the former use of a house. Many homes were once places of trade. A name may also help you to date your home. 'Railway Cottage' is likely to have been built for a family of railway workers and so can be dated to the mid 19th century onwards.

Local namesakes

A good line of research to pursue is the name of the house or street (see pages 224-225), which can give clues to its age and previous use. Many roads are named after famous people or battles, which can give you an idea of when they were built. But you should exercise caution, because a road name could have been based on a character or event from a more distant past. The names of people who exerted local influence or owned land were often used to describe property. The district of Brighton known as Kemptown was named after the principal architect who designed the building façades, Thomas Kemp. Sometimes road names can give you clues about local industries, such as Brick Pit Lane, or old landmarks that may no longer be standing, such as Gallows Corner.

A step back Taking a good look at your home from the front and back can reveal much about how the house has changed. The arched window (above) looks as though it may once have been a doorway. At the back of the house (below) the window frames look original (unlike the white, modern replacements at the front).

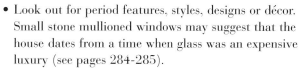

Surveying your land

You should also explore the extent of your property and the land surrounding it.

- Inspect any odd lumps and bumps in your garden; they may be remnants of former structures such as outhouses, sheds or stabling, all of which can be checked on maps and plans. You may even find the remains of an air-raid shelter, many of which were filled in and buried after the Second World War.
- Outbuildings or extensions may help to date your property. Coal sheds were introduced in late Victorian times while houses with attached garages are likely to date from the 20th century.
- If you have a garden, check to see how old the trees are; recent planting indicates a more modern development, whereas large, ancient trees suggest an older property or one that was built on woodland or an old orchard.
- The boundaries of your house can tell you about its age. Look at whether modern fencing or young hedging has been used. Flint walls and mature hedgerows indicate older boundaries.

What the interior can tell you

You are not restricted to the outside of the house. The design, layout, fixtures and fittings on the inside of your house will also yield clues about the age of the property (see pages 306-309, 316-317, 320-321, 323).

- Look out for period features, styles, designs or décor. Small stone mullioned windows may suggest that the house dates from a time when glass was an expensive luxury (see pages 284-285).
- Consider where the stairs are, and how they are constructed. By the Georgian period, grand or large staircases were often placed centrally in the entrance hall compared to earlier houses when staircases were placed at the side.
- The height, size and shape of a room are revealing as fashions changed over time, leading to different periods being associated with certain designs and layouts.
- Interior doors, door frames, window frames, picture rails, position of fireplaces and use of tiles can also indicate when the room was originally furnished.

Houses that were something else

All kinds of buildings that once served a functional purpose have been turned into homes. Converted mills, barns, oast houses and railway stations are fairly easy to spot, but less obvious are the former post offices, shops and public houses.

The past lives of buildings

Upheavals in agriculture and industry have often left buildings devoid of a purpose. The decline in traditional farming, particularly after the Second World War, made many farm buildings redundant. Some decayed, but others were sold and converted into houses. Similarly, in the cities, large warehouses stood empty for years before their potential as flats was spotted by developers in the 1970s. Almost anywhere you go, you will spot practical buildings of bygone eras now being used as homes.

Country converts

Perhaps the most common rural conversions are barns that have become surplus to a farmer's requirements. Their imposing exteriors and cavernous interiors with huge old beams open up many possibilities for those who like unrestricted space. Look for barn conversions close to farm buildings. But bear in mind that the barn could have been part of a farm that has long been demolished.

Drive around the southeastern counties of Essex, Suffolk, Norfolk and Lincolnshire and you will come across plenty of windmills. Their corn-grinding or

Rooms with a view A converted lighthouse makes the perfect living space for those who like curves, and its position almost guarantees peace and quiet. Fixtures and fittings are necessarily made to measure to cope with the circular layout. This lighthouse near lonely Guy's Head in Lincolnshire looks out over The Wash.

pumping days now over, most have been converted into a particularly romantic kind of accommodation. A good example is the mill at Cley-next-the-Sea in north Norfolk, which is now a guesthouse with its former stables and boatshed turned into self-catering units.

Look out also for oast houses, especially in Kent. With their distinctive conical tops they are more likely to be homes these days than places to dry hops. But the ultimate in high living is the lighthouse (above), with rooms far above ground and walls up to 1m (3ft) thick.

HOMES THAT HIDE THEIR PAST

It is usually straightforward to work out if a building was once a windmill or a railway station. But what if your home was once a post office, bakery, vicarage or public house? Sometimes there are clues in the structure of the building itself. Look at the layout and how it differs from other houses in the same street. Does it have a large window at the front, where the others have smaller windows (it may once have been the display window of a shop)?

You should also consider a building's location, such as a vicarage sited close to a church or a forge at the heart of a village. The house in Stedham, Sussex (right), at first betrays little of its former use, but the stone name plaque and the covered entrance porch, now a window, are clues to what was once a pub. Other clues may be more subtle, such as a blocked up posting box indicating a former post office.

If you suspect that your home once had a commercial use, you will need to do some research in local archives. A good place to start is with local directories (see page 217).

Recycling the Industrial Revolution

In towns and cities the warehouses, textile mills and factories have been snapped up for development, mostly because of the grandeur imparted by their enormous proportions. The old run-down dock area of east London, re-christened Docklands as part of its late 20th-century clean-up, yielded hundreds of handsome large warehouses that had been empty for years. They have been quickly converted into flats, townhouses and lofts for artists, film-makers and workers in the City.

The Stroud Valley in south Gloucestershire is another area that has undergone rapid redevelopment. It was once lined with textile works, such as the late-Victorian Hill Paul clothing factory and the enormous early 19th-century Dunkirk Mill, that are now well-appointed apartments.

Following the railways

Hundreds of rural railway stations were closed in the 1960s under the notorious 'Beeching Axe' (see page 85). Most have been demolished or lie ruined, but some have been converted into private houses. At Lynton in Devon even the goods shed has become a home, and at Dent on the Settle & Carlisle line, high in the moorlands of east Cumbria, a three-bedroomed house stands right on the platform, the decorative bargeboards of its twin gables revealing its railway company origin. At Great Moulton, between Diss and Norwich in Norfolk, the former level-crossing keeper's cottage has become a two-bedroomed house, while the old signal box at Shelley in west Yorkshire is now a house with three bedrooms.

FIND OUT MORE

- www.diydoctor.org.uk/projects/barn_conversion.htm Tips on converting a barn.
- www.shipleywindmill.org.uk Website for Shipley Windmill.
- www.property.org.uk/unique/rail.html Converted railway buildings.
- www.martello-towers.co.uk Martello tower conversions.
- www.ecastles.co.uk/albert.html Website for Fort Albert, Isle of Wight.
- www.sealandgov.org Website of the Principality of Sealand.

Towers and forts

Former military buildings seem to exert endless fascination. It is hard to make a home in a Napoleonic-era Martello Tower because of its inherent cold, damp and dark, not to mention the awkward elliptical shape. But that has not deterred the owners of towers at Folkestone, Sandwich and Dymchurch in Kent, and Pevensey in East Sussex. Likewise the immense and formidably grim-looking Fort Albert was built in 1856 to glower threateningly across The Solent at any potential invaders. It looks the least likely place to be turned into cosy apartments, but that is exactly what has happened to it.

Perhaps the most bizarre story of all belongs to Roughs Tower, a Second World War gun platform measuring just 137m x 43m (450ft x 140ft), situated in the North Sea, some 6 miles off the Essex coast. It has been converted not only into a comfortable home but also into a self-proclaimed sovereign state, the Principality of Sealand, complete with its own head of state, currency, flag and passports.

All change Brentor Station, near Tavistock, Devon, was built by the London and South Westen Railway Company in 1890. Made from local granite and carefully restored, it is now a charming and unusual setting for a guesthouse.

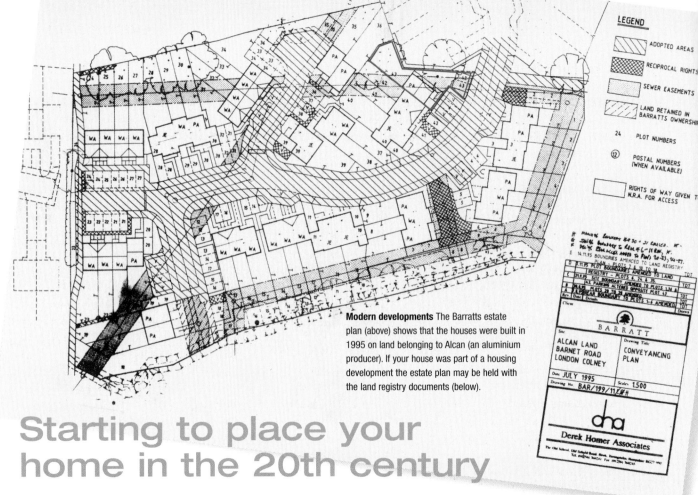

Modern developments The Barratts estate plan (above) shows that the houses were built in 1995 on land belonging to Alcan (an aluminium producer). If your house was part of a housing development the estate plan may be held with the land registry documents (below).

Starting to place your home in the 20th century

Many of us live in a house or flat that dates from the 20th century, probably from the 1920s onwards. To discover when the property was built, who built it and who lived in it you can take a clear series of fairly straightforward steps. If your home is older, you can follow the same path to see what was happening to it over the past 100 years.

Your first ports of call

There are two initial steps you can take to start to fill in the story of your home.

Title deeds First, try to track down your title deeds, which will give you information about the names of previous owners. If you have a mortgage, your lender will hold these documents, so you will need to make a formal approach to view them. Many companies charge a fee for access.

Land Registry records Next approach the Land Registry (see DIRECTORY) and request (for a small fee) the latest registered title (see right) along with the plan accompanying the registration. The plan will show the extent of the property – a useful document that you can use during your research to compare with older maps (see pages 26–27). The registered title may refer to former owners, although it will probably simply mention yourself since the Land Registry only holds details relating to the date of the last sale. The

Land Registry was not set up to hold historic records, and you will need to search for earlier title deeds in local archives, or in the possession of former owners.

Property registration in Scotland Transfers of land in Scotland are carried out by a deed called an Instrument of Sasine (see pages 318–319). The Register of Sasines has printed summaries of transactions in the 20th century arranged by county and year. Indexes of places and names also help to speed up your search. The register is held at the National Archives of Scotland (see DIRECTORY).

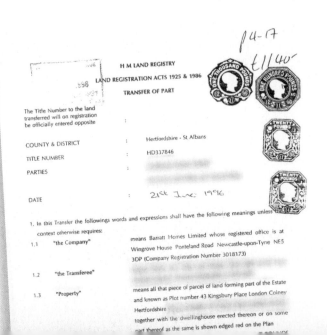

Slum clearance developments

In the 1920s successive legislation gave powers to local authorities to demolish unsanitary dwellings and create modern housing for the working classes in urban areas (see pages 188-189). The planning regulations are well documented in local records, including planning schemes, local authority orders and legal documents.

Where to find records Search in local records and the National Archives (see DIRECTORY), particularly among the records of the Ministry of Health (Housing Department).

Post-war redevelopment records

After the Second World War, plans were drawn up for large-scale reconstruction of the towns and cities damaged by bombing (see pages 198-199). Following the Town and Country Planning Act in 1947, developers had to seek planning permission from local authorities before any building could go ahead. Similarly, all local authorities were required to prepare a development plan for their local area.

Where to find records Many of these records are held in county archives. Duplicate plans and paperwork were also passed on to the Ministry of Town and Country

Planning whose records can be viewed at the National Archives (see DIRECTORY). Bomb census maps and papers (see below) are also stored at the National Archives.

The birth of new towns

As new housing developments sprang up they created a mass of documentation, held in local record offices.

Local government and planning records Your local council should hold records of planning applications (after 1947, following the Town and Country Planning Act). These consist of plans, maps and building specifications relating to advice on street layout, materials to be used, planting of trees and landscaping, the provision of public utilities and even street lighting. These records can also be found at the National Archives (see DIRECTORY). Some local authorities have databases that contain planning and building details of each property in the district.

Records of services Utility company records include maps and plans showing when houses were connected to gas mains, water supplies or the National Grid. Many refer by name to the occupiers or owners of the house. These are stored at your local record office.

Construction company brochures These brochures can be linked to a precise construction date. Also look out for advertisements in local newspapers (see pages 216-217).

After the bombs Thousands of properties were rebuilt following the damage caused by the Blitz. Bomb census maps will show you how the war affected your area, while accompanying reports can add details such as how many bombs were dropped and when. The map below shows the destruction in part of Lambeth, London. Walcot Square (circled) was badly hit; today (inset) it is much restored, but the light-coloured bricks give a clue to where new properties were erected on top of bomb sites.

FIND OUT MORE

• www.landreg.gov.uk On-line access to the Land Registry.

Key

- Total destruction
- Damage beyond repair
- Seriously damaged but doubtful if repairable
- Seriously damaged but repairable at cost
- General blast damages, minor in nature
- Blast damages, minor in nature
- Clearance areas
- V1 bomb

Filling in the 20th-century story of your home

Logging the streets Old Post Office directories from the 20th century (right) exist for most towns. If you follow the street names back from year to year, you could find when a street was built.

If you live in a 20th-century house or flat you may think there is little history to uncover, but whatever the age or style of a property, there is much to learn. You can find details of a property when first built, or learn out about the site on which it was constructed – perhaps an earlier property stood there, or the land could have been part of a farm or estate.

What used to be there?

To find out what was once on the site your home now occupies, look at Ordnance Survey (OS) maps (see pages 26-27) dating from before the property was built. The 1910-15 Valuation Office Survey (see page 310) or earlier records such as tithe and enclosure maps (see pages 26-27) will also show you how an area has changed, and where your home fits in to the story.

Digging for Britain

If your home was built in the latter part of the 20th century on what was previously agricultural land, you should look up the area in the National Farm Survey records (see page 130). The survey was carried out in 1941-3 to assess the productivity of farms in order to help the war effort. Copies of OS maps were marked up to show the boundary of each farm, with a code assigned to every individual holding. Assessment forms include details of the size and extent of the property, the name and address of the owner, the name of the tenant farmer (if applicable), and information on the quality of the farm and how the land was being used.

Where to find the records The records are stored at the National Archives (see DIRECTORY) for England and Wales, with limited records for Scotland in the National Archives of Scotland (see DIRECTORY).

What did your house look like?

Perhaps your house has been modernised and you wish to see what it looked like when it was new. There are several types of record that will help you.

• Old sales catalogues belonging to local estate agents often contain photographs of exteriors and specify the internal period features of houses, so you may be able to see how your house looked when it was brand new.

• Local newspapers (see pages 216-217) often carry advertisements for property sales or rentals. You will need to have a rough idea of when a sale took place.

• Auctioneers' records are worth checking as they list sales and sometimes the contents of the property, which may have been sold at the same time.

Studying the property market A 1930 brochure for Huxley Road on the Grove Park Estate in Welling, Kent, gives detailed information on how a property on this estate would have looked when it was first built, including specifications for the rooms and even fixtures and fittings.

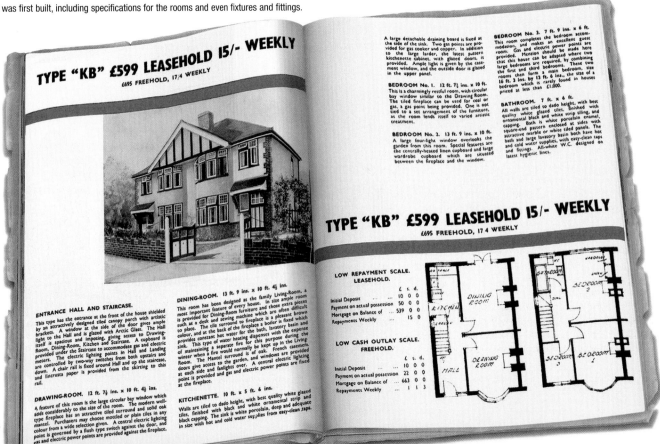

could also check whether your home is mentioned in the Pevsner architectural guide for your area (held at your library). Each volume describes local notable buildings, and includes a gazetteer arranged alphabetically by place.

Where to find the records Look for architectural records in your county record office. In Scotland the Royal Commission on the Ancient and Historical Monuments (see DIRECTORY) has a wide collection of architects' papers.

Local directories

Many local trade, postal and telephone directories cover the 20th century. The volumes will usually include a street index, and often have a map. They can be found at local record offices and reference libraries.

Trade directories Properties that were associated with a trade or profession, such as shops or inns, can be traced in trade or commercial directories (see page 217). You can find out the names of the occupants and the business that was run from the property. Then it should be possible to cross-reference with trade licences, local newspaper advertisements, trade journals and photographs (all at local archives) to find when it was converted to a domestic property.

at any Post Office 1'6

Where to find the records Estate agents' catalogues may have been deposited in your local studies library or at the county record office. Local newspapers are stored in local archives, with copies at British Library Newspapers (see DIRECTORY). Check for local auctioneers' records in local archives.

Architectural records

If your home is architecturally imposing or has an unusual design, it is worth checking at the Royal Institute of British Architects (see DIRECTORY) to see if any building accounts or architects' plans have been deposited. You

FIND OUT MORE

• www.catalogue.nationalarchives. gov.uk/RdLeaflet.asp?sLeafletID=309 Advice on how to use the National Farm Survey.
• www.pevsner.co.uk Website giving information about architectural guides to Britain.
• www.bl.uk/collections/newspapers. html An on-line catalogue of national and local papers.
• www.historicaldirectories.org An on-line catalogue of national and local directories.

When research takes you back to bare land

As you look back to a period before your home was built, you will need to keep in mind the social history of your area. In the 1920s and 30s there was a rapid expansion of the suburbs, and land from large estates was often sold off and developed. Your street could be one of the many thousands built at this time on what was then the rural fringes of a town. In many cases the large estate house was converted to flats, or a non-domestic use such as a hotel or residential home. Sometimes it was demolished to make way for more housing. You can find demolition orders and slum clearance files at the National Archives (see DIRECTORY) or in local archives. You do not have to restrict your searches to 'wordy' documents. Most local study centres have extensive photographic archives. The photograph on the right shows the junction of Pinner Road and Headstone Lane in North Harrow, where Aish & Cartwright were building 'labour-saving' semis in 1924.

Interior clues in post-war homes

The home in the 1950s, 60s and 70s cast aside the austere look of the pre-war period. New properties were often smaller than their predecessors, so built-in furniture was used to make the most of the space. Modern living demanded flexible use of living areas and the convenience of easy-clean surfaces. Key features to look out for in the post-war home are room partitions, fitted kitchens with Formica worktops, linoleum floors and washable vinyl wallpaper.

Room partition

Formica worktop

Open-tread staircase

1970s bathroom suite

The open plan room

The concept of 'open planning' was widely adopted providing a feeling of increased space and light, with interior walls kept to a minimum, large picture windows and open-tread staircases. Room partitions or dividers acted as a wall substitute.

- **Room partitions or dividers** If you have an open-plan living, kitchen or dining area, you may still have in place the original 1950s or 60s open storage units which acted as 'room dividers'. These were usually finished in teak, or in a plastic veneer if adjoining the kitchen. Built-in sliding screens or 'foldaway' room partitions also became popular, allowing for a more flexible approach to space. Look out for those made from imitation leather, which covered collapsible partitions in a wide range of colours and patterns.
- **Windows** Large, single-pane floor-to-ceiling windows, known as 'picture windows', are a good indication that a property was built in the later 1950s or 60s. Pilkington made double-glazed units as large as 10ft by 6ft (3m by 1.8m). You may also find original sliding windows or patio doors, again double-glazed and often mahogany framed.
- **Staircases** Look at the location and style of your staircase. Stairs in 1950s homes generally rose directly from the open-plan living room and were a wooden open-tread ladder design to enhance the effect of light and space.

Built-in aesthetics

Modernist styling called for furniture and fittings that saved space. Look out for built-in cupboards in the hall, fitted wardrobes in the bedroom or fitted units in the kitchen or bathroom. You should examine the finishes and surfaces carefully, as they are the key to dating your interiors accurately.

- **Fitted kitchens** Worktops with plastic laminates from companies such as Formica and Warerite were popular in the 1950s and 60s. These materials were hard-wearing, easy to clean and readily manufactured in the latest decorative colours and patterns, including fashionable fake leather and wood finishes. A pressed steel or coloured enamel sink unit is also a clue to a 1950s or 60s kitchen.
- **Bathrooms** Look out for the panelled baths and built-in storage ('vanity') units found in many post-war bathrooms. Baths, toilets and wash basins were increasingly being made of Fibreglass or Perspex from the mid 1960s onwards, usually in colour co-ordinated pastel shades, particularly pink, blue and 'avocado'.
- **Fitted wardrobes** Veneers in teak, maple or mahogany were a strong element in designs of 1960s and early 70s, as were louvered doors. Wardrobes might also form part of a built-in bedroom suite, or act as a room partition.

HEATING

Increasingly sophisticated plumbing and heating systems provided the standard of comfort demanded by the modern consumer in the 1950s and 60s. As a result there was less reliance on the fireplace as a form of heating.

- **Fireplaces** With the increasing popularity of the television, a fire ceased to be the focal point of the living-room. Fireplaces became decorative rather than functional. If your home has one dating from the 1950s or 60s, it will probably be faced in stone or brick. Sometimes a built-in storage or shelving unit would be incorporated.
- **Central heating** Most new homes built from the 1960s onwards had central heating installed, giving a better standard of all-over draught-free warmth.

Exposed brickwork

Vinyl flooring

FIND OUT MORE

• Museum of Domestic Design and Architecture Collection includes 1950s wallpapers and textiles and trade catalogues. www.moda.mdx.ac.uk
• The Twentieth Century Society www.c20society.org.uk
• Geffrye Museum Has a 1950s-60s room set. www.geffrye-museum.org.uk
• *Fiftiestyle: Home Decorating and Furnishing from the 1950s* (Lesley Hoskins, Middlesex University Press, 2004)
• *Sixtiestyle: Home Decoration and Furnishings from the 1960s* (David Heathcote, Middlesex University Press, 2004)
• *Contemporary: Architecture and Interiors of the 1950s* A survey of trends in taste and interior design (Lesley Jackson, Phaidon Press, 1998)
• *Decorative Arts, 1970s* (Charlotte and Peter Fiell, Taschen, 2000)
• *Formica and Design* (S.G. Lewin, Rizzoli International Publications, 1991)

Poly-flor flexible vinyl floor tiles, 1960

Wallpaper 1958, by Shand Kydd

Textured 1960 wallpaper, by Lightbown Aspinall

'Spartacus', 1970s vinyl wallpaper, by Mayfair

Floors

If you have a 1950s, 60s or 70s home, man-made fibre tufted carpets may still exist in some areas. But a more likely survivor is the synthetic floor tile, in vinyl or linoleum. Look for these in hallways, landings, kitchens and bathrooms, and also for surviving pieces inside cupboards and fitted wardrobes or beneath fitted carpets.

• **Linoleum** Lino was commonly used as a floor covering in post-war homes, especially in the kitchen, and came in an array of mottled patterns designed not to show dirt.
• **Vinyl tiles** These tiles were hard-wearing and easy to install and keep clean. They were also very cheap, and in the 1950s and 60s gradually replaced lino as the material of choice for areas that were in constant use. Tiles with a faux marbling effect were available in a range of colours. Chequerboard vinyl floors in combinations of black and white, red and white, and yellow and white were popular during the 1950s.
• **Rubber or cork tiles, or hardwood block or strip** By the mid 1960s and in the 70s, these were considered a more stylish alternative to vinyl tiles for flooring, giving a room a more sophisticated, ultra-modern look.

Walls and wallpaper

Although there were fewer internal walls in homes of this era, walls still had an important role to play, giving a sense of space through surface texture, colour and pattern. Dados and picture rails disappeared and the decorative border or frieze became obsolete. The ceilings of the period were plain, with no mouldings to cover awkward edges.

• **Wall finishes** Look out for exposed brick and tongue-and-groove pine panelling, which were both popular in the 1960s and early 70s, as were textured wall finishes such as hessian and the more synthetic products such as textured paint and wallpapers, or vinyl wall tiles. Often a variety of textures – both natural and simulated – were used together.
• **Wallpaper** Washable vinyl-coated papers were commonly used in bathrooms and kitchens in the 1960s, but you are more likely to find textured 'woodchip' wallpaper which was widely used throughout the home in the 1960s and 70s and remains in many today. Remnants of screen-printed contemporary patterns may also survive. These were often bold and colourful, in abstract or geometric designs, inspired by graphic art.

Early 20th-century interior clues

The Edwardian home had many similarities to that of the Victorian era. But after the upheaval of the First World War ideas about living space took a new turn, bringing in the elegant, functional fashions of Art Deco. Change did not happen overnight. So when you try to date aspects of your home between 1900 and 1945, remember that the original features you see will owe as much to tradition as they do to the fashions of the day.

FIND OUT MORE

• *20s and 30s Style* (M. Horsham, Grange Books, 1989)
• *The 1930s Home* (G. Stephenson, Shire, 2000)
• www.bbc.co.uk/homes/design/period_index.shtml An introduction to period styles of the early 20th century.
• www.bricksandbrass.co.uk Information on how to identify the designs of elements such as wallpaper, stained glass and fireplaces in homes built in the 1920s and 30s.
• The Twentieth Century Society See DIRECTORY.
• The Bakelite Museum See DIRECTORY.

Art Nouveau

Art Deco

1930s stained glass

Bakelite switches

1930s bellboard

Fireplaces

If your home has original fireplaces, you can get close to establishing the decade in which it was built. The elaborate decoration of the late Victorian period was not repeated in 20th-century fireplaces. Instead of fussy little bouquets, representations of flowers were elongated, curved and stylised in the Art Nouveau fashion, which began in the 1890s and took off in the early 1900s. A fireplace installed in the decade before the First World War is more likely to be made of brightly burnished steel or copper than the black-leaded cast-iron of the late 19th century. In the 1920s and 30s, Art Deco style brought long straight lines and bold patterns. Not much then changed until the 1950s.

• **Art Nouveau** Like their Victorian predecessors, the Edwardians used tiles in fire surrounds, but the colours were bright and the floral imagery kept simple. Look for flowers that are more a brief freehand sketch in ceramic than an oil painting on clay. This style was popular until the 1920s.
• **Art Deco** The geometric, angular and functional lines of Art Deco are quite distinctive. If your fireplace has a chunky, stepped profile (see above), it is likely to be 1930s or possibly later. Typically the tiles are shades of pink, green or beige. Look out for Art Deco motifs such as shells, foliage, flowers and the more abstract designs such as the sunburst. An Art Deco fireplace in your home suggests that the house was built in the 1920s or 30s.
• **Tudorbethan fireplaces** An imposing inglenook fireplace featuring large expanses of tiling is likely to date from the 1920s and 30s, when there was a retrospective fashion for mock-Tudor detail in newly built large suburban houses.

Windows

The style of windows in your home can give a clue to its age. Painted steel-framed windows became popular in the 1920s and 30s, and were widely used into the 1960s, although by then the frames enclosed larger, single planes of glass. It was thought that the steel frames would be more durable than old-fashioned wood, but in fact they were prone to condensation and rust. Many have been replaced.

• **Stained glass** Art Nouveau or Art Deco motifs can be seen in many early 20th-century homes. Leaded stained glass door panels were popular, featuring colourful images of flora and fauna or stylised images such as the galleon ship or sunburst motif (see pages 288-289)

Fixtures

If your home has Bakelite doorknobs, escutcheons and light switches, it is a clear indication that the property dates from the early 20th century, particularly the 1920s and 30s. Bakelite, first introduced in the USA in 1909, was a popular material for electrics because it was totally non-conductive and practically indestructible. 'It will not burn; it will not melt,' declared *Time* magazine in 1924. Anyone who carries out wiring work in a pre-Second World War house may well find a jumble of brown Bakelite junction boxes beneath the floorboards.

Design for living Signs of a typical 1930s lounge might include large metal-framed windows, flush-fitting cupboards, tiled fireplace and unadorned Art Deco furnishings.

Art Nouveau wallpaper 1902, Silver Studio

Wallpaper c.1910, Silver Studio

Art Deco wallpaper c.1935

Floors

In the early 20th century, floorboards went out of fashion and linoleum and parquet floors were all the rage. Take a look under your carpet and see what is there. A design may be incorporated around the edge of the floor to frame a centrally placed rug.

• **Parquet floors** These were made in oak or walnut and laid in 9in by 2in blocks. A common pattern was 'herringbone' – a repeating series of v-shapes. Although they were fashionable in the 1920s and 30s, many parquet floors have not survived because they were ripped up in the 1940s and 50s by homeowners who needed to get beneath the floor to install central heating pipes.
• **Linoleum floors** The pattern will indicate the linoleum's age. Subtle colours belong to the Edwardian era and bold geometric designs to the 1930s.

Walls and ceilings

Does your home have oak panelling? This form of decoration was adopted after 1905, as it gave an appearance of comfort and luxury. It was a feature of the Tudorbethan style of the 1920s and 30s that aimed to recreate a medieval look.

• **False oak beams** Should your home have such beams it is likely that it was built in the 1920s or 30s when the Tudorbethan style was popular. The beams, in-filled with plaster, play no structural role and have a purely decorative purpose.

Wallpaper

When stripping wallpaper, it is common to find layers of old wallpaper underneath. You can literally peel back the years as you strip off the layers. Wallpaper designs can readily be linked to a certain period and go right back to Edwardian times, when wallpapered friezes were fashionable (as were stencils).

• **Muted colours and flat, curving patterns** The Art Nouveau style in the early 1900s favoured scenes from nature with stylised flowers, birds, plants and peacock feathers.
• **Moulded papers** Imitation exotic woods or simulated fabric finishes were popular in the Edwardian period. Designs were generally plain and patterns simple.
• **Bold motifs** Bright colours and geometric patterns are typical of Art Deco wallpapers from the 1920s and 30s. Their popularity persisted into the 1950s.

The home scene at the turn of the 20th century

Between 1910 and 1915 the surveyors of the Inland Revenue compiled the most comprehensive set of property records that had ever been made for the whole of Britain. If your home was built at or before this time you will be able to find out who was living there, how much the property was worth and much more besides.

The Valuation Office Survey

Between 1910 and 1915 the government carried out a national survey to assess the value of property for tax purposes. The records consist of valuation books, Ordnance Survey (OS) maps and field books.

The valuation books summarise the ownership and value of the property. OS maps record the extent of each property, and assign each one a 'hereditament number' marked in red. These numbers can be looked up in the field books, which describe each property, recording the number and uses of rooms and outbuildings. They also comment on the general condition, water supply and sanitation of each property (see also pages 130-131).

The records can show you where your property boundaries were, or indeed whether your house had even been built by this date. In some areas, proposed housing developments were drawn in pencil on the maps, which may help you to work out the construction date of a house. Most of the survey records survive although there are occasional gaps due to accidental loss.

Where to find the records The English and Welsh records are held at the National Archives (see DIRECTORY), in classes IR 58, 121 and 124-135. The Scottish records are stored at the National Archives in Edinburgh (see DIRECTORY) as field books (IRS 51-87), maps (IRS 101-133) and a few on-site notebooks for the Dundee area (IRS 88). A set of valuation books were also made for local record offices.

Lack of title deeds

Title deeds are usually a good way to find out who owned your home in the past. But in 1925 the Law of Property Act stated that deeds had to be held for only 30 years, so many were simply thrown away, which means that deeds dating from before the 20th century are scarce. Some were deposited at local record offices, while others may survive in private hands, with the former owners of the property.

Valuable survey If your property is part of a Victorian terrace, it may well be listed in the Valuation Office Survey. Find its hereditament number on the OS map and cross-reference it with the relevant field book. The field book entries (right) list the name and address of the owner, the occupier (if different) and whether the property is freehold, copyhold or leasehold.

The story of 14 Walcot Square

In the Victorian era huge numbers of properties were built to cater for the growing urban populations. Walcot Square in Lambeth, London, is one such development and a good example of how you can follow the history of a house through the 19th century and into the 20th.

Early history
In 1667 Edmund Walcott bequeathed the land on which Walcot Square stands to a charity, in order to raise money for the poor of the area. This information can be found in probate records of the Prerogative Courts of Canterbury (see pages 324-325). By searching in the Walcot Charity estate papers, held at the Lambeth archives and a local reference library, we know that by 1837 the trustees of the charity had decided to develop the site. They wanted to build housing for people who sought accommodation within easy reach of the City of London.

A Victorian redevelopment
Plans stored with the charity's estate papers show that between 1837 and 1839 Walcot Square was designed and constructed by the architect John Woodward. The first lease for No. 1 Walcot Square in 1837 was granted to a local builder, Charles Newnham. This indicates that well-to-do, professional people were taking up residence in the square. The property remained in the Newnham family until the late 1890s, by which time it had been renumbered as No. 14. The occupations recorded for residents in the census returns from 1881 and 1891 indicate that the area in general was by then home to people from lower levels of society (see pages 218-219 for information on using census records).

Walcot Square in the 20th century
The 1901 census and tenancy papers show that predominantly working class tenants were living at the property until it was damaged during the Blitz in 1940 (see page 303). The building was renovated after the war and today has one owner-occupier.

No. 1 or 14? When researching the history of a property you should keep in mind that the street number may have changed. No. 14 Walcot Square was No. 1 when Charles Newnham took up the first lease (below). Old leases can also give you an idea of a tenant's social standing, since class was closely associated with a person's job at the turn of the 20th century. As a builder, Mr Newnham was middle class.

Leases (continued)

FIND OUT MORE

• *Old Title Deeds* (N.W. Alcock, Phillimore, 2001)
• www.nationalarchives.gov. uk/pathways/localhistory/ gallery1/valuation.htm
Information on how to find and use the Valuation Office maps and field books.

Homes for the working class The 1901 census return shows that No. 14 had been converted to flats, with three separate households, 14 people in all, inhabiting the building (see below). The flats were let out to working-class tenants, including a labourer, messenger, porter and, more exotically, an Italian mosaic layer and a feather curler.

Victorian home comforts

Today it is hard to imagine life without central heating, electric lighting, flushing toilets and hot running water. Yet all these appliances were unavailable to our ancestors at the turn of the 19th century. It was the innovative, practical and optimistic Victorians who either invented them or persevered in making them work properly. The arrival of these 'mod cons' gradually changed the way people lived and had an impact on the way houses were constructed and furnished.

RIPPINGILLE'S PATENT Oil Warming STOVES *The Best in the World.*

FOR SALE HERE

Turning up the heat

Gas was available from the early 19th century, but it was not introduced into many homes until the 1830s. A welcome invention for the better-off householder was the gas-fired water heater, in which a gas burner heated water flowing through a copper pipe. There were snags – it was hard to regulate the temperature and flow of the water, so that the contraption could become overheated to the point of explosion. Once the public water supply at a regulated pressure had been introduced, it became possible to develop the storage tank water heater, which was more reliable. Heating by means of steam pipes had been introduced into factories decades before Victorian pioneers began experimenting with domestic central heating. By

Domestic bliss The well-to-do Victorian was keen to make her home a haven with the latest gadgets. An 1894 advertisement (above) for oil-warming stoves seems to offer the way to a contented family, not just better heating. Gas lamps (right) also offered a happier home – they were brighter and safer than candles and cleaner than paraffin.

the end of the 19th century cast iron radiators were being mass-produced, and most affluent householders had installed a heating system based on the circulation of hot water.

Cast-iron monsters Rosser & Russell's advertisement for hot water, steam and gas radiators in an 1888 issue of *The Builder* was aimed at the wealthier Victorian. Central heating would not be widely available until the 1950s.

Estimates for Heating Apparatus, Ventilation, Hot-Water Supply, Cooking Apparatus, &c.

RADIATORS,
HOT WATER, STEAM, AND GAS.
ROSSER & RUSSELL,
OFFICES—
22, CHARING CROSS, LONDON.
WORKS—
Queen's Wharf, Hammersmith, W.
PATENTEES & MANUFACTURERS
Have in stock or progress in various sizes from 10 ft. to 200 ft. superficial heating surface each.
BOILERS, PIPES, STEAM-WATER HEATERS.
TRADE SUPPLIED.   PRICE LISTS FREE.

Let there be light

After the flickering light of candles, the introduction of gas lighting was a boon to the Victorians. Gas lighting was far brighter than candle-light, especially after the invention in the 1880s of the incandescent gas mantle, consisting of a skirt of silk or cotton soaked in soluble salts (thorium and cerium), and suspended over a fierce flame. The light shone upwards rather than downwards, but this disadvantage was

FLUSHED WITH PRIDE
Contrary to general belief and despite his name, the London plumber Thomas Crapper (1836-1910) did not give us the flush lavatory. In 1775 Alexander Cummings invented a flush mechanism, and three years later Joseph Bramah produced the first effective flush water closet, although the sewers at the time were unable to cope with the waste. The Victorians provided the necessary sewerage, and even applied their love of decoration to the lavatory itself (right, the Humber bowl of 1880).

overcome late in the 1890s with the introduction of the inverted mantle. Many homes used both gas lights and paraffin lamps, introduced in the 1860s. Paraffin gave a better light than candles, but it was smokier, smellier and more dangerous than gas.

By the turn of the 20th century, electric lighting was beginning to appear in the home. The carbon filament bulbs burned with a soft light but because they gave out negligible heat and no fumes, unlike gas and paraffin, they could be positioned anywhere within a room.

Brightening up the walls

In the early 19th century, interior wall coverings (see page 321) were often made of expensive fabrics such as silk, satin or cotton, and restricted to the better-off households. In the 1830s cheaper roller-printed wallpapers became available, and more houseowners could afford to cover their walls in bright, cheerful paper with printed designs (see page 317).

These wallpapers were shown off to best advantage in natural light, and technological advances in glass-making meant that larger pieces of plate glass, rather than many smaller panes, became the window glazing of choice.

Windows themselves became more numerous after the heavy tax on glass was abolished in 1845, followed by the window tax in 1851 (see also pages 281, 285).

Damp and drains

Most early Victorian houses suffered from rising damp. Damp-proof courses – initially a layer of slates 15cm (6in) above ground level, and later a layer of bitumen – started to be incorporated into new buildings after the Public Health Act of 1875. The Act laid down statutory requirements for public health that included the provision of unpolluted water, rubbish collection, street cleaning and the hygienic sewage disposal. It was the culmination of 27 years of legislation that began with an Act of 1848 that established a General Board of Health for London. Soon similar local Boards spread across Britain, responding to a growing public concern about the disgusting state of many rivers, wells and streets, which had become the unregulated sewage and garbage dumps of overcrowded cities, causing outbreaks of cholera, typhoid and diarrhoea.

The 1875 Act also decreed that every house should have either a flush lavatory, a privy or an ash pit. By the late 19th century every household that could afford it had an indoor lavatory with a high-level flush cistern and a dispenser full of lavatory paper (invented in America in 1857). The houses of the poorest still made do with an outside hut in which there was an earth or ash closet. The human waste, dirty water and other liquid sewage was carried away, and fresh water brought in, through cast-iron, lead or glazed ceramic piping.

FIND OUT MORE

• The Gas Museum, Leicester Includes displays on the use of gas in the home. www.gasmuseum.co.uk
• Abbey Pumping Station Museum Covers the history of plumbing and sewage control. www.leicestermuseums.ac.uk
• www.periodproperty.co.uk/article018.htm Information about lighting in the Victorian home.

Bright idea Although he did not invent the lightbulb, Thomas Edison made it considerably more efficient and long-lasting in the 1880s by using first a carbon and then a tungsten filament. By 1926 electricity networks were gradually linking up the country to power stations so that every home could enjoy the benefits of clean, safe lighting at the flick of a switch.

Charting your home through Victorian times

Throughout the 19th century there was a huge movement of people from the countryside into the towns and as a result thousands of houses were built to accommodate them. Whether you live in a detached 'villa', terraced house, 'two-up-two-down' worker's cottage or converted flat, there is an array of documents that can help you to find out when your house was built.

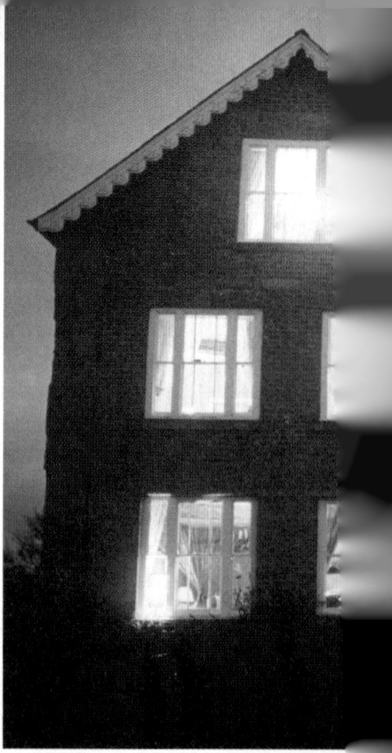

Mapping evidence

Victorian houses have distinctive architectural styles (see pages 276-283), but if you want to find out the precise year in which your home was built you will need to begin by searching through maps (see pages 26-27). By looking at the various types of map made in the 19th century you will be able to see when your home first appears. You will need to work back in time, in roughly the following order:

- town plans
- Ordnance Survey (OS) maps
- tithe maps
- enclosure maps.

Victorian town plans If you live in an urban area, look up some old town plans. These started to be produced during the Victorian period in great numbers by urban district councils, which used the maps when designing sewers and implementing improvements such as gas street lights and pedestrian paving. In many cases, maps are detailed enough to be able to identify individual properties.

Town plans are often held in local and city archives and county record offices. Between 1847 and 1895, the OS mapped 61 Scottish towns in great detail and the maps can be seen at the National Library of Scotland and on-line (see DIRECTORY).

Ordnance Survey maps You will be able to find OS maps at a scale of six inches to the mile going back decade by decade to the 1850s. (There are earlier OS sheets going back to 1801, but the scale of one inch to the mile means that they are unhelpful for locating individual properties.) Most county or local archives have a good selection. The British Library in London (see DIRECTORY) holds a copy of all OS maps, while the National Archives and the National Library of Scotland also hold OS material as part of their collections (see DIRECTORY).

Tithe awards If your home is still on an OS map of the 1850s, the next step is to see if it appears on a tithe map of the area (see pages 27, 215). Drawn up between 1836 and 1852, following the Tithe

Northop Township

OCCUPIERS.	Numbers referring to the Plan.	NAME AND DESCRIPTION of LANDS AND PREMISES.	STATE of CULTIVATION.
Seary Mr Maurice	b365	House yard &c near Boars Head	Homestead
	b367	Garden	Arable
	b198	Ponly field	do
	b199	Small do	do
	b207	Large do	do
	b210	Field by Swndwfr	Pasture
	b361	Cae cithin	do
	b362	Nant	do
	b363	Cae Caul	
	b366	Caer coed gellig	Pool
	"	Pool in do	Coal Wash
	b364	Coal Waste	
	383	Part of the ddôl	Pasture
Webster Sarah	384	Part of Weirglawdd y Sarn	do
Williams Edward Grocer	b33	House yard and Garden in Northop	Homestead
	b111	Croft	Pasture
Cartwright Margaret & another	b37	House garden & Smithy in Northop	Homestead & Smithy
	b51	House and Garden do	do
Davies Anne	b321	Garden near Swndwfr	Arable
Evans John	b43	House and Garden	Homestead
Wynne Margaret	b21	House and Garden	Homestead
Williams John	b27	House and Garden	do
Foulkes Thomas			
Blackwell Robert	b28	Croft	Arable
Joynson Joseph	b38	Public house yard & Cyatch	Homestead
		Orchard	Arable
	b112	Little field and road	Pasture & road
		Cae crwn	do

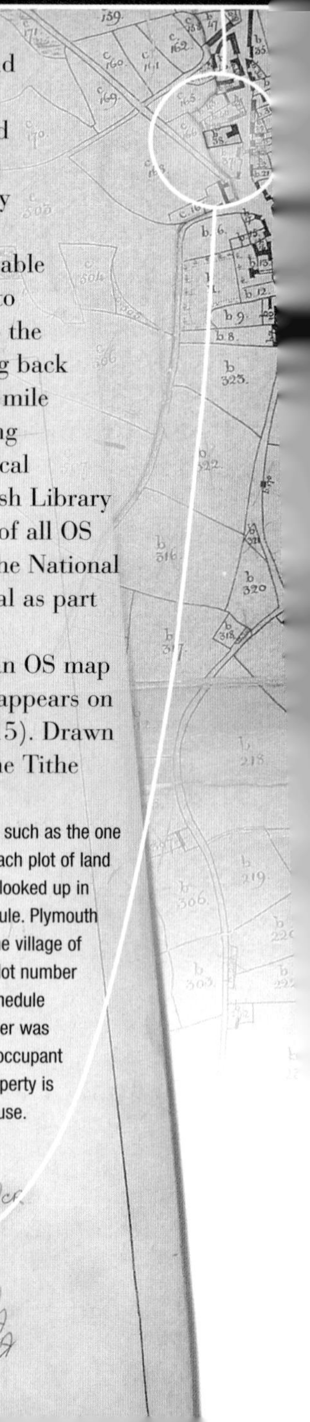

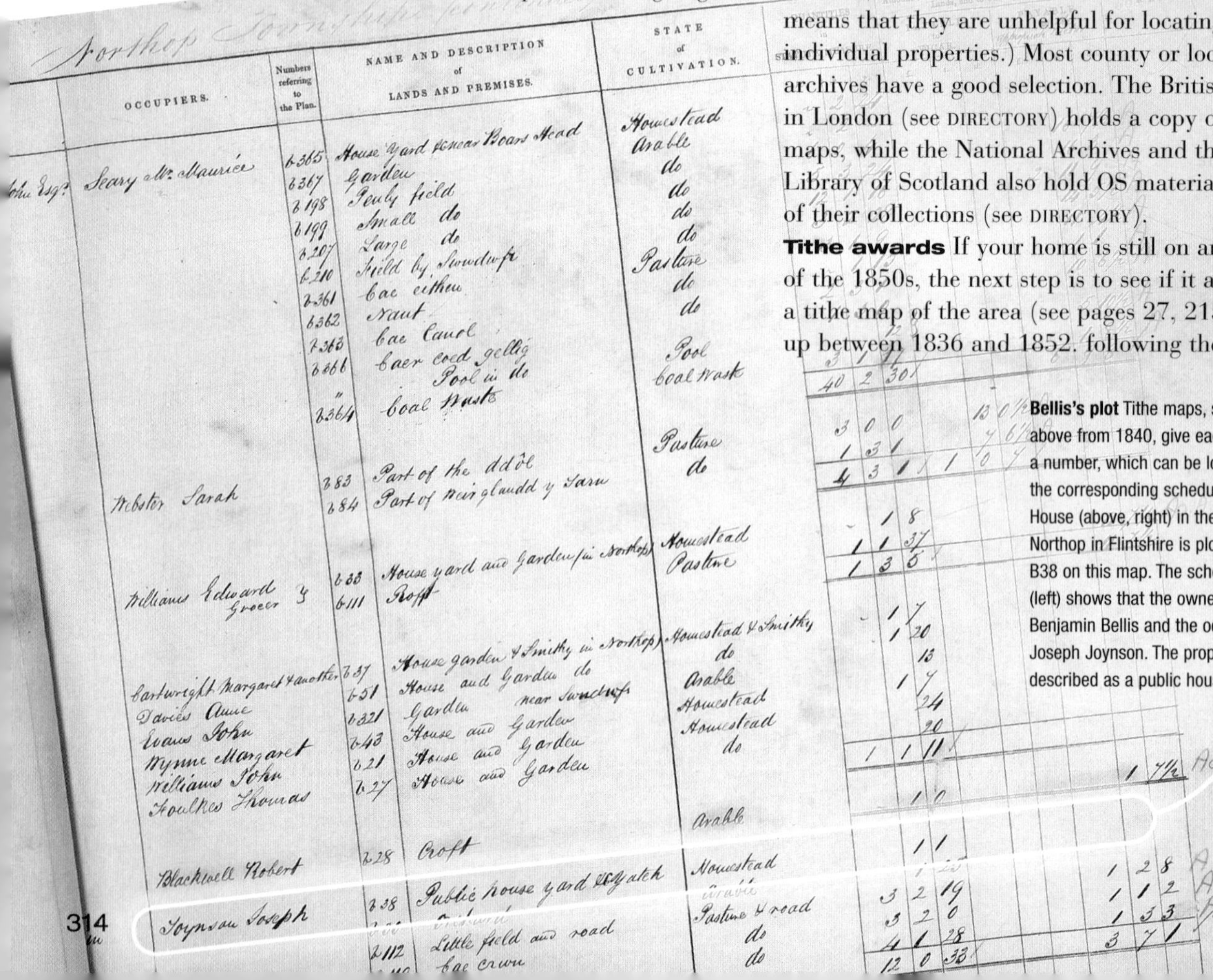

Bellis's plot Tithe maps, such as the one above from 1840, give each plot of land a number, which can be looked up in the corresponding schedule. Plymouth House (above, right) in the village of Northop in Flintshire is plot number B38 on this map. The schedule (left) shows that the owner was Benjamin Bellis and the occupant Joseph Joynson. The property is described as a public house.

Past life as a pub Tithe records and trade directories from the 19th century reveal that Plymouth House in Northop, Flintshire, was a public house called the Yacht Inn, providing accommodation for travellers on the Chester to Holyrood coach route.

Commutation Act of 1836, tithe maps and schedules detail each parcel of land, house and outbuilding within more than 11,000 parishes in England and Wales. If your home was built after 1836, a tithe map can also show who owned the land and how it was worked previously.

Three sets of maps and schedules were made, with one set deposited at the National Archives (see DIRECTORY) and other copies usually sent to the relevant county record office. The National Library of Wales (see DIRECTORY) also has an extensive collection of tithe documents.

Enclosure maps These maps can take you back even further. From 1750 to around 1850, numerous Acts of Parliament authorised the enclosure of open-fields and common land into smaller rectangular fields (see page 62). The enclosure awards (see pages 27, 215) incorporate a map and index book or schedule where you can identify who owned your property or the land on which it would later be built. These records are deposited at the National Archives (see DIRECTORY) or in local record offices.

Now for some lateral thinking

After tracing your home on the various maps, you may be left with a gap in its history due to incomplete records. For example, your home may appear on OS maps for the

FIND OUT MORE

• www.historicaldirectories.org An on-line library of local and trade directories for England and Wales (1750-1919).
• www.nls.uk/digitallibrary/map/townplans/ An on-line collection of Victorian Scottish town plans.
• www.old-maps.co.uk An on-line collection of late 19th-century OS maps, searchable by county, place name or grid reference.

1890s, but not on a map of 1870. Now you need to think of ways to narrow down your search.

Census records The Victorians carried out a census every ten years (see pages 218-219), listing every household and its occupants. These records will narrow your search to within ten years. Using the example above, you would look up the 1871, 1881 and 1891 census records. If your home is not in the census for 1871 or 1881 but appears in the 1891 census, then you can deduce that it was built between 1881 and 1891.

Directories As a final way of pinpointing the date your home was built you can use old local directories (see page 217). From the later 19th century most local directories list house numbers and street names. In the above example you would need to look at directories between 1881 and 1891. This should give you the year of construction.

Health and sanitation records

The work carried out to improve living standards in the Victorian era generated plenty of records in which your home may be listed (see pages 258-259). In London the Metropolitan Board of Works was set up in 1855 to build a network of sewers and install paving and lighting. It even assigned road names and numbers to individual properties. The records of the Metropolitan Board of Works are held at the London Metropolitan Archives (see DIRECTORY). You will find similar resources for other cities and towns in your local record office.

OTHER USEFUL SOURCES OF INFORMATION
Estate papers If your house was part of an estate you may find these records of interest. They often contain maps and written surveys of properties, as well as correspondence, leases and rentals. See page 329.
Old photographs Use these to see what your house once looked like. See pages 212-213.

For sale notices Old local newspapers can reveal gems of information about a home. The advertisement above for Cliff House, in Cullercoats, Northumberland, appeared in the *Shields Daily News* in 1868. It gives an illuminating room-by-room description of the house, even down to its 'spacious wine, beer and coal cellars'. Newspaper clippings can be found at local archives (see pages 216-217).

Victorian interior clues

The Victorians liked to adorn their houses with ironmongery, ceramics and woodwork. These fittings, including tiles, dado rails, ceiling roses and doorknobs, were mass-produced and so affordable to all. They followed the fashion, so the smallest surviving feature in your home can help to pinpoint its age, and even give an insight into the tastes and aspirations of owners long ago.

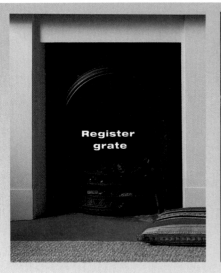

Register grate

Tile surrounds

Brass finger-plate and door knob

Four-panelled door

Fireplaces

If your house is Victorian, it is likely to have cast-iron fireplaces. The drawing room – the place for entertaining – would have had the most impressive arrangement, with surrounds of black or grey slate, veined or painted marbles, or painted tiles. The bedrooms had smaller, simpler hearths. Fireplace technology evolved during the 19th century and you can tell whether a fireplace is early, mid or late Victorian from the style of the grate.

• **Cast-iron hob grate** Early Victorian fireplaces had square or rectangular openings and the decoration was restrained, with classical motifs.
• **Cast-iron register grate** This type of fireplace, with an arched top, was introduced in about 1850. The grate had a moveable iron plate to adjust the flue.
• **Straight-topped register grate** In the 1870s and 1880s fireplaces went back to having square openings and cast-iron surrounds. But they featured splayed sides, or 'cheeks', bearing tiles that would reflect heat into the room. The ceramic tiles were highly decorative, showing stylised flowers and animals.

Windows

Victorian houses were built with large-paned sash windows. You may also come across panels of stained glass in fanlights, front doors and landings. Typical motifs were floral, geometric or medieval, such as the fleurs-de-lys.

Interior shutters These were popular in the 19th century because the Victorians were concerned about the damaging effects on sunlight on their furniture.

Fixtures

The Victorians embellished their homes with brass fittings, leaded lights and mouldings. The amount of decoration reflected the importance of the room, with more elaborate designs in rooms used for entertaining.

• **Doors** In the 1960s internal doors were often covered over to create a more modern look. Look beneath the plywood to see if an original four-panelled Victorian door survives.
• **Fingerplates** These were brass, and screwed to doors above the knob to stop the paintwork getting dirty. Early Victorian fingerplates were plain, but as the century progressed they became more ornate. After the 1850s there were Japanese-style and mock-rococo fingerplates.
• **Door knobs** These have often been replaced many times, but you may still find Victorian doorknobs made of brass, bronze or porcelain.

Floors

The Victorians continued the Georgian practice of showcasing the parts of the house where visitors would be received (see pages 320-321). A tiled hallway is a strong indication that your home dates from the Victorian era.

Tiled floors From the 1850s through to the end of the Edwardian era, there was a vogue for encaustic tiles – coloured tiles in geometric shapes which were laid in intricate mosaic patterns. These tiles often survive because they are so hardy and practical. Common colours were reds, browns and buffs, with the occasional green, blue or white tile thrown in for relief. Tiles were only ever laid in the front hallway, so if you see a mosaic kitchen floor in a late Victorian house it can only be a modern attempt to introduce period flavour into the kitchen.

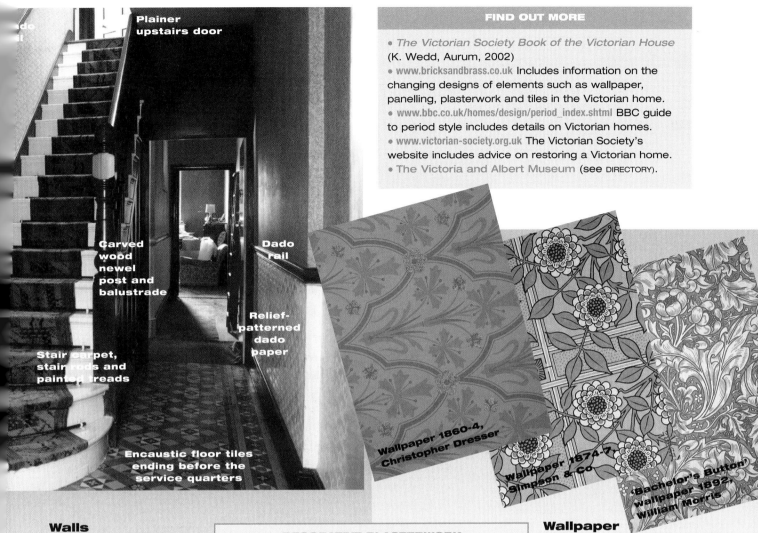

Plainer upstairs door

Carved wood newel post and balustrade

Dado rail

Relief-patterned dado paper

Stair carpet, stair rods and painted treads

Encaustic floor tiles ending before the service quarters

Wallpaper 1860-4, Christopher Dresser

Wallpaper 1874-7, Simpson & Co

'Bachelor's Button' wallpaper 1892, William Morris

FIND OUT MORE

• *The Victorian Society Book of the Victorian House* (K. Wedd, Aurum, 2002)
• www.bricksandbrass.co.uk Includes information on the changing designs of elements such as wallpaper, panelling, plasterwork and tiles in the Victorian home.
• www.bbc.co.uk/homes/design/period_index.shtml BBC guide to period style includes details on Victorian homes.
• www.victorian-society.org.uk The Victorian Society's website includes advice on restoring a Victorian home.
• The Victoria and Albert Museum (see DIRECTORY).

Walls

A wooden rail fixed to the wall at about waist height (a dado rail) was a universal feature. Below the rail the wall was panelled or, in halls and passageways, tiled so that it could be easily washed. A cheap alternative was a relief-patterned paper such as Lincrusta (from 1877) or Anaglypta (from 1887) – mixtures of wood pulp, linseed oil, gums, resin and wax. They were so hard wearing that many survive. The space above the dado – the field – was then free to be decorated with wallpaper. Dado rails (and picture rails) became less common in dining and drawing rooms from the 1890s and were often removed in the 20th century. But when you strip a wall in a Victorian house you can usually see the old scars in the plaster where the rails used to be.

DECORATIVE PLASTERWORK

Ready-made decorative plasterwork for walls and ceilings proliferated in the Victorian period, such as the ceiling rose, a circular feature from which a chandelier or a crystal lantern would hang. Handmade plaster or timber ceiling roses (see a selection of designs below from the 1830s) were typical of the early Victorian period. They used naturalistic designs and were more delicate and flatter than later counterparts.

Intricately detailed garlands of oakleaves began to appear on ceilings and cornices in the 1850s. Sculpted ceilings, painted salmon pink and pale green, were common in the 1860s. The mouldings became increasingly bulky and more ornate and stretched across the whole ceiling with plaster ribs or vaulting in Gothic revival styles.

Factory-made cardboard ceiling roses date from the 1880s. These were much simpler in style with little floral embellishment. Such roses survive in many late Victorian houses, where, despite bright electric light, they can still easily be mistaken for plaster versions.

Wallpaper

Check inside cupboards and behind plasterwork and you may find some original Victorian wallpaper. From the 1830s patterned fabrics became widely available, and cheap mass-produced papers were used in every room in every home by the 1870s. Wallpaper borders and friezes were also common.

• **Moiré wallpaper** A wall covering popular in early Victorian times that imitated textiles or panelling and featured sprig and trellis designs. It was a style hangover from the Georgian period.
• **Strong geometric patterns** Inspired by the Gothic Revival of the mid-Victorian period, wallpaper was produced in rich colours such as dark greens and burgundy. The patterns were elaborate, often flock or velvet-textured. Christopher Dresser was one of the most popular designers.
• **Detailed naturalistic plant-inspired designs** Willow and acanthus leaves were popular in the late Victorian period. William Morris-style flowers or large dahlias and hydrangeas were typical.
• **Embossed wallpapers** At the end of the Victorian era, wallpapers began to imitate moulded plaster, wainscot, carved wood and stamped leather.

Taking the story back to the 18th century

The 18th century was a time of increasing commercial prosperity, as trade links developed across the world. The newly rich poured their wealth into impressive homes. Towns such as Bath, Bristol and Newcastle underwent large-scale redevelopment during the Georgian period, and many of the houses are still standing. Outside the towns, grand houses were built in country estates, some of which have since been converted into flats. If you live in a town house, flat or more modest Georgian building, there is much you can discover about its history.

Georgian property deeds

In the early years of the 18th century several local deed registries were established by Acts of Parliament. They were the forerunners of the national Land Registry established in 1862. The local registries enabled people to record property transactions, although the records created were not deeds as such, merely the memorial of when and how a property changed hands. The registries are an important resource, as they allow you to trace the history of houses for which original title deeds no longer survive (see page 310). The parts of England covered by these local registries are London and Middlesex, the 'Bedford level' (including Bedfordshire and extending across neighbouring counties), as well as the North, East and West Ridings of Yorkshire.

Further deed registration took place in many of the central English courts, often by way of a fictitious lawsuit. The buyer – in full knowledge of the landowner – would come up with some reason why the landowner should be removed from his land and then take him to court. The dispute would inevitably be 'settled out of court', but it would leave an official record of a property transaction. The documents can tell you the names of owners and the dates the property changed hands.

Where to find the records The National Archives (see DIRECTORY) holds a variety of property records, including title deeds. You will also find title deeds and court records (quarter sessions) in local or county record offices.

Property registration in Scotland Scotland operated a different system of property registration. Transfers and mortgages of property were carried out by a deed called an Instrument of Sasine. After 1617 copies of the records have been kept in a central Register of Sasines. From 1783, detailed summaries of the documents, known as abridgements, were created. They are arranged by county and year. These, and name indexes, will speed up your search and can be viewed at the National Archives of Scotland (see DIRECTORY).

Estate records

Many town or country estates were built during the Georgian and Regency periods. Some of the estates were so large that they included whole villages (see

Scottish sasine Property transfers after 1617 in Scotland were recorded in the Register of Sasines. Summaries of these documents are fully indexed by place and partly by name.

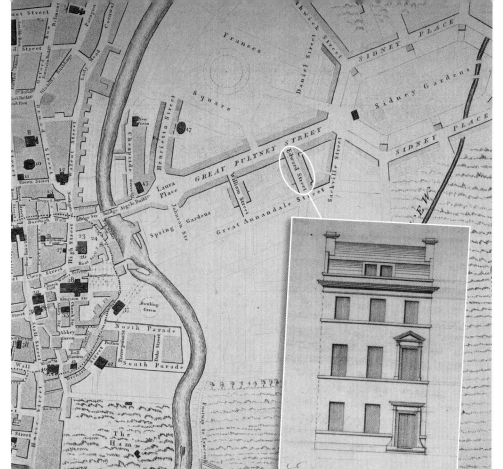

Bath estate records Landowners' estate papers can tell you much about urban properties built during the speculative housing boom in the Georgian period. The detailed 1799 estate plan (left) shows the position of Edward Street, where the terraced house (inset) was built during the development of Bath to the east of the River Avon.

See you in court

One underused but rich source for 18th-century property history is equity court records (see page 331). Many people contested property inheritance, and brought civil actions to court. Sometimes the cases dragged on for years, and generated piles of documents that reveal details about house occupancy, ownership and even construction. Sometimes the papers include details of furniture and other possessions.

The two main equity courts active during the 18th century were those of Chancery and Exchequer. Equity court records include:
- bills of complaint filed by the plaintiff
- answers from the defendants
- decrees and orders made by the judges
- depositions supplied by witnesses
- evidence supporting rival cases.

Supporting documents were also archived, so you may find title deeds, property plans, marriage settlements and building contracts among the records.

Where to find the records Equity court records are stored at the National Archives (see DIRECTORY).

pages 112-113). If your house was part of such an estate you will need to locate the estate papers. The following records may turn up in estate papers (see page 113) and can help you to build up a picture of how and when your house was designed and who commissioned the work.

Estate records will also give you the names of the first owners or tenants, and how much it cost to build the property or rent it from the owners. Records include:
- architects' plans and drawings
- building leases and contracts
- tenancy agreements
- schedules of rent and payments
- stewards' accounts
- penalties for non-maintenance of property
- accounts for repairs and improvements
- estate maps.

Where to find the records Since estate papers and accounts are private property you are only likely to see them if they have been deposited in a local archive or county record office.

Georgian interior clues

The guiding principles of interior design in the Georgian period were symmetry and proportion, combined with a desire to display wealth and status. Money and attention were lavished on the rooms used by guests, most on the ground floor. You are likely to find the fireplaces, the plaster cornices, even the architrave around the doors to be more elaborate in these rooms than in the upper rooms or basement – the domain of children and servants.

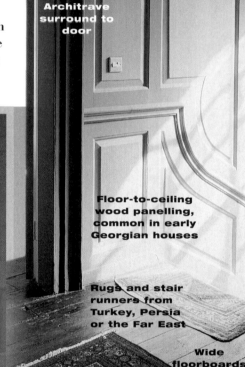

Chandelier, originally lit using candles

Architrave surround to door

Carved mahogany first-floor balustrade

Floor-to-ceiling wood panelling, common in early Georgian houses

Rugs and stair runners from Turkey, Persia or the Far East

Wide floorboards

Mid-Georgian fireplace

Simple Georgian upper room fireplace

Fireplaces

The Georgian period extends over more than 100 years, but by looking at the fireplaces you can date a home to within a few decades. The grandest houses had white marble surrounds with inlays of coloured marble. The less well off made do with 'scagliola' – plaster mixed with marble chips and polished to resemble the real thing. These faux-marble fittings were light and easy to install.

Over the years many Georgian fireplaces, particularly the grandest marble examples, will have been ripped out and sold, often replaced with a more modern imitation. The fireplaces that are more likely to have survived are the simple, functional surrounds on an upper floor that was not used for entertaining.

• **Early Georgian** Palladian-style fireplaces were popular from around 1714 to 1760. These featured columns, swags, scrolls and shells. The mantelpieces were narrow and supported by brackets or pairs of carved figures. The grates began as free-standing wrought-iron baskets. But these were soon eclipsed by cast-iron 'hob grates'. The flat-topped hobs, on which pots and kettles were kept warm, were introduced in the 1720s and widespread by 1780.

• **Mid Georgian** The Neo-Classical period (from 1750) favoured more delicate designs, using figures from Greek mythology and other Classical motifs. Delftware imitation fireplace tiles were popular by 1750.

• **Regency** Late Georgian fireplaces were simpler than their predecessors, with few adornments and decoration.

Floors

The type of flooring indicated the homeowner's affluence. If you have a floor made of wide planks of English oak – more than 30cm (12in) wide and fitted tightly with tongue-and-groove joints – you can assume the Georgian homeowner was fairly wealthy. Many people saved money by using pine or fir wood, imported in vast quantities from Scandinavia and around the Baltic. These floors were nailed down in narrower planks (oak trees are thicker than pine) and scrubbed with lime and sand until they shone. Boards became increasingly narrow over time, down to 20cm (10in), and more uniform in width as machines for planing timber were introduced. Floorboards were made to be seen, with rugs placed in the centre of rooms. Wilton carpets date from 1655, but it was not until the mid to late 18th century that fitted carpets came into fashion.

Ceilings

The Georgians applied decorative mouldings to their ceilings in abundance. The mouldings were originally made from wood – by 1720 plaster was also used.

• **Early Georgian** Early 18th-century designs followed Classical styles and were large and chunky, such as the egg-and-dart moulding – alternating egg and dart-shaped figures – often seen on cornices.
• **Mid Georgian** Mouldings became progressively more subtle with a lower profile and the details were Classically inspired.
• **Regency** By the end of the 18th century mouldings were light and simple. Bead moulding was popular, and known as 'reeding', where several beads were linked together to mimic the ornamentation on Classical columns. Look for reeding on cornices, fireplaces, door surrounds, dados and skirting.

FIND OUT MORE

• **The Georgian Group** Charity dedicated to preserving Georgian buildings and gardens. www.georgiangroup.org.uk
• *The Georgian Group Book of the Georgian House* (S. Parissien, Aurum, 1995)
• *Georgian House Style* (I. Cranfield, David & Charles, 2001)

Classical wallpaper 1769

Georgian dining room interior

Chinoiserie wallpaper 1740

Wallpaper

It is possible to find a scrap of Georgian wallpaper in the back of a fitted cupboard, underneath newer layers of plaster, or behind a patch of skirting board. Wallpaper was a luxury item until the production process was mechanised in the Victorian era, and Georgian patterns were as flamboyant as a peacock's tail. The common themes included Grecian pillars and arches (above, top), Classical motifs featuring urns, swags and niches, and Chinese birds and fishes (reflecting the fashion for chinoiserie – above, bottom). Flock wallpaper was also the height of fashion.

Walls

Wood panelling to the full height of the room was fashionable until the 1740s. After that point, panelling stopped at the dado rail and the walls above would be papered or painted. Common colour schemes were sage green, blue grey or oxblood red. The wooden panels were usually made from cheap pine rather than pricey oak. There was no point in using expensive wood because panelling was never left bare. Pine panels were painted in colours to mimic more prestigious woods such as mahogany or cedar. Panelling was often removed in later years, and usually leaves little trace.

Doors

The ground and first floor rooms of early 18th-century town houses often had mahogany double panelled doors. They gave an impression of space and light, and lent the rooms an air of grandeur. The number of panels in doors varied. Six was the norm on early Georgian doors; by the end of the period two or three-panel doors were common.

• **Doorframes** Compare the mouldings on the doorframes of rooms upstairs to those in the main reception rooms and you may find that they are different. The entrance to an upper room might be as plain and rectilinear as a matchbox, while the lower doorway is framed in an elaborate moulding made up of ovolos (convex shapes), fillets (flat surfaces) and beads (cylindrical shapes). In the grandest houses the doorframes to the best rooms resemble the porticos of Greek temples with Classical pediments and architrave mouldings displaying Classical motifs such as ancathus leaves, shells and scrolling foliage.
• **Glazing** Internal doors were sometimes glazed – usually with four or six panes in the upper half of the door.
• **Door furniture** Rooms reserved for entertaining might have brass or bronze fittings, with glass, ebony and white china also used for door handles. Elsewhere handles and hinges were usually made of cast iron painted black.

TIPS ON DATING WALLPAPER

• Blue wallpapers date from the first half of the 18th century as an embargo to protect the indigo-dying trade prevented the use of any other colours.
• The quality of Georgian handblocked wallpaper is a clue to its age. The paper is thick and is watermarked. It may even have a tax stamp on the back.

Following the story of a home back to its earliest days

Most simple early medieval homes have disappeared because the organic materials used to build them have perished, but many later timber-framed houses have survived. You may find that an apparently Georgian or Victorian building hides an older core or that your home was once part of a larger structure now demolished. Even if your home is modern, it can be intriguing to find out what was once on the site it now occupies.

Mapped out Landowners sometimes created detailed maps of their estates to keep track of tenants. The 1665 estate map of Bidston, Cheshire (above), includes the church, a useful marker for surrounding buildings.

Manorial records

Whether you live in a medieval structure or just want to know what the landscape around your home looked like in medieval times, your first port of call should be manorial records. These go back to the introduction of the feudal system to England and Wales in the 11th century. Under this system the basic unit of land was called a manor (see pages 146–147). The lord of the manor leased property to individuals in return for a service or money. The transaction was recorded in the manor court roll and copies of the entry were handed to each new tenant, or 'copyholder'. Copyholders had to seek the approval of the lord before they sold, inherited or mortgaged their property and this, too, was recorded in court rolls. Bear in mind that up to around 1733 the documents were written in Latin (see pages 22–23). Most archives have Latin dictionaries and guides to help you with interpretation.

The Manorial Register at the National Archives (see DIRECTORY) lists the manors of a particular parish. It will tell you what manorial records survive for your area.

What the court rolls tell you Surviving court rolls, dating from the 1230s, describe the property in some detail and name previous occupants. By the 17th century place name indexes start to appear more frequently and can help you to track property occupancy quickly. If you find the name or a description of your home in the court rolls, you can work backwards and forwards among surviving rolls to compile a list of tenants.

Estate maps and surveys Often the lord of the manor made maps of his estate, cross-referenced to survey books, to keep track of who rented which property. Owners also made lists of tenants and freeholders in their manor. The maps (see page 27) can show you the position of your home (or its absence) within the manor and whether the house was part of a larger property that has since been demolished.

Where to find manorial records The National Archives (see DIRECTORY) has a wide collection of court rolls, estate maps and surveys, although most are stored in county record offices. Some manorial records are available from the internet (see 'Find out more' box).

Dividing up the manor

When the lord of the manor died an 'inquisition post mortem' would take place to identify what lands were held and who should succeed to them. Local residents were asked to provide information on property held by the deceased, including houses, tenements or cottages. Inquisitions post mortem can also provide information (called an assignment of dower) about what part of an estate had been set aside for the lord's widow. In many cases specific rooms are mentioned and listed. These documents can be found at the National Archives (see DIRECTORY) as well as at local record offices.

Old timers Black-and-white, half-timbered houses are typical of Montgomeryshire. The style indicates that they were built between the 15th and 17th century.

Medieval interior clues

Most medieval houses will have undergone considerable structural and cosmetic changes over the years, but you can sometimes find clues to their original structure and design, especially in attics and cellars.

Changes in floor level Check if part of the house is lower at one end: this may indicate that it was originally a medieval longhouse, where animals were kept in a byre. The byre was on a lower level to prevent animal slurry from seeping into the living quarters.

Examine the rafters The heavier the timbers, the older the house is likely to be. Also note the type of wood: oak was the most common material until the late 17th century. If there is a complex skeleton of rafters they may have been the original structure of a medieval timber-framed house. Look out for blackened timbers: these indicate the house was an old medieval hall with a central, open hearth.

Check for old beams

Many early beams were hidden during the 18th and 19th centuries behind false lowered ceilings, or were cased in plaster cornices. If you can get access to beams, look for chamfering on the outer corners (left) which was pronounced in the 16th century and before but became more subtle over time.

Medieval signs The fine mullioned window on the right is medieval. It has original bars but no shutters. Also look out for chamfered beams (below left) where a large amount of the edge has been cut away. These were a common embellishment in medieval houses.

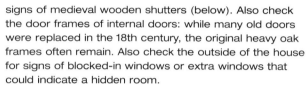

Filled-in doors and windows Examine any recesses in walls and cracks in the plaster that may indicate former windows and doors (right). Check the windows for signs of medieval wooden shutters (below). Also check the door frames of internal doors: while many old doors were replaced in the 18th century, the original heavy oak frames often remain. Also check the outside of the house for signs of blocked-in windows or extra windows that could indicate a hidden room.

Fixtures and fittings
Look for clues around windows and doors. Slots and holes on the original heavy exterior oak beam of a window (right) show where wooden shutters were once attached.

A licence to trade

Medieval housing in urban areas tended to combine a place of trade or shop with a dwelling area above. You might find information in title deeds, leases, records of boroughs and corporations, or even in the records of local courts if shopholders breached the numerous regulations about what they could sell. Most buildings required licences before they could be used for trade, so look for applications in local sources such as quarter session records, which are held at county records offices. The owners of alehouses or taverns had to apply to the local magistrates for bonds guaranteeing good behaviour.

FIND OUT MORE

- *Manorial Records* (D. Stuart, Phillimore, 1992)
- www.mdr.nationalarchives.gov.uk/mdr/ An on-line catalogue of manorial records covering Hampshire, Norfolk, Surrey, Middlesex, Yorkshire and Wales.
- www.catalogue.nationalarchives.gov.uk/ Rdleaflet.asp?sLeafletID=226 On-line guide to pre-1689 taxation records held at the National Archives.

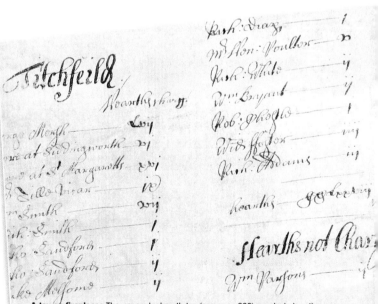

A tax on fireplaces The unpopular hearth tax (see page 330) was levied on the number of hearths in a property. The tax returns list the liable houses in each parish and the name of the owner. The one above of around 1665 is for Titchfield, Hampshire. Comparing hearth tax returns with manorial records can help you to establish the rough size of a property and its owner's means. Wealthier people could afford more hearths.

Through the keyhole: looking at previous owners' possessions

If your house is more than a century old, you might have trouble envisaging how it was furnished. Wills and probate inventories can help tremendously here. They list previous owners' possessions and can help you to picture how the rooms once looked based on objects that were actually there.

Where there's a will...

In 1540 the Statute of Wills allowed property to be given to a person of a man's choosing (and not automatically to his heir). But wills tell you more than simply who owned or inherited your home. They often contain specific instructions about the disposal of household possessions, clothing and heirlooms.

Worldly goods A will may be accompanied by a probate inventory itemising all the deceased's possessions complete with valuations. These lists were made to assist the executors of a will in carrying out final bequests, and to protect them against claims of fraud. From 1530 to 1750 many probate courts required inventories, but later they were not mandatory. So you are less likely to find a probate inventory for someone who died in the 19th or 20th centuries, although inventories were sometimes made to avoid disputes among relatives. If you are lucky enough to find a probate inventory for a previous owner of your home, you may be able to deduce how the house was furnished since many inventories list goods room by room.

Finding names of previous owners Before you start looking for a particular property in a will, you need the names of previous owners. You can find these out using census records (see pages 218-219), title deeds (see pages 302, 310, 318, 329) or rate books (see page 327). You can then start to look for the death of the owner in parish records or in civil records held at the Family Records Centre (see DIRECTORY), and check to see if a will was left.

Where to find wills

A will may be held in local archives or personal papers, but should also be registered with the court that had responsibility for 'proving' its authenticity.

Before 1858

- Wills were registered with the church courts (the main ones being the Prerogative Courts of Canterbury and the Prerogative Courts of York).

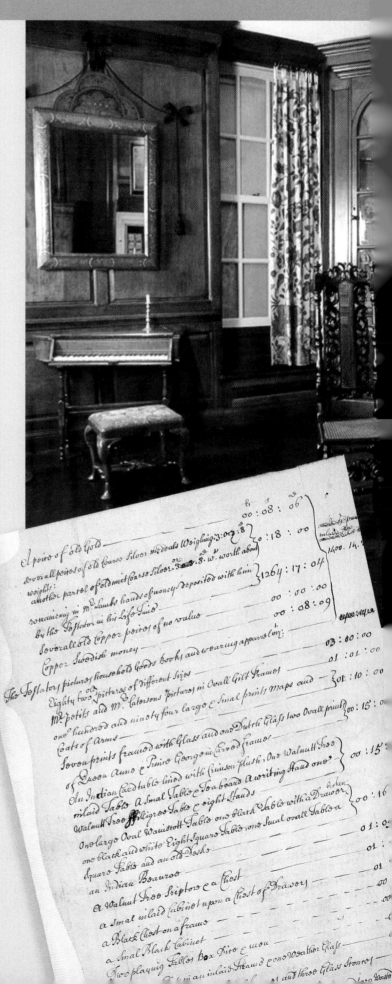

Designs of the day The National Archives (see DIRECTORY) holds collections of registered designs for a huge array of domestic items, ranging from wallpaper samples to drawings and photographs of furniture, lamps and household appliances. They will help you to picture any items listed in an inventory. So if you wanted to find out about fixtures from 1868, for example, you would need to look through the registered designs for that year.

- Records of the Prerogative Courts of Canterbury (for southern England and Wales) are held at the National Archives (see DIRECTORY).
- Records of the Prerogative Courts of York (for northern England) are held at the Borthwick Institute, York (see DIRECTORY).
- Local record offices and probate registries also hold probate information.

After 1858
- English and Welsh wills were registered at the Court of Probate, later the Principal Registry, London (see DIRECTORY). You can order copies of wills from the registry or arrange a visit in person.
- A detailed index to wills – the National Probate Calendar – is available at the National Archives, Family Records Centre and the Guildhall Library (see DIRECTORY).

Scotland

Until 1868 land and buildings were inherited by the eldest son alone. Personal property could be left in a 'testamentary dispensation'. The National Archives of Scotland (see DIRECTORY) is the best place to start researching bequests.

In case of fire

Fire insurance records can provide a list of household items that would have been insured against loss. They survive from the 17th century onwards, although only in large numbers from the 18th and 19th centuries. The records are not easy to use without a policy number, but if you have a fire mark on the outside of your home – placed there to alert the insurance company's fire brigade that the householder was insured – the policy number should be inscribed on it.

Where to find fire insurance records The records are usually held in local archives. The City of Westminster Archives (see DIRECTORY, under 'London boroughs') has a particularly fine collection for London companies.

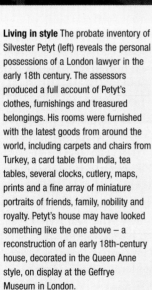

Living in style The probate inventory of Silvester Petyt (left) reveals the personal possessions of a London lawyer in the early 18th century. The assessors produced a full account of Petyt's clothes, furnishings and treasured belongings. His rooms were furnished with the latest goods from around the world, including carpets and chairs from Turkey, a card table from India, tea tables, several clocks, cutlery, maps, prints and a fine array of miniature portraits of friends, family, nobility and royalty. Petyt's house may have looked something like the one above – a reconstruction of an early 18th-century house, decorated in the Queen Anne style, on display at the Geffrye Museum in London.

FIND OUT MORE

• Geffrye Museum The museum, sited within a set of 18th-century almshouses in Shoreditch, London, shows the changing style of English domestic interiors from 1600 to the present day. Reconstructed period rooms contain collections of furniture, textiles, paintings and decorative arts. www.geffrye-museum.org.uk

• *Probate jurisdictions: where to look for wills* (ed. J. Gibson and B. Langston, 5th ed., FFHS, 1995)

• *Prerogative Court of Canterbury wills and other probate records* (M. Scott, National Archives, 1997)

• *Index to the Probate Accounts of England and Wales* (ed. P. Spufford, London, British Record Society, 1999)

• www.nationalarchives.gov.uk/househistory/guide/probate.htm National Archives leaflet on where to find probate records.

• www.documentsonline.nationalarchives.gov.uk/wills.asp Information about using the records of the Prerogative Courts of Canterbury.

• www.scottishdocuments.com Advanced search option allows you to search for Scottish wills by name, court and place.

Who lived where you live in the Victorian period?

Thanks to census records you can discover more about Victorian inhabitants than those at any other time. The first census took place in 1801 and from then on was carried out every ten years. The earliest censuses were intended merely as population counts but from 1841 the returns include names, addresses, ages and occupations, and from 1851, relationships and places of birth, too.

Census returns

If you want to find out about the people who lived in your home from the mid to late 19th century, the first place to look is the census returns that were taken every ten years throughout the 19th century (see pages 218-219 for more details).

- The 1841 census is the first where you can discover who were the occupants of homes. It also includes an indication (within five years) of their ages, as well as providing information on occupations, and house and street names.

- From 1851 census records are more useful as they include greater detail on each inhabitant, such as a full name, marital status, exact age, relationship to the head of the household and place of birth.

- The 1901 census (see page 218) is available on-line, with a facility to search by property.

Note that because of the personal nature of the content, census returns for England, Wales and Scotland are closed to the public for 100 years. The 1901 census is the most recent record available. When using census returns it is best to start with the most recent records and then work backwards in time.

Life downstairs If your home is a large Victorian house a variety of servants may have lived there, cooking, cleaning amd minding children for the family upstairs.

> **TIP FOR USING THE 1901 CENSUS**
> In the 1901 returns your house may have had a different street number, or it may have had a name instead of a number. If so, you might be able to locate the property by comparing the occupants in the street or neighbourhood with other records, such as rate books (see page 327), the 1910 Valuation Office Survey (see page 310) or old directories (see pages 217, 315). This will help you to fill in the gaps.

How did previous occupants earn their living?

Census returns from 1841 onwards list occupations, and so you can start to build a picture of the type of people who lived in your home during the 19th century, and how the use of the house and status of the area changed over time. If you found that the people living in your property were associated with a particular trade, you could then start to search for employment documents (often in local archives) such as factory staff ledgers, trade union membership, pay books and disciplinary committees (see pages 240-241). Remember that as most businesses were privately owned, there is no guarantee that records will survive. Another source worth checking is a museum dedicated to the particular trade or industry.

Crowded homes You may be surprised at the number of people living in your house at the same time. In the 19th century many properties were the homes of extended families, with in-laws and grandparents all

Designs of the day The National Archives (see DIRECTORY) holds collections of registered designs for a huge array of domestic items, ranging from wallpaper samples to drawings and photographs of furniture, lamps and household appliances. They will help you to picture any items listed in an inventory. So if you wanted to find out about fixtures from 1868, for example, you would need to look through the registered designs for that year.

- Records of the Prerogative Courts of Canterbury (for southern England and Wales) are held at the National Archives (see DIRECTORY).
- Records of the Prerogative Courts of York (for northern England) are held at the Borthwick Institute, York (see DIRECTORY).
- Local record offices and probate registries also hold probate information.

After 1858
- English and Welsh wills were registered at the Court of Probate, later the Principal Registry, London (see DIRECTORY). You can order copies of wills from the registry or arrange a visit in person.
- A detailed index to wills – the National Probate Calendar – is available at the National Archives, Family Records Centre and the Guildhall Library (see DIRECTORY).

Scotland
Until 1868 land and buildings were inherited by the eldest son alone. Personal property could be left in a 'testamentary dispensation'. The National Archives of Scotland (see DIRECTORY) is the best place to start researching bequests.

In case of fire
Fire insurance records can provide a list of household items that would have been insured against loss. They survive from the 17th century onwards, although only in large numbers from the 18th and 19th centuries. The records are not easy to use without a policy number, but if you have a fire mark on the outside of your home – placed there to alert the insurance company's fire brigade that the householder was insured – the policy number should be inscribed on it.

Where to find fire insurance records The records are usually held in local archives. The City of Westminster Archives (see DIRECTORY, under 'London boroughs') has a particularly fine collection for London companies.

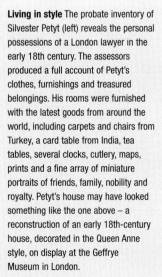

Living in style The probate inventory of Silvester Petyt (left) reveals the personal possessions of a London lawyer in the early 18th century. The assessors produced a full account of Petyt's clothes, furnishings and treasured belongings. His rooms were furnished with the latest goods from around the world, including carpets and chairs from Turkey, a card table from India, tea tables, several clocks, cutlery, maps, prints and a fine array of miniature portraits of friends, family, nobility and royalty. Petyt's house may have looked something like the one above – a reconstruction of an early 18th-century house, decorated in the Queen Anne style, on display at the Geffrye Museum in London.

Who lived where you live over the past 100 years?

There is more to tracing the history of your home than simply finding out how old the property is – you can put its history into context by digging up some information about the people who used to live there before you did. Find out about the lives they led and where they came from and you can begin to see how they turned the bricks and mortar of a house into a home.

Ask the neighbours

Your first step is to undertake some local detective work. Ask your neighbours about your house, especially if they have been in the area for a number of years. If the property was built within living memory, they may even remember when it was first erected and who the first occupant was. At the least you should be able to obtain a list of names of former owners or occupants that can help you with your research.

Questions to ask Try to adopt a diplomatic approach when making enquiries. People may be suspicious of your motives at first and your questions may seem intrusive. Explain what you are trying to achieve and they will be more likely to open up. The following questions should start you off:
• What sort of people lived in the house?
• How many people lived there?
• What jobs did they do?

• What were their backgrounds?
• When did they move there?
• Where did they move to when they left?
• Are there any interesting stories and legends about the house or the people who lived there?

Local societies Try asking local history groups (see page 17) about the people who lived in your house. Many groups have collated gravestone information from local cemeteries and graveyards, which may be of use to you.

Registered to vote

Electoral lists (see pages 222-223) record the names of all residents who were eligible to vote and a description of the property. They should help you to compile a list of previous inhabitants of your home. It is best to start with the most recent records and work backwards in time, because modern lists tend to include street indexes, house numbers or names and reflect modern parliamentary boundaries, making them easier to use.

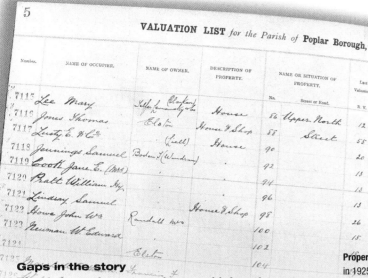

Property values The local authority rate book for Upper North Street, Poplar, London, in 1925, gives a description of the properties and the level of rate due, information that can reveal the wealth and status of the inhabitants of the houses.

Gaps in the story

Electoral records may not always yield the information you hoped for. Bear the following points in mind.

- There may be people missing from the list because they were ineligible to vote. The vote was extended to women over 30 only in 1918 and to women over 21 in 1928.
- Some people may have been registered elsewhere and so your house may not always appear in the lists. This may well be an indication that your home was once used as a commercial site or had a non-domestic use, which may require further research in other records (see pages 302–305).

Where to find the records Most main reference libraries hold current electoral lists, although you may need to go to a county record office or local studies library to track down older lists. The British Library in London (see DIRECTORY) holds an extensive collection for the 20th century. Some 19th-century Scottish electoral registers are held at the National Archives of Scotland (see DIRECTORY). The National Library of Scotland (see DIRECTORY) has 20th-century material, dating from the 1940s.

Checking title deeds

If you can obtain the title deeds of your property – usually held by your mortgage provider (see page 302) – you should be able to see the names of former owners. Remember that since 1970 title deeds need only extend back 15 years (between 1925 and 1970, they had to go back 30 years). If you know where the previous owners moved to, you might be able to track them down through phone books or other local directories. Ask them if they have any interesting stories about your house, or whether they recall the name of the people from whom they purchased the property.

Rate books

Over the last century rates were allocated based on the size of property and location. Rate books (Valuation Rolls from 1854 in Scotland) recorded the level of tax to be paid to each local authority. They often give the name of both the owner and occupier of the property, as well as the contemporary value of the house. Look for rate books in county or city archives. In 1989 (Scotland) and 1990 (England and Wales), the poll tax (later community charge) briefly replaced property rates as a way of generating revenue for local authorities. It was superseded in 1993 by the Council Tax.

Using directories

Trade directories were introduced to help people find local businesses (see pages 216–217). Publishers such as Kelly's and the Post Office added street and name indexes to their volumes as well as lists of trades, making them excellent sources for finding out who lived in your house, and what occupations they had.

Where to find the records Look for directories in local reference libraries or local and county record offices.

Names and numbers Working through a series of Post Office directories, such as this one for London dating from 1968, can help you track down who was living in your house and when they moved out.

FIND OUT MORE

- *Electoral Registers Since 1832 and Burgess Rolls* (J. Gibson and C. Rogers, FFHS, 1990)
- www.genealogysupplies.com Provides a list of county directories available on CD.

Who lived where you live in the Victorian period?

Thanks to census records you can discover more about Victorian inhabitants than those at any other time. The first census took place in 1801 and from then on was carried out every ten years. The earliest censuses were intended merely as population counts but from 1841 the returns include names, addresses, ages and occupations, and from 1851, relationships and places of birth, too.

Census returns

If you want to find out about the people who lived in your home from the mid to late 19th century, the first place to look is the census returns that were taken every ten years throughout the 19th century (see pages 218-219 for more details).

- The 1841 census is the first where you can discover who were the occupants of homes. It also includes an indication (within five years) of their ages, as well as providing information on occupations, and house and street names.
- From 1851 census records are more useful as they include greater detail on each inhabitant, such as a full name, marital status, exact age, relationship to the head of the household and place of birth.
- The 1901 census (see page 218) is available on-line, with a facility to search by property.

Note that because of the personal nature of the content, census returns for England, Wales and Scotland are closed to the public for 100 years. The 1901 census is the most recent record available. When using census returns it is best to start with the most recent records and then work backwards in time.

Life downstairs If your home is a large Victorian house a variety of servants may have lived there, cooking, cleaning amd minding children for the family upstairs.

> ### TIP FOR USING THE 1901 CENSUS
> In the 1901 returns your house may have had a different street number, or it may have had a name instead of a number. If so, you might be able to locate the property by comparing the occupants in the street or neighbourhood with other records, such as rate books (see page 327), the 1910 Valuation Office Survey (see page 310) or old directories (see pages 217, 315). This will help you to fill in the gaps.

How did previous occupants earn their living?

Census returns from 1841 onwards list occupations, and so you can start to build a picture of the type of people who lived in your home during the 19th century, and how the use of the house and status of the area changed over time. If you found that the people living in your property were associated with a particular trade, you could then start to search for employment documents (often in local archives) such as factory staff ledgers, trade union membership, pay books and disciplinary committees (see pages 240-241). Remember that as most businesses were privately owned, there is no guarantee that records will survive. Another source worth checking is a museum dedicated to the particular trade or industry.

Crowded homes You may be surprised at the number of people living in your house at the same time. In the 19th century many properties were the homes of extended families, with in-laws and grandparents all

The Vicar's household The number of live-in servants shown on a census return can be a clue to the wealth of the owners, as the 1901 return for The Vicarage in Great Yarmouth illustrates. There are five servants – a lady's maid, cook, parlour maid, house maid and kitchen maid – to administer to the small family of Francis Godolphin Pelham, his wife and daughter.

sharing the same roof as their children and grandchildren. Tenements (see page 283) and multi-storied properties often contained several families living together in shared accommodation. Higher up the class system, you might also find domestic servants, such as housemaids, cooks or, in more prosperous establishments, butlers, coachmen and governesses. These clues all provide rich detail about the former uses of your home and the status of the people who lived there.

Victorian title deeds

When the Law of Property Act was introduced in 1925, the requirement to prove ownership as far back as possible was reduced to only 30 years. Consequently, large numbers of title deeds were destroyed. But if you are lucky enough to find any at your local county record office, you will see that they often tell you more than just the names of previous owners. The status and sometimes profession of the buyer and seller are normally recorded, along with their usual address if they were not actually living in the house in question. Note the date of the sale and price paid as well as any sub-leases or loans raised against the property. Constant re-mortgaging would suggest that the owner was in need of money.

Estate papers

If your property was once part of a larger estate, you may be able to find some useful information in estate papers – usually deposited in local archives (see pages 113, 318-319). Documents may include account books, schedules, ledgers or pay books for rented houses. From such material you can learn more about the type of person who owned or lived in your property. Records relating to the management of an estate often reveal what mix of people were employed to keep things running smoothly. Although many people listed in estate rentals and surveys will simply be tenant farmers, who rented property and

land as smallholders, other specialist occupations such as estate bailiff or steward might be recorded as well. Many properties for agricultural workers or tenant farmers were built on rural estates, and improvements to the houses are often reflected in increased rents or expenditure in the accounts of the estate steward.

REGULATIONS

The stairs to be swept every morning, and washed at least twice a week by the Tenants—week about—Tenants upstairs sweeping and washing the stairs below the flat in which they reside; and the Tenants on the ground floor sweeping and washing the close, the paint work of lower walls of stairs to be washed down regularly, also lower walls of closes. The staircase windows to be cleaned regularly by the Tenants in turn.

No clothes will be allowed to be hung out at the windows to dry.

Tenants must be careful not to allow their Children to break the staircase windows, or otherwise injure the property; and to keep clean and well-aired houses; and not to give offence or annoyance to their neighbours in any way; as none but cleanly and respectable persons will be allowed to remain Tenants.

Rugs and Mats only to be beaten between the hours of 8 a.m. and 12 noon, at back of property.

Any person casting filth over the window or laying it in any other place than the ashpit will be removed from the Property at the first terms of removal. **No Dogs allowed.**

Following the rules Regulation cards issued to tenants can give an insight into their lives. An early 20th-century card (above) sets out a rigorous timetable of cleaning required, and even specifies when and where rugs may be beaten.

FIND OUT MORE

- www.bricksandbrass.co.uk/people/people.htm
A description of the daily lives of a late Victorian family living in a suburban home, describing clothes, room furnishings and daily routines.
- www.1901census.nationalarchives.gov.uk
On-line 1901 census for England and Wales (pay per view).
- www.scotlandspeople.gov.uk
On-line Scottish registers (pay per view).

Who lived where you live in Georgian days and beyond?

If your home was built in the Georgian period, or even earlier, many generations of people will have lived there before you. You can trace their names through tax records, and if they entered into a property dispute you may be able to find out much more about their personalities and the way they lived.

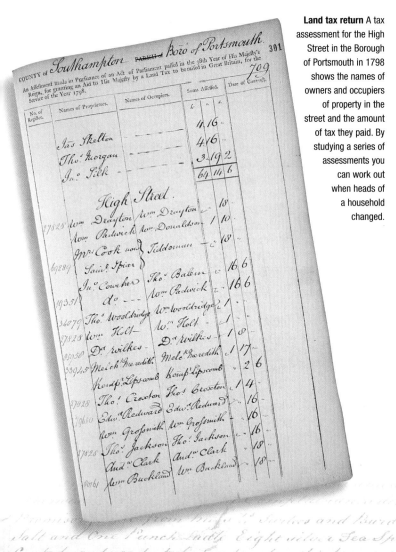

At home with the Georgians The Hoare family relax in the study of their Hampstead house around 1820. Their names may appear in a will or tax records.

Land tax return A tax assessment for the High Street in the Borough of Portsmouth in 1798 shows the names of owners and occupiers of property in the street and the amount of tax they paid. By studying a series of assessments you can work out when heads of a household changed.

Death and taxes

The two unavoidable aspects of life are good starting points when searching for names of previous owners of your home. A will can tell you what a person left behind, while tax records show how they lived.

The land tax This was a tax on the value of land in England and Wales, levied between 1692 and 1963. The annual assessments usually list both owners and occupiers, and many records survive, particularly between 1780 and 1832, when they were used to prove the entitlement to vote. From 1798 the returns often include a brief description of the property. Land tax returns are usually held at county record offices among quarter session records, and a complete set for 1798 is available at the National Archives (see DIRECTORY).

Hearth tax This tax – levied from 1662 to 1688 in England and Wales, and from 1691 to 1695 in Scotland – was based on the number of hearths in a property (see pages 219, 323). As well as the name of the owner or occupier, the records will give you an indication of the person's affluence and the size of the property.

Window tax Levied from 1696 to 1851, the window tax was always unpopular since it seemed to be a tax on fresh air, light and health. Blocked-in windows indicate where a previous owner reduced his tax bill. Records are held mostly at the National Archives (see DIRECTORY).

Local rates These were essentially taxes on property and they vary depending on where you live. Early church rates were levied on householders to help the poor in a particular parish, while in towns corporations taxed their citizens to raise money for improving local facilities. Look for rate returns in local record offices.

Last will and testament

If you are searching for an owner who lived 200 years ago or more, you may well unearth a probate inventory associated with the person's will (see pages 324-325). If one exists it will give you valuable information about a previous owner or occupier's work and belongings. From these scraps you can start to build up a picture of the person's social standing and circle of friends. Registered wills for southern England and Wales can be accessed on the National Archives website, while material for northern England is stored at the Borthwick Institute, York. Scottish testaments are housed at the National Archives of Scotland (see DIRECTORY).

Legal wrangles

Equity court records generated by property disputes can provide a colourful insight into the character of people who once lived in your home. The equity law courts were established as a system of justice based on conscience rather than the strict rules of law. All used the 'pleading' system, whereby an original bill of complaint was brought into the court by the plaintiff and was answered by the defendant. The Court of Chancery records go back to 1386, while the Court of Exchequer did not become an equity court until the mid 16th century. Other courts provided access to justice for lower ranks of society, such as the Court of Requests and the Court of Star Chamber.

Evidence often describes a property in detail, or at least names the owner or occupier. In many cases the contents of a property are itemised, showing you how the house was originally furnished or used.

Where to find records All surviving court records are held at the National Archives (see DIRECTORY).

FIND OUT MORE

• *Land and window tax assessments* (J. Gibson, M. Medleycott and D. Mills, 2nd ed., FFHS, 1998)
• *The Hearth Tax, other Later Stuart Tax Lists and the Association Oath Rolls* (J. Gibson, FFHS, 1985)
• www.nationalarchives.gov.uk/e179
An on-line catalogue of taxation records, some of which refer to property.
• www.scottishdocuments.com
An on-line index to Scottish wills from 1515 to 1823.
• www.nas.gov.uk/miniframe/fact_sheet/taxation.pdf
A National Archives of Scotland fact sheet on taxation records.

An 18th-century property dispute

From the 17th century onwards people seemed to delight in bringing lawsuits against each other to settle grievances over an inheritance. A good example concerns Thomas Armstrong, a customs officer who built Cliff House in Cullercoats, Northumberland, during the 1750s. Armstrong's father-in-law, William Allison, died at sea in mysterious circumstances, and as executor Armstrong moved quickly to carry out what he claimed to be the terms of Allison's will. Allison's property in Cullercoats (left) was seized and placed under Armstrong's control, while Allison's widow Jane was forcibly ejected from the family home. We know of these events because Jane Allison brought a lawsuit against Armstrong in the Court of Chancery. The story sheds light on the lengths that feuding families would go to in the search for material wealth. While Jane Allison travelled to London to make her complaint in the Court of Chancery, the devious customs officer took advantage of her absence and filed a complaint against her in the local courts. She was arrested on her return to Cullercoats and thrown into Northumberland gaol. The last we hear of Jane Allison is in a further petition to Chancery, where she claims one of Armstrong's men had stolen the paperwork she needed to prove her innocence. The document mentions some of the personal possessions she 'rescued' from her late husband's house, including 'six chairs, two tables, a looking glass, a tea box, a pair of bellows, a tea kettle, six china cups and saucers ... a tea pot and two silver spoons'. Although this level of detail is rare, you never know what you may uncover in your searches.

Directory of sources

The directory lists sources of information mentioned in the book and other useful addresses. They are arranged alphabetically, including county and city record offices, except for London boroughs, which appear under 'L'.

Aberdeen City Archives
Town House, Broad Street
Aberdeen AB10 1AQ
Tel. 01224 522513
and
Old Aberdeen House Branch
Dunbar Street
Aberdeen AB24 3UJ
Tel. 01224 481775

Anglesey County Record Office
Shire Hall, Glanhwfa Road
Llangefni LL77 7TW
Tel. 01248 752080
www.anglesey.gov.uk

Angus Archives
Montrose Library
214 High Street
Montrose DD10 8PH
Tel. 01674 671415
www.angus.gov.uk/history

Argyll and Bute Council Archives
Manse Brae
Lochgilphead PA31 8QU
Tel. 01546 604774
www.argyll-bute.gov.uk

Ayrshire Archives
Ayrshire Archives Centre
Craigie Estate
Ayr KA8 0SS
Tel. 01292 287584
www.south-ayrshire.gov.uk

North Ayrshire Libraries
Local History Library
39-41 Princes Street
Ardrossan KA22 8BT
Tel. 01294 469137
www.learning-north-ayrshire.com

b

The Bakelite Museum
Orchard Mill
Williton
Somerset TA4 4NS
Tel. 01984 632133
www.bakelitemuseum.co.uk

Bath and North East Somerset Record Office
Guildhall, High Street
Bath BA1 5AW
Tel. 01225 477421
www.batharchives.co.uk

Bath Central Library
19 The Podium
Northgate Street
Bath BA1 5AN
Tel. 01225 787400
www.foursite.somerset.gov.uk

Bedfordshire and Luton Archives and Record Service
County Hall, Cauldwell Street
Bedford MK42 9AP
Tel. 01234 228833/228777
www.bedfordshire.gov.uk/archives

Berkshire Record Office
9 Coley Avenue
Reading RG1 6AF
Tel. 0118 901 5132
www.berkshirerecordoffice.org.uk

Birmingham City Archives
Floor 7, Central Library
Chamberlain Square
Birmingham B3 3HQ
Tel. 0121 303 4217
www.birmingham.gov.uk/archives

Blackburn with Darwen *see*
LANCASHIRE RECORD OFFICE

Black Country Living Museum
Dudley
West Midlands DY1 4SQ
Tel. 0121 557 9643
www.bclm.co.uk

Bodleian Library
Broad Street
Oxford OX1 3BG
Tel. 01865 277180
www.bodley.ox.ac.uk

Bolton Archives and Local Studies
Central Library, Civic Centre
Le Mans Crescent
Bolton BL1 1SE
Tel. 01204 332185
http://bold.bolton.gov.uk

Borthwick Institute for Archives
University of York
Heslington
York YO10 5DD
Tel. 01904 321166
www.york.ac.uk/inst/bihr

Bournemouth Heritage Zone
Bournemouth Library
22 The Triangle
Bournemouth BH2 5RQ
Tel. 01202 454844
www.bournemouth.gov.uk/
residents/libraries

Bracknell Record Office *see*
BERKSHIRE RECORD OFFICE

Bristol Record Office
'B' Bond Warehouse
Smeaton Road
Bristol BS1 6XN
Tel. 0117 922 4224
www.bristol-city.gov.uk/recordoffice

British Association for Local History
BALH PO Box 6549
Somersal Herbert
Ashbourne DE6 5WH
Tel. 01283 585947
www.balh.co.uk

British Library
96 Euston Road
London NW1 2DB
Tel. 020 7412 7000/
020 7412 7702 (map library)
www.bl.uk

British Library Newspapers
Colindale Avenue
London NW9 5HE
Tel. 020 7412 7353
www.bl.uk/collections/
newspapers.html

British Telecom Archives
Holborn Telephone Exchange
268-270 High Holborn
London WC1V 7EE
Tel. 020 7440 4220

British Trust for Conservation Volunteers
Conservation Centre
163 Balby Road
Doncaster DN4 0RH
Tel. 01302 572244
www.btcv.org

Centre for Buckinghamshire Studies
County Hall, Walton Street
Aylesbury HP20 1UU
Tel. 01296 382587
www.buckscc.gov.uk/archives

Bury Archive Service
Moss Street
Bury BL9 0DG
Tel. 0161 797 6697
www.bury.gov.uk/archives

Business Archives of Scotland
c/o Glasgow University Archives
and Business Record Centre
77-87 Dumbarton Road
Glasgow G11 6PW
Tel. 0141 330 4159
www.archives.gla.ac.uk

c

Cadw
Plas Carew
Unit 5-7 Cefn Coed
Parc Nantgarw
Cardiff CF15 7QQ
Tel. 01443 336000
www.cadw.wales.gov.uk

Caerphilly Archives
Bargoed Library, The Square
Bargoed CF81 8QQ
Tel. 01443 875548
www.caerphilly.gov.uk/learning/
libraries

Cambridgeshire County Record Office
Shire Hall, Castle Hill
Cambridge CB3 0AP
Tel. 01223 717281
www.camcnty.gov.uk

Carmarthenshire Archives Service
Parc Myrddin
Richmond Terrace
Carmarthen SA31 1DA
Tel. 01267 228232
www.carmarthenshire.gov.uk/
archives

Catholic Central Library
www.catholic-library.org.uk

Catholic Record Society
(*publication enquiries only*)
12 Melbourne Place
Wolsingham
Co Durham DL13 3EH
Tel. 01388 527747
www.catholic-history.org.uk/crs

Ceredigion Archives
County Offices, Marine Terrace
Aberystwyth SY23 2DE
Tel. 01970 633697/8
www.ceredigion-archives.org.uk

**Cheshire and Chester Archives
and Local Studies Service**
Duke Street
Chester CH1 1RL
Tel. 01244 602574
www.cheshire.gov.uk/recoff

Church of England Record Centre
15 Galleywall Road
London SE16 3PB
Tel. 020 7898 1030
www.church-of-england.org

Clackmannan Local Studies
Library Services Library
Drysdale Street
Alloa FK10 1JL
Tel. 01259 722262
www.clacksweb.org.uk/culture/
localhistoryandlocalstudies/

Conwy Record Office
The Old Board School
Lloyd Street
Llandudno LL30 2YG
Tel. 01492 860882
www.conwy.gov.uk

Cornwall Record Office
County Hall
Truro TR1 3AY
Tel. 01872 323127
www.cornwall.gov.uk

**Corporation of London
Records Office**
PO Box 270, Guildhall
London EC2P 2EJ
Tel. 020 7332 1251
www.corpoflondon.gov.uk

**Council for the Protection
of Rural England**
CPRE National Office
128 Southwark Street
London SE1 0SW
Tel. 020 7981 2800
www.cpre.org.uk

The Countryside Agency
John Dower House
Crescent Place
Cheltenham
Gloucestershire GL50 3RA
Tel. 01242 533222
www.countryside.gov.uk

Cumbria Record Office (Carlisle)
The Castle
Carlisle CA3 8UR
Tel. 01228 607284/5
www.cumbria.gov.uk/archives/
recordoffices

COMPANY REGISTRIES

Companies House
(*Main office for England
and Wales*)
Crown Way
Cardiff CF14 3UZ
Tel. 029 2038 8588
www.companieshouse.gov.uk

Companies House
21 Bloomsbury Street
London WC1B 3XD
Tel. 029 2038 8588
www.companieshouse.gov.uk

Companies House
37 Castle Terrace
Edinburgh EH1 2EB
Tel. 029 2038 8588
www.companieshouse.gov.uk

---

 d

Cumbria Record Office (Kendal)
County Offices
Kendal LA9 4RQ
Tel. 01539 773540
www.cumbria.gov.uk/archives/
recordoffices

Denbighshire Record Office
46 Clwyd Street
Ruthin LL15 1HP
Tel. 01824 708250
www.denbighshire.gov.uk

Derby Local Studies Library
25B Irongate
Derby DE1 3GL
Tel. 01332 255393
www.derby.gov.uk/libraries/
about/localstudies

Derbyshire Record Office
County Offices, New Street
Matlock DE4 3AG
Tel. 01629 580000/
01629 585347 (search room)
www.derbyshire.gov.uk

Devon Record Office
Great Moor House
Bittern Road, Sowton
Exeter EX2 7NL
Tel. 01392 384253
www.devon.gov.uk/
record_office.htm

**North Devon Library
and Record Office**
Tuly Street
Barnstaple EX31 1EL
Tel. 01271 388607
www.devon-cc.gov.uk/dro

**West Devon and Plymouth
Record Office**
Unit 3, Clare Place
Coxside, Plymouth Pl4 0JW
Tel. 01752 305940
www.plymouth.gov.uk

Dorset Record Office
Bridport Road
Dorchester DT1 1RP
Tel. 01305 250550
www.dorsetcc.gov.uk/records.htm

Dry Stone Walling Association
Westmorland County
Showground
Lane Farm, Crooklands
Milnthorpe
Cumbria LA7 7NH
Tel. 01539 567953
www.dswa.org.uk

Dudley Archives
Mount Pleasant Street
Roseville, Coseley
West Midlands WV14 9JR
Tel. 01384 812770
www.dudley.gov.uk

Dumfries and Galloway Archives
Archive Centre
33 Burns Street
Dumfries DG1 2PS
Tel. 01387 269254
www.dumgal.gov.uk/services/depts/
comres/library/archives.htm

Durham County Record Office
County Hall
Durham DH1 5UL
Tel. 0191 383 3253
www.durham.gov.uk/recordoffice

e

East Dunbartonshire Archives
William Patrick Library
2-4 West High Street
Kirkintilloch G66 1AD
Tel. 0141 776 8090
or
Brookwood Library
166 Drymen Road
Bearsden G61 3RJ
Tel. 0141 942 6811
www.eastdunbarton.gov.uk

East Lothian Local History Centre
Haddington Library
Newton Port
Haddington EH41 3NA
Tel. 01620 823307
www.eastlothian.gov.uk

East Renfrewshire Heritage Centre
Giffnock Library
Station Road, Giffnock
East Renfrewshire G46 6JF
Tel. 0141 577 4976
www.eastrenfrewshire.gov.uk

East Sussex Record Office
The Maltings, Castle Precincts
Lewes BN7 1YT
Tel. 01273 482349
www.eastsussexcc.gov.uk/
useourarchives

Edinburgh City Archives
Dept of Corporate Services
City of Edinburgh Council
City Chambers, High Street
Edinburgh EH1 1YJ
Tel. 0131 529 4616
www.edinburgh.gov.uk

English Heritage
PO Box 569
Swindon SN2 2YP
Tel. 0870 333 1181
www.english-heritage.org.uk

The English Place-Name Society
School of English Studies
University of Nottingham
Nottingham NG7 2RD
Tel. 0115 951 5919
www.nottingham.ac.uk/english/
research/EPNS

Essex Record Office
Wharf Road
Chelmsford CM2 6YT
Tel. 01245 244 644
www.essexcc.gov.uk/ero

 f

Falkirk History Research Centre
Callendar House
Callendar Park
Falkirk FK1 1YR
Tel. 01324 503778
www.falkirk.gov.uk

Family Records Centre
1 Myddelton Street
London EC1R 1UW
Tel. 020 8392 5300/
0845 603 7788 (certificates)
www.familyrecords.gov.uk/frc

**Federation of Family History
Societies (FFHS)**
Administrator
PO Box 2425
Coventry CV5 6YX
Tel. 07041 492032
www.ffhs.org.uk

FFHS (Publications) Ltd
Units 15 and 16
Chesham Industrial Centre
Oram Street
Bury BL9 6EN
Tel. 0161 797 3843
www.genfair.com

The Federation of Synagogues
65 Watford Way
London NW4 3AQ
Tel. 020 8202 2263

Fife Archives
Carleton House
The Haig Business Park
Balgonie Road
Markinch KY7 6AQ
Tel. 01592 416504
www.fife.gov.uk

Flintshire Record Office
The Old Rectory, Hawarden
Deeside CH5 3NR
Tel. 01244 532364
www.flintshire.gov.uk

**General Register Office
for Scotland**
New Register House
3 West Register Street
Edinburgh EH1 3YT
Tel. 0131 314 4433
www.gro-scotland.gov.uk

Glamorgan Record Office
Glamorgan Building
King Edward VII Avenue
Cathays Park
Cardiff CF10 3NE
Tel. 029 2078 0282
www.glamro.gov.uk

Glasgow City Archives
The Mitchell Library
North Street
Glasgow G3 7DN
Tel. 0141 287 2910
www.glasgow.gov.uk

Gloucestershire Record Office
Clarence Row
Alvin Street
Gloucester GL1 3DW
Tel. 01452 425295
www.gloucestershire.gov.uk

Guildhall Library
Aldermanbury
London EC2P 2EJ
Tel. 020 7332 1868/1870
**www.cityoflondon.gov.uk/
guildhalllibrary**

Gwent Record Office
County Hall
Cwmbran NP44 2XH
Tel. 01633 644886
www.llgc.org.uk/cac/cac0004.htm

**Gwynedd Archives and
Museums Service**
Caernarfon Record Office
County Offices, Shirehall Street
Caernarfon LL55 1SH
Tel. 01286 679095/679088
www.llgc.org.uk/cac/cac0053.htm

Halton Local History Service
Halton Lea Library
Halton Lea, Runcorn
Cheshire WA7 2PF
Tel. 01928 715351
www.halton.gov.uk

Hampshire Record Office
Sussex Street
Winchester SO23 8TH
Tel. 01962 846154
**www.hants.gov.uk/
record-office/index.html**

Herefordshire Record Office
Harold Street
Hereford HR1 2QX
Tel. 01432 260750
www.herefordshire.gov.uk

Heritage Motor Centre
Banbury Road
Gaydon
Warwickshire CV35 0BJ
Tel. 01926 641188
www.heritage-motor-centre.co.uk

**Hertfordshire Archives
and Local Studies**
County Hall, Pegs Lane
Hertford SG13 8EJ
Tel. 01438 737333
www.hertsdirect.org

North Highland Archive
Wick Library
Sinclair Terrace
Wick KW1 5AB
Tel. 01955 606432
www.highland.gov.uk

Highland Council Archive
Cultural and Leisure Services
Inverness Library
Farraline Park
Inverness IV1 1NH
Tel. 01463 220330
www.highland.gov.uk

Historic Scotland
Longmore House
Salisbury Place
Edinburgh EH9 1SH
Tel. 0131 668 8600
www.historic-scotland.gov.uk

House of Lords Record Office
House of Lords, Westminster
London SW1A 0PW
Tel. 020 7219 3074
www.parliament.uk

**Huguenot Society of Great
Britain and Ireland**
Huguenot Library
University College London
Gower Street
London WC1E 6BT
Tel. 020 7679 5199
www.huguenotsociety.org.uk

**Huntingdonshire County
Record Office**
Grammar School Walk
Huntingdon
Cambridgeshire PE29 3LF
Tel. 01480 375842
www.cambridgeshire.gov.uk

Imperial War Museum
Lambeth Road
London SE1 6HZ
Tel. 020 7416 5000/5320
www.iwm.org.uk

Imperial War Museum Duxford
Duxford
Cambridgeshire CB2 4QR
Tel. 01223 835000
www.iwm.org.uk

Inverclyde Local History Library
The Watt Library
9 Union Street
Greenock PA16 9JH
Tel: 01475 715628
www.inverclyde.gov.uk/Libraries

Isle of Man Public Record Office
Unit 40A
Spring Valley Industrial Estate
Braddan, Douglas IM2 2QS
Tel. 01624 693569

Isle of Wight Record Office
26 Hillside, Newport
Isle of Wight PO30 2EB
Tel. 01983 823820/1
**www.iwight.com/library/
record_office**

j, k, l

Jewish Chronicle
25 Furnival Street
London EC4A 1JT
Tel. 020 7415 1500
www.thejc.co.uk

**Jewish Historical Society
of England**
33 Seymour Place
London W1H 6AT
Tel. 020 7723 5852
www.jhse.org

Jewish Museum
80 East End Road
London N3 2SY
Tel. 020 8349 1143
www.jewishmuseum.org.uk

Centre for Kentish Studies
Sessions House, County Hall
Maidstone ME14 1XQ
Tel. 01622 694363
www.kent.gov.uk/archives

Knowsley Local Studies
Huyton Library
Civic Way, Huyton
Knowsley L36 9GD
Tel. 0151 443 3738
**www.knowsley.gov.uk/leisure/
libraries**

Lambeth Palace Library
Lambeth Palace Road
London SE1 7JU
Tel. 020 7898 1400
www.lambethpalacelibrary.org

Lancashire Record Office
Bow Lane
Preston PR1 2RE
Tel. 01772 263039
www.archives.lancashire.gov.uk

Land registers (for Scotland)
see REGISTERS OF SCOTLAND
EXECUTIVE AGENCY

LONDON BOROUGHS

Barking and Dagenham
Valence House Museum
Becontree Avenue
Dagenham
Essex RM8 3HT
Tel. 020 8270 6896
www.barking-dagenham.gov.uk

Barnet
Local Studies and
Archives Centre
80 Daws Lane, Mill Hill
London NW7 4SL
Tel. 020 8959 2876
www.barnet.gov.uk

**Bexley Local Studies and
Archive Centre**
Manor House
Grassington Road
Sidcup DA14 6BW
Tel. 020 8301 1545
www.bexley.gov.uk/localstudies

Brent
Brent Community History
Library and Archive
Cricklewood Library
152 Olive Road
London NW2 6UY
Tel. 020 8937 3541
www.brent.gov.uk

Bromley
Local Studies and Archives
Central Library, High Street
Bromley
Kent BR1 1EX
Tel. 020 8461 7170
www.bromley.gov.uk

Camden
Camden Local Studies and
Archives Centre
Holborn Library
32-38 Theobald's Road
London WC1X 8PA
Tel. 020 7974 6342
www.camden.gov.uk/localstudies

Croydon
Local Studies Library
Central Library
Croydon Clocktower
Katharine Street
Croydon CR9 1ET
Tel. 020 8760 5400 Ext.
61112
www.croydon.gov.uk

Ealing
Local History Library
and Archives
Central Library
103 Ealing Broadway Centre
London W5 5JY
Tel. 020 8825 8194
www.ealing.gov.uk

Enfield
Archives and Local
History Unit
Southgate Town Hall
Green Lanes
Palmers Green
London N13 4XD
Tel. 020 8379 2724
www.enfield.gov.uk

Greenwich
Greenwich Local History
and Archives Library
Woodlands
90 Mycenae Road
London SE3 7SE
Tel. 020 8854 2452
www.greenwich.gov.uk

Hackney
Hackney Archives
Department
43 De Beauvoir Road
London N1 5SQ
Tel. 020 7241 2886
www.hackney.gov.uk

Hammersmith and Fulham
Archives and Local
History Centre
The Lilla Huset
191 Talgarth Road
London W6 8BJ
Tel. 020 8741 5159
www.lbhf.gov.uk

Haringey
Haringey Archive Service
Bruce Castle Museum
Lordship Lane
London N17 8NU
Tel. 020 8808 8772
www.haringey.gov.uk

Harrow
Harrow Reference Library
Civic Centre
Station Road
Harrow HA1 2UU
Tel. 020 8424 1056
www.harrow.gov.uk

Havering
Reference and Information
Library
St Edward's Way
Romford
Essex RM1 3AR
Tel. 01708 432 3943
www.havering.gov.uk

Hillingdon
Hillingdon Heritage Service
Central Library
14-15 High Street
Uxbridge
Middlesex UB8 1HD
Tel. 01895 250702
www.hillingdon.gov.uk

Hounslow
Chiswick Local Studies
Department
Duke's Avenue
Chiswick
London W4 2AB
Tel. 020 8994 5295
 and
Hounslow Library
Local Studies Department
24 Treaty Centre
High Street
Hounslow
Middlesex TW3 1ES
Tel. 0845 456 2800
www.hounslow.info

Islington
Islington History Collection
Central Reference Library
2 Fieldway Crescent
London N5 1PF
Tel. 020 7527 6900
www.islington.gov.uk/council/
library/history.htm

**Royal Borough of
Kensington and Chelsea**
Local Studies Section
Kensington Central Library
Phillimore Walk
London W8 7RX
Tel. 020 7361 3038
www.rbkc.gov.uk

**Royal Borough of Kingston
upon Thames**
Kingston Local History Room
North Kingston Centre
Richmond Road
Kingston KT2 5PE
Tel. 020 8547 6738
www.kingston.gov.uk

Lambeth
Lambeth Archives
Department
52 Knatchbull Road
London SE5 9QY
Tel. 020 7926 6076
www.lambethlandmark.com

Lewisham
Lewisham Local
Studies Centre
Lewisham Library
199-201 Lewisham
High Street
London SE13 6LG
Tel. 020 8297 0682
www.lewisham.gov.uk

Merton
Local Studies Centre
Merton Civic Centre
London Road, Morden
Surrey SM4 5DX
Tel. 020 8545 3239
www.merton.gov.uk

Newham
Archives and Local
Studies Library
Stratford Library
3 The Grove
Stratford
London E15 1EL
Tel. 020 8557 8856
www.newham.gov.uk

Redbridge
Archives Service
Central Library
Clements Road
Ilford
Essex IG1 1EA
Tel. 020 8708 2414
www.redbridge.gov.uk

Richmond upon Thames
Local Studies Collection
Albert Barkas Room
Old Town Hall
Whittaker Avenue
Richmond TW9 1TP
Tel. 020 8332 6820
www.richmond.gov.uk

Southwark
Southwark Local
Studies Library
211 Borough High Street
London SE1 1JA
Tel. 020 7403 3507
www.southwark.gov.uk

continued overleaf

335

continued from overleaf

LONDON BOROUGHS

Sutton
Local Studies Centre
Sutton Central Library
St Nicholas Way
Sutton SM1 1EA
Tel. 020 8770 4747
www.sutton.gov.uk

Tower Hamlets
Local History Library
and Archives
Bancroft Library
277 Bancroft Road
London E1 4DQ
Tel. 020 7364 1289
www.towerhamlets.gov.uk

Waltham Forest
Local History Library
Vestry House Museum
Vestry House, Walthamstow
London E17 9NH
Tel. 020 8509 1917
www.lbwf.gov.uk

Wandsworth
Local History Service
Battersea Library
265 Lavender Hill
London SW11 1JB
Tel. 020 8871 7753
www.wandsworth.gov.uk

Westminster
Westminster Archives
Centre, 10 St Ann's Street
London SW1P 2DE
Tel. 020 7641 5180
www.westminster.gov.uk/
archives

Land Registry
Lincoln's Inn Fields
London WC2A 3PH
Tel. 020 7917 8888
www.landreg.gov.uk

**Latter-Day Saints
Distribution Centre (LDS)**
399 Carretts Green Lane
Birmingham B33 0UH
www.familysearch.org

**Record Office for Leicestershire,
Leicester and Rutland**
Long Street, Wigston Magna
Leicester LE18 2AH
Tel. 0116 257 1080
www.leics.gov.uk

Lincolnshire Archives
St Rumbold Street
Lincoln LN2 5AB
Tel. 01522 526204
www.lincolnshire.gov.uk/archives

North East Lincolnshire Archives
Town Hall, Town Hall Square
Grimsby DN31 1HX
Tel. 01472 323585
www.nelincs.gov.uk

**Liverpool Record Office and
Local Studies Service**
Central Library
William Brown Street
Liverpool L3 8EW
Tel. 0151 233 5817
http://archives.liverpool.gov.uk

London Library
14 St James' Square
London SW1Y 4LG
Tel. 020 7930 7705
www.londonlibrary.co.uk

London Metropolitan Archives
Corporation of London
40 Northampton Road
London EC1R 0HB
Tel. 020 7332 3820
www.cityoflondon.gov.uk/archives

m

Manchester City Archives
Archives and Local Studies
Central Library
St Peter's Square
Manchester M2 5PD
Tel. 0161 234 1979
www.manchester.gov.uk/
libraries/arls

**Greater Manchester County
Record Office**
56 Marshall Street, New Cross
Manchester M4 5FU
Tel. 0161 832 5284
www.gmcro.co.uk

**Medway Archives and
Local Studies Centre**
Civic Centre
Strood, Rochester
Kent ME2 4AU
Tel. 01634 332714
www.medway.gov.uk/index/
leisure/archives.htm

Merseyside
see LIVERPOOL RECORD OFFICE

MAGAZINES

Ancestors
PO BOX 38
Richmond
TW9 4AJ
Tel. 020 8392 5370

**The Local Historian
(journal of BALH)**
and
Local History News
see BRITISH ASSOCIATION FOR
LOCAL HISTORY

Local History Magazine
Local History Press Ltd
3 Devonshire Promenade
Lenton
Nottingham NG7 2DS
Tel. 0115 970 6473
www.local-history.co.uk

Scottish Local History Journal
Department of
Scottish History
University of Edinburgh
17 Buccleuch Place
Edinburgh EH8 9LN
Tel. 0131 650 4030
www.slhf.gcal.ac.uk

Merthyr Tydfil Archives
Central Library
High Street
Merthyr Tydfil CF47 8AF
Tel. 01685 723057
www.merthyr.gov.uk

Metropolitan Police Archives
see NATIONAL ARCHIVES

Middlesex *for records of the
former county see* LONDON
BOROUGH OF WESTMINSTER *and*
LONDON METROPOLITAN ARCHIVES

Midlothian Council Archives
Library Headquarters
2 Clerk Street
Loanhead EH22 9DR
Tel. 0131 271 3976
www.midlothian.gov.uk

Modern Records Centre
University Library
University of Warwick
Coventry CV4 7AL
Tel. 02476 524219
www.warwick.ac.uk/services/
library/mrc

Moray Archives
Grant Lodge Local
Heritage Centre
Elgin Library
Cooper Park
Elgin
www.moray.gov.uk

Museum of English Rural Life
see RURAL HISTORY CENTRE

Museum of Scottish Country Life
Kittochside
Philipshill Road
East Kilbride G76 9HR
Tel. 01355 224 181
www.nms.ac.uk/countrylife

Museum of Welsh Life
St Fagan's Castle
Cardiff CF5 6XB
Tel. 029 2057 3500
www.nmgw.ac.uk

n

National Archives
Ruskin Avenue
Kew
Surrey TW9 4DU
Tel. 020 8876 3444
www.nationalarchives.gov.uk

National Archives of Scotland
HM General Register House
2 Princes Street
Edinburgh EH1 3YY
Tel. 0131 535 1314
and
West Search Room
West Register House
Charlotte Square
Edinburgh EH2 4DJ
Tel. 0131 535 1413
www.nas.gov.uk

National Army Museum
Department of Archives,
Photographs, Film and Sound
Royal Hospital Road
London SW3 4HT
Tel. 020 7730 0717
Ext. 2214/2
www.national-army-museum.ac.uk

National Hedgelaying Society
Queenwood Bungalow
Hollandridge Lane
Christmas Common
Watlington OX49 5HW
Tel. 01491 613 501
www.hedgelaying.org.uk

National Library of Scotland
Department of Manuscripts
George IV Bridge
Edinburgh EH1 1EW
Tel. 0131 632 3700
www.nls.uk

National Library of Wales
Department of Manuscripts
and Records
Penglais, Aberystwyth
Ceredigion SY23 3BU
Tel. 01970 632 800
www.llgc.org.uk

National Maritime Museum
Park Row, Greenwich
London SE10 9NF
Tel. 020 8858 4422
www.nmm.ac.uk

**National Monuments
Record Centre**
Kemble Drive
Swindon SN2 2GZ
Tel. 01793 414600
www.english-heritage.org.uk

**National Monuments Record
of Scotland** *see* ROYAL COMMISSION
ON THE ANCIENT AND HISTORICAL
MONUMENTS OF SCOTLAND

National Museums of Scotland
Chambers Street
Edinburgh EH1 1JF
Tel. 0131 247 4422
www.nms.ac.uk

National Trust
PO Box 39
Warrington WA5 7WD
Tel. 0870 458 4000
www.nationaltrust.org.uk

National Trust for Scotland
Wemyss House
28 Charlotte Square
Edinburgh EH2 4ET
Tel. 0131 243 9300
www.nts.org.uk

Neath-Port Talbot Archives
Neath Library
Victoria Gardens
Neath SA11 3BA
Tel. 01639 644604
www.neath-porttalbot.gov.uk

Norfolk Record Office
The Archive Centre
Martineau Lane
Norwich NR1 2DQ
Tel. 01603 222599
www.archives.norfolk.gov.uk

Northamptonshire Record Office
Wootton Hall Park
Northampton NN4 8BQ
Tel. 01604 762129
www.northamptonshire.gov.uk

North Lanarkshire Archives
10 Kelvin Road
Lenziemill Road
Cumbernauld
Glasgow G67 2BA
Tel. 01236 737114
www.northlan.gov.uk

Northumberland Record Office
Melton Park
North Gosforth
Newcastle upon Tyne NE3 5QX
Tel. 0191 2362680
www.northumberland.gov.uk

Nottinghamshire Archives
County House
Castle Meadow Road
Nottingham NG2 1AG
Tel. 0115 958 1634/950 4524
www.nottinghamshire.gov.uk

O

Office for National Statistics
Cardiff Road
Newport NP10 8XG
Tel. 0845 601 3034
www.statistics.gov.uk

**Oldham Local Studies
and Archives**
84 Union Street
Oldham OL1 1DN
Tel. 0161 911 46545
www.oldham.gov.uk/community/
local_studies

Orkney Library and Archives
Junction Road
Kirkwall
Orkney KW15 1AG
Tel. 01856 873166/875260
www.orkneylibrary.org.uk

Oxfordshire Record Office
St Luke's Church
Temple Road
Cowley
Oxford OX4 2HT
Tel. 01865 398200
www.oxfordshire.gov.uk/oro

p,q

Pembrokeshire Record Office
The Castle
Haverfordwest SA61 2EF
Tel. 01437 763707
www.llgc.org.uk

Perth and Kinross Council Archive
AK Bell Library
2-8 York Place, Perth PH2 8EP
Tel. 01738 477012
www.pkc.gov.uk

Poole Local History Centre
Waterfront Museum
4 High Street
Poole BH15 1BW
Tel. 01202 262600
www.poole.gov.uk

Portsmouth Archives
Central Library
Guildhall Square
Portsmouth PO1 2DX
Tel. 023 9281 9311
www.portsmouth.gov.uk

PROBATE OFFICES

Birmingham
The Priory Courts
33 Bull Street
Birmingham B4 6DU
Tel. 0121 681 3400

Brighton
William Street
Brighton BN2 2LG
Tel. 0127 368 4071

Bristol
The Crescent Centre
Temple Back
Bristol BS1 6EP
Tel. 0117 927 3915/
0117 926 4619

Cardiff
PO Box 474
2 Park Street
Cardiff CF10 1TB
Tel. 029 2037 6467

Ipswich
Ground Floor
8 Arcade Street
Ipswich IP1 1EJ
Tel. 01473 280260

Isle of Man
General Registry
Isle of Man Courts of Justice
Deemsters Walk
Bucks Road
Douglas IM1 3AR
Tel. 01624 685 242

Leeds
3rd Floor, Coronet House
Queen Street
Leeds LS1 2BA
Tel. 0113 386 3540

Liverpool
Queen Elizabeth II
Law Courts
Derby Square
Liverpool L2 1XA
Tel. 0151 236 8264

London
Principal Registry of the
Family Division
First Avenue House
42-49 High Holborn
London WC1V 6NP
Tel. 020 7947 6000

Manchester
9th Floor, Astley House
23 Quay Street
Manchester M3 4AT
Tel. 0161 837 6070

Newcastle upon Tyne
2nd Floor, Plummer House
Croft Street
Newcastle NE1 6NP
Tel. 0191 261 8383

Oxford
St Aldates
Oxford OX1 1LY
Tel. 01865 793050

Winchester
4th Floor, Cromwell House
Andover Road
Winchester SO23 7EW
Tel. 01962 897029

**Scotland: HM General
Register Office**
(probate up to 1985)

HM Register Office
HM Register House
Princes Street
Edinburgh EH1 3YY
Tel. 0131 535 1352

HM Commissary Office
(probate after 1985)
Sheriff Court House
27 Chambers Street
Edinburgh EH1 1LB
Tel. 0131 247 2850

Stirling Council Archives Services
Unit 6
Burghmuir Industrial Estate
Stirling FK7 7PY
Tel. 01786 450745
www.stirling.gov.uk

Stockport
see CHESHIRE, DERBYSHIRE OR
LANCASHIRE ARCHIVES

Suffolk
*County archives are in three
locations and share a website*:
www.suffolkcc.gov.uk/libraries

Suffolk Record Office
77 Raingate Street
Bury St Edmunds IP33 2AR
Tel. 01284 352352

Suffolk Record Office
Gatacre Road
Ipswich IP1 2LQ
Tel. 01473 584541

Suffolk Record Office
Central Library
Clapham Road
Lowestoft NR32 1DR
Tel. 01502 405358

Surrey History Centre
130 Goldsworth Road
Woking GU21 1ND
Tel. 01483 518737
www.surreycc.gov.uk/
surreyhistoryservice

Sussex
see EAST SUSSEX *and* WEST
SUSSEX RECORD OFFICES

Swansea
see WEST GLAMORGAN
ARCHIVE SERVICE

t

**Tameside Local Studies
and Archives Centre**
Tameside Central Library
Old Street
Ashton-under-Lyne
Tameside OL6 7SG
Tel. 0161 342 4242
www.tameside.gov.uk

Teesside Archives
*Holds archives for Stockton-
on-Tees and Middlesbrough*
Exchange House
6 Marton Road
Middlesbrough TS1 1DB
Tel. 01642 248321
www.middlesbrough.gov.uk

Thurrock Archives
Grays Library
Orsett Road, Grays
Essex RM17 5DX
Tel. 01375 383611
www.thurrock.gov.uk/libraries

Torfaen Local Studies Centre
Abersychan Library
Brynteg, Abersychan
Pontypool NP4 7BG
Tel. 01495 772261
www.torfaen.gov.uk

Trafford Local Studies Centre
Sale Library, Sale Waterside
Sale M33 7ZF
Tel. 0161 912 3013
www.trafford.gov.uk

Twentieth Century Society
70 Cowcross Street
London EC1M 6EJ
Tel. 020 7250 3857
www.c20society.org.uk

Tyne & Wear Archive Service
Blandford House
Blandford Square
Newcastle upon Tyne NE1 4JA
Tel. 0191 232 6789
www.thenortheast.com/archives

v,w

Victoria and Albert Museum
Cromwell Road
London SW7 2RL
Tel. 020 7942 2000
www.vam.ac.uk

Walsall Local History Centre
Essex Street, Walsall WS2 7AS
Tel. 01922 721305
www.walsall.gov.uk

Warrington Archives
Central Library, Museum Street
Warrington WA1 1JB
Tel. 01925 442889/90
www.warrington.gov.uk

**Warwickshire County
Record Office**
Priory Park, Cape Road
Warwick CV34 4JS
Tel. 01926 412735
www.warwickshire.gov.uk/
general/rcindex.htm

**Weald and Downland
Open Air Museum**
Singleton Park, Chichester
West Sussex PO18 0EU
Tel. 01243 811 363
www.wealddown.co.uk

Wesley Historical Society Library
Wesley Centre
Oxford Brookes University
Harcourt Hill
Oxford OX2 9AT
Tel. 01865 488319

West Country Studies Library
Castle Street, Exeter EX4 3PQ
Tel. 01392 384216
www.devon-cc.gov.uk/
library/locstudy

West Dunbartonshire Archives
Strathleven Place
Dunbarton G82 1BD
Tel. 01389 733273
www.wdcweb.info/library

West Glamorgan Archive Service
County Hall
Oystermouth Road
Swansea SA1 3SN
Tel. 01792 636589
www.swansea.gov.uk/
westglamorganarchives

West Lothian Council Archives
Local History Library
Library HQ, Hopefield Road
Blackburn
West Lothian EH47 7HZ
Tel. 01506 776331
www.westlothian.gov.uk/libraries

Westmorland *see* CUMBRIA
RECORD OFFICE

West Sussex Record Office
County Hall
Chichester PO19 1RQ
Tel. 01243 777100
www.westsussex.gov.uk

Wigan Archive Service
Town Hall, Leigh
Lancashire WN7 2DY
Tel. 01942 404430
www.wlct.org

**Wiltshire and Swindon
Record Office**
County Hall East
Bythesea Road
Trowbridge BA14 8BS
Tel. 01225 713138
www.wiltshire.gov.uk

Windsor and Maidenhead Archives
Maidenhead Library
St Ives Road,
Maidenhead SL6 1QU
Tel. 01628 796 969
www.rbwm.gov.uk/libraries/
maidenhead.htm

Wokingham
see BERKSHIRE RECORD OFFICE

**Wolverhampton Archive and
Local Studies**
42-50 Snow Hill
Wolverhampton WV2 4AG
Tel. 01902 552480
www.wolverhampton.gov.uk

Women's Library
London Metropolitan University
Old Castle Street
London E1 7NT
Tel. 020 7320 2222
www.thewomenslibrary.ac.uk

Worcestershire Record Office
Headquarters Branch
County Hall, Spetchley Road
Worcester WR5 2NP
Tel. 01905 766351
www.worcestershire.gov.uk/records

**Workers Educational
Association (WEA)**
Quick House
65 Clifton Street
London EC2A 4JE
Tel. 020 7375 3092
www.wea.org.uk

y

York City Archives
Art Gallery Building
Exhibition Square
York YO1 7EW
Tel. 01904 551878/9
www.york.gov.uk/heritage/
museums/index

East Riding of Yorkshire Archives
County Hall, Beverley
East Riding of Yorkshire
HU17 9BA
Tel. 01482 392790
www.eastriding.gov.uk/libraries/
archives/archives.html

**North Yorkshire County
Record Office**
County Hall
Northallerton
North Yorkshire DL7 8AF
Tel. 01609 777585
www.northyorks.gov.uk

West Yorkshire Archive Service
Wakefield Headquarters
Registry of Deeds
Newstead Road
Wakefield WF1 2DE
Tel. 01924 305980
www.archives.wyjs.org.uk

Index

Page numbers in *italic* refer to illustrations and captions.

Acknowledgments

Illustrations in *The Story of Where You Live* were supplied by the following.
Some short forms of suppliers have been used: BAL – The Bridgeman Art Library, London; LRL – © Last Refuge Limited, Dae Sasitorn & Adrian Warren; MEPL – Mary Evans Picture Library; SSPL – Science and Society Picture Library; TSP – The Skyscan Photolibrary. The following abbreviations are also used: T top; C centre; B bottom; L left; R right. © RD indicates images that are copyright of The Reader's Digest Association Limited.

Cover TL The Francis Frith Collection, Salisbury, Wiltshire SP3 5QP TC Edifice BL Popperfoto BC Popperfoto BR Woodfall Wild Images **Endpapers** © RD/London Topographical Society **2-3** Hulton Getty Images **4** CL © RD/Jason Smalley B Popperfoto **4-5** T © RD/Jason Smalley **5** TR Aerofilms BL Topham Picture Library BR Edifice **6** (both) © RD/Jason Smalley **7** See pgs 261-2, 68-9 and 192 **8** BL Collections/Graeme Pocock BC Topham Picture Library/British Museum BR The Art Archive, London/Bodleian Library, Oxford **9** T AKG London/Musee de la Tapisserie, Bayeux B Collections/Roy Stedall-Humphryes **10** TL The Art Archive, London/John Webb TR Neil Holmes BL AKG London/British Library **11** CL © RD CR Christie's Images BC Colin Molyneux **12** C MEPL CR MEPL BL Mick Sharp and Jean Williamson/Jean Williamson **13** CL The Art Archive, London B SSPL **14** CR AKG London BL SSPL BR SSPL **15** CR www.arcaid.co.uk/Martin Jones BL Topham Picture Library BR Eye Ubiquitous/R.D. Battersby **16** (both)© RD/Jason Smalley **17** TL & TR © RD/Jason Smalley B © RD **18** C Powys County Archives Office B www.cornwall.gov.uk **18-19** © RD/Jason Smalley **19** TR © RD/Jason Smalley BR © RD **20** © RD/Jon Bouchier **21** © RD **22-23** The National Archives **23** L The National Archives R www.balh.co.uk **23-24** The National Archives **24** www.balh.co.uk **25** TR www.scotlandspeople.gov.uk B www.old-maps.co.uk **26** (all) Ordnance Survey/ © Crown Copyright **27** T The National Archives B © RD **28** T LRL B © RD/David Tarn **29** (all) © RD **30** © RD **31** © RD TR John Cleare/Mountain Camera **32** © RD **33** T © RD BL Collections/Chris Blyth BR © RD **34** BL English Heritage/Bob Skingle BR © RD **35** TR The Travelsite/Jarrold Publishing CR BAL/Philip Mould, Historical Portraits. London UK BL TSP **36** BL BAL **36-37** LRL **37** © RD/Jason Smalley **38** T Collections/Lawrence Englesberg **38-39** TSP/Edmund Nagele **39** T Tom Mackie C © RD CR Collections/Paul Felix **40** T Collections/Andria Massey B TSP/Bob Evans **41** T © RD/Jon Wyand C Collections/David M. Hughes **42** T English Heritage/Skyscan Balloon Photography **42-43** B TSP **43** T Neil Holmes B Collections **44** L LRL TR The Photolibrary Wales BR TSP/Westair **45** T Collections/George Wright BR TSP **46** © RD **47** L TSP/Flashpoint TR Ordnance Survey/ © Crown Copyright B © RD **48** B © RD **48-49** T Scottish Borders Council **49** CR Ecclesiastical & Eccentricities Picture Library/Anson BC Ordnance Survey/ © Crown Copyright B Mick Sharp and Jean Williamson **50** TSP **51** TL © RD TR BAL/Private Collection BL © RD BR © RD **52** BL © RD/Richard Turpin BC Ordnance Survey/ © Crown Copyright **52-53** T TSP/Colour Library Books B © RD **53** TR Collections/Graeme Peacock **54** L Aerofilms **54-55** T John Cleare/Mountain Camera **55** TR BAL/Musee Condee, Chantilly **56** L BAL/Osterreichische Nationalbibliothek, Vienna **56-57** C TSP/Peter Smith **57** BC © RD **58** T BAL/British Library, London BL Collections/David Lyons **58-59** B The Photolibrary Wales **59** TR © RD BR Collections/Andrew Baskott **60** TL The Art Archive, London **60-61** TSP **61** TL Ordnance Survey/ © Crown Copyright TR By Kind Permission of Historic Scotland **62** C BAL/New Walk Museum, Leicester City Museum Service CR BAL **62-63** Topham Picture Library B TSP/Bracegirdle **63** TR Kevin Allen Photography **64** L BAL/Ashmolean Museum, University of Oxford BR Garden Picture Library **64-65** The National Trust/Andrew Butler **65** C RIBA Library Photographs Collection/Dr Jane Ridley BR Garden Picture Library/Clive Nichols **66** TL TSP/Pitkin Unichrome Ltd B BAL/Private Collection TC Collections/Michael St Maur Sheil **67** TC By Courtesy of the National Portrait Gallery, London/067BSWYL B Tamar Valley AONB Service/Countryside Agency/Chris Chapman **68** L © RD **68-69** T SSPL B © RD **69** BAL/Ironbridge Gorge Museum, Telford **70** BL BAL **71** TL Topham Picture Library TR © RD BL Tom Mackie **72** TL BAL/Private Collection R © RD **73** TL SSPL BR Collections/Dennis Barnes **74** C © RD CR © RD BL SSPL **74-75** T © RD **75** T SSPL B LRL/Dae Sasitorn **76** TL © RD BL & BR By permission of the Board of the British Library, London **77** T TSP BL SSPL BR Ordnance Survey/ © Crown Copyright **78** BL Collections/Liz Stares **78-79** Colin Molyneux **79** TR Topham Picture Library BR TSP **80** B The National Archives **80-81** TSP **81** B Topham Picture Library **82** T TSP BL © RD BC © RD **83** TL The National Archives C Neil Holmes CR Collections BR Collections B Mick Sharp and Jean Williamson **84** T Topham Picture Library B Popperfoto **85** T LRL L SSPL **86** CR SSPL BL Topham Picture Library **86-87** TSP **87** B Collections/Ross Graham **88** BL Hulton Getty Images **88-89** Carol Freer, PDC painters/Carol Freer, PDC Painters **89** Collections/Alan Barnes **90** TL Collections BR Premaphotos Wildlife/Ken Preston-Mafham **90-91** Tony Bates **91** TR Photofusion/Bob Watkins CR Countryside Agency/Charlie Hedley **92** T Carnegie Publishing Ltd/Sheffield Central

Library, Local Studies Department BL Collections/Ian Walker **93** T © RD/Jason Smalley **94** Reproduced with the permission of the County Archivist, Lancashire Record Office/County Archivist, Lancashire Record Office (P29) **95** (map) Trustees of The National Library of Scotland/Trustees of the National Library of Scotland (photograph) Air Photo Library, University of Cambridge/Tillhill & Stirling Council CR © RD **96** L Carnegie Publishing Ltd/Sheffield Central Library, Local Studies Department R Carnegie Publishing Ltd/Sheffield Central Library, Local Studies Department **96-97** BAL/Sheffield Galleries and Museums Trust **97** TL Sheffield Central Library,/Local Studies Department TR Sheffield Industrial Museums Trust **98** T LRL **99** TC Ordnance Survey/ © Crown Copyright TR Neil Holmes B © RD/Jason Smalley **100** T Ordnance Survey/ © Crown Copyright B TSP/Kevin Allen **101** TL © RD/Jason Smalley CR Ecclesiastical & Eccentricities Picture Library/Dorothy Burrows B John Cleare/Mountain Camera **102** T Cath Marsh B Roger G Howard/Photographers Direct **103** TL The National Trust/Nick Meers R © RD **104** Collections/Robin Weaver **105** T © RD/Jason Smalley B West Glamorgan Archive Service **106** L Colin Molyneux R © RD/Eric Meacher **107** L David Hey/George Redmonds R Ordnance Survey/ © Crown Copyright **108** NHPA/David Woodfall **108-109** Ardea, London/Adrian Warren **109** T NHPA/Guy Edwards CR © RD/ Jason Smalley **110** B © RD **111** B St.Andrews University Library **112** BR Collections/Robin Weaver **112-113** © RD/Roger Hutchins **113** T By permission of the Trustees of the Chatsworth Settlement CL Garden Picture Library/Clive Boursnell R Topham Picture Library **114** T Institute of Agricultural History and Museum of English Rural Life, Reading C & B Hulton Getty Images **115** T Institute of Agricultural History and Museum of English Rural Life, Reading/Topical Press Agency Ltd B Hulton Getty Images **116** L Woodfall Wild Images R Woodfall Wild Images/Bob Gibbons **116-117** © RD/Jason Smalley **117** T Ordnance Survey/ © Crown Copyright L Natural Visions R Ardea, London/David Dixon **118** T David Hey C Edifice/Philippa Lewis B Topham Picture Library **119** T © RD/Jason Smalley B Nottinghamshire County Council: Culture and Community **120** (maps) © Crown copyright. Reproduced with permission of the Forestry Commission BL Woodfall Wild Images/Mark Hamblin **121** T Woodfall Wild Images TL Ardea, London B Forestry Commission/Neil Campbell **122** L Ordnance Survey/ © Crown Copyright TL Collections/David McGill BL © RD **122-123** John Cleare/Mountain Camera **123** TR Ecclesiastical & Eccentricities Picture Library/Dorothy Burrows C Collections CR © RD **124** C Ecclesiastical & Eccentricities Picture Library/Dorothy Burrows CR Ecclesiastical & Eccentricities Picture Library/Dorothy Burrows BL Neil Holmes BR © RD/Richard Turpin **124-125** Neil Holmes **125** C Alvey & Towers Picture Library BR © RD/Jason Smalley **126** R © RD **127** T © RD/Jason Smalley **128** TL Friends of Three Sisters/Wigan Leisure & Culture Trust CL Phil Jones Photography/photographersdirect.com **128-129** LRL **129** TL Cotswold Water Park Society TR Photograph © English Nature/Peter Wakely **130** (both) The National Archives **130-131** John Cleare/Mountain Camera **131** BC © RD BR The Illustrated London News Picture Library **132** Popperfoto **132-133** Photofusion/Martin Bond **133** © RD/Jason Smalley **134** T Butser Ancient Farm BL Scottish Viewpoint/Paul Tomkins BR (c)Fenland Archaelogical Trust/John Byford **135** © RD **136** © RD **137** By permission of the Board of the British Library, London TR TSP BR The Travelsite/Neil Setchfield **138** T Doncaster Record Office BL Courtesy of the Wiltshire & Swindon Record Office/Derek Parker B Edifice/Philippa Lewis **139** TL © RD C © RD BR LRL **140** T Neil Holmes B Collections/Gary Smith **141** T Collections/Alan Creeley C The Art Archive, London/University Library, Prague/ Dagli Orti B National Centre for Early Music **142** L TSP/B.Croxford R © RD **143** TL The National Trust/Mathew Antrobus CR Collections BR Collections **144** TR Ordnance Survey/ © Crown Copyright C © RD CR Ordnance Survey/ © Crown Copyright B AKG London/British Library **145** TR Mike Kipling Photography C Ordnance Survey/ © Crown Copyright B Ordnance Survey/ © Crown Copyright B The National Archives **146** AKG London/British Library **146-147** © RD **147** T English Heritage BR The National Archives **148** T © RD B BAL/Bibliotheque Royale de Belgique **149** L © RD R (all) Surname Atlas CD Rom/www.archersoftware.co.uk **150** CL © RD C © RD BR BAL/Guildhall Library, Corporation of London **151** T © John Allen C Neil Holmes B Newcastle Libraries and Information Service **152** TR The Art Archive, London/Eileen Tweedy BL Manchester Local Studies Unit BR Manchester City Art Galleries/Gallery of Costume **153** L BAL/Yale, Paul Mellon Collection R Collections/Ashely Cooper B © RD **154** C Liverpool Record Office B Liverpool Record Office **154-155** T Carnegie Publishing Ltd/Liverpool Record Office C Liverpool Record Office **155** BL Ron Davies Photography BR Edifice/Lewis-Darley **156** TR National Trust for Scotland/David Robertson B BAL/O'Shea Gallery, London **157** C English Heritage/Paul Higham R TSP BC Topham Picture Library **158** T www.donaldheald.com B SSPL **159** T David Hey B National Trust for Scotland **160** SSPL **161** TL BAL TR Archive held for the Arkwright Society by Trevor Steed (CM&TS) BL (c) Trustees of the National Museums of Scotland **162** © RD L © RD **163** (all) © RD **164** T Hammersmith & Fulham archives & local history centre/from 'Living London' George R.Sims C Birmingham Central Library BR Martyn Chillmaid Photography **165** MEPL **166** T The Illustrated London News Picture Library B Topham Picture Library **167** Topham Picture Library **168** L www.arcaid.co.uk/David Churchill R www.arcaid.co.uk/David Churchill **169** T Ian Butterfield Photography B Leeds City Council **170** T The Illustrated London News Picture Library B By Courtesy of the National Portrait Gallery, London **171** (both) www.raggedschoolmuseum.org.uk **172** TL www.arcaid.co.uk/Richard Waite BR The Marks & Spencer Company Archive **172-173** The Marks & Spencer Company Archive **173** C The Marks & Spencer Company Archive BL The Sainsbury Archive **174** T SSPL B The Francis Frith Collection, Salisbury, Wiltshire SP3 5QP **174-175** Popperfoto **175** B © RD/Julie Bennett **176** T Popperfoto **177** T MEPL BL Topham Picture Library BR English Heritage **178** Museum of London R © RD/London Topographical Society **179** T The National Trust, Northern Ireland B Bolton and Bury Treasures in Trust **180** C MEPL BL Topham Picture Library **180-185** Crossness Engines Trust **181** SSPL **182** BL Topham Picture Library **183** R Museum of London **184** T Mick Sharp and Jean Williamson B SSPL **185** L Getty Images R Topham Picture Library **186** C MEPL BL MEPL **187** TL © RD TR Collections/Nigel Hawkins CR © RD BR Popperfoto **188** TL By permission of the Board of the British Library, London CL The Advertising Archives **188-189** © RD/Julie Bennett **189** T The London Borough of Barking & Dagenham Local Studies Library CR TSP/© lapl **190** BL BAL/John Bethell BR London Transport Museum **190-191** T SSPL B © RD **191** TR Edifice/Tom Thistlethwait **192** L Angelo Hornak **192-193** Topham Picture Library **193** T Edifice B Aidan O'Rourke **194** T © RD B Mirrorpix **195** T www.artofthes-tate.co.uk B www.islandimages.org.uk **196** L SSPL BR © RD **196-197** Topham Picture Library **197** T © RD **198** L © Glasgow City Council (Museums) R English Heritage/Nigel Corrie **199** TL The National Archives TR © RD CR Topham Picture Library **200** L Popperfoto R Hulton Getty Images **201** TR Michael E.Ware B Mirrorpix **202** L Hulton Getty Images R © RD **203** T Rex Features Ltd/Alisdair Macdonald CL © RD BL © RD BR Hulton Getty Images **204** T Hulton Getty Images B Popperfoto **205** T Copyright Sylvia Cordaiy Photo Library Ltd/Glyn Edmunds B LRL **206-207** The Francis Frith Collection, Salisbury, Wiltshire SP3 5QP **207** T Popperfoto CR Rex Features Ltd/Organic Picture Lib **208** TL BAL/Musee d'Orsay, Paris BR The Anthony Blake Photo Library/Anthony Blake **209** TL Harry Ramsden's TR Londonstills.com BL Pizza Express (Restaurants) Ltd BR Vintage Magazine Co **210** T The John Frost Historical Newspaper Service BL © RD/Jason Smalley **211** Wandsworth Museum **212** B © RD **212-213** Historystore **213** C A Photograph from work by Frank Meadow Sutcliffe,Hon.F.R.P.S. (1853-1941) Copyright The Sutcliffe Gallery,Whitby, YO21 3BA/by agreement with Whitby Literary and Philosophical Society B © RD/Jason Smalley **214** T © RD/Jason Smalley BL Ordnance Survey/ © Crown Copyright **215** T Berkshire Record Office C Berkshire Record Office BL David Hey **216** B The John Frost Historical Newspaper Service **216-217** The National Archives **217** B © 2001 Archive CD Books. All rights reserved **218** C The National Archives B © RD/Jason Smalley Jason Smalley B The National Archives **218-219** The National Archives **219** B The National Archives **220** T Rex Features Ltd/GMC C www.scan.org.uk B Jonathan Smith/photographersdirect.com **221** T © National Library of Scotland B © RD **222** C Birmingham Central Library **222-223** T Alan Godfrey Maps/Sandwell Local History Library C © RD B Birmingham Central Library **224** T Collections/Michael Nicholson CR Alamy Images BL © RD/Jason Smalley BR Salisbury District Council **225** T Stan Kujawa Images/photographersdirect.com CL The Art Archive, London CR Hulton Getty Images BR Sithean Photo/photographersdirect.com **226** TL Liz King Media/photographersdirect.com C Stanley Pritchard/photographersdirect.com CR & BR www.oldbaileyonline.org **227** L © RD 228 L © RD/Jason Smalley BR www.churchplansonline.org.uk **228-229** Collections/Robert Hallmann **229** (all) © RD **230** L © RD/Jon Wyand **230-231** © RD/Roger Hutchins **231** T © RD/Jason Smalley B MEPL **232** T Neil Holmes B Neil Holmes **233** BAL **234** L The Photolibrary Wales TR Meirion Record Office BR National Library of Wales **235** (both) Nigel Roberson/photographersdirect.com **236** CL 'Royal Pavilion, Libraries and Museums, Brighton & Hove'/Royal Pavilion, Libraries and Museums, Brighton & Hove B © RD/Angelo Hornak/East Sussex Record Office ESC 24/2/1 **236-237** T © RD/Angelo Hornak **237** T © RD/Angelo Hornak/Middle Street Primary School/East Sussex Record Office (ESC 24/1/1) C © RD/Angelo Hornak/Middle Street Primary School/East Sussex Record Office ESC (24/7/73-73) B © RD/Angelo Hornak/Middle Street Primary School/East Sussex Record Office (ESC 82/A) **238** T Andrew Lawson C John Heseltine B Greenwich Heritage Centre **239** L © RD TR Beamish North of England Open Air Museum **240** T Jaguar Daimler Heritage Trust B The Advertising Archives **241** © RD/Jason Smalley **242** L National Coal Mining Museum for England R The Museum of Lead Mining-Wanlockhead **243** T The National Trust/Keith Hewitt L The National Trust/Dennis Gilbert R Bryan & Cherry Alexander **244** T © RD/John Andrews B © RD/John Andrews **244-245** © RD/John Andrews **245** TL © RD TR © RD B The National Archives **246** L Adrian Japp Photography, photographersdi-rect.com **247** T BAL B The National Archives **248** TL Hulton Getty Images BR Hammersmith & Fulham archives & local history centre **249** © RD/Roger Hutchins/Stoke Bruerne Canal Museum **250** L Milepost Ninety-Two and a Half **250-251** Rail Images **251** T © RD CR Milepost Ninety-Two and a Half **252** TR Collections/Liz Stares C The National Motor Museum, Beaulieu **253** T SSPL B MEPL **254** L The Travelsite/Jarrold Publishing R Pictures courtesy of Bradford Council **255** TL Collections/Archie Young TR City of Newcastle Upon Tyne BR Newcastle Libraries and Information Service **256** T © RD/Jason Smalley B Imperial War Museum **257** TR Popperfoto BR (both) Collections/Dorothy Burrows **258** TL © RD/Julie Bennett **258-259** © RD/from Walls across the valley by Brian Robinson © RD/from Walls across the valley by Brian Robinson **259** (post boxes) © RD TL Collections/Barbara West B © Michael Melbourne/Papplewick Pumping Station Trust **260** ArenaPAL T Collections/Dorothy Burrows **261** T Sheffield Wednesday FC B Sheffield Wednesday FC **262** T Collections/Andria Massey CR © RD/Guildhall Library, Corporation of London/Geremy Butler B Edifice/Philippa Lewis **263** TC Edifice/Philippa Lewis TR Edifice/Philippa Lewis B Collections/Kim Naylor **264** TR Neil Holmes C & BL Ecclesiastical & Eccentricities Picture Library/John Turner **265** T Ecclesiastical & Eccentricities Picture Library/H. Harrison L Edifice/Tom Thistlethwaite BR MEPL **266** Museum of Garden History **266-267** © RD/Julie Bennett **267** Postal Heritage Trust **268** T Pictures of Britain (rest) © RD **269** (window) Edifice/Phillipa Lewis (cruck frame) Edifice/Lewis-Darley (rest) © RD **270** TR © RD B David Williams/David Williams Picture Library **270-271** Collections/Roger Scruton **271** Edifice/Gillian Darley **272** TC © RD/Roger Hutchins TR © RD C © RD/Roger Hutchins CR © RD BL © RD **273** TR Edifice B Edifice/Philippa Lewis (rest) © RD **276** Collections/Michael Burgess **277** T Institute of Agricultural History and Museum of English Rural Life, Reading **278-279** The National Trust **279** TL The National Trust/Dennis Gilbert TR The National Trust C The National Trust/Birmingham City Council BR The National Trust/John Bingham **280** © RD/Roger Hutchins **281** T Edifice B RIBA Library Photographs Collection **282** BAL **283** T www.arcaid.co.uk/David Mark Soulsby B www.arcaid.co.uk/Gillian Darley **284** (all) Edifice **285** TL Edifice/Gillian Darley CL Edifice CR Edifice/Gillian Darley BL & BR Edifice **286** © RD/Roger Hutchins **287** T The Advertising Archives B © RD/Julie Bennett **288** T The Art Archive, London/Eileen Tweedy C & B Museum of Garden History **289** BL © RD/Julie Bennett BR Edifice/Gillian Darley **290** © RD **290-291** www.galinsky.com **291** B The Advertising Archives **292** View/Raf Makda **293** T Countryside Properties plc C & B Erskine Tovatt **294** T The Advertising Archives **294-295** B Reproduced with the permission of the County Archivist, Lancashire Record Office **295** © RD/Jason Smalley **296** T © RD/Angelo Hornak CL Phil Flowers **297** TL & TC © RD/Angelo Hornak BC © RD/Angelo Hornak/East Sussex Record Office, SAU/669 BR © RD/Paul Manners **298** TR Edifice C © RD BL © RD/Julie Bennett **299** L © RD/Jason Smalley R © RD/Jason Smalley **300** T Elizabeth Whiting & Associates B Edifice/Philippa Lewis **301** Travel Ink **302** T © RD B © RD **303** L London Metropolitan Archives B © RD **304** Harrow Local Studies **305** T Postal Heritage Trust B Harrow Local Studies **306** C The Advertising Archives **306-307** Elizabeth Whiting & Associates **307** C © RD CR & R Museum on Domestic Design and Architecture, Middlesex University/Angelo Hornak BR © RD/Angelo Hornak **308** CL The National Trust/Keith Paisley CR & BR The National Trust/Dennis Gilbert **309** T Martin Black (rest), Museum on Domestic Design and Architecture, Middlesex University **310** L Edifice R The National Archives **311** T Minet Library C Minet Library B The National Archives **312** T The National Archives BL © RD BR SSPL **313** T SSPL B SSPL **314** (both) The National Archives **314-315** The Photolibrary Wales **315** BR © RD **316** L Interior Archive Limited/Edina van der Wyck CR © RD CR Copyright Sylvia Cordaiy Photo Library Ltd **316-317** Elizabeth Whiting & Associates **317** C The National Archives CR The National Archives R The National Trust B © RD **318** T Edifice B The Scottish Record Office **319** Inset Bath Record Office TL Bath Record Office **320** CL Elizabeth Whiting & Associates C Elizabeth Whiting & Associates CR www.arcaid.co.uk/Benedict Luxmoore **321** TR Courtesy of the Trustees of the Victoria and Albert Museum, London CL Elizabeth Whiting & Associates CR Courtesy of the Trustees of the Victoria and Albert Museum, London **322** T Cheshire Record Office B © RD **323** TR, CL & CR Amy Browne BR The National Archives **324** B The National Archives **324-325** Geffrye Museum, London **325** T The National Archives **326** Hulton Getty Images **327** T Tower Hamlets Local History Library & Archives B BT Archives **328** Popperfoto **328-329** The National Archives **329** © Glasgow City Council (Museums) **330** T The Art Archive, London L The National Archives **330-331** The National Archives **331** The National Archives

The Story of Where You Live was designed and edited by The Reader's Digest Association Limited, London.

First edition copyright © 2005
The Reader's Digest Association Limited,
11 Westferry Circus, Canary Wharf,
London E14 4HE

We are committed to both the quality of our products and the service we provide to our customers. We value your comments, so please feel free to contact us on **08705 113366** or via our website at: **www.readersdigest.co.uk**
If you have any comments or suggestions about the content of our books, email us at gbeditorial@readersdigest.co.uk

This product includes mapping data licensed from Ordnance Survey © Crown Copyright and/or database right 2005. Licence number PU 100018100.

Maps on pages 29, 30, 31, 32, 33, 34, 46, 51 (left), 57, 59, 68, 71, 72, 74, 82, 110, 122 (top), 131, 136, 142, 144 (centre), 148, 149 (left), 150, 153, 162, 187, 190-1, 194, 196, 197, 199, 268, 269 © 2005 Cartographica Limited

Concept code UK1773/IC
Book code 400-179-01
ISBN 0 276 42959 1
Oracle code 250009012H.00.24

READER'S DIGEST PROJECT TEAM

Editor
John Andrews

Art Editor
Julie Bennett

Senior Designer
Austin Taylor

Assitant Editors
Caroline Boucher
Liz Clasen
Celia Coyne
Jane Hutchings
Cécile Landau

Editorial Assistant
Gail Paten

Picture Research
Elizabeth Loving
Rosie Taylor

Proofreader
Ron Pankhurst

Indexer
Hilary Bird

READER'S DIGEST GENERAL BOOKS

Editorial Director
Cortina Butler
Art Director
Nick Clark
Executive Editor
Julian Browne
Managing Editor
Alastair Holmes
Picture Resource Manager
Martin Smith
Pre-press Account Manager
Penny Grose
Origination
Colour Systems Limited, London
Printing and binding
Partenaires-Livres, France

CONTRIBUTORS

Chief Consultant
David Hey
Emeritus Professor of Local and Family History, The University of Sheffield

Consultants
Sonia Baker
Peter Christian

Writers
Sonia Baker
Nick Barratt
Jonathan Bastable
Peter Christian
David Hey
Roger Hunt
Alice McEwan
Christopher Somerville

Photography
Angelo Hornak
Jason Smalley

Maps
Cartographica Limited

Illustration
Roger Hutchins

Digital Imaging
Ian Atkinson

Reader's Digest would like to thank the following for their help in the preparation of this book:

Andrew Bennett, East Sussex County Archives; Martin Bennett; Chorley Borough Council; Jane McKenna; Paul Manners and Marietta Van Dyck; The Museum of Science & Industry in Manchester; Diane Naylor, Andrew Petit and Stewart Mann, Chatsworth House, Derbyshire; Alison Smith, The Canal Museum, Stoke Bruerne; Donna Steele and David Dyer, Middle Street School, Brighton; Kingston Local History Room, Kingston upon Thames